Helene de F. Rothwell is a retired educator and former Assistant Coordinator of Media Services for Peel Board of Education.

This basic, annotated bibliography of Canadian-produced filmstrips lists approximately 1800 significant items, in both English and French, produced in Canada for children and young adults up to August, 1978.

Compiled as a previewing and selection guide for schools and libraries and as a basic bibliography for international reference, this volume lists the filmstrips by Dewey Decimal classification number and incorporates a new approach to subject access by using the Preserved Context Index System (PRECIS), a computer-generated system founded on linguistic principles. It also contains a key to abbreviations, a title index, a series list, and a directory of distributors.

Ministry of Education, Ontario
Information Centre, 13th Floor,
Mowat Block, Queen's Park,
Toronto, Ont.　　　M7A 1L2

Canadian Selection:
Filmstrips

Compiled by
HELENE de F. ROTHWELL

University of Toronto Press
Toronto   Buffalo   London

© University of Toronto Press 1980
Toronto Buffalo London
Printed in Canada

ISBN 0-8020-4586-3

Canadian Cataloguing in Publication Data

Rothwell, Helene de F., 1914-
Canadian selection

ISBN 0-8020-4586-3

1. Filmstrips - Catalogs.   I. Title.
LB1043.8Z9R67   017'.437   C80-094472-0

The production of this book was made possible by grants from the Ontario Ministry of Education and the National Film Board of Canada.

The University of Toronto Library Automation Systems (UTLAS) was responsible for the computer print-out.

Contents

Preface   vii

Introduction   ix

Acknowledgements   xiii

Abbreviations   xv

Part One
The Classified Catalogue   1

Part Two
PRECIS Subject Index   271

Part Three
Title Index   425

Part Four
Series List   457

Part Five
Distributors' Directory   497

Addendum   501

Preface

When Helene Rothwell first approached the Centre for Research in Librarianship more than two years ago with her ideas for a selective, annotated catalogue of Canadian-produced non-print materials, she argued cogently that no general guide to such materials then existed; and that the resulting lack of criteria for the evaluation and selection of Canadian materials was not only hampering Canadian efforts to purchase Canadian-produced filmstrips, films, and cassettes, but was also tending to blur the distinction between well-produced and poorly produced Canadian non-print materials. Far more money was being wasted in poor selection, argued Ms Rothwell, than would be spent on the preparation of the catalogue which had been her life-long dream.

The Centre and the Government of Ontario found her arguments persuasive. The present pilot study on Canadian-produced filmstrips is the result, funded by a $30,000 grant from the Ontario Ministry of Education and by an additional $7050 from the National Film Board of Canada.

If further evidence of the urgent need to realize Ms Rothwell's dream is needed, it is surely provided by the findings of the Report of the Commission on Canadian Studies, chaired by the distinguished founding president of Trent University, Professor T.H.B. Symons. That report, thought by the Canadian Book and Periodical Development Council to be of such importance that the Council voluntarily undertook to publish an abridged version, devotes an entire segment of its limited space to an analysis of audio-visual resources and Canadian Studies. The report (in its abridged version) reminds us that media can be very important tools. 'Eighteen-year-olds entering university have seen about 15,000 hours of television; they have seen over 500 feature films. Yet they have perhaps read only fifty books on their own initiative.' The report, however, notes further that, 'There is also a serious lack of Canadian electronic materials ('software'). Some 80 per cent of films and audiovisual aids used in Canadian schools come from foreign sources ...

A vast opportunity exists for the use of electronic materials in the teaching and research of Canadian studies.'

A large part of the problem, as the Commission sees it, is that 'Most of this [Canadian-produced educational audiovisual products] material remains within the province of origin and must surely represent much unnecessary duplication. However, little has been done to provide effective distribution ... A national study should be undertaken of media resources ... There is also a need for a standard procedure across Canada for the classification and retrieval of media materials.'

Helene Rothwell has gone far with respect to filmstrips towards redressing the adverse balance described by the Commission on Canadian Studies. She has provided the first reasonably objective access to Canadian-produced strips. She has incorporated a dynamic new approach to subject access by using the Preserved Context Index System (PRECIS) recently developed in Great Britain. She has surmounted provincialism by searching untiringly across Canada for material from local producers. She has identified and evaluated some 2200 filmstrips and, of these, has selected, annotated, and classified approximately 2000, many heretofore relatively unknown. And this is only a beginning; for Ms Rothwell and her team of dedicated associates intend, if funding is forthcoming, to carry their project much further and, with the co-operation of the National Computerized Information System of the National Film Board and other non-print agencies, to do for almost all Canadian non-print materials what she has so ably done for Canadian-produced filmstrips.

The Centre for Research in Librarianship is proud to be associated with this at least partial realization of Helene Rothwell's dream. It believes, as must the Commission on Canadian Studies and indeed all learning Canadians, in the absolute importance and urgency of Ms Rothwell's undertaking; and it hopes very much to help her to expand and complete her work to the overall benefit of Canadian education and culture.

John P. Wilkinson
Director
Centre for Research in Librarianship
Faculty of Library Science
University of Toronto

Introduction

Purpose

The objective of the Canadian Non-Print Project is to compile and publish a standard catalogue of the most significant non-print materials (in both English and French) that have been produced in Canada for children and young adults, and, as a by-product, to produce a machine-readable data base which could be used for updating purposes and/or as the foundation of a computerized retrieval service. The full catalogue will ultimately provide a selective, annotated bibliography designed as a working tool for Canadian schools and libraries. Phase 1 of this project, as now published, provides a basic guide for the previewing and selection of Canadian-produced filmstrips in all schools and libraries, both new and established; serves as a tool to systematically assess and develop school and library collections; provides a source of cataloguing and classification information by presenting Dewey Decimal Classification numbers and appropriate PRECIS-generated subject headings; provides assistance to educators in the presentation of reference service and advice; and serves internationally as a basic, annotated bibliography of Canadian-produced filmstrips.

Scope

The items included in Phase 1 of the project were restricted to filmstrips (both silent and with accompanying sound) suitable for use by children and young adults from Kindergarten to Grade 13. The catalogue is for individual filmstrips only; therefore, filmstrips sold *only* as a set have been excluded. Approximately 1800 filmstrips have been included in this edition. Those items that were rejected either did not meet the criteria set for selection or could not be sold separately. All items were produced prior to August 1978. Unless otherwise stated all filmstrips listed are useful both as teaching aids and for independent study.

Methodology and criteria for title selection

Contact was made with all known commercial companies and with those institutions producing filmstrips at a 'local' level. This included boards of education, universities and colleges, departments of education, and various museums. Although many items were located among the latter sources, only a few of them were for sale and thus eligible for inclusion in our buying guide. All materials to be considered were shipped to the Centre for Research in Librarianship, where they were re-examined or assigned for evaluation if they were new productions.

Evaluative lists of non-print materials secured from institutions across Canada were examined for recommended titles. If there was doubt about the acceptance of an item, it was again submitted to the evaluation teams set up in Metro Toronto schools. New materials were examined several times by teams of educators with their students. Final selection was made on the basis of organization of content, bias, currency, and technical quality. Descriptive annotations were completed by a team of both English- and French-speaking educators, and a final check was made by the central staff. Each item was then classified, subject headings were selected, and a PRECIS string assigned. It is important to note that sound filmstrips are listed as filmstrips with accompanying sound and not as kits.

Arrangement

Part I   contains a key to abbreviations used in the catalogue.
Part II   is a classified catalogue arranged by Dewey Decimal Classification number.
Part III   is a PRECIS-generated subject index.
Part IV   is a title index arranged alphabetically.
Part V   is an alphabetical list of important series with representative titles of each.
Part VI   is a list of distributors whose titles appear in the catalogue including the initials used to represent the distributors.

Form of entry

The catalogue has been compiled as a buying guide for Canadian-produced filmstrips and not as a cataloguing guide. Therefore, a bibliographic form rather than a cataloguing form has been used for each entry. Some of the information, however, could be an aid to simple cataloguing procedures if used with caution.

Both the producer and the current distributor are listed with the date of production. Occasionally both production and copyright dates appear. If a title is part of a series, the title of the series is placed in parentheses. In addition, a Dewey Decimal Classification number, suggested subject headings, accompanying materials, grade levels, and the most recent prices are given. Descriptive annotations are included with each entry.

In some cases the title used in the catalogue does not appear on the item itself but has been assigned by the producer, usually to facilitate ordering.

Classification and subject headings

The suggested subject headings given with each entry are from *Sears List of Subject Headings, 11th edition*. Sears was chosen because it was felt its headings would best suit small school libraries. In a few instances *Canadiana* was used when it seemed more appropriate for the peculiarly Canadian subject matter.

Classification of entries is by numbers from *The Abridged Dewey Decimal Classification and Relative Index, 10th edition*.

PRECIS subject index

The subject index is an example of the use of the Preserved Context Index System (PRECIS), a computer-generated system founded on linguistic principles.

PRECIS was developed at the British National Bibliography in the early 1970s. It has been adopted by a number of institutions around the world, including the National Film Board of Canada, Aurora High School Library, and the ONTERIS Project of the Ontario Ministry of Education. Current research and development is progressing towards translingual indexing, a refinement which should be of considerable value in a bilingual country.

The user can consult the index through specific access points (lead terms), and will find a specific entry, co-extensive with one subject of the filmstrip, which includes grade levels. *See* and *See also* references facilitate retrieval.

The use of PRECIS has been welcomed by specialists in non-book materials. The great general systems of subject representation and retrieval were designed to cope with commercial monographs. They are frequently unsuitable for such items as four-minute filmloops.

In most cases, the indexing has been done from the annotations. We have concentrated on the question 'What is this filmstrip about?' and not on the question 'What can this filmstrip be used for?' The latter has many answers, not all of which can be anticipated. We have pursued even vestigial subjects. Indexing by purpose has been allowed in a few cases - for example, language teaching materials.

The subject of the filmstrip as a whole was indexed, except where a filmstrip concerned two or more legitimate subjects. In these cases, we indexed all themes.

An open-ended vocabulary has been used throughout. Spelling controversies were referred to the *Gage Senior Dictionary of Canadian English*.

In order to avoid over-long columns of entries, the terms 'Canada' and 'North America' have been used as access points when their sole function in the subject statement is to serve as geographical location.

The subject index was developed by C.D. Robinson, one of the very few persons in Canada with the necessary expertise. Mr Robinson has worked with Derek Austin (who invented the system) at the British National Bibliography, and was responsible for the *College Bibliocentre Film Catalogue* published in Toronto.

Acknowledgements

The compilation of this catalogue could not have been accomplished without the assistance of many persons.

An Advisory Committee, appointed from across Canada, consisted of the following members: Professor Larry Amey, Dalhousie University, School of Library Service; Elizabeth Avison, University of Toronto, Media Centre; D. Pauline Fennell, Ontario Ministry of Education, Professional Development Branch; Dean Francess G. Halpenny, University of Toronto, Faculty of Library Science; Ken Haycock, Vancouver School Board, Co-ordinator of Library Services; Professor Edith Jarvi, University of Toronto, Faculty of Library Science; Jean B. Weihs, Seneca College, Director of Library Techniques; Dr John P. Wilkinson, Director of the University of Toronto's Centre for Research in Librarianship. The support and advice of this committee were invaluable.

Special acknowledgement must be given to the four assistants whose contributions to the cataloguing, annotating, and general organization of materials made this entire project possible. These staff members were Janet Blue, Jane Coventry, Anita McCallum, and Pat Tomey. Without the dedicated contribution and support of these assistants the project never would have been completed.

For the development of the PRECIS subject index we are greatly indebted to C.D. Robinson, whose description of the subject index appears in the introduction.

Contributions to the evaluation and the selection of materials were made by educators from the following institutions and Boards of Education: Calgary Board of Education, Edmonton Board of Education, Peel Board of Education, North York Board of Education, Scarborough Board of Education, Borough of York Board of Education, Toronto Board of Education, Metropolitan Toronto Separate School Board, Dufferin-Peel Separate School Board, Etobicoke Board of Education, Queen's University Faculty of Education, Province of Alberta Department of Education.

Individual educators who assisted with annotations include Sheila Bishop, Sheila Cook, Eileen Daniels, Gabby Heinrich, Nancy Tong, Dorothy Tuddenham, and Sarah Vanderburgh.

Others whose special assistance was most appreciated include Helen Coffey, Nancy Deline, Grace Funk, Yvonne Hurst, Joan Kerrigan, Bill Porter, Cay Schaffter, Gwen Washburn, Judy Gardhouse, and Colin Neale.

Funding for this pilot project came from the Ontario Ministry of Education and from the National Film Board of Canada. To both these institutions I wish to express my gratitude for their financial support and for their encouragement in this first phase of the selective guide to Canadian audio-visual materials.

A special word of thanks must be made to all the producers of Canadian materials who so willingly offered their support and co-operation. Their confidence in the project was demonstrated when shipments of all their productions were made, free of charge, to the Centre for Research in Librarianship, where they remained with us for approximately one year.

The National Computerized Information System of the National Film Board was responsible for the input of all data to University of Toronto Library Automation Systems (UTLAS) that gave us the final computer print-out.

To Dr John Wilkinson, Director of the Centre for Research in Librarianship, my personal gratitude is extended for his sound professional advice, his untiring patience and encouragement, and for his vision, without which this project would never have been launched.

To all who have contributed in any measure to the production of the Canadian Non-Print Project, I extend my sincere gratitude.

Helene de F. Rothwell

Abbreviations

adv.	advance
aud.	audible
auto.	automatic
avail.	available
b & w	black and white
cap.	captions
cass.	cassette
col.	colour
dist.	distributor
Eng.	English
fr.	frames
Fr.	French
I.	Intermediate
i.	intermediate
J.	Junior
j.	junior
K.	Kindergarten
k.	kindergarten
man.	manual
min.	minutes
P.	Primary
p.	primary
prod.	producer
read. script	reading script
S.	Senior
s.	senior
sec.	seconds
sig.	signals
supp. mat.	supplementary material
teach.	teacher's
w/	with
AUE	Atlantic Underwater Enterprises
BH	Bellhaven House Ltd.
CFM	Canfilm Media
FMS	Falcon Media Systems
Int. Cin.	International Cinemedia

M-L	Moreland-Latchford
NCM	NC Multimedia
NFB	National Film Board
R.Q.M.	Robert Q. Millman
SHN	See! Hear! Now!
VCI	Visual Communications International
UEVA	Universal Education & Visual Arts (Canada)
WCL	William Clare Ltd.

Part One

The Classified Catalogue

The Classified Catalogue

001.54
A Book is a friend.
   prod. [Toronto] : B&R, 1976.- dist. B&R 27 fr. : col. : 35 mm. & captions & teacher's manual. $10.00 p

   1. Books - Care and treatment.

   Captioned cartoons provide a light approach to the serious topic of the careful handling of books. Emphasizes the interesting things books can show and tell and illustrates several specific ways to care for a book properly.-

024
Discovering your library.
   prod. [Toronto] : M-L, 1974.- dist. Sch. Ser. or Vint. 53 fr. : col. : 35 mm. & cassette (9 min.) : auto. & aud. adv. sig. & teacher's guide. $16.50 (Your library : how to use it : $75.00) j

   1. Libraries and readers.

   A new girl in school is introduced to all the resource material, equipment, and facilities in the school library. Illustrates the library as a place for reading, research, and activities, such as puppetry. Emphasizes careful handling of equipment and checking out materials.-

024
How do you share your library?
   prod. [Toronto] : M-L, 1974.- dist. Sch. Ser. or Vint. 53 fr. : col. : 35 mm. & cassette (10 min.) : auto. & aud. adv. sig. & teacher's guide. $16.50 (Your library : how to use it : $75.00) j

   1. Libraries and readers.

   A comprehensive outline of responsible library behavior. Stresses care of books, consequences of abuse, returning books on time, bringing writing materials to the library, taking turns, respecting others, returning materials to their place, proper use of av material.-

025
What's white and yellow and read all over?
   prod. [Toronto] : 1976.- dist. VEC 94 fr. : col. : 35 mm. & cassette (14 min.) : auto. & aud. adv. sig. & teacher's guide, 4 posters, and 12 activity masters. $24.00 (Hello! Getting together with the telephone : $96.00) pi

   1. Directoriees. 2. Telephone.

   Explains how the white and yellow telephone directories may be used in a variety of situations as well as step-by-step instructions in locating information in these directories. French title available : QU'EST-CE QUI BLANC OU JAUNE ET QUI FAIT MARCHER LES DOIGTS.-

028.7
Doing a project.
   prod. [Toronto] : M-L, 1974.- dist. Sch. Ser. or Vint. 54 fr. : col. : 35 mm. & cassette (7 min.) : auto. & aud. adv. sig. & teacher's guide. $16.50 (Your library : how to use it : $75.00) j

   1. Libraries and readers.

   Describes use of resources in school and public libraries for project material. Explains notemaking during research stage, and organization of materials.-

028.7
Have you a book about?
   prod. [Toronto] : B & R, 1973.- dist. B & R 45 fr. : b&w & col. : 35 mm. & captions & teacher's manual. $10.00 (Finding material in the resource centre : $27.00) pj

   1. Libraries and readers.

   Portrays a child in search of material "about" birds. Illustrates each of the steps necessary to locate information, both print and non-print, on a particular subject in the library resource centre. Emphasizes and illustrates the use of the card catalogue.-

The Classified Catalogue

028.7
    Have you a book by?
        prod. [Toronto] : B & R, 1973.- dist. B & R 45 fr. : b&w & col. : 35 mm. & captions & teacher's manual. $10.00 (Finding material in the resource centre : $27.00) pj

        1. Libraries and readers.

        Shows the steps followed by two children looking for material (both print and non-print) by a particular Canadian author in the library resource centre. Emphasizes and illustrates the use of the card catalogue.-

028.7
    Have you a book called?
        prod. [Toronto] : B & R, 1973.- dist. B & R 45 fr. : b&w & col. : 35 mm. & captions & teacher's manual. $10.00 (Finding material in the resource centre : $27.00) pj

        1. Libraries and readers.

        Illustrates the steps followed by a child trying to locate a particular title in the library resource centre. Emphasizes and descusses use of the card catalogue.-

028.7
    The Library. (Or, how I learned to love Melvil Dewey).
        prod. [Scarborough, Ont.] : SHN, 1976. dist. PHM 65 : 69 fr. : col. : 35 mm. & cassette (12 min.) : auto. & aud. adv. sig. & teacher's guide. $48.00 ji

        1. Libraries and readers.

        Uses cartoons, background music, and sound effects for a light approach to the basics of effective library use. Discusses the reason for the development of library practices, and describes the use of the card catalogue, encyclopedias, and periodical indexes. Title has two parts.-

070
    The Newspaper : part 2.
        prod. [Toronto] : Int. Cin., 1975.- dist. VEC 66 fr. : col. : 35 mm. & cassette (8 min.) : auto. & aud. adv. sig. & teacher's guide. $24.00 (Community close-ups : $192.00) pj

        1. Newspapers.

        Provides a detailed explanation of the printing process by showing how a news story is composed, typeset, proofread, pasted, and finally printed.-

070
    The Newspaper : part 1.
        prod. [Toronto] : Int. Cin., 1975.- dist. VEC 66 fr. : col. : 35 mm. & cassette (8 min.) : auto. & aud. adv. sig. & teacher's guide. $24.00 (Community close-ups : $192.00) pj

        1. Newspapers.

        An introduction into various departments in a newspaper building, discussing how reporters gather information for a story, and the various stages of a newspaper article from its first draft until it appears in print.-

152.1
    Colour sets.
        prod. [Oakville, Ont.] : SC, 1971.- dist. SC 56 fr. : col. : 35 mm. & cassette (7 min.) : auto. adv. sig. only. $35.00 s

        1. Color sense.

        A variety of visual examples accompany narration on colour sense and its application to artwork. Encourages recognition of and experimentation with colour and colour sets.-

152.1
    Listen to my world.
        prod. [Toronto] : B&R, 1974.- dist. B&R 20 fr. : col. : 35 mm. & captions & teacher's manual. $10.00 (This is my world : $27.00) pj

        1. Hearing.

        A small boy discovers the many interesting sounds he can hear. The basic vocabulary would allow this material to be used as a supplement to a grade one reading programme.-

152.1
    Look at my world.
        prod. [Toronto] : B&R, 1974.- dist. B&R 20 fr. : col. : 35 mm. & captions & teacher's manual. $10.00 (This is my world : $27.00) pj

        1. Vision.

        Gaining awareness of the world through the sense of sight is the theme as a small boy discovers where and how he can look and what he can see. The basic vocabulary would allow this material to be used as a supplement to a grade one reading programme.-

The Classified Catalogue

152.1
    Observing by hearing, tasting, smelling, touching.
        prod. [Hamilton, Ont.] : VCI, 1977.- dist. MHR 34 fr. : col. : 35 mm. & captions & teacher's guide. $35.00 (Thinking skills : observing) p

    1. Senses and sensation.

    Introduces the four senses, discussing what can be observed by using each sense and situations where these senses are used in the environment. Produced in 4 parts.-

152.1
    Observing by seeing : colours purple, orange, green.
        prod. [Hamilton, Ont.] : VCI, 1977.- dist. MHR 28 fr. : col. : 35 mm. & captions & teacher's guide. $35.00 (Thinking skills : observing) p

    1. Purple. 2. Orange. 3. Green.

    Introduces the basic colours of purple, orange, and green, identifies the words naming these colours, and discusses the occurrence of the colours in everyday life. Produced in 3 parts.-

152.1
    Observing by seeing : colours black, white, brown.
        prod. [Hamilton, Ont.] : VCI, 1977.- dist. MHR 28 fr. : col. : 35 mm. & captions & teacher's guide. $35.00 (Thinking skills : observing) p

    1. Black. 2. White. 3. Brown.

    Introduces the basic colours of black, white, and brown, identifies the words naming these colours, and discusses the occurrence of these colours in everyday life. Produced in 3 parts.-

152.1
    Touch my world.
        prod. [Toronto Ont.] :B & R, 1974.- dist. B & R   20 fr. : col. : 35 mm. & teacher's manual & captions. $10.00 (This is my world : $27.00) pj

    1. Touch.

    Introduces the sense of touch as an aid in learning about the world, while also mentioning the use of sight and hearing. The basic vocabulary would allow this material to be used as a supplement to a grade one reading programme.-

152.4
    But I don't know how.
        prod. [Toronto] : Int. Cin., 1977.- dist. VEC 47 fr. : col. : 35 mm. & cassette (5 min.) : auto. & aud. adv. sig. & teacher's guide. $24.00 (Feelings : $154.00) pj

    1. Emotions.

    Children discuss their self-doubts about living as an adult in a grown-up world. They then discover that as children they possess certain skills and talents that adults do not have. French title available : JE NE PEUX PAS.-

152.4
    Ce n'est pas juste.
        prod. [Toronto] : Int. Cin., 1977.- dist. VEC 52 fr. : col. : 35 mm. & cassette (5 min.) : auto. & aud. adv. sig. & teacher's guide. $24.00 (Sentiments : $154.00) pj

    1. Emotions.

    Illustrates that children are not alone in thinking they have not been treated fairly in given number of situations. Shows that everyone at one time or another feels he or she has been treated unfairly. English title available : THAT'S NOT FAIR.-

152.4
    Cesse de faire le bébé.
        prod. [Toronto] : Int. Cin., 1977.- dist. VEC 46 fr. : col. : 35 mm. & cassette (4 min.) : auto. & aud. adv. sig. & teacher's guide. $24.00 (Sentiments : $154.00) pj

    1. Behavior. 2. Emotions.

    A series of anecdotes where both children and adults act "just like a baby". Illustrates that there is still a baby inside all of us needing attention, comforting, and an occasional chance to act childish. English title available :STOP ACTING LIKE A BABY.-

The Classified Catalogue

152.4
C'est frustrant.
  prod. [Toronto] : M-L, 1975.- dist. Sch. Ser. or Vint. 56 fr. : col. : 35 mm. & cassette (7 min.) : auto. & aud. adv. sig. & teacher's guide. $16.50 (Mes sentiments : $65.00) j

  1. Emotions.

  Describes Greg's difficulties when he cannot remember his lines in the class play, even with help from his teacher and parents. Viewers are asked what they would do in Greg's situation and to discuss frustrating experiences they have had. English title available : YOUR FRUSTRATION.-

152.4
Everybody's afraid of something.
  prod. Int. Cin., 1977.- dist. VEC 53 fr. : col. : 35 mm. & cassette (6 min.) : auto. & aud. adv. sig. & teacher's guide. $24.00 (Feelings : $154.00) pj

  1. Fear.

  By showing situations in which children and even adults admit to being afraid, children learn that everyone has a fear of something and that it is nothing to be ashamed of. French title available : TOUT LE MONDE A PEUR DE QUELQUE CHOSE.-

152.4
Gr-r-r-r.
  prod. [Toronto] : Int. Cin., 1977.- dist. VEC 48 fr. : col. : 35 mm. & cassette (4 min.) : auto. & aud. adv. sig. & teacher's guide. $24.00 (Feelings : $154.00) pj

  1. Anger.

  Describes how anger is contagious, and how one instance of anger can set off a chain reaction of hurt and angry feelings amongst others. Designed to encourage discussion about inner concerns. French title available : Rrrrr.-

152.4
Inside outside.
  prod. [Toronto] : Int. Cin., 1977.- dist. VEC 50 fr. : col. : 35 mm. & cassette (5 min.) : auto.& aud. adv. sig. &teacher's guide. $24.00 (Feelings : $154.00) pj

  1. Emotions.

  An amusing anecdote shows how our exterior behavior often contradicts real, inner feelings. Develops an awareness of why people display contempt when frightened, anger when startled, and laughter when nervous. Cartoons illustrate. French title available : LES MASQUES.-

152.4
J'ai peur.
  prod. [Toronto] : M-L, 1975.- dist. Sch. Ser. or Vint. 52 fr. : col. : 35 mm. & cassette (6 min.) : auto. & aud. adv. sig. & teacher's guide. $16.50 (Mes sentiments : $65.00) j

  1. Fear.

  Uses a classroom situation to illustrate childhood fears. Nancy, afraid to give a book report in front of the class, explores ways to escape from it. The conclusion is open-ended to encourage group discussion. English title available : YOUR FEAR.-

152.4
Je l'envie.
  prod. [Toronto] : M-L, 1975.- dist. Sch. Ser. or Vint. 54 fr. : col. : 35 mm. & cassette (7 min.) : auto. & aud. adv. sig. & teacher's guide. $16.50 (Mes sentiments : $65.00) j

  1. Envy. 2. Ethics.

  Envious of a friend's new bicycle, Robbie hesitates to offer a clue when it is stolen. Viewers are asked to decide what they would do in Robbie's place, and to discuss attitudes. English title available : YOUR ENVY.-

The Classified Catalogue

152.4
  Je me mets en colère.
    prod. [Toronto] : M-L, 1975.- dist. Sch. Ser. or Vint. 51 fr. : col. : 35 mm. & cassette (7 min.) : auto. & aud. adv. sig. & teacher's guide. $16.50 (Mes sentiments : $65.00) j

    1. Anger. 2. Ethics.

    An enactment of a typical family situation underling the consequences of losing one's temper. Tom does not want to share his new radio with his brother, and blames the latter when it breaks. As punishment for losing his temper, Tom's father confiscates the radio. Viewers are then asked to discuss Tom's behaviour. English title available : YOUR ANGER.-

152.4
  Je ne peux pas.
    prod. [Toronto] : Int. Cin., 1977.- dist. VEC 47 fr. : col. : 35 mm. & cassette (4 min.) : auto. & aud. adv. sig. & teacher's guide. $24.00 (Sentiments : $154.00) pj

    1. Emotions.

    Children discuss their self-doubts about living as an adult in a grown-up world. They then discover that as children they possess certain skills and talents that adults do not have. English title available : BUT I DON'T KNOW HOW.-

152.4
  Many different me-s.
    prod. [Toronto] : Int. Cin., 1977.- dist. VEC 50 fr. : col. : 35 mm. & cassette (6 min.) : auto. & aud. adv. sig. & teacher's guide. $24.00 (Feelings : $154.00) pj

    1. Emotions.

    Cartoon characters portray the "many different me's" inherent in an individual, and how a person is viewed in different ways by different people. Stimulates discussion on conflicts created when one tries to live up to several expectations. French title available : MOI ET MES DIVERSES PERSONALITES.-

152.4
  Les Masques.
    prod. [Toronto] : Int. Cin., 1977.- dist. VEC 50 fr. : col. : 35 mm. & cassette (5 min.) : auto. & aud. adv. sig. & teacher's guide. $24.00 (Sentiments : $154.00) pj

    1. Emotions.

    An amusing anecdote shows how our exterior behaviour often contradicts real, inner feelings. Develops an awareness of why people display contempt when frightened, anger when startled, and laughter when nervous. Cartoons illustrate. English title available : INSIDE OUTSIDE.-

152.4
  Moi et mes diverses personalités.
    prod. [Toronto] : Int. Cin., 1977.- dist. VEC 50 fr. : col. : 35 mm. & cassette (6 min.) : auto. & aud. adv. sig. & teacher's guide. $24.00 (Sentiments : $154.00) pj

    1. Emotions.

    Cartoon characters portray the "many different me's" inherent in an individual, and how a person is viewed in different ways by different people. Stimulates discussion on conflicts created when one tries to live up to several expectations. English title available : MANY DIFFERENT ME-S.-

152.4
  Quand je serai grand.
    prod. [Toronto] : Int. Cin., 1977.- dist. VEC 58 fr. : col. : 35 mm. & cassette (6 min.) : auto. & aud. adv. sig. & teacher's guide. $24.00 (Sentiments : $154.00) pj

    1. Emotions.

    Magic turns an unhappy child into an adult, teaching him that grownups have problems too. Emphasizes adult responsibilities. Good example of roleplaying technique. Illustrated with cartoons. English title available : WHEN I GROW UP.-

The Classified Catalogue

152.4
    Rrrrr.
        prod. [Toronto] : Int. Cin., 1977.- dist. VEC 48 fr. : col. : 35 mm. & cassette (4 min.) : auto. & aud. adv. sig. & teacher's guide. $24.00 (Sentiments : $154.00) pj

        1. Anger.

        Describes how anger is contagious, and how one instance of anger can set off a chain reaction of hurt and angry feelings amongst others. Designed to encourage discussion about inner concerns. English title available : Gr-r-r-r.-

152.4
    Stop acting like a baby.
        prod. Int. Cin., 1977.- dist. VEC 46 fr. col. : 35 mm. & cassette (5 min.) : auto. & aud. adv. sig. &dteacher's guide. $24.00 (Feelings : $154.00) pj

        1. Behavior. 2. Emotions.

        A series of anecdotes where both children and adults act "just like a baby". Illustrates that there is still a baby inside all of us needing attention, comfort, and an occasional chance to act childish. French title available : CESSE DE FAIRE LE BEBE.-

152.4
    That's not fair.
        prod. [Toronto] : Int. Cin., 1977.- dist. VEC 52 fr. : col. : 35 mm. & cassette (6 min.) : auto. & aud. adv. sig. & teacher's guide. $24.00 (Feelings : $154.00) pj

        1. Emotions

        Illustrates that children are not alone in thinking they have not been treated fairly in a given number of situations. Shows that everyone at one time or another feels he or she has been treated unfairly. French title available : CE N'EST PAS JUSTE.-

152.4
    To be alone.
        prod. [Montreal?] : NFB, 1974.- dist. McI. 141 fr. : b&w & col. : 35 mm. & cassette (28 min.) : auto. & aud. adv. sig. & teacher's guide. $18.00 (A Question of values) s

        1. Loneliness. 2. Single women. 3. Divorce.

        Re-enactments of actual case studies reflect three different viewpoints on being alone. Shown is a man suffering from severe depression, a woman coping with seperation and a single individual happily unattached. Useful for discussion on loneliness, depression, separation, divorce, and on changing attitudes toward single women. French title available : VIVRE SEULE.-

152.4
    Tout le monde a peur de quelque chose.
        prod. [Toronto] : Int. Cin., 1977.- dist. VEC 53 fr. : col. : 35 mm. & cassette (6 min.) : auto. & aud. adv. sig. & teacher's guide. $24.00 (Sentiments : $154.00) pj

        1. Fear.

        By showing situations in which children and even adults admit to being afraid, children learn that everyone has a fear of something and that it is nothing to be ashamed of. English title available : EVERYBODY'S AFRAID OF SOMETHING.-

152.4
    Vivre seule.
        prod. [Montreal?] : NFB, 1974.- dist. SEC 141 fr. : b&w & col. : 35 mm. & cassette (28 min.) : auto. & aud. adv. sig. & teacher's guide. $18.00 (Points de vue) s

        1. Loneliness. 2. Single women. 3. Divorce.

        Re-enactments of actual case studies reflect three different viewpoints on being alone. Shown is a man suffering from severe depression, a woman coping with seperation and a single individual happily unattached. Useful for discussion on loneliness, depression, separation, divorce, and on changing attitudes toward single women. English title available : TO BE ALONE .-

152.4
When I grow up.
prod. [Toronto] : Int. Cin., 1977.- dist. VEC or Vint. 58 fr. : col. : 35 mm. & cassette (6 min.) : auto. & aud. adv. sig. & teacher's guide. $24.00 (Feelings : $154.00) pj

1. Emotions.

Magic turns an unhappy child into an adult, teaching him that grownups have problems too. Emphasizes adult responsibilities. Good example of roleplaying technique. Illustrated with cartoons. French title available : QUAND JE SERAI GRAND.-

152.4
Your anger.
prod. [Toronto] : M-L, 1973.- dist. Sch. Ser. or Vint. 51 fr. : col. : 35 mm. & cassette (7 min.) : auto. & aud. adv. sig. & teacher's guide. $16.50 (Your emotions : $65.00) j

1. Anger. 2. Ethics.

An enactment of a typical family situation underlining the consequences of losing one's temper. Tom does not want to share his new radio with his brother, and blames the latter when it breaks. As punishment for losing his temper, Tom's father confiscates the radio. Viewers are then asked to discuss Tom's behaviour. French title available : JE ME METS EN COLERE.-

152.4
Your envy.
prod. [Toronto] : M-L, 1973.- dist. Sch. Ser. or Vint. 54 fr. : col. : 35 mm. & cassette (7 min.) : auto. & aud. adv. sig. & teacher's guide. $16.50 (Your emotions : $65.00) j

1. Envy. 2. Ethics.

Envious of a friend's new bicycle, Robbie hesitates to offer a clue when it is stolen. Viewers are asked to decide what they would do in Robbie's place, and to discuss attitudes. French title available : JE L'ENVIE.-

152.4
Your fear.
prod. [Toronto] : M-L, 1973.- dist. Sch. Ser. or Vint. 52 fr. : col. : 35 mm. & cassette (6 min.) : auto. & aud. adv. sig. & teacher's guide. $16.50 (Your emotions : $65.00) j

1. Fear.

Uses a classroom situation to illustrate childhood fears. Nancy, afraid to give a book report in front of the class, explores ways to escape from it. The conclusion is open-ended to encourage group discussion. French title available : J'AI PEUR.-

152.4
Your frustration.
prod. [Toronto] : M-L, 1973.- dist. Sch. Ser. or Vint. 56 fr. : col. : 35 mm. & cassette (7 min.) : auto. & aud. adv. sig. & teacher's guide. $16.50 (Your emotions : $65.00) j

1. Emotions.

Describes Greg's difficulties when he cannot remember his lines in the class play, even with help from his teacher and parents. Viewers are asked what they would do in Greg's situation and to discuss frustrating experiences they have had. French title available : C'EST FRUSTRANT.-

155.2
Vous et votre personnalité.
prod. [Toronto] : M-L, 1974.- dist. Sch. Ser. or Vint. 44 fr. : col. : 35 mm. & cassette (10 min.) : auto. & aud. adv. sig. & teacher's guide. $16.50 (Vie de famille et éducation sexuelle série C : $85.00) pj

1. Personality.

Photographs and graphics are used to explain the effects of hereditary characteristics, environment and physical and emotional differences on personality development. Emphasizes understanding of self and others. English title available :YOU AND YOUR PERSONALITY.-

The Classified Catalogue

155.2
    You and your personality.
        prod. [Toronto] : M-L, 1973.- dist. Sch. Ser. or Vint. 44 fr. : col. : 35 mm. & cassette (10 min.) : auto. & aud. adv. sig. & teacher's guide. $16.50 (Family living and sex education series C : $85.00) ji

        1. Personality.

        Photographs and graphics are used to explain the effects of hereditary characteristics, environment, and physical and emotional differences on personality development. Emphasizes understanding of self and others. French title available : VOUS ET VOTRE PERSONNALITE.-

158
    Le Comportement humain.
        prod. [Toronto] : M-L, 1974.- dist. Sch. Ser. or Vint. 42 fr. : col. : 35 mm. & cassette (7 min.) : auto. & aud. adv. sig. & teacher's guide. $16.50 (Vie de famille et éducation sexuelle série C : $85.00) pj

        1. Human relations.

        Photographs are used to create an understanding of inter-personal relationships. Attempts to develop an awareness of self and a respect for the differences in others. English title available : HUMAN BEHAVIOUR.-

158
    Human behaviour.
        prod. [Toronto] : M-L, 1973.- dist. Sch. Ser. or Vint. 42 fr. : col. : 35 mm. & cassette (7 min.) : auto. & aud. adv. sig. & teacher's guide. $16.50 (Family living and sex education series C : $85.00) ji

        1. Human relations.

        Photographs are used to create an understanding of inter-personal relationships. Attempts to develop an awareness of self and a respect for the differences in others. French title available : LE COMPORTEMENT HUMAIN.-

160.76
    A quoi cela ressemble-t-il?
        prod. [Toronto] : Int. Cin., 1976.- dist. VEC 78 fr. : col. : 35 mm. & cassette (5 min.) : auto. & aud. adv. sig. & teacher's guide. $24.00 (Ouvre l'oeil et le bon... : $230.00) pj

        1. Reasoning - Problems, exercises, etc.

        Children are presented with differently shaped pieces of paper, and through the process of deduction are asked to predict the kinds of geometric shapes and designs that may be created by folding the paper in various ways. Part of a series designed to stimulate thinking and perceptive skills. Useful for Special Education students as well. English title available : HOW WILL IT LOOK?

160.76
    Can you find them?
        prod. [Toronto] : Int. Cin., 1976.- dist. VEC 55 fr. : col. : 35 mm. & cassette (5 min.) : auto. & aud. adv. sig. & teacher's guide, two activity sheets and ten activity cards. $24.00 (Look, listen, discover! : $230.00) pj

        1. Reasoning - Problems, exercise, etc.

        Viewers are shown various objects and shapes, then practise visual recall by locating the object amongst others. Part of a series, designed to involve children in problem-solving activities to challenge thinking powers. Although developed for Special Education classes, it may be used at all elementary levels. French title available : LES OBJETS DISPARUS.-

160.76
    Classons, classons!
        prod. [Toronto] : Int. Cin., 1976.- dist. VEC 57 fr. : col. : 35 mm. & cassette (4 min.) : auto. & aud. adv. sig. & teacher's guide. $24.00 (Ouvre l'oeil et le bon... : $230.00) pj

        1. Reasoning - Problems, exercises, etc.

        Shows how to place groups of objects in order numerically, alphabetically, by size and by colour. Teaches relational and comparative terms. Would be useful for Special Education students as well. English title available : PUT THEM IN ORDER.-

The Classified Catalogue

160.76
    Does it belong?
        prod. [Toronto] : Int. Cin., 1976.- dist. VEC 70 fr. : col. : 35 mm. & cassette (7 min.) : auto. & aud. adv. sig. & teacher's guide, two activity sheets and ten activity cards. $24.00 (Look, listen, discover! : $230.00) pj

        1. Reasoning - Problems, exercises, etc.

        Asks viewers to identify the inconsistency in each of several sequences of pictures. Would be useful for Special Education students. French title available : JE ME SUIS TROMPE DE GROUPE : QUE SUIS-JE?-

160.76
    Ecoute bien...
        prod. [Toronto] : Int. Cin., 1976.- dist. VEC 66 fr. : col. : 35 mm. & cassette (9 min.) : auto. & aud. adv. sig. & teacher's guide. $24.00 (Ouvre l'oeil et le bon... : $230.00) pj

        1. Reasoning - Problems, exercises, etc.

        A game is played where children are asked to pick out the object in the picture from clues given by the narrator. Useful for Special Education students as well. English title available : LISTEN FOR THE CLUES.-

160.76
    How will it look?
        prod. [Toronto] : Int. Cin., 1976.- dist. VEC 78 fr. : col. : 35 mm. & cassette (5 min.) : auto. & aud. adv. sig. & teacher's guide, two activity sheets and ten activity cards. $24.00 (Look, listen, discover! : $230.00) pj

        1. Reasoning - Problems, exercises, etc.

        Children are presented with differently shaped pieces of paper, and through the process of deduction are asked to predict the kinds of geometric shapes and designs that may be created by folding the paper in various ways. Part of a series designed to stimulate thinking and perceptive skills. Useful for Special Education Students as well. French title available : A QUOI CELA RESSEMBLE-T-IL?-

160.76
    Je me suis trompé de groupe : que suis-je?
        prod. [Toronto] : Int. Cin., 1976.- dist. VEC 70 fr. : col. : 35 mm. & cassette (7 min.) : auto. & aud. adv. sig. & teacher's guide. $24.00 (Ouvre l'oeil et le bon... : $230.00) pj

        1. Reasoning - Problems, exercises, etc.

        Asks viewers to identify the inconsistency in each of several sequences of pictures. Would be useful for Special Education students. English title available : DOES IT BELONG?

160.76
    Listen for the clues.
        prod. [Toronto] : Int. Cin., 1976.- dist. VEC 66 fr. : col. : 35 mm. & cassette (9 min.) : auto. & aud. adv. sig. & teacher's guide, two activity sheets and ten activity cards. $24.00 (Look, listen, discover! : $230.00) pj

        1. Reasoning - Problems, exercises, etc.

        A game is played where children are asked to pick out he object in the picture from clues given by the narrator. Useful for Special Education students as well. : ECOUTE BIEN... .-

160.76
    Mets-toi à ma place!
        prod. [Toronto] : Int. Cin., 1976.- dist. VEC 56 fr. : col. : 35 mm. & cassette (5 min.) : auto. & aud. adv. sig. & teacher's guide. $24.00 (Ouvre l'oeil et le bon... : $230.00) pj

        1. Reasoning - Problems, exercises , etc.

        Children watch as a photographer moves around three objects on a table, photographing them from various angles. The children are asked to visualize what each picture will look like, which introduces them to spatial relationships between objects, and an awareness of viewpoint. Useful for Special Education Students as well. English title available : PICK THE PICTURE.-

160.76
    Les Objets disparus.
        prod. [Toronto] : Int. Cin., 1976.- dist. VEC 55 fr. : col. : 35 mm. & cassette (5 min.) : auto. & aud. adv. sig. & teacher's guide. $24.00 (Ouvre l'oeil et le bon... : $230.00) pj

        1. Reasoning - Problems, exercises, etc.

        Viewers are shown various objects and shapes, then practise visual recall by locating the object amongst others. Part of a series, designed to involve children in problem-solving activities to challenge thinking powers. Although developed for Special Education classes, it may be used at all elementary levels. English title available : CAN YOU FIND THEM?

The Classified Catalogue

160.76
    Pick the picture.
        prod. [Toronto] : Int. Cin., 1976.- dist. VEC 56 fr. : col. : 35 mm. & cassette (5 min.) : auto. & aud. adv. sig. & teacher's guide, two activity sheets and ten activity cards. $24.00 (Look, listen, discover! : $230.00) pj

        1. Reasoning - Problems, exercises, etc.

        Children watch as photographer moves around three objects on a table, photographing them from various angles. The children are asked to visualize what each picture will look like, which introduces them to spatial relationships between objects, and an awareness of viewpoint. Useful for special education students as well. French title available : METS-TOI A MA PLACE!-

160.76
    Put them in order.
        prod. [Toronto] : Int. Cin., 1976- dist. VEC 57 fr. : col. : 35 mm. & cassette (5 min.) : auto. & aud. adv. sig. & teacher's guide, two activity sheets and ten activity cards. $24.00 (Look, listen, discover! : $230.00) pj

        1. Reasoning - Problems, exercises, etc.

        Shows how to place groups of objects in order numerically, alphabetically, by size and by colour. Teaches relational and comparative terms. Would be useful for Special Eduation Students as well. French title available : CLASSONS, CLASSONS!-

160.76
    Qu'est-ce qui manque?
        prod. [Toronto] : Int. Cin., 1976.- dist. VEC 53 fr. : col. : 35 mm. & cassette (7 min.) : auto. & aud. adv. sig. & teacher's guide. $24.00 (Ouvre l'oeil et le bon... : $230.00) pj

        1. Reasoning - Problems, exercises, etc.

        Children identify items which have been removed from a group of objects. Would be useful for Special Education students as well. English title available : WHAT'S MISSING?-

160.76
    Qu'est-ce qui ne va pas?
        prod. [Toronto] : Int. Cin., 1976.- dist. VEC 47 fr. : col. : 35 mm. & cassette (5 min.) : auto. & aud. adv. sig. & teacher's guide. $24.00 (Ouvre l'oeil et le bon... : $230.00) pj

        1. Reasoning - Problems, exercises, etc.

        Children examine various situations where something has been done incorrectly. They are encouraged to determine what is wrong, thereby learning about order, sequence and noticing detail. Useful for Special Education students as well. English title available : WHAT'S WRONG HERE?-

160.76
    Trouvons les ressemblance.
        prod. [Toronto] : Int. Cin., 1976.- dist. VEC 59 fr. : col. : 35 mm. & cassette (6 min.) : auto. & aud. adv. sig. & teacher's guide. $24.00 (Ouvre l'oeil et le bon... : $230.00) pj

        1. Reasoning - Problems, exercises, etc.

        Encourages children to look for and identify the common element in a series of pictures. Useful for Special Education students as well. English title available : WHAT DO THEY HAVE IN COMMON?-

160.76
    What do they have in common.
        prod. [Toronto] : Int. Cin., 1976.- dist. VEC 59 fr. : col. : 35 mm. & cassette (6 min.) : auto. & aud. adv. sig. & teacher's guide, two activity sheets and ten activity cards. $24.00 (Look, listen, discover! : $230.00) pj

        1. Reasoning - Problems, exercises, etc.

        Encourages children to look for and identify the common element in a series of pictures. Useful for special education students as well. French title available : TROUVONS LA RESSEMBLANCE.-

The Classified Catalogue

160.76
What's missing?
prod. [Toronto] : Int. Cin., 1976.- dist. VEC 53 fr. : col. : 35 mm. & cassette (7 min.) : auto. & aud. adv. sig. & teacher's guide, two activity sheets and ten activity cards. $24.00 (Look, listen, discover! : $230.00) pj

1. Reasoning - Problems, exercises, etc.

Children identify items which have been removed from a group of objects. Would be useful for Special Education Students as well. French title available : QU'EST-CE QUI MANQUE?-

160.76
What's wrong here?
prod. [Toronto] : Int. Cin., 1976.- dist. VEC 47 fr. : col. : 35 mm. & cassette (4 min.) : auto. & aud. adv. sig. & teacher's guide, two activity sheets and ten activity cards. $24.00 (Look, listen, discover! : $230.00) pj

1. Reasoning - Problems, exercises, etc.

Children examine various situations where something has been done incorrectly. They are encouraged to determine what is wrong, there by learning about order, sequence and noticing detail. Useful for Special Education students as well. French title available : QU'EST-CE QUI NE VA PAS?

160.76
Which group will they go to?
prod. [Toronto] : Int. Cin., 1976.- dist. VEC 54 fr. : col. : 35 mm. & cassette (5 min.) : auto. & aud. adv. sig. & teacher's guide, two activity sheets and ten activity cards. $24.00 (Look, listen, discover! : $230.00) pj

1. Reasoning - Problems, exercises, etc.

Six cartoon characters group and re-group themselves according to different classification principles, such as colour of clothing and size. Children are asked to identify type of classification being used, and how characters will be split up. Would be useful for special education students as well. French title available : LES ENSEMBLES.-

173
Ce qu'est la maturite.
prod. [Toronto] : M-L, 1974.- dist. Sch. Ser. or Vint. 43 fr. : col. : 35 mm. & cassette (7 min.) : auto. & aud. adv. sig. & teacher's guide. $16.50 (Vie de famille et éducation sexuelle série C : $85.00) pj

1. Family life education.

Uses photos and graphics to encourage discussion on factors necessary for being responsible parents. English title available : THE MEANING OF MATURITY.-

173
The Meaning of maturity.
prod. [Toronto] : M-L, 1973.- dist. Sch. Ser. or Vint. 43 fr. : col. : 35 mm. & cassette (11 min.) : auto. & aud. adv. sig. & teacher's guide. $16.50 (Family living and sex education series C : $85.00) ji

1. Family life education.

Uses photos and graphics to encourage discussion on factors necessary for being responsible parents. French title available : CE QU'EST LA MATURITE.-

174
Values : yours and theirs.
prod. [Toronto] : M-L, 1975.- dist. Sch. Ser. or Vint. 52 fr. : col. : 35 mm. & cassette (8 min.) : auto. & aud. adv. sig. & teacher's guide. $16.50 (Maturity : options and consequences : $85.00) is

1. Business ethics.

Depicts the problem encountered by two young men in their summer jobs when the dishonesty of their employer's working procedures becomes apparent.-

176
Growing up.
prod. [Toronto] : M-L, 1975.- dist. Sch. Ser. or w Vint. 60 fr. : col. : 35 mm. & cassette (8 min.) : auto. & aud. adv. sig. & teacher's guide. $16.50 (Maturity : options and consequences : $85.00) is

1. Sexual ethics. 2. Unmarried couples. 3. Dating (Social customs).

Discussion between a teen-age girl and her father, and with her girl friend. Points out the problems of teen-age intimacy. Promotes consideration of several moral issues facing today's teen-agers.-

The Classified Catalogue

176
    To be together.
        prod. [Montreal?] : NFB, 1974.- dist. McI. 137 fr. : b&w & col. : 35 mm. & cassette (26 min.) : auto. & aud. adv. sig. & teacher's guide. $18.00 (A Question of values) s

        1. Sexual ethics.   2. Marriage.
        3. Homosexuality.   4. Life styles.

        Explores effect of changing social and sexual values upon Canadian lifestyles. Featured are a married couple, a common-law couple, and a gay couple. Re-enactments of actual case studies encourages further discussion on pros and cons of traditional and alternative lifestyles. French title available : VIVRE ENSEMBLE.-

176
    Vivre ensemble.
        prod. [Montreal?] : NFB, 1974.- dist. SEC 137 fr. : b&w & col. : 35 mm. & cassette (26 min.) : auto. & aud. adv. sig. & teacher's guide. $18.00 (Points de vue) s

        1. Sexual ethics.   2. Marriage.
        3. Homosexuality.   4. Life styles.

        Explores effect of changing social and sexual values upon Canadian lifestyles. Featured are a married couple, a common-law couple, and a gay couple. Re-enactments of actual case studies encourages further discussion on pros and cons of traditional and alternative lifestyles. English title available : TO BE TOGETHER.-

177
    Deceit.
        prod. [Toronto] : M-L, 1975.- dist. Sch. Ser. or Vint. 54 fr. : col. : 35 mm. & cassette (10 min.) : auto. & aud. adv. sig. & teacher's guide. $16.50 (Character awareness : $85.00) is

        1. Truthfulness and falsehood.

        A comprehensive picture of the motivation for and the results of lying. At a new high school a student lies about his ability as a swimmer to impress a girl. The other students become angry when the student fails to show up for team practices.-

177
    La générosité.
        prod. [Toronto] : M-L, 1975.- dist. Sch. Ser. or Vint. 47 fr. : col. : 35 mm. & cassette (10 min.) : auto. & aud. adv. sig. & teacher's guide. $16.50 (Attitudes morales : $75.00) pj

        1. Behavior.

        Dramatic presentation of a situation involving a young girl who must decide whether or not to share with others. Four alternative solutions to the situation encourage children to reach their own decision avoiding simplistic solutions. Of most value in a classroom situation where discussion can take place. English title available : GENEROSITY.-

177
    The Grocery cart and noise.
        prod. [Edmonton] : PPH, 1974.- dist. PPH 10 fr. : col. : 35 mm. & teacher's guide. (Now what : $35.00) pj

        1. Behavior.

        Two stories about children misusing a grocery cart and playing loudly near a sleeping baby. Format promotes discussion on responsibility and consideration for others. Illustrated with cartoons. To be used with manual. Part of a series.-

177
    The Living room and clothes.
        prod. [Edmonton] : PPH, 1974.- dist. PPH 9 fr. : col. : 35 mm. & teacher's guide. (Now what : $35.00) pj

        1. Behavior.

        Justice, equality and freedom are themes in these two stories where a clean room is mussed and well-dressed children poke fun at a child in patched clothes. Teacher's manual to be used in leading discussion about feelings and values. Illustrated with cartoons. Part of a series.-

The Classified Catalogue

179

The Chocolate bar and the bicycle.
  prod. [Edmonton] : PPH, 1974.- dist. PPH 19 fr. : col. : 35 mm. & teacher's guide. (Now what : $35.00) pj

  1. Behavior.

  Uses cartoons to illustrate two stories about consideration, honesty and justice. One story concerns carelessness with a bicycle, the other illustrates stealing. Encourages children to consider consequences of an action. Part of a series.-

179

Courage.
  prod. [Toronto] : M-L, 1975.- dist. Sch. Ser. or Vint. 52 fr. : col. : 35 mm. & cassette (10 min.) : auto. & aud. adv. sig. & teacher's guide. $16.50 (Character awareness : $85.00) is

  1. Courage.

  The quality of courage is examined in a realistic situation. Emphasizes the difference between showing off in a careless way and a courageous act that is carefully thought out.-

179

La culpabilité.
  prod. [Toronto] : M-L, 1975.- dist. Sch. Ser. or Vint. 49 fr. : col. : 35 mm. & cassette (10 min.) : auto. & aud. adv. sig. & teacher's guide. $16.50 (Attitudes morales : $75.00) pj

  1. Behavior.

  A young girl narrates a familiar situation which involves problem-solving and moral decision-making. Four alternative solutions are presented which demonstrate different ways of handling the situation. Each ending provides an opportunity for class discussion of personal moral values. English title available : GUILT.-

179

Guilt.
  prod. [Toronto] : M-L, 1973.- dist. Sch. Ser. or Vint. 49 fr. : col. : 35 mm. & cassette (10 min.) : auto. & aud. adv. sig. & teacher's guide. $16.50 (Moral decision-making : $75.00) kpi

  1. 2. Ethics. 3. Guilt.

  A young girl narrates a familiar situation which involves problem-solving and moral decision-making. Four alternative solutions are presented which demonstrate different ways of handling the situation. Each ending provides an opportunity for class discussion of personal moral values. French title available : LA CULPABILITE.-

179

L'honnêteté.
  prod. [Toronto] : M-L, 1975.- dist. Sch. Ser. or Vint. 51 fr. : col. : 35 mm. & cassette (10 min.) : auto. & aud. adv. sig. & teacher's guide. $16.50 (Attitudes morales : $75.00) pj

  1. Honesty.

  Dramatic presentation of a realistic situation concerning honesty. Narrated by a young boy who is overpaid by a paper route customer and must then decide what to do with the extra money. Five different solutions are presented in sequence to allow for class discussion. English title available: HONESTY.-

179

L'Hostilité.
  prod. [Toronto] : M-L, 1975.- dist. Sch. Ser. or Vint. 47 fr. : col. : 35 mm. & cassette (10 min.) : auto. & aud. adv. sig. & teacher's guide. $16.50 (Attitudes morales : $75.00) pj

  1. Behavior.

  The dramtic presentation of a hostile situation in which a young boy must make a moral decision. Five alternative endings are shown of possible ways in which the boy might react to the situations in order to select an appropriate solution. Suitable for class presentation where discussion can take place. English title availabe : HOSTILITY.-

The Classified Catalogue

179
Hostility.
  prod. [Toronto] : M-L, 1973.- dist. Sch. Ser. or Vint. 47 fr. : col. : 35 mm. & cassette (10 min.) : auto. & aud. adv. sig. & teacher's guide. $16.50 (Moral decision making : $75.00) kpi

  1. Behavior.

  The dramatic presentation of a hostile situation in which a young boy must make a moral decision. Five alternative endings are shown of possible ways in which the boy might react to the situation. A realistic and interesting means of encouraging children to analyse situations in order to select an appropriate solution. Suitable for class presentation where discussion can take place. French title available: L'HOSTILITE.-

179
L'intégrité.
  prod. [Toronto] : M-L, 1975.- dist. Sch. Ser. or Vint. 39 fr. : col. : 35 mm. & cassette (7 min.) : auto. & aud. adv. sig. & teacher's guide. $16.50 (Attitudes morales : $75.00) pj

  1. Behavior.

  A dramatic presentation of a realistic situation where a young boy is presented with an opportunity to cheat on a test. Four alternative endings follow with opportunity for discussion. A thought-provoking presentation of the concept of right and wrong which avoids simplistic solutions. English title available : INTEGRITY.-

179
Integrity.
  prod. [Toronto] : M-L, 1973.- dist. Sch. Ser. or Vint. 39 fr. : col. : 35 mm. & cassette (7 min.) : auto. & aud. adv. sig. & teacher's guide. $16.50 (Moral decision-making : $75.00) kpi

  1. Behavior.

  A dramatic presentation of a realistic situation where a young boy is presented with an opportunity to cheat on a test. Four alternative endings follow with an opportunity for discussion. A thought-provoking presentation of the concept of right and wrong which avoids simplistic solutions. French title available : L'INTEGRITE.-

179
Jealousy.
  prod. [Toronto] : M-L, 1975.- dist. Sch. Ser. or Vint. 63 fr. : col. : 35 mm. & cassette (9 min.) : auto. & aud. adv. sig. & teacher's guide. $16.50 (Character awareness : $85.00) is

  1. Jealousy.

  A presentation of several realistic situations that give rise to feelings of jealousy. Students are encouraged to see these as natural feelings and to appreciate their own good attributes.-

179
Loyalty.
  prod. [Toronto] : M-L, 1975.- dist. Sch. Ser. or Vint. 53 fr. : col. : 35 mm. & cassette (9 min.) : auto. & aud. adv. sig. & teacher's guide. $16.50 (Character awareness : $85.00) is

  1. Loyalty.

  A student is torn between loyalty to her friend who is workig hard for an essay contest and to her brother who is paying a college student to write the essay for him. Presents problems that could confront students.-

179
Perseverance.
  prod. [Toronto] : M-L, 1975.- dist. Sch. Ser. or Vint. 55 fr. : col. : 35 mm. & cassette (10 min.) : auto. & aud. adv. sig. & teacher's guide. $16.50 (Character awareness : $85.00) is

  1. Behavior.

  The story of two boys, one a fine athlete and the other, his friend, who is learning gymnastics. Emphasizes that persistence and hard work are important in learning a new skill. Includes a discussion of Mary who overcame a leg injury to become a fine athlete. A useful aid to encourage students in their endeavours.-

The Classified Catalogue

179
    The Test and bottles.
        prod. [Edmonton] : PPH, 1974.- dist. PPH 10 fr. : col. : 35 mm. & teacher's guide. (Now what : $35.00) pj

        1. Behavior.

        Cartoons illustrate stories of a child cheating during an exam and a child caught breaking bottles. Viewers are asked to express opinions and discuss feelings of those involved in situation. Brings out values of honesty, loyalty, justice and pride. To be used with manual. Part of a series.-

179
    Vanity.
        prod. [Toronto] : M-L, 1975.- dist. Sch. Ser. or VInt. 78 fr. : col. : 35 mm. & cassette (12 min.) : auto. & aud. adv. sig. & teacher's guide. $16.50 (Character awareness : $85.00) is

        1. Behavior.

        Presents many sides of a realistic situation involving a student who is excessively vain about her talents as a dancer. All the participants in a musical show learn valuable lessons.-

179
    Wet cement and the radio.
        prod. [Edmonton] : PPH, 1974.- dist. PPH 9 fr. : col. : 35 mm. & teacher's guide. (Now what : $35.00) pj

        1. Behavior.

        Two stories about a boy who steals a radio and runs through a recently laid sidewalk. The manual encourages discussion on honesty and justice. Illustrated with cartoons. Part of a series.-

232.9
    Super Jesus.
        prod. [Toronto] : M-L, 1974.- dist. Sch. Ser. or VInt. 72 fr. : col. : 35 mm. & cassette (13 min.) : auto. & aud. adv. sig. & teacher's guide. $16.50 (Famous stories of great courage : $85.00) i

        1. Jesus Christ - Biography.

        Outlines the events in Jesus' life from the age of thirty until his death. Includes his entrance into Jerusalem on Palm Sunday, the Last Supper, his arrest, and his death. Stresses Jesus' great courage and kindness. French title available : JESUS : HOMME-DIEU.-

289.9
    Hutterite persecution : 1526-1917.
        prod. [Scarborough] : R.B.M., 1978.- dist. ETHOS 46 fr. : b&w & col. : 35 mm. & cassette (12 min.) : auto. & aud. adv. sig. & reading script. $21.50 (Canadian folk culture : the Hutterites : $79.00) is

        1. Hutterites - History.

        Persecution of this non-violent religious group in Europe and United States is examined. Shows Hutterites' continuation of European heritage through communal lifestyle, beliefs, dress and crafts. Comprehensive treatment with drawings, photographs of communities, artwork and religious artifacts.-

292
    Noble Hercules.
        prod. [Toronto] : M-L, 1974.- dist. Sch. Ser. or Vint. 58 fr. : col. : 35 mm. & cassette (16 min.) : auto. & aud. adv. sig. & teacher's guide. $16.50 (Famous stories of great courage :$85.00) i

        1. Mythology, Classical.

        Uses expressive drawings to tell the story of Hercules, Son of Zeus. Describes how Hercules strangles two snakes with his bare hands, his victory over King Erginus, and liberation of Thebes. An interesting introduction to Greek mythology. French title available : LE GRAND HERCULE.-

296.4
    The Jewish people.
        prod. [Edmonton] : PPH, 1974.- dist. PPH 40 fr. : col. : 35 mm. & cassette (13 min.) : auto. & aud. adv. sig. & teacher's guide. $27.50 pj

        1. Judaism.

        An introduction to Jewish religious practices, describing and explaining the synagogue, some of the religious services and holidays, a traditional Sabbath, a Bar-Mitzvah, and the importance of Israel to the Jewish people.-

The Classified Catalogue

296.4
    Passover.
        prod. [Edmonton] : PPH, 1974.- dist. PPH 41 fr. : col. : 35 mm. & cassette (11 min.) : auto. & aud. adv. sig. & teacher's guide. $27.50 pj

        1. Passover. 2. Fasts and feasts - Judaism.

        Describes and explains the customs and tradition of the Passover ceremony. Includes a script in simpler terms for elementary children, and one suitable for older students and adults.-

299
    Drugs and religious ritual.
        prod. [Montreal?] : NFB, 1972.- dist. McI. 51 fr. : b&w & col. : 35 mm. & disc (33 1/3 rpm. mono. 12 min.) : auto. & aud. adv. sig. $9.00 s

        1. Indians of North America - Religion. 2. Indians of South America - Religion. 3. Drug abuse - History.

        A comprehensive account of the origins and development of drug use in North and South America. Drawings, historical photographs and prints illustrate the plants used by native peoples to achieve an altered state of consiousness, and role of the Shaman, Medicine man and priest in directing the use of these drugs for medical and religious purposes. Indicates how this aspect of native life was eliminated through introduction of distilled liquor to the cultures.-

299
    Mother Earth : an Indian view.
        prod. [Scarborough, Ont.] : R.B.M., 1974.- dist. ETHOS 76 fr. : b&w & col. : 35 mm. & cassette (18 min.) : auto. & aud. adv. sig. & reading script. $19.00 (Indian culture in Canada : $69.00) jis

        1. Indians of North America - Canada - Religion.

        A combination of photographs and artwork illustrate the four roles played by the earth in the Canadian Indian's concept of life : as a home, as an actual being, as a teacher, and as a community made up of all things, living and inanimate.-

299
    Spirits and monsters.
        prod. [Toronto] : Int. Cin., 1975.- dist. VEC 55 fr. : col. : 35 mm. & cassette (5 min.) : auto. & aud. adv. sig. & teacher's guide. $24.00 (The Arctic through Eskimo eyes : $86.00) ji

        1. Eskimos - Religion. 2. Folklore, Eskimo.

        Using authentic drawings, music, and translations of their tales, Cape Dorset Eskimos illustrate the role the shaman, spirits and monsters played, and still play, in the day-to-day business of survival.-

301.31
    The City : laboratory of history.
        prod. [Scarborough, Ont.] : R.B.M., 1975.- dist. ETHOS 46 fr. : col. : 35 mm. & cassette (12 min.) : auto. & aud adv. sig. & teacher's manual. $19.00 (Urban studies : $103.50) ji

        1. Metropolitan areas.

        Presents the changing city as an opportunity for observing history first hand. Illustrated with photographs showing changes in transportation, neighborhoods and architecture over the years.-

301.34
    Aging of the urban site.
        prod. [Scarborough, Ont.] : R.B.M., 1974.- dist. ETHOS 92 fr. : col. : 35 mm. & cassette (11 min.) : auto. & aud. adv. sig. & teacher's guide. $19.00 (Urbanism in Canada) ji

        1. Metropolitan areas.

        Introduces the concentric ring, sector, and multiple nuclei theories of urban growth, illustrating each of these theories with diagrams and photographs. Also discusses the effects of centripetal forces on urban change.-

301.34
    City life.
        prod. [Toronto] : Int. Cin., 1975.- dist. VEC 70 fr. : col. : 35 mm. & cassette (7 min.) : auto. & aud. adv. sig. & teacher's manual. $24.00 (Cityscapes : $64.00) pjis

        1. City life.

        An unusual introduction to a study of the city and urban geography. Its imaginative approach, photography and musical score make it also useful for art, and language as well as remedial and special education.-

The Classified Catalogue

301.34
  City moods.
    prod. [Toronto] : Int. Cin., 1975.- dist. VEC 70 fr. : col. : 35 mm. & cassette (7 min.) : auto. & aud. adv. sig. & teacher's manual. $24.00 (Cityscapes : $64.00) pjis

    1. City life.

    An interesting collection of people, architecture, colours, textures, and seasons in the city, showing how they create various city moods. Its imaginative approach, photography and music make it useful for art and language as well as remedial and special education.-

301.34
  City patterns.
    prod. [Toronto] : Int. Cin., 1975.- dist. VEC 70 fr. : col. : 35 mm. & cassette (5 min.) : auto. & aud. adv. sig. & teacher's manual. $24.00 (Cityscapes : $64.00) pjis

    1. City life.

    A display of both old and new in the city, pointing out continuing similarities in shapes and designs of city architecture. Its imaginative approach, photography and music make it useful for art and language as well as remedial and special education.-

301.34
  Industrial community 1 : patterns of growth.
    prod. [Don Mills, Ont.] : F & W, 1973.- dist. F & W 25 fr. : col.: 35 mm. & captions & teacher's guide. $7.20 (Man in his world) ji

    1. Metropolitan areas.

    Illustrates how modern industrial communities grow due to certain natural advantages related to agriculture and communications. Also shows the similar growth patterns of an industrialized community.-

301.34
  Problems of urban environment.
    prod. [Scarborough, Ont.] : R.B.M., 1975.- dist. ETHOS 49 fr. : col. : 35 mm. & cassette (14 min.) : auto. & aud. adv. sig. & teacher's manual. $19.00 (Urban studies : $103.50) ji

    1. Metropolitan areas.

    Discusses urban problems such as the automobile, polluted air and water, noise, congestion, urban sprawl, as well as the need to provide services and recreational opportunities.-

301.34
  Recreation : the Canadian city.
    prod. [Scarborough, Ont.] : R.B.M., 1974.- dist. ETHOS 49 fr. : col. : 35 mm. & cassette (12 min.) : auto. & aud. adv. sig. & teacher's guide. $19.00 (Urbanism in Canada) ji

    1. City life.

    Records the various types of seasonal recreational activities available to the Canadian city dweller, such as shopping, cultural events, and sports of all kinds.-

301.34
  Suburban site.
    prod. [Scarborough, Ont.] : R.B.M., 1974.- dist. ETHOS 75 fr. : col. : 35 mm. &dcassette (8 min.) : auto. & aud. adv. sig. & teacher's guide. $19.00 (Urbanism in Canada) ji

    1. Metropolitan areas.

    An introduction to the modern-day suburb. Includes the advantages and disadvantages associated with suburban living, types of suburban housing developments, and the role of transportation in the creation of suburbs.-

301.34
  Urban culture.
    prod. [Scarborough, Ont.] : R.B.M., 1975.- dist. ETHOS 82 fr. : col. : 35 mm. & cassette (12 min.) : auto. & aud. adv. sig. & teacher's manual. $19.00 (Urbanism in Canada) ji

    1. Metropolitan areas. 2. City life.

    Identifys and illustrates, with photographs from across Canada, some of the cultural aspects found in urban centres. Includes literature, the arts, science, museums, government, sports, religion, entertainment, and markets.-

301.34
  The Urban revolution : the first cities.
    prod. [Montreal?] : NFB, 1972.- dist. McI. 86 fr. : b&w & col. : 35 mm. & captions & cassette (15 min.) : auto. & aud. adv. sig. $18.00 is

    1. Metropolitan areas.

    Considers the origin and development of cities, providing a detailed description of the beginning of cities in the Middle East.-

The Classified Catalogue

301.34
  Urbanization : the new accent on cities.
    prod. [Toronto] : Int. Cin., 1978.- dist. VEC 81 fr. : b&w & col. : 35 mm. & cassette (15 min.) : auto. & aud. adv. sig. & teacher's guide. $24.00 (Canada and its regions : the geography of a changing land : $155.00) ji

    1. Cities and towns - Canada.

    An analysis of urbanization and growth of suburbs in Canada. Indicates factors which determine location of major Canadian cities and which contribute to or hinder growth. Outlines advantages and disadvantages of city living and need to use city space wisely avoiding inadequate planning.-

301.34
  What is a community?
    prod. [Scarborough, Ont.] : R.B.M., 1975.- dist. ETHOS 53 fr. : col. : 35 mm. & cassette (12 min.) : auto. & aud. adv. sig. & teacher's manual. $19.00 (Community studies : $69.00) i

    1. Cities and towns.

    Identifies and describes characteristics common to any community. Factors covered in the discussion include commercial, recreational, and industrial areas, production of goods and services, government, transportation and communication, and history.-

301.340971
  Kinds of Canadian communities.
    prod. [Scarborough, Ont.] : R.B.M., 1975.- dist. ETHOS 53 fr. : col. : 35 mm. & cassette (12 min.) : auto. & aud. adv. sig. & teacher's manual. $19.00 (Community studies : $69.00) i

    1. Cities and towns - Canada.

    Discusses Canadian communities of many kinds. Included are those with an agricultural or industrial base, those serving special purposes, such as tourist centers and historical replicas, and those in remote areas or special locations, such as fishing ports, northern settlements and island communities.-

301.340971
  Kinds of urban centres.
    prod. [Scarborough, Ont.] : R.B.M., 1974.- dist. ETHOS 93 fr. : col. : 35 mm. & cassette (13 min.) : auto. & aud. adv. sig. & teacher's guide. $19.00 (Urbanism in Canada) ji

    1. Metropolitan areas.

    Illustrates the various kinds of urban centres in Canada today with photographs of London, Ontario, a market and service centre, Kitchener, a market and manufacturing centre, Winnipeg and Montreal, route centres, Halifax, Thunder Bay, and Vancouver, transportation terminals, Hamilton, an industrial centre, Elliott Lake and Sudbury, resource centres.-

301.41
  C'est pas facile!
    prod. [Montreal?] : NFB, 1975.- dist. SEC 77 fr. : b&w & col. : 35 mm. & cassette (16 min.) : auto. & aud. adv. sig. & teacher's guide. $18.00 (Savoir ... sentir) is

    1. Sex discrimination.

    A presentation designed to stimulate discussion on new options open to men and women as a result of change in traditional social values. Compares past and present attitudes toward the sexes, to reflect changing social atmosphere. Illustrated with collages. English title available : IT ISN'T EASY.-

301.41
  It isn't easy.
    prod. [Montreal?] : NFB, 1975.- dist. McI. 77 fr. : b&w & col. : 35 mm. & cassette (16 min.) : auto. & aud. adv. sig. & teacher's guide. $18.00 (Facts and feelings) is

    1. Sex discrimination.

    A presentation designed to stimulate discussion on new options open to men and women as a result of change in traditional social values. Compares past and present attitudes toward the sexes, to reflect changing social atmosphere. Illustrated with collages. French title available : C'EST PAS FACILE.-

The Classified Catalogue

301.41
    Teenage father.
        prod. [Toronto] : M-L, 1975.- dist. Sch. Ser. or Vint. 52 fr. : col. : 35 mm. & cassette (7 min.) : auto. & aud. adv. sig. & teacher's guide. $16.50 (Maturity : options & consequences : $85.00) is

        1. Unmarried mothers. 2. Unmarried couples.

        Illustrates the problems facing an unwed teen-age couple expecting a baby. Includes discussions between Ted and Jeannie (the father and mother to be) and a discussion with an adoption agency counsellor. Stresses that decisions cannot be easily made.-

301.41
    Teenage mother.
        prod. [Toronto] : M-L, 1975.- dist. Sch. Ser. or Vint. 47 fr. : col. : 35 mm. & cassette (7 min.) : auto. & aud. adv. sig. & teacher's guide. $16.50 (Maturity : options & consequences : $85.00) is

        1. Unmarried mothers.

        A doctor presents the alternative open to Jeannie, an unmarried pregnant 15 year old. Reluctant to face the problems, Jeannie finally realizes the importance of the decisions she has to make, and how they will affect her family.-

301.410971
    From Europe to Parliament Hill.
        prod.]Scarborough] : SHN, 1973.- dist. PHM 93 fr. : b&w & col. : 35 mm. & cassette (25 min.) : auto. & aud. adv. sig. & study guide. $39.60 (Women in Canada : $63.30) s

        1. Women - Canada. 2. Women - Suffrage.

        Examines the contributions of Canadian women. Includes Madeleine de Vercherres, Laura Secord, Emily Stowe, Pauline Johnson, and Emily Carr. Discusses Nellie McClung and the Suffragette Movement.-

301.410971
    From franchise to freedom.
        prod. [Scarborough] : SHN, 1973.- dist. PHM 91 fr. : b&w & col. : 35 mm. & cassette (27 min.) : auto. & aud. adv. sig. & study guide. $39.60 (Women in Canada : $63.30) s

        1. Women - Civil rights. 2. Women - Canada.

        Outlines development of women's rights. Shows accomplishments of many Canadian women in the fields of politics, law, engineering, and theatre. Presents many successful women of today, including Charlotte Whitton, Judy LaMarsh, Kate Reid, and Margaret Atwood.-

301.42
    Backwards is forwards in reverse.
        prod. [Montreal?] : NFB, 1974.- dist. McI. 29 fr. : col. : 35 mm. & cassette (8 min.) : auto. & aud. adv. sig. & manual. $18.00 (Living and growing) p

        1. Family.

        Conversation during a family gathering of the cartoon characters brings out role of the family in continuing life. Explains generation concept, reproduction, growth and change within a family. Mentions how families differ in number of parents, grandparents, and children. French title available : DERRIERE EST DEVANT SENS DEVANT DERRIERE.-

301.42
    Derriere est devant sens devant derriere.
        prod. [Montreal?] : NFB, 1974.- dist. SEC 29 fr. : col. : 35 mm. & cassette (8 min.) : auto. & aud. adv. sig. & manual. $18.00 (La vie qui pousse) p

        1. Family.

        Conversation during a family gathering of the cartoon characters brings out role of the family in continuing life. Explains generation concept, reproduction, growth and change within a family. Mentions how families differ in number of parents, grandparents, and children. English title available : BACKWARDS IS FORWARDS IN REVERSE.-

The Classified Catalogue

301.450971
    Black Canadians.
        prod. [Toronto] : M-L, 1976.- dist. Sch. Ser. or Vint. 63 fr. : b&w & col. : 35 mm. & cassette (13 min.) : auto. & aud. & adv. sig. & teacher's guide. $16.50 (The Canadian mosaic : $105.00) is

        1. Blacks in Canada - History.

        Explores the history of black people in Canada, and creates an awareness of the existence of racial prejudice both in the past and present. Describes slavery in Canada in the 1700's and how the efforts of heroic black Canadians of such as Josiah Henson and Mary Ann Chad helped improve the black image in Canada. Reviews Canada's changing racial situation today.-

301.450971
    British Canadians.
        prod. [Toronto] : M-L, 1976.- dist. Sch. Ser. or Vint. 62 fr. : b&w & col. : 35 mm. & cassette (13 min.) : auto. & aud. adv. sig. & teacher's guide. $16.50 (The Canadian mosaic : $105.00) is

        1. British in Canada - History. 2. Canada - Immigration and emigration - History.

        Uses paintings and photographs, to examine the effects of British culture on the development of Canada as an independent nation. Explains reasons for various waves of British immigration.-

301.450971
    Chinese and Japanese Canadians.
        prod. [Toronto] : M-L, 1976.- dist. Sch. Ser. or Vint. 67 fr. : b&w & col. : 35 mm. & cassette (19 min.) : auto. & aud. adv. sig. & teacher's guide. $16.50 (The Canadian mosaic : $105.00) is

        1. Japanese in Canada - History. 2. Chinese inCanada - History.

        A detailed look at Canada's treatment of its Chinese and Japanese citizens in the past. Explains the internment of the Japanese living on the British Columbia coast during World War II.-

301.450971
    Chinese contribution to Canadian life.
        prod. [Scarborough, Ont.] : RBM, 1978.- dist. ETHOS 44 fr. : b&w & col. : 35 mm. & cassette (10 min.) : auto. & aud. adv. sig. & reading script. $19.00 (Canadian folk culture : the Chinese : $79.00) s

        1. Chinese in Canada.

        An analysis of the thriving Chinese communities found in Canada today. Gives examples of adaptation and contribution to Canadian lifestyle and retention of traditions and beliefs. Improved social status exemplified by several well-known Chinese Canadians in variety of careers are featured. Includes photographs of Chinatowns in Toronto and Vancouver.-

301.450971
    Difficulties of Chinese immigrants.
        prod. [Scarborough, Ont.] : RBM, 1978.- dist. ETHOS 46 fr. : b&w & col. : 35 mm. & cassette (11 min.) : auto. & aud. adv. sig. & reading script. $19.00 (Canadian folk culture : the Chinese : $79.00) s

        1. Chinese in Canada - History. 2. Canada - Race relations - History. 3. Canada - Immigration and emigration - History.

        Recounts anti-Asiatic feelings toward Chinese immigrants from their first arrival in Canada in 1858. Discusses their role as labourers during gold rush and building of CPR. Describes efforts of British Columbia government to impose immigration restrictions.-

301.450971
    The First Chinese communities in British Columbia.
        prod. [Scarborough, Ont.] : RBM, 1978.- dist. ETHOS 46 fr. : b&w & col. : 35 mm. & cassette (13 min.) : auto. & aud. adv. sig. & reading script. $19.00 (Canadian folk culture : the Chinese : $79.00) s

        1. Chinese in British Columbia - History. 2. Canada - Race relations - History. 3. Canada - Immigration and emigration - History.

        Focuses on construction of isolated Chinese communities as a result of prejudice and government-imposed restrictions. Describes crude living conditions, and growth of benevolent societies to alleviate problems. Illustrated with archival photographs.-

The Classified Catalogue

301.450971
  French Canadians.
    prod. [Toronto] : M-L, 1976.- dist. Sch. Ser. or Vint. 73 fr. : b&w & col. : 35 mm. & cassette (13 min.) : auto. & aud. adv. sig. & teacher's guide. $16.50 (The Canadian mosaic : $105.00) is

  1. Canadians, French-speaking - History.

  Considers the survival and growth of French Canadian culture and French Canadian contributions to the political and economic life of Canada. Examines the difficulties faced during the Seven Years War, the Durham Report and the Conscription Issues. Deals with the concept of separatism and possible alternatives for the future of French Canada. Illustrated with historical paintings and photographs.-

301.450971
  Hutterite contribution to Canadian society.
    prod. [Scarborough, Ont.] : R.B.M., 1978.- dist. ETHOS 44 fr. : b&w & col. : 35 mm. & cassette (7 min.) : auto. & aud. adv. sig. & reading script. $21.50 (Canadian folk culture : the Hutterites : $79.00) is

  1. Hutterites. 2. Collective settlements - Canada.

  Hutterite communes located in western provinces serve as examples of successful cooperative farming and peaceful communal living. Accounts for religious group's lack of social problems inherent in modern society and comments upon their serious commitments to community's welfare.-

301.450971
  Hutterite way of life.
    prod. [Scarborough, Ont.] : R.B.M., 1978.- dist. ETHOS 55 fr. : b&w & col. : 35 mm. & cassette (13 min.) : auto. & aud. adv. sig. & reading script. $21.50 (Canadian folk culture : the Hutterites : $79.00) is

  1. Hutterites - Social life and customs. 2. Collective settlements - Canada.

  An introduction to the Hutterite's cooperative lifestyle as exemplified by their self-sufficient communities. Includes schooling and raising of children, housing, recreation and farm management. Shows group's adaptation to modern society while co-existing with traditional customs and beliefs. Photographed at a Hutterite commune in Western Canada.-

301.450971
  The Hutterite ways.
    prod. [Edmonton] : PPH, 1978.- dist. ETHOS 30 fr. : col. : 35 mm. & cassette (5 min.) : auto. & aud. adv. sig. & teacher's guide. $19.00 pj

  1. Hutterites. 2. Collective settlements - Alberta.

  An introduction to the communal lifestyle of the Hutterites briefly describing their background, the division of duties on the bruderhof, educational system, and clothing.-

301.450971
  Hutterites in Canada : 1917 - present.
    prod. [Scarborough, Ont.] : R.B.M., 1978.- dist. ETHOS 50 fr. : b&w & col. : 35 mm. & cassette (11 min.) : auto. & aud. adv. sig. & reading script. $21.50 (Canadian folk culture : the Hutterites : $79.00) is

  1. Hutterites - History. 2. Collective settlements - Canada.

  Traces Hutterites' history in Canada, as seen in conflicts with Canadian government over land, schooling and other issues. Gives reason for migration and discusses diverse Canadian reactions to them. Uses archival and modern photographs to contrast early Canadian Hutterite communities with communes existing today.-

301.450971
  I come from Jamaica.
    prod. [Toronto] : McI. 1978.- dist. McI. 46 fr. : col. : 35 mm. & cassette (9 min.) : auto. & aud. adv. sig. & teacher's guide. $19.00 (The People we are : $95.00) pj

  1. Jamaicans in Canada.

  Melaine and her sister have just arrived at Toronto airport from Jamaica to join their parents. Records Melaine's initial impressions of Canada, the people and the homes. Shows her adapting to a new school and her first experiences with snow. Reveals little Jamaican culture or traditions.-

The Classified Catalogue

301.450971
　　I was born in Portugal.
　　　　prod. [Toronto, Ont.] : McI. 1978.- dist. McI. 52 fr. : col. : 35 mm. & cassette (10 min.) : auto. & aud. adv. sig. & teacher's guide. $19.00 (The People we are : $95.00) pj

　　1. Portuguese in Canada.

　　Eleven-year-old Mary Coehlo from Lisbon, Portugal, describes how she helps to prepare traditional Portuguese dishes, and enjoys reading and playing the piano. Other pictures show a television station where Mary's father has a radio and television show geared toward Portuguese listeners. Ends with photographs of her family at the swearing-in ceremony at the Court of Canadian citizenship.-

301.450971
　　Irish contributions to Canadian life.
　　　　prod. [Scarborough, Ont.] : R.B.M., 1978.- dist. ETHOS 52 fr. : b&w & col. : 35 mm. & cassette (12 min.) : auto. & aud. adv. sig. & reading script. $21.50 (Canadian folk culture : the Irish : $79.00) s

　　1. Irish in Canada.

　　An overview of the numerous Canadians of Irish descent who have contributed to country's growth in a variety of careers. Featured are prominent business people, clergy, poets and authors from the past and present. Well illustrated with paintings and photographs.-

301.450971
　　The Japanese come to Canada.
　　　　prod. [Scarborough, Ont.] : R.B.M., 1978.- dist. ETHOS 45 fr. : b&w & col. : 35 mm. & cassette (9 min.) : auto. & aud. adv. sig. & manual. $21.50 (Canadian folk culture : the Japanese : $79.00) s

　　1. Japanese in Canada - History. 2. Canada - Race relations - History. 3. Canada - Immigration and emigration - History.

　　An analysis of anti-Asiatic feelings in Canada toward Japanese immigrants from turn of the century to Second World War. Photographs depict difficulties of Japanese to integrate while hampered by prejudice and Federal Government policy. Would provoke preliminary discussion of war as it shows origins of tension leading to eventual evacuation of Japanese.-

301.450971
　　Japanese contribution to Canadian society.
　　　　prod. [Scarborough, Ont.] : R.B.M., 1978.- dist. ETHOS 48 fr. : b&w & col. : 35 mm. & cassette (9 min.) : auto. & aud. adv. sig. & manual. $21.50 (Canadian folk culture : the Japanese : $79.00) s

　　1. Japanese in Canada.

　　Documents the emergence of Japanese Canadians as a strong, hardworking ethnic group following their forced evacuation from west coast during Second World War. Shows influence of Japanese culture upon Canadian lifestyle in architecture, horticulture, culinary and martial arts.-

301.450971
　　The Japanese during World War II.
　　　　prod. [Scarborough, Ont.] : R.B.M., 1978.- dist. ETHOS 49 fr. : b&w & col. : 35 mm. & cassette (12 min.) : auto. & aud. adv. sig. & manual. $21.50 (Canadian folk culture : the Japanese : $79.00) s

　　1. Japanese in Canada - History. 2. Canada - Race relations - History.

　　Describes wartime treatment of Japanese Canadians following bombing of Pearl Harbour. Discusses anti-Asiatic tensions and government policies leading to impoundment of Japanese property and evacuation to interior relocation camps. Indicates post-war implications of War Measures Act upon Japanese. Photographs show evacuation and camp conditions.-

301.450971
　　My birthplace was India.
　　　　prod. [Toronto] : McI. 1978.- dist. McI. 45 fr. : col. : 35 mm. &dcassette (9 min.) : auto. & aud. adv. sig. & teacher's guide. $19.00 (The People we are : $95.00) pj

　　1. Indians in Canada.

　　Features 13-year old John D'Souza and his family from Goa, India. John talks of differences between Canadian schools and those of India, his personal interests and his plans for the future. Pictures of him at home with his brothers and sisters, and at his father's restaurant and catering business indicate his place and responsibility within the family. Also included are photographs of John and his sisters performing a traditional dance in costume.-

The Classified Catalogue

301.450971
    My family is Chinese.
        prod. [Toronto, Ont.] : McI. 1978.- dist. McI. 55 fr. : col. ; 35 mm. & cassette (10 min.) : auto. & aud. adv. sig. & teacher's guide. $19.00 (The People we are ; $95.00) pj

        1. Chinese in Canada.

Nine-year-old Larry Chan describes his Chinese family from Hong Kong, now living in Canada. Shows Larry painting at his grandmother's art studio, taking T'ai Chi lessons, writing Chinese and attending the Buddist church. Emphasis is on adaptation to Canadian lifestyle, while retaining cultural heritage.-

301.450971
    My Italian heritage.
        prod. [Toronto] : McI. 1978.- dist. McI. 51 fr. : col. ; 35 mm. & cassette (12 min.) : auto. & aud. adv. sig. & teacher's guide. $19.00 (The People we are ; $95.00) pj

        1. Italians in Canada.

Ten-year-old Monique Camarra describes her life as a child of Italian heritage and as a daughter of restaurant owners in Canada. She is seen helping to prepare Italian foods in the restaurant kitchen, and explaining what she is doing. Included are photographs of Monique at school, her impressions of life and her hopes and ambitions. Stresses the importance of family ties amongst Italians and the association of large family celebrations with good food.-

301.450971
    Prairie homestead.
        prod. [Scarborough, Ont.] : R.B.M., 1975.- dist. ETHOS 44 fr. : b&w & col. ; 35 mm. & cassette (13 min.) : auto. & aud. adv. sig. & teacher's manual. $19.00 (The Ukranians-Canadian homesteaders ; $34.50) is

        1. Ukranians in Canada - History. 2. Prairie Provinces - History. 3. Canada - Immigration and emigration - History.

Describes the hardships faced by the early Ukranian immigrants to Canada. These included immigration procedures, travel, finding and clearing land, and building homes.-

301.450971
    Strangers to Canada.
        prod. [Scarborough, Ont.] : R.B.M., 1975.- dist. ETHOS 30 fr. : b&w & col. ; 35 mm. & cassette (14 min.) : auto. & aud. adv. sig. & teacher's manual. $19.00 (The Ukranians-Canadian homesteaders ; $34.50) is

        1. Ukranians in Canada - History. 2. Canada - Immigration and emigration - History.

Studies the Ukranian immigrants to Canada, the conditions under which they emigrated, their origins, and reasons for immigrating. Photos, diagrams, charts and maps, and Ukranian songs.-

301.4509711
    Doukhobor contribution to Canadian society.
        prod. [Scarborough, Ont.] : R.B.M., 1978.- dist. ETHOS 50 fr. : b&w & col. ; 35 mm. & cassette (15 min.) : auto. & aud. adv. sig. & reading script. $21.50 (Canadian folk culture ; the Doukhobors ; $79.00) s

        1. Dukhobors - History.

A descriptive account of the Doukhobors' gradual acculturation process divided into three stages of development. Briefly covers persecution and conflicts with Canadian government. Shows their adoption of Canadian agricultural technology and integration into businesses while retaining traditional religious practices.-

301.4509711
    Doukhobor immigrants in the West.
        prod. [Scarborough, Ont.] : R.B.M., 1978.- dist. ETHOS 52 fr. : b&w & col. ; 35 mm. & cassette (18 min.) : auto. & aud. adv. sig. & reading script. $21.50 (Canadian folk culture ; the Doukhobors ; $79.00) s

        1. Dukhobors - History. 2. Canada - Immigration and emigration - History.

Presentation relates extreme hardships endured by Doukhobors who first arrived in Saskatchewan in 1899. A brief history of persecution in Russia and United States is followed by account of Canadian provincial hostilities which resulted in migration to British Columbia.-

The Classified Catalogue

301.4509711
    Doukhobor way of life.
        prod. [Scarborough, Ont.] : R.B.M., 1978.- dist. ETHOS 62 fr. : b&w & col. : 35 mm. & cassette (16 min.) : auto. & aud. adv. sig. & reading script. $21.50 (Canadian folk culture : the Doukhobors : $79.00) s

        1. Dukhobors - Social life and customs. 2. Collective settlements - Canada.

        A look at modern day Doukhobor lifestyle. Analyzes effect of internal conflict upon disintegration of traditional communal living. Contrasts original dress, language, attitude and religion with present assimilation into Canadian society.-

301.4509711
    A Time of migration and troubles.
        prod. [Scarborough, Ont.] : R.B.M., 1978.- dist. ETHOS 61 fr. : b&w & col. : 35 mm. & cassette (21 min.) : auto. & aud. adv. sig. & reading script. $21.50 (Canadian folk culture : the Doukhobors : $79.00) s

        1. Dukhobors - History. 2. British Columbia - History.

        Documentary focuses on turbulent history of Doukhobors living in British Columbia. Shows destruction of the community in Brilliant, B.C. by the terrorist radical group, Sons of Freedom. Describes subsequent re-adjustment of independent Doukhobors into Canadian society. Illustrated with historical photographs.-

301.4509713
    Irish feuds and quarrels.
        prod. [Scarborough, Ont.] : R.B.M., 1978.- dist. ETHOS 53 fr. : b&w & col. : 35 mm. & cassette (14 min.) : auto. & aud. adv. sig. & reading script. $21.50 (Canadian folk culture : the Irish : $79.00) s

        1. Irish in Canada - History. 2. Ontario - History.

        Traces revival of hostilities among Irish immigrants in Ontario to their origins in mother country. Provides descriptive accounts of three major events - Fenian raids, Donnelly massacres and organization of Ontario Orangemen: Uses sketches, newspaper clippings and photographs to illustrate these more violent moments in province's history.-

301.5
    Housing : the Canadian city.
        prod. [Scarborough, Ont.] : R.B.M., 1975.- dist. ETHOS 41 fr. : col. : 35 mm. & cassette (12 min.) : auto. & aud. adv. sig. & teacher's manual. $19.00 (Urban studies : $103.50) ji

        1. Housing.

        An over-all study of the various types of housing - old and new - and the influence of urban growth on the Canadian community.-

320.50971
    The Rise of Socialism in Canada.
        prod. [Scarborough, Ont.] : SHN, 1976.- dist. PHM 151 fr. : col. : 35 mm. & cassette (28 min.) : auto. & aud. adv. sig. & teacher's guide. $39.60 s

        1. Socialism - Canada - History.

        Outlines history and aims of socialism, particularly in Canada, when C.C.F. Party was founded. Includes J.S. Woodsworth, Tommy Douglas and David Lewis.-

320.951
    Political life.
        prod. [Kitchener, Ont.] : EDU, 1974.- dist. EDU 25 fr. : col. : 35 mm. & cassette (8 min.) : auto. & aud. adv. sig. & teacher's guide. $15.95 (China : $79.95) jis

        1. China - Politics and government.

        Deals with the importance of the theories of Mao Tse-tung and the Cultural Revolution. Describes the New Red Guards, Neighbourhood Committees that pass on government instructions and organize political study groups, the Little Red Book, the School for Cultural Minorities, and memorials to the "People".-

323.40971
    Le Canada, pays de liberté.
        prod. [Montreal?] : NFB, made 1958 : 1968.- dist. SEC. 24 fr. : col. : 35 mm. & captions & texte. $9.00 ;

        1. Civil rights.

        Uses drawings to illustrate the concepts of the basic rights and freedoms of Canadians such as feedom of speech, and of the press.-

The Classified Catalogue

324.71
    Get out and vote! election campaigns and issues.
        prod. [Toronto] : Int. Cin., 1978.- dist. VEC 87 fr. : col. : 35 mm. & casstte (15 min.) : auto. & aud. adv. sig. & teacher's guide. $24.00 (How Canada is governed : $130.00) ji

        1. Elections - Canada.

    Follows the campaign of a local candidate from when election first announced to voting procedures and tabulation of results. Explains rules that govern elections at all levels such as who may vote and eligibility to run for office. Photographs clearly illustrate all aspects of elections and voting.-

324.71
    The Municipal election.
        prod. [Scarborough, Ont.] : R.B.M., 1975.- dist. ETHOS 42 fr. : col. : 35 mm. & cassette (9 min.) : auto. & aud. adv. sig. & teacher's manual. $19.00 (Urban studies : $103.50) ji

        1. Elections - Canada. 2. Municipal government - Canada.

    Surveys the steps necessary to elect a new municipal government, including calling the election, enumeration of voters, choosing candidates for each ward, the campaign itself, and the vote on election day.
    Illustrated with photographs of a recent municipal election in Toronto.-

324.71
    Le vote au Canada.
        prod. [Montreal?] : NFB, 1973.- dist. SEC 61 fr. : col. : 35 mm. & captions & manual. $9.00 j

        1. Elections - Canada.

    A general overview of Canadian voting procedures from calling an election to tabulation of results. With photographs shot on location, discusses role of chief electoral officer and describes electoral districts, eligibility, marking ballots, etc. English title available : VOTING IN CANADA.-

324.71
    Voting in Canada.
        prod. [Montreal?] : NFB, 1972.- dist. McI. 56 fr. : col. : 35 mm. & captions & manual. $9.00 (Government of Canada) j

        1. Elections - Canada.

    A general overview of Canadian voting procedures from calling an election to tabulation of results. With photographs shot on location, discusses role of chief electoral officer and describes electoral districts, eligibility, marking ballots, etc. French title available : LA VOTE AU CANADA.-

325.71
    Changing profile.
        prod. [Scarborough, Ont.] : SHN, 1976.- dist. PHM 89 fr. : b&w & col. : 35 mm. & cassette (22 min.) : auto. & aud. adv. sig. & teacher's guide. $39.60 (The Peoples of Canada - our multicultural heritage : $82.00) is

        1. Canada - Immigration and emigration - History.

    Black and white photos and documents supplement colour photos to provide a frank view of some problems of immigration since 1945. Leads students to draw their own conclusions about immigration policies for the future.-

325.71
    European Canadians.
        prod. [Toornto] : M-L, 1976.- dist. Sch. Ser. or Vint. 60 fr. : b&w & col. : 35 mm. & cassette (13 min.) : auto. & aud. adv. sig. & teacher's guide. $16.50 (The Canadian mosaic : $105.00) is

        1. Canada - Immigration and emigration - History. 2. Canada - Foreign population - History.

    Explores in detail the reasons for European immigration to Canada, including Clifford Sifton's immigration polilcty in 1896. Describes the difficulties encountered by immigrants and outlines positive contributions to Canadian society. Encourages further study of effects of European immigration on Canadian culture.-

The Classified Catalogue

325.71
    The Fourth wave.
        prod. [Toronto] : NCM, 1977.- dist. I.T.F. 2 filmstrips (91:93 fr.) : b&w & col. : 35 mm. & 2 cassettes (12:14 min.) : auto. & aud. adv. sig. & script. $57.50 s

        1. Canada - Immigration and emigration - History.

        A chronological account of social and economic problems faced by immigrants arriving in Canada 1896-1914. Contrasts federal government's promotion of immigration with subsequent exploitation of immigrants by Canadians. Archival photographs illustrate problems with homesteading, finances, education, and mass movements to cities. Produced in two parts for viewing convenience.-

325.71
    Irish immigration.
        prod. [Scarborough, Ont.] : R.B.M., 1978.- dist. ETHOS 49 fr. : b&w & col. : 35 mm. & cassette (14 min.) : auto. & aud. adv. sig. & reading script. $21.50 (Canadian folk culture : the Irish : $79.00) s

        1. Canada - Immigration and emigration - History. 2. Ireland - History.

        Drawings, sketches, photographs provide additional insights into social conditions in Ireland which prompted mass migration to North America from mid-1700's to 1910. Shows how Canadians' impressions of Irish immigrants were influenced by the poverty and disease brought with them.-

325.71
    Two cultures.
        prod. [Scarborough, Ont.] : SHN, 1976.- dist. PHM 126 fr. : b&w & col. : 35 mm. & cassette (30 min.) : auto. & aud. adv. sig. & teacher's guide. $39.60 (The Peoples of Canada - our multicultural heritage : $82.00) is

        1. Canada - Immigration and emigration - History.

        Traces immigration patterns in Canada from early explorers to European groups searching for land. Discusses hardships and problems endured by immigrants. Uses historic paintings, etchings, portraits, documents and early photos.-

327.71
    Canadian-American relations : part 2 :
        prod. [Scarborough, Ont.] : SHN, 1977.- dist. PHM 78 fr. : col. : 35 mm. & cassette (17 min.) : auto. & aud. adv. sig. & study guide. $39.60 (Canadian-American relations : $82.00) s

        1. Canada - Foreign relations - United States. 2. United States - Foreign relations - Canada.

        A comprehensive look at the changing Canadian policies from World War 1 to 1963. Discusses Prohibition, the slow-down of trade during the Depression, aid of the U.S.A. at the onset of World War 11, and common defense projects following the war. Also includes formation of the United Nations, N.A.T.O., the AVRO Arrow conflict, and the Cuban Missile Crisis. Illustrated with photographs and drawings.-

327.71
    Canadian-American relations : part 1 :
        prod. [Scarborough, Ont.] : SHN, 1977.- dist. PHM 84 fr. : col. : 35 mm. & cassette (22 min.) : auto. & aud. adv. sig. & study guide. $39.60 (Canadian-American relations : $82.00) s

        1. Canada - Foreign relations - United States. 2. United States - Foreign relations - Canada.

        A comprehensive summary of early relations with the United States. Covers American Revolution, War of 1812, 49th Parallel Dispute, and the American Civil War. Describes how these events fostered much anti-American feeling in Canada. Includes Confederation, Loyalist Movement, Alaska Boundary Dispute and establishment of several International Joint Commissions to assist in common interests. Uses historical drawings and photographs.-

The Classified Catalogue

327.71
Canadian-American relations : part 3 :
prod. [Scarborough, Ont.] : SHN, 1977.- dist. PHM 84 fr. : col. : 35 mm. & cassette (21 min.) : auto. & aud. adv. sig. & study guide. $39.60 (Canadian-American relations : $82.00) s

1. Canada - Foreign relations - United States. 2. United States - Foreign relations - Canada.

Describes the unique relationship of co-operation and good-neighbourliness between Canada and the U.S.A. Discusses similarities and differences in foreign policies, stressing the Pearson-Johnson confrontation over Vietnam, Canada's commitment to N.O.R.A.D., expansion of trade between the two countries, and increased American investment in Canada. Discusses in detail Canadian dependence upon the U.S.A. Includes the Watkins Report and the Foreign Investment Review Act. Uses photographs and drawings.-

328.71
Federal government.
prod. [Montreal?] : NFB, 1965.- dist. McI. 44 fr. : col. : 35 mm. & captions. $9.00 (Government of Canada.) is

1. Canada. Parliament.

Uses photographs of the Pearson era to study the principles of the Canadian federal government. Examines the role of the Governor-General, the House of Commons, the Cabinet, the Senate, and the Prime Minister. Traces the steps in passing a bill. French title available : LE GOUVERNEMENT FEDERAL.-

328.71
Le gouvernement fédéral.
prod. [Montreal?] : NFB, 1965.- dist. SEC 46 fr. : col. : 35 mm. & captions. $9.00 (Le gouvernement au Canada) is

1. Canada. Parliament.

Uses photographs of the Pearson era to study the principles of the Canadian federal government. Examines the role of the Governor General, the House of Commons, the Cabinet, the Senate, and the Prime Minister. Traces the steps in passing a bill. English title available : FEDERAL GOVERNMENT.-

328.71
Parliament : making and changing laws.
prod. [Toronto] : Int. Cin., 1978.- dist. VEC 53 fr. : col. : 35 mm. & cassette (15 min.) : auto. & aud. adv. sig. & teacher's guide. $24.00 (How Canada is governed : $130.00) ji

1. Parliamentary practice. 2. Canada. Parliament.

Explains origins of Canada's federal system and how organization of Parliament reinforces concept of federalism. Using passing of a gun law as an example, outlines note of Senate and House of Commons in introducing, discussing and passing a bill. Makes use of sketches, with some photographs of Parliament.-

328.71
Parliament buildings.
prod. [Stratford, Ont.] : Sch. Ch., 1976.- dist. Sch. Ch. 46 fr. : b&w & col. : 35 mm. & captions & teacher's manual. $7.95 (Our national capital : $39.75) ji

1. Canada. Parliament. 2. Canada - Politics and government.

An informative presentation of the Federal Parliament buildings in Ottawa. Discusses the construction of the original Parliament buildings, the fire and reconstruction of the present buildings, using authentic photographs. Explains the roles of the Governor-General, the Prime Minister, the Senate and the House of Commons. Shows the more important wings of the Parliament Buildings, and historic photos, such as the raising of the new Canadian flag, and visits by Premier Kosygin and President Nixon.-

328.71
Parliamentary government.
prod. [Montreal?] : NFB, 1965.- dist. McI. 46 fr. : col. : 35 mm. & captions. $9.00 (Government of Canada) j

1. Canada. Parliament. 2. Representative government and representation. 3. Parliamentary practice.

Major roles of the Cabinet and the House of Commons are shown in this descriptive overview of the Canadian parliamentary system. Includes how Cabinet members are chosen, types of isssues discussed, Orders-in-Council, Acts of Parliament and passing of bills. French title available : LE REGIME PARLEMENTAIRE.-

The Classified Catalogue

328.71
Le régime parlementaire.
prod. [Montreal?] : NFB, 1965.- dist. SEC 48 fr. : col. : 35 mm. & captions. $9.00 (Le gouvernement au Canada) j

1. Representative government and representation. 2. Canada. Parliament. 3. Parliamentary practice.

Major roles of the Cabinet and the House of Commons are shown in this descriptive overview of the Canadian parliamentary system. Includes how Cabinet members are chosen, types of issues discussed, Orders-in-Council, Acts of Parliament and passing of bills. English title available : PARLIAMENTARY GOVERNMENT.-

328.71
Une visite au Palais du Parlement.
prod. [Montreal?] : NFB, [1959] dist. SEC 46 fr. : col. : 35 mm. & captions & manual. $9.00 j

1. Canada. Parliament.

A tour of the Parliament buildings by two children. Focusses on the Senate, the House of Commons and the Library. Text and comments in accompanying booklet are useful for pre-teaching vocabulary. Suitable for immersion classes or extended French classes in social science.-

329
Electronic politics.
prod. [Montreal?] : NFB, made 1971 : 1972.- dist. McI. 40 fr. : b&w & col. : 35 mm. & captions. $9.00 is

1. Television in politics.

Photographs and cartoons, but few captions in the discussion of how traditional patterns of politics are being reshaped by the electronic marketplace of television and related media. For classroom instruction by a well-informed teacher. French title available : L'ELECTRONIQUE EN POLITIQUE.-

329
L'Electronique en politique.
prod. [Montreal?] : NFB, made 1971 : 1972.- dist. SEC 40 fr. : b&w & col. : 35 mm. & captions. $9.00 is

1. Television in politics.

Photographs and cartoons, but few captions in this discussion of how traditional patterns of politics are being reshaped by the electronic marketplace of television and related media. For classroom instruction by a well-informed teacher. English title available : ELECTRONIC POLITICS.-

329.971
Parties and elections.
prod. [Montreal?] : NFB, 35 mm. dist. McI. 43 fr. : col. : 35 mm. & captions. $9.00 (Government of Canada) j

1. Political parties - Canada. 2. Television in politics.

Examines role of political parties in democratic governments, using Canadian politics as example. Shows inside workings of parties from local to national level and discusses effects of mass media on electoral system. French title available : PARTIS ET ELECTIONS.-

329.971
Partis et elections.
prod. [Montreal?] : NFB, 1965.- dist. SEC 43 fr. : col. : 35 mm. & captions. $9.00 (Le gouvernement au Canada) j

1. Political parties. 2. Television in politics.

Examines roles of political parties in democratic governments, using Canadian politics as example. Shows inside workings of parties from local to national level and discusses effects of mass media on electoral system. English title available : PARTIES AND ELECTIONS.-

The Classified Catalogue

330.12
Urban economy.
prod. [Scarborough, Ont.] : R.B.M., 1974.- dist. ETHOS 80 fr. : col. : 35 mm. & cassette (9 min.) : auto. & aud. adv. sig. & teacher's guide. $19.00 (Urbanism in Canada) ji

1. Economics.

Uses photographs to illustrate the four major levels of the economic system: primary (extractive or resource-based); secondary (manufacturing and transportation); tertiary (service industries, wholesaling and retailing); quartenary (administrative or office-oriented).-

330.9
I was asked to draw this picture : children's views on world development.
prod. [Montreal?] : NFB, 1975.- dist. McI. 74 fr. : col. : 35 mm. & cassette (13 min.) : auto. & aud. adv. sig. & reading script. $9.00 ji

1. Developing areas.

Examines the problems of poverty and hunger in the world's developing nations from the viewpoint of junior-intermediate children. Posters drawn by children across Canada together with photographs of the Third World help to emphasize the theme of contrast between the have and have-not nations. Useful as an introduction to the topic.-

330.971
Introduction : the people and the land.
prod. [Toronto] : Int. Cin., 1978.- dist. VEC 84 fr. : col. : 35 mm. & cassette (15 min.) : auto. & aud. adv. sig. & teacher's guide. $24.00 (Canada and its regions : the geography of a changing land : $155.00) ji

1. Canada - Economic conditions. 2. Canada - Geography.

Identifies physiographical regions, climate, vegetation, and major resources of each of Canada's geographic areas. Uses a geographical approach to interpret economic and social changes in Canada's past, present and future. Can be used as introduction to Canada's geography but is primarily designed to give an overview of concepts presented in series "Canada and its regions".-

330.9711
The Mountainous West.
dist. [Toronto] : Int. Cin., 1978.- 78 fr. : b&w & col. : 35 mm. & cassette (15 min.) : auto. & aud. adv. sig. $24.00 (Canada and its regions : the geography of a changing land : $155.00) ji

1. British Columbia - Geography. 2. British Columbia - Economic conditions.

A chronological account of region showing influence of geographical factors such as the mountains and sea access upon industrial growth. Describes natural resources, early settlement, gold rush days, transportation and industry.-

330.9712
The Northland.
prod. [Toronto] : Int. Cin., 1978.- dist. VEC 77 fr. : b&w & col. : 35 mm. & cassette (15 min.) : auto. & aud. adv. sig. $24.00 (Canada and its regions : the geography of a changing land : $155.00) ji

1. Arctic regions - Economic conditions.

Presents North as new industrial frontier owing to energy supplies and other natural resources. Discusses consequences of developing north such as damage to native peoples' lifestyle, environment and wildlife. Comments on governmental structure which involves inhabitants in future of region.-

330.9713
Central Canada : the people.
prod. [Toronto] : Int. Cin., 1978.- dist. VEC 76 fr. : b&w & col. : 35 mm. & cassette (15 min.) : auto. & aud. adv. sig. $24.00 (Canada and its regions : the geography of a changing land : $155.00) ji

1. Ontario - Economic conditions. 2. Quebec - Economic conditions.

A summary of human and environmental factors which have contributed to central Canada's importance as an economic and political centre. Covers diverse topics such as climate, evolution of trade and water routes, growth of urban environment, pollution, and influence of United States upon region's industrial system.-

The Classified Catalogue

330.9713
    Central Canada : the place.
        prod. [Toronto] : Int. Cin., 1978.- dist. VEC 73 fr. : col. : 35 mm. & cassette (15 min.) : auto. & aud. adv. sig. $24.00 (Canada and its regions : the geography of a changing land : $155.00) ji

        1. Montreal, Que. - Economic conditions.
        2. Toronto, Ont. Economic conditions.

    Compares and contrasts growth of Montreal and Toronto as leading commercial centres.-

330.9715
    Atlantic Canada.
        prod. [Toronto] : Int. Cin., 1978.- dist. VEC 70 fr. : b&w & col. : 35 mm. & cassette (15 min.) : auto. & aud. adv. sig. & teacher's guide. $24.00 (Canada and its regions : the geography of a changing land :$155.00) ji

        1. Atlantic Provinces - Geography.
        2. Atlantic Provinces - Economic conditions.

    Uses history and geography of region to explain Atlantic provinces' present high unemployment rate and lack of industrial development. Lists factors which have contributed to problems in economy and outlines plans to alleviate situation.-

330.9715
    Atlantic Canada : New Brunswick.
        prod. [Montreal?] : NFB, 1973.- dist. McI. 57 fr. : col. : 35 mm. & captions & notes & teacher's guide. $9.00 (Atlantic Canada : $63.00) jis

        1. New Brunswick - Economic conditions.
        2. New Brunswick - Industries.

    Uses photographs, maps and charts to examine the economic conditions and industries of New Brunswick. Describes the foresty, mining, agriculture, fishing, and hydro-electric industries. Discusses the expansion of small secondary industries. French title available : LE CANADA ATLANTIQUE : LE NOUVEAU-BRUNSWICK.-

330.9715
    Atlantic Canada : economy.
        prod. [Montreal?] : NFB, 1973.- dist. McI. 64 fr. : col. : 35 mm. & captions & notes & teacher's guide. $9.00 (Atlantic Canada : $63.00) jis

        1. Atlantic Provinces - Economic conditions.
        2. Atlantic Provinces - Industries.

    Uses photographs, maps, and charts to describe and locate the various industries of the Atlantic Provinces of Canada, such as fishing, forestry, agriculture, mining, and promise of off-shore oil deposits. Points out Maritime problems of isolation and unemployment, and how they are being solved with increased transportation and encouragement of new business. French title available : LE CANADA ATLANTIQUE : ECONOMIE.-

330.9715
    Le Canada atlantique : le Nouveau-Brunswick.
        prod. [Montreal?] : NFB, 1973.- dist. SEC 61 fr. : col. : 35 mm. & notes, teacher's guide & captions. $9.00 (Le Canada Atlantique) jis

        1. New Brunswick - Economic conditions.
        2. New Brunswick - Industries.

    Uses photographs, maps and charts to examine the economic conditions and industries of New Brunswick. Describes the forestry, mining, agriculture, fishing and hydro-electric industries. Discusses the expansion of small secondary industries. English title available : ATLANTIC CANADA : NEW BRUNSWICK.-

330.9715
    Le Canada atlantique : économie.
        prod. [Montreal?] : NFB, 1973.- dist. SEC 65 fr. : col. : 35 mm. & notes, teacher's guide & captions. $9.00 (Le Canada Atlantique) jis

        1. Atlantic Provinces - Economic conditions.
        2. Atlantic Provinces - Industries.

    Uses photographs, maps and charts to describe and locate the various industries of the Atlantic Provinces of Canada, such as fishing, forestry, agriculture, mining, and promise of off-shore oil deposits. Points out Maritime problems of isolation and unemployment, and how they are being solved with increased transportation and encouragement of new business. English title availalbe : ATLANTIC CANADA : ECONOMY.-

The Classified Catalogue

330.9716
Atlantic Canada : Nova Scotia.
prod. [Montreal?] : NFB, 1973.- dist. McI. 62 fr. : col. : 35 mm. & captions & teacher's guide. $9.00 (Atlantic Canada : $63.00) jis

1. Nova Scotia - Economic conditions.
2. Nova Scotia - Industries.

An overview of the economic conditions of Nova Scotia. Contrasts large industries in populated Halifax with less populated areas, such as Cape Breton Island. Discusses importance of steel and coal production to the Sydney-Glace Bay area and many small manufacturers throughout Nova Scotia. Describes agriculture and fishing industries. French title available : LE CANADA ATLANTIQUE : LA NOUVELLE ECOSSE.-

330.9716
Le Canada atlantique : la Nouvelle Ecosse.
prod. [Montreal?] : NFB, 1973.- dist. SEC 67 fr. : col. : 35 mm. & captions & teacher's guide. $9.00 (Le Canada atlantique) jis

1. Nova Scotia - Economic conditions.
2. Nova Scotia - Industries.

An overview of the economic conditions of Nova Scotia. Contrasts large industries in populated Halifax with less populated areas, such as Cape Breton Island. Discusses the importance of steel and coal production to the Sydney-Glace Bay area and many small manufacturers throughout Nova Scotia. Describes agriculture and fishing industries. English title available : ATLANTIC CANADA : NOVA SCOTIA.-

330.9716
Cape Breton Island : industrial regions.
prod. [Scarborough, Ont.] : R.B.M., 1976.- dist. ETHOS 44 fr. : b&w & col. : 35 mm. & cassette (10 min.) : auto. & aud. adv. sig. & teacher's manual. $19.00 (Regional studies : $138.00) ji

1. Cape Breton Island, N.S. - Economic conditions.

The two main industrial regions of Cape Breton, the Strait of Canso, and the Sydney area, are emphasized in the study of the Island's present-day economy and problems.-

330.9717
Atlantic Canada : Prince Edward Island.
prod. [Montreal?] : NFB, 1972.- dist. McI. 56 fr. : col. : 35 mm. & captions & notes & teacher's guide. $9.00 (Atlantic Canada : $63.00) jis

1. Prince Edward Island - Economic conditions. 2. Prince Edward Island - Industries.

Photographs, maps and charts describe the economic conditions of Prince Edward Island. Fishing, tourism, and the Canadian Forces Base are briefly referred to. Shows harvesting and storing potatoes on a potato farm, and points out how some farmers are diversifying their crops. Best suited for teaching situation because of lack of relation of notes to particular frames. French title available : LE CANADA ATLANTIQUE : L'ILE DU PRINCE EDOUARD.-

330.9717
Le Canada atlantique : l'Ile du Prince-Edouard.
prod. [Montreal?] : NFB, 1973.- dist. SEC 58 fr. : col. : 35 mm. & captions & notes & teacher's guide. $9.00 (Le Canada Atlantique) jis

1. Prince Edward Island - Economic conditions. 2. Prince Edward Island - Industries.

Photographs, maps and charts describe the economic conditions of Prince Edward Island. Fishing, tourism, and the Canadian Forces Base are briefly referred to. Shows harvesting and storing potatoes on a potato farm, and points how some farmers are diversifying their crops. English title available : ATLANTIC CANADA : PRINCE EDWARD ISLAND.-

330.9718
Atlantic Canada : Island of Newfoundland.
prod. [Montreal?] : NFB, 1973.- dist. McI. 54 fr. : col. : 35 mm. & captions & notes. $9.00 (Atlantic Canada : $63.00) jis

1. Newfoundland - Industries.
2. Newfoundland - Economic conditions.

Photographs with maps and diagrams describe the city of St. John's and examine the fishing industry, including Canadian fishing territories. Compares traditional fishing methods with modern practises. Mentions the annual seal hunt and the mining, forestry, manufacturing and service industries. French title available : LE CANADA ATLANTIQUE : L'ILE DE TERRE-NEUVE.-

The Classified Catalogue

330.9718
Le Canada atlantique : L'Ile de Terre-Neuve.
prod. [Montreal?] : NFB, 1973.- dist. SEC 56 fr. : col. : 35 mm. & notes, teacher's guide & captions. $9.00 (Le Canada Atlantique) jis

1. Newfoundland - Economic conditions. 2. Newfoundland - Industries.

Photographs with maps and diagrams describe the city of St. John's and examine the fishing industry, including Canadian fishing territories. Compares traditional fishing methods with modern practices. Mentions the annual seal hunt and the mining, forestry, manufacturing and service industries. English title available : ATLANTIC CANADA : ISLAND OF NEWFOUNDLAND.-

330.9719
Atlantic Canada : Labrador.
prod. [Montreal?] : NFB, 1973.- dist. McI. 55 fr. : col. : 35 mm. & captions & notes & teacher's guide. $9.00 (Atlantic Canada : $63.00) jis

1. Labrador - Industries. 2. Labrador - Economic conditions.

Photographs and maps describe the logging, fishing, and mining industries of Labrador. Deals with the hydro-electric development at Churchill Falls in detail. French title available : LE CANADA ATLANTIQUE : LE LABRADOR.-

330.9719
Le Canada atlantique : le Labrador.
prod. [Montreal?] : NFB, 1973.- dist. SEC 57 fr. : col. : 35 mm. & notes, teacher's guide & captions. $9.00 (Le Canada Atlantique) jis

1. Labrador - Industries. 2. Labrador - Economic conditions.

Photographs and maps describe the logging, fishing and mining industries of Labrador. Deals with the hydro-electric development at Churchill Falls in detail. English title available : ATLANTIC CANADA : LABADOR.-

331.40971
Bread and roses : the struggle of the Canadian working women.
prod. [Toronto] : NCM, 1978.- dist. I.T.F. 2 parts (92 : 75 fr.) : b&w & col. : 35 mm. & 2 cassettes (18 : 17 min.) : auto. & aud. adv. sig. & reading script. $57.50 (Canadians in conflict) s

1. Woman - Employment - History. 2. Woman - Civil rights - History. 3. Women in Canada - History.

A chronological account of the Canadian working woman's fight for equal rights in the work force. Shows organization and growth of women's movements from the turn of the century to the present, in opposition to sub-standard working conditions, low pay and lack of voting privileges. Produced in two parts for viewing convenience.-

331.880971
Beginnings.
prod. [Scarborough Ont.] : SHN, 1976.- dist. PHM 105 fr. : b&w & col. : 35 mm. & cassette (26 min.) : auto. & aud. adv. sig. & teacher's guide. $39.60 (Trade unions : the Canadian experience : $65.00) s

1. Labour unions - Canada - History.

Traces the origins of organized labour in Canada explaining the reasons for unions and strikes includes many recent labour disputes.-

331.880971
Development.
prod. [Scarborough Ont.] : SHN, 1976.- dist. PHM 99 fr. : b&w & col. : 35 mm. & cassette (24 min.) : auto. adv. sig. & teacher's guide. $39.60 (Trade unions : the Canadian experience : $65.00) s

1. Labor unions - Canada - History.

Deals with the development of small trade unions into larger groups, and their struggles with employees. Describes the effect of the A.F.L. on Canadian unions. Explains aims of trade unions using many actual examples of their success.-

The Classified Catalogue

331.890971
    Winnipeg General Strike, 1919.
        prod. [Toronto] : NCM, 1978.- dist. I.T.F. 2 parts (73 : 77 fr.) : b&w : 35 mm. & 2 cassettes (16 : 17 min.) : auto. & aud. adv. sig. & manual. $57.50 (Canadians in conflict) s

    1. Strikes and lockouts. 2. Canada - History - 1914-1945.

    Original black and white photographs plus the viewpoints of a Winnipeg businessman, female reformer, and older unionist describe the conditions and circumstances in Winnipeg that led up to this important social, political and economic event of the post World War 1 era. Second part of filmstrip summarizes the mechanics of the strike itself and the major events of its six week duration that led to "Bloody Sunday". Produced in two parts for viewing convenience.-

332.024
    Money : how much do you need?
        prod. [Toronto] : M-L, 1974.- dist. Sch. Ser. or Vint. 37 fr. : col. : 35 mm. & cassette (5 min.) : auto. & aud. adv. sig. teacher's guide. $16.50 (Learning about money : $65.00) pj

    1. Finance, Personal.

    In this introduction to income planning the importance of living within your means is demonstrated with definitions of credit, credit ratings, credit cards, loans, buying on time or installment buying, down payments, and interest.-

332.024
    Money : planning a budget.
        prod. [Toronto] : M-L, 1974.- dist. Sch. Ser. or Vint. 36 fr. : col. : 35 mm. & cassette (6 min.) : auto. & aud. & adv. sig. & eacher's guide. $16.50 (Learning about money : $65.00) pj

    1. Finance, Personal.

    Illustrates and discusses budgeting, saving, and earning money. Also provides an excellent introduction to the history and function of banks, stocks, and bonds.-

332.024
    Money : how to spend it.
        prod. [Toronto] : M-L, 1974.- dist. Sch. Ser. or Vint. 39 fr. : col. : 35 mm. & cassette (8 min.) : auto. & aud. adv. sig. & teacher's guide. $16.50 (Learning about money : $65.00) pj

    1. Finance, Personal. 2. Consumer education.

    An introduction to saving and spending money wisely. Using examples with which a child can identify, special means of getting the most value for money are described. These include price-comparing, selective shopping, waiting for sales, and buying in quantities.-

332.1
    Creation of money by the banking system.
        prod. [Oakville, Ont.] : SC, 1971.- dist. SC 81 fr. : col. : 35 mm. & cassette (22 min.) : auto. adv. sig. only& worksheet. $35.00 s

    1. Banks and banking. 2. Money.

    Amusing illustrations depict techniques used by banks to 'create' money by expanding upon existing deposits Explains concepts such as cash reserves, money supply and vote of increase. Filmstrip designed to be viewed in conjunction with worksheet.-

332.4
    What is money?
        prod. [Oakville, Ont.] : SC, 1971.- dist. Sheridan College 48 fr. : col. : 35 mm. & cassette (17 min.) : auto. adv. sig. only& worksheet. $35.00 s

    1. Money.

    Presents concepts behind present day monetary system. Briefly discusses evolution of money economy and comments upon our moving to a "cashless" society. Illustrated with chartss and diagrams.-

The Classified Catalogue

333.3
    Les censitaires.
        prod. [Montreal?] : NFB, 1963.- dist. SEC 34 fr. : col. : 35 mm. & captions. $9.00 ji

        1. Land tenure. 2. Frontier and pioneer life - Quebec. 3. Canada - History - To 1763 (New France).

        A study of the seigneural system of landholding in New France. Drawings illustrate ways that settlers were introduced to the new land, the responsibilities of the habitant to his community and to his seigneur, and some daily activities that the habitant enjoyed. Describes some social customs and religious holidays.-

333.3
    The Habitants.
        prod. [Montreal?] : NFB, 1963.- dist. McI. 30 fr. : col. : 35 mm. & captions & teacher's manual. $9.00 (New France : segneurial system : $45.00) ji

        1. Land tenure. 2. Frontier and pioneer life - Quebec. 3. Canada - History - To 1763 (New France).

        A study of the seigneurial system of land holding in New France. Drawings illustrate ways that settlers were introduced to the new land, the responsibilites of the habitant to his community and to his seigneur, and some daily activities that the habitant enjoyed. Describes some social customs and religious holidays. French title available : LES CENSITAIRES.-

333.3
    Seigneurs and seigneuries.
        prod. [Montreal?] : NFB, 1977.- dist. McI. 36 fr. : col. : 35 mm. & captions & teaching guide. $9.00 (New France : seigneurial system : $45.00) ji

        1. Land tenure. 2. Frontier and pioneer life - Quebec. 3. Canada - History - To 1763 (New France).

        Drawings and maps illustrate and describe the Seigneurial System. Explains how seigneuries were granted, their location and size, the duties of the Seigneur and the growth of parishes. French title available : SEIGNEURS ET SEIGNEURIES.-

333.3
    Seigneurs et seigneuries.
        prod. [Montreal?] : NFB, 1963.- dist. SEC 38 fr. : col. : 35 mm. & captions & teacher's guide. $9.00 ji

        1. Land tenure. 2. Frontier and pioneer life - Quebec. 3. Canada - History - To 1763 (New France).

        Drawings and maps illustrate and describe the Seigneurial System. Explains how seigneuries were granted, their location of the Seigneur and the growth of parishes. English title available : SEIGNEURS AND SEIGNEURIES.-

333.7
    Alternatives for the future.
        prod. [Toronto] : M-L, 1974.- dist. Sch. Ser. or Vint. 59 fr. : col. : 35 mm. & cassette (14 min.) : auto. & aud. adv. sig. & teacher's guide. $16.50 (Energy : crisis and resolution : $85.00) i

        1. Power resources.

        Discusses the dilemma created by man's quest for a complex technological society. Examines the reasons for the scarcity of traditional natural energy resources and explores the new types of energy that are being developed, such as nuclear, solar and geo-thermal power. Encourages discussion about man's energy needs, methods of conservation and plans for future supplies.-

333.7
    The Energy crisis?
        prod. [Montreal?] : NFB, 1974.- dist. McI. 64 fr. : col. : 35 mm. & captions. $9.00 ji

        1. Power resources.

        Discusses reasons for potential energy crisis in Canada. Explores coal, oil, natural gas, and electrical industries, and their effects on agriculture, transportation, urban life, and industry. Suggests alternatives to avoid severe shortages. Points out ecological hazards of energy production.-

The Classified Catalogue

333.7
　　Fruit Belt preservation and regional planning.
　　　　prod. [Scarborough, Ont.] : FCC, 1976.- 10 fr. : col. : 35 mm. & cassette (23 min.) : auto. & aud. adv. sig. & teacher's guide and reading script. $9.95 (Niagara Fruit Belt : $29.85) jis

　　　　1. Land use.　2. Niagara Peninsula, Ont.

　　　　Considers the problem of urban encroachment on valuable tender-fruit lands in the Niagara region, discussing the role played by regional planning and the changes it has brought about. Includes maps and photos. Repeats information given in "An Overview of the Niagara Fruit Belt" but in greater detail. A condensed version of the narration is provided. Material packaged in clear vinyl envelope that would fit a legal-size filing cabinet.-

333.7
　　Introduction to energy.
　　　　prod. [Toronto] : M-L, 1974.- dist. Sch. Ser. or Vint. 55 fr. : col. : 35 mm. & cassette (12 min.) : auto. & aud. adv. sig. & teacher's guide. $16.50 (Energy : crisis and resolution : $85.00) i

　　　　1. Power resources.

　　　　Examines energy resources of the past and the development of man's present energy resources. Using photography and diagrams, takes an objective look at the crisis of our dwindling energy supplies, and explores new alternatives for the future.-

333.7
　　An Overview of the Niagara Fruit Belt.
　　　　prod. [Scarborough, Ont.] : FCC, 1977.- dist. FCC 49 fr. : b&w & col. : 35 mm. & cassette (21 min.) : auto. & aud. adv. sig. & teacher's guide. $16.95 is

　　　　1. Land use.　2. Niagara Peninsula, Ont.

　　　　Discusses four topics : the distribution, topography, and soil of the Niagara fruit lands; the land use and layouts of two fruit farms; problems of urban competition for fruit land; and, the effects of regional planning. Repeats some of the Niagara Fruit Belt series, but in less detail.-

333.7
　　Problems of land use in urban fringe - urban shadow areas.
　　　　prod. [Scarborough, Ont.] : FCC, 1976.- dist. FCC 10 fr. : col. : 35 mm. & cassette (23 min.) : auto. & aud. adv. sig. & teacher's guide and reading script. $9.95 (Niagara Fruit Belt : $29.85) jis

　　　　1. Land use.　2. Niagara Peninsula, Ont.

　　　　Illustrates a variety of fringe and shadow land-use problems. While relating to the Niagara Fruit Belt, the problems are similar to those of fringe and shadow areas surrounding other cities and towns. Includes maps and photos. Repeats information given in "An Overview of the Niagara Fruit Belt" but with greater detail. A condensed version of the narration is provided. Material packaged in a clear vinyl envelope to fit legal-size filing cabinet.-

333.7
　　Sources of power.
　　　　prod. [Toronto] : RQM, 1975.- dist. Lea. 40 fr. : col. : 35 mm. & captions & teacher's guide. $9.00 (An Introduction to : sources of power) ji

　　　　1. Power resources.

　　　　A clear, concise explanation of the four basic sources of power: Water, thermal, oil-gas and nuclear, relating them to the everyday needs of people.-

333.8
　　Fossil fuels : coal.
　　　　prod. [Toronto] : M-L, 1974.- dist. Sch. Ser. or Vint. 63 fr. : col. : 35 mm. & cassette (13 min.) : auto. & aud. adv. sig. & teacher's guide. $16.50 (Energy : crisis and resolution : $85.00) i

　　　　1. Coal.

　　　　Uses photographs and diagrams to explain the formation of coal, various mining methods, locations of major coal deposits in North America, and the use of coal as a form of energy. Thoroughly discusses the importance of coal as an energy source in the past, the present, and the future.-

333.8
Fossil fuels : oil and natural gas.
prod. [Toronto] : M-L, 1974.- dist. Sch. Ser. or Vint. 61 fr. : col. : 35 mm. & cassette (14 min.) : auto. & aud. adv. sig. & teacher's guide. $16.50 (Energy : crisis and resolution : $85.00) i

1. Petroleum. 2. Gas, Natural.

Traces the evolution and history of oil and gas production. Explains the importance of oil and gas as energy sources, and the need for conservation. Explores new energy sources and looks at exploration, drilling and marketing of oil and gas today. Illustrated with photos and diagrams.-

333.9
La crise de l'environnement.
prod. [Montreal?] : NFB, 1972.- dist. SEC 47 fr. : col. : 35 mm. & captions & notes. $9.00 is

1. Environmental policy. 2. Ecology. 3. Conservation of natural resources.

Cartoons provide a starting point for discussion of the causes of our environment crisis - concentrations of people, demand for resources, and the results - pollution and depletion of resources. Part of a multi-media kit titled "La protection de l'environnement". English title available : ENVIRONMENT CRISIS.-

333.9
Environment : biosphere.
prod. [Montreal?] : NFB, 1972.- dist. McI. 41 fr. : col. : 35 mm. & captions & notes. $9.00 is

1. Ecology. 2. Environmental policy.

Captions with Peter Whalley's cartoons succintly describe biosphere, the sun's energy, nature's cycles, ecosystems and pollution when man overloads the cycles. Designed to provoke discussion. Part of a multi-media kit titled "Environmental protection". French title available : L'ENVIRONNEMENT ET LA BIOSPHERE.-

333.9
Environment crisis.
prod. [Montreal?] : NFB, 1972.- dist. McI. 47 fr. : col. : 35 mm. & captions & notes. $9.00 is

1. Environmental policy. 2. Ecology. 3. Conservation of natural resources.

Cartoons provide a starting point for discussion of the causes of our environment crisis, - concentrations of people, demand for resources, and the result - pollution and depletion of resources. Part of a multi-media kit titled "Environmental protection". French title available : LA CRISE DE L'ENVIRONNEMENT.-

333.9
Environment protection.
prod. [Montreal?] : NFB, 1972.- dist. McI. 46 fr. : col. : 35 mm. & captions & printed notes. $9.00 is

1. Environmental policy.

Designed to provoke discussion, cartoons and captions outline "care less" attitudes to environment protection, the need for co-ordinated action, and realistic solutions such as limits on consumer goods and recycling. Part of a multi-media kit titled "Environmental policy". French title available : LA PROTECTION DE L'ENVIRONNEMENT.-

333.9
L'environnement et la biosphère.
prod. [Montreal?] : NFB, 1972.- dist. SEC 41 fr. : col. : 35 mm. & captions & notes. $9.00 is

1. Ecology. 2. Environmental policy.

Captions with Peter Whalley's cartoons succinctly describe biosphere, the sun's energy, nature's cycles, ecosystems and pollution when man overloads the cycles. Designed to provoke discussion. Part of a kit titled "La protection de l'environnement". English title available : ENVIRONMENT BIOSPHERE.-

The Classified Catalogue

333.9
    La protection de l'environnement.
        prod. [Montreal?] : NFB. made 1972 : 1976.- dist. SEC 46 fr. : col. : 35 mm. & captions & printed notes. $9.00 jis

        1. Environmental policy.

        Designed to provoke discussion, cartoons and captions outline "care less" attitudes to environment protection, the need for co-ordinated action, and realistic solutions such as limits on consumer goods and recycling. Part of a multi-media kit titled "La protection de l'environnement." English title available : ENVIRONMENT PROTECTION.-

335
    A Kibbutz in Israel.
        prod. Edmonton] : PPH. 1976.- dist. PPH 39 fr. : col. : 35 mm. & cassette (11 min.) : auto. & aud. adv. sig. & teacher's guide. pj

        1. Collective settlements - Israel.

        Describes the daily activities and way of life at Kibbutz Yavneh, an example of communal living based on the ideals of equality, democracy, co-operation, and responsibility.-

336.20971
    The History of income tax in Canada.
        prod. [Montreal?] : NFB. 1975.- dist. McI. 61 fr. : b&w & col. : 35 mm. & captions & notes. $9.00 is

        1. Income tax - History. 2. Taxation - Canada - History.

        Cartoons by Peter Whalley contribute to a survey of taxes in Canada from 1650 to the 1972 Income Tax Act. Suggested vocabulary study and useful additional information are contained in the guide.-

338.10971
    Le blé canadien : de la ferme au marché.
        prod. [Montreal?] : NFB. 1967.- dist. SEC 45 fr. : col. : 35 mm. & captions & teacher's manual. $9.00 jis

        1. Wheat.

        A description of wheat production in the Canadian Prairie provinces, stressing the high quality of Canadian grain. Discusses quantity shipped for export and the rigid controls which keep the quality high. Studies the importance and duties of the Canadian Wheat Board. Traces production and handling methods throughout the year. English title available : CANADIAN WHEAT : FROM FARM TO MARKET.-

338.10971
    Canadian wheat : from farm to market.
        prod. [Montreal?] : NFB. 1967.- dist. McI. 45 fr. : col. : 35 mm. & captions & teacher's manual. $9.00 jis

        1. Wheat.

        A description of wheat production in the Canadian Prairie provinces, stressing the high quality of Canadian grain. Discusses quantity shipped for export and the rigid controls which keep the quality high. Studies the importance and duties of the Canadian Wheat Board. Traces production and handling methods throughout the year. French title available : LE BLE CANADIEN : DE LA FERME AU MARCHE.-

338.10971
    L'economie forestière.
        prod. [Montreal?] : NFB. 1971.- dist. SEC 43 fr. : b&w & col. : 35 mm. & captions. $9.00 jis

        1. Forests and forestry - Canada.

        Photographs, maps, and charts provide detailed information about the development of Canada's forest industry to its present economic value, and what is being done to ensure the future of the industry. The economic, ecological, and recreational importance of our forests is also stressed. Part of a multi-media kit titled "Les forêts du Canada". English title available : THE FOREST ECONOMY.-

The Classified Catalogue

338.10971
    The Forest economy.
        prod. [Montreal?] : NFB, 1971.- dist. McI. 43 fr. : b&w & col. : 35 mm. & captions. $9.00 jis

        1. Forests and forestry - Canada.

        Photographs, maps, and charts provide detailed information about the development of Canada's forest industry to its present economic value, and what is being done to ensure the future of the industry. The economic, ecological, and recreational importance of our forests is also stressed. Part of a multi-media kit titled "Canada's forests". French title available : L'ECONOMIE FORESTIERE.-

338.10971
    Timber.
        prod. [Toronto] : McI., 1969.- dist. McI. 36 fr. : col. : 35 mm. & captions & study guide. $10.00 (Canada : a nation built on trade : $60.00) ji

        1. Forests and forestry - Canada.

        Traces the historical importance of forestry in the Canadian economy and its role in the growth of Canada's trade. The transportation of timber and its usage is portrayed in sketches, with questions in some captions to stimulate thought. Includes the development of pulp and paper industry, B.C. timber industry and conversation problems.-

338.10971
    Wheat.
        prod. [Toronto] : McI., 1969.- dist. McI. 38 fr. : col. : 35 mm. & captions & study guide. $10.00 (Canada : a nation built on trade : $60.00) ji

        1. Wheat. 2. Prairie Provinces - History.

        Traces the historical development of wheat production and trade in the Prairie Provinces, with emphasis on the importance of wheat in Canada's trade. Explains the importance of transportation facilities, building of railways, Port of Churchill and Seaway. Illustrated with artwork, maps, and charts.-

338.20971
    Les Canadiens et leurs minéraux.
        prod. [Montreal?] : NFB, 1973.- dist. SEC 50 fr. : col. : 35 mm. & captions $9.00 is

        1. Mines and mineral resources - Canada.

        Drawings provide a contemporary view of the Canadian mining industry, examining the roles of various levels of government in management of mineral resources. Explains financial distribution of government funds, land conservation, and recycling efforts. English title available : MINERALS FOR CANADIANS.-

338.20971
    Minerals.
        prod. [Toronto] : McI., 1969.- dist. McI. 38 fr. : col. : 35 mm. & captions & study guide. $10.00 (Canada : a nation built on trade : $60.00) ji

        1. Mines and mineral resources - Canada.

        Outlines the role played by mineral resources in the development of Canada's trade and economy. Emphasizes gold, coal, copper, and nickel, and discusses recent development of oil, gas, and potash.-

338.20971
    Minerals for Canadians.
        prod. [Montreal?] : NFB, 1973.- dist. McI. 50 fr. : col. : 35 mm. & captions. $9.00 is

        1. Mines and minerals resources - Canada.

        Drawings provide a contemporary overview of the Canadian mining industry, examining the roles of various levels of government in management of mineral resources. Explains financial distribution of government funds, land conservation, and recycling efforts. French title available : LES CANADIENS ET LEURS MINERAUX.-

The Classified Catalogue

338.30971
Fish.
prod. [Toronto] : McI., 1969.- dist. McI. 36 fr. : col. : 35 mm. & captions & study guide. $10.00 (Canada : a nation built on trade : $60.00) ji

1. Fisheries - Canada - History.

Uses artwork, maps, and charts to trace the history of the fishing trade from the time of John Cabot. Describes how the English method of curing fish led to settlements in Newfoundland, and discusses changes in fishing techniques. Illustrates the three main fishing areas of Canada.-

338.30971
Fur.
prod. [Toronto] : McI., 1969.- dist. McI. 36 fr. : col. : 35 mm. & captions & study guide. $10.00 (Canada : a nation built on trade : $60.00) ji

1. Fur trade - History.

A survey of the growth and the importance of the fur industry to Canada's trade using artwork and maps. Explains how fur trading with Indians and desire for beaver pelts led to exploration of the country, formation of Hudson's Bay and Northwest Companies. Concludes by reviewing present day fur industry.-

338.40971
L'industrie du fer et de l'acier au Canada.
prod. [Montreal?] : NFB, made 1969 : 1971.- dist. SEC 52 fr. : b&w & col. : 35 mm. & captions. $9.00 ji

1. Iron industry and trade. 2. Steel industry and trade.

An overview of the development of iron and steel industry, showing mine locations, types of mines, iron smelting, steelmaking. Includes maps, black and white and colour photos at Algoma Steel. Questions on filmstrip and lack of manual make teacher preparation
necessary before classroom use. English title available : IRON AND STEEL INDUSTRY IN CANADA.-

338.40971
Iron and steel industry in Canada.
prod. [Montreal?] : NFB, 1969.- dist. McI. 52 fr. : b&w & col. : 35 mm. & captions. $9.00 ji

1. Iron industry and trade. 2. Steel industry and trade.

An overview of the development of iron and steel industry, showing mines, iron smelting, steelmaking. Includes maps, black and white and colour photos at Algoma Steel. Questions on filmstrip and lack of manual make teacher preparation necessary before classroom use. French title available : L'INDUSTRIE DU FER ET DE L'ACIER AU CANADA.-

338.91
Let's talk about it.
prod. [Montreal?] : NFB, 1977.- dist. McI. 39 fr. : col. : 35 mm. & captions. $9.00 s

1. Developing areas. 2. International economic relations. 3. Economic assistance.

Designed to elicit discussion about the unequal distribution of the world's resources. Cartoons organize the issues under five basic themes: commodities, tariff and trade preferences, technology and multinational corporations, international monetary reform, and aid. French title available : UN NOUVEL ORDRE ECONOMIQUE INTERNATIONAL : "PARLONS-EN".-

338.91
Un nouvel ordre economique international : "parlons-en".
prod. [Montreal?] : NFB, 1977.- dist. SEC 39 fr. : col. : 35 mm. & captions. $9.00 s

1. Developing areas. 2. International economic relations. 3. Economic assistance.

Designed to elicit discussion about the unequal distribution of the world's resources. Cartoons organize the issues under five basic themes : commodities, tariff and trade preferences, technology and multinational corporations, international monetary reform, and aid. English title available : LET'S TALK ABOUT IT.-

The Classified Catalogue

338.91
Qu'est-ce que l'aide au developpement international?
prod. [Montreal?] : NFB, 1970.- dist. SEC 48 fr. : b&w & col. : 35 mm. & captions. $9.00 s

1. Economic assistance.   2. Developing areas.

A provocative introduction to all aspects of aid to developing countries. Suggests reasons for Canada to be concerned, and possible rationales for Canada in providing development assistance. Poses cogent questions for discussion - what types of aid, administration and efficiency of aid, reasons for past failures, and future goals. Uses drawings and photos. English title available : WHAT IS INTERNATIONAL DEVELOPMENT ASSISTANCE?-

338.91
What is international development assistance?
prod. [Montreal?] : NFB, made 1969 : 1974.- dist. McI. 53 fr. : b&w & col. : 35 mm. & captions. $9.00 s

1. Economic assistance.   2. Developing areas.

A provocative introduction to all aspects of aid to developing countries. Suggests reasons for Canada to be concerned, and possible rationales for Canada in providing development assistance. Poses cogent questions for discussion - what types of aid, administration and eficieny of aid, reasons for past failures, and future goals. Uses drawings and photos. French title available : QU'EST-CE QUE L'AIDE AU DEVELOPPEMENT INTERNATIONAL?-

338.988
I can see clearly now.
prod. [Scarborough, Ont.] : SFM, 1974.- dist. SFM 85 fr. : col. : 35 mm. & cassette (25 min.) : auto. & aud. adv. sig. & reading script. $17.00 is

1. Government ownership.   2. Guyana - Economic policy.

Explores social, economic and political implications of Guyana's decision to nationalize its Demba bauxite company owned by Montreal-based Alcan. Describes the country's history of slavery under colony rule, and its attempts as a republic to end exploitation by wealthy nations through assuming ownership of its natural resources.-

339.3
National output and its measurement.
prod. [Oakville, Ont.] : SC, 1971.- dist. SC 44 fr. : col. : 35 mm. & cassette (21 min.) : auto. & aud. adv. sig. $35.00 s

1. Economics.

Defines and explains the G.N.P. by describing generation and measurement of production. Indicates role of consumption, investment, government, net exports real growth and inflation. Worksheet included for use with filmstrip.-

339.4
The Determination of the levels of gross national product and incomes.
prod. [Oakville, Ont.] : SC, 1971.- dist. SC 60 fr. : col. : 35 mm. & cassette (20 min.) : auto. & aud. adv. sig. & worksheet. $35.00 s

1. Economics.

A detailed analysis of factors determining levels of G.N.P. and total income. Diagrams, charts are used to interpret relationship between G.N.P. and total income, and to describe effects of external forces such as consumption, income flow, savings, investment, inflation, etc.-

339.5
Economic policy in perspective.
prod. [Oakville, Ont.] : SC, 1971.- dist. SC 53 fr. : col. : 35 mm. & cassette (14 min.) : auto. sig. & worksheet. $35.00 s

1. Inflation.   2. Canada - Economic policy.

An analysis of major monetary and fiscal policies used by Canadian government. Questions posed throughout filmstrip and on accompanying worksheet encourage understanding of relationship between unemployment, inflation and recession. Illustrated with graphs, charts, drawings.-

340
How does the law work?
prod. [Toronto] : Int. Cin., 1977.- dist. VEC 72 fr. : col. : 35 mm. & cassette (8 min.) : auto. & aud. adv. sig. & teacher's guide. $24.00 (Why do we have laws? : $86.00) i

1. Law - Canada.

An overview of how the law works in court: civil trials, criminal trials with discussion of the role of judge, jury, lawyers, defendents. Designed for classroom use and discussion.-

The Classified Catalogue

340
Too many laws... or too few?
   prod. [Toronto] : Int. Cin., 1977.- dist. VEC 75 fr. : col. ; 35 mm. & cassette (9 min.) : auto. & aud. adv. sig. & teacher's guide. $24.00 (Why do we have laws? : $86.00) i

   1. Law - Canada.

   Illustrates how laws protect our property and rights, sometimes at the expense of individual freedom. Raises questions about group protection vs. individual freedom. Designed for classroom use and discussion with teachers.-

340
What are laws?
   prod. [Toronto] : Int. Cin., 1977.- dist. VEC 82 fr. : col. ; 35 mm. & cassette (12 min.) : auto. & aud. adv. sig. & teacher's guide. $24.00 (Why do we have laws? : $86.00) i

   1. Law - Canada.

   Uses examples to raise questions about the role of the law in the life of the average citizen. Discusses laws as reflection of society's values, law makers, origins of Canadian law and types of laws and statutes. For classroom use and discussion with teachers.-

342
How do we make laws?
   prod. [Toronto] : Int. Cin. 1977.- dist. VEC 74 fr. : col. ; 35 mm. & cassette (10 min.) : auto. & aud. adv. sig. & teacher's guide. $24.00 (Why do we have laws? : $86.00) i

   1. Canada - Constitutional law.

   Uses examples to raise questions that will encourage follow-up discussion about the role of the law in the life of the average citizen. Discusses the B.N.A. Act, federal and provincial jurisdictions, how laws can be changed by political pressure, and role of public servants in enforcing regulations. Suggests follow-up classroom discussion.-

342
Why governments?
   prod. [Toronto] : Int. Cin., 1978.- dist. VEC 71 fr. : b&w & col. ; 35 mm. & cassette (15 min.) : auto. & aud. adv. sig. $24.00 (How Canada is governed : $130.00) ji

   1. Canada - Constitutional law. 2. Canada - Politics and government.

   Presentation discusses the decision-making process in Canadian government. Pinpoints people involved in law-making, the division of federal and provincial powers, application and interpretation of laws. Encourages discussion on why societies need rules and whether or not governments serve interests of all its citizens.-

342.4
Constitutional development.
   prod. [Montreal?] : NFB, 1964.- dist. McI. 43 fr. : col. ; 35 mm. & captions & teacher's guide. $9.00 (Government of Canada) is

   1. Canada. Constitution. 2. Canada - Politics and government.

   Cartoon strip outlining federal and provincial responsibilities in 1867 and today, including problems that have arisen. Amusing drawings with generally simple captions. Open-ended to lead to discussion. French title available : L'EVOLUTION CONSTITUTIONNELLE.-

342.4
L'Evolution constitutionelle.
   prod. [Montreal?] : NFB, 1964.- dist. SEC 45 fr. : col. ; 35 mm. & captions & teacher's guide. $9.00 (Le gouvernement au Canada) is

   1. Canada - Constitutional law - History. 2. Canada - Politics and government.

   Cartoon strip outlining federal and provincial responsibilities in 1867 and today, including problems that have arisen. Amusing drawings with generally simple captions. Open-ended to lead to discussion. Very suitable for immersion classes or extended French classes in Social Science. English title available : CONSTITUTIONAL DEVELOPMENT.-

The Classified Catalogue

342.4
    Ottawa and the provinces : issues, choices and values.
        prod. [Toronto] : Int. Cin., 1978.- dist. VEC 72 fr. : b&w & col. : 35 mm. & cassette (15 min.) : auto. & aud. adv. sig. $24.00 (How Canada is governed : $130.00) ji

        1. Canada - Constitutional law. 2. Canada - Politics and government.

        Provides a humorous photographic approach to describe the Canadian federal/provincial relationship in the past, present and future. Indicates division of responsibility and discusses the present power struggle inherent in move toward provincial autonomy.-

350.971
    The Role of the Public Service.
        prod. [Toronto] : Int. Cin., 1978.- dist. VEC 62 fr. : b&w & col. : 35 mm. & cassette (15 min.) : auto. & aud. adv. sig. & teacher's guide. $24.00 (How Canada is governed : $130.00) ji

        1. Civil service - Canada.

        An overview of the governmental departments, commissions, boards, agencies and crown corporations which employ public servants. Gives examples of various responsibilities of public service in meeting needs of Canadians. Comments on implications of ever-increasing public service upon government and public.-

352.071
    Go fight City Hall! local decision making.
        prod. [Toronto] : Int. Cin., 1978.- dist. VEC 82 fr. : b&w & col. : 35 mm. & cassette (15 min.) : auto. & aud. adv. sig. & teacher's guide. $24.00 (How Canada is governed : $130.00) ji

        1. Municipal government - Canada.

        Describes role of municipal governments in providing services required daily by residents. Identifies these services and indicates areas of overlapping between provincial and municipal governments. Emphasizes effectiveness of citizens' pressure groups in combating problems of urbanization.-

352.071
    Le gouvernement local.
        prod. [Montreal?] : NFB, 1965.- dist. SEC 38 fr. : col. : 35 mm. & captions. $9.00 (Le gouvernement au Canada) is

        1. Local government.

        A lighthearted approach illustrating pros and cons of local government. Indicates numerous services provided by government to taxpayers. Students encouraged to participate in discussion during viewing. English title available : LOCAL GOVERNMENT.-

352.071
    Local government.
        prod. [Montreal?] : NFB, 1965.- dist. McI. 36 fr. : col. : 35 mm. & captions. $9.00 (Government of Canada) is

        1. Local government.

        A lighthearted approach illustrating pros and cons of local government. Indicates *numerouse services provided by government to taxpayers. Students encouraged to participate in discussion during viewing. French title available : LE GOUVERNEMENT LOCAL.-

352.071
    Urban government.
        prod. [Scarborough, Ont.] : R.B.M., 1975.- dist. ETHOS 39 fr. : col. : 35 mm. & cassette (11 min.) : auto. & aud. adv. sig. & teacher's manual. $19.00 (Urban studies : $103.50) ji

        1. Municipal government - Canada.

        Photographs of Toronto illustrate this outline of the many questions faced by a municipal government, including transportation, the environment, urban growth, and provision of essential services.-

The Classified Catalogue

354.71
    Le gouvernement provincial.
        prod. [Montreal?] : NFB, 1965.- dist. SEC 47 fr. : col. : 35 mm. & captions. $9.00 (Le gouvernement au Canada.) is

        1. Canada - Politics and government.

        Photographs and cartoon drawings describe the role of the Provincial government and compare its responsibilities with those of the Federal government. Explains duties of members of Parliament and powers of Provincial government in education, health, and justice. Discusses provincial and federal taxation system. Although photos are dated, the information is still valid. English title available : PROVINCIAL GOVERNMENT.-

354.71
    Provincial government
        prod. [Montreal?] : NFB, 1965.- dist. McI. 42 fr. : col. : 35 mm. & captions. $9.00 (Government of Canada) is

        1. Canada - Politics and government.

        Photographs and cartoon drawings describe the role of the provincial government and compare its responsibilites with those of the federal government. Explains duties of members of parliament and powers of Provincial government in education, health, and justice. Discusses provincial and federal taxation systems. Although photos are dated, the information is still valid. French title available : LE GOUVERNEMENT PROVINCIAL.-

354.712
    The Structure of government.
        prod. [Montreal?] : NFB, made 1966 : 1968.- dist. McI. 32 fr. : col. : 35 mm. & captions. $9.00 ji

        1. Northwest Territories - Politics and government.

        Photographs, maps and cartoon drawings describe the operation of government in the Northwest Territories. Explains federal representation by one MP and one Cabinet Minister, and Territorial Government of 12 members. The roles of the Department of Indian Affairs and Northern Development and other departments are shown.-

362.7
    Children's hospital : in-patient.
        prod. [Toronto] : Int. Cin., 1977.- dist. VEC 70 fr. : col. : 35 mm. & cassette (6 min.) : auto. & aud. adv. sig. & teacher's guide. $24.00 (Community close-ups : $192.00) pj

        1. Children's hospitals.

        Explains operation procedures and subsequent convalescence in a hospital. French title available : UN HOPITAL POUR ENFANTS : PATIENT HOSPITALISE.-

362.7
    Children's hospital : check-ups and emergencies.
        prod. [Toronto] : Int. Cin., 1977.- dist. VEC 77 fr. : col. : 35 mm. & cassette (8 min.) : auto. & aud. adv. sig. & teacher's guide. $24.00 (Community close-ups : $192.00) pj

        1. Children's hospitals.

        Focusses on the different out-patient departments and facilities, showing how a large hospital deals with common maladies which afflict young children. French title available : UN HOPITAL POUR ENFANTS : EXAMENS ET URGENCES.-

362.7
    Un Hôpital pour enfants : examen et urgences.
        prod. [Toronto] : Int. Cin., 1975.- dist. VEC 77 fr. : col. : 35 mm. & cassette (9 min.) : auto. & aud. adv. sig. & teacher's guide. $24.00 (Un Hôpital pour enfants : $45.00) pj

        1. Children's hospitals.

        Focusses on the different our-patient departments and facilities, showing how a large hospital deals with common maladies which afflict young children. English title available : CHILDREN'S HOSPITAL : CHECK-UPS AND EMERGENCIES.-

362.7
    Un Hôpital pour enfants : patient hospitalisé.
        prod. [Toronto] : Int. Cin., 1976.- dist. VEC 70 fr. : col. : 35 mm. & cassette (8 min.) : auto. & aud. adv. sig. & teacher's guide. $24.00 (Un Hôpital pour enfants : $45.00) pj

        1. Children's hospitals.

        Explains operation procedures and subsequent convalesence in a hospital. English title available : CHILDREN'S HOSPITAL : IN-PATIENT.-

The Classified Catalogue

362.7
Jimmie to the rescue.
prod. [London, Ont.] : LBE, 1977.- dist. LBE 24 fr. : col. : 35 mm. & cassette (4 min.) : auto. & aud. adv. sig. (Block parent : $20.00) pj

1. Block parent (Program). 2. Child welfare.

When two boys become frightened by a large, unfriendly dog, they go to a Block Parent house for help. Enactment of the situation reinforces the Block Parent logo, and the role of the Block Parent in seeing children home safely. Part of a series.-

362.7
June's narrow escape.
prod. [London, Ont] : LBE, 1977.- dist. LBE 26 fr. : col. : 35 mm. & cassette (5 min.) : auto. & aud. adv. sig. (Block parent : $20.00) pj

1. Block Parent (Program). 2. Child welfare.

Shows a young girl getting into a strange man's car, effectively warning against this type of behavior. Girl's subsequent decision to leave car and inform Block Parent indicates parent and police role in handling the situation. Part of a series.-

362.7
Short cut to trouble.
prod. [London, Ont.] : LBE, 1977.- dist. LBE 27 fr. : col. : 35 mm. & cassette (5 min.) : auto. & aud. adv. sig. (Block parent : $20.00) pj

1. Block Parent (Program). 2. Child welfare.

Shows a boy who senses that he is being followed while taking a shortcut, in order to show children how they may go to a Block Parent for help in a similar situation. Explains how this type of incident can be avoided if children are warned against travelling through dense bush alone. Part of a series.-

362.706
Qu'est-ce qu'UNICEF?
prod. [Montreal?] : NFB, 1967.- dist. SEC 29 fr. : col. : 35 mm. & cassette (5 min.) : auto. & aud. adv. sig. $18.00 pji

1. United Nations International Children's Emergency Fund.

Cartoons and photographs illustrate multiple uses of UNICEF in underdeveloped countries. Traces historical development and shows how money, collected for Hallowe'en, is used for medicine, food and schooling. Only the voices of young children are featured on the record. English title available : WHAT IS UNICEF?-

362.706
What is UNICEF?
prod. [Montreal?] : NFB, 1967.- dist. McI. 30 fr. : col. : 35 mm. & cassette (5 min.) : auto. & aud. adv. sig. $18.00 pji

1. United Nations International Children's Emergency Fund.

Cartoons and photographs illustrate multiple uses of UNICEF in underdeveloped countries. Traces historical development and shows how money, collected for Hallowe'en, is used for medicine, food, and schooling. Only the voices of young children are featured on the record. French title available : QU'EST-CE QU' UNICEF?-

362.8
Love and marriage.
prod. [Toronto] : M-L, 1975.- dist. Sch. Ser. or Vint. 52 fr. : col. : 35 mm. & cassette (8 min.) : auto. & aud. adv. sig. & teacher's guide. $16.50 (Maturity : options & consequences : $85.00) is

1. Marriage counselling.

Discusses the issues of teen-age marriage, some of its problems, and possible reasons for and against it. Illustrates the factors that affect an important decision. Discussion points are included in guide.-

The Classified Catalogue

363.2
  The Police force : behind the scenes.
    prod. [Toronto] : Int. Cin., 1977.- dist. VEC
    63 fr. : col. ; 35 mm. & cassette (8 min.) :
    auto. & aud. adv. sig. & teacher's guide.
    $24.00 (Community close-ups : $192.00) j

    1. Police.

    Discusses some of the techniques used by a
    modern police force with emphasis on the
    need for patience and skill. Illustrations
    include booking procedures, the ballistics
    department, the identification kit, and the
    canine rescue squad.-

363.2
  The Police force : part of the community.
    prod. [Toronto] : Int. Cin., 1977.- dist. VEC
    54 fr. : col. ; 35 mm. & cassette (7 min.) :
    auto. & aud. adv. sig. & teacher's guide.
    $24.00 (Community close-ups : $192.00) pj

    1. Police.

    Emphasizes that the police and the
    community must work together. Illustrates the
    many facets of a large metropolitan police
    force - the communications centre, the
    emergency task force and its equipment, the
    firing range, the mounted patrol stables, and
    the continuing education of policemen.
    Introduced with a brief look at
    peace-keeping in the past and the role of
    the Mounties today.-

363.2
  The Police officer.
    prod. [Scarborough, Ont.] : FCC, 1978.- dist.
    FCC 24 fr. : col. ; 35 mm. & cassette (6
    min.) : auto. & aud. adv. sig. & teacher's
    guide. $12.95 (The Community helpers :
    $25.90) p

    1. Police.

    Shows police officers performing a variety of
    duties and in a number of situations familiar
    to children, - directing traffic, on
    motorcycles or horseback, helping lost
    children, teaching bicycle safety. Emphasizes
    their concern for safety and their
    friendliness.-

363.20971
  The Beginning of a new era.
    prod. [Scarborough, Ont.] : R.B.M., 1976.- dist.
    ETHOS 44 fr. : b&w & col. ; 35 mm. &
    cassette (13 min.) : auto. & aud. adv. sig. &
    teacher's manual. $19.00 (Royal Canadian
    Mounted Police : $69.00) ji

    1. Canada. Royal Canadian Mounted Police -
    History.

    Describes the work of the R.C.M.P. from the
    arrival of the settlers at the close of the
    19th century to the formation of the Air
    Section in 1937. Photographs depict the
    historical journey of their ship "St. Roch".-

363.20971
  The Force keeps the peace.
    prod. [Toronto] : Int. Cin., 1976.- dist. VEC
    57 fr. : col. ; 35 mm. & cassette (10 min.) :
    auto. & aud. adv. sig. & teacher's guide.
    $24.00 (The Scarlet force : the story of the
    North West Mounted Police : $45.00) ji

    1. Canada. North West Mounted Police -
    History.

    A continuation of the history of the
    Northwest Mounted Police, discussing how the
    force grew in numbers, responsibilities, and
    reputation as Canada expanded to the west
    and north.-

363.20971
  The Force rides west.
    prod. [Toronto] : Int. Cin., 1976.- dist. VEC
    64 fr. : b&w & col. ; 35 mm. & cassette (8
    min.) : auto. & aud. adv. sig. & teacher's
    guide. $24.00 (The Scarlet force : the story
    of the North West Mounted Police : $45.00) ji

    1. Canada. North West Mounted Police -
    History.

    An informative history of the origin of the
    Northwest Mounted Police, and how the
    concept of a Canadian military police force
    was designed to maintain law and order in
    the West.-

The Classified Catalogue

363.20971
    La Gendarmerie du Nord-Ouest : la rébellion de 1885.
        prod. [Montreal?] : NFB, 1961.- dist. SEC 49 fr. : b&w : 35 mm. & captions & teacher's guide. $9.00 ji

    1. Riel Rebellion, 1885. 2. Canada. North West Mounted Police - History.

    Authentic black and white photographs trace the economic conditions of the Indians and Métis in the West, leading up to the Rebellion of 1885. Actual period newspaper drawings examine the phases of the Rebellion and how the Police tried to prevent an uprising. Discusses Louis Riel and his Métis Bill of Rights. English title available : THE NORTH WEST MOUNTED POLICE : THE REBELLION OF 1885.-

363.20971
    La Gendarmerie du Nord-Ouest : la longue marche vers l'Ouest.
        prod. [Montreal?] : NFB, 1961.- dist. SEC 45 fr. : b&w : 35 mm. & captions & teacher's manual. $9.00 jis

    1. Canada. Northwest Mounted Police - History.

    Black and white drawings from period newspapers emphasize the need for a police force in the early years of Canada's west. Traces the organization of the Northwest Mounted Police and records the trip west to round up whiskey traders and outlaws. Features sketches by an artist who was on the trip. English title available : NORTH WEST MOUNTED POLICE : THE LONG MARCH WEST.-

363.20971
    History of the Royal Canadian Mounted Police.
        prod. [Scarborough] : SHN, 1972.- dist. PHM 123 fr. : col. : 35 mm. & cassette (10 min.) : auto. & aud. adv. sig. & teaching guide. $39.60 is

    1. Canada. Royal Canadian Mounted Police - History.

    Describes the formation of the Northwest Mounted Police in early 1870's. Discusses the relationship with Chief Crowfoot, the coming of the railroad, the Riel Rebellion, and the Yukon Gold Rush. Continues into the 20th century.-

363.20971
    North West Mounted Police : the Klondike Gold Rush.
        prod. [Montreal?] : NFB, 1961.- dist. McI. 49 fr. : b&w : 35 mm. & captions & teacher's manual. $9.00 ji

    1. Klondike gold fields. 2. Canada. North West Mounted Police - History.

    Early black and white photographs trace the history of the Royal Canadian Mounted Police during the Klondike Gold Rush of 1896. Examines duties of the police force and how they helped prospectors prepare for excursions into the gold field.-

363.20971
    North West Mounted Police : the long march west.
        prod. [Montreal?] : NFB, 1961.- dist. McI. 45 fr. : b&w : 35 mm.& captions & teacher's manual. $9.00 jis

    1. Canada. Northwest Mounted Police - History.

    Black and white drawings from period newspapers emphasize the need for a police force in the early years of Canada's west. Traces the organization of the Northwest Mounted Police and records the trip West to round up whiskey traders and outlaws. Features sketches by an artist who was on the trip. French title available : LA GENDAMERIE DU NORD-OUEST LA LONGUE MARCHE VERS L'OUEST.-

363.20971
    The North West Mounted Police - the Rebellion of 1885.
        prod. [Montreal?] : NFB, 1961.- dist. McI. 50 fr. : b&w : 35 mm. & captions & teacher's guide. $9.00 ji

    1. Riel Rebellion, 1885. 2. Canada. North West Mounted Police - History.

    Authentic black and white photographs trace the economic conditions of the Indians and Métis in the West, leading up to the Rebellion of 1885. Actual period newspaper drawings examine the phases of the Rebellion and how the Police tried to prevent an uprising. Discusses Louis Riel and his Métis Bill of Rights. French title available : LA GENDARMERIE DU NORD-OUEST - LA REBELLION DE 1885.-

The Classified Catalogue

363.20971
  The Northwest Mounted Police.
   prod. [Scarborough, Ont.] : R.B.M., 1976.- dist. ETHOS 47 fr. : b&w & col. : 35 mm. & cassette (14 min.) : auto. & aud. adv. sig. & teacher's manual. $19.00 (Royal Canadian Mounted Police : $69.00) ji

   1. Canada. North West Mounted Police - History.

   Traces the growth of Canada's national police force, the R.C.M.P. from its establishment in 1873 as the Northwest Mounted Police. Photographs depict episodes from the early days.-

363.3
  The Firefighter.
   prod. [Scarborough, Ont.] : FCC., 1978.- dist. FCC 24 fr. : col. : 35 mm & cassette (5 min.) : auto. & aud. adv. sig. & teacher's guide. $12.95 (The Community helpers : $25.90) p

   1. Fire fighters.

   Follows the steps taken when an emergency call is received at a fire station. Also illustrates firefighting equipment, and emphasizes the willingness of firemen to answer children's questions.-

363.3
  My father the fireman.
   prod. [Toronto] : Lea., 1973.- dist. Lea. 42 fr. : col. : 35 mm. & captions. $9.00 p

   1. Fire fighters.

   Focuses on an actual employee of the Richmond Hill Fire Department to show the daily life of a fireman. Outlines procedures used from when firehall first receives alarm, to fighting the fire. Photographs illustrate types of fires, trucks and equipment used and interior of station.-

365
  A Captive society.
   prod. [Montreal?] : NFB, 1970.- dist. McI. 52 fr. : col. : 35 mm. & captions & printed notes. $9.00 is

   1. Prisons - Canada.

   Illustrates life in Canada's prisons. Provides actual facts and data on prisoners including types of people who become prisoners. Compares maximum security institution with medium and minimum security ones. An inquiry approach encourages group discussion and suggestions from viewers on objectives of our prison system and ways in which it could be improved. French title available : UN MONDE FERMÉ.-

365
  Un monde fermeś.
   prod. [Montreal?] : NFB, made 1970 : 1971.- dist. SEC 52 fr. : col. : 35 mm. & captions & printed notes. $9.00 is

   1. Prisons - Canada.

   Illustrates life in Canada's prisons. Provides actual facts and data on prisoners including types of people who become prisoners. Compares maximum security institutions with medium and minimum security ones. An inquiry approach encourages group discussion and suggestions from viewers on objectives of our prison system and ways in which it could be improved. English title available : A CAPTIVE SOCIETY.-

370.19
  City students visit Ogoki.
   prod. [Toronto] : RQM, 1975.- dist. Lea. 42 fr. : col. : 35 mm. & captions & teacher's guide. $9.00 (An Exchange with people of native ancestry : $18.00) is

   1. Students, Interchange of. 2. Exhange of persons programs. 3. Ogoki, Ont.

   An account of city students' visit to the remote native village of Ogoki. Photographs show the initial preparations, such as lessons in first aid, snowshoeing, and shooting. Activities experienced during the exchange include hunting, snowmobiling, fishing, ad cooking various types of native food.-

370.19
Ogoki native people visit the city.
   prod. [Toronto] : RQM, 1975.- dist. Lea. 45 fr. : col. : 35 mm. & captions & teacher's guide. $9.00 (An Exchange with people of native ancestry : $18.00) is

   1. Students, Interchange of. 2. Exchange of persons programs.

   Photographs of Ogoki natives in Toronto. Provides candid shots of the young people enjoying the sights and sounds of Toronto. 2nd in series.-

371.33
The Diazo process.
   prod. [Oakville, Ont.] : SC, 1972.- dist. SC 60 fr. : col. : 35 mm. & cassette (8 min.) : auto. & aud. adv. sig. $35.00 s

   1. Overhead transparencies. 2. Teaching - Audio-visual aids.

   Step by step instructions show production of overhead transparency using Diazo process. Discusses materials used, lettering techniques, exposure time, master preparation, film development and mounting. Best used under teacher's direction.-

371.33
Handmade overhead transparencies and their use.
   prod. [Oakville, Ont.] : SC, 1972.- dist. SC 61 fr. : col. : 35 mm. & cassette (10 min.) : auto. adv. sig. only. $35.00 is

   1. Overhead transparencies. 2. Teaching - Audio-visual aids.

   Diagrams and photographs are used to examine the advantages of using overhead projectors in group situations. Discusses the methods of preparing handmade visuals and provides detailed steps to follow to ensure an effective result. Includes reducing visuals by reverse projection and mounting transparencies.-

371.33
Producing your own instructional audio-visual programme.
   prod. [Oakville, Ont.] : SC, 1972.- dist. SC 57 fr. : col. : 35 mm. & cassette (7 min.) : auto. adv. sig. only. $35.00 is

   1. Teaching - Audio-visual aids.

   Photographs and diagrams trace the steps in producing a programme. Includes script writing, production, and presentation. Explains use of storyboards, colour coding slides for effective and varied visual display, and importance of simple concise language. Provides method of timing production and balancing sound with visual display.-

371.33
Producing your own slide program.
   prod. [Oakville, Ont.] : SC, 1972.- dist. SC 50 fr. : col. : 35 mm. & cassette (8 min.) : auto. adv. sig. only. $35.00 s

   1. Teaching - Audio-visual aids.

   Outlines the production of a slide programme, using carousel projector and tape cassette. Shows proper use of projector, setting up and pulsing of tape recorder to synchronize with programme. Included is example of short slide/tape showing demonstrating skills.-

372.6
The Absent-minded Mr. Villoughby.
   prod. [Toronto] : M-L, 1973.- dist. Sch. Ser. or Vint. 51 fr. : col. : 35 mm. & cassette (11 min.) : auto. & aud. adv. sig. & teaching guide. $16.50 (Open-ended multiple/endings : $75.00) j

   1. Storytelling - Study and teaching.

   Photographs show the adventures of a young boy, Jamie, as he tries to return a bag to an absent-minded friend. Encourages viewers to create their own endings to the story and to discuss the two alternative endings suggested. French title available : LE SAC DE M. DARLUNE.-

The Classified Catalogue

372.6
    The Adventures of bunny rabbit.
        prod. [Toronto] : M-L, 1974.- dist. Sch. Ser. or Vint. 53 fr. : col. : 35 mm. & cassette (7 min.) : auto. & aud. adv. sig. & teacher's guide. $16.50 (Animal adventures with two endings : $49.50) p

        1. Storytelling - Study and teaching.
        2. Rabbits - Fiction.

        Photos and dramatization are used to tell the story of a greedy rabbit who escapes from his hutch and confronts the dangers of the outside world. Two alternative endings are suggested-children are invited to create their own endings.-

372.6
    The Adventures of kitty cat.
        prod. [Toronto] : M-L, 1974.- dist. Sch. Ser. or Vint. 57 fr. : col. : 35 mm. & cassette (11 min.) : auto. & aud. adv. sig. & teacher's guide. $16.50 (Animal adventures with two endings : $49.50) p

        1. Storytelling - Study and teaching.
        2. Cats - Fiction.

        Dramatized story of a cat who tries to dog. Photos are used to show humourous consequences. Story has two alternative endings and invites children to create their own endings.-

372.6
    The Adventures of puppy dog.
        prod. [Toronto] : M-L, 1974.- dist. Sch. Ser. or Vint. 54 fr. : col. : 35 mm. & cassette (8 min.) : auto. & aud. adv. sig. & teacher's guide. $16.50 (Animal adventures with two endings : $49.50) p

        1. Storytelling - Study and teaching.
        2. Dogs - Fiction.

        Dramatized story, using photos, of a puppy and his adventures when he gets lost in the city. Two alternative endings are suggested and children are invited to create their own endings.-

372.6
    L'aventure de Robert.
        prod. [Toronto] : M-L, 1974.- dist. Sch. Ser. or Vint. 50 fr. : col. : 35 mm. & cassette (11 min.) : auto. & aud. adv. sig. & teacher's guide. $16.50 (Histoires à dénouements multiples : $75.00) j

        1. Storytelling - Study and teaching.

        Invites viewers to create and discuss their own endings for a story about a boy and the adventures he has when he hides in the back of a delivery truck. Three possible endings are suggested. English title available : SURPRISE ADVENTURE.-

372.6
    La chasse aux trésors.
        prod. [Toronto] : M-L, 1974.- dist. Sch. Ser. or Vint. 52 fr. : col. : 35 mm. & cassette (12 min.) : auto. & aud. adv. sig. & teacher's guide. $16.50 (Histoires à dénouements multiples : $75.00) j

        1. Storytelling - Study and teaching.
        2. Buried treasure - Fiction.

        An imaginative story of four children, an old map, and a giant old key. Encourages viewers to create their own endings before the story continues to suggest three alternative endings. English title available : THE OLD MAP MYSTERY.-

372.6
    Le déménagement.
        prod. [Toronto] : M-L, 1974.- dist. Sch. Ser. or Vint. 44 fr. : col. : 35 mm. & cassette (7 min.) : auto. & aud. adv. sig. & teacher's guide. $16.50 (Histoires à dénouements multiples : $75.00) j

        1. Storytelling - Study and teaching.

        The story of Mike, and his adventures en route to his new home. Encourages viewers to create their own endings, before the story continues to suggest two possible endings. English title available : MOVING DAY MIX-UP.-

The Classified Catalogue

372.6
  The Great horse contest.
    prod. [Toronto] : M-L, 1973.- dist. Sch. Ser. or Vint. 80 fr. : col. : 35 mm. & cassette (10 min.) : auto. & aud. adv. sig. & teacher's guide. $16.50 (New children's stories : $65.00) pj

    1. Storytelling - Study and teaching.
    2. Horses - Fiction.

    The story of Natalie, who enters a long-distance horse race with the assistance of her grandmother. Illustrates that playing fair is more important than winning.-

372.6
  La maison aux fantômes.
    prod. [Toronto] : M-L, 1974.- dist. Sch. Ser. or Vint. 46 fr. : col. : 35 mm. & cassette (10 min.) : auto. & aud. adv. sig. & teacher's guide. $16.50 (Histoires à dénouements multiples : $75.00) j

    1. Storytelling - Study annd teaching.
    2. Ghosts - Fiction.

    A suspenseful story of three children in a haunted house who meet a charming ghost who provides them with a picnic. Viewers are invited to discuss their own solutions to the story before other possible endings are suggested. English title available : THREE IN A HAUNTED HOUSE.-

372.6
  Moving day mix-up.
    prod. [Toronto] : M-L, 1973.- dist. Sch. Ser. or Vint. 44 fr. : col. : 35 mm. & cassette (7 min.) : auto. & aud. adv. sig. & teaching guide. $16.50 (Open-ended multiple/endings : $75.00) j

    1. Story telling - Study and teaching.

    The story of Mike, and his adventures en route to his new home. Encourages viewers to create their own endings, before the story continues to suggest two possible endings. French title available : LE DEMENAGEMENT.-

372.6
  The Old map mystery.
    prod. [Toronto] : M-L, 1973.- dist. Sch. Ser. or Vint. 52 fr. : col. : 35 mm. & cassette (12 min.) : auto. & aud. adv. sig. & teacher's guide. $16.50 (Open-ended multiple/endings : $75.00) ji

    1. Storytelling - Study and teaching.

    An imaginative story of four children, an old map, and a giant old key. Encourages viewers to create their own endings before the story continues to suggest three alternative endings. French title available : LA CHASSE AUX TRESORS.-

372.6
  Une promenade en traineau.
    prod. [Montreal?] : NFB, 1975.- dist. SEC 51 fr. : col. : 35 mm. $9.00 p

    1. Language arts - Study and teaching.
    2. Winter sports. 3. Outdoor recreation.

    Captionless filmstrip to be used to develop conversation, comprehension skills, storytelling and crafts, and to serve as a field trip for the primary class. Photographs show the barn, grooming the horse, hitching to the sleigh. Winter activities such as sliding, ice fishing, skating, snow building, and dog sledding are included. English title available : SLEIGH RIDE.-

372.6
  The Rescue of Julius the donkey.
    prod. [Toronto] : M-L, 1973.- dist. Sch. Ser. or Vint. 67 fr. : col. : 35 mm. & cassette (11 min.) : auto. & aud. adv. sig. & teacher's guide. $16.50 (New children's stories : $65.00) pj

    1. Storytelling - Study and teaching.
    2. Donkeys - Fiction.

    The adventures of young Nancy as she attempts to rescue Julius, the donkey, from an abandoned farm. Nancy realizes the worry she is causing her parents and learns the meaning of responsibility.-

The Classified Catalogue

372.6
  The Runaway.
    prod. [Toronto] : M-L, 1973.- dist. Sch. Ser. or Vint. 54 fr. : col. : 35 mm. & cassette (6 min.) : auto. & aud. adv. sig. & teacher's guide. $16.50 (New children's stories : $65.00) pj

    1. Storytelling - Study and teaching.
    2. Runaways - Fiction.

    The story of ten-year old Mark who, having just moved from the country to the city, decides to run away from home. Tells of his experiences with a youth gang, his problems, his wanderings, and the friend he finds along the way.-

372.6
  Le sac de M. Danlune.
    prod. [Toronto] : M-L, 1974.- dist. Sch. Ser. or Vint. 51 fr. : col. : 35 mm. & cassette (11 min.) : bauto. & aud. adv. sig. & teacher's guide. $16.50 (Histoires à dénouements multiples : $75.00) j

    1. Storytelling - Study and teaching.

    Photographs show the adventures of a young boy, Jamie, as he tries to return a bag to an absent-minded friend. Encourages viewers to create their own endings to the story and to discuss the two alternative endings suggested. English title available : THE ABSENT-MINDED MR. WILLOUGHBY.-

372.6
  The Sparkling imagination.
    prod. [Toronto] : M-L, 1973.- dist. Sch. Ser. or Vint. 95 fr. : col. : 35 mm. & cassette (13 min.) : auto. & aud. adv. sig. & teacher's guide. $16.50 (New children's stories : $65.00) pj

    1. Storytelling - Study and teaching.

    Illustrates the adventure of two children who plan to write a story using a typewriter. The spirit of the typewriter helps their thinking by appearing as the characters in their stories. Guides students to plan the structure and plot of their own stories.-

372.6
  Surprise adventure.
    prod. [Toronto] : M-L, 1973.- dist. Sch. Ser. or Vint. 50 fr. : col. : 35 mm. & cassette (11 min.) : auto. & aud. adv. sig. & teaching guide. $16.50 (Open-ended multiple/endings : $75.00) j

    1. Storytelling - Study and teaching.

    Invites viewers to create and discuss their own endings for a story about a boy and the adventures he has when he hides in the back of a delivery truck. Three possible endings are suggested. French title available : L'AVENTURE DE ROBERT.-

372.6
  Three in a haunted house.
    prod. [Toronto] : M-L, 1973.- dist. Sch. Ser. or Vint. 46 fr. : col. : 35 mm. & cassette (10 min.) : auto. & aud. adv. sig. & teacher's guide. $16.50 (Open-ended multiple/endings : $75.00) ji

    1. Storytelling - Study and teaching.

    A suspenseful story of three children in a haunted house who meet a charming ghost who provides them with a picnic. Viewers are invited to discuss their own solutions to the story before other possible endings are suggested. French title available : LA MAISON AUX FANTOMES.-

379.51
  Education.
    prod. [Kitchener, Ont.]: EDU, 1974.- dist. EDU 25 fr. : col. : 35 mm. & cassette (9 min.) : auto. & aud. adv. sig. & teacher's guide. $15.95 (China : $79.95) jis

    1. Education - China.

    Describes the education system of China which stresses the importance of manual labour, practical and physical skills. Discusses how the elderly help children understand the past, the importance of political theories, the teaching of industrial skills, and equality of boys and girls in all areas.-

The Classified Catalogue

379.51
    Education and health.
        prod. [Toronto] : CFM, 1975.- dist. BAM 41 fr. : col. : 35 mm. & cassette (13 min.) : auto. & aud. adv. sig. & teacher's guide. $15.50 (China : $89.00) i

        1. Education - China. 2. Medicine - China.

        A detailed look at the modern Chinese educational system, highlighting the new work-study program of combining education with meaningful productive labour at all age levels. Also outlines major aspects of the Chinese medical system, emphasizing the use of acupuncture treatments.-

380
    Our shrinking world.
        prod. [Montreal?] : NFB, made 1966 : 1967.- dist. McI. 37 fr. : col. : 35 mm. & captions. $9.00 ji

        1. Transportation - History. 2. Communication - History.

        Ancient methods of sending goods and messages are illustrated with drawings. Discusses time-saving inventions of the wheel, electricity, internal combustion, and steam power, as well as newer forms of transportation and communication. Photos show trucks, trains, piggybacks, containers, as well as undersea cables and satellites.-

380
    Transportation and communication in Japan.
        prod. [Hamilton, Ont.] : VCI, 1977.- dist. MHR 39 fr. : col. : 35 mm. & teacher's guide & captions. $12.85 (Japan : $72.00) j

        1. Communication. 2. Japan - Transportation.

        Discusses vital roles of shipping, railway networks, trucks, cars, bicycles, buses, taxis, road systems, telephones, radio, television, and of air transport in this country of many islands.-

380.5
    Age of steam and the automobile.
        prod. [Scarborough, Ont.] : R.B.M., 1976.- dist. ETHOS 39 fr. : b&w & col. : 35 mm. & cassette (9 min.) : auto. & aud. adv. sig. & teacher's manual. $19.00 (Transportation in Canada) jis

        1. Railroads - Canada - History.
        2. Automobiles - History.

        Examines railroads and motor vehicles, the new technologies developed in the latter part of the 19th century and the first of the 20th.-

380.5
    Le Bouclier canadien - moyens de transport.
        prod. [Montreal?] : NFB, 1966.- dist. SEC 40 fr. : col. : 35 mm. & captions & teacher's manual. $9.00 jis

        1. Canadian Shield - Transportation.

        Maps and photos illustrate transportation in the Canadian Shield and its problems, with many of the captions posing questions to encourage discussion. Road building and maintenance, use of rivers and lakes, railway and air transportation are illustrated. Review frames are included. English title available : TRANSPORTATION IN THE CANADIAN SHIELD.-

380.5
    China II - transportation.
        prod. [Don Mills, Ont.] : F & V, 1973.- dist. F & V 26 fr. : col. : 35 mm. & teacher's guide. $7.20 (Man in his world) ji

        1. Transportation. 2. China.

        Illustrates the gamut of transportation means in China. Emphasizes that, in addition to conventional modes, people, both men and women also provide a source of transportation.-

The Classified Catalogue

380.5
De la terre à l'air.
   prod. [Toronto] : Int. Cin., 1975.- dist. VEC 51 fr. : b&w & col. : 35 mm. & cassette (12 min.) : auto. & aud. adv. sig. & teaching guide. $24.00 (Transport : l'aventure Canadienne : $86.00) ij

   1. Transportation - History.

   Describes the development of electric powered urban rail systems and discusses development of the automobile and the airplane with special reference to the history of Canadian air transportation. English title avilable : WHEELS AND WINGS.-

380.5
De la traction animal à la vapeur.
   prod. [Toronto] : Int. Cin., 1975.- dist. VEC 53 fr. : b&w & col. : 35 mm. & cassette (12 min.) : auto. & aud. adv. sig. & teaching guide. $24.00 (Transport : l'aventure Canadienne : $86.00) ij

   1. Transportation - History.

   Authentic drawings and photographs of early stage coaches and steamengines illustrate the use of horse and steam power in the development of Canadian overland transportation. English title available : MUSCLE AND STEAM.-

380.5
Japan II : transportation and communication.
   prod. [Don Mills, Ont.] : F & W, 1976.- dist. F & W 25 fr. : col. : 35 mm. & teacher's guide. $7.20 (Man in his world) ji

   1. Transportation. 2. Japan.

   A comprehensive summary of the variety of ways people, goods, and ideas are moved about in Japan. The important role of the Tokaido Express, the subways, and the commuter trains in densely populated areas, bicycles, buses, cars, trucks, ferry boats, ships, and planes in transportation are all discussed. For classroom use.-

380.5
Today and tomorrow.
   prod. [Toronto] : Int. Cin., 1974.- dist. VEC 59 fr. : col. : 35 mm. & cassette (12 min.) : auto. & aud. adv. sig. & teaching manual. $24.00 (Transporation : the Canadian adventure: $86.00) ij

   1. Transportation.

   Discusses transportation of the future. Describes STOL aircraft, monorails, hovercraft, and SST'S. Shows how nature of the environment will be the cause of and remedy for man's transportation problems. French title available : LE PRESENT ET LE FUTUR.-

380.5
Transportation.
   prod. [Toronto] : M-L, 1973.- dist. Sch. Ser. or Vint. 49 fr. : col. : 35 mm. & cassette (9 min.) : auto. & aud. adv. sig. & teacher's guide. $16.50 (Settlers of North America : $75.00) pji

   1. Transportation - History.

   The development of travel from the time of the settlers' arrival in North America, - walking, canoes, wagons, trains, steam engines, etc. Demonstrates the effects that improved transportation had on settlement patterns and civilization.-

380.5
Transportation in the Canadian Shield.
   prod. [Montreal?] : NFB, 1966.- dist. McI. 35 fr. : col. : 35 mm. & captions & teacher's manual. $9.00 (Canadian Shield) jis

   1. Canadian Shield - Transportation.

   Maps and photos illustrate transportation in the Canadian Shield and its problems, with many of the captions posing questions to encourage discussion. Road building and maintenance, use of rivers and lakes, railway and air transportation are illustrated. Review frames are included. French title available : LE BOUCLIER CANADIEN : MOYENS DE TRANSPORT.-

The Classified Catalogue

380.5
    Transportation today : by air and water.
        prod. [Scarborough, Ont.] : R.B.M., 1976.- dist. ETHOS 46 fr. : col. : 35 mm. & cassette (10 min.) : auto. & aud. adv. sig. & teacher's manual. $19.00 (Transportation in Canada) ji

        1. Transportation.

    A general overview of the many ways used by Canadians for travelling by air and by water.-

380.5
    Wheels and wings.
        prod. [Toronto] : Int. Cin., 1974.- dist. VEC 51 fr. : b&w & col. : 35 mm. & cassette (11 min.) : auto. & aud. adv. sig. & teaching guide. $24.00 (Transportation : the Canadian adventure : $86.00) ij

        1. Transportation - History.

    Describes the development of electric powered urban rail systems and discusses development of the automobile and the airplane with special reference to the history of Canadian air transportation. French title available : DE LA TERRE A L'AIR.-

382.0971
    A Survey.
        prod. [Toronto] : McI., 1969.- dist. McI. 36 fr. : col. : 35 mm. & captions & study guide. $10.00 (Canada : a nation built on trade : $60.00) ji

        1. Canada - Commerce - History.

    Describes Canada's historical dependence on trade, showing how the natural resources of fish, fur, timber, wheat, and minerals have been developed as important trading commodities. Uses artwork, graphs, photographs and questions in captions to evoke discussion.-

382.1
    Toward a new international economic order.
        prod. [Montreal?] : NFB, 1977.- dist. McI. 56 fr. : b&w & col. : 35mm. & cassette (12 min.) : auto. & aud. adv. sig. $18.00 s

        1. International economic relations.
        2. Developing areas.

    An analysis of economic relations existing between wealthy powers and developing nations. Explains how past exploitation of colonies by Europe and North America has led to present trade imbalance. Describes Third World's attempts to control their own resources through nationalization of industry and exportation of manufactured goods. Illustrated with photographs, drawings, charts. French title available : VERS UN NOUVEL ORDRE ECONOMIQUE INTERNATIONAL.-

383
    Anna sends a letter.
        prod. [Montreal?] : NFB, 1975.- dist. McI. 49 fr. : col. : 35 mm. & captions. $9.00 pj

        1. Postal service - Canada.

    An explanation of Canada's postal code to a little girl. Cartoons show how computers sort the coded mail, how to remember a postal code, the code, and its importance in prompt delivery.-

383
    A Day in the life of a letter carrier.
        prod. [Stratford, Ont.] Sch. Ch., 1975.- dist. Sch. Ch. 41 fr. : col. : 35 mm. & captions. $7.95 (Canadian community helpers : $15.90) ji

        1. Postal service.

    A letter carrier for the post office explains the variety of duties a postman performs : sorting and packaging mail at the post office, delivering mail to stores, apartment buildings, and homes. The day ends with the postman at home with his family.-

383
    How a letter travels.
        prod. [Stratford, Ont.] : Sch. Ch., 1975.- dist. Sch. Ch. 29 fr. : col. : 35 mm. & captions. $7.95 (Canadian community helpers : $15.90) ji

        1. Postal service.

    Children follow the travels of a letter written by a boy - from mailbox to sorting bags, to delivery trucks and letter carriers - until its safe arrival at his grandmother's in another city.-

The Classified Catalogue

384
    Principaux signaux de détresse.
        prod. [Toronto] : M-L. 1975.- dist. Sch. Ser. or Wint. 47 fr. : col. : 35 mm. & cassette (10 min.) : auto. & aud. adv. sig. & teacher's guide. $16.50 (Activités de plein air : survie : $85.00) i

        1. Signals and signaling. 2. Wilderness survival.

        Describes basic distress signals to be understood by rescue pilots. Includes using life jackets, reflections of sunlight, fire at night and smoke by day, groupings of three of anything, or shaping peeled logs into symbols to convey needs. Good information for any trek into the bush. English title available : BASIC DISTRESS SIGNALS.-

384.6
    Allô, Monsieur Bell!
        prod. [Toronto] : Int. Cin., 1976.- dist. VEC 87 fr. : col. : 35 mm. & cassette (16 min.) : auto. & aud. adv. sig. & teacher's guide, posters and activity masters. $24.00 (Allô! Parlons téléphone : $96.00) pj

        1. Telephone.

        Alexander Granham Bell, impersonated by an actor, shows us the development of the telephone from his early model to the ones presently used. English title available : HELLO, MR BELL.-

384.6
    Et maintenant, tous ensemble.
        prod. [Toronto] : Int. Cin., 1976.- dist. VEC 76 fr. : col. : 35 mm. & cassette (5 min.) : auto. & aud. adv. sig. & teacher's guide, posters and activity masters. $24.00 (Allô! Parlons téléphone : $96.00) pj

        1. Telephone.

        A brief look at the communication needs of a community and the role of the telephone in fulfilling these needs. English title available : GETTING TOGETHER.-

384.6
    Les Experts en téléphonie.
        prod. [Toronto] : Int. Cin., 1976.- dist. VEC 80 fr. : col. : 35 mm. & cassette (9 min.) : auto. & aud. adv. sig. & teacher's guide, posters and activity masters. $24.00 (Allô! Parlons téléphone : $96.00) pj

        1. Telephone.

        Introduces young children to the proper use of the telephone, teaching them to be skillful and effective. Includes how to use the telephone in an emergency. English title available : NOW YOU'RE TALKING.-

384.6025
    Qu'est-ce qui est blanc ou jaune, et qui fait marcher les doigts?
        prod. [Toronto] : Int. Cin., 1976.- dist. VEC 93 fr. : col. : 35 mm. & cassette (14 min.) : auto. & aud. adv. sig. & teacher's guide, posters and activity masters. $24.00 (Allô! Parlons téléphone : $96.00) pj

        1. Telephone.

        Explains how the white and yellow telephone directories may be used in a variety of situations, as well as step-by-step instructions in locating information in these directories. English title available : WHAT'S WHITE AND YELLOW AND READ ALL OVER?-

385
    Rail transportation in Canada : today.
        prod. [Scarborough, Ont.] : R.B.M. 1976.- dist. ETHOS 51 fr. : b&w & col. : 35 mm. & cassette (10 min.) : auto. & aud. adv. sig. & teacher's manual. $19.00 (Transportation in Canada : $276.00) jis

        1. Railroads - Canada.

        Explores the role of railways in transportation an communication in Canada today, with a look at the variety of rolling stock and motive power being used.-

385.0971
    Inter-city train.
        prod. [Toronto] : Int. Cin., 1977.- dist. VEC 66 fr. : col. : 35 mm. & cassette (8 min.) : auto. & aud. adv. sig. & teacher's guide. $24.00 (Community close-ups : $192.00) pj

        1. Railroads - Canada.

        Modern, inter-city travel by train is described as a young girl tells of her first train ride. Features photos of Toronto's Union Station and CN'S Turbo train.-

The Classified Catalogue

385.0971
    Rail transportation in Canada : the early days.
        prod. [Scarborough, Ont.] : R.B.M., 1976.- dist. ETHOS 45 fr. : b&w & col. : 35 mm. & cassette (11 min.) : auto. & aud. adv. sig. & teacher's manual. $19.00 (Transportation in Canada) jis

        1. Railroads - Canada - History.

        Describes the development of railroading in Canada from the inaugural run of the Champlain and St. Lawrence railroad in 1836, with emphasis on changes brought about by the new technology.-

385.0971
    Rails across Canada.
        prod. [Toronto] : McI. 1977.- dist. McI. 56 fr. : col. : 35 mm. & cassette (18 min.) : auto. & aud. adv. sig. & teacher's guide. $19.00 (Canada on the move : $76.00) ji

        1. Railroads - Canada - History.

        History of railroading in Canada. Shows importance of railway building boom to immigration, settlement and Confederation, and uses of railways today. Indicates new emphasis on commuter service instead of long-distance passenger service.-

386.0971
    The Great Lakes - St. Lawrence Seaway.
        prod. [Scarborough, Ont.] : R.B.M., 1976.- dist. ETHOS 48 fr. : col. : 35 mm. & cassette (12 min.) : auto. & aud. adv. sig. & teacher's manual. $19.00 (Transportation in Canada) ji

        1. St. Lawrence Seaway.

        A survey of one of the world's famous inland waterways showing cargoes, types of ships, and various landmarks.-

386.0971
    Un Monde nouveau, des méthodes nouvelles.
        prod. [Toronto] : Int. Cin., 1975.- dist. VEC 46 fr. : b&w & col. : 35 mm. & cassette (6 min.) : auto.& aud. adv. sig. & teaching guide. $24.00 (Transport : l'aventure Canadienne : $86.00) ij

        1. Shipping - Canada - History.

        Photographs and paintings show the development of water transportation in Canada, from rafts and canoes with portages to steamboats and ships using canals. English title available : NEW WAYS IN A NEW LAND.-

386.0971
    New ways in a new land.
        prod. [Toronto] : Int. Cin., 1974.- dist. VEC 46 fr. : b&w & col. : 35 mm. & cassette (11 min.) : auto. & aud. adv. sig. & teacher's manual. $24.00 (Transportation : the Canadian adventure : $86.00) ji

        1. Shipping - Canada - History.

        Photographs and paintings show the development of water transportation in Canada, from rafts and canoes with portages to steamboats and ships using canals. French title available : UN MONDE NOUVEAU DES METHODES NOUVELLES.-

386.0971
    On Canadian waters.
        prod. [Toronto] : McI. 1977.- dist. McI. 45 fr. : col. : 35 mm. & cassette (10 min.) : auto. & aud. adv. sig. & teacher's guide. $19.00 (Canada on the move : $76.00) ji

        1. Shipping - Canada - History.

        A look at past and present use of water transportation in Canada's major industries. Shows types of watercraft from those used by Indians to modern vessels of today, and indicates use. Provides authentic sounds.-

386.0971
    The Seaway.
        prod. [Montreal?] : NFB, made 1959 : 1964.- dist. McI. 51 fr. : col. : 35 mm. & captions & teacher's manual. $9.00 ji

        1. St. Lawrence Seaway - History.

        Drawings trace the history of the St. Lawrence River as a trade route, the building of canals and dams to allow passage through the Great Lakes. Photos show the Seaway project, completed in 1959 and its importance to trade.-

386.0971
    The Seaway and its ships.
        prod. [Scarborough, Ont.] : R.B.M., 1974.- dist. ETHOS 89 fr. : b&w & col. : 35 mm. & cassette (14 min.) : auto. & aud. adv. sig. & teacher's manual. $19.00 (Transportation in Canada) jis

        1. Shipping - Canada. 2. St. Lawrence Seaway - Economic aspects.

        An account of the economic importance of the St. Lawrence Seaway, showing the many types of ships that make use of it.-

The Classified Catalogue

386.0971
  Ships and power.
    prod. [Montreal?] : NFB, made 1958 : 1974.- dist. McI. 42 fr. : col. : 35 mm. & captions & teacher's manual. $9.00 ji

    1. Shipping - Canada. 2. St. Lawrence River. 3. St. Lawrence Seaway.

    Shows the importance of the St. Lawrence River system as a water route into the continent and as a source of hydro-electric power. Drawings illustrate early travel by canoe, the need for larger cargo boats, and the building of canals and locks. Photographs show modern ships, the Welland canal, and the expansion of the Seaway.-

386.09713
  Le Canal Rideau.
    prod. [Montreal?[: NFB, 1970.- dist. SEC 46 fr. : col. : 35 mm. & captions & printed notes. $9.00 (Image du Canada) ji

    1. Rideau Canal, Ont. - History.

    A general overview of the Rideau Canal, beginning with a map of the Canal and its locks. Photographs and sketches provide historical background to this waterway built for defense purposes after the War of 1812, to connect Kingston and Montreal. Shows the various falls, dams, and locks along its length. English title available : RIDEAU CANAL.-

386.09713
  Port of Thunder Bay.
    prod. [Stratford, Ont.] : Sch. Ch., 1974.- dist. Sch. Ch. 48 fr. : b & w & col. : 35 mm. & captions. $7.95 (Canadian ports : $31.80) ji

    1. Shipping - Canada. 2. Thunder Bay, Ont. - Harbor.

    Explores the relationship between the port of Thunder Bay and the Great Lakes region it serves. Early and present day photos of the harbour are included to show how grain and iron ore are transported to Thunder Bay, stored, loaded on ships, and sent to other parts of Canada. Lakers and ocean-going freighters are compared.-

386.09713
  Port of Toronto.
    prod. [Scarborough, Ont.] : R.B.M., 1974.- dist. ETHOS 76 fr. : b&w & col. : 35 mm. & cassette (14 min.) : auto. & aud. adv. sig. & teacher's manual. $19.00 (Transportation in Canada) jis

    1. Toronto, Ont. - Harbor. 2. Shipping - Canada.

    A description of this seaway port. Gives a brief history of its development. Includes description of vessels and cargo, both foreign and domestic.-

386.09713
  The Port of Toronto.
    prod. [Winnipeg] : VCL, 1972.- dist. Sch. Ch. 45 fr. : b&w &col. : 35 mm. & captions. $7.95 (Canadian ports : $31.80) ji

    1. Toronto, Ont. - Harbor.

    Drawings, sketches and photographs depict the growth of Toronto's harbour, as well as the changes made to accomodate the ships using this port. Aspects of Toronto harbour life are discussed, such as the different types of ships and cargo, the methods of moving and shipping goods, and the responsibility of the Harbour Police toward protecting the harbour.-

386.09713
  Rideau Canal.
    prod. [Montreal?] : NFB, 1970.- dist. McI. 46 fr. : col. : 35 mm. & captions & printed notes. $9.00 (Image Canada : $45.00) ji

    1. Rideau Canal, Ont. - History.

    A general overview of the Rideau Canal, beginning with a map of the Canal and its locks. Photographs and sketches provide historical background to this waterway built for defense purposes after the War of 1812, to connect Kingston and Montreal. Shows the various falls, dams, and locks along its length. French title available : LE CANAL RIDEAU.-

The Classified Catalogue

386.09713
    A Seaway port.
        prod. [Scarborough, Ont.] : R.B.M., 1976.- dist. ETHOS 52 fr. : col. : 35 mm. & cassette (11 min.) : auto. & aud. adv. sig. & teacher's manual. $19.00 (Transportation in Canada) ji

        1. Shipping - Canada. 2. Toronto, Ont. - Harbor.

        Included in this look at Toronto's busy harbour are the kinds of vessels to be found, their cargoes, the recreational use made of the harbour, and containerization as a factor in its development as a port.-

386.09713
    Thunder Bay's industrial harbour.
        prod. [Thunder Bay, Ont.] : CP, 1975.- dist. CP 51 fr. : col. : 35 mm. & cassette (22 min.) : auto. & aud. adv. sig. & reading script. $14.50 i

        1. Thunder Bay, Ont. - Harbour.
        2. Thunder Bay, Ont. - Industries.

        A detailed statistical study of the major industries of Thunder Bay's harbour. Also provides information on the harbour's historical background and its physical development.-

386.09713
    The Welland Canal (historical).
        prod. [Scarborough, Ont.] : FCC, 1978.- dist. FCC 10 fr. : b&w & col. : 35 mm. & cassette (10 min.) : auto. & aud. adv. sig. & teacher's guide and narration card. $9.95 (The Welland Canal : $19.90) jis

        1. Welland Canal - History.

        Traces the development of the four stages of the Welland Canal, describing the reasons for its construction, its influence on neighbouring towns, and the traffic it has carried. Photographs and sketches. Material packaged in clear vinyl envelope that would fit a legal-size filing cabinet.-

386.09713
    The Welland Canal (today).
        prod. [Scarborough, Ont.] : FCC, 1978.- dist. FCC 10 fr. : col. : 35 mm. & cassette (10 min.) & auto. & aud. adv. sig. & teacher's guide and reading script. $9.95 (The Welland Canal : $19.90) jis

        1. Welland Canal - History.

        The growth and development of the Welland Canal as an international transportation route and its present-day commercial uses are described with photos, maps and charts. Material packaged in clear vinyl envelope that would fit a legal-sized filing cabinet.-

387.109711
    The Port of Vancouver.
        prod. [Stratford, Ont.] : Sch. Ch., 1974.- dist. Sch. Ch. 46 fr. : b&w & col. : 35 mm. & captions. $7.95 (Canadian ports : $31.80) ji

        1. Shipping - Canada. 2. Vancouver, B.C. - Harbor.

        A history of Vancouver's port from early exportation of lumber to its present important status in Canada. Discusses exporting of lumber, newsprint, grain and minerals, the machinery used to load ships, and the many different types of ships seen in the port.-

387.109715
    The Port of St. John.
        prod. [Scarborough, Ont.] : R.B.M., 1976.- dist. ETHOS 46 fr. : b&w & col. : 35 mm. & cassette (8 min.) : auto. & aud. adv. sig. & teacher's manual. $19.00 (Cities of Canada) ji

        1. Shipping - Canada. 2. Saint John, N.B. - Harbor. 3. Saint John, N.B. - History.

        Traces the role of Saint John, New Brunswick, as an important Canadian seaport from its early history to present. Indicates types of industries using harbour and variety of cargo. Illustrated with both archival and modern photographs.-

The Classified Catalogue

387.109716
    Port city : Halifax.
        prod. [Montreal?] : NFB, 1973.- dist. McI. 43 fr. : col. : 35 mm. & captions. $9.00 (Canadian cities) jis

        1. Halifax, N.S. - Harbor. 2. Halifax, N.S. - History. 3. Shipping - Canada.

        Traces the history of Halifax from the 1700's to its present status as an important naval base, and one of Canada's principal ports for foreign trade. The significance of the city's railway service and container port facilities is also explained. Includes photographs of the natural harbour and historic sites. French title available : VILLE PORTUAIRE (HALIFAX).-

387.109716
    Port of Halifax.
        prod. [Stratford, Ont.] : Sch. Ch., 1974.- dist. Sch. Ch. 48 fr. : b&w & col. : 35 mm. & captions. $7.95 (Canadian ports : $31.80) ji

        1. Shipping - Canada. 2. Halifax, N.S. - Harbor.

        Discusses development of the port of Halifax from British naval base to its present role as an important Canadian port. Discusses harbour industries and types of ships seen in the harbour. Includes photographs of machinery for loading and moving cargo.-

387.109716
    Ville portuaire (Halifax).
        prod. [Montreal?] : NFB, 1973.- dist. SEC 67 fr. : b&w & col. : 35 mm. & captions. $9.00 jis

        1. Shipping - Canada. 2. Halifax, N.S. - Harbor. 3. Halifax, N.S. - History.

        Traces the history of Halifax from the 1700's to its present status as an important naval base, and one of Canada's principal ports for foreign trade. The significance of the city's railway service and container port facilities is also explained. Includes photographs of the natural harbour and historic sites. English title available : PORT CITY : HALIFAX.-

387.7
    International airport.
        prod. [Toronto] : Int. Cin., 1975.- dist. VEC 76 fr. : col. : 35 mm. & cassette (6 min.) : auto. & aud. adv. sig. & teacher's guide. $24.00 (Community close-ups : $192.00) pj

        1. Airports.

        With no narration, this filmstrip immerses children in daily life at an airport through actual sounds and pictures taken at Toronto International Airport.-

387.7
    A Visit to the airport.
        prod. [Montreal?] : NFB, made 1964; 1966.- dist. McI. 34 fr. : col. : 35 mm. & captions. $9.00 pj

        1. Airports.

        Photographs and captions show the activities at a large airport. Includes the terminal, flight crew, groundcrew, passengers, and controllers. Baggage is shown being loaded, the fuel being pumped into the plane, and the instruments being checked. Includes questions for viewers and a review section. French title available : UNE VISITE A L'AEROPORT.-

387.7
    Une visite á l'aéroport.
        prod. [Montreal?] : NFB, made 1964 : 1966.- dist. SEC 34 fr. : col. : 35 mm. & captions. $9.00 pj

        1. Airports.

        Photographs and captions show the activities at a large airport. Includes the terminal, flight crew, ground crew, passengers, and controllers. Baggage is shown being loaded, the fuel being pumped into the plane, and the instruments being checked. Includes questions for viewers and a review section. English title available : A VISIT TO THE AIRPORT.-

The Classified Catalogue

387.70971
    Aviation in Canada.
        prod. [Scarborough, Ont.] : R.B.M., 1976.- dist. ETHOS 79 fr. : col. : 35 mm. & cassette (19 min.) : auto. & aud. adv. sig. & teacher's manual. $19.00 (Transportation in Canada) ji

        1. Aeronautics - History. 2. Aeronautics - Commercial.

        An overview of the role of aviation in Canadian transportation today. Shows great variety of airplanes and their uses. Discusses growth of DeHavilland and Canadian Air Force. Emphasizes Canada's contributions to airplane design.-

387.70971
    Aviation in Canada : the early days.
        prod. [Scarborough, Ont.] : R.B.M., 1976.- dist. ETHOS 49 fr. : col. : 35 mm. & cassette (12 min.) : auto. & aud. adv. sig. & teacher's manual. $19.00 (Transportation in Canada) ji

        1. Aeronautics - History.

        A look at the early days of flying in Canada - through old photographs - airplane flight at Baddeck, the influence of World War 1 on the development of aviation, and the growth of bush flying in the 1920's and 30's.-

387.70971
    Aviation in Canada - today.
        prod. [Scarborough, Ont.] : R.B.M., 1976.- dist. ETHOS 54, fr. : col. : 35 mm. & cassette (14 min.) : auto. & aud. adv. sig. & teacher's manual. $19.00 (Transportation in Canada) ji

        1. Aeronautics.

        Describes Canada's large and diversified aviation industry. Includes the role it plays in Canada's transportation system, as a communications link with the north, and its importance in the development of natural resources.-

387.70971
    Histoire de l'aviation au Canada.
        prod. [Montreal?] : NFB, made 1964 : 1972.- dist. SEC 44 fr. : b&w & col. : 35 mm. & captions. $9.00 ji

        1. Aeronautics - History.

        Drawings, black and white and colour photos plus captions provide history of military and commercial air travel in Canada. Includes photos of all types of aircraft, and questions for discussion and further study. For classroom use. English title available : HISTORY OF FLIGHT IN CANADA.-

387.70971
    History of flight in Canada.
        prod. [Montreal?] : NFB, made 1964 : 1972.- dist. McI. 44 fr. : col. : 35 mm. & captions. $9.00 ji

        1. Aeronautics - History.

        Drawings, black and white and colour photos plus captions provide history of military and commerical air travel in Canada. Includes photos of all types of aircraft, and questions for discussion and further study. For classroom use. French title available : HISTOIRE DE L'AVIATION AU CANADA.-

387.70971
    Wings over Canada.
        prod. [Toronto] : McI., 1977.- dist. McI. 58 fr. : b&w & col. : 35 mm. & cassette (15 min.) : auto. & aud. adv. sig. & teacher's guide. $19.00 (Canada on the move : $76.00) ji

        1. Aeronautics - History.

        A chronological look at aviation in Canada from 1903 to present. Indicates role of prominent individuals and institutions in promoting aircraft as means of transportation. Shows increased use of airplanes in industry, exploration and passenger service. Photographs feature all types of aircraft including the Concord.-

The Classified Catalogue

388
Transportation today : by land.
prod. [Scarborough, Ont.] : R.B.M., 1976.- dist. ETHOS 53 fr. : col. : 35 mm. & cassette (11 min.) : auto. & aud. adv. sig. & teacher's manual. $19.00 (Transportation in Canada) ji

1. Transportation.

A look at the many ways of travelling on land in Canada today - from motor vehicles of all descriptions to cable cars, elevators and escalators.-

388.30971
On Canadian roads.
prod. [Toronto] : McI., 1977.- dist. McI. 53 fr. : b&w & col. : 35 mm. & cassette (11 min.) : auto. & aud. adv. sig. & teacher's guide. $19.00 (Canada on the move : $76.00) ji

1. Transportation, Highway - History.

A history of land travel in Canada. Discusses and illustrates modes of transportation used by Indians and early settlers. Traces evolution of the automobile to the cars, trucks, vans, buses seen today. Comments upon role of land transportation in modern urban community.-

388.34
Trucks in Canada.
prod. [Scarborough, Ont.] : R.B.M., 1976.- dist. ETHOS 42 fr. : col. : 35 mm. & reading script. $19.00 (Facts on Canada) pj

1. Trucks.

Looks at the great variety in shapes, sizes, and purposes of trucks which are available for almost every job.-

388.409713
Public transportation in the city.
prod. [Scarborough, Ont.] : FCC, 1978.- dist. FCC 36 fr. : b&w & col. : 35 mm. & cassette (9 min.) : auto. & aud. adv. sig. & teacher's guide. $12.95 (The Urban community) p

1. Local transit. 2. Toronto, Ont. - Transit system.

Describes in simple terms four modes of public transportation used in Toronto - the subway, diesel bus, trolley bus, and street car. Carefully explains how to use the subway and bus, and the differences in the three forms of surface transportation. Useful for introducing young children to public transportation.-

388.409713
Transportation.
prod. [Scarborough, Ont.] : R.B.M., 1974.- dist. ETHOS 66 fr. : col. : 35 mm. & cassette (12 min.) : auto. & aud. adv. sig. & teacher's guide. $19.00 (Urbanism in Canada) ji

1. Local transit. 2. Toronto, Ont. - Transit systems.

Illustrates some important aspects of urban transportation with photos of the Toronto area and cartoon-style sketches. Roads (local, collector, artery and expressway), rail transportation (Go train, Union station), subways, streetcars, diesel buses and facilities for air and water transportation are discussed.-

388.409713
Transportation in Toronto.
prod. [Winnipeg] : VCL 1972.- dist. Sch. Ch. 45 fr. : b&w & col. : 35 mm. & captions. $7.95 ji

1. Toronto, Ont. - Transit systems - History.

A history of public transportation systems in Toronto from 1849 to the present complex network serving the city today. Excellent photographs of Toronto, past and present, depict the growth from horse-drawn trolleys to the electric trolley cars, trolley buses and motor buses. Additional photos of subway and Go transit help illustrate the interdependence between subways and surface public transportation to move people.-

389
Area.
prod. [Scarborough, Ont.] : R.B.M., 1974.- dist. ETHOS 70 fr. : col. : 35 mm. & cassette (14 min.) : auto. & aud. adv. sig. & teacher's manual. $19.00 (Metric measurement for primary children : $69.00) pj

1. Metric system.

Uses a circus theme with artwork, to develop the concepts of surface and area and how to measure area using metric units.-

The Classified Catalogue

389
    Area units.
        prod. [Toronto] : M-L, 1974.- dist. Sch. Ser. or Vint. 49 fr. : col. : 35 mm. & cassette (13 min.) : auto. & aud. adv. sig. & teacher's guide. $16.50 (Metric measurement : $65.00) j

        1. Metric system.

        Diagrams are used to provide a clear discussion of area. Shows relationship between length, height and area, how to estimate and calculate exact areas of rectangles, triangles and circles using formulas for each. French title available : UNITES DE SURFACE.-

389
    Capacity counts.
        prod. [Don Mills, Ont.] : ADD, 1975.- dist. ADD 51 fr. : col. : 35 mm. & cassette (15 min.) : auto. & aud. adv. sig. & teacher's manual. $30.25 (It's a metric world : $164.71) ji

        1. Metric system.

        While planning a party Mary learns importance of accurate capacity measurement. Discusses liters, milliliters, kiloliters, and capacity sizes measured by each. Students asked to estimate capacity of both liquids and solids from numerous examples given, such as eyedropper and railway tank car. Illustrated with photographs and cartoons. Includes test on side B of cassette.-

389
    Celsius scenes.
        prod. [Don Mills, Ont.] : ADD, 1975.- dist. ADD 61 fr. : col. : 35 mm. & cassette (15 min.) : auto. & aud. adv. sig. & teacher's manual. $30.25 (It's a metric world : $164.71) ji

        1. Metric system. 2. Temperature.

        Photographs and cartoons humourously illustrate measurement of hotness and coldness with a celsius thermometer. Shows use of thermometer, such as determining body and seasonal temperatures. Students participate by estimating temperatures in various situations. Includes test on side B of cassette.-

389
    Cubic concepts.
        prod. [Don Mills, Ont.] : ADD, 1975.- dist. ADD 43 fr. : col. : 35 mm. & cassette (15 min.) : auto. & aud. adv. sig. & teacher's manual. $30.25 (It's a metric world : $164.71) ji

        1. Metric system.

        Concept of cubic meters, centimeters and decimeters in volume measurement. Examples include measuring volumes of objects using either one or all three standard units. Objects featured vary from volume of ping pong ball to volume of moon. Illustrated with cartoons and photographs. Includes test on side B of cassette.-

389
    Lengthy tales.
        prod. [Don Mills, Ont.] : ADD, 1975.- dist. ADD 47 fr. : col. : 35 mm. & cassette (13 min.) : auto. & aud. adv. sig. & teacher's manual. $30.25 (It's a metric world : $164.71) ji

        1. Metric system.

        Cartoons with captions and photographs show use of meters, centimeters and kilometers to measure length of various sized objects. Different objects with same length are grouped together to help students estimate length and see relationship between standard units. Includes test on side B of cassette.-

389
    Une Ligne - une surface.
        prod. [Toronto] : M-L, 1975.- dist. Sch. Ser. or Vint. 55 fr. : col. : 35 mm. & cassette (11 min.) : auto. & aud. adv. sig. & teacher's guide. $16.50 (Le système International : $65.00) j

        1. Metric system.

        Introduces the metre and the use of prefixes to make multiples and submultiples of this basic unit. Practical uses are shown for measuring length. Scale on maps is studied. Demonstrates the finding of area of various sized objects. Explains the importance of the SI system of measurement in the world today. English title available : MEASURING LENGTH AND AREA.-

389

Linear - area.
prod. [Scarborough, Ont.] : R.B.M., 1974.- dist. ETHOS 67 fr. : col. : 35 mm. & cassette (10 min.) : auto. & aud. adv. sig. & teacher's manual. $19.00 (Metric measurement : $69.00) jis

1. Metric system.

Introduces the common units of length, their interrelationships and their application in measuring area.-

389

Linear measurement.
prod. [Scarborough, Ont.] : R.B.M., 1974.- dist. ETHOS 61 fr. : col. : 35 mm. & cassette (10 min.) : auto. & aud. adv. sig. & teacher's manual. $19.00 (Metric measurement for primary children : $69.00) pj

1. Metric system.

Develops the concept of length, height, width, then introduces the measurement of length, first by using non-standard units, then the common metric units. Uses a circus theme with cartoon illustrations.-

389

Linear units.
prod. [Toronto] : M-L, 1974.- dist. Sch. Ser. or Vint. 54 fr. : col. : 35 mm. & cassette (16 min.) : auto. & aud. adv. sig. & teacher's guide. $16.50 (Metric measurement : $65.00) j

1. Metric system.

Introduces the meter, kilometer, centimeter and millimeter. Shows conversion from one to the other and when to use each unit. Defines perimeter, circumference, radius, diameters, and discusses how to find each. Provides classroom activities that can be done during the filmstrip. French title available : UNITES DE LONGUER.-

389

Mass.
prod. [Scarborough, Ont.] : R.B.M., 1974.- dist. ETHOS 51 fr. : col. : 35 mm. & cassette (9 min.) : auto. & aud. adv. sig. & teacher's manual. $19.00 (Metric measurement : $69.00) jis

1. Metric system.

Introduces the concept of mass, the common units for measuring mass and their interrelationships, and the use of these measurements in everyday life.-

389

Mass matters.
prod. [Don Mills, Ont.] : ADD, 1975.- dist. ADD 43 fr. : col. : 35 mm. & cassette (12 min.) : auto. & aud. adv. sig. & teacher's manual. $30.25 (It's a metric world : $164.71) ji

1. Metric system.

Shows how to measure mass of an object using the common mass units kilograms, grams, milligrams, and tonnes. Students asked to estimate masses of different sized objects from a dollar bill to an elephant. Stresses difference between mass and size. Illustrated with captioned cartoons and photographs. Includes test on side B of cassette.-

389

Measuring length and area.
prod. [Toronto] : M-L, 1974.- dist. Sch. Ser. or Vint. 55 fr. : col. : 35 mm. & cassette (11 min.) : auto. & aud. adv. sig. & teacher's guide. $16.50 (SI - the metric system : $65.00) i

1. Metric system.

Introduces the metre and the use of prefixes to make multiples and submultiples of this basic unit. Practical uses are shown for measuring length. Scale on maps is studied. Demonstrates the finding of area of various sized objects. Explains the importance of the SI system of measurement in the world today. French title available : UNE LIGNE : UNE SURFACE.-

389

Measuring mass.
prod. [Toronto] : M-L, 1974.- dist. Sch. Ser. or Vint. 41 fr. : col. : 35 mm. & cassette (8 min.) : auto. & aud. adv. sig. & teacher's guide. $16.50 (SI - the metric system : $65.00) i

1. Metric system.

Presents kilograms as the standard unit of measurement of mass. Reviews briefly area, perimeter, volume. Introduces the hectogram, decagram, gram, decigram, centigram, miligram. Defines mass and weight. Describes how balance scales work to determine mass. Stresses necessity of a single, simple, logical, international system of measurement. French title available : UN POIDS : UNE MASSE.-

The Classified Catalogue

389
> Measuring volume.
>   prod. [Toronto] : M-L, 1974.- dist. Sch. Ser. or Wint.   40 fr. : col. : 35 mm. & cassette (8 min.) : auto. & aud. adv. sig. & teacher's guide. $16.50 (SI - the metric system : $65.00) i
>
> 1. Metric system.
>
> Visual explanation of the formula for finding the volume of a rectangle, using coloured cubes. Conversion tables are given involving hectolitres, kilolitres, decalitres, litres, decilitres, centilitres, millilitres. Uses examples from supermarket of volumes of commonly purchased commodities. French title available : UN VOLUME : UNE CAPACITE.-

389
> Mesure de volumes.
>   prod. [Montreal?] : NFB, 1969.- dist. SEC   35 fr. : col. : 35 mm. & captions & printed notes. $9.00 (Science à l'élémentaire) pj
>
> 1. Weights and measures - Experiments.
> 2. Science - Experiments.
>
> Pictorial instructions for an experiment illustrating measurement of volume of different shaped containers by the amount of liquid each holds. English title available : TO MEASURE VOLUME.-

389
> The Metric system : why?
>   prod. [Scarborough, Ont.] : SHN, 1974.- dist. PHM   80 fr. : col. : 35 mm. & cassette (12 min.) : auto. & aud. adv. sig. & reading script. $39.60 (Why go metric? : man & measurement : $64.00) jis
>
> 1. Metric system.
>
> Designed as motivation for the study of the Metric system, uses simple drawings to illustrate man's need to communicate and the desirability of a standard measurement.-

389
> The Metric system : a better way .... for all!
>   prod. [Scarborough, Ont.] : SHN, 1974.- dist. PHM   80 fr. : col. : 35 mm. & cassette (12 min.) : auto. & aud. adv. sig. & reading script. $39.60 (Why go metric? : man and measurement : $64.00) jis
>
> 1. Metric system - History.
>
> Traces the establishment of the Metric system. Details of all units of measurement are covered. Includes conversion system. Drawings used as illustrations.-

389
> The Metric system : how?.
>   prod. [Scarborough, Ont.] : SHN, 1974.- dist. PHM   80 fr. : col. : 35 mm. & cassette (12 min.) : auto. & aud. adv. sig. & reading script. $39.60 (Why go metric? : man & measurement : $64.00) jis
>
> 1. Weights and measures - History.
>
> Describes the development of standard units of measurement including the Imperial system. Discusses length, volume, weight and area and considers the need for a simpler system of measurement. Illustrated with diagrams.-

389
> The Metric system : a better way ... for some.
>   prod. [Scarborough, Ont.] : SHN, 1974.- dist. PHM   80 fr. : col. : 35 mm. & cassette (12 min.) : auto. & aud. adv. sig. & reading script. $39.60 (Why go metric? : man & measurement : $64.00) jis
>
> 1. Metric system.
>
> Uses drawings to describe the problems of communicating in a metric world using the customary system. Outlines the changes that industries and people will need to make the conversion.-

389
Le Monde à l'heure du système international.
prod. [Toronto] : M-L. 1975.- dist. Sch. Ser. or Vint. 44 fr. : col. : 35 mm. & cassette (11 min.) : auto. & aud. adv. sig. & teacher's guide. $16.50 (Usage du Système International : $65.00) i

1. Metric system.

Introduction to International System: meters, centimeters, millimeters, kilometers, grams, kilograms, hectares, etc. Gives examples of everyday usefulness for measuring mass, volume, area, distance. English title available : THE METRIC WORLD.-

389
Un Poids - une masse.
prod. [Toronto] : M-L. 1975.- dist. Sch. Ser. or Vint. 41 fr. : col. : 35 mm. & cassette (8 min.) : auto. & aud. adv. sig. & teacher's guide. $16.50 (Le Système International : $65.00) j

1. Metric system.

Presents kilograms as the standard unit of measurement of mass. Reviews briefly area, perimeter, volume. Introduces the hectogram, decagram, gram, decigram, centigram, miligram. Defines mass and weight. Describes how balance scales work to determine mass. Stresses the necessity of a single, logical, international system of measurement. English title available : MEASURING MASS.-

389
Square stories.
prod. [Don Mills, Ont.] : ADD. 1975.- dist. ADD 57 fr. : col. : 35 mm. & cassette (15 min.) : auto. & aud. adv. sig. & teacher's manual. $30.25 (It's a metric world : $164.71) ji

1. Metric system.

Measurement of area by standard units, square meters, millimeters, and kilometers. Students calculate large and small areas from photographs of different sized objects. Clearly indicates relationship between units. Also introduces hectares. Uses cartoons and photographs to illustrate. Includes test on side B of cassette.-

389
Standardizing measurement.
prod. [Toronto] : M-L. 1974.- dist. Sch. Ser. or Vint. 51 fr. : col. : 35 mm. & cassette (9 min.) : auto. & aud. adv. sig. & teacher's guide. $16.50 (SI - the metric system : $65.00) j

1. Weights and measures - History

A demonstration of the practical problems caused by the lack of a standard system of measurement is followed by a history of the development of the Imperial system of measurement and the SI system of units. French title available : UN SYSTEME DE MESURE.-

389
Un Système de mesure.
prod. [Toronto] : M-L. 197 .- dist. Sch. Ser. or Vint. 51 fr. : col. : 35 mm. & cassette (9 min.) : auto. & aud. adv. sig. & teacher's guide. $16.50 (Le Système International : $65.00) j

1. Weights and measures - History.

A demonstration of the practical problems caused by the lack of a standard system of measurement is followed by a history of the development of the Imperial System of Measurement and the SI system of units. English title available : STANDARDIZING MEASUREMENT.-

389
Temperature.
prod. [Scarborough, Ont.] : R.B.M., 1974.- dist. ETHOS 63 fr. : col. : 35 mm. & cassette (14 min.) : auto. & aud. adv. sig. & teacher's manual. $19.00 (Metric measurement : $69.00) jis

1. Metric system. 2. Temperature.

Discusses the use of Celsuis scale to measure temperature, introducing some common temperatures as a guide to better understanding the less familiar.-

The Classified Catalogue

389
    Temperature and mass.
        prod. [Scarborough, Ont.] : R.B.M., 1974.- dist. ETHOS 60 fr. : col. : 35 mm. & cassette (11 min.) : auto. & aud. adv. sig. & teacher's manual. $19.00 (Metric measurement for primary children : $69.00) pj

    1. Metric system. 2. Temperature.

    A circus theme is used to develop basic concepts relating to temperature and mass. Illustrated with cartoons.-

389
    To measure volume.
        prod. [Montreal?] : NFB, 1969.- dist. McI. 33 fr. : col. : 35 mm. & captions & printed notes. $9.00 (Elementary science) pj

    1. Weights and measures - Experiments. 2. Science - Experiments.

    Pictorial instructions for an experiment illustrating measurement of volume of different shaped containers by the amount of liquid each holds. French title available : MESURE DE VOLUMES.-

389
    Unité de surface.
        prod. [Toronto] : M-L, 1975.- dist. Sch. Ser. or Vint. 49 fr. : col. : 35 mm. & cassette (13 min.) : auto. & aud. adv. sig. & teacher's guide. $16.50 (Usage du Système International : $65.00) i

    1. Metric system.

    Diagrams are used to provide a clear discussion of area. Shows relationship between length, height and area, how to estimate and calculate exact areas of rectangles, triangles and circles using formulas for each. English title available : AREA UNITS.-

389
    Les Unités de volume.
        prod. [Toronto] : M-L, 1975.- dist. Sch. Ser. or Vint. 50 fr. : col. : 35 mm. & cassette (14 min.) : auto. & aud. adv. sig. & teacher's guide. $16.50 (Usage du Système International : $65.00) i

    1. Metric system.

    Relationship between length, area and volume provides introduction of cubic centimeter. Looks at rectangular solids, rectangular, triangular and octagonal prisms, cones, spheres, cylinders and pyramids: how to find volume of each and interrelationship of their volumes. English title available : VOLUME UNITS.-

389
    Un Volume - une capacité.
        prod. [Toronto] : M-L, 1975.- dist. Sch. Ser. or Vint. 37 fr. : col. : 35 mm. & cassette (5 min.) : auto. & aud. adv. sig. & teacher's guide. $16.50 (Le Système International : $65.00) j

    1. Metric system.

    Visual explanation of the formula for finding the volume of a rectangle, using coloured cubes. Conversion tables are given involving hectolitres, kilolitres, decalitres, litres, decilitres, centilitres, millilitres. Uses examples from supermarket of volumes of commonly purchased commodities. English title available : MEASURING VOLUME.-

389
    Volume - capacity.
        prod. [Scarborough, Ont.] : R.B.M., 1974.- dist. ETHOS 62 fr. : col. : 35 mm. & cassette (9 min.) : auto. & aud. adv. sig. & teacher's manual. $19.00 (Metric measurement : $69.00) jis

    1. Metric system.

    Introduces the concepts of volume as a measurement for dry materials and capacity as a measurement for liquids. The use of these units of measurement in everyday life is discussed.-

The Classified Catalogue

389
    Volume and capacity.
        prod. [Scarborough, Ont.] : R.B.M., 1974.- dist. ETHOS 75 fr. : col. : 35 mm. & cassette (16 min.) : auto. & aud. adv. sig. & teacher's manual. $19.00 (Metric measurement for primary children : $69.00) pj

        1. Metric system.

        A visit to the circus provides the opportunity to learn about capacity and its standard unit, the litre, and to review the other concepts of length, area, temperature, and mass. Illustrated with cartoons.-

389
    Volume units.
        prod. [Toronto] : M-L, 1974.- dist. Sch. Ser. or Vint. 50 fr. : col. : 35 mm. & cassette (14 min.) : auto. & aud. adv. sig. & teacher's guide. $16.50 (Metric measurement : $65.00) j

        1. Metric system.

        Relationship between length, area and volume provides introduction of cubic centimeter. Looks at rectangular solids, rectangular, triangular and octagonal prisms, cones, spheres, cylinders and pyramids; how to find volume of each and interrelationship of their volumes. French title available : LES UNITES DE VOLUME.-

391.09701
    Masks of the North American Indians.
        prod. [Montreal?] : NFB, 1965.- dist. McI. 40 fr. : col. : 35 mm. & reading script. $9.00 (Native arts : $35.00) jis

        1. Indians of North America - Costume and adornment. 2. Indians of North America - Art.

        Pictures of imaginative masks including those of Eskimo, Haida, Tsimshian, Nootka, Kwakiutl, and Iroquois. Manual essential for detailed information. Good for art class. French title available : MASQUES DES INDIENS DE L'AMERIQUE DU NORD.-

391.09701
    Masques des Indiens de l'Amérique du Nord.
        prod. [Montreal?] : NFB, 1953.- dist. SEC 40 fr. : col. : 35 mm. & reading script. $9.00 (L'art indigène) jis

        1. Indians of North America - Costume and adornment. 2. Indians of North America - Art.

        Pictures of imaginative masks including those of Eskimo, Haida, Tsimshian, Nootka, Kwakiutl, and Iroquois. Manual essential for detailed information. Good for art class. English title available : MASKS OF THE NORTH AMERICAN INDIANS.-

391.09701
    Native clothing.
        prod. [Toronto] : RQM, 1973.- dist. Lea. 33 fr. : col. : 35 mm. & captions & teacher's guide. $9.00 (Our native people : customs and legends) js

        1. Indians of North America - Costume and adornment.

        Describes native dress, using photos of types of garments worn by different Indian tribes. Outlines methods of construction, materials used, and adornment.-

391.0971
    Historic costumes : part 1.
        prod. [Toronto] : TBE, 1975.- dist. TBE 8 fr. : b&w : 35 mm. & captions. $2.00 (Canadian history pictures) jis

        1. Costume. 2. Frontier and pioneer life.

        Drawings by C.W. Jefferys of costumes from nineteenth century to mid-Victoria era depict different Canadian lifestyles. Includes dancing apparel, habitant attire, and strolling costumes of Victorian upper elite. Contrasts this with simpler dress of early French and English settlers.-

394.09713
    The Day Santa came to town.
        prod. [Scarborough, Ont.] : R.B.M., 1975.- dist. ETHOS 60 fr. : col. : 35 mm. & cassette (12 min.) : auto. & aud. adv. sig. & teacher's manual.- $19.00 (Special occasions) pj

        1. Parades.

        All the fun and excitement of that special day when Santa Claus arrives in town is captured in photographs of Eatn's Santa Claus parade in Toronto.-

The Classified Catalogue

394.09713
    La Parade du Père Noël à Toronto.
        prod. [Toronto] : TBE, 197] dist. TBE 38 fr. : col. : 35 mm. $8.00 pj

        1. Parades.

    A series of photographs taken during a Toronto Santa Claus parade. Focuses on colours, costumes, performers, floats and crowds. No captions, designed for oral discussion. -

394.2
    Canadian Christmas : traditions of Christmas.
        prod. [Toronto] : B & R, 1973.- dist. B & R 30 fr. : col. : 35 mm. & cassette (9 min.) : auto. & aud. adv. sig. & script & teacher's manual. $16.00 (Canadian holidays : $180.00) pj

        1. Christmas - Canada.

    Presents an overview of the origins of many popular Canadian Christmas traditions, such as gift-giving, Yule logs, pageants, carols, Christmas trees, Christmas cards, foods and games.-

394.2
    Christmas today.
        prod. [Toronto] : B & R, 1973.- dist. B & R 20 fr. : col. : 35 mm. & cassette (5 min.) : auto. & aud. adv. sig. & script & teacher's manual. $16.00 (Canadian holidays : $180.00) pj

        1. Christmas - Canada.

    Summarizes the activities and events which lead up to Christmas today, beginning with the Santa Claus parade. Also includes sending cards, getting and decorating a tree, buying a turkey, and hanging the stockings.-

394.2
    Dominion Day.
        prod. [Scarborough, Ont.] : R.B.M., 1975.- dist. ETHOS 39 fr. : b&w & col. : 35 mm. & cassette (7 min.) : auto. & aud. adv. sig. & teacher's guide. $19.00 pj

        1. Dominion Day.

    A brief summary of events leading to Confederation, the eventual inclusion of ten provinces, and the celebration of Canada's centennial in 1967. Uses photographs, artwork, and sound effects, including the call of a loon. Ends with the singing of "O CANADA".-

394.2
    Dominion Day.
        prod. [Toronto] : B & R, 1976.- dist. B & R 25 fr. : b&w & col. : 35 mm. & cassette (10 min.) : auto. & aud. adv. sig. & teacher's guide & reading script. $16.00 (Canadian holidays : $180.00) pj

        1. Dominion Day.

    Traces Canada's gradual development from a loosely-connected group of colonies to one country. Explains the meaning of Dominion Day and introduces the terms Prime Minister, Confederation, and Parliament Buildings.-

394.2
    Easter in Canada.
        prod. [Toronto] : B & R, 1975.- dist. B & R 23 fr. : col. : 35 mm. & cassette (8 min.) : auto. & aud. adv. sig. & teacher's manual & script. $16.00 (Canadian holidays : $180.00) pj

        1. Easter.

    Outlines the reasons behind the symbols associated with Easter, including eggs, rabbits, lilies, and special foods such as hot-cross buns.-

394.2
    Hallowe'en in Canada.
        prod. [Toronto] : B & R, 1975.- dist. B & R 36 fr. : col. : 35 mm. & cassette (12 min.) : auto. & aud. adv. sig. & script & teacher's manual. $16.00 (Canadian holidays : $180.00) pj

        1. Halloween.

    Sound effects help to create an eerie atmosphere in this explanation of the traditions underlying our Hallowe'en customs and symbols. Includes the modern "tradition" of collecting for UNICEF.-

394.2
Inventing a heritage.
 prod. [Toronto] : McI. 1977.- dist. McI. 27 fr. : col. : 35 mm. & cassette (9 min.) : auto. & aud. adv. sig. & teacher's guide. $19.00 (Canada's heritage today : $102.00) ji

1. Holidays.

Relates an imaginary holiday where children are asked to invent symbols, decorations, foods, activities, etc. that would reflect the story of the holiday. Teaches that the traditional activities and items associated with a holiday stem from the meaning behind the day, or its purpose.-

394.2
Remembrance Day.
 prod. [Toronto] : B & R. 1975.- dist. B & R 22 fr. : b&w & col. : 35 mm. & cassette (8 min.) : auto. & aud. adv. sig. & teacher's manual & reading script. $16.00 (Canadian holidays : $180.00) pj

1. Remembrance Day.

The underlying reasons for Remembrance Day and its symbols are discussed. Photographs of the National War Memorial in Ottawa and Remembrance Day ceremonies, as well as several war photographs provide illustration.-

394.2
St. Valentine's Day.
 prod. [Toronto] : B & R. 1975.- dist. B & R 26 fr. : col. : 35 mm. & cassette (8 min.) : auto. & aud. adv. sig. & teacher's manual & reading script. $16.00 (Canadian holidays : $180.00) pj

1. Valentine's Day.

An overview of the origin and symbols associated with St. Valentine's Day. Concludes with a mention of St. Patrick's Day, briefly contrasting its traditional symbols with those of St. Valentine's Day.-

394.2
The Story of Thanksgiving.
 prod. [Toronto] : B & R. 1973.- dist. B & R 23 fr. : col. : 35 mm. & cassette (7 min.) : auto. & aud. adv. sig. & teacher's guide. $18.00 (Canadian holidays : $180.00) pj

1. Thanksgiving Day - History.

Discusses the development of the Canadian Thanksgiving tradition. Includes several of the original reasons for thecelebration, and mentions the shifting of the holiday's date over the years.-

394.2
Thanksgiving today.
 prod. [Toronto] : B & R. 1973.- dist. B & R 32 fr. : col. : 35 mm. & cassette (8 min.) : auto. & aud. adv. sig. & teacher's manual & script. $16.00 (Canadian holidays : $180.00) pj

1. Thanksgiving Day.

Highlights several activities and foods of today's Thanksgiving season. Includes football, gardening, fruits and vegetables, and turkey, and illustrates the influence seasons can have on the type of activities pursued.-

394.2
Victoria Day.
 prod. [Toronto] : B & R. 1975.- dist. B & R 35 fr. : b&w & col. : 35 mm. & cassette (16 min.) : auto. & aud. adv. sig. & script & teacher's manual. $16.00 (Canadian holidays : $180.00) pj

1. Victoria Day.

Photographs, paintings and sketches of Queen Victoria illustrate the story of her life and the ideals she promoted. Suggests reasons for celebrating a holiday in her honour, and discusses activities common at this time of year.-

The Classified Catalogue

398.2
    The Angekkok of Thule.
        prod. [Scarborough, Ont.] : R.B.M., 1974.- dist. ETHOS 41 fr. : col. : 35 mm. & cassette (9 min.) : auto. & aud. adv. sig. & teacher's manual. $19.00 (Eskimo myths and legends : $69.00) pj

        1. Folklore, Eskimo.

        Artwork is used to illustrate the legend of Signuk's journey to Tomatik to find a cure for the sickness and death sweeping her camp. Shared with each other is the advice she is given. When this is done, her people quickly recover.-

398.2
    Attituk and the caribou.
        prod. [Scarborough, Ont.] : R.B.M., 1974.- dist. ETHOS 58 fr. : col. : 35 mm. & cassette (15 min.) : auto. & aud. adv. sig. & teacher's manual. $19.00 (Eskimo myths and legends : $69.00) pj

        1. Folklore, Eskimo.

        The story of the greedy Eskimo hunter who learns that unless he slaughters only enough caribou to meet the needs of his people, the caribou herds will cease to return each year. Illustrated with artwork, and includes authentic background sounds.-

398.2
    Le chasseur qui partit.
        prod. [Toronto] : Int. Cin., 1974.- dist. VEC 56 fr. : col. : 35 mm. & cassette (8 min.) : auto. & aud. adv. sig. & teacher's guide. $24.00 (Les arbres m'ont raconté : $86.00) pji

        1. Folklore, Eskimo.

        An Eskimo story about a hunter, who, unhappy with his own life, lives the life of an animal, and learns that, like man, animals, have problems, too. Seed collages illustrate the legend, with narration by Chief Dan George. English title available : THE HUNTER WHO WENT AWAY.-

398.2
    Le Festival des phoques.
        prod. [Toronto] : M-L, 1975.- dist. Sch. Ser. or Vint. 49 fr. : col. : 35 mm. & cassette (8 min.) : auto. & aud. adv. sig. & teacher's guide. $16.50 (Légendes Amérindiennes : $85.00) j

        1. Folklore, Eskimo.

        A young Inuit boy accompanies the village medicine man to the ocean bottom to see how seal bladders which had been inflated and put back into the water by the seal hunters become new seals. English title available : THE FESTIVAL OF THE SEALS.-

398.2
    The Festival of the seals.
        prod. : M-L, 1973.- dist. Sch. Ser. or Vint. 49 fr. : col. : 35 mm. & cassette (8 min.) : auto. & aud. adv. sig. & teacher's guide. $16.50 (Indian legends : $85.00) j

        1. Folklore, Eskimo.

        A young Inuit boy accompanies the village medicine man to the ocean bottom to see how seal bladders which have been inflated and put back into the water by the seal hunters become new seals. French title available : LE FESTIVAL DES PHOQUES.-

398.2
    Good King Arthur.
        prod. [Toronto] : M-L, 1974.- dist. Sch. Ser. or Vint. 67 fr. : col. : 35 mm. & cassette (12 min.) : auto. & aud. adv. sig. & teacher's guide. $16.50 (Famous stories of great courage : $85.00) i

        1. Arthur, King.

        The story of King Arthur and his courage when facing the Sable Knight (King Pellinore). With the sword Excalibur, Arthur is able to defeat Pellinore and chooses to offer him friendship. French title available : LE BON ROI ARTHUR.-

398.2
> Le hibou et le lemming : une légende eskimo.
> prod. [Montreal?] : NFB, 1973.- dist. SEC 59 fr. : col. : 35 mm. & disc (33 1/3 rpm. 7 min.) : auto. & aud. adv. sig. $18.00 p
>
> 1. Folklore, Eskimo.
>
> Sealskin puppets have been photographed for this version of an Eskimo legend about a lemming who escapes from a hungry owl by using flattery. Authentic Eskimo dialogue and chants accompany the narration. English title available : THE OWL AND THE LEMMING : ESKIMO LEGEND.-

398.2
> The Hunter who went away.
> prod. [Toronto] : Int. Cin., 1973.- dist. VEC 56 fr. : col. : 35 mm. & cassette (8 min.) : auto. & aud. adv. sig. & teacher's guide. $24.00 (Tales from the treetops : $86.00) pji
>
> 1. Folklore, Eskimo.
>
> An Eskimo story about a hunter, who, unhappy with his own life, lives the life of an animal and learns that, like man, animals have problems, too. Seed collages illustrate the legend, with narration by chief Dan George. French title available: LE CHASSEUR QUI PARTIT.-

398.2
> The Legend of the flying canoe.
> prod. [Montreal?] : NFB, 1965.- dist. McI. 29 fr. : col. : 35 mm. & captions. $9.00 (Canadian stories and legends series) pj
>
> 1. Folklore, Canadian (French).
>
> Colourful art work complements this subtle French Canadian legend of groups of men who dared to ride in a flying canoe, piloted by Satan.-

398.2
> The Legend of the raven who flew backwards.
> prod. [Scarborough, Ont.] : R.B.M., 1974.- dist. ETHOS 39 fr. : col. : 35 mm. & cassette (10 min.) : auto. & aud. sig. & teacher's manual. $19.00 (Eskimo myths and legends : $69.00) pj
>
> 1. Folklore, Eskimo.
>
> Artwork illustrates the legend of Cree, the raven, who, lacking any foresight and preferring to look backwards, end up simply as a mysterious pile of feathers.-

398.2
> The Owl and the lemming : Eskimo legend.
> prod. [Montreal?] : NFB, 1972.- dist. McI. 59 fr. : col. : 35 mm. & cassette (6 min.) : auto. & aud. adv. sig. $18.00 p
>
> 1. Folklore, Eskimo.
>
> Sealskin puppets have been photographed for this version of an Eskimo legend about a lemming who escapes from a hungry owl by using flattery. Authentic Eskimo dialogue and chants accompany the English narration. French title available : LE HIBOU ET LE LEMMING : UNE LEGENDE ESKIMO.-

398.2
> The Shaman goes to the moon.
> prod. [Scarborough, Ont.] : R.B.M., 1974.- dist. ETHOS 51 fr. : col. : 35 mm. & cassette (12 min.) : auto. & aud. adv. sig. & teacher's manual. $19.00 (Eskimo myths and legends : $69.00) pj
>
> 1. Folklore, Eskimo.
>
> Two white visitors at an Eskimo camp learn that, depending on one's point of view, there may be more than one way to reach the moon.-

398.2
> Ti-Jean and the lumberjacks.
> prod. [Montreal?] : NFB, made 1960 : 1974.- dist. McI. 31 fr. : col. : 35 mm. & captions & teacher's manual. $9.00 p
>
> 1. Folklore - Canadian (French).
>
> Ti-Jean, a small boy from Quebec, who is very strong, helps the lumberjacks and shows off his amazing strength by chopping trees, eating, and log-cutting. Cartoon characters and captions are used. French title available : TI-JEAN ET LES BUCHERONS.-

398.2
> Ti-Jean saves the harvest.
> prod. [Montreal?] : NFB, made 1960 : 1975.- dist. McI. 34 fr. : col. : 35 mm. & captions & teacher's manual. $9.00 pj
>
> 1. Folklore - Canadian (French).
>
> A cartoon presentation of a trip to the Canadian West, featuring Ti-Jean, a strong little boy from Quebec. Using a railway handcar, he travels through Quebec and Ontario to the prairies, where he quickly cuts wheat by hand and drives the harvest machine. French title available : LES EXPLOITS DE TI-JEAN DANS L'OUEST.-

The Classified Catalogue

398.209415
    Ireland : O'Reilly's Christmas cap.
        prod. [Toronto] M-L, 1976.- dist. Sch. Ser. or Vint. 58 fr. : col. : 35 mm. & cassette (9 min.) : auto. & aud. adv. sig. & teacher's guide. $16.50 (Christmas tales from many lands : $75.00) pj

        1. Christmas stories. 2. Folklore - Ireland.

        Colourful hand puppets depict the tale of O'Reilly, an Irish Scrooge who learns of kindness and generosity on Christmas eve. The narrator, with his Irish lilt, provides a unique voice for each character of the story. French title available : L'IRLANDE : LA CASQUETTE DE O'REILLY.-

398.20943
    Baron Münchhausen in a whale of a tale : a German legend.
        prod. [Montreal?] : NFB, made 1974 : 1975.- dist. McI. 34 fr. : col. : 35 mm. & captions. $9.00 (Stories and legends from other lands series) j

        1. Legends - Germany.

        A humourously exaggerated tale of a ship's encounter with a whale, and how the baron saved the day, illustrated with artwork. French title available : LE BARON MUNCHHAUSEN DANS UNE HISTOIRE CHAVIRANTE : UN CONTE ALLEMAND.-

398.20943
    Germany : the nutcracker's happy Christmas.
        prod. [Toronto] : Moreland-Latchford, 1976.- dist. School Services or Vintergreen Communications 65 fr. : col. : 35 mm. & cassette (14 min.) : auto. & aud. adv. sig. & teacher's guide. $16.50 (Christmas tales from many lands : $75.00) kpi

        1. Folklore - Germany. 2. Christmas stories.

        The famous German nutcracker legend is recaptured through colorful original drawings. The narrator's German accent and his ability to create a different voice for each character capture attention as does the familiar background music from the Nutcracker suite ballet. A familiar tale of interest to young children. French title available : L'ALLEMAGNE : LE PLUS BEAU NOEL DE CASSE-NOIX.-

398.209438
    Bartek l'étourdi : un conte polinais.
        prod. [Montreal?] : NFB, 1976.- dist. SEC 44 fr. : col. : 35 mm. & captions. $9.00 p

        1. Folklore - Poland.

        The story of a kind but foolish peasant who tries to find a present to please his wife and discovers that the "greatest magic is the goodness in one's heart". Artwork illustrations. English title available : FOOLISH BARTEK : A POLISH TALE.-

398.209438
    Foolish Bartek : (a Polish tale).
        prod. [Montreal?] : NFB, 1976.- dist. McI. 44 fr. : col. : 35 mm. & captions. $9.00 (Stories and legends from other lands series) p

        1. Folklore - Poland.

        The story of a kind but foolish peasant who tries to find a present to please his wife and discovers that the "greatest magic is the goodness in one's heart." Artwork illustrations. French title available : BARTEK L'ETOURDI : UN CONTE POLINAIS.-

398.209439
    La biche miraculeuse : une légende hongroise.
        prod. [Montreal?] : NFB, 1971.- dist. SEC 46 fr. : col. : 35 mm. & captions & printed notes. $9.00 (Contes et légends d'ailleurs) pj

        1. Legends - Hungary.

        In their search for a miraculous hind, two young men and their followers find wives, and the area they discover and settle in later becomes the country of Hungary. Story re-telling and illustrations by Elizabeth Cleaver. English title available : THE MIRACULOUS HIND : A HUNGARIAN LEGEND.-

398.209439
    The Miraculous hind : a hungarian legend.
        prod. [Montreal?] : NFB, 1971.- dist. McI. 50 fr. : col. : 35 mm. & captions & printed notes. $9.00 (Stories and legends from other lands series) pj

        1. Legends - Hungary.

        In their search for a miraculous hind, two young men and their followers find wives, and the area they discover and settle in later becomes the country of Hungary. Story re-telling and illustrations by Elizabeth Cleaver. French title available : LA BICHE MIRACULEUSE.-

The Classified Catalogue

398.20944
  La belle au bois dormant.
   prod. [Montreal?] : NFB, 1972.- dist. SEC 40 fr. : col. : 35 mm. & captions. $9.00 (Contes et légendes d'ailleurs) pj

  1. Legends - France.

  Stylized drawings by Carel Moiseiwitsch illustrate the popular French legend of a princess destined to sleep for one hundred years. English title available : SLEEPING BEAUTY : A FRENCH LEGEND.-

398.20944
  Puss 'n Boots.
   prod. [Toronto] : M-L, 1974.- dist. Sch. Ser. or Vint. 74 fr. : col. : 35 mm. & cassette (14 min.) : auto. & aud. adv. sig. & teacher's guide. $16.50 (Animal stories from other lands : $85.00) pj

  1. Folklore - France.

  A clever cat rewards a poor but kind woodchopper - first by bringing him food and good fortune, then by bringing him riches and a princess for his wife. Illustrated with drawings.-

398.20944
  Sleeping Beauty : a French legend.
   prod. [Montreal?] : NFB, 1972.- dist. McI. 36 fr. : col. : 35 mm. & captions. $9.00 (Stories and legends from other lands series) pj

  1. Legends - France.

  Stylized drawings by Carel Moiseiwitsch illustrate the popular French legend of a princess destined to sleep for one hundred years. French title available : LA BELLE AU BOIS DORMANT.-

398.20945
  L'Italie : la legende de Dame la Befana.
   prod. [Toronto] : M-L, 1976.- dist. Sch. Ser. or Vint. 56 fr. : col. : 35 mm. & cassette (11 min.) : auto. & aud. adv. sig. & teacher's guide. $16.50 (Les Légendes de Noël des pay étrangers : $75.00) pj

  1. Folklore - Italy. 2. Christmas stories.

  Portrays the traditional legend of the immortal Christmas wanderer - La Befana. Characters fashioned of wood, cloth, pipe cleaners, spools and other common household materials, are creatively photographed, and the tale is related by a narrator with an Italian accent. English title available: ITALY-THE LEGEND OF LA BEFANA.-

398.20945
  The Silliest man in Italy.
   prod. [Toronto] : M-L, 1974.- dist. Sch. Ser. or Vint. 64 fr. : col. : 35 mm. & cassette (10 min.) : auto. & aud. adv. sig. & teacher's guide. $16.50 (Folk tales around the world : $85.00) pj

  1. Folklore - Italy.

  An Italian folktale illustrated with drawings and accompanied by appropriate music.-

398.20947
  The Firebird and the magic horse.
   prod. [Toronto] : M-L, 1974.- dist. Sch. Ser. or Vint. 61 fr. : col. : 35 mm. & cassette (11 min.) : auto. & aud. adv. sig. & teacher's guide. $16.50 (Folk tales around the world : $85.00) pj

  1. Folklore - Russia.

  A Russian folktale shows how ingratitude can be harmful to others. Illustrated with drawings and includes appropriate background music.-

398.20947
  Ilia le Grans : une légende Ukrainienne.
   prod. [Montreal?] : NFB, 1976.- dist. SEC 37 fr. : col. : 35 mm. & captions. $9.00 pj

  1. Legends - Ukrainian.

  A poor young peasant becomes a mighty and courageous warrior slaying giants, dragons, and wicked Bohatyrs, and marrying the princess. Artwork with captions. English title available : ILIA THE MIGHTY : A UKRAINIAN LEGEND.-

The Classified Catalogue

398.20947
    Ilia the mighty : a Ukrainian legend.
        prod. [Montreal?] : NFB, 1976.- dist. McI. 39 fr. : col. : 35 mm. & captions. $9.00 (Stories and legends from other lands series) pj

        1. Legends - Ukranian.

    A poor young peasant becomes a mighty and courageous warrior slaying giants, dragons, and wicked Bohatyrs, and marrying the princess. Artwork with captions. French title available : ILIA LE GRANS : UNE LEGENDE UKRANIENNE.-

398.20947
    Peter and the wolf.
        prod. [Toronto] : M-L, 1974.- dist. Sch. Ser. or Wint. 68 fr. : col. : 35 mm. & cassette (13 min.) : auto. & aud. adv. sig. & teacher's guide. $16.50 (Animal stories from other lands : $85.00) pj

        1. Folklore - Russia.

    The classic Russian tale of a young boy who learns the value of friends when he is caught in a difficult situation with a wolf. Illustrated with drawings.-

398.20951
    The Mandarin and the butterflies.
        prod. [Toronto] : M-L, 1974.- dist. Sch. Ser. or Wint. 72 fr. : col. : 35 mm. & cassette (13 min.) : auto. & aud. adv. sig. & teacher's guide. $16.50 (Animal stories from other lands : $85.00) pj

        1. Folklore - China.

    Mandarin Wang, a judge in ancient China, exiled because of his son's cruelty to butterflies, is allowed by the Butterfly Princess to return home once he has learned the value of kindness.-

398.20951
    The Superlative horse.
        prod. [Toronto] : M-L, 1974.- dist. Sch. Ser. or Wint. 77 fr. : col. : 35 mm. & cassette (12 min.) : auto. & aud. adv. sig. & teacher's guide. $16.50 (Folk tales around the world : $85.00) pj

        1. Folklore - China.

    A Chinese folktale demonstrating the futility of envy. Story is accompanied by drawings and appropriate music.-

398.20951
    The Wishing bowl (China).
        prod. [Toronto] : Int. Cin., 1975.- dist. VEC 65 fr. : col. : 35 mm. & cassette (8 min.) : auto. & aud. adv. sig. & teacher's guide. $24.00 (Folktales from the ancient East) pj

        1. Folklore - China.

    A folktale from ancient China tells the story of a landlord whose jealousy of a young boy and his magic bowl drives him to evil deeds. Detail of artwork and music add to the ethnic flavour.-

398.20952
    The Two frogs : a Japanese legend.
        prod. [Montreal?] : NFB, 1973.- dist. McI. 41 fr. : col. : 35 mm. & captions. $9.00 (Stories and legends from other lands series) p

        1. Folklore - Japan.

    Water colour illustrations enhance this tale of two frogs, one from Kyoto and the other from Osaka, who decide to travel and meet each other on a mountain top. French title available : LES DEUX GRENOUILLES : UN CONTE JAPONAIS.-

398.20952
    Urashima Taro the fisherlad.
        prod. [Toronto] : M-L, 1974.- dist. Sch. Ser. or Wint. 69 fr. : col. : 35 mm. & cassette (11 min.) : auto. & aud. adv. sig. & teacher's guide. $16.50 (Folk tales around the world : $85.00) pj

        1. Folklore - Japan.

    The importance of personal integrity is illustrated in this Japanese folktale. Narration is accompanied by drawings and appropriate music.-

398.20954
    The Rajah's garden.
        prod. [Toronto] : Int. Cin., 1975.- dist. VEC 62 fr. : col. : 35 mm. & cassette (9 min.) : auto. & aud. adv. sig. & teacher's guide. $24.00 (Folktales from the ancient East) pj

        1. Folklore - India.

    Jealousy and forgiveness are illustrated in this Indian tale of a jealous princess who commits an evil deed and is forgiven by the Rajah's beautiful wife. Artwork and music blend with Indian setting.-

The Classified Catalogue

398.209561
Foolish friends : Turkey.
prod. [Toronto] : Int. Cin., 1975.- dist. VEC 61 fr. : col. : 35 mm. & cassette (8 min.) : auto.& aud. adv. sig. & teacher's guide. $24.00 (Folktales from the ancient East) pj

1. Folklore - Turkey.

Two friends living in ancient Turkey play a cruel joke on each other with serious consequences. Colourful drawings and music add to the story.-

398.2095691
Syria : the little camel.
prod. [Toronto] : M-L, 1973.- dist. Sch. Ser. or Vint. 51 fr. : col. : 35 mm. & cassette (8 min.) : auto. & aud. adv. sig. & teacher's guide. $16.50 (Christmas tales from many lands : $75.00) kpi

1. Folklore - Syria. 2. Christmas stories.

A Christmas legend recounting the relationship that developed between the youngest of the three wise men and his tiny camel during their trip to Bethlehem. The tale demonstrates courage and determination. Three-dimensional characters sculpted from clay illustrate the story, and the background music is characteristic of the Syrian setting. French title available : LA SYRIE : LE PETIT CHAMEAU.-

398.2095694
The Lost wisdom (Israel).
prod. [Toronto] : Int. Cin., 1975.- dist. VEC 61 fr. : col. : 35 mm & cassette (9 min.) : auto. & aud. adv. sig. & teacher's guide. $24.00 (Folktales from the ancient East) j

1. Folklore - Israel.

Artwork and music enhance this folktale from ancient Israel in which a cruel, wealthy young man comes to realize the importance of treating others as you would want to be treated.-

398.2095694
The Value of a boiled egg.
prod. [Toronto] : M-L, 1974.- dist. Sch. Ser. or Vint. 68 fr. : col. : 35 mm. & cassette (11 min.) : auto. & aud. adv. sig. & teacher's guide. $16.50 (Folk tales around the world : $85.00) pj

1. Folklore, Jewish.

A Jewish folktale illustrating the value of wisdom. Drawings and appropriate music support the narration.-

398.2096
How the leopard got its spots.
prod. [Toronto] : M-L, 1974.- dist. Sch. Ser. or Vint. 61 fr. : col. : 35 mm. & cassette (10 min.) : auto. & aud. adv. sig. & teacher's guide. $16.50 (Animal stories from other lands : $85.00) pj

1. Folklore - Africa.

An African tale, illustrated with line-drawings, explains why the leopard needed to have spots and how he managed to get them.-

398.2096
Why the spider has a narrow waist.
prod. [Toronto] : M-L, 1974.- dist. Sch. Ser. or Vint. 58 fr. : col. : 35 mm. & cassette (10 min.) : auto. & aud. adv. sig. & teacher's guide. $16.50 (Folk tales around the world : $85.00) pj

1. Folklore - Africa.

An African folktale illustrates the folly of greed. Story uses humourous drawings accompanied by background music.-

398.209701
Au tout début.
prod. [Toronto] : M-L, 1975.- dist. Sch. Ser. or Vint. 49 fr. : col. : 35 mm. & cassette (9 min.) : auto. & aud. adv. sig. & teacher's guide. $16.50 (Légendes amérindiennes : $85.00) j

1. Indians of North America - Legends.

A tale which parallels the Fall of Man, using animals instead of people. Suitable for classroom discussion of how evil begins and spreads. English title available : HOW IT ALL BEGAN.-

The Classified Catalogue

398.209701
    Le Bouc à une corne.
        prod. [Toronto] : M-L, 1975.- dist. Sch. Ser. or Vint. 49 fr. : col. : 35 mm. & cassette (10 min.) : auto. & aud. adv. sig. & teacher's guide. $16.50 (Légendes Amérindiennes : $85.00) j

        1. Indians of North America - Legends.

        An Indian who obeyed the old hunting laws is worthy to learn the mountain goat songs and dances to pass on to his descendants. Discusses immorality of killing more game than necessary for survival. Particularly suitable for classroom discussion. English title available : THE ONE-HORNED MOUNTAIN GOAT.-

398.209701
    La danse du soleil des Amérindiens de Plaines.
        prod. [Toronto] : M-L, 1975.- dist. Sch. Ser. or Vint. 49 fr. : col. : 35 mm. & cassette (10 min.) : auto. & aud. adv. sig. & teacher's guide. $16.50 (Légendes Amérindiennes : $85.00) j

        1. Indians of North America - Legends.

        The story of Star Boy, and how he came to initiate the festival of the Sun Dance in honour of his grandfather, the Sun. English title available : THE SUN DANCE OF THE PLAINS INDIANS.-

398.209701
    The First salmon.
        prod. [Montreal?] : NFB, 1971.- dist. McI. 77 fr. : col. : 35 mm. & cassette (6 min.) : auto. & aud. adv. sig. $18.00 pj

        1. Haida Indians - Legends.

        Drawings illustrate this West Coast Indian tale. The spirit fog woman magically produces salmon for her husband Raven. When he becomes ungrateful she takes the salmon with her into the sea forever. French title available : LE PREMIER SAUMON.-

398.209701
    Glooscap and the four wishes.
        prod. [Montreal?] : NFB, made 1966 : 1976.- dist. McI. 34 fr. : col. : 35 mm. & captions. $9.00 (Canadian stories and legends series) p

        1. Indians of North America - Legends.

        Four Indian braves ask Glooscap to grant their wishes and he obliges. Artwork enhances the story line. French title available : GLOOSCAP ET LES QUATRE VOEUX.-

398.209701
    Glooscap et les quatre voeux : [légende indienne].
        prod. [Montreal?] : NFB, 1966.- dist. SEC 34 fr. : col. : 35 mm. & captions. $9.00 (Légendes indiennes) p

        1. Indians of North America - Legends.

        Four Indian braves ask Glooscap to grant their wishes and he obliges. Artwork enhances the story line. English title available : GLOOSCAP AND THE FOUR WISHES : AN INDIAN LEGEND.-

398.209701
    Glooskap brings summer.
        prod. [Toronto] : M-L, 1973.- dist. Sch. Ser. or Vint. 49 fr. : col. : 35 mm. & cassette (10 min.) : auto. & aud. adv. sig. & teacher's guide. $16.50 (Indian legends : $85.00) j

        1. Indians of North America - Legends.

        An allegorical explanation of the seasons. Suitable for classroom discussion of seasons, or discussion of allegory. French title available : GLOOSKAP NOUS A DONNE L'ETE.-

398.209701
    L'histoire de Pan de Glouton.
        prod. [Toronto] : Int. Cin., 1974.- dist. VEC 64 fr. : col. : 35 mm. & cassette (7 min.) : auto. & aud. adv. sig. & teaching guide. $24.00 (Les arbres m'ont raconté : $86.00) pj

        1. Indians of North America - Legends.

        A story, illustrated with seed pictures, about two brothers, Greedy Pan and Curious Eye, whose differing attitudes about life affect the outcome of their own. English title available : THE STORY OF GREEDY PAN.-

398.209701
    How it all began.
        prod. [Toronto] : M-L, 1973.- dist. Sch Ser. or Vint. 49 fr. : col. : 35 mm. & cassette (9 min.) : auto. & aud. adv. sig. & teacher's guide. $16.50 (Indian legends : $85.00) j

        1. Indians of North America - Legends.

        A tale which parallels the Fall of Man, using animals instead of people. Suitable for classroom discussion of how evil begins and spreads. French title available : AU TOUT DEBUT.-

The Classified Catalogue

398.209701
How summer came to our land.
prod. [Toronto] : Int. Cin., 1976.- dist. VEC 71 fr. : col. : 35 mm. & cassette (8 min.) : auto. & aud. adv. sig. & teacher's guide. $24.00 (Legends of the Micmac : $86.00) pji

1. Micmac Indians - Legends.

Using beautifully decorated puppets tells how Queen Summer broke Winter's spell and brought summer to the Micmac land.-

398.209701
How the deer got fire.
prod. [Toronto] : M-L, 1974.- dist. Sch. Ser. or Vint. 78 fr. : col. : 35 mm. & cassette (13 min.) : auto. & aud. adv. sig. & teacher's guide. $16.50 (Animal stories from other lands : $85.00) pj

1. Indians of North America - Legends.

A legend from Canada telling how Little Deer brings fire from the Wolf people to his friends the Deer People, who then share it with all the other Indian nations. Illustrated with drawings.-

398.209701
The Legend of the loon.
prod. [Toronto] : Int. Cin., 1976.- dist. VEC 64 fr. : col. : 35 mm. & cassette (7 min.) : auto. & aud. adv. sig. & teacher's guide. $24.00 (Legends of the Micmac : $86.00) pji

1. Micmac Indians - Legends.

The story of how the loon became a water bird and why it has a haunting cry.-

398.209701
The Medicine that restores life.
prod. [Toronto] : M-L, 1973.- dist. Sch. Ser. or Vint. 49 fr. : col. 35 mm. & cassette (8 min.) : auto. & aud. adv. sig. & teacher's guide. $16.50 (Indian legends : $85.00) j

1. Indians of North America - Legends.

A wise hunter, killed in battle, is restored to life by a medicine concocted by the animals of the forest who loved him. French title available : LE REMEDE DE LA VIE.-

398.209701
Naba-Cha and the Rocky Mountains.
prod. [Montreal?] : NFB, 1966.- dist. McI. 28 fr. : col. : 35 mm. & captions. $9.00 (Canadian stories and legends series) p

1. Indians of North America - Legends.

Stylized drawings complement the story of an Indian boy's escape from a giant and how the mountains, swamps and forests were formed to assist his escape.-

398.209701
The One-horned mountain goat.
prod. [Toronto] : M-L, 1973.- dist. Sch. Ser. or Vint. 49 fr. : col. : 35 mm. & cassette (10 min.) : auto. & aud. adv. sig. & teacher's guide. $16.50 (Indian legends : $85.00) j

1. Indians of North America - Legends.

An Indian who obeyed the old hunting laws is worthy to learn the mountain goat songs and dances to pass on to his descendants. Discusses immorality of killing more game than necessary for survival. Particularly suitable for classroom discussion. French title available : LE BOUC A UNE CORNE.-

398.209701
Les piquants du Porc-Epic.
prod. [Montreal?] : NFB, 1966.- dist. SEC 29 fr. : col. : 35 mm. & captions. $9.00 (Légendes indiennes) p

1. Indians of North America - Legends.

Artwork depicts the Indian legend of Porcupine who escapes Bear and Wolf by covering himself with thorns. English title available : WHY A PORCUPINE HAS QUILLS.-

398.209701
Pourquoi les pieds-noirs ne font jamais de mal aux souris.
prod. [Toronto] : Int. Cin., 1974.- dist. VEC 45 fr. : col. : 35 mm. & cassette (6 min.) : auto. & aud. adv. sig. & teacher's guide. $24.00 (Les arbres m'ont raconté : $86.00) pj

1. Indians of North America - Legends.

An Indian legend telling why the Blackfeet never hurt a mouse, and why Man is chief of all the animals in the forest. Illustrated with seed collages. English title available : WHY THE BLACKFEET NEVER HURT A MOUSE.-

398.209701
    Le premier saumon.
        prod. [Montreal?] : NFB, 1971.- dist. SEC 77 fr. : col. : 35 mm. & cassette (6 min.) : auto. & aud. adv. sig. $9.00 (Légendes indiennes) pj

    1. Haida Indians - Legend.

    Drawings illustrate this West Coast Indian tale. The spirit fog woman magically produces salmon for her husband Raven. When he becomes ungrateful she takes the salmon with her into the sea forever. English title available : THE FIRST SALMON : HAIDA INDIAN LEGEND.-

398.209701
    Le remède de la vie.
        prod. [Toronto] : M-L, 1975.- dist. Sch. Ser. or Vint. 49 fr. : col. : 35 mm. & cassette (8 min.) : auto. & aud. adv. sig. & teacher's guide. $16.50 (Légendes amérindiennes : $85.00) j

    1. Indians of North America - Legends.

    A wise hunter, killed in battle, is restored to life by a medecine concocted by the animals of the forest who loved him. English title available : THE MEDICINE THAT RESTORES LIFE.-

398.209701
    The Story of Greedy Pan.
        prod. [Toronto] : Int. Cin., 1973.- dist. VEC 64 fr. : col. : 35 mm. & cassette (7 min.) : auto. & aud. adv. sig. & teaching guide. $24.00 (Tales from the treetops : $86.00) pji

    1. Indians of North America - Legends.

    A story, illustrated with seed pictures, about two brothers, Greedy Pan and Curious Eye, whose differing attitudes about life affect the outcome of their own. Narrated by Chief Dan George. French title available : L'HISTOIRE DE PAN LE GLOUTON.-

398.209701
    The Sun dance of the Plains Indians.
        prod. [Toronto] : M-L, 1973.- dist. ssch. ser. or Vint. 49 fr. : col. : 35 mm. & cassette (10 min.) : auto. & aud. adv. sig. & teacher's guide. $16.50 (Indian legends : $85.00) j

    1. Indians of North America - Legends.

    The story of Star Boy, and how he came to initiate the festival of the Sun Dance in honour of his grandfather, the Sun. French title available : LA DANSE DU SOLEIL DES AMERINDIENS DE PLAINES.-

398.209701
    Why a porcupine has quills.
        prod. [Montreal?] : NFB, made 1966 : 1976.- dist. McI. 27 fr. : col. : 35 mm. & captions. $9.00 (Canadian stories and legends series) p

    1. Indians of North America - Legends.

    Artwork depicts the Indian legend of Porcupine Bear who escapes Bear and Wolf by covering himself with thorns. French title available : LES PIQUANTS DU PORC.-

398.20971
    La mouette et la baleine.
        prod. [Montreal?] : NFB, made 1966 : 1967. dist. SEC 32 fr. : col. : 35 mm. & captions. $9.00 p

    1. Folklore - Canada.

    A Maritime legend of the seagull who finds her lost egg in the stomach of a whale. Illustrations add humour. English title available : THE SEAGULL AND THE WHALE.-

398.20972
    Mexico : the humblest gift.
        prod. [Toronto] : M-L, 1976.- dist. Sch. Ser. or Vint. 67 fr. : col. : 35 mm. & cassette (13 min.) : auto. & aud. adv. sig. & teacher's guide. $16.50 (Christmas tales from many lands : $75.00) kpi

    1. Folklore - Mexico. 2. Christmas stories.

    Expressive and colourful cut-out figures are photographed in front of a three-dimensional background in this depiction of the traditional Mexican Christmas legend of the Flor de la Nochebuena, the poinsettia. The story, along with the narrator's Spanish accent and the music soundtrack provide a realistic glimpse into the culture of Mexico. French title available : LE MEXIQUE : L'HUMBLE PRESENT.-

The Classified Catalogue

398.20972
    La Mexique : l'humble présent.
       prod. [Toronto] : M-L, 1976.- dist. Sch. Ser. or Vint. 67 fr. : col. : 35 mm. & cassette (13 min.) : auto. & aud. adv. sig. & teacher's guide. $16.50 (Les Légendes de Noël des pay étrangers : $75.00) pj

       1. Folklore - Mexico. 2. Christmas stories.

       Expressive and colourful cut-out figures are photographed in front of a three-dimensional background in this depiction of the traditional Mexican Christmas legend of the Flor de la Nochebuena, the poinsettia. The story, along with the narrator's Spanish accent and the music soundtrack provide a realistic glimpse into the culture of Mexico. English title available : MEXICO - THE HUMBLEST GIFT.-

398.2097295
    The Tiger and the rabbit.
       prod. [Toronto] : M-L, 1974.- dist. Sch. Scr. or Vint. 68 fr. : col. : 35 mm. & cassette (13 min.) : auto. & aud. adv. sig. & teacher's guide. $16.50 (Animal stories from other lands : $85.00) pj

       1. Folklore - Puerto Rico.

       A Puerto Rican tale, illustrated with simple drawings, of a clever rabbit who outwits his enemy, the tiger, time and time again. The tiger, tiring of being alone, changes his ways and is accepted as a friend by all the forest creatures.-

401
    Introduction to language study.
       prod. [Toronto] : Int. Cin., 1970? dist. VEC 67 fr. : col. : 35 mm. & cassette (11 min.) : auto. & aud. adv. sig. & teacher's guide. $24.00 (The History of the English language : $65.00) is

       1. Language and languages.

       Intended to stimulate students to consider language as a whole and to notice language patterns. Deals with the need to communicate and the history of language. Time is allowed for students to respond immediately to questions and activities in the filmstrip.-

407
    Of the farm.
       prod. [Montreal?] : NFB, 1975.- dist. McI. 36 fr. : col. : 35 mm. & printed notes. $9.00 ("Of the" : $27.00) pji

       1. Language arts - Study and teaching.
       2. Farms - Pictorial works.

       A semi-abandoned farm as seen through the eyes of a photographer. A study of form, shape and contrast, this visual essay expresses a moment of the present through elements of the past. A useful filmstrip for a language arts programme.-

407
    Of the horse.
       prod. [Montreal?] : NFB, 1974.- dist. McI. 39 fr. : col. : 35 mm. & printed notes. $9.00 ("Of the" : $27.00) pji

       1. Language arts - Study and teaching.

       An experience of form and movement is the photographer's perception of the horse frozen in moments of changing time. Portrays the beauty of the horse from many unusual angles. Of most use in a language arts programme to stimulate discussion. French title available : DU CHEVAL.-

407
    Of the land.
       prod. [Montreal?] : NFB, 1974.- dist. McI. 54 fr. : col. : 35 mm. & printed notes. $9.00 ("Of the" : $27.00) pji

       1. Language arts - Study and teaching.
       2. Canadian Shield - Pictorial works.

       Photographs portray the wild landscapes of the Canadian Shield region of Canada. Emphasizes the order and design found in untouched wilderness. Of most use in a language arts programme to stimulate discussion. French title available : DE LA TERRE.-

The Classified Catalogue

407
    Sleigh ride.
        prod. [Montreal?] : NFB, 1975.- dist. McI. 51 fr. : col. : 35 mm. $9.00 (Fieldtrips on filmstrips series) p

        1. Language arts - Study and teaching. 2. Winter sports. 3. Outdoor recreation.

        Captionless filmstrip to be used to develop conversation, comprehension skills, storytelling and crafts, and to serve as a field trip for the primary class. Photographs show the barn, grooming the horse, hitching to the sleigh. Winter activities such as sliding, ice fishing, skating, snow building, and dog sledding are included. French title available : UNE PROMENADE EN TRAINEAU.-

411
    The Bungler.
        prod. [Toronto] : M-L, 1975.- dist. Sch. Ser. or Vint. 42 fr. : col. : 35 mm. & cassette (6 min.) : auto. & aud. adv. sig. & teacher's guide. $16.50 (Reading readiness : $85.00) p

        1. Alphabet. 2. Reading.

        Promotes the recognition of the letter B and auditory awareness of B sound through a cartoon story of a wind-up toy that carries a bag full of objects beginning with B.-

411
    The Cowboy.
        prod. [Toronto] : M-L, 1975.- dist. Sch. Ser. or Vint. 63 fr. : col. : 35 mm. & cassette (10 min.) : auto. & aud. adv. sig. & teacher's guide. $16.50 (Reading readiness : $85.00) p

        1. Alphabet. 2. Reading.

        A cowboy and a talking horse are used to promote recognition of the letter C and auditory awareness of the hard C sound. Story presents pictures and printed words of objects beginning with this sound.-

411
    The Doodler.
        prod. [Toronto] : M-L, 1975.- dist. Sch. Ser. or Vint. 45 fr. : col. : 35 mm. & cassette (9 min.) : auto. & aud. adv. sig. & teacher's guide. $16.50 (Reading readiness : $85.00) p

        1. Alphabet. 2. Reading.

        Story of two children meeting a doodler who draws pictures of things beginning with D. Promotes recognition of the letter D and its sound. Illustrated with cartoons and accompanied by original music.-

411
    The Gobbler.
        prod. [Toronto] : M-L, 1975.- dist. Sch. Ser. or Vint. 57 fr. : col. : 35 mm. & cassette (11 min.) : auto. & aud. adv. sig. & teacher's guide. $16.50 (Reading readiness : $85.00) p

        1. Alphabet. 2. Reading.

        Cartoon story of a creature who gobbles G objects. Promotes recognition of letter G and auditory awareness of sound.-

411
    The Puffer.
        prod. [Toronto] : M-L, 1975.- dist. Sch. Ser. or Vint. 49 fr. : col. : 35 mm. & cassette (8 min.) : auto. & aud. adv. sig. & teacher's guide. $16.50 (Reading readiness : $85.00) p

        1. Alphabet. 2. Reading.

        Cartoon characters present a story of a town invaded by Purple P bubbles. Promotes recognition of letter P and its sound. Lists words beginning with P.-

411
    The Ticker.
        prod. [Toronto] : M-L, 1975.- dist. Sch. Ser. or Vint. 52 fr. : col. : 35 mm. & cassette (10 min.) : auto. & aud. adv. sig. & teacher's guide. $16.50 (Reading readiness : $85.00) p

        1. Alphabet. 2. Reading.

        Cartoon story about toys to promote recognition of letter T and its sound. Includes printed words under all pictures starting with T.

411
    Writing systems.
        prod. [Toronto] : Int. Cin., 1970? dist. VEC 64 fr. : col. : 35 mm. & cassette (14 min.) : auto. & aud. adv. sig. & teacher's guide. $24.00 (The History of the English language : $65.00) is

        1. Alphabet. 2. Hieroglyphics. 3. Picture writing.

        Deals with the need for recording messages. Includes several writing systems, such as picture writing, pictographs, locographs, hieroglyphs, and alphabets. Points out the variations of symbols in writing systems.-

The Classified Catalogue

411.09701
    Cree syllabary.
        prod. [Toronto] : RQM, 1973.- dist. Lea. 37 fr. : col. : 35 mm. & captions & teacher's guide. $9.00 (Our native people - customs and legends) ji

        1. Cree Indians. 2. Alphabet.

        A comprehensive summary in graphic form of the commonly used Cree symbols and the resulting syllabic alphabet. Several examples of the use of this alphabet to form words are given.-

411.09701
    Native picture writing.
        prod. [Toronto] : RQM., 1973.- dist. Lea. 34 fr. : col. : 35 mm. & captions & teacher's guide. $9.00 (Our native people - customs and legends) ji

        1. Picture writing.

        Describes the purpose of native writings and presents authentic graphics of various symbols used in written communication.-

420.9
    Origins and early history of English.
        prod. [Toronto] : Int. Cin., 1970? dist. VEC 82 fr. : col. : 35 mm. & cassette (15 min.) : auto. & aud. adv. sig. & teacher's guide. $24.00 (The History of the English language : $65.00) is

        1. English language - History.

        Traces development of English from its earliest beginnings to modern times. Discusses Old and Middle English and the Indo-European theory of language.-

421
    Commas.
        prod. [Toronto] : M-L, 1975.- dist. Sch. Ser. or Vint. 46 fr. : col. : 35 mm. & cassette (8 min.) : auto. & aud. adv. sig. & teacher's guide. $16.50 (Basic punctuation : $85.00) j

        1. Punctuation.

        Two cartoon characters demonstrate usage of the comma. Illustrates importance of pauses indicated by commas in written English.-

421
    Periods, question marks, and exclamation marks.
        prod. [Toronto] : M-L, 1975.- dist. Sch. Ser. or Vint. 46 fr. : col. : 35 mm. & cassette (9 min.) : auto. & aud. adv. sig. & teacher's guide. $16.50 (Basic punctuation : $85.00) j

        1. Punctuation.

        Explains the use of periods, question marks, and exclamation marks, and their effects on the meaning of a sentence. Compares punctuation to traffic signs.-

421
    Pitch, stress and juncture.
        prod. [Toronto] : M-L, 1975.- dist. Sch. Ser. or Vint. 44 fr. : col. : 35 mm. & cassette (7 min.) : auto. & aud. adv. sig. & teacher's guide. $16.50 (Basic punctuation : $85.00) j

        1. Rhetoric.

        Demonstrates effectively how to use the voice in order to change the meaning of a word or sentence. Stresses the importance of proper punctuation. Introduces the words : pitch, stress, and juncture.-

421
    Quotation marks and the apostrophe.
        prod. [Toronto] : M-L, 1975.- dist. Sch. Ser. or Vint. 48 fr. : col. : 35 mm. & cassette (9 min.) : auto. & aud. adv. sig. & teacher's guide. $16.50 (Basic punctuation : $85.00) j

        1. Punctuation.

        Comprehensive discussion of the use of these punctuation marks. Stresses importance of correct punctuation to aid understanding of written and spoken language.-

421
    Using capital letters.
        prod. [Toronto] : M-L, 1975.- dist. Sch. Ser. or Vint. 39 fr. : col. : 35 mm. & cassette (7 min.) : auto. & aud. adv. sig. & teacher's guide. $16.50 (Basic punctuation : $85.00) j

        1. Punctuation.

        Cartoon characters teach the important conventions of capitalization: to begin a sentence, a proper noun, a quotation, days, months, and holidays, as well as titles and the word "I".-

421
    Using punctuation marks.
       prod. [Toronto] : M-L, 1975.- dist. Sch. Ser. or Wint. 44 fr. : col. : 35 mm. & cassette (10 min.) : auto. & aud. adv. sig. & teacher's guide. $16.50 (Basic punctuation : $85.00) j

       1. Punctuation.

       Cartoon drawings and narration are used to introduce the colon, semicolon, hyphen, dash, and brackets, and to explain the usage of each.-

440.7
    Les aventures de Léo à la ferme.
       prod. [Montreal?] : NFB, 1955.- dist. SEC 34 fr. : col. : 35 mm. & captions & disc (33 1/3 rpm. 9 min.) : aud. adv. sig. & teacher's guide. $18.00 pj

       1. French language - Study and teaching.
       2. Farm life - Fiction.

       Leo the mouse, a cartoon character, has many accidents on his cousin's farm. French captions and narration tell of his day. He has problems with horses, a bull, an old pump, jumping into hay, and standing under a tree during a storm. For French language instruction.-

440.7
    La cigale et la fourmi.
       prod. [Toronto] : CFM, 1976.- dist. BAM 41 fr. : col. : 35 mm. & cassette (6 min.) : auto. & aud. adv. sig. & teacher's guide. $15.50 (Conversational French for beginners : les fables de la Fontaine : $149.00) ji

       1. French language - Study and teaching.

       The fable by La Fontaine about the cicada (grasshopper) and the ant provides the basis for this humourous cartoon story with a modern setting. Basic structures are designed for beginners in French.-

440.7
    Conseil tenu par les rats.
       prod. [Toronto] : CFM, 1976.- dist. BAM 45 fr. : col. : 35 mm. & cassette (11 min.) : auto. & aud. adv. sig. & teacher's guide. $15.50 (Conversational French for beginners : les fables de la Fontaine : $149.00) ji

       1. French language - Study and teaching.

       A cartoon story based on La Fontaine's fable about a meeting of rats who propose solutions but cannot implement them.
Situations are invented to include modern vocabulary. Basic structures are designed for beginners in French with only the present tense used. There are some variations in pronunciation.-

440.7
    Le corbeau et le renard.
       prod. [Toronto] : CFM, 1976.- dist. BAM 43 fr. : col. : 35 mm. & cassette (10 min.) : auto. & aud. adv. sig. & teacher's guide. $15.50 (Conversational French for beginners : les fables de la Fontaine : $149.00) ji

       1. French language - Study and teaching.

       La Fontaine's fable of the crow and the fox provides the framework for this basic cartoon story with situations invented to include modern vocabulary. Basic structures are designed for beginners in French with present tense mainly used; but there are some advanced structures, such as subjunctive. Vocabulary level is more difficult than the structure level.-

440.7
    Le cordonnier et le banquier
       prod. [Toronto] : CFM, 1976.- dist. BAM 46 fr. : col. : 35 mm. & cassette (8 min.) : auto. & aud. adv. sig. & teacher's guide. $15.50 (Conversational French for beginners : les fables de la Fontaine : $149.00) ji

       1. French language - Study and teaching.

       La Fontaine's fable of the rich man and the poor man, illustrated with cartoons, is used as a framework and situations are expanded to include modern vocabulary. Basic structures are designed for beginners in French; but the narration contains some low frequency vocabulary and complex structures.-

The Classified Catalogue

440.7
    Les deux chevres.
        prod. [Toronto] : CFM, 1976.- dist. BAM 42 fr. : col. : 35 mm. & cassette (8 min.) : auto. & aud. adv. sig. & teacher's guide. $15.50 (Conversational French for beginners : les fables de la Fontaine : $149.00) ji

        1. French language - Study and teaching.

        La Fontaine's fable about two goats provides the basis for a cartoon story with additional dialogue using modern vocabulary. Basic structures and vocabulary are designed for beginners of French with only the present tense used. No reading script is provided in the guide.-

440.7
    Les exploits de Ti-Jean dans l'Ouest.
        prod. [Montreal?] : NFB, 1960.- dist. McI. 32 fr. : col. : 35 mm. & captions & disc (33 1/3 rpm. 8 min.) & teacher's manual. $$9.00 pj

        1. Folklore - Canadian (French).

        A cartoon presentation of a trip to the Canadian West, featuring Ti-Jean, a strong little boy from Quebec. Using a railway handcar, he travels through Quebec and Ontario to the prairies, where he quickly cuts wheat by hand and drives the harvest machine. English title available : TI-JEAN SAVES THE HARVEST.-

440.7
    Le lion et le rat.
        prod. [Toronto] : CFM, 1976.- dist. BAM 44 fr. : col. : 35 mm. & cassette (8 min.) : auto. & aud. adv. sig. & teacher's manual. $15.50 (Conversational French for beginners : les fables de la Fontaine : $149.00) ji

        1. French language - Study and teaching.

        La Fontaine's fable of the lion and the rat provides the framework for a cartoon story with situations invented to bring in modern vocabulary. Basic structures are designed for beginners in French with the present tense mainly used. Stresses learning of moderate-frequency vocabulary.-

440.7
    L'ours et les deux compagnons.
        prod. [Toronto] : CFM, 1976.- dist. BAM 42 fr. : col. : 35 mm. & cassette (7 min.) : auto. & aud. adv. sig. & teacher's guide. $15.50 (Conversational French for beginners : les fables de la Fontaine : $149.00) ji

        1. French language - Study and teaching.

        La Fontaine's story of the bear and the two hunters is used as a framework and situations are invented to use modern vocabualry. Basic structures are designed for beginners of French.-

440.7
    Le rat de ville et le rat des champs.
        prod. [Toronto] : CFM, 1976.- dist. BAM 41 fr. : col. : 35 mm. & cassette (7 min.) : auto. & aud. adv. sig. & teacher's guide. $15.50 (Conversational French for beginners : les fables de la Fontaine : $149.00) ji

        1. French language - Study and teaching.

        Humorous cartoons are used to illustrate La Fontaine's fable of the city mouse and country mouse. The story is used as a framework only and situations are invented to bring in modern vocabulary. Basic structures are designed for beginners in French; but the narration contains some low-frequency vocabulary and more complex structurres.-

440.7
    Le renard et la cigogne.
        prod. [Toronto] : CFM, 1976.- dist. BAM 42 fr. col. :$35 mm. & cassette (7 min.) : auto. & aud. adv. sig. & teacher's guide. $15.50 (Conversational French for beginners : les fables de la Fontaine : $149.00) ji

        1. French language - Study and teaching.

        La Fontaine's fable of the scheming fox and the stork who outwits him is illustrated with attractive cartoons. The story is used as a framework only and situations are invented to bring in modern vocabulary. Basic structures are designed for beginners in French; but the narrative contains some low-frequency vocabulary and more complex structures.-

The Classified Catalogue

440.7

Le renard et le bouc.
prod. [Toronto] : CFM, 1976.- dist. BAM 41 fr. : col. : 35 mm. & cassette (11 min.) : auto. & aud. adv. sig. & teacher's guide. $15.50 (Conversational French for beginners : les fables de la Fontaine : $149.00) ji

1. French language - Study and teaching.

La Fontaine's fable of the fox and the billy goat is used as a framework only and situations are invented to introduce modern vocabulary. Basic structures are designed for beginners in French with only the present tense used.-

440.7

Ti-Jean et les bûcherons.
prod. [Montreal?] : NFB, 1960.- dist. SEC 30 fr. : col. : 35 mm. & captions & disc (33 1/3 rpm, 8 min.) : auto. & aud. adv. sig. & teacher's manual. $18.00 p

1. Folklore - Canadian (French).

Ti-Jean a small boy from Quebec, who is very strong, helps the lumberjacks and shows off his amazing strength by chopping trees, eating, and log-cutting. Cartoon characters and captions are used. English title available : TI-JEAN AND THE LUMBERJACKS.-

507

5 sens + mésures = observation.
prod. [Montreal?] : NFB, 1969.- dist. SEC 33 fr. : col. : 35 mm. & captions & teacher's manual. $9.00 (Science à l'élémentaire) pj

1. Science - Experiments. 2. Weights and measures - Experiments.

A step-by-step guide to an experiment on weight measurement, comparison and classification. Encourages student participation. Emphasizes use of senses, accurate scientific observation, use of tools, and careful recording of measurement. Illustrated with photographs. English title available : 5 SENSES + MEASUREMENT = OBSERVATION.-

507

5 senses + measurement = observation.
prod. [Montreal?] : NFB, 1969.- dist. McI. 33 fr. : col. : 35 mm. & captions & teacher's manual. $9.00 (Elementary science) pj

1. Science - Experiments. 2. Weights and measures - Experiments.

A step-by-step guide to an experiment on weight measurement, comparison and classification. Encourages student participation. Emphasizes use of senses, accurate scientific observation, use of tools, and careful recording of measurement. Illustrated with photographs. French title available : 5 SENS + MESURE = OBSERVATION.-

507.4

The Science Centre.
prod. [Toronto] : RQM, 1975.- dist. Lea. 48 fr. : col. : 35 mm. & captions & teacher's guide. $9.00 (An Introduction to : Ontario Science Centre) ji

1. Science - Exhibitions. 2. Ontario Science Centre.

Highlights of a visit to the Ontario Science Centre. Background information about the building of the centre, its location and physical layout are given. Photographs show children exploring the engineering and science arcades, and the space section.-

516

Observing by seeing : shapes and sizes.
prod. [Hamilton] : VCI, 1977.- dist. MHR 6 parts (62 fr.) : col. : 35 mm. & captions & teacher's guide. $12.85 (Thinking skills : observing) p

1. Size and shape.

Introduces the basic shapes, circle, square, triangle, and rectangle, discussing the occurence of the shapes in everyday life. The concepts of size : big-small, long-short, wide-narrow, and comparative and superlative terms such as smaller and smallest are also introduced. Produced in six parts for viewing convenience.-

516
    Shapes designed by man.
        prod. [Scarborough, Ont.] : R.B.M., 1976.- dist. ETHOS 58 fr. : col. : 35 mm. & cassette (9 min.) : auto. & aud. adv. sig. & reading script. $19.00 (Enrichment mathematics : $39.00) ji

        1. Size and shape.

        Explores the many geometric shapes found originally in nature and adapted by man. Among the shapes studied are the circle, triangle, straight line, quadrilateral, cylinder, cone and sphere.-

516
    Shapes in nature.
        prod. [Scarborough, Ont.] : R.B.M., 1976.- dist. ETHOS 67 fr. : col. : 35 mm. & cassette (8 min.) : auto. & aud. adv. sig. & reading script. $19.00 (Enrichment mathematics : $39.00) ji

        1. Size and shape.

        Explores the occurence of many geometric shapes in the natural world. Included in the discussion are circles, triangles, cylinders, cones, spheres, and the straight line.-

523.1
    Our discovery of the universe.
        prod. [Toronto] : Int. Cin., 1977.- dist. VEC 70 fr. : col. : 35 mm. & cassette (11 min.) : auto. & aud. adv. sig. & teacher's guide and 17 student activity cards. $24.00 (Exploring our solar system : $86.00) jis

        1. Astronomy - History. 2. Universe.

        An historical look at man's changing concepts of the earth and the universe. Discusses how theories of early European astronomers and their inventions, like the telescope, have led to the more sophisticated concepts of the universe.-

523.1
    Our place in the universe.
        prod. [Toronto] : Int. Cin., 1977.- dist. VEC 69 fr. : col. : 35 mm. & cassette (11 min.) : auto. & aud. adv. sig. & teacher's guide and 17 student activity cards. $24.00 (Exploring our solar system : $86.00) jis

        1. Universe. 2. Solar system.

        An introduction to the solar system discussing the earth in relation to the universe, and explaining how the universe began. Explains present day methods of charting distant galaxies.-

523.3
    La Lune : ses phases.
        prod. [Toronto] : M-L, 1975.- dist. Sch. Ser. or Vint. 31 fr. : col. : 35 mm. & cassette (6 min.) : auto. & aud. adv. sig. & teacher's guide. $16.50 (La Terre et l'univers : $85.00) ji

        1. Moon.

        Models are used to show the different phases of the moon. Explains how the sun lights the moon creating the phases from New Moon to Full Moon. These phases are shown on a calendar. English title available : PHASES OF THE MOON.-

523.3
    The Moon's position in space.
        prod. [Toronto] : M-L, 1973.- dist. Sch. Ser. or Vint. 35 fr. : col. : 35 mm & cassette (6 min.) : auto. & aud. adv. sig. & teacher's guide. $16.50 (Learning about our universe $85.00) ij

        1. Moon.

        A comprehensive study of the moon. Actual pictures of the moon's surface are included. Uses models to show the rotation and revolution of the moon and earth around the sun. Compares the relative size of the moon, earth, and sun. French title available: LA POSITION DE LA LUNE.-

The Classified Catalogue

523.3
    Phases of the moon.
        prod. [Toronto] : M-L, 1973.- dist. Sch. Ser. or Vint. 31 fr. : col. : 35 mm. & cassette (6 min.) : auto. & aud. adv. sig. & teacher's guide. $16.50 (Learning about our universe : $85.00) ij

        1. Moon.

        Models are used to show the different phases of the moon. Explains how the sun lights the moon creating the phases from new moon to full moon. These phases are shown on a calendar. French title available : LA LUNE : SES PHASES.-

523.3
    La position de la lune.
        prod. [Toronto] : M-L, 1975.- dist. Sch. Ser. or Vint. 35 fr. : col. : 35 mm. & cassette (6 min.) : auto. & aud. adv. sig. & teacher's guide. $16.50 (La Terre et l'univers : $85.00) ji

        1. Moon.

        A comprehensive study of the moon. Actual pictures of the moon's surface are included. Uses model to show the rotations and revolutions of the moon and earth around the sun. Compares the relative size of the moon, earth, and sun. English title available : THE MOON'S POSITION IN SPACE.-

523.4
    Our journey into space.
        prod. [Toronto] : Int. Cin., 1977.- dist. VEC 65 fr. : col. : 35 mm. & cassette (12 min.) : auto. & aud. adv. sig. & teacher's guide and 17 student activity cards. $24.00 (Exploring our solar system : $86.00) jis

        1. Planets

        Photographs of Venus, Jupiter, Mars, Mercury, Saturn, and the moon, taken by the astronauts during the Apollo voyages and by the Viking space vehicle now in orbit. Illuminates the results of modern space exploration and informs us of the latest findings about the planets in our solar system.-

523.7
    Influence du soleil sur la terre.
        prod. [Toronto] : M-L, 1975.- dist. Sch. Ser. or Vint. 40 fr. : col. : 35 mm. & cassette (6 min.) : auto. & aud. adv. sig. & teacher's guide. $16.50 (La Terre et l'univers : $85.00) ji

        1. Sun. 2. Solar system.

        A comprehensive view of the sun's importance to earth. Places the sun in space. Explains the size, composition and some uses of the sun to the earth. Suggests two experiments to conductwith students. English title availalbe : WHAT THE SUN MEANS TO THE EARTH.-

523.7
    Light from the sun.
        prod. [Toronto] : M-L, 1973.- dist. Sch. Ser. or Vint. 32 fr. : col. : 35 mm. & cassette (6 min.) : auto. & aud. adv. sig. & teacher's guide. $16.50 (Learning about our universe : $85.00) ij

        1. Sun. 2. Solar system.

        Explains the sun's role in causing day and night. Shows how shadows occur and demonstrates the changes that occur as the sun's position alters. Suggests that the students experiment with shadows. French title available : LA LUMIERE DU SOLEIL.-

523.7
    La Lumière du soleil.
        prod. [Toronto] : M-L, 1975.- dist. Sch. Ser. or Vint. 32 fr. : col. : 35 mm. & cassette (6 min.) : auto. & aud. adv. sig. & teacher's guide. $16.50 (La Terre et l'univers : $85.00) ji

        1. Sun. 2. Solar system.

        Explains the sun's role in causing day and night. Shows how shadows occur and demonstrates the changes that occur as the sun's position alters. Suggests that the students experiment with shadows. English title available : LIGHT FROM THE SUN.-

523.7
What the sun means to the earth.
 prod. [Toronto] : M-L, 1973.- dist. Sch. Ser. or Vint. 40 fr. : col. : 35 mm. & cassette (6 min.) : auto. & aud. adv. sig. & teacher's guide. $16.50 (Learning about our universe : $85.00) ij

1. Sun 2. Solar system.

A comprehensive view of the sun's importance to earth. Places the sun in space. Explains the size, composition and some uses of the sun to the earth. Suggests two experiments to conduct with students. French title available : INFLUENCE DU SOLEIL SUR LA TERRE.-

523.8
Looking at the stars.
 prod. [Toronto] : M-L, 1973.- dist. Sch. Ser. or Vint. 39 fr. : col. : 35 mm. & cassette (6 min.) : auto. & aud. adv. sig. & teacher's guide. $16.50 (Learning about science : $75.00) p

1. Stars.

Uses photographs and diagrams to examine the stars in the night sky. Traces the history of the constellations and origins of their names. Outline shapes point out the more common constellations. French title available : REGARDANT LES ETOILES.-

523.8
Les Millions d'etoiles.
 prod. [Toronto] : M-L, 1975.- dist. Sch. Ser. or Vint. 34 fr. : col. : 35 mm. & cassette (6 min.) : auto. & aud. adv. sig. & teacher's guide. $16.50 (La Terre et l'univers : $85.00) ji

1. Stars. 2. Telescope. 3. Astronomy.

Demonstrates the vastness of space and the millions of stars that are present in it. Shows telescope and explains its use for astronomers. The Milky Way Galaxy is featured. English title available : MILLIONS OF STARS IN THE UNIVERSE.-

523.8
Regardent les étoiles.
 prod. [Toronto] : M-L, 1975.- dist. Sch. Ser. or Vint. 39 fr. : col. : 35 mm. & cassette (7 min.) : auto. & aud. adv. sig. & teacher's guide. $16.50 (Les Saisons, la terre, l'espace : $75.00) p

1. Stars.

Uses photographs and diagrams to examine the stars in the night sky. Traces the history of the constellations and origins of their names. Outline shapes point out the more common constellations. English title available : LOOKING AT THE STARS.-

525
L'Automme et l'hiver : ce qu'ils sont.
 prod. [Toronto] : M-L, 1975.- dist. Sch. Ser. or Vint. 42 fr. : col. : 35 mm. & cassette (6 min.) : auto. & aud. adv. sig. & teacher's guide. $16.50 (Les Saisons, la terre, l'espace : $75.00) p

1. Autumn. 2. Winter.

Illustrates the signs and activities of Autumn and Winter - harvesting wheat, football games, preparing the house for cold weather, snow covered fields, and children playing games in the snow. Also discusses bird feeding stations and hibernation. English title available : AUTUMN AND WINTER : WHAT THEY MEAN.-

525
Autumn.
 prod. [Toronto] : Int. Cin., 1974.- dist. VEC 48 fr. : col. : 35 mm. & cassette (7 min.) : auto. & aud. adv. sig. & teacher's guide. $24.00 (The Seasons : a journey through the year : $86.00) j

1. Autumn.

Photographs portray the colours and signs of Autumn in Eastern Canada. Discusses how animals prepare for winter, changes in plants, and how students can feed birds in winter.-

The Classified Catalogue

525
Autumn and winter : what they mean.
prod. [Toronto] : M-L, 1973.- dist. Sch. Ser. or Vint. 42 fr. : col. : 35 mm. & cassette (6 min.) : auto. & aud. adv. sig. & teacher's guide. $16.50 (Learning about science : $75.00) p

1. Autumn. 2. Winter.

Illustrates the signs and activities of autumn and winter - harvesting wheat, football games, preparing the house for cold weather, snow-covered fields, and children playing games in the snow. Also discusses bird feeding stations and hibernation. French title available : L'AUTOMNE ET L'HIVER : CE QU'ILS SONT.-

525
La Forme de la terre.
prod. [Toronto] : M-L, 1975.- dist. Sch. Ser. or Vint. 38 fr. : col. : 35 mm. & cassette (6 min.) : auto. & aud. adv. sig. & teacher's guide. $16.50 (Les Saisons, la terre, l'espace : $75.00) p

1. Earth.

Discusses the travels of early explorers, such as Columbus, and their belief that the world was flat. Examines the relationship between size and distance as shown by the size of the sun. Photos show several experiments to help prove these concepts. English title available : THE SHAPE OF THE EARTH.-

525
Laurentian winter.
prod. [Montreal?] : NFB, 1972.- dist. McI. 57 fr. : col. : 35 mm. & captions. $9.00 pjis

1. Language arts - Study and teaching. 2. Laurentides region, Que. 3. Winter.

Illustrates winter in the Laurentians in Quebec. Includes views of ice patterns, evergreens, winter streams, birds, animals, snowmobilers and tobogganers. A legend is quoted describing the sharing of Winter and Summer. Classroom use could include creative writing, artwork, and discussion of various aspects of winter.-

525
Notre planète : la terre.
prod. [Toronto] : M-L, 1975.- dist. Sch. Ser. or Vint. 37 fr. : col. : 35 mm. & cassette (7 min.) : auto. & aud. adv. sig. & teacher's guide. $16.50 (La Terre et l'univers : $85.00) ji

1. Earth.

Demonstrates why man cannot feel the roundness of the earth by comparing man's size. Pictures some geographic features of the earth. Explains the solar system. A comprehensive introduction to several aspects of the earth. English title available : THE PLANET WE LIVE ON.-

525
The Planet we live on.
prod. [Toronto] : M-L, 1973.- dist. Sch. Ser. or Vint. 37 fr. : col. : 35 mm. & cassette (7 min.) : auto. & aud. adv. sig. & teacher's guide. $16.50 (Learning about our universe : $85.00) ij

1. Earth.

Demonstrates why man cannot feel the roundness of the earth by comparing man's size to the earth's size. Pictures some geographic features of the earth. Explains the solar system. A comprehensize introduction to several aspects of the earth. French title available : NOTRE PLANETE : LA TERRE.-

525
Le Printemps et l'été : ce qu'ils sont.
prod. [Toronto] : M-L, 1975.- dist. Sch. Ser. or Vint. 49 fr. : col. : 35 mm. & cassette (6 min.) : auto. & aud. adv. sig. & teacher's guide. $16.50 (Les Saisons, la terre, l'espace : $75.00) p

1. Spring. 2. Summer.

The sights and activities of Spring and Summer - spring flowers, children playing outdoors, preparing house and garden for Summer, and animals shedding winter coats. Discusses summer activities in the city and on the farm, mentioning the dangers of forest fires. English title available : SPRING AND SUMMER : WHAT THEY MEAN.-

The Classified Catalogue

525

The Shape of the earth.
    prod. [Toronto] : M-L, 1973.- dist. Sch. Ser. or Vint. 38 fr. : col. : 35 mm. & cassette (6 min.) : auto. & aud. adv. sig. & teacher's guide. $16.50 (Learning about science : $75.00) p

1. Earth.

Discusses the travels of early explorers, such as Columbus, and their belief that the world was flat. Examines the relationship between size and distance as shown by the size of the sun. Photos show several experiments to help prove these concepts. French title available : LA FORME DE LA TERRE.-

525

Spring.
    prod. [Toronto] : Int. Cin., 1974.- dist. VEC 55 fr. : col. : 35 mm. & cassette (6 min.) : auto. & aud. adv. sig. & teacher's guide. $24.00 (The Seasons : a journey through the year : $86.00) j

1. Spring.

Uses an original song to describe spring in Eastern Canada. Includes activities of spring animals and birds, flow of maple sugar, earliest plants and wildflowers.-

525

Spring and summer : what they mean.
    prod. [Toronto] : M-L, 1973.- dist. Sch.Ser. or Vint. 43 fr. : col. : 35 mm. & cassette (6 min.) : auto. & aud. adv. sig. & teacher's guide. $16.50 (Learning about science : $75.00) p

1. Spring. 2. Summer.

The sights and activities of spring and summer - spring flowers, children playing for summer, and animals shedding winter coats. Discusses summer activities in the city and on the farm, mentioning the dangers of forest fires. French title available : LE PRINTEMPS ET L'ETE : CE QU'ILS SONT.-

525

Spring is coming.
    prod. [Montreal?] : NFB, 1975.- dist. McI. 45 fr. : col. : 35 mm. $9.00 (Fieldtrips on filmstrips series) p

1. Spring.

Illustrates spring activities, such as gathering maple sap to make maple syrup, bicycle riding, baseball, and shows the danger of spring flooding. Bilingual introduction. French title available : LE PRINTEMPS S'EN VIENT.-

525

Summer.
    prod. [Toronto] : Int. Cin., 1974.- dist. VEC 56 fr. : col. : 35 mm. & cassette (7 min.) : auto. & aud. adv. sig. & teacher's guide. $24.00 (The Seasons : a journey through the year : $86.00) j

1. Summer.

Song and manual explain the summer photographs. Discusses many wildflowers of summer, nesting of birds, weather cycles, insects and butterflies that emerge in late summer.-

525

Summer - reflections on Lake Blue Water.
    prod. [Toronto] : M-L, 1973.- dist. Sch. Ser. or Vint. 58 fr. : col. : 35 mm. & cassette (11 min.) : auto. & aud. adv. sig. & teaching guide. $16.50 (Season stories) pj

1. Summer. 2. Canoes and canoeing.

A young Ojibway boy living near Georgian Bay in Ontario tells of his summers spent canoeing with his father and learning from him the ancient art of making a birch bark canoe. Outlines the basic steps in canoe construction.-

525

Winter.
    prod. [Toronto] : Int. Cin., 1974.- dist. VEC 44 fr. : col. : 35 mm. & cassette (8 min.) : auto. & aud. adv. sig. & teacher's guide. $24.00 (The Seasons : a journey through the year : $86.00) j

1. Winter.

Song and manual describe development of ice, frost, and snow. Explains how snow protects plants, how to identify animal tracks, and habits of many winter birds and animals.-

The Classified Catalogue

525
    Winter - ice fire lights.
        prod. [Toronto] : M-L, 1973.- dist. Sch. Ser. or Vint. 54 fr. : col. : 35 mm. & cassette (12 min.) : auto. & aud. adv. sig. & teaching guide. $16.50 (Season stories) pj

        1. Winter.

    A young country boy explains what he enjoys about winter - sliding on the river, helping the local stationmaster, working with his father at their country zoo. Includes photos of some of the inhabitants of the zoo, such as llamas and pheasants.-

526
    The Earth grid.
        prod. [Scarborough, Ont.] : BH, 1970.- dist. BSC 20 fr. : col. : 35 mm. & captions & manual. $7.00 (Understanding the earth grid : $20.00) pji

        1. Geodesy.

    Diagrams are used to show how to calculate positions on the earth's surface using longitude and latitude, degrees, minutes and seconds.-

526
    Latitude.
        prod. [Scarborough, Ont.] : BH, 1970.- dist. BSC 16 fr. : col. : 35 mm. & captions & manual. $7.00 (Understanding the earth grid : $20.00) pji

        1. Latitude.

    Diagrams are used to demonstrate the purpose of latitude, its measurement, and to illustrate the concept "parallel of latitude".-

526
    Longitude.
        prod. [Scarborough, Ont.] : BH, 1970.- dist. BSC 18 fr. : col. : 35 mm. & captions & manual. $7.00 (Understanding the earth grid : $20.00) pji

        1. Longitude.

    Diagrams are used to illustrate the concept of longitude and its measurement, and to demonstrate the meaning of meridian anti-meridian.-

528.09713
    Spring wildflowers : southern Ontario and Quebec.
        prod. [Montreal?] : NFB, made 1963 : 1972.- dist. McI. 46 fr. : col. : 35 mm. & captions. $9.00 (Common Canadian wildflowers) pjis

        1. Wild flowers. 2. Botany - Ontario. 3. Botany - Quebec.

    Close-up photographs and captions identify wildflowers and where they may be found. Includes skunk cabbage, hepatica, spring beauty, trillium, etc. Includes index of Latin names. French title available : FLEURS SAUVAGES PRINTANIERES : SUD DE L'ONTARIO ET DU QUEBEC.-

535
    The Microscope - a delicate tool.
        prod. [Scarborough, Ont.] : R.B.M., 1975.- dist. ETHOS 39 fr. : col. : 35 mm. & cassette (8 min.) : auto. & aud. adv. sig. & teacher's manual. $19.00 (Science) ji

        1. Microscope and microscopy.

    Introduces this essential scientific tool, discussing parts, care, handling, and storage.-

535
    The Microscope - its operation.
        prod. [Scarborough, Ont.] : R.B.M., 1975.- dist. ETHOS 42 fr. : col. : 35 mm. & cassette (7 min.) : auto. & aud. adv. sig. & teacher's manual. $19.00 (Science) ji

        1. Microscope and microscopy.

    Discusses the correct operation of a microscope, outlining each step in the process.-

537.2
    Fundamentals of electricity.
        prod. [Toronto] : M-L, 1973.- dist. Sch. Ser. or Vint. 48 fr. : col : 35 mm. & cassette (9 min.) : auto. & aud. adv. sig. & teacher's guide. $16.50 (Principles of electricity : $75.00) ji

        1. Electricity.

    Uses familiar examples to demonstrate the various ways of producing static electricity. Diagrams and experiments show the law of electrical charges, electron transfer, electrical attraction and repulsion. Atoms are defined and their composition is explained. The parts and function of an electroscope are discussed.-

537.5
General electronics.
prod. [Toronto] : M-L, 1973.- dist. Sch. Ser. or Wint. 36 fr. : col. : 35 mm. & cassette (9 min.) : auto. & aud. adv. sig. & teacher's guide. $16.50 (Principles of electricity : $75.00) is

1. Electronics.

A moderately technical discussion of the fundamentals of electronics. Demonstrations are used in explaining the principle of the vacuum tube. The diode and triode are defined and their differences explained. The vacuum tube is compared to the transistor.-

538.01
Principles of magnetism.
prod. [Toronto] : M-L, 1973.- dist. Sch. Ser. or Wint. 49 fr. : col. : 35 mm. & cassette (9 min.) : auto. & aud. adv. sig. & teacher's guide. $16.50 (Principles of electricity : $75.00) ji

1. Magnetism. 2. Compass.

Introduces the basic laws of magnetism, explaining natural and artifical magnets. The construction and principle of a compass are carefully outlined. Experiments are used to demonstrate attraction and repulsion, magnetic fields, and the value of magnetic poles.-

538.028
The Compass.
prod. [Willowdale, Ont.] : UEVA (Can), 1975.- dist. BAM 45 fr. : col. : 35 mm. & cassette (19 min.) : auto. & aud. adv. sig. & teacher's guide. $15.50 (Adventures with map and compass : $65.95) j

1. Compass.

A discussion of the basics of compass use. Details include the major compass points in degrees, compass functions, setting a compass, declination, and finding bearings with and without a map. Breaks in narration for practice exercises would allow this to be used for several lessons.-

548
Croissance de cristaux.
prod. [Montreal?] : NFB, 1967.- dist. SEC 34 fr. : col. : 35 mm. & captions & printed notes. $9.00 (Science à l'élémentaire) ji

1. Crystallography - Experiments.

Illustrates the steps in an experiment to grow crystals, including photographs of all the materials needed. Encourages viewer to participate and record different ingredients used for growing crystals. Requires instructor preparation and research before proceeding with the experiment. English title available : HOW TO GROW CRYSTALS.-

548
How to grow crystals.
prod. [Montreal?] : NFB, 1967.- dist. McI. 35 fr. : col. : 35 mm. & captions & printed notes. $9.00 (Elementary science) ji

1. Crystallography - Experiments.

Illustrates the steps in an experiment to grow crystals, including photographs of all the materials needed. Encourages viewer to participate and record different ingredients used for growing crystals. Requires instructor preparation and research before proceeding with the experiment. French title available : CROISSANCE DE CRISTAUX.-

549
Learning about rocks and minerals.
prod. [Montreal?] : NFB, 1964.- dist. McI. 47 fr. : col. : 35 mm. & captions & teacher's manual. $9.00 ji

1. Rocks. 2. Mineralogy.

Drawings and photographs are used to show the presence of rocks and minerals around us. Three basic rock types, igneous, sedimentary, and metamorphic rocks are shown with examples and properties of each. Minerals are divided into metallic and non-metallic, identifiable by the shape of the crystal. Experiments, suggestions for collecting, and resource materials are contained in the manual. Part of a multi-media kit titled "Rocks and minerals". French title available : LES ROCHES ET LES MINERAUX.-

The Classified Catalogue

549

Les roches et les minéraux.
prod. [Montreal?] : NFB, 1964.- dist. SEC 47 fr. : col. : 35 mm. & captions & teacher's manual. $9.00 ji

1. Rocks.

Drawings and photographs are used to show the presence of rocks and minerals around us. Three basic rock types, igneous, sedimentary, and metamorphic rocks are shown with examples and properties of each. Minerals are divided into metallic and non-metallic, identifiable by the shape of the crystal. Experiments, suggestions for collecting, and resource materials are contained in the manual. Part of a multi-media kit titled "Les roches et les minéraux". English title available : LEARNING ABOUT ROCKS AND MINERALS.-

551

Our ever-changing earth.
prod. [Toronto] : Int. Cin., 1977.- dist. VEC 68 fr. : col. : 35 mm. & cassette (12 min.) : auto. & aud. adv. sig. & teacher's guide and 17 student activity cards. $24.00 (Exploring our solar system : $86.00) jis

1. Geology.

Uses photographs of the earth to discuss the effect of the ice age, volcanic eruptions, earthquakes, and meteorites upon the earth's surface. Also briefly discusses evolution of plant life and other living organisms and how pollution disrupts the balance of our environment.-

551.2

Geomorphologie volcanique.
prod. [Montreal?] : NFB, 1970.- dist. SEC 51 fr. : col. : 35 mm. & captions & printed notes. $9.00 ji

1. Volcanoes.

Uses photographs, including some close-ups shots, to illustrate the different types of volcanic activity and the various landforms that result. Technical vocabulary requires preliminary research before viewing. Detailed and comprehensive, including most of the famous volcanoes in the world. English title available : VOLCANIC LANDFORMS.-

551.2

Volcanic landforms.
prod. [Montreal?] : NFB, 1970.- dist. McI. 51 fr. : col. : 35 mm. & captions & printed notes. $9.00 ji

1. Volcanoes.

Uses photographs, including some close-up shots, to illustrate the different types of volcanic activity and the various landforms that result. Technical vocabulary requires preliminary research before viewing. Detailed and comprehensive, including most of the famous volcanoes in the world. French title available : GEOMORPHLOGIC VOLCANIQUE.-

551.3

Les formes de relief glaciaire.
prod. [Montreal?] : NFB, 1966.- dist. SEC 46 fr. : col. : 35 mm. & captions & teacher's guide. $9.00 ji

1. Glaciers. 2. Geology.

Field photography and maps illustrate the many different features that result from glacial erosion, transport and deposition. Manual provides vital accompaniment for teaching and classroom discussion. Comprehensive treatment compensates for the technical quality of the film. Part of a multi-media kit titled "Les glaciers". English title available : GLACIAL LANDFORMS.-

The Classified Catalogue

551.3
Glacial landforms.
prod. [Montreal?] : NFB, 1966.- dist. McI. 46 fr. : col. : 35 mm. & captions & teacher's guide. $9.00 ji

1. Glaciers. 2. Geology.

Field photography and maps illustrate the many different features that result from glacial erosion, transport and deposition. Manual provides vital accompaniment for teaching and classroom discussion.
Comprehensive treatment compensates for the technical quality of the film. Part of a multi-media kit titled "Glaciation." French title available : LES FORMES DE RELIEF GLACIAIRE.-

551.3
Glacier land deposits.
prod. [Toronto] : B & R, 1974.- dist. B & R 47 fr. : col. : 35 mm. & cassette (16 min.) : auto. & aud. adv. sig. & teacher's manual. $32.00 (Landforms from the Ice Age. : $32.00) is

1. Glaciers. 2. Geology.

Using both diagrams and photographs, shows how the continental ice sheet altered the topography, first through erosion, then by depositing glacial debris in such formations as drumlins and moraines.-

551.3
Glacier water deposits.
prod. [Toronto] : B & R, 1974.- dist. B & R 33 fr. : col. : 35 mm. & cassette (9 min.) : auto. & aud. adv. sig. & teacher's manual. $32.00 (Landforms from the Ice Age : $32.00) is

1. Glaciers. 2. Geology.

The structure of delta kames, eskers, and clay and sand plains, formations created by glacial deposits in bodies of water that later drained away, are described and illustrated with diagrams and photographs.-

551.3
Les glaciers.
prod. [Montreal?] : NFB, made 1965 : 1967.- dist. SEC 40 fr. : col. : 35 mm. & captions & manual. $9.00 jis

1. Glaciers.

Artwork, maps, diagrams supplement photographs to provide a comprehensive study of the kinds of glaciers, how they are formed and behave. Part of a multi-media kit titled "Les glaciers." English title available : GLACIERS.-

551.3
Glaciers.
prod. [Montreal?] : NFB, made 1965 : 1973.- dist. McI. 40 fr. : col. : 35 mm. & captions & manual. $9.00 jis

1. Glaciers.

Artwork, maps, diagrams supplement photographs to provide a comprehensive study of the kinds of glaciers, how they are formed and behave. Part of a multi-media kit titled "Glaciation". French title available : LES GLACIERS.-

551.6
Starting your own weather station.
prod. [Toronto] : M-L, 1974.- dist. Sch. Ser. or Vint. 50 fr. : col. : 35 mm. & cassette (7 min.) : auto. & aud. adv. sig. & teacher's guide. $16.50 (Inquiry into weather : $85.00) j

1. Weather forecasting.

Describes how to make a weather station. Explains the need to measure amount of cloud cover, wind speed, temperature, humidity, rainfall, air pressure, and the use of various homemade instruments.-

The Classified Catalogue

574.1
The Beginning of life : plants and fish.
prod. [Toronto] : M-L, 1973.- dist. Sch. Ser. or Vint. 36 fr. : col. : 35 mm. & cassette (6 min.) : auto. & aud. adv. sig. & teacher's guide. $16.50 (Family living and sex education series A : $75.00) pj

1. Reproduction. 2. Sex education.

Photographs used to show how life begins for a plant, a tree and a fish. As each matures it produces its own new egg, seed or sperm - demonstrating reproduction. The process of fertilization is explained in detail using fish as the example. French title available : LA VIE COMMENCE - PLANTES ET POISSONS.-

574.1
La Vie commence - plantes et poissons.
prod. [Toronto] : M-L, 1974.- dist. Sch. Ser. or Vint. 36 fr. : col. : 35 mm. & cassette (6 min.) : auto. & aud. adv. sig. & teacher's guide. $16.50 (Vie de famille et éducation sexuelle série A : $75.00) pj

1. Reproduction. 2. Sex education.

Photographs are used to show how life begins for a plant, a tree, and a fish. As each matures it produces its own new egg, seed or sperm - demonstrating reproduction. The process of fertilization is explained in detail using fish as the example. English title available : THE BEGINNING OF LIFE - PLANTS AND FISH.-

574.3
Comes from ... grows to.
prod. [Montreal?] : NFB, 1974.- dist. McI. 30 fr. : col. : 35 mm. & cassette (9 min.) : auto. & aud. adv. sig. & manual. $18.00 (Living and growing) pj

1. Growth.

Cartoon characters play a game where each identifies origins of animals and plants and what they grow to be. Does not discuss human reproduction but stresses that humans and all other living things start from seed and grow into something different.
Emphasizes change that comes with growth by encouraging children to imagine themselves in later years. French title available : VIENT DE ... DEVIENT.-

574.3
Vient de - devient .
prod. [Montreal?] : NFB, 1974.- dist. McI. 30 fr. : col. : 35 mm. & cassette (9 min.) : auto. & aud. adv. sig. & manual. $18.00 (La vie qui pousse) pj

1. Growth.

Cartoon characters play a game where each identifies origins of animals and plants and what they grow to be. Does not discuss human reproduction but stresses that humans and all other living things start from seed and grow into something different.
Emphasizes change that comes with growth by encouraging children to imagine themselves in later years. English title available : COMES FROM ... GROWS TO.-

574.5
City habitats.
prod. [Georgetown, Ont.] : FMS, 1976.- dist. McI. 50 fr. : col. : 35 mm. & cassette (13 min.) : auto. & aud. adv. sig. & teacher's guide. $10.00 (Nature in the city : $57.00) ji

1. Ecology. 2. Animals - Habitation.

Describes the large variety of natural habitats for living things in the cities, water habitats for ducks, turtles, muskrats, water plants; woodlots for owls, squirrels, deer, and open grassy areas for kildeer and groundhogs.-

574.5
Les communantés végétales et animales.
prod. [Toronto] : M-L, 1975.- dist. Sch. Ser. or Vint. 53 fr. : col. : 35 mm. & cassette (7 min.) : auto. & aud. adv. sig. & teacher's guide. $16.50 (A la découverte de l'écologie : $85.00) j

1. Ecology.

An exploration of a forest community showing the interdependence of plant and animal populations and the physical elements of their environment. Traces the delicate natural balances which compose an ecosystem. English title available : PLANT AND ANIMAL COMMUNITIES.-

The Classified Catalogue

574.5
Les cycles de nourriture.
  prod. [Toronto] : M-L, 1975.- dist. Sch. Ser. or Vint. 52 fr. : col. : 35 mm. & cassette (7 min.) : auto. & aud. adv. sig. & teacher's guide. $16.50 (A la découverte de l'écologie : $85.00) j

  1. Food chains (Ecology).

  Studies the basic feeding relationships between plant and animals. Illustrates sample experiments that can be set up in a clasroom to show the food chain in an aquarium and a terrarium, and includes photos of microscope slides. English title available : FOOD CHAINS.-

574.5
Les ecosystèmes.
  prod. [Toronto] : M-L, 1975.- dist. Sch. Ser. or Vint. 51 fr. : col. : 35 mm. & cassette (6 min.) : auto. & aud. adv. sig. & teacher's guide. $16.50 (A la découverte de l'écologie : $85.00) j

  1. Ecology. 2. Man - Influence on nature.

  Explores the environmental, physical and organic elements that compose an ecosystem. Encourages viewers to discuss the prevention of the harm done by man to natural habitats and ecosystems. Broad scope allows this to be used as an introduction to man's effect on natural balance of nature. English title available : ECOSYSTEMS.-

574.5
Explorons la forêt.
  prod. [Montreal?] : NFB, 1965.- dist. SEC 33 fr. : col. : 35 mm. & captions & teacher's guide. $9.00 p

  1. Forest ecology.

  Drawings portray the woods and its inhabitants during summer, fall, winter and spring. Students are asked to identify many of the creatures, whose names are supplied in the guide. English title available : A VISIT TO THE WOODS.-

574.5
Food chains.
  prod. [Toronto] : M-L, 1975.- dist. Sch. Ser. or Vint. 52 fr. : col. : 35 mm. & cassette (8 min.) : auto. & aud. adv. sig. & teacher's guide. $16.50 (Ecology : exploration and discovery : $85.00) j

  1. Food chains (Ecology).

  Studies the basic feeding relationships between plants and animals. Illustrates sample experiments that can be set up in a classroom to show the food chain in an aquarium and terrarium, and includes photos of microscope slides. French title available : LES CYCLES DE NOURRITURE.-

574.5
The Natural ecology of water.
  prod. [Scarborough, Ont.] : R.B.M., 1975.- dist. ETHOS 41 fr. : col. : 35 mm. & cassette (8 min.) : auto. & aud. adv. sig. & reading script. $18.50 (Science) ji

  1. Water.

  Shows multiple uses of water by plants, animals and man. Describe's water's components and how destroyed by pollution. Stresses need to make best use of water in industry and recreation taking into consideration our dependence upon it.-

574.5
Nature adapts to the city.
  prod. [Georgetown, Ont.] : FMS, 1976.- dist. McI. 49 fr. : col. : 35 mm. & cassette (10 min.) : auto. & aud. adv. sig. & teacher's guide. $19.00 (Nature in the city : $57.00) ji

  1. Adaptation (Biology).

  Describes how nature can exist in the city, if it has the ability to adapt to new conditions. Shows the adaptation of Canada geese and ducks to city parks, variety of hawks and owls who eat the rodents in meadows near airports, pigeons that roost on any building, and how some plants have survived adverse conditions.-

The Classified Catalogue

574.5
Nature in the neighbourhood.
prod. [Georgetown, Ont.] : FMS, 1976.- dist. McI. 57 fr. : col. ; 35 mm. & cassette (13 min.) : auto. & aud. adv. sig. & teacher's guide. $19.00 (Nature in the city : $57.00) ji

1. Ecology. 2. Animals - Habitations.

Shows how city neighbourhoods with shade trees, lawns, ponds, ravines, and empty lots, provide habitats for birds, frogs, mushrooms, insects, animals, wild and cultivated plants. Explains how many birds and animals have learned to take advantage of man's presence.-

574.5
Les Organismes et le milieu.
prod. [Toronto] : M-L, 1975.- dist. Sch. Ser. or Vint. 57 fr. : col. ; 35 mm. & cassette (8 min.) : auto. & aud. adv. sig. & teacher's guide. $16.50 (A la découverte de l'écologie : $85.00) j

1. Ecology. 2. Adaptation (Biology).

A detailed examination of the ways living organisms interact with and are adapted to their environment. Explains the terms organism, environment, matter and illustrates conditions for optimum growth of plants and animals. Photos show actual classroom experience. English title available : ORGANISMS AND ENVIRONMENT.-

574.5
A Visit to the woods.
prod. [Montreal?] : NFB, 1975.- dist. McI. 28 fr. : col. ; 35 mm. & captions & teacher's guide. $9.00 (Discovering life around us : $45.00) p

1. Forest ecology.

Drawings portray the woods and its inhabitants during summer, fall, winter and spring. Students are asked to identify many of the creatures, whose names are supplied in the guide. French title available : EXPLORONS LA FORET.-

574.509712
Ecology of the Arctic.
prod. [Georgetown, Ont.] : FMS, 1971.- dist. McI. 52 fr. : col. ; 35 mm. & cassette (12 min.) : auto. & aud. adv. sig. & teacher's guide. $10.00 (The Living Arctic : $57.00) ji

1. Ecology. 2. Arctic regions.

A detailed study of the Arctic regions illustrating the relationship of the climate to plant and animal life, with photos supported by commentary and appropriate bird and animal sounds. Presents Arctic topography, climate, and plant and animal characteristics.-

574.509712
Life on the Barren Lands.
prod. [Georgetown, Ont.] : FMS, 1976.- dist. McI 43 fr. : col. ; 35 mm. & cassette (13 min.) : auto. & aud. adv. sig. & teacher's manual. $19.00 (Wildlife of North America : the mammals : $95.00) ji

1. Ecology. 2. Mammals. 3. Arctic regions.

Examines the basic ecology of the Arctic tundra, describing the mammals that live there, such as polar bears, Arctic hares, and squirrels, lemming, caribou. Photographs and commentary explain survival techniques of wildlife and the importance of an available food supply.-

574.509712
Patterns of life.
prod. [Toronto] : Int. Cin., 1971.- dist. VEC 45 fr. : col. ; 35 mm. & 4 pamphlets, 2 maps, 1 teacher's guide, 1 transparency & captions. $12.00 (The Living Arctic : $54.00) ji

1. Ecology. 2. Man - Influence on nature. 3. Arctic regions.

Shows how the white man and modern machinery are upsetting the balance of nature in the Arctic. Describes controls designed to reduce ecological damage.-

The Classified Catalogue

574.509759
Ecology of the Everglades.
prod. [Georgetown, Ont.] : FMS, 1971.- dist. McI. 47 fr. : col. : 35 mm. & cassette (14 min.) : auto. & aud. adv. sig. $19.00 (The Everglades : $38.00) ji

1. Ecology.   2. Marshes.   3. Everglades, Fla.

Examines the ecological roles of animals, birds and plant life found in Florida Everglades. Identifies wildlife and shows feeding habits. Authentic sounds accompany narration.-

574.92
Explorons le bord de la mer.
prod. [Montreal?] : NFB, made 1965 : 1977.- dist. SEC 35 fr. : col. : 35 mm. & captions & teacher's manual. $9.00 p

1. Seashore.   2. Marine ecology.

Uses drawings to portray life at the edge of the sea. Includes birds, shelled animals, plants, mammals, and microscopic plant and animal life, emphasizing their interdependence. Identifications are supplied in the guide. English title available : A VISIT TO THE SEASHORE.-

574.92
Explorons l'etang.
prod. [Montreal?] : NFB, 1965.- dist. SEC 33 fr. : col. : 35 mm. & captions & teacher's manual. $9.00 p

1. Ponds.   2. Fresh water biology.

Artwork is used to depict creatures of the pond, and how man uses the pond. The names of the plants, animals, birds, and insects are contained in the guide for identification. Designed for classroom use. English title available : A VISIT TO A POND.-

574.92
Plants, sponges, coelenterates.
prod. [Dartmouth, N.S.] : AEU, [1977] dist. Sch. Ser. 43 fr. : col. : 35 mm. & cassette (14 min.) : auto. & aud. adv. sig. & teacher's guide. $25.00 (Ocean bottom dwellers : $60.00) is

1. Marine plants.   2. Invertebrates.

Examines rockweeds, sea wracks, laminaria, the sea anemone, sponges, hydroids, and tunicates. Describes their structure, adaptations, feeding habits and relationship with other organisms. Illustrated with photos of these organisms in their natural habitat.-

574.92
Plants, sponges, coelenterates.
prod. [Dartmouth, N.S.] : AEU, 1977.- dist. Sch. Ser. 43 fr. : col. : 35 mm. & cassette (14 min.) : auto. & aud. adv. sig. & teacher's guide. $25.00 (Ocean bottom dwellers : $60.00) is

1. Marine plants.   2. Invertebrates.

Examines rockweeds, sea wracks, laminaria, the sea anemone, sponges, hydroids, and tunicates. Describes their structure, adaptations, feeding habits and relationships with other organisms. Illustrated with photos of these organisms in their natural habitat.-

574.92
A Visit to a pond.
prod. [Montreal?] : NFB, 1965.- dist. McI. 28 fr. : col. : 35 mm. & captions & teacher's manual. $9.00 (Discovering life around us : $45.00) p

1. Ponds.   2. Fresh water biology.

Artwork is used to depict creatures of the pond, and how man uses the pond. The names of the plants, animals, birds, and insects are contained in the guide for identification. Designed for classroom use. French title available : EXPLORONS L'ETANG.-

574.92
A Visit to the seashore.
prod. [Montreal?] : NFB, 1965.- dist. McI. 30 fr. : col. : 35 mm. & captions & teacher's manual. $9.00 (Discovering life around us : $45.00) p

1. Seashore.   2. Marine ecology.

Uses drawings to portray life at the edge of the sea. Includes birds, shelled animals, plants, mammals, and microscopic plant and animal life, emphasizing their interdependence. Identifications are supplied in the guide. French title available : EXPLORONS LE BORD DE LA MER.-

The Classified Catalogue

578
    Making your own microscopic slides.
        prod. [Scarborough, Ont.] : R.B.M., 1975.- dist. ETHOS 40 fr. : col. : 35 mm. & cassette (7 min.) : auto. & aud. adv. sig. & teacher's manual. $19.00 (Science) ji

        1. Microscope and microscopy.

        Students are given instruction in the preparation of their own microscopic slides using, among other things, materials from their own bodies.-

578
    The World of microscopy.
        prod. [Scarborough, Ont.] : R.B.M., 1975.- dist. ETHOS 38 fr. : col. : 35 mm. & cassette (8 min.) : auto. & aud. adv. sig. & teacher's manual. $19.00 (Science) ji

        1. Microscope and microscopy.

        Shows how familiar objects take on new dimensions when examined under a microscope. Uses examples of plant and animal cells to illustrate their similarities and differences. Introduces the terms algae, nucleus, cytoplasm.-

581.3
    Nutrition et croissance de l'arbre.
        prod. [Montreal?] : NFB, made 1965 : 1967.- dist. SEC 47 fr. : col. : 35 mm. & captions. $9.00 pji

        1. Trees. 2. Growth (Plants).
        3. Photosynthesis.

        An inquiry approach leads the viewer to study the ways in which plants grow and best conditions for growth. Uses photographs and diagrams of cross-sections of leaf, stem and root cells to explain photosynthesis. English title available : WHY DO TREES GROW?-

581.3
    Why do trees grow?
        prod. [Montreal?] : NFB, made 1965 : 1966. dist. McI. 47 fr. : col. : 35 mm. & captions. $9.00 pji

        1. Trees. 2. Growth (Plants).
        3. Photosynthesis.

        An inquiry approach leads the viewer to study the ways in which plants grow and the best conditions for growth. Uses photographs and diagrams of cross-sections of leaf, stem, and root cells to explain photosynthesis. French title available : NUTRITION ET CROISSANCE DE L'ARBRE.-

581.5
    Coast and montane forest : a comparison.
        prod. [Montreal?] : NFB, 1970.- dist. McI. 47 fr. : col. : 35 mm. & captions. $9.00 is

        1. Forests and forestry - Canada.
        2. Forest ecology.

        Uses photographs and diagrams to compare the geography and climate of a coastal forest near Alberni, British Columbia, with a montane forest near Kamloops, British Columbia. Investigates the ecosystem of each forest and lists data in detail. Part of a multi-media kit titled "Canada's forests". French title available : LA FORET DES MONTAGNES ET LA FORET COTIERE : UNE COMPARAISON.-

581.5
    Deciduous and boreal forests : a comparison.
        prod. [Montreal?] : NFB, 1969.- dist. McI. 44 fr. : col. : 35 mm. & captions. $9.00 is

        1. Forests and forestry - Canada.
        2. Forest ecology.

        Maps, tables, and photographs are used to compare the characteristics of Canadian deciduous and boreal forest and to examine ecological variations of the regions that contribute to their differences. Part of a multi-media kit titled "Canada's forests". French title available : LA FORET FEUILLUE ET LA FORET BOREALE : UNE COMPARAISON.-

581.5
    Discovering plants in winter.
        prod. [Scarborough, Ont.] : R.B.M., 1975.- dist. ETHOS 35 fr. : col. : 35 mm. & cassette (8 min.) : auto. & aud. adv. sig. & teacher's manual. $19.00 (Science) ji

        1. Plants. 2. Winter.

        Signs of life can be found, even in the dead of winter. Evergreens, bracken, fungus, lichens, ferns, and mullein are among the plants mentioned.-

The Classified Catalogue

581.5
La forêt feuille et la forêt boréale : une comparaison.
prod. [Montreal?] : NFB, 1969.- dist. SEC 44 fr. : col. : 35 mm. & captions. $9.00 is

1. Forests and forestry - Canada.
2. Forest ecology.

Maps, tables, and photographs are used to compare the characteristics of Canadian deciduous and boral forests and to examine ecological variations of the regions that contribute to their differences. Part of a multi-media kit titled "Les forêts du Canada. English title available : DECIDUOUS AND BOREAL FORESTS : A COMPARISON.-

581.6
Eating out I.
prod. [Toronto] : RQM, 1974.- dist. Lea. 37 fr. : col. : 35 mm. & captions & teacher's guide. $9.00 (Living in the outdoors) jis

1. Plants, Edible. 2. Outdoor life.

An introduction to wild, edible plants according to use, - salads, seasonings, hot and cold beverages. Stresses which part of the plant to eat and any necessary preparation.-

581.6
Eating out II.
prod. [Toronto] : RQM, 1974.- dist. Lea. 36 fr. : col. : 35 mm. & captions & teacher's guide. $9.00 (Living in the outdoors) jis

1. Plants, Edible. 2. Outdoor life.

Photos illustrate edible fruit, leaves, bark and berries of the various woodland plants and trees.-

581.6
La forêt des montagnes et la forêt côtière : une comparaison .
prod. [Montreal?] : NFB, 1970.- dist. SEC 47 fr. : col. : 35 mm. & captions. $9.00 is

1. Forest ecology. 2. Forests and forestry - Canada.

Uses photographs and diagrams to compare the geography and climate of a coastal forest near Alberni, British Columbia, with a montane forest near Kamloops, British Columbia. Investigates the ecosystem of each forest and lists data in detail. Part of a multi-media kit titled "Les forêts du Canada. English title available : COAST AND MONTANE FORESTS : A COMPARISON.-

581.97
What on earth! : a look at plants.
prod. [Georgetown, Ont.] : FMS, 1971.- dist. McI. 45 fr. : col. : 35 mm. & captions & teacher's guide. $10.00 (Wildflowers of North America : $50.00) ji

1. Botany - North America.

Photographs of a variety of plants, berries, seeds, lichen and mushrooms are presented without captions in order to stimulate the child's senses and imagination. The teacher's guide offers provocative questions for discussion with younger student groups, cautioning that the frame identification guide is included only for curious older students and adults.-

581.971
Canadian wildlife - flora.
prod. [Scarborough, Ont.] : R.B.M., 1976.- dist. ETHOS 44 fr. : col. : 35 mm. & reading script. $19.00 (Facts on Canada) pj

1. Botany - Canada.

A look at some of the most common wildflowers and plants found in Canada. Included are some members of the daisy and lily families, thistles, conifers, and some fruit-bearing plants.-

581.971
Plant communities, woodlot and wetlands.
prod. [Scarborough, Ont.] : R.B.M., 1975.- dist. ETHOS 48 fr. : col. : 35 mm. & cassette (10 min.) : auto. & aud. adv. sig. & teacher's manual. $19.00 (Outdoor education) ji

1. Botany - Canada.

Many familiar plants most often found in Canadian wooded and wetland areas are identified and described. These included the dogtooth violet, wild ginger, columbine, Joe-Pye weed, marsh marigold, water lily, and pitcher plant.-

The Classified Catalogue

581.9712
    Plants of the Arctic.
        prod. [Toronto] : Int. Cin., 1974.- dist. Sch. Ch. 53 fr. : col. : 35 mm. & cassette (9 min.) : auto. & aud. adv. sig. & teacher's manual. $16.95 (Arctic portrait : $49.00) ji

        1. Botany - Arctic regions. 2. Adaptation (Biology).

        A description of the flowers, lichen, mosses, and trees that cover the Arctic ground during the short summer growing season. Covers what each plant is, where it grows, and how it adapts to the cold weather conditions. Also includes a discussion of the plants interdependence with Arctic animals, and how the Eskimo uses certain plants for various purposes.-

582
    Deciduous trees.
        prod. [Weston, Ont.] : B & R, 1973.- dist. Lea. 55 fr. : col. : 35 mm. & teacher's manual. $9.00 (Nature study : $51.00) is

        1. Trees.

        For each deciduous tree there is a photograph of its overall shape plus close-ups of the leaf structure, berries, flowers, and bark. The companion guide lists the trees with botanical names, explains the difference between deciduous and evergreen, and the importance of the individual leaf in identifying the tree.-

582
    La dissémination des graines.
        prod. [Montreal?] : NFB, made 1965 : 1967.- dist. SEC 47 fr. : col. : 35 mm. & captions. $9.00 pj

        1. Seeds.

        Uses an inquiry approach to study the various ways that seeds travel to find proper growing conditions. Discusses seed spread by plant mechanisms, animals, water and wind. Specific seeds are illustrated. English title available : HOW SEEDS ARE SPREAD.-

582
    Garden flowers of spring.
        prod. [Weston, Ont.] : & R, 1973.- dist. Lea. 65 fr. : col. : 35 mm. & teacher's guide. $9.00 (Nature study : $51.00) is

        1. Flowers.

        Vivid photographs of spring garden flowers. The accompanying guide lists the flowers alphabetically with botanical names. Data on the care of such flowers, the soil preference, season and length of bloom, height, colour, and foliage description is given.-

582
    Garden flowers of summer and autumn.
        prod. [Weston, Ont.] : B & R, 1973.- dist. Lea. 62 fr. : col. : 35 mm. & teacher's guide. $9.00 (Nature study : $51.00) is

        1. Flowers.

        Acquaints the viewer with some common varieties of cultivated flowers found in gardens during summer and fall. The guide's arrangement of the flowers is alphabetical, and includes descriptions of appearance, best planting location, soil type, propagation and any unique characteristics.-

582
    How seeds are spread.
        prod. [Montreal?] : NFB, 1965.- dist. McI. 40 fr. : col. : 35 mm. & captions. $9.00 pj

        1. Seeds.

        Uses an inquiry approach to study the various ways that seeds travel to find proper growing conditions. Discusses seeds spread by plant mechanisms, animals, water and wind. Specific seeds are illustrated. French title available : LA DISSEMINATION DES GRAINES.-

582
    Plant communities, wasteland wildflowers.
        prod. [Scarborough, Ont.] : R.B.M., 1975.- dist. ETHOS 44 fr. : col. : 35 mm. & cassette (10 min.) : auto. & aud. adv. sig. & teacher's manual. $19.00 (Outdoor education) ji

        1. Wild flowers.

        Identifies many of the most common wildflowers found in waste areas, their habitats, and their usefulness to man and animals. Included are the daisy, buttercup, dandelion, goldenrod, milkweed, Queen Anne's lace, thistle, yarrow, etc.-

The Classified Catalogue

582
    Wild flowers of spring.
        prod. [Weston, Ont.] : B & R, 1973.- dist. Lea. 44 fr. : col. : 35 mm. & teacher's guide. $9.00 (Nature study : $51.00) is

    1. Wild flowers.

    Photographs of spring wildflowers in their natural habitat. The utilization guide suggests an introduction to the class. Defines terms such as orders, families, species, genera, and outlines factors in identifying wildflowers. Includes family habitat and general description for each flower, with some of its uses.-

582
    Wild flowers of summer & autumn.
        prod. [Weston, Ont.] : B & R, 1973.- dist. Lea. 48 fr. : col. : 35 mm. & teacher's guide. $9.00 (Nature study : $51.00) is

    1. Wild flowers.

    Although the format of this filmstrip is similar to Wild flowers of spring, the introduction in the utilization guide is more ecologically orientated, stressing the concept of wildflowers as living creatures for conservation.-

582.097
    Autumn wildflowers of eastern North America.
        prod. [Georgetown, Ont.] : FMS, 1971.- dist. McI.- 52 fr. : col. : 35 mm. & captions and teacher's guide. $10.00 (Wildflowers of North America : $50.00) ji

    1. Wild flowers. 2. Botany - North America.

    Flowers of late summer and autumn are photographed in the meadows, bogs, swamps and woodlands of eastern United Statesand Canada. The 36 species are briefly described in the Teacher's Identification List, in addition to a list of names in the final frame.-

582.097
    Spring wildflowers of eastern North America.
        prod. [Georgetown, Ont.] : FMS, 1971.- dist. McI. 50 fr. : col. : 35 mm. & captions and teacher's guide. $10.00 (Wildflowers of North America : $50.00) ji

    1. Wild flowers. 2. Botany - North America.

    A photographic guide to 43 common wildflowers that bloom from March to June in eastern North America. An accompanying list provides names and brief descriptions.-

582.097
    Summer wildflowers of eastern North America.
        prod. [Georgetown, Ont.] : FMS, 1971.- dist. McI. 51 fr. : col. : 35 mm. & captions and teacher's guide. $10.00 (Wildflowers of North America : $50.00) ji

    1. Wildflowers. 2. Botany - North America.

    A photographic guide to summer wildflowers presented in order of blossoming time. The close-ups illustrate the plant characteristics and habitat, described in the separate identification list. A frame identification list appears at the end of the filmstrip.-

582.0971
    Fleurs sauvages diverses : l'est du Canada.
        prod. [Montreal?] : NFB, 1963.- dist. SEC 53 fr. : col. : 35 mm. & captions. $9.00 (Les fleurs sauvages communes du Canada) pjis

    1. Wild flowers.

    Captioned photos illustrate and give brief descriptions of Eastern Canada wildflowers. Includes lady's slipper, pitcher plant, water lily, buttercups, Indian pipe, yarrow, fireweed, Queen Anne's lace and many others. An index of Latin names is included. English title available : SELECTED WILDFLOWERS : EASTERN CANADA.-

582.0971
    Fleurs sauvages printanières : sud des provinces des Prairies.
        prod. [Montreal?] : NFB, 1963.- dist. SEC 45 fr. : col. : 35 mm. & captions. $9.00 (Les fleurs sauvages communes du Canada) pjis

    1. Wild flowers. 2. Botany - Prairie Provinces.

    Close-up photographs describe many common wildflowers of the southern regions of the Prairie provinces. Examines habitat and flowering period, as well as unusual information about some wildflowers. Latin names are provided in index. English title available : SPRING WILDFLOWERS : SOUTHERN PRAIRIE PROVINCES.-

The Classified Catalogue

582.0971
>Selected wildflowers : eastern Canada.
>prod. [Montreal?] : NFB, 1963.- dist. McI. 53 fr. : col. ; 35 mm. & captions. $9.00 (Common Canadian wildflowers) pjis
>
>1. Wild flowers. 2. Botany - Eastern Canada.
>
>Captioned photos illustrate and give brief descriptions of Eastern Canada wildflowers. Includes lady's slipper, pitcher plant, water lily, buttercups, Indian pipe, yarrow, fireweed, Queen Anne's lace and many others. An index of Latin names is included. French title available : FLEURS SAUVAGES DIVERSES : EST CANADA.-

582.09711
>Fleurs sauvages printanières : Colombie-Britannique.
>prod. [Montreal?] : NFB, 1963.- dist. SEC 48 fr. : col. ; 35 mm. & captions. $9.00 (Les fleurs sauvages communes du Canada) pjis
>
>1. Wild flowers. 2. Botany - British Columbia.
>
>A photographic study of wildflowers common to British Columbia. Information is provided on colour, habitat and flowering period of these wildflowers, as well as other unusual or interesting facts. Latin names are listed in index. English title available : SPRING WILDFLOWERS : BRITISH COLUMBIA.-

582.09711
>Spring wildflowers : British Columbia.
>prod. [Montreal?] : NFB, 1963.- dist. McI. 48 fr. : col. ; 35 mm. & captions. $9.00 (Common Canadian wildflowers) pjis
>
>1. Wild flowers. 2. Botany - British Columbia.
>
>A photographic study of wildflowers common to British Columbia. Information is provided on colour, habitat and flowering period of these wildflowers, as well as other unusual or interesting facts. Latin names are listed in index. French title available : FLEURS SAUVAGES PRINTANIERES : COLOMBIE - BRITANNIQUE.-

582.09712
>Arctic wildflowers.
>prod. [Montreal?] : NFB, 1963.- dist. McI. 30 fr. : col. ; 35 mm. & captions. $9.00 (Common Canadian wildflowers) pjis
>
>1. Wild flowers. 2. Botany - Arctic regions.
>
>Captioned photographs illustrate and give brief descriptions of Arctic wildflowers and their locations. Includes yellow saxifrage, sweet coltsfoot, cottongrass, labrador tea, snow buttercup, cloudberry, chickweed, mountain cranberry, etc. Index of Latin names at end. French title available : FLEURS SAUVAGES DE L'ARCTIQUE.-

582.09712
>Fleurs sauvages de l'Arctique.
>prod. [Montreal?] : NFB, 1963.- dist. SEC 39 fr. : col. ; 35 mm. & captions. $9.00 (Les fleurs sauvages communes du Canada) pjis
>
>1. Wild flowers. 2. Botany - Arctic regions.
>
>Captioned photographs illustrate and give brief descriptions of Arctic wildflowers and their locations. Includes yellow saxifrage, sweet coltsfoot, cottongrass, labrador tea, snow buttercup, cloudberry, chickweed, mountain cranberry, etc. Index of Latin names at end. English title available : ARCTIC WILDFLOWERS.-

582.09712
>Fleurs sauvages diverses : l'ouest du Canada.
>prod. [Montreal?] : NFB, 1963.- dist. SEC 43 fr. : col. ; 35 mm. & captions. $9.00 (Les fleurs sauvages communes du Canada) pjis
>
>1. Wild flowers. 2. Botany - Prairie Provinces.
>
>Photographs depict variety of wildflowers found in Western Canada, with captions describing the environment of each flower. An index of Latin names is provided at the end of filmstrip. English title available : SELECTED WILDFLOWERS : WESTERN CANADA.-

The Classified Catalogue

582.09712
    Fleurs sauvages printanières : nord des provinces des Prairies.
        prod. [Montreal?] : NFB, 1963.- dist. SEC 50 fr. : col. : 35 mm. & captions. $9.00 (Les fleurs sauvages communes du Canada) pjis

    1. Wild flowers. 2. Botany - Prairie Provinces.

    Close-up photographs illustrate spring wildflowers of the Northern Prairie provinces and their most common habitat. The few measurements are not metric. Provides unusual information about several flowers, includes provincial flowers of the Prairie provinces, and stresses conservation. Provides a list of Latin names at the end. English title available : SPRING WILDFLOWERS : NORTHERN PRAIRIE PROVINCES.-

582.09712
    Selected wildflowers : Western Canada.
        prod. [Montreal?] : NFB, 1963.- dist. McI. 43 fr. : col. : 35 mm. & captions. $9.00 (Common Canadian wildflowers) pjis

    1. Wild flowers. 2. Botany - Prairie Provinces.

    Photographs depict variety of wildflowers found in Western Canada, with captions describing the environment of each flower. An index of Latin names is provided at the end of filmstrip. French title available : FLEURS SAUVAGES DIVERSES : L'OUEST DU CANADA

582.09712
    Spring wildflowers : southern Prairie provinces.
        prod. [Montreal?] : NFB, made 1963 : 1965.- dist. McI. 45 fr. : col. : 35 mm. & captions. $9.00 (Common Canadian wildflowers) pjis

    1. Wild flowers. 2. Botany - Prairie Provinces.

    Close-up photographs describe many common wildflowers of the southern regions of the Prairie provinces. Examines habitat and flowering period, as well as unusual information about some wildflowers. Latin names are provided in index. French title available : FLEURS SAUVAGES PRINTANIERES : SUD DES PROVINCES DES PRAIRIES.-

582.09712
    Spring wildflowers : northern Prairie provinces.
        prod. [Montreal?] : NFB, made 1963 : 1972.- dist. McI. 50 fr. : col. : 35 mm. & captions. $9.00 (Common Canadian wildflowers) pjis

    1. Wild flowers. 2. Botany - Prairie Provinces.

    Close-up photographs illustrate spring wildflowers of the Northern Prairie provinces and their most common habitat. The few measurements are not metric. Provides unusual information about several flowers, includes provincial flowers of the Prairie provinces, and stresses conservation. Provides a list of Latin names at the end. French title available : FLEURS SAUVAGES PRINTANIERES : NORD DES PROVINCES DES PRAIRIES.-

582.09713
    Fleurs sauvages printanières : sud de l'Ontario et du Québec.
        prod. [Montreal?] : NFB, 1963.- dist. SEC 46 fr. : col. : 35 mm. & captions. $9.00 (Les fleurs sauvages communes du Canada) pjis

    1. Wild flowers. 2. Botany - Ontario. 3. Botany - Quebec.

    Close-up photographs and captions identify wildflowers and where they may be found. Includes skunk cabbage, hepatica, spring beauty, trillium, etc. Includes index of Latin names. English title available : SPRING WILDFLOVERS : SOUTHERN ONTARIO AND QUEBEC.-

582.09713
    Fleurs sauvages printanières : nord de l'Ontario et du Québec.
        prod. [Montreal?] : NFB, 1963.- dist. SEC 47 fr. : col. : 35 mm. & captions. $9.00 (Les fleurs sauvages communes du Canada) pjis

    1. Wild flowers. 2. Botany - Ontario. 3. Botany - Quebec.

    Captioned photographs illustrate spring wildflowers and their location. Includes bloodroot, trailing arbutus, blue violet, Canada violet, dandelion, marsh marigold, Canada anemone, white daisy, etc. Index of Latin names at end. English title available : SPRING WILDFLOVERS : NORTHERN ONTARIO AND QUEBEC.-

582.09713
Spring wildflowers : Northern Ontario and Quebec.
prod. [Montreal?] : NFB, 1963.- dist. McI. 47 fr. : col. : 35 mm. & captions. $9.00 (Common Canadian wildflowers) pjis

1. Wild flowrs.   2. Botany - Ontario.
3. Botany - Quebec.

Captioned photographs illustrate spring wildflowers and their location. Includes bloodroot, trailing arbutus, blue violet, Canada violet, dandelion, marsh marigold, Canada anemone, white daisy, etc. Index of Latin names at end. French title available : FLEURS SAUVAGES PRINTANIERES : NORD DE L'ONTARIO ET DU QUEBEC.-

582.09715
Fleurs sauvages printaniéres : les Maritimes.
prod. [Montreal?] : NFB, 1963.- dist. SEC 48 fr. : col. : 35 mm. & captions. $9.00 (Les fleurs sauvages communes du Canada) pjis

1. Wild flowers.   2. Botany - Maritime Provinces.

Uses close-up photographs and captions to identify forty spring wildflowers of the Maritime Provinces. Provides basic information on the environment in which each one grows. Includes a list of the Latin names for all the flowers illustrated. Useful as an introduction to further study of wildflowers. English title available : SPRING WILDFLOWERS : THE MARITIMES.-

582.09715
Spring wildflowers : the Maritimes.
prod. [Montreal?] : NFB, 1963.- dist. McI. 48 fr. : col. : 35 mm. & captions. $9.00 (Common Canadian wildflowers) pjis

1. Wild flowers.   2. Botany - Maritime Provinces.

Uses close-up photographs and captions to identify forty spring wildflowers of the Maritime Provinces. Provides basic information on the environment in which each one grows. Includes a list of the Latin names for all the flowers illustrated. Useful as an introduction to further study of wildflowers. French title available : FLEURS SAUVAGES PRINTANIERES : LES MARITIMES.-

582.09718
Fleurs sauvages printanières : Terre-Neuve.
prod. [Montreal?] : NFB, 1963.- dist. SEC 46 fr. : col. : 35 mm. & captions. $9.00 (Les fleurs sauvages communes du canada) pjis

1. Wild flowers.   2. Botany - Newfoundland.

Captioned photos illustrate Newfoundland wildflowers and where they may be found. Includes rhodora, cloudberry, wild iris, bluebells, etc. Latin names in index. English title available : SPRING WILDFLOWERS : NEWFOUNDLAND.-

582.09718
Spring wildflowers : Newfoundland.
prod. [Montreal?] : NFB, 1963.- dist. McI. 46 fr. : col. : 35 mm. & captions. $9.00 (Common Canadian wildflowers) pjis

1. Wild flowers.   2. Botany - Newfoundland.

Captioned photos illustrate Newfoundland wildflowers and where they may be found. Includes rhodora, cloudberry, wild iris, bluebells, etc. Latin names in index. French title available : FLEURS SAUVAGES PRINTANIERES : TERRE-NEUVE.-

584
Orchids of Eastern North America.
prod. [Georgetown, Ont.] : FMS, 1971.- dist. McI. 52 fr. : col. : 35 mm. & captions & teacher's guide. $10.00 (Wildflowers of North America :$50.00) ji

1. Orchids.   2. Wild flowers.   3. Botany - North America.

Photographs of 33 types of orchids found in woods and bogs of eastern United States and Canada. A separate identification list gives names and brief descriptions of each orchid in addition to a list of names at the end of the filmstrip.-

The Classified Catalogue

585
    Evergreen trees.
        prod. [Veston, Ont.] : B & R, 1973.- dist. Lea. 44 fr. : col. : 35 mm. & teacher's guide. $9.00 (Nature study : $51.00) is

        1. Evergreens.

        A systematic presentation of fifteen different kinds of evergreen trees. Photographs of the entire tree are followed by excellent close-ups of the leaf and cone structure. The utilization guide provides detailed information of the location, use, height, and leaf composition of evergreens. Basic differences between the trees are outlined.-

590.74
    At the zoo.
        prod. [Montreal?] : NFB, 1975.- dist. McI. 49 fr. : col. : 35 mm. $9.00 (Fieldtrips on filmstrips series) p

        1. Zoological gardens.

        Photographs without captions illustrate a children's field trip to the zoo. A preliminary note on the filmstrip in English and French suggests its potential use as a stimulus to oral and written language, as well as an introduction or follow-up to an actual class trip. French title available : AU ZOO.-

590.74
    Au zoo.
        prod. [Montreal] : NFB, 1975.- dist. SEC 49 fr. : col. : 35 mm. $9.00 p

        1. Zoological gardens.

        Photographs without captions illustrate a children's field trip to the zoo. A preliminary note on the filmstrip in English and French suggests its potential use as a stimulus to oral and written language, as well as an introduction or follow-up to an actual class trip. English title available : AT THE ZOO.-

591
    Animal tracks.
        prod. [Montreal?] : NFB, 1953.- dist. McI. 39 fr. : b&w : 35 mm. & captions & teacher's manual. $9.00 pj

        1. Tracking and trailing.

        Uses black and white drawings to classify common Canadian domestic and wild animals as flat-foots, toe-walkers, and toe-nail walkers. Shows detailed illustrations of the tracks they make and how to identify them. French title available : IMPREINTES D'ANIMAUX.-

591.1
    Birth.
        prod. [Toronto] : M-L, 1973.- dist. Sch. Ser. or Vint. 25 fr. : col. : 35 mm. & cassette (5 min.) : auto. & aud. adv. sig. & teacher's guide. $16.50 (Family living and sex education series A : $75.00) pj

        1. Reproduction. 2. Sex education.

        Explains growth of kittens inside a mother cat's body, and their birth. Photos and graphics are used to explain parts of the mother's body, and for comparison between anatomy of female cats and humans. French title available : LA NAISSANCE.-

591.1
    Les Cellules reproductives.
        prod. [Toronto] : M-L, 1974.- dist. Sch. Ser. or Vint. 26 fr. : col. : 35 mm & cassette (5 min.) : auto. & aud. adv. sig. & teacher's guide. $16.50 (Vie de famille et éducation sexuelle série B : $75.00) pj

        1. Reproduction. 2. Sex education.

        Photographs and graphics are used to explain origins and functions of egg and sperm cells, and the reproductive process in cats. Picture of animal and human parents with their offspring reinforce the concept that each species reproduces only its own kind. English title available : THE REPRODUCTIVE CELLS.-

591.1
    From two to one.
        prod. [Toronto] : M-L, 1973.- dist. Sch. Ser. or Vint. 35 fr. : col. : 35 mm. & cassette (7 min.) : auto. & aud. adv. sig. & teacher's guide. $16.50 (Family living and sex education series A : $75.00) pj

        1. Reproduction. 2. Sex education.

        Photographs and graphics demonstrate fertilization and reproduction in mammals. The production of egg and sperm cells is explained using cats as emamples. Introduces proper terminology for male and female reproductive organs. French title available : UN DE DEUX.-

The Classified Catalogue

591.1
 Le Mâle - la femelle
  prod. [Toronto] : M-L, 1974.- dist. Sch. Ser. or Vint. 37 fr. : col. : 35 mm. & cassette (5 min.) : auto. & aud. adv. sig. & teacher's guide. $16.50 (Vie de famille et éducation sexuelle série A : $75.00) pj

  1. Reproduction. 2. Sex education.

  Photographs and graphics demonstrate fertilization, reproduction and development using gulls and chickens as examples. The development of a chick from a fertilized egg is seen as it grows inside the shell. English title available : MALE AND FEMALE.-

591.1
 Male and female.
  prod. [Toronto] : M-L, 1973.- dist. Sch. Ser. or Vint. 35 fr. : col. : 35 mm. & cassette (5 min.) : auto. & aud. adv. sig. & teacher's guide. $16.50 (Family living and sex education series A : $75.00) pj

  1. Reproduction. 2. Sex education.

  Photographs and graphics demonstrate fertilization, reproduction and development using gulls and chickens as examples. The development of a chick from a fertilized egg is seen as it grows inside the shell. French title available : LA MALE - FEMELLE.-

591.1
 La Naissance.
  prod. [Toronto] : M-L, 1974.- dist. Sch. Ser. or Vint. 25 fr. : col. : 35 mm. & cassette (5 min.) : auto. & aud. adv. sig. & teacher's guide. $16.50 (Vie de famille et éducation sexuelle série A : $75.00) pj

  1. Reproduction. 2. Sex education.

  Explains growth of kittens inside a mother cat's body, and their birth. Photos and graphics are used to explain parts of the mother's body, and for comparison between anatomy of female cats and humans. English title available : BIRTH.-

591.1
 Ovulation - mammifères.
  prod. [Toronto] : M-L, 1974.- dist. Sch. Ser. or Vint. 30 fr. : col. : 35 mm. & cassette (6 min.) : auto. & aud. adv. sig. & teacher's guide. $16.50 (Vie de famille et éducation sexuelle série B : $75.00) pj

  1. Reproduction. 2. Sex education.

  Describes the differing female reproductive cycles of several mammalian species. Includes discussion of the fertilization of the egg and growth of an embryo in the uterus of a human mother. Illustrated with photos and graphics. English title available : OVULATION - MAMMALS.-

591.1
 The Process of reproduction.
  prod. [Toronto] : M-L, 1973.- dist. Sch. Ser. or Vint. 47 fr. : col. : 35 mm. & cassette (8 min.) : auto. & aud. adv. sig. & teacher's guide. $16.50 (Family living and sex education series C : $85.00) ji

  1. Reproduction. 2. Sex education.

  Photographs and diagrams are used to explain the processes of external and internal fertilization and development in serveral different animals including humans. Varying degrees of parental care of young among different species are compared to human parents and children. French title available : LE PROCESSUS DE REPRODUCTION.-

591.1
 Le Processus de reproduction.
  prod. [Toronto] : M-L, 1974.- dist. Sch. Ser. or Vint. 42 fr. : col. : 35 mm. & cassette (11 min.) : auto. & aud. adv. sig. & teacher's guide. $16.50 (Vie de famille et éducation sexuelle série C : $85.00) pj

  1. Reproduction. 2. Sex education.

  Photographs and diagrams used to explain process of external and internal fertilization and development in several different animals including humans. Varying degrees of parental care of young among different species are compared to human parents and children. English title available : THE PROCESS OF REPRODUCTION.-

The Classified Catalogue

591.1
Un de deux.
prod. [Toronto] : M-L, 1974.- dist. Sch. Ser. or Vint. 35 fr. : col. : 35 mm. & cassette (7 min.) : auto. & aud. adv. sig. & teacher's guide. $16.50 (Vie de famille et éducation sexuelle série A : $75.00) pj

1. Reproduction. 2. Sex education.

Photographs and graphics demonstrate fertilization and reproduction in mammals. The Production of egg and sperm cells is explained using cats as examples. Introduces correct terminology for male and female reproductive organs. English title available : FROM TWO TO ONE.-

591.5
Discovering animals in winter.
prod. [Scarborough, Ont.] : R.B.M., 1975.- dist. ETHOS 37 fr. : col. : 35 mm. & cassette (8 min.) : auto. & aud. adv. sig. & teacher's manual. $19.00 (Science) ji

1. Animals - Habits and behavior. 2. Vinter.

A winter walk provides insight into the habits of winter's animals and birds. Among those mentioned are rabbits, deer, chickadees, mice, owls, and hawks.-

591.5
L'Habitat.
prod. [Toronto] : M-L, 1975.- dist. Sch. Ser. or Vint. 44 fr. : col. : 35 mm. & cassette (6 min.) : auto. & aud. adv. sig. & teacher's guide. $16.50 (A la découverte de l'écologie : $85.00) j

1. Ecology. 2. Adaptation (Biology).

Explains the term "habitat" clearly and studies several animals, suggesting ways in which each animal is adapted to its environment. Broad scope makes it useful as an introduction to further studies of animals and their environment. English title available : HABITAT AND ADAPTATION.-

591.5
Habitat and adaptation.
prod. [Toronto] : M-L, 1975.- dist. Sch. Ser. or Vint. 44 fr. : col. : 35 mm. & cassette (6 min.) : auto. & aud. adv. sig. & teacher's guide. $16.50 (Ecology : exploration and discovery : $85.00) j

1. Ecology. 2. Adaption (Biology).

Explains the term "habitat" clearly and studies several animals, suggesting ways in which each animal is adapted to its environment. Broad scope makes it useful as an introduction to further studies of animals and their environment. French title available : L'HABITAT.-

591.5
Life on the Prairies.
prod. [Georgetown, Ont.] : FMS, 1976.- dist. McI 59 fr. : col. : 35 mm. & cassette (14 min.) : auto. & aud. adv. sig. & teacher's manual. $19.00 (Wildlife of North America : the mammals : $95.00) ji

1. Ecology. 2. Wildlife - Conservation. 3. Mammals.

Compares the prairie ecosystem before 1800 with the situation today, explaining why so many mammals such as bisons, prairie dogs and pronghorn antelopes nearly became extinct. Encourages an awareness of problems for wildlife when civilization advances and advocates the need for protection measures.-

591.5
Les populations.
prod. [Toronto] : M-L, 1975.- dist. Sch. Ser. or Vint. 62 fr. : col. : 35 mm. & cassette (8 min.) : auto. & aud. adv. sig. & teacher's guide. $16.50 (A la découverte de l'écologie : $85.00) j

1. Ecology.

Uses an actual classroom group to demonstrate and explain an animal population survey. Thoroughly discusses the factors affecting the size and survival of a population, emphasizing the interdependence of plants and animals in the same habitat. English title available : POPULATIONS.-

The Classified Catalogue

591.5
  Populations.
    prod. [Toronto] : M-L, 1975.- dist. Sch. Ser. or Vint. 62 fr. : col. : 35 mm. & cassette (9 min.) : auto. & aud. adv. sig. & teacher's guide. $16.50 (Ecology : exploration and discovery : $85.00) j

    1. Ecology.

    Uses an actual classroom group to demonstrate and explain an animal population survey. Thoroughly discusses the factors affecting the size and survival of a population, emphasizing the interdependence of plants and animals in the same habitat. French title available : LES POPULATIONS.-

591.96
  African meat-eaters.
    prod. [Georgetown, Ont.] : FMS, 1970.- dist. McI. 34 fr. : col. : 35 mm. & captions. $10.00 (Africa : $30.00) j

    1. Animals - Africa.

    Shows what animals certain larger animals kill for food and other animals who eat what has already been killed. Also describes birds and insects as meat-eaters and their methods of killing prey.-

591.96
  Animals together.
    prod. [Georgetown, Ont.] : FMS, 1970.- dist. McI. 35 fr. : col. : 35 mm. & captions. $10.00 (Africa : $30.00) j

    1. Animals - Africa.

    An overview of the social behaviour of African animals. Shows loners (such as leopards and crocodiles), families of lions and elephants, family groups of baboons and large herds of antelopes, gazelles, flamingos and vultures.-

591.96
  Grassland 1 : animals of the African Grasslands.
    prod. [Don Mills, Ont.] : F & V, 1973.- dist. F & V 23 fr. : col. : 35 mm. & teacher's guide. $7.20 (Man in his world) ji

    1. Animals - Africa. 2. Adaptation (Biology).

    Photos of about fifteen animals living in a reserve in Tanzania. The accompanying guide points out the unique features of each animal and the physical characteristics that allow each creature to survive in its particular environment. Designed for instructional use since all information must be read from the guide.-

591.96
  Large animals of Africa.
    prod. [Georgetown, Ont.] : FMS, 1970.- dist. McI. 31 fr. : col. : 35 mm. & captions. $10.00 (Africa : $30.00) j

    1. Animals - Africa.

    Shows large mammals, birds and reptiles of Africa, pointing out physical characteristics, temperament, social behaviour and feeding habits of different specific animals.-

591.9712
  Animals of the Arctic.
    prod. [Toronto] : Int. Cin., 1974.- dist. Sch. Ch. 52 fr. : col. : 35 mm. & cassette (10 min.) : auto. & aud. adv. sig. & teacher's manual. $16.95 (Arctic portrait : $49.00) ji

    1. Animals - Arctic regions. 2. Adaptation (Biology).

    A look at the numerous sea, land and air creatures and the ways in which they have adapted to their northern environment. Close-ups show the animals and their young in their natural habitat. Covers eating habits, nesting, migration patterns, and how the animal's exterior coat changes to suit the environment. Actual sound of the animals placed at appropriate spots in the audio cassette.-

The Classified Catalogue

591.9712

The Arctic animals.
prod. [Georgetown, Ont.] : FMS 1971.- dist. McI. 48 fr. : col. : 35 mm. & cassette (13 min.) : auto. & aud. adv. sig. & teacher's guide. $19.00 (The Living Arctic : $57.00) ji

1. Animals - Arctic regions.

Photographs of land and water animals are accompanied by commentary enlivened with sounds recorded on location. Migratory habits of musk ox and caribou are described, as are adaptations of fox, bear, wolf, seal, hare and lemming to the seasons. Interdependence of plant and animal life is also shown.-

593

Echinoderms.
prod. [Darthmouth, N.S.] : AEU. [1977] dist. Sch. Ser. 43 fr. : col. : 35 mm. & cassette (10 min.) : auto. & aud. adv. sig. & teacher's guide. $25.00 (Ocean bottom dwellers : $60.00) is

1. Protozoa.

Uses underwater photographs to describe in detail the structure, locomotive techniques, and feeding habits of the sea urchin and the starfish. The camouflage technique, destructive power and predators of the sea urchin are also discussed.-

593

Echinoderms.
prod. [Dartmouth, N.S.] : AEU. 1977.- dist. Sch. Ser. 43 fr. : col. : 35 mm. & cassette (10 min.) : auto. & aud. adv. sig. & teacher's guide. $25.00 (Ocean bottom dwellers : $60.00) is

1. Protozoa.

Uses underwater photographs to describe in detail the structure, locomotive techniques, and feeding habits of the sea urchin and the starfish. The camouflage technique, destructive power and predators of the sea urchin are also discussed.-

594

Crustaceans, molluscs.
prod. [Dartmouth, N.S.] : AEU. 1977.- dist. Sch. Ser. 63 fr. : col. : 35 mm. & cassette (17 min.) : auto. & aud. adv. sig. & teacher's guide. $25.00 (Ocean bottom dwellers : $60.00) is

1. Crustacea. 2. Mollusks.

Discusses the structure, feeding habits, and means of locomotion of various crustaceans and molluscs, including limpets, mussels, oysters and scallops, periwinkles, moon snails, whelk, barnacles, and hermit crabs. Illustrated with photos of these organisms in their natural habitat.-

595

Les araignées.
prod. [Montreal?] : NFB. made 1965 : 1967.- dist. SEC 42 fr. : col. : 35 mm. & captions. $9.00 pji

1. Spiders.

Examines spiders and their habitat. Contrasts spiders with insects, providing details of specific spiders and how to identify them and their webs. Examines the structure and use of the spider's web. Details of the life cycle are illustrated. English title available : SPIDERS.-

595

La croissance du homard.
prod. [Montreal?] : NFB. made 1955 : 1972.- dist. SEC 35 fr. : col. : 35 mm. & captions & teacher's guide. $9.00 pji

1. Lobsters.

Clear drawings illustrate the cycle of growth, egg laying, egg hatching, stages of development in free-swimming lobsters, the moulting process and its appearance at maturity. English title available : HOW LOBSTERS GROW.-

The Classified Catalogue

595
How lobsters grow.
   prod. [Montreal?] : NFB, made 1955 : 1976.- dist. McI. 35 fr. : col. : 35 mm. & captions & teacher's guide. $9.00 pji

   1. Lobsters.

   Clear drawings illustrate the cycle of growth, egg laying, egg hatching, stages of development in free-swimming lobsters, the moulting process and its appearance at maturity. French title available : LA CROISSANCE DU HOMARD.-

595
Spider ecology.
   prod. [Scarborough, Ont.] : R.B.M., 1975.- dist. ETHOS 35 fr. : col. : 35 mm. & cassette (7 min.) : auto. & aud. adv. sig. & teacher's manual. $19.00 (Science) ji

   1. Spiders.

   Examines the role played by spiders within their surroundings: obtaining food and shelter, controlling insects, and providing a food source for larger animals.-

595
Spiders.
   prod. [Montreal?] : NFB, 1965.- dist. McI. 38 fr. : col. : 35 mm. & captions. $9.00 (Insects and spiders : $54.00) pji

   1. Spiders.

   Examines spiders and their habitat. Contrasts spiders with insects, providing details of specific spiders and how to identify them and their webs. Examines the structure and use of the spider's web. Details of the life cycle are illustrated. French title available : LES ARAIGNEES.-

595
What is a spider?
   prod. [Scarborough, Ont.] : R.B.M., 1975.- dist. ETHOS 36 fr. : col. : 35 mm. & cassette (8 min.) : auto. & aud. adv. sig. & teacher's manual. $19.00 (Science) ji

   1. Spiders.

   Details the anatomy of a spider, outlining the functions of each part.-

595.7
L'abeille.
   prod. [Montreal?] : NFB, 1963.- dist. SEC 39 fr. : col. : 35 mm. & captions. $9.00 pj

   1. Bees.

   Photographs illustrate the life cycle of the honeybee. Includes views of a beehive, worker, drone and queen bees, and workers gathering nectar and pollen. Review questions are included in the captions. English title available : THE HONEYBEE.-

595.7
The Cecropia moth.
   prod. [Montreal?] : NFB, 1971.- dist. McI. 44 fr. : col. : 35 mm. & captions. $9.00 (Insects and spiders : $54.00) jis

   1. Moths.

   Uses many close-up shots to describe the life cycle of the cecropia moth and its habitat. Illustrates the steps of the development of the egg, larva and pupa stages. Shows step-by-step photographs of emerging adult in spring. French title available : LE PAON DE NUIT.-

595.7
Les coléoptères.
   prod. [Montreal?] : NFB, 1963.- dist. SEC 46 fr. : col. : 35 mm. & captions. $9.00 p

   1. Beetles.

   Shows identifying characteristics of beetles, and gives the life cycle of four types of beetle: the potato beetle, ladybug, flour beetle and June bug. Shows also how they can be kept to be studied. Simple explanations with questions presented at intervals. Pictures accompany most of the difficult vocabulary.-

595.7
Le criquet (sauterrelle).
   prod. [Montreal?] : NFB, 1963.- dist. SEC 36 fr. : col. : 35 mm. & captions. $9.00 pj

   1. Grasshoppers. 2. Terrariums.

   Illustrates the unique features and characteristic habitat, and shows the stages in their life cycle. Demonstrates the construction and use of a simple terrarium. Drawings, diagrams, and photographs. English title available : THE GRASSHOPPER.-

The Classified Catalogue

595.7
Dragonflies and damselflies.
  prod. [Montreal?] : NFB, 1963.- dist. McI. 39 fr. : col. ; 35 mm. & captions. $9.00 (Insects and spiders : $54.00) pj

  1. Dragonflies. 2. Damselflies.

  Photographs and drawings are used to depict the life cycle of the dragonfly and of the damselfly. The differences between the two are shown. French title available : LIBELLULES ET DEMOISELLES.-

595.7
The Fantastic world of insects (A).
  prod. [Scarborough, Ont.] : R.B.M., 1975.- dist. ETHOS 37 fr. : col. ; 35 mm. & cassette (8 min.) : auto. & aud. adv. sig. & teacher's manual. $19.00 (Science) ji

  1. Insects.

  Introduces the vast and varied world of insects. Covers how to identify insects, their forms and habits, their advantages and disadvantages, and discusses bugs and beetles as two subgroups of this world.-

595.7
The Fantastic world of insects (B).
  prod. [Scarborough, Ont.] : R.B.M., 1975.- dist. ETHOS 35 fr. : col. ; 35 mm. & cassette (8 min.) : auto. & aud. adv. sig. & teacher's manual. $19.00 (Science) ji

  1. Insects.

  Discusses the characteristics of particular insects using close-up photography of the insect world. Includes moths and butterflies, ants, aphids and bees, and flies.-

595.7
The Grasshopper.
  prod. [Montreal?] : NFB, 1963.- dist. McI. 33 fr. : col. ; 35 mm. & captions. $9.00 (Insects and spiders : $54.00) pj

  1. Grasshoppers. 2. Terrariums.

  Illustrates the unique features and characteristic habitat, and shows stages in their life cycle. Demonstrates the construction and use of simple terrarium. Drawings, diagrams and photographs. French title available : LE CRIQUET (SAUTERRELLE).-

595.7
The Honeybee.
  prod. [Montreal?] : NFB, 1963.- dist. McI. 35 fr. : col. ; 35 mm. & captions. $9.00 (Insects and spiders : $54.00) pj

  1. Bees.

  Comprehensive photographic coverage of the life cycle of the honeybee. Includes views of a beehive, worker, drone and queen bees, and workers gathering nectar and pollen. Review questions are included in the captions. French title available : L'ABEILLE.-

595.7
Libellules et demoiselles.
  prod. [Montreal?] : NFB, 1963.- dist. SEC 42 fr. : col. ; 35 mm. & captions. $9.00 pj

  1. Dragonflies. 2. Damselflies.

  Photographs and drawings are used to depict the life cycle of the dragonfly and the damsefly. The differences between the two are shown. English title available : DRAGONFLIES AND DAMSELFLIES.-

595.7
Life in a beehive.
  prod. [Montreal?] : NFB, 1970.- dist. McI. 47 fr. : col. ; 35 mm. & captions. $9.00 jis

  1. Bees.

  Uses an inquiry approach to examine life inside the beehive. Describes the three different types of bees and the work each one performs. Illustrates the many activities of the worker bees. Traces the life cycle of the bee and the manner in which a new colony is established. French title available : LA VIE DANS LA RUCHE.-

595.7
The Monarch butterfly.
  prod. [Montreal?] : NFB, [1962?] dist. McI. 36 fr. : col. ; 35 mm. & captions. $9.00 (Insects and spiders : $54.00) pji

  1. Butterflies.

  An inquiry approach encourages the viewer to study the life cyle of the Monarch Butterfly and its habitat. Provides information for experiments to help observe the changes in the cycle. Photographs record the changes step-by-step. French title available : LE PAPILLON MONARQUE.-

The Classified Catalogue

595.7
    Le paon de nuit.
        prod. [Montreal?] : NFB, 1971.- dist. SEC 46 fr. : col. : 35 mm. & captions. $9.00 jis

        1. Moths.

        Uses many close-up shots to describe the life cycle of the cecropia moth and its habitat. Illustrates all the steps of the development of the egg, larva and pupa stages. Shows step-by-step photographs of emerging adult in spring. Measurements not metric. English title available : THE CECROPIA MOTH.-

595.7
    Le papillon monarque.
        prod. [Montreal?] : NFB, 1962.- dist. SEC 30 fr. : col. : 35 mm. & captions. $9.00 pji

        1. Butterflies.

        An inquiry approach encourages the viewer to study the life cycle of the Monarch Butterfly and its habitat. Provides information for experiment to help observe the changes step-by-step in the cycle. Photographs record the changes . English title available : THE MONARCH BUTTERFLY.-

595.7
    La vie dans la ruche.
        prod. [Montreal?] : NFB, 1970.- dist. SEC 47 fr. : col. : 35 mm. & captions. $9.00 jis

        1. Bees.

        Uses an inquiry approach to examine life inside the beehive. Describes the three different types of bees and the work each one performs. Illustrates the many activites of the worker bees. Traces the life cycle of the bee and the manner in which a new colony is established. English title available :LIFE IN A BEEHIVE.-

597
    The Frog.
        prod. [Montreal?] : NFB, made 1953 : 1975.- dist. McI. 27 fr. : col. : 35 mm. & captions & manual. $9.00 pji

        1. Frogs.

        Drawings illustrate the life cycle of the bull frog as an example for other species of frogs. Most frames have no captions: detailed information is in manual. Discusses enemies of frogs at both egg and tadpole stages, and points out the benefits of frogs to the balance of nature. French title available : LA GRENOUILLE.-

597
    La grenouille.
        prod. [Montreal?] : NFB, made 1953 : 1965.- dist. SEC 27 fr. : col. : 35 mm. & captions & manual. $9.00 pji

        1. Frogs.

        Drawings illustrate the life cycle of the bull frog as an example for other species of frogs. Most frames have no captions: detailed information is in manual. Discusses enemies of frogs at both egg and tadpole stages, and points out the benefits of frogs to the balance of nature. English title available : THE FROG.-

597
    Le saumon atlantique.
        prod. [Montreal?] : NFB, 1972.- dist. SEC 37 fr. : col. : 35 mm. & captions & manual. $9.00 pji

        1. Salmon.

        Drawings, diagrams, and photographs combine to describe the life cycle of the Atlantic salmon and the various stages of development. Discusses predators and man-made obstacles. Studies fish hatcheries and advantages of increasing salmon stock in this manner. Measurements not metric. English title available : THE STORY OF ATLANTIC SALMON.-

The Classified Catalogue

597
    Le saumon du Pacifique.
        prod. [Montreal?] : NFB, made 1959 : 1963.- dist. SEC 40 fr. : col. : 35 mm. & captions & teacher's guide. $9.00 pji

        1. Salmon.

        Drawings and diagrams describe the life cycle of the Pacific salmon and spawning habits of the sockeye salmon. Examines methods whereby salmon are assisted upstream to spawn. Studies enemies and hazards which endanger the salmon, feeding and travelling habits, and stresses the importance of maintaining this valuable resource.
        Measurements are not metric. English title available : THE STORY OF PACIFIC SALMON.-

597
    The Story of Atlantic salmon.
        prod. [Montreal?] : NFB, 1972.- dist. McI. 37 fr. : col. : 35 mm. & captions & manual. $9.00 pji

        1. Salmon.

        Drawings, diagrams, and photographs combine to describe the life cycle of the Atlantic salmon and the various stages of development. Discusses predators and man-made obstacles. Studies fish hatcheries and advantages of increasing salmon stock in this manner. Measurements are not metric. French title available : LE SAUMON ATLANTIQUE.-

597
    The Story of Pacific salmon.
        prod. [Montreal?] : NFB, made 1959 : 1963.- dist. McI. 40 fr. : col. : 35 mm. & captions & teacher's guide. $9.00 pji

        1. Salmon.

        Drawings and diagrams describe the life cycle of the Pacific salmon and spawning habits of the sockeye salmon. Examines methods whereby salmon are assisted upstream to spawn. Studies enemies and hazards which endanger the salmon, feeding and travelling habits, and stresses the importance of maintaining this valuable resource.
        Measurements are not metric. French title available : LE SAUMON DU PACIFIQUE.-

597
    Toads and frogs of Eastern Canada.
        prod. [Montreal?] : NFB, made 1957 : 1974.- dist. McI. 35 fr. : col. : 35 mm. & captions & teacher's manual. $9.00 pji

        1. Frogs.

        Drawings illustrate physical characteristics and various habitats of amphibians. Compares frogs with toads, and provides particular details of ten frogs and two toads. Measurements are not given in metric.-

597
    La Vie commence - grenouilles.
        prod. [Toronto] : M-L, 1974.- dist. Sch. Ser. or Vint. 29 fr. : col. : 35 mm. & cassette (5 min.) : auto. & aud. adv. sig. & teacher's guide. $16.50 (Vie de famille et éducation sexuelle série B : $75.00) pj

        1. Frogs.   2. Reproduction.

        A detailed discussion of the reproductive process and life cycle of frogs. The stages of development from embryo to tadpole to frog are included. English title available : THE BEGINNING OF LIFE : FROGS.-

598.2
    The Arctic birds.
        prod. [Georgetown, Ont.] : FMS 1971.- dist. McI. 48 fr. : col. : 35 mm. & cassette (13 min.) : auto. & aud. adv. sig. & teacher's guide. $19.00 (The Living Arctic : $57.00) ji

        1. Birds - Arctic regions.

        A detailed examination of the homes and habits of land and water birds of Canada's far north, with adaptations necessary for survival there. Photographs and authentic sounds of loons, cranes, whistling swans, ptarmigans, golden plovers, gulls, and terns nesting, feeding, etc.-

598.2
    La bernache canadienne.
        prod. [Montreal?] : NFB, 1953.- dist. SEC 29 fr. : col. : 35 mm. & printed notes & captions. $9.00 pj

        1. Canada goose.

        Detailed drawings illustrate the life, habits and habitat of the Canada goose. Notes game laws which ensure preservation of this bird; discusses migratory habits. English title available : THE CANADA GOOSE.-

598.2
Birds and their environment.
prod. [Toronto] : M-L, 1975.- dist. Sch. Ser. or Wint. 59 fr. : col. : 35 mm. & cassette (13 min.) : auto. & aud. adv. sig. & teacher's guide. $16.50 (Bird life of North America : $85.00) ji

1. Birds. 2. Evolution. 3. Adaptation (Biology).

Traces the evolution of birds from the reptilian stage to the many species of today. Stresses adaptation for survival, giving specific examples.-

598.2
Birds, in wetlands.
prod. [Scarborough, Ont.] : R.B.M., 1975.- dist. ETHOS 39 fr. : col. : 35 mm. & cassette (8 min.) : auto. & aud. adv. sig. & teacher's manual. $19.00 (Science) ji

1. Birds - Habits and behaviour.

Explores the nesting and feeding habits of several common species to be found in wetland areas. Included in the discussion are the mallard duck, marsh hawk, swamp sparrow, Canada goose, tern and kildeer.-

598.2
Birds of the city.
prod. [Montreal?] : NFB, made 1960 : 1973.- dist. McI. 42 fr. : col. : 35 mm. & captions & teacher's manual. $9.00 pj

1. Birds - Canada.

Drawings of common birds found in the city. Includes pigeons, house sparrows, gulls and ducks. Studies birds that are attracted to city gardens and those that stop on their migration south in autumn. Useful as an introduction to bird study. Measurements are not metric. French title available : LES OISEAUX DES VILLES.-

598.2
Birds of the Everglades.
prod. [Georgetown, Ont.] : FMS, 1971.- dist. McI. 51 fr. : col. : 35 mm. & cassette (11 min.) : auto. & aud. adv. sig. $19.00 (The Everglades : $38.00) ji

1. Birds - Florida - Habits and behavior.

Colourful photographs combine with authentic sounds in this introduction to birds living in the Florida Everglades. Identifies each bird, and points out its physical adaptation to the environment, nesting and feeding habits.-

598.2
Birds, their upland homes and habits.
prod. [Scarborough, Ont.] : R.B.M., 1975.- dist. ETHOS 38 fr. : col. : 35 mm. & cassette (9 min.) : auto. & aud. adv. sig. & teacher's manual. $19.00 (Science) ji

1. Birds - Habits and behaviour.

Shows how birds make use of their surroundings and natural materials to make safe shelters for their families. Robins, starlings, sparrows, hawks, owls and warblers are among the birds briefly mentioned.-

598.2
The Canada goose.
prod. [Montreal?] : NFB, made 1953 : 1970.- dist. McI. 26 fr. : col. : 35 mm. & captions & printed notes. $9.00 (Birds of Canada : $54.00) pj

1. Canada goose.

Detailed drawings illustrate the life, habits, and habitat of the Canada goose. Notes game laws which ensure preservation of this bird: discusses migratory habits. French title available : LA BERNACHE CANADIENNE.-

598.2
Comment les oiseaux élèvent leur petits.
prod. [Toronto] : Int. Cin., 1975.- dist. VEC 59 fr. : col. : 35 mm. & cassette (9 min.) : auto. & aud. adv. sig. & teacher's guide. $24.00 (Le Monde des oiseaux : $64.00) ji

1. Birds - Habits and behavior.

Shows courting rituals, nest-building, and egg-laying of several species of birds, and includes hatching, feeding and development of young chicks. English title available : HOW BIRDS RAISE THEIR YOUNG.-

598.2
Comment les oiseaux s'adaptent pour survivre.
prod. [Toronto] : Int. Cin., 1975.- dist. VEC 59 fr. : col. : 35 mm. & cassette (8 min.) : auto. & aud. adv. sig. & teacher's guide. $24.00 (La Monde des oiseaux : $64.00) ji

1. Birds. 2. Adaptation (Biology).

Reveals some of the dangers birds face in their natural habitat: ways in which birds have adapted to survive, and how man has aided in their survival. English title available : HOW BIRDS ADAPT TO SURVIVE.-

The Classified Catalogue

598.2
Common birds of Canada.
prod. [Montreal?] : NFB, made 1953 ; 1966.- dist. McI. 33 fr. : col. : 35 mm. & captions & teacher's manual. $9.00 pj

1. Birds - Canada.

Detailed drawings portray some of the more common birds of Canada, presented in the order of the evolutionary scale from primitive to advanced species. Measurements are not metric. Filmstrip only provides information on the name and size of birds; detailed notes are found in the manual. Best if used with groups. French title available : LES OISEAUX COMMUNS DU CANADA.-

598.2
The Common loon.
prod. [Montreal?] : NFB, 1956.- dist. McI. 32 fr. : col. : 35 mm. & captions & print notes. $9.00 (Birds of Canada : $54.00) pj

1. Loons.

Detailed drawings portray the physical characteristics and habitat of loons. Describes life cycle, main food supply, fishing methods, nesting habits, migratory routes and raising of the young. French title available : LE PLONGEON A COLLIER.-

598.2
Les faucons.
prod. [Montreal?] : NFB, 1960.- dist. SEC 35 fr. : col. : 35 mm. & printed notes & captions. $9.00 pj

1. Hawks.

Photographs illustrate the habits and characteristics of day time birds of prey. Studies the Marsh hawk and Sparrow hawk as typical examples of hawks; discussing hunting techniques, nesting habits and main food source. Measurements not metric. English title available : HAWKS.-

598.2
Fowl-like birds.
prod. [Toronto] : M-L, 1975.- dist. Sch. Ser. or Vint. 62 fr. : col. : 35 mm. & cassette (14 min.) : auto. & aud. adv. sig. & teacher's guide. $16.50 (Bird life of North America : $85.00) ji

1. 2. Birds - Habits and behavior. 3. Birds - North America.

Uses sound effects and photography to describe features of fowl-like birds in great detail. Discusses camouflage, courtship practices, and the hazards facing these birds.-

598.2
La grue blanche d'Amérique.
prod. [Montreal?] : NFB, made 1959 ; 1968.- dist. SEC 35 fr. : col. : 35 mm. & printed notes & captions. $9.00 pj

1. Whooping cranes.

Detailed drawings portray the physical characteristics, habitat, and behaviour of whooping cranes. Discusses why they have become an endangered species. English title available : THE WHOOPING CRANE.-

598.2
Hawks.
prod. [Montreal?] : NFB, 1960.- dist. McI. 30 fr. : col. : 35 mm. & captions & printed notes. $9.00 (Birds of Canada : $54.00) pj

1. Hawks.

Photographs illustrate the habits and characteristics of daytime birds of prey. Studies the Marsh hawk and Sparrow hawk as typical examples of hawks; discussing hunting techniques, nesting habits and main food source. Measurements not metric. French title available : LES FAUCONS.-

598.2
Les hiboux.
prod. [Montreal?] : NFB, made 1960 ; 1972.- dist. SEC 27 fr. : col. : 35 mm. & printed notes & captions. $9.00 pj

1. Owls.

Depicts the environment and habits of several species of owls including the barn owl, snowy owl, screech owl, and great horned owl. English title available : OWLS.-

598.2
How birds adapt to survive.
prod. [Toronto] : Int. Cin., 1975.- dist. VEC 59 fr. : col. : 35 mm. & cassette (8 min.) : auto. & aud. adv. sig. & teacher's manual. $24.00 (The World of birds : $64.00) ji

1. Birds. 2. Adaptation (Biology).

Reveals some of the dangers birds face in their natural habitat; ways in which birds have adapted to survive, and how man has aided in their survival. French title available :COMMENT LES OISEAUX S'ADAPTENT POUR SURVIVRE.-

598.2
How birds find food.
prod. [Toronto] : Int. Cin., 1975.- dist. VEC 57 fr. : col. :$35 mm. & cassette (8 min.) : auto. & aud. adv. sig. & teacher's manual. $24.00 (The World of birds : $64.00) ij

1. Birds - Habits and behavior.

How and where birds find nourishment in their natural habitat, and how each kind of bird is physically adapted to eat the different types of food in its environment. French title available : COMMENT LES OISEAUX SE PROCURENT LEUR NOURRITURE.-

598.2
How birds raise their young.
prod. [Toronto] : Int. Cin., 1975.- dist. VEC 59 fr. : col. : 35 mm. & cassette (9 min.) : auto. & aud. adv. sig. & teacher's manual. $24.00 (The World of birds : $64.00) ij

1. Birds - Habits and behavior.

Shows courting rituals, nest-building, and egg-laying of several species of birds, and includes hatching, feeding and development of young chicks. French title available : COMMENT LES OISEAUX ELEVENT LEUR PETITS.-

598.2
The Kingfisher.
prod. [Montreal?] : NFB, made 1957 : 1975.- dist. McI. 22 fr. : col. : 35 mm. & captions & printed notes. $9.00 (Birds of Canada : $54.00) pj

1. Kingfishers.

Detailed drawings describe the appearance, habitat, and nesting habits of kingfishers. Discusses their food, migration areas, and how they raise their young.-

598.2
Les oiseaux des villes.
prod. [Montreal?] : NFB, made 1960 : 1964.- dist. SEC 42 fr. : col. : 35 mm. & captions & teacher's manual. $9.00 pj

1. Birds - Canada.

Drawings of common birds found in the city. Includes pigeons, house sparrows, gulls and ducks. Studies birds that are attracted to city gardens and those that stop on their migration south in autumn. Useful as an introduction to bird study. Measurements are not metric. English title available : BIRDS OF THE CITY.-

598.2
Perching birds.
prod. [Toronto] : M-L, 1975.- dist. Sch. Ser. or Vint. 64 fr. : col. : 35 mm & cassette (15 min.) : auto. & aud. adv. sig. & teacher's guide. $16.50 (Bird life of North America : $85.00) ji

1. Birds - Habits and behavior. 2. Birds - North America.

Uses specific examples to explain the physical characteristics and habits of perching birds. Deals with natural and man-made hazards they face.-

598.2
Le plongeon à collier.
prod. [Montreal?] : NFB, made 1956 : 1970.- dist. SEC 36 fr. : col. : 35 mm. & printed notes & captions. $9.00 pj

1. Loons.

Detailed drawings portray the physical characteristics and habitat of loons. Describes life cycle, main food supply, fishing methods, nesting habits, migratory routes and raising of the young. English title available : THE COMMON LOON.-

598.2
The Predators.
prod. [Scarborough, Ont.] : R.B.M., 1975.- dist. ETHOS 47 fr. : col. & cassette (12 min.) : auto. & aud. adv. sig. & teacher's manual. $19.00 (Science) ji

1. Birds of prey.

A tour of southern Ontario bird sanctuary, visiting those birds commonly regarded as predators, which have been rescued and cared for by the sanctuary.-

598.2
    Predators.
        prod. [Toronto] : M-L, 1975.- dist. Sch. Ser. or Vint. 62 fr. : col. : 35 mm. & cassette (15 min.) : auto. & aud. adv. sig. & teacher's guide. $16.50 (Bird life of North America : $85.00) ji

        1. Birds of prey - Habits and behavior. 2. Birds - North America.

        Uses photographs and specific examples to examine predatory birds, their nesting habits, feeding methods and adaptations for survival. Stresses their importance in the balance of nature.-

598.2
    Shorebirds.
        prod. [Toronto] : M-L, 1975.- dist. Sch. Ser. or Vint. 62 fr. : col. : 35 mm. & cassette (13 min.) : auto. & aud. adv. sig. & teacher's guide. $16.50 (Bird life of North America : $85.00) ji

        1. Birds - Habits and ebhavior. 2. Birds - North America.

        A detailed presentation of the physical characteristics of shorebirds and their adaptation to various environments. Uses photography and sound effects to illustrate nesting, feeding, and migratory habits of shorebirds.-

598.2
    Waterfowl.
        prod. [Toronto] : M-L, 1975.- dist. Sch. Ser. or Vint. 50 fr. : col. : 35 mm. & cassette (11 min.) : auto. & aud. adv. sig. & teacher's guide. $16.50 (Bird life of North America : $85.00) ji

        1. Water birds - Habits and behavior.
        2. Birds - North America.

        A comprehensive presentation of the physical features and habits of specific waterfowl species. Stresses migration patterns, location of territories, food supply and incubation processes.-

598.2
    The Whooping crane : [a study of a vanishing species].
        prod. [Montreal?] : NFB, made 1959 : 1968.- dist. McI. 32 fr. : col. : 35 mm. & captions & printed notes. $9.00 (Birds of Canada : $54.00) pj

        1. Whooping cranes.

        Detailed drawings portray the physical characteristics, habitat, and behavior of whooping cranes. Discusses why they have become an endangered species. French title available : LA GRUE BLANCHE D'AMERIQUE : [ETUDE D'UNE ESPECE EN VOIE D'EXTINCTION].-

599
    Les Anes domestiques.
        prod. [Toronto] : M-L, 1975.- dist. Sch. Ser. or Vint. 40 fr. : col. : 35 mm. & cassette (7 min.) : auto. & aud. adv. sig. & teacher's guide. $16.50 (Les Animaux - tableaux réalists : $75.00) kpji

        1. Donkeys.

        A description of the physical characteristics and habits of donkeys. Provides detailed narration on one side of cassette, music and sound effects on the other. Would be useful in a language arts programme. English title available : DONKEYS, DONKEYS, DONKEYS.-

599
    The Beaver.
        prod. [Montreal?] : NFB, made 1953 : 1973.- dist. McI. 30 fr. : col. : 35 mm. & captions & reading script. $9.00 (Animals of Canada : $72.00) pj

        1. Beavers.

        Accurate drawings examine the physical features and habits of the beaver. Explains in detail the construction of the beaver lodge. Discusses ways in which beavers aid in conservation of animals, and also some damage caused by beavers.-

The Classified Catalogue

599

Les Bestiaux de l'ouest.
   prod. [Toronto] : M-L, 1975.- dist. Sch. Ser.
   or Vint. 65 fr. : col. : 35 mm. & cassette
   (9 min.) : auto. & aud. adv. sig. & teacher's
   guide. $16.50 (Les Animaux - tableaux
   réalistes : $75.00) kpji

   1. Cattle.

   Uses close-up photography to examine the
   beef cattle that roam the grasslands of the
   foothills of the Rocky Mountains. Describes
   the physical features of beef cattle, how
   they are herded by cowboys, and why they
   are branded. Narration on one track, natural
   sounds and music on the other. Would be
   useful in a language arts programme. English
   title available : CATTLE, CATTLE, CATTLE.-

599

Le bison d'Amérique.
   prod. [Montreal?] : NFB, made 1959 : 1966.-
   dist. SEC 36 fr. : col. : 35 mm. & captions &
   reading script. $9.00 pj

   1. Bison.   2. Wildlife - Conservation.

   Uses drawings to describe the physical
   features, habits and habitat of the North
   American buffalo. Examines the reasons for
   decreased numbers of these animals and how
   they are protected today. Follows the habits
   of buffalo throughout the seasons and
   discusses their natural enemies. Weights and
   sizes are not metric. English title available :
   THE NORTH AMERICAN BUFFALO.-

599

Les Bisons des plaines.
   prod. [Toronto] : M-L, 1975.- dist. Sch. Ser.
   or Vint. 50 fr. : col. : 35 mm. & cassette
   (7 min.) : auto. & aud. adv. sig. & teacher's
   guide. $16.50 (Les Animaux - tableaux
   réalistes : $75.00) kpji

   1. Bison.   2. Wildlife - Conservation.

   Describes the physical characteristics of the
   bison that roam the national parklands of
   North America under conservation protection,
   explaining how they became an endangered
   species. Examines their eating habits, social
   habits and relationship to smaller animals and
   birds. Explanatory sound track on one side
   of the cassette, music and sound effects on
   the other. Would be useful in a language
   arts programme. English title available :
   BUFFALO, BUFFALO, BUFFALO.-

599

The Black bear.
   prod. [Montreal?] : NFB, made 1956 : 1975.-
   dist. McI. 41 fr. : col. : 35 mm. & captions
   & reading script. $9.00 (Animals of Canada :
   $72.00) pj

   1. Bears.

   Studies the habits and habitat of the black
   bear. Accurate drawings illustrate the
   physical features and eating habits. Examines
   the life cycle of the black bear and role of
   the mother in raising cubs. Sizes are not
   metric. French title available : L'OURS NOIR.-

599

Buffalo, buffalo, buffalo.
   prod. [Toronto] : M-L, 1973.- dist. Sch. Ser.
   or Vint. 50 fr. : col. : 35 mm. & cassette
   (7 min.) : auto. & aud. adv. sig. & teacher's
   guide. $16.50 (Animals - a close-up look :
   $75.00) kpij

   1. Bison.   2. Wildlife - Conservation.

   Describes the physical characteristics of the
   bison that roam the national parklands of
   North America under conservation protection,
   explaining how they became an endangered
   species. Examines their eating habits, social
   habits and relationship to smaller animals and
   birds. Explanatory sound track on one side
   of the cassette, music and sound effects on
   the other. Would be useful in a language
   arts programme. French title available : LES
   BISONS DES PLAINES.-

599

The Cat family.
   prod. [Montreal?] : NFB, 1961.- dist. McI. 28
   fr. : col. : 35 mm. & captions & reading
   script. $9.00 (Animals of Canada : $72.00) pj

   1. Cats.

   Illustrates with drawings the common
   characteristics of all members of the cat
   family. Measurements and weight are not
   provided in metric. Studies the lynx, bobcat,
   and mountain lion in detail. Examines their
   life cycles, their habits and environment.
   French title available : FELINS DU CANADA.-

The Classified Catalogue

599

Les Chèvres en vedette.
prod. [Toronto] : M-L, 1975.- dist. Sch. Ser. or Vint. 42 fr. : col. : 35 mm. & cassette (8 min.) : auto. & aud. adv. sig. & teacher's guide. $16.50 (Les Animaux - tableaux réalistes : $75.00) kpji

1. Goats.

Describes the characteristics and habits of goats, examining their relationship to the environment. Narration on one side of the cassette, music and sound effects on the other. Would be useful in a language arts programme. English title available : GOATS, GOATS, GOATS.-

599

Donkeys, donkeys, donkeys.
prod. [Toronto] : M-L, 1973.- dist. Sch. Ser. or Vint. 40 fr. : col. : 35 mm. & cassette (7 min.) : auto. & aud. adv. sig. & teacher's guide. $16.50 (Animals - a close-up look : $75.00) kpij

1. Donkeys.

A description of the physical characteristics and habits of donkeys. Provides detailed narration on one side of cassette, music and sound effects on the other. Would be useful in a language arts programme. French title available : LES ANES DOMESTIQUES.-

599

Félins du Canada.
prod. [Montreal?] : NFB, made 1961 : 1965.- dist. SEC 34 fr. : col. : 35 mm. & captions & reading script. $9.00 pj

1. Cats.

Illustrates with drawings the common characteristics of all members of the cat family. Measurements and weight are not provided in metric. Studies the lynx, bobcat and mountain lion in detail. Examines their life cycles, their habits and environment. English title available : THE CAT FAMILY.-

599

Le gaufre á poches.
prod. [Montreal?] : NFB, made 1956 : 1965. dist. SEC 33 fr. : col. : 35 mm. & captions & reading script. $9.00 pj

1. Gophers.

Drawings illustrate the habits and behavior of the pocket gopher and provide a cross-section of a gopher tunnel. Traces the life cycle of the gopher and discusses his main enemies. Explains some useful and harmful aspects of the gopher's burrowing habits. Sizes are not metric. English title available : THE POCKET GOPHER.-

599

Goats, goats, goats.
prod. [Toronto] : M-L, 1973.- dist. Sch. Ser. or Vint. 42 fr. : col. : 35 mm. & cassette (8 min.) : auto. & aud. adv. sig. & teacher's guide. $16.50 (Animals - a close-up look : $75.00) kpij

1. Goats.

Describes the characteristics and habits of goats, examining their relationship to bhe environment. Narration on one side of the cassette, music and side effects on the other. Would be useful in a language arts programme. French title available : LES CHEVRES EN VEDETTE.-

599

Hoofed mammals of Canada.
prod. [Montreal?] : NFB, 1975.- dist. McI. 30 fr. : col. : 35 mm. & captions. $9.00 (Mammals of Canada : $45.00) ji

1. Pronghorns. 2. Deer. 3. Bovines.

Uses drawings and photographs to examine the pronghorns, the deer, and the bovine. Describes habits and habitats of mammals in each group, including adaptation to environment.-

599

Insectivores and bats.
prod. [Montreal?] : NFB, 1975.- dist. McI. 44 fr. : col. : 35 mm. & captions. $9.00 (Mammals of Canada : $45.00) j

1. Bats. 2. Moles. 3. Shrews.

Drawings, diagrams and photographs with captions provide a good summary of the different types of bats, moles and shrews, their general location in Canada and their habits.-

599

Les mammifères marins du Canada.
prod. [Montreal?] : NFB, 1973.- dist. SEC 44 fr. : col. : 35 mm. & captions. $9.00 ji

1. Whales. 2. Seals.

Examines the two orders of mammals that live in the oceans off Canada - the pinnipedia (seals) and the cetacea (whales). Size (not in S.I. units), food, enemies, common features and specific characteristics are included. Drawings used throughout. English title available : MARINE MAMMALS OF CANADA.-

599

Marine mammals of Canada.
prod. [Montreal?] : NFB, 1973.- dist. McI. 39 fr. : col. : 35 mm. & captions. $9.00 (Mammals of Canada : $45.00) ji

1. Seals. 2. Whales.

Examines the two orders of mammals that live in the oceans off Canada - the pinnipedia (seals) and the cetacea (whales). Size (not S.I. units), food, enemies, common features and specific characteristics are included. Drawings used throughout. French title available : LES MAMMIFERES MARINS DU CANADA.-

599

The North American buffalo.
prod. [Montreal?] : NFB, made 1959 : 1976.- dist. McI. 32 fr. : col. : 35 mm. & captions & reading script. $9.00 (Animals of Canada : $72.00) pj

1. Bison. 2. Wildlife - Conservation.

Uses drawings to describe the physical features, habits and habitat of the North American buffalo. Examines the reasons for decreased numbers of these animals and how they are protected today. Follows the habits of buffalo throughout the seasons and discusses their natural enemies. Weights and sizes are not metric. French title available : LE BISON D'AMERIQUE.-

599

L'ours noir.
prod. [Montreal?] : NFB, made 1956 : 1976.- dist. SEC 45 fr. : col. : 35 mm. & captions & reading script. $9.00 pj

1. Bears.

Studies the habits and habitat of the black bear. Accurate drawings illustrate the physical features and eating habits. Examines the life cycle of the black bear and role of the mother in raising cubs. Sizes are not metric. English title available : THE BLACK BEAR.-

599

L'ours polaire.
prod. [Montreal?] : NFB, made 1959 : 1964.- dist. SEC 35 fr. : col. : 35 mm. & captions & reading script. $9.00 pj

1. Polar bears.

Describes the habitat of the polar bear and traces its life cycle including the activities of the mother and cubs. Detail is given to the search for food and importance of the polar bear to the Eskimos. Sizes are not given in metric. Illustrated with drawings. English title available : THE POLAR BEAR.-

599

The Pocket gophers.
prod. [Montreal?] : NFB, made 1956 : 1973.- dist. McI. 30 fr. : col. : 35 mm. & captions & reading script. $9.00 (Animals of Canada : $72.00) pj

1. Gophers.

Drawings illustrate the habits and behavior of the pocket gopher and provide a cross-section of a gopher tunnel. Traces the life cycle of the gopher and discusses his main enemies. Explains some useful and harmful aspects of the gopher's burrowing habits. Sizes are not metric. French title available : LE GAUFRE A POCHES.-

599

The Polar bear.
   prod. [Montreal?] : NFB, made 1959 : 1974.- dist. McI.   31 fr. : col. : 35 mm. & captions & reading script. $9.00 (Animals of Canada : $72.00) pj

   1. Polar bears.

   Describes the habitat of the polar bear and traces its life cycle including the activities of the mother and cubs. Detail is given to the search for food and the importance of the polar bear to the Eskimos. Sizes are not given in metric. Illustrated with drawings. French title available : L'OURS POLAIRE.-

599

Les poneys : petits et grands.
   prod. [Toronto] : M-L, 1975.- dist. Sch. Ser. or Vint.   46 fr. : col. : 35 mm. & cassette (7 min.) : auto. & aud. adv. sig. & teacher's guide. $16.50 (Les animaux - tableaux réalistes : $75.00) kpji

   1. Ponies.

   Depicts the physical characteristics, habits, and environment of Velsh ponies. Includes photos of competition jumping. Narration on one sound track, music and sound effects on the other. Would be useful in a language arts programme. English title available: PONIES, PONIES, PONIES.-

599

The Raccoon.
   prod. [Montreal?] : NFB, 1957.- dist. McI.   22 fr. : col. : 35 mm. & captions & reading script. $9.00 (Animals of Canada : $72.00) pj

   1. Raccoons.

   Uses drawings to describe physical features and characteristics of the raccoon. Sizes are not provided in metric. Examines the four types of raccoons in Canada. Traces the raccoon's life cycle and the type of home they prefer, as well as their eating habits.-

599

Rodents, rabbits and hares.
   prod. [Montreal?] : NFB, 1972.- dist. McI.   39 fr. : col. : 35 mm. & captions. $9.00 (Mammals of Canada : $45.00) j

   1. Rodents.   2. Rabbits.

   Exmphasizes the difference between the order rodentia (rodents) and the order lagamorpha (rabbits and hares). Examines the characteristics of rodents and their various habitats, then the habits of rabbits and hares and their environments, explaining how these two groups fit into the balance of nature. Illustrated with coloured drawings. Encourages further research by viewers. French title available : RONGEURS, LAPINS ET LIEVRES.-

599

Rongeurs, lapins et lièvres.
   prod. [Montreal?] : NFB, 1972.- dist. SEC   42 fr. : col. : 35 mm. & captions. $9.00 pj

   1. Rodents.   2. Rabbits.

   Emphasizes the difference between the order rodentia rodents) and the order lagamorpha (rabbits and hares). Examines the characteristics of rodents and their various habitats, then the habits of rabbits and hares and their environments, explaining how these two groups fit into the balance of nature. Illustrated with coloured drawings. Encourages further research by viewers. English title available : RODENTS, RABBITS AND HARES.-

599

Squirrels.
   prod. [Montreal?] : NFB, 1960.- dist. McI.   24 fr. : col. : 35 mm. & captions & reading script. $9.00 (Animals of Canada : $72.00) pj

   1. Squirresl.

   Drawings illustrate the many types of squirrels and their relatives, as well as mapping out their territories. Discusses the habits of city squirrels, points out his enemies and describes his preparations for winter. Sizes not metric.-

The Classified Catalogue

599
   The Story of mammals.
      prod. [Georgetown, Ont.] : FMS 1976.- dist. McI. 55 fr. : col. : 35 mm. & cassette (13 min.) : auto. & aud. adv. sig. & teacher's manual. $19.00 (Wildlife of North America : the mammals : $95.00) ji

   1. Mammals.   2. Adaptation (Biology).

   Illustrates and describes physical features common to all mammals, and differences that distinguish them from other vertebrates. Discusses adaptation of mammals to habitats and how they have assisted man's survival through the ages. Also points out effects of civilization on the mammal population and its requirements for survival.-

599
   Wiggle nose and long ears.
      prod. [Scarborough, Ont.] : FCC, 1976.- dist. FCC 10 fr. : col. : 35 mm. & cassette (6 min.) : auto. & aud. adv. sig. & reading script. $8.85 (Farm life : $35.40) p

   1. Rabbits.

   Describes the ways in which a rabbit protects himself and learns from his surroundings. Discusses a litter, how the doe prepares for the birth of the litter, and how she looks after them. Material packaged in clear vinyl envelope that would fit a legal-size filing cabinet.-

599.097
   The Eastern forest.
      prod. [Georgetown, Ont.] : FMS, 1971.- dist. McI. 42 fr. : col. : 35 mm. & captions. $10.00 (Mammals of North America : $40.00) pj

   1. Mammals.   2. Adaptation (Biology).

   Animals originally found in forest and meadows are photographed in wooded areas of suburbs. Included are deer, porcupine, bear, oppossum, woodchuck and coyote. Water attracts the beaver, muskrat, moose and otter. Fields and woods support mice, squirrels, skunks and racoons.-

599.097
   The Grasslands.
      prod. [Georgetown, Ont.] : FMS, 1971.- dist. McI. 42 fr. : col. : 35 mm. & captions. $10.00 (Mammals of North America : $40.00) pj

   1. Mammals.   2. Adaptation (Biology).

   Animals living in the Grasslands or Prairie require special adaptation to survive. Prairie dogs, pronghorns and bison are seen roaming across the plains. Included with the familiar pocket gopher, squirrels and other rodents, are the coyote, badger, weasel, raccoon, hare, porcupine and bobcat.-

599.097
   Life in the boreal forest.
      prod. [Georgetown, Ont.] : FMS 1976.- dist. McI. 56 fr. : col. : 35 mm. & cassette (14 min.) : auto. & aud. adv. sig. & teacher's manual. $19.00 (Wildlife of North America : the mammals : $95.00) ji

   1. Mammals.   2. Adaptation (Biology).

   Examines the huge wilderness areas in the northern part of the continent and the mammals that have managed to survive there. Includes photographs of animals of the rodent family, the largest group, and types of deer, and wolves that have overcome their harsh environments.-

599.097
   The Rocky Mountains.
      prod. [Georgetown, Ont.] : FMS, 1971.- dist. McI. 40 fr. : col. : 35 mm. & captions. $10.00 (Mammals of North America : $40.00) pj

   1. Mammals.   2. Adaptation (Biology).

   Mammals inhabiting the Rocky Mountains are examined in detail emphasizing the adaptations of each to the habitat selected. Small and large animals are included living in grasslands or mountain ice fields. Mountain sheep and goats are pictured with the lynx, coyote, weasel, bear, deer, and moose of the forests and alpine meadows.-

599.0971
    Carnivores : the flesh eaters.
        prod. [Montreal?] : NFB, 1975.- dist. McI. 35 fr. : col. : 35 mm. & captions. $9.00 (Mammals of Canada : $45.00) ji

    1. Mammals.

    Uses drawings and photographs to describe the habits of the five groups of carnivores - cats, bears, dogs, raccoons, and weasles and their relatives. Examines the various methods of hunting these mammals and their place in the balance of nature. States size and weight of each animal illustrated. Not metric. French title available : LES CARNIVORES.-

599.09712
    The Arctic.
        prod. [Georgetown, Ont.] : FMS, 1971.- dist. 44 fr. : col. : 35 mm. & captions. $10.00 (Mammals of North America : $40.00) pj

    1. Mammals. 2. Adaptation (Biology).
    3. Arctic regions.

    A description of Arctic mammals and how they adapt to long, harsh winters and short summers. Includes caribou travelling north, and musk-ox shedding coats in the spring, rabbits and foxes growing new fur, and seal and walrus basking in the summer sun.-

607
    National Research Council.
        prod.]Winnipeg] : WCL, 1972.- dist. Sch. Ch. 46 fr. : b&w & col. : 35 mm. & captions. $7.95 (Our national capital : $39.75) ji

    1. National Research Council of Canada.

    An overview of the kinds of problems the scientists at the National Research Council investigate to make life safer and better for Canadians. Photographs of experiments in progress illustrate the variety of interests, from more effective ways of fighting house fires to studies of wind flow around tall city buildings. Concludes with a discussion of the National Science Library's role in gathering, storing, and distributing scientific information.-

607.4
    Le Canada à Osaka '70.
        prod. [Montreal?] : NFB, 1971.- dist. SEC 79 fr. : col. : 35 mm. & captions & notes. $9.00 pji

    1. Expo '70.

    A brief view of modern Japan and Osaka, the site of Expo '70, and the four main areas of the fair. The four Canadian pavilions are displayed in great detail. Discusses the success of the Canadian pavilions and the effect on world visitors of the displays. English title available : CANADA AT OSAKA '70.-

607.4
    Canada at Osaka '70.
        prod. [Montreal?] : NFB, 1971.- dist. McI. 79 fr. : col. : 35 mm. & captions & notes. $9.00 pji

    1. Expo '70.

    A brief view of modern Japan and Osaka, the site of Expo '70 and the four main areas of the fair. The Four Canadian pavilions are displayed in great detail. Discusses the success of the Canadian pavilions and the effect on world visitors of the displays. French title available : LE CANADA A OSAKA '70.-

607.4
    Expo 67 : Montreal, Canada.
        prod. [Montreal?] : NFB, 1968.- dist. McI. 47 fr. : col. : 35 mm. & script. $9.00 jis

    1. Expo 67.

    A comprehensive tour of the Expo '67 site showing many of the many spectacular buildings with innovative architecture, adornments, and special displays. French title available : EXPO '67.-

607.4
    Expo '67 : [Montreal, (Canada)].
        prod. [Montreal?] : NFB, 1968.- dist. SEC 47 fr. : col. : 35 mm. & script. $9.00 jis

    1. Expo '67

    A comprehensive tour of the Expo '67 site showing many of the spectacular buildings with innovative architecture, adornments, and special displays. English title available : EXPO '67.-

The Classified Catalogue

607.4
Let's go to the fair.
   prod. [Scarborough, Ont.] : R.B.M., 1975.- dist. ETHOS 62 fr. : col. : 35 mm. & cassette (13 min.) : auto. & aud. adv. sig. & teacher's manual.- $19.00 (Special occasions) pj

   1. Fairs.

   The colour and fun of a fall country fair are captured in photographs of its many attractions. These include the food, the rides and games, and the exhibits of farm animals, produce, arts and crafts, baking, and farm machinery.-

610.73
Nursing : the challenge of caring.
   prod. [Toronto] : Int. Cin., 1976.- dist. VEC 80 fr. : col. : 35 mm. & cassette (7 min.) : auto. & aud. adv. sig. & teacher's guide. $24.00 is

   1. Nursing.   2. Nurses.

   An overall view of various aspects of nursing as a profession in Canada, and the changing role of the nurse both in and out of the hospital situation in today's society.-

612
The Biology of taste and smell.
   prod. [Scarborough, Ont.] : R.B.M., 1975.- dist. ETHOS 41 fr. : col. : 35 mm. & cassette (9 min.) : auto. & aud. adv. sig. & teacher's manual. $19.00 (Science) ji

   1. Taste.   2. Smell.

   Examines the closely-linked mechanisms for tasting and smelling developed by all animals, with emphasis on humans.-

612
Exercise - a new look.
   prod. [Toronto] : M-L, 1973.- dist. Sch. Ser. or Vint. 43 fr. : col. : 35 mm. & cassette (6 min.) : auto. & aud. adv. sig. & teacher's guide. $16.50 (Health - a new look : $65.00) kp

   1. Muscles.   2. Exercise.

   Describes how humans move, and illustrates the functions of various muscles. Encourages discussion of several sports and whether they are good exercise. Examines the importance of the heart muscle.-

612
Hearing.
   prod. [Toronto] : M-L, 1976.- dist. Sch. Ser. or Vint. 56 fr. : col. : 35 mm. & cassette (10 min.) : auto. & aud. adv. sig. & teacher's guide. $16.50 (Learning about the human body : $85.00) j

   1. Ear.   2. Hearing.

   Describes the parts of the ear, their functions and importance. Also shows how to care for ears, and introduces sound waves. Diagrams, cartoons and photos.-

612
Our five senses of touch.
   prod. [Scarborough, Ont.] : R.B.M., 1975.- dist. ETHOS 40 fr. : col. : 35 mm. & cassette (9 min.) : auto. & aud. adv. sig. & teacher's manual. $19.00 (Science) ji

   1. Senses and sensations.

   Discusses how animals and humans use well-developed cells sensitive to heat and cold, touch, pressure and pain to provide information about their environment, as an aid to survival.-

612
Smell, taste and touch.
   prod. [Toronto] : M-L, 1976.- dist. Sch. Ser. or Vint. 42 fr. : col. : 35 mm. & cassette (8 min.) : auto. & aud. adv. sig. & teacher's guide. $16.50 (Learning about the human body : $85.00) j

   1. Smell.   2. Taste.   3. Touch.

   Detailed description of the functioning of smell, taste, and touch, showing how they complement each other and convey pleasure or warning of danger. Uses diagrams, cartoons and photos.-

612
Vision.
   prod. [Toronto] : M-L, 1976.- dist. Sch. Ser. or Vint. 49 fr. : col. : 35 mm. & cassette (10 min.) : auto. & aud. adv. sig. & teacher's guide. $16.50 (Learning about the human body : $85.00) j

   1. Vision.

   Uses diagrams and photos to explain the process of seeing, and to describe its use in interpreting the environment.-

The Classified Catalogue

612.6
   Being born.
      prod. [Montreal?] : NFB, 1974.- dist. McI. 25 fr. : col. : 35 mm. & cassette (7 min.) : auto. & aud. adv. sig. & teacher's guide. $18.00 (Living and growing) pj

      1. Reproduction. 2. Sex education.

      Describes joining of sperm and egg in human conception, growth of egg inside mother, and birth. Compares this to fertilization and growth of other living things, such as pollination of flowers. Drawings show position of baby during pregnancy and external effects on mother. Introduces terms, womb, uterus, umbilical cord and vagina. Illustrations simple, avoiding detail. Does not show birth process. French title available : IL ETAIT UNE FOISE UNE OEUF.-

612.6
   Conception and birth.
      prod. [Montreal?] : NFB, 1974.- dist. McI. 51 fr. : col. : 35 mm. & captions. $9.00 (Sex education : $45.00) is

      1. Sex education. 2. Reproduction.

      Stylized graphics of male and female sex organs, sexual intercourse, conception, growth of the embryo, and birth. Captions are brief and the filmstrip is designed as a teaching aid to be used by a teacher with training in sex education.-

612.6
   Le développement et l'apprentissage.
      prod. [Toronto] : M-L, 1974.- dist. Sch. Ser or Vint. 50 fr. : col. : 35 mm. & cassette (7 min.) : auto. & aud. adv. sig. & teacher's guide. $16.50 (Vie de famille et éducation sexuelle série A : $75.00) pj

      1. Growth.

      Photographs of children from different ethnic backgrounds are used to show the gradual development of a human being - especially stressing physical growth, personality development and learning processes. English title available : GROWING AND LEARNING.-

612.6
   Développement pré-natal.
      prod. [Toronto] : M-L, 1974.- dist. Sch. Ser. or Vint. 24 fr. : col. : 35 mm. & cassette (6 min.) : auto. & aud. adv. sig. & teacher's guide. $16.50 (Vie de famille et éducation sexuelle série A : $75.00) pj

      1. Reproduction. 2. Sex education.

      Explains gestation, pregnancy, development of the human embryo, and nourishment of a human baby. Illustrated with photos and graphics. English title available : PRE-NATAL DEVELOPMENT.-

612.6
   L'Embryon se développe.
      prod. [Toronto] : M-L, 1974.- dist. Sch. Ser. or Vint. 41 fr. : col. : 35 mm & cassette (11 min.) : auto. & aud. adv. sig. & teacher's guide. $16.50 (Vie de famille et éducation sexuelle série C : $85.00) pj

      1. Reproduction. 2. Sex education.

      Reproductive cells and their functions are explained. Graphics and photos show how the human fertilized egg divides into three layers of cells and how the different body parts develop from them. English title available : PATTERN OF EMBRYO DEVELOPMENT.-

612.6
   Etre pubère.
      prod. [Toronto] : M-L, 1974.- dist. Sch. Ser. or Vint. 43 fr. : col. : 35 mm. & cassette (8 min.) : auto. & aud. adv. sig. & teacher's guide. $16.50 (Vie de famille et éducation sexuelle série C $85.00) pj

      1. Adolescence. 2. Sex education.

      Provides information about male and female sexual development through puberty. Also attempts to explain the psychological and emotional changes that occur during this time. Photos and graphs are used. English title available : THE MEANING OF PUBERTY.-

The Classified Catalogue

612.6
    Growing and learning.
        prod. [Toronto] : M-L, 1973.- dist. Sch. Scr. or Vint. 54 fr. : col. : 35 mm. & cassette (5 min.) : auto. & aud. adv. sig. & teacher's guide. $16.50 (Family living and sex education series A : $75.00) pj

        1. Growth.

    Photographs of children from different ethnic backgrounds are used to show the gradual development of a human being - especially stressing physical growth, personality development and learning processes. French title available : LE DEVELOPPEMENT ET L'APPRENTISSAGE.-

612.6
    Il etait une fois un oeuf.
        prod. [Montreal?] : NFB, 1974.- dist. SEC 25 fr. : col. : 35 mm. & cassette (7 min.) : auto. & aud. adv. sig. & teacher's guide. $18.00 (La vie qui pousse) pj

        1. Reproduction. 2. Sex education.

    Describes joining of sperm and egg in human conception, growth of egg inside mother, and birth. Compares this to fertilization and growth of other living things, such as pollination of flowers. Drawings show position of baby during pregnancy and external effects on mother. Introduces terms, womb, uterus, umbilical cord and vagina. Illustrations simple, avoiding detail. Does not show birth process. English title available : BEING BORN.-

612.6
    The Meaning of puberty.
        prod. [Toronto] : M-L, 1973.- dist. Sch. Ser. or Vint. 43 fr. : col. : 35 mm. & cassette (8 min.) : auto. & aud. adv. sig. & teacher's guide. $16.50 (Family living and sex education series C : $85.00) ji

        1. Adolescence. 2. Sex instruction.

    Provides information about male and female sexual development through puberty. Also attempts to explain the psychological and emotional changes that occur during this time. Photos and graphics are used. French title available :ETRE PUBERE.-

612.6
    La Naissance d'un être humain.
        prod. [Toronto] : M-L, 1974.- dist. Sch. Ser. or Vint. 32 fr. : col. : 35 mm. & cassette (5 min.) : auto. & aud. adv. sig. & teacher's guide. $16.50 (Vie de famille et éducation sexuelle série B : $75.00) pj

        1. Childbirth. 2. Reproduction. 3. Sex education.

    Uses diagrams and photos to demonstrate the process of childbirth and to explain the male and female reproductive systems. English title available : A HUMAN BEING IS BORN.-

612.6
    Pattern of embryo development.
        prod. [Toronto] : M-L, 1973.- dist. Sch. Ser. or Vint. 41 fr. : col. : 35 mm. & cassette (11 min.) : auto. & aud. adv. sig. & teacher's guide. $16.50 (Family living and sex education series C : $85.00) ji

        1. Reproduction. 2. Sex education.

    Reproductive cells and their functions are explained. Graphics and photos show how the human fertilized egg divides into three layers of cells and how the different body parts develop from them. French title available : L'EMBRYON SE DEVELOPPE.-

612.6
    Pre-natal development.
        prod. [Toronto] : M-L, 1973.- dist. Sch. Ser. or Vint. 29 fr. : col. : 35 mm. & cassette (5 min.) : auto. & aud. adv. sig. & teacher's guide. $16.50 (Family living and sex education series B : $75.00) j

        1. Reproduction. 2. Sex education.

    Explains gestation, pregnancy, development of the human embryo, and nourishment of a human baby. Illustrated with photos and graphics. French title available : DEVELOPPEMENT PRE-NATAL.-

The Classified Catalogue

612.6
    Puberty.
        prod. [Montreal?] : NFB, 1974.- dist. McI. 62 fr. : col. : 35 mm. & captions. $9.00 (Sex eduxation : $45.00) is

        1. Adolescence. 2. Menstruation.

        Silhouettes of males and females, with diagrams of organs, are used to illustrate physical external and internal changes that occur with puberty. The nature of menstruation and menstrual cycle are shown. French title available : PUBERTE.-

613
    Cleanliness - anew look.
        prod. [Toronto] : M-L, 1973.- dist. Sch. Ser. or Vint. 45 fr. : col. : 35 mm. & cassette (5 min.) : auto. & aud. adv. sig. & teacher's guide. $16.50 (Health - a new look : $65.00) kp

        1. Hygiene.

        Describes the relationship between germs and disease. Illustrates that germs are one of the many living things on earth. Discusses ways in which we can control germs by washing and avoiding infections.-

613.6
    Faire un feu et construire un abri.
        prod. [Toronto] : M-L, 1975.- dist. Sch. Ser. or Vint. 41 fr. : col. : 35 mm. & cassette (9 min.) : auto. & aud. adv. sig. & teacher's guide. $16.50 (Activités de plein air : survie : $85.00) i

        1. Wilderness survival.

        Detailed instructions on how to build an emergency lean-to and fir bough bed, how to build a safe reflector fire, and how to use the bow and drill method of lighting a fire. Stresses safety, preservation and conservation. English title available : HOW TO MAKE A FIRE AND SHELTER.-

613.6
    How to make a fire and shelter.
        prod. [Toronto] : M-L, 1974.- dist. Sch. Ser. or Vint. 41 fr. : col. : 35 mm. & cassette (9 min.) : auto. & aud. adv. sig. & teacher's guide. $16.50 (Outdoor survival : $85.00) j

        1. Wilderness survival.

        Detailed instructions on how to build an emergency lean-to and fir bough bed, how to build a safe reflector fire, and how to use the bow and drill method of lighting a fire. Stresses safety, preservation and conservation. French title available : FAIRE UN FEU ET CONSTRUIRE UN ABRI.-

613.6
    Outdoor cooking.
        prod. [Toronto] : M-L, 1975.- dist. Sch. Ser. or Vint. 43 fr. : col. : 35 mm. & cassette (9 min.) : auto. & aud. adv. sig. & teaching guide. $16.50 (Outdoor education) is

        1. Wilderness survival.

        Detailed description and photographs of survival requirements and techniques for obtaining food, and cooking and preserving it in a winter wilderness. Some teacher preparation required before group viewing and discussion.-

613.6
    Outdoor survival kit.
        prod. [Toronto] : M-L, 1974.- dist. Sch. Ser. or Vint. 42 fr. : col. : 35 mm. & cassette (9 min.) : auto. & aud. adv. sig. & teacher's guide. $16.50 (Outdoor survival : $85.00) j

        1. Wilderness survival.

        Lists the contents of a compact survival kit showing how these items can be used effectively to survive in the bush. Two stranded girls demonstrate hunting and fishing techniques, cooking, using available food from trees and rock faces, and setting up proper distress signs. French title available : TROUSSE DE SURVIE.-

The Classified Catalogue

613.6
    Summer survival.
        prod. [Scarborough, Ont.] : R.B.M., 1975.- dist. ETHOS 53 fr. : col. : 35 mm. & cassette (11 min.) : auto. & aud. adv. sig. & teacher's manual. $19.00 (Outdoor education) is

        1. Wilderness survival.

        Offers pointers on building shelters, making a fire, and gathering edible plants and animals, when one is lost.-

613.6
    Survival in the bush.
        prod. [Toronto] : R.Q.M, 1973.- dist. Lea. 47 fr. : col. : 35 mm. & captions. $9.00 (Survival & safety in the outdoors) jis

        1. Wilderness survival.

        Features the basic rules for survival in the bush. Photographs cover the building of shelters, fires, the foods available, plant remedies for cuts, insect bites, and poison ivy. Warns against eating unknown plants and trapping small animals unless in an emergency.-

613.6
    Trousse de survie.
        prod. [Toronto] : M-L, 1975.- dist. Sch. Ser. or Wint. 42 fr. : col. : 35 mm. & cassette (9 min.) : auto. & aud. adv. sig. & teacher's guide. $16.50 (Activités de plein air : survie : $85.00) j

        1. Wilderness survival.

        Lists the contents of a compact survival kit showing how these items can be used effectively to survive in the bush. Two stranded girls demonstrate hunting and fishing techniques, cooking, using available food from trees and rock faces, and setting up distress signs. English title available : OUTDOOR SURVIVAL KIT.-

613.6
    Winter survival.
        prod. [Scarborough, Ont.] : R.B.M., 1975.- dist. ETHOS 61 fr. : col. : 35 mm. & cassette (12 min.) : auto. & aud. adv. sig. & teacher's manual. $19.00 (Outdoor education) is

        1. Wilderness survival.

        Offers pointers on how to survive if one becomes lost on a winter camping trip. Tips include how to establish a shelter, build a fire, and how to find some sources of food.-

613.8
    Alcohol.
        prod. [Montreal?] : NFB, 1973.- dist. McI. 48 fr. : col. : 35 mm. & captions. $9.00 jis

        1. Alcohol. 2. Alcoholism.

        Cartoons are used to illustrate the various aspects of alcohol, its history, its positive uses and effects, its negative effects and the causes of alcoholism. Part of a multi-media kit titled "Drugs and the human body". French title available : L'ALCOOL.-

613.8
    L'alcool.
        prod. [Montreal?] : NFB, 1973.- dist. SEC 48 fr. : col. : 35 mm. & captions. $9.00 jis

        1. Alcohol. 2. Alcoholism.

        Cartoons are used to illustrate the various aspects of alcohol, its history, its positive uses and effects, its negative effects and the causes of alcoholism. Part of a multi-media kit titled "Les drogues et le corps humain". English title available : ALCOHOL.-

613.8
    Effects of misuse.
        prod. [Toronto] : M-L, 1974.- dist. Sch. Ser. or Wint. 63 fr. : col. : 35 mm. & cassette (10 min.) : auto. & aud. adv. sig. & teacher's guide. $16.50 (Drugs, medicines, and you : $75.00) j

        1. Drugs and youth.

        Discusses the effects of drug abuse on the family of a user. Misuse of drugs by a teenager prompts his younger brother to visit a nearby hospital drug clinic. Photographs of the boy talking with a social worker and psychiatrist familiarize students with a hospital setting and indicate the roles of these professionals in educating both youths and parents on symptoms of drug abuse.-

The Classified Catalogue

613.8
   Le fumeur est une victime.
      prod. [Montreal?] : NFB, 1967.- dist. SEC 34 fr. : col. : 35 mm. & captions. $9.00 jis

      1. Smoking.

      Through the use of cartoons this filmstrip discusses why people smoke, the influence of T.V. commercials, the social disadvantages, and the physically harmful effects of this activity. English title available : THE SMOKING EPIDEMIC.-

613.8
   Pourquoi prend-on de la drogue?
      prod. [Montreal?] : NFB, 1972.- dist. SEC 31 fr. : col. : 35 mm. & captions. $9.00 ji

      1. Drug abuse.

      Captioned drawings and photos suggest many possible reasons for taking drugs. 22 unlabelled duplicate frames are included for individual mounting as slides to be arranged in order of importance. Designed to stimulate discussion. Part of a multi-media kit titled "Les drogues et le corps humain". English title available : WHY DO PEOPLE TAKE DRUGS?-

613.8
   The Smoking epidemic.
      prod. [Montreal?] : NFB, 1967.- dist. McI. 34 fr. : col. : 35 mm. & captions. $9.00

      1. Smoking.

      Through the use of cartoons this filmstrip discusses why people smoke, the influence of T.V. commercials, the social disadvantages and physically harmful effects of tis activity. French title available : LE FUMEUR EST UNE VICTIME.-

613.8
   Les solvants.
      prod. [Montreal?] : NFB, 1972.- dist. SEC 33 fr. : col. : 35 mm. & captions. $9.00 ji

      1. Solvents.

      Produced in collaboration with Addiction Research Foundation. Uses drawings to emphasize the danger in sniffing solvents, including physical, legal, and psychological aspects. A factual and unemotional treatment. Part of a multi-media kit titled : "Les drogues et le corps humain". English title available : SOLVENTS.-

613.8
   Solvents.
      prod. [Montreal?] : NFB, 1972.- dist. McI. 27 fr. : col. : 35 mm. & captions. $9.00 ji

      1. Solvents.

      Produced in collaboration with Addiction Research Foundation. Uses drawings to emphasize the danger in sniffing solvents, including physical, legal, and psychological aspects. A factual and unemotional treatment. Part of a multi-media kit titled "Drugs and the human body". French title available : LES SOLVANTS.-

613.8
   The Trouble with alcohol.
      prod. [Toronto] : M-L, 1975.- dist. Sch. Ser. or Vint. 50 fr. : col. : 35 mm. & cassette (8 min.) : auto. & aud. adv. sig. & teacher's guide. $16.50 (Maturity : options and consequences : $85.00) is

      1. Alcoholism.

      Discusses the way a young man's excessive drinking affects his life, his job, and his marriage.-

613.8
   Why do people take drugs?
      prod. Montreal?] : NFB, 1972.- dist. McI. 31 fr. : b&w & col. : 35 mm. & captions. $9.00 ji

      1. Drug abuse.

      Captioned drawings and photos suggest many possible reasons for taking drugs. 22 unlabelled duplicate frames are included for individual mounting as slides to be arranged in order of importance. Designed to stimulate discussion. Part of a multi-media kit titled "Drugs and the human body". French title available : POURQUOI PREND-ON DE LA DROGUE?-

613.9
   Contraception.
      prod. [Montreal?] : NFB, 1974.- dist. McI. 95 fr. : col. : 35 mm. & captions. $9.00 (Sex education : $45.00) is

      1. Birth control.

      Stylized graphics show how the commonly recommended methods of contraception are used and how they work. Recommended for group use by a teacher or sex education instructor.-

The Classified Catalogue

613.9
>The Diaphragm.
>>prod. [Toronto] : M-L, 1974.- dist. Sch. Ser. or Vint. 46 fr. : col. : 35 mm. & cassette (9 min.) : auto. & aud. adv. sig. & teacher's guide. $16.50 (Family planning methods : $85.00) is
>
>>1. Birth control.
>
>>Clear, simple narration, using diagrams, discusses conception and use of diaphragm in prevention of pregnancy. Emphasizes choosing a method of contraception to meet individual needs, stressing that success of any method depends upon careful use by individual.-

613.9
>Un historique de la contraception.
>>prod. [Montreal?] : NFB, made 1974 : 1977.- 128 fr. : b&w & col. : 35 mm. & cassette (23 min.) : auto. & aud. adv. sig. & teacher's manual. $18.00 (Point de vue) s
>
>>1. Birth control - History. 2. Sexual ethics.
>
>>A history of the relationship between social values and birth control in Europe and North America. Discusses primitive and modern methods and stresses importance of birth control in fight against poverty, child labour, infanticide, and abortion. Traces Canadian efforts to legalize contraceptives. Well illustrated with historic photographs and drawings. English title available : A HISTORY OF CONTRACEPTION.-

613.9
>A history of contraception.
>>prod. [Montreal?] : NFB, made 1974 : 1977.- 128 fr. : b&w & col. : 35 mm. & cassette (23 min.) : auto. & aud. adv. sig. & teacher's manual. $18.00 (A question of values) s
>
>>1. Birth control - History. 2. Sexual ethics.
>
>>A history of the relationship between social values and birth control in Europe and North America. Discusses primitive and modern methods and stresses importance of birth control in fight against poverty, child labour, infanticide, and abortion. Traces Canadian efforts to legalize contraceptives. Well illustrated with historic photographs and drawings. French title available : UN HISTORIQUE DE LA CONTRACEPTION.-

613.9
>The Intrauterine device.
>>prod. [Toronto] : M-L, 1974.- dist. Sch. Ser. or Vint. 57 fr. : col. : 35 mm. & cassette (8 min.) : auto. & aud. adv. sig. & teacher's guide. $16.50 (Family planning methods : $85.00) is
>
>>1. Birth control.
>
>>Different intrauterine devices are illustrated, and purpose and use described, following a concise discussion of how pregnancy occurs. Outlines advantages and disadvantages, using diagrams and photos to illustrate.-

613.9
>The Pill.
>>prod. [Toronto] : M-L, 1974.- dist. Sch. Ser. or Vint. 56 fr. : col. : 35 mm. & cassette (10 min.) : auto. & aud. adv. sig. & teacher's guide. $16.50 (Family planning methods : $85.00) is
>
>>1. Birth control.
>
>>Uses diagrams to show how oral contraceptives act to inhibit ovulation and prevent pregnancy. Emphasizes choosing a method of contraception to suit individual, stressing that success of any method depends upon careful use. Mentions disadvantages of the pill, but does not describe or discuss them.-

613.9
>The Rhythm and sympto-thermal methods.
>>prod. [Toronto] : M-L, 1974.- dist. Sch. Ser. or Vint. 55 fr. : col. : 35 mm. & cassette (9 min.) : auto. & aud. adv. sig. & teacher's guide. $16.50 (Family planning methods : $85.00) is
>
>>1. Birth control.
>
>>Diagrams and photos describe clearly and simply how pregnancy occurs. Explains use of rhythm and sympto-thermal methods. Stresses that high motivation on part of both partners is necessary for methods to be effective.-

613.9
   Tubal ligation and vasectomy.
      prod. [Toronto] : M-L, 1974.- dist. Sch. Ser. or Vint. 50 fr. : col. : 35 mm. & cassette (10 min.) : auto. & aud. adv. sig. & teacher's guide. $16.50 (Family planning methods : $85.00) is

      1. Sterilization (Birth control).

      An illustrated discussion of these two permanent surgical methods preceded by a brief description of conception. Emphasizes simplicity and permanency of operations, and need for emotional maturity and careful consideration beforehand.-

613.9
   Vaginal spermicides and the condom.
      prod. [Toronto] : M-L, 1974.- dist. Sch. Ser. or Vint. 48 fr. : col. : 35 mm. & cassette (10 min.) : auto. & aud. adv. sig. & teacher's guide. $16.50 (Family planning methods : $85.00) is

      1. Birth control.

      Describes the correct use of vaginal spermicides and condoms as methods for preventing pregnancy, preceded by a brief explanation of how pregnancy occurs. Suggests combined use of both methods for greatest effectiveness, and consultation with a doctor. Stresses that success depends on careful use. Diagrams and photos.-

614.3
   Aliments classés du Canada.
      prod. [Montreal?] : NFB, 1971.- dist. SEC 52 fr. : col. : 35 mm. & captions & teacher's manual. $9.00 jis

      1. Food adulteration and inspection. 2. Food - Quality.

      A comprehensive photographic coverage of Canada's grading system for different foods. Includes meat, poultry, eggs, diary products, and fruits, vegetables, jam, honey and maple products. An informative guide for consumers of all ages. English title available : CANADA'S GRADED FOODS.-

614.3
   Canada's graded foods.
      prod. [Montreal?] : NFB, 1971.- dist. McI. 52 fr. : b&w : 35 mm. & captions & teacher's manual. $9.00 jis

      1. Food adulteration and inspection. 2. Food - Quality.

      A comprehensive photographic coverage of Canada's grading system for different foods. Includes meat, poultry, eggs, dairy products, fruits, vegetables, jam, honey and maple products. An informative guide for consumers of all ages. French title available : ALIMENTS CLASSES DU CANADA.-

614.7
   Qu'est-ce que la fumée?
      prod. [Montreal?] : NFB, made 1969 : 1971.- dist. SEC 45 fr. : col. : 35 mm. & captions. $9.00 jis

      1. Air - Pollution. 2. Smoke.

      Cartoons and photographs explain briefly the history of smoke, how it is formed and its chemical components. Most of the information provided concerns air pollution, a by-product of man's progress, and smoke from cigarettes. The effects of them on the body and the body's reaction are also discussed. English title available : WHAT IS SMOKE?-

614.7
   What is smoke?
      prod. [Montreal?] : NFB, 1969.- dist. McI. 45 fr. : col. : 35 mm. & captions. $9.00

      1. Smoke. 2. Air - Pollution

      Cartoons and photographs explain briefly the history of smoke, how it is formed and its chemical components. Most of the information provided concerns air pollution, a by-product of man's progress, and smoke from cigarettes. The effects of them on the body and the body's reaction are also discussed. French title available : QU'EST-CE QUE LA FUMEE?-

614.8
Bicycle safety.
   prod. [Toronto] : Int. Cin., 1976.- dist. VEC 38 fr. : col. : 35 mm. & cassette (6 min.) : auto. & aud. adv. sig. & teacher's guide. $24.00 (Safety songs and stories : $130.00) pj

   1. Bicycles and bicycling - Safety measures.

   Cartoons show how unsafe conduct on a bicycle can result in the "unsafe bikerider blues." Accompanied by original music and words.-

614.8
Dangers fréquents en atelier.
   prod. [Toronto] : M-L, 1972.- dist. Sch. Ser. or Vint. 52 fr. : col. : 35 mm. & cassette (13 min.) : auto. & aud. adv. sig. & teacher's guide. $16.50 (Sécurité dans l'atelier : $85.00) is

   1. Machine shop practice. - Safety measures.

   Discusses the dangerous situations that can arise in a shop situation. Examines problems caused by clutter, carrying and lifting heavy objects, defective tools, and combustible gas. Stresses knowledge of emergency switches, first aid kits and fire extinguishers. English title available : GENERAL SHOP HAZARDS.-

614.8
First aid in the bush.
   prod. [Toronto] : M-L, 1974.- dist. Sch. Ser. or Vint. 45 fr. : col. : 35 mm. & cassette (11 min.) : auto. & aud. adv. sig. & teacher's guide. $16.50 (Outdoor survival : $85.00) j

   1. First aid. 2. Wilderness survival.

   Emphasizes necessity of a complete first aid kit, immediate medical attention if possible, and cleanliness. Itemizes articles in first aid kit. Describes various bush injuries and techniques, and supplies to treat injuries. Describes different types of slings, bandages, and provides information on treating shock and other serious injuries. Excellent for use with a group planning bush travel. French title available : PREMIERS SOINS EN FORET.-

614.8
"Flashy" the fire bug.
   prod. [Montreal?] : NFB, made 1953 : 1975.- dist. McI. 46 fr. : col. : 35 mm. & captions & disc (9 min. mono.) : aud. & adv. sig. & manual. $9.00 p

   1. Fire prevention.

   Presents many potential fire hazards and fire prevention. Features cartoon characters - Flashy, who starts fires, and Fire Lore, who knows how to prevent them. Illustrates three types of fire extinguishers.-

614.8
General shop hazards.
   prod. [Toronto] : M-L, 1970.- dist. Sch. Ser. or Vint. 52 fr. : col. : 35 mm. & cassette (10 min.) : auto. & aud. adv. sig. & teacher's guide. $16.50 (Shop safety : $85.00) is

   1. Machine shop practice - Safety measures.

   Discusses the dangerous situations that can arise in a shop situation. Examines problems caused by clutter, carrying and lifting heavy objects, defective tools, and combustible gas. Stresses knowledge of emergency switches, first aid kits and fire extinguishers. French title available : DANGERS FREQUENTS EN ATELIER.-

614.8
Home safety.
   prod. [Toronto] : Int. Cin., 1976.- dist. VEC 37 fr. : col. : 35 mm. & cassette (5 min.) : auto. & aud. adv. sig. & teacher's guide. $24.00 (Safety songs and stories : $130.00) pj

   1. Accidents - Prevention.

   Through the use of original words, music, and art work the dangerous antics of Careless Clyde point out home hazards to children.-

614.8
Home safety.
   prod. [Toronto] : M-L, 1974.- dist. Sch. Ser. or Vint. 54 fr. : col. : 35 mm. & cassette (8 min.) : auto. & aud. adv. sig. & teacher's guide. $16.50 (Safety : a way of life : $65.00) pj

   1. Accidents - Prevention.

   Demonstrates correct behavior in the home, encouraging viewers to spot safety errors. Includes medicine chest safety and safe behavior with electricity.-

614.8
> Pensez "sécurité".
> prod. [Toronto] : M-L, 1972.- dist. Sch. Ser. or Vint. 46 fr. : col. : 35 mm. & cassette (10 min.) : auto. & aud. adv. sig. & teacher's guide. $16.50 (Sécurité dans l'atelier : $85.00) is
>
> 1. Machine shop practice - Safety measures.
>
> Examines the proper safety attitude in a shop. Discusses working defensively, practising tidiness, using the correct tools and material for the situation. Points out importance of planning ahead and wearing protective clothing. English title available : THINK SAFETY.-

614.8
> Premiers soins en forêt.
> prod. [Toronto] : M-L, 1975.- dist. Sch. Ser. or Vint. 45 fr. : col. : 35 mm. & cassette (11 min.) : auto. & aud. adv. sig. & teacher's guide. $16.50 (Activités de plein air : survie : $85.00) i
>
> 1. First aid. 2. Wilderness survival.
>
> Itemizes the articles in a first aid kit, describing different types of slings and bandages. Included information on treating shock and other serious injuries, emphasizing the need for immediate medical attention, if available, and cleanliness. English title available : FIRST AID IN THE BUSH.-

614.8
> Ride safely to school.
> prod. [Montreal?] : NFB, made1957 : 1973.- dist. McI. 37 fr. : col. : 35 mm. & captions & teacher's manual & script. $9.00 (Junior safety) pj
>
> 1. Accidents - Preventions.
>
> Cartoons demonstrate safety rules on the street. Can be presented as a play, with children playing the parts. Mr. Scarecrow leads the discussion of rules for riding in the car, crossing at the corner, carrying books in a bicycle basket, and others.-

614.8
> Safety on the slopes.
> prod. [Montreal?] : NFB, 1962.- dist. McI. 32 fr. : col. : 35 mm. & captions. $9.00 ji
>
> 1. Skis and skiing - Safety measures.
>
> Uses cartoons to illustrate the proper preparations for downhill skiing including choice of correct equipment, physical exercises and safety rules while at the slopes. Also gives advice on using ski lifts and correct procedures in case of an accident.-

614.8
> Safety on the street.
> prod. [Toronto] : Int. Cin., 1976.- dist. VEC 37 fr. : col. : 35 mm. & cassette (4 min.) : auto. & aud. adv. sig. & teacher's guide. $24.00 (Safety songs and stories : $130.00) pj
>
> 1. Accidents - Prevention.
>
> Original music, words and cartoons reveal how Dangerous Django suffers the consequences of ignoring safety rules on the street.-

614.8
> School bus safety.
> prod. [Toronto] : Int. Cin., 1976.- dist. VEC 38 fr. : col. : 35 mm & cassette (6 min.) : auto. & aud. adv. sig. & teacher's guide. $24.00 (Safety songs and stories : $130.00) pj
>
> 1. Accidents - Prevention.
>
> Tom sets the example for everything a school boy and girl should not do on a school bus. Cartoons, original words and music.-

614.8
> School safety.
> prod. [Toronto] : M-L, 1974.- dist. Sch. Ser. or Vint. 56 fr. : col. : 35 mm. & cassette (8 min.) : auto. & aud. adv. sig. & teacher's guide. $16.50 (Safety : a way of life : $65.00) pj
>
> 1. Accidents - Prevention.
>
> Examines safety rules for travelling to school, on the playground, and in the school. Discusses traffic safety, bicycle safety and fire safety. Encourages viewers to spot safety mistakes and how to correct them.-

The Classified Catalogue

614.8
    Sécurité en hiver.
        prod. [Montreal?] : NFB, 1965.- dist. SEC 31 fr. : col. : 35 mm. & captions. $9.00 pj

        1. Accidents - Prevention. 2. Winter - Safety measures.

        Drawings in cartoon form provide information on winter safety. Covers traffic safety, such as not hitching a ride or playing on the road, natural ice safety such as testing thin ice and wearing hockey helmets, safety on skis and toboggans. Discusses dangers of icy steps and walks. English title available : WINTER SAFETY.-

614.8
    Small boat safety.
        prod. [Toronto] : Int. Cin., 1976.- dist. VEC 32 fr. : col. : 35 mm. & cassette (5 min.) : auto. & aud. adv. sig. & teacher's guide. $24.00 (Safety songs and stories : $130.00) pj

        1. Boats and boating - Safety measures.

        The do's and don'ts of small boat safety are explained through the use of cartoons, original words and music.-

614.8
    Swimming safety.
        prod. [Toronto] : Int. Cin., 1976.- dist. VEC 38 fr. : col. : 35 mm. & cassette (5 min.) : auto. & aud. adv. sig. & teacher's guide. $24.00 (Safety songs and stories : $130.00) pj

        1. Swimming - Safety measures.

        Using cartoons, (accompanied by original words and music) the artist illustrates how Calypso Kitty ignores water safety rules while at the beach and finds herself in very dangerous situations.-

614.8
    Techniques antinoyade.
        prod. [Toronto] : M-L, 1975.- dist. Sch. Ser. or Vint. 38 fr. : col. : 35 mm. & cassette (8 min.) : auto. & aud. adv. sig. & teacher's guide. $16.50 (Activités de plein air : survie : $85.00) i

        1. Swimming - Safety measures. 2. Artificial respiration.

        Step-by-step description of drownproofing, stressing conservation of energy, and relaxation. Also describes mouth-to-mouth resuscitation and Sylvester Method of artificial respiration stressing immediate and continuous action. Should be previewed by teacher before classroom use. English title available : WATER RESCUE.-

614.8
    Things dangerous to eat.
        prod. [Toronto, Ont.] : McI., 1977.- dist. McI. 26 fr. : col. : 35 mm. & cassette (8 min.) : auto. & aud. adv. sig. & teacher's manual. $19.00 (Sam Slice tells the story of food : $95.00) pj

        1. Accidents - Preventions. 2. Poisons.

        Shows the dangers of tasting unknown things such as pills, cleaning materials, insecticides, etc. Also presents words, POISON, DANGER, CAUTION, and symbols that might appear on dangerous products.-

614.8
    Think safety.
        prod. [Toronto] : M-L, 1970.- dist. Sch. Ser. or Vint. 46 fr. : col. : 35 mm. & cassette (10 min.) : auto. & aud. adv. sig. & teacher's guide. $16.50 (Shop safety : $85.00) is

        1. Machine shop practice - Safety measures.

        Examines the proper safety attitude in a shop. Discusses working defensively, practising tidiness, using the correct tools and material for the situation. Points out importance of planning ahead and wearing protective clothing. French title available : PENSEZ "SECURITE".-

The Classified Catalogue

614.8
    Traffic safety.
        prod. [Toronto] : M-L, 1974.- dist. Sch. Ser. or Vint. 55 fr. : col. : 35 mm. & cassette (8 min.) : auto. & aud. adv. sig. & teacher's guide. $16.50 (Safety : a way of life : $65.00) pj

        1. Accidents - Prevention. 2. Bicycles and bicycling - Safety measures.

        A discussion of safety rules and accident prevention on the street. Examines bicycle safety. Photographs and sound track encourage viewers to spot the traffic safety errors. Reviews the mistakes and corrects them.-

614.8
    Transit safety.
        prod. [Toronto] : M-L, 1974.- dist. Sch. Ser. or Vint. 54 fr. : col. : 35 mm. & cassette (7 min.) : auto. & aud. adv. sig. & teacher's guide. $16.50 (Safety : a way of life : $65.00) pj

        1. Accidents - Prevention.

        An examination of safe behavior when using public transportation. Includes a discussion of safety on the subway, reviewing safety mistakes and how to correct them.-

614.8
    Water rescue.
        prod. [Toronto] : M-L, 1974.- dist. Sch. Ser. or Vint. 38 fr. : col. : 35 mm. & cassette (7 min.) : auto. & aud. adv. sig. & teacher's guide. $16.50 (Outdoor survival : $85.00) j

        1. Swimming - Safety measures. 2. Artificial respiration.

        Step-by-step description of drownproofing, stressing conservation of energy, and relaxation. Also describes mouth-to-mouth resuscitation and Sylvester method of artificial respiration stressing immediate and continuous action. Should be previewed by a teacher before classroom use. French title available : TECHNIQUES ANTIOYADE.-

614.8
    Water safety.
        prod. [Montreal?] : NFB, 1966.- dist. McI. 32 fr. : col. : 35 mm. & captions. $9.00 pj

        1. Swimming - Safety measures.

        A cartoon character, Rusty the Mechanical Boy, is used to portray the danger of some swimming situations. Pool, river, and beach swimming are covered separately. Each frame is captioned with a question to answer regarding dangerous or correct behaviour.-

614.8
    Winter safety.
        prod. [Montreal?] : NFB, 1965.- dist. McI. 31 fr. : col. : 35 mm. & captions. $9.00 pj

        1. Accidents - Prevention. 2. Winter - Safety measures.

        Drawings in cartoon form provide information on winter safety. Covers traffic safety, such as not hitching a ride or playing on the road, natural ice safety, such as testing thin ice and wearing hockey helmets, safety on skis and toboggans. Discusses dangers of icy steps and walks. French title available : SECURITE EN HIVER.-

615
    Amphetamines and barbiturates.
        prod. [Montreal?] : NFB, 1972.- dist. McI. 40 fr. : col. : 35 mm. & captions. $9.00 is

        1. Amphetamines. 2. Barbiturates.

        Produced in collaboration with Addiction Research Foundation, this deals with the effects, medical uses, dependency, potential withdrawal symptoms, and legality of the two drugs. Part of a multi-media kit titled "Drugs and the human body". French title available : AMPHETAMINES BARBITURIQUES.-

615
    Les amphétamines et les barbituriques.
        prod. [Montreal?] : NFB, 1972.- dist. SEC 48 fr. : col. : 35 mm. & captions. $9.00 is

        1. Amphetamines. 2. Barbiturates.

        Produced in collaboration with Addiction Research Foundation, this deals with the effects, medical uses, dependency, potential withdrawal symptoms, and legability of the two drugs. Part of a multi-media kit titled "Les drogues et les corps humain". English title available : AMPHETAMINES AND BARBITURATES.-

615

How people misuse them.
  prod. [Toronto] : M-L, 1974.- dist. Sch. Ser. or Wint. 52 fr. : col. : 35 mm. & cassette (8 min.) : auto. & aud. adv. sig. & teacher's guide. $16.50 (Drugs, medicines, and you : $75.00) j

1. Drugs.

A drug store scene between a pharmacist and his young part-time assistant provides information on drug misuse by careless people. Cites examples of misuse of headache and sleeping pills, cough medicines, and continual use of drugs, without consulting a doctor. Also warns against sharing prescribed drugs with another individual.-

615

LSD.
  prod. [Montreal?] : NFB, 1972.- dist. McI. 37 fr. : col. : 35 mm. & captions. $9.00 is

1. Lysergic acid diethylamide.

Cartoon drawings are used in this discussion of the drug : its chemical make-up, the legal penalties for possessing, trafficking, or making it, and the physical and psychological effects from taking it. Explains factors that may change the effects of LSD, such as amount, mood, previous experience, and purity of the drug. Discussion points are included in the filmstrip. Part of a multi-media kit title "Drugs and the human body". French title available : LSD.-

615

LSD.
  prod. [Montreal?] : NFB, 1972.- dist. SEC 44 fr. : col. : 35 mm. & captions. $9.00 is

1. Lysergic acid diethylamide.

Cartoon drawings are used in this discussion of the drug: its chemical make-up, the legal penalties for possessing, trafficking, or making it, and the physical and psychological effects from taking it. Explains factors that may change the effect of LSD, such as amount, mood, previous experience, and purity of the drug. Discussion points are included in the filmstrip. Part of a multi-media kit titled "Les drogues et le corps humain." English title available : LSD.-

615

La marijuana : quelques vérités.
  prod. [Montreal?] : NFB, 1972.- dist. SEC 58 fr. : col. : 35 mm. & cassette (12 min.) : auto. & aud. adv. sig. $18.00 is

1. Marihuana.

Photograhs show the plant, its habitat, history and uses. Cartoons provide good coverage of the physical, social and emotional reasons for the drug's use, its known effect on the human body, as well as its legal aspects. Part of a multi-media kit titled "Les drogues et le corps humain". English title available : SOME KNOWN FACTS ABOUT MARIJUANA.-

615

Opiates.
  prod. [Montreal?] : NFB, 1973.- dist. McI. 40 fr. : b&w & col. : 35 mm. & captions. $9.00 is

1. Narcotics. 2. Narcotic habit.

Discusses history and use of opium, morphine, codeine, and heroin for treatment of severe pain. Shows the misuse of opiates by sniffing or injecting them to get "high" and possible effects, such as death, malnutrition, hepatitis, and drug use are discussed. Photographs and cartoon drawings. Part of a multi-media kit titled "Drugs and the human body". French title available : LES STUPEFIANTS OPIACES.-

615

Les stupéfiants opiacés.
  prod. [Montreal?] : NFB, 1973.- dist. SEC 46 fr. : col. : 35 mm. & captions. $9.00 is

1. Narcotics. 2. Narcotic habit.

Discusses history and use of opium, codeine, and heroin for treatment of severe pain. Shows the misuse of opiates by sniffing or injecting them to get "high" and possible effects, such as death, malnutrition, hepatitis, and drug dependence. Legal problems of drug use are discussed. Photographs and cartoon drawings. Part of a multi-media kit titled "Les drogues et le corps humain". English title available : OPIATES.-

The Classified Catalogue

615
    Using them safely.
        prod. [Toronto] : M-L, 1974.- dist. Sch. Ser. or Vint. 57 fr. : col. : 35 mm. & cassette (10 min.) : auto. & aud. adv. sig. & teacher's guide. $16.50 (Drugs, medicines, and you : $75.00) j

        1. Drugs - Safety measures.

        A discussion of safety precautions taken by drug manufacturers, doctors, and pharmacists to protect consumers of prescription and non-prescription drugs and medicines. Illustrates a family situation where the user of a prescription allows the drug to fall into the hands of a young child. Emphasizes the rules of safety, such as accurate reading of directions and storage in a safe place.-

615
    What they do.
        prod. [Toronto] : M-L, 1974.- dist. Sch. Ser. or Vint. 55 fr. : col. : 35 mm. & cassette (10 min.) : auto. & aud. adv. sig. & teacher's guide. $16.50 (Drugs, medicines, and you : $75.00) j

        1. Drugs.

        Introduces and describes drugs and medicines that combine with the natural resources of the body to fight disease. Uses photographs and diagrams to explain local and general anaesthetics, vaccines, antihistamines, and antiseptics. Indicates how each drug relieves pain in the body and its effect on brain activity.-

615
    Where they come from.
        prod. [Toronto] : M-L, 1974.- dist. Sch. Ser. or Vint. 65 fr. : col. : 35 mm. & cassette (10 min.) : auto. & aud. adv. sig. & teacher's guide. $16.50 (Drugs, medicines, and you : $75.00) j

        1. Drugs.

        Identifies healing properties inherent in natural substances from the environment and from animals, which are used in preparation of drugs and medicines. Photographs show how natural substances, such as seaweed and petroleum are refined and used to treat, cure or prevent disease. Cites use of animal secretions in man's use of insulin. Explains how the development of man-made synthetics has guaranteed a sufficent quantity of drugs to the consumer.-

616.9
    About V.D. - gonorrhea.
        prod. [Montreal?] : NFB, 1974.- dist. McI. 66 fr. : col. : 35 mm. & captions. $9.00 (Sex education : $45.00) is

        1. Gonorrhea.

        Stylized graphics show how gonorrhea is contracted, the specific symptoms in men as contrasted with those in women, how the disease spreads, and the damage that can occur if treatment is delayed. For group use by a teacher or sex education instructor.-

616.9
    About V.D. - syphilis.
        prod. [Montreal?] : NFB, 1974.- dist. McI. 57 fr. : col. : 35 mm. & captions. $9.00 (Sex education : $45.00) is

        1. Syphilis.

        Stylized graphics are used to explain how the disease is contracted, symptoms as the disease progresses, and the ultimate damage to heart and nnervous system if not treated at an early stage. For classroom use as a teaching aid for sex education teacher.-

616.9
    The History of venereal disease.
        prod. [Toronto] : M-L, 1974.- dist. Sch. Ser. or Vint. 52 fr. : col. : 35 mm. & cassette (11 min.) : auto. & aud. adv. sig. & teacher's guide. $16.50 (Venereal disease : what I need to know : $85.00) is

        1. Venereal diseases - History.

        Traces existance of V.D. from earliest times, naming famous people through the ages believed to have been victims of this disease. Covers probable origins of disease, and contracts early cures and remedies with modern clinical diagnosis and antibiotics. Suggests combating increasing incidence of V.D. with informal discussion of the facts. Illustrated with photos, diagrams, and sketches.-

The Classified Catalogue

616.9
    The Facts about venereal disease.
       prod. [Montreal?] : NFB, 1967.- dist. McI. 40 fr. : col. : 35 mm. & cassette (12 min.) : auto. & aud. ad. sig. $9.00 is

       1. Venereal diseases.

       Cartoon drawings, photographs, and diagrams present the facts about syphilis and gonorrhea. Discusses the transmission, its symptoms and its effects. stresses that early treatment is essential.-

617.6
    Awareness of dental problems.
       prod. [Toronto] : B&R, 1973.- dist. B&R 28 fr. : col. : 35 mm. & cassette (9 min.) : auto. & aud. adv. sig. & teacher's manual & reading script. $18.00 (Preventive dental health : $72.00) jis

       1. Teeth - Care and treatment.

       Photos supplemented with some cartoon-style drawings are used to identify gum disease, plaque, and decay. The inteeraction of saliva, plaque and sugar is shown as the cause of decay.-

617.6
    Dental aids and trends in dentistry.
       prod. [Toronto] : B & R, 1973.- dist. B & R 1 filmstrip : col. : 35 mm. & cassette (16 min,) : auto. & aud. adv. sig. $10.00 (Preventive dental health : $72.00) jis

       1. Teeth - Care and treatment.

       Covers the pros and cons of a variety of dental health aids, including electric toothbrushes, water irrigators and piks, mouthwashes and toothpaste. and stimudents. New trends in dentistry and the history and benefits of fluoridation are discussed.-

617.6
    Details of brushing, disclosing & flossing.
       prod. [Toronto] : B&R, 1973.- dist. B&R 27 fr. : col. : 35 mm. & cassette (9 min.) : auto. & aud. sig. & teacher's manual & reading script. $18.00 (Preventive dental health : $72.00) jis

       1. Teeth - Care and treatment.

       The characteristics of an acceptable toothbrush, the target areas and proper techniques for brushing are illustrated. The use of disclosure tablets (dyes) to reveal the location of plaque on teeth is discussed as an aid to thorough brushing and flossing.-

617.6
    Flossing vs. gum disease.
       prod. [Toronto] : B&R, 1973.- dist. B&R 30 fr. : col. : 35 mm. & cassette (9 min.) : auto. & aud. adv. sig. & teacher's manual & reading script. $18.00 (Preventive dental health : $72.00) jis

       1. Teeth - Care and treatment.

       Illustrates the details of correct flossing procedures. Gingivitis and pyorrhea or periodontitus are shown, and healthy and diseased gums compared.-

617.6
    Summary and conclusion.
       prod. [Toronto] : B&R, 1973.- dist. B&R 23 fr. : col. : 35 mm. & cassette (7 min.) : auto. & aud. adv. sig. & teacher's manual, & reading script. $18.00 (Preventive dental health : $72.00) jis

       1. Teeth - Care and treatment.

       Reviews the role of the dental hygienist, the importance of checkups and home care, and the significance of health gums and teeth to personal appearance.-

The Classified Catalogue

617.6
    Teeth : anew look.
        prod. [Toronto] : M-L, 1973.- dist. Sch. Ser. or Vint. 42 fr. : col. : 35 mm. & cassette (5 min.) : auto. & aud. adv. sig. & teacher's guide. $16.50 (Health : a new look : $65.00) p

    1. Teeth - Care and treatment.

    Uses photographs and drawings to explain the reasons for brushing teeth. Shows germs at work that cause tooth decay and explains in detail the proper way to brush teeth.-

621.3
    Sources of electricity.
        prod. [Toronto] : M-L, 1973.- dist. Sch. Ser. or Vint. 50 fr. : col. : 35 mm. & cassette (10 min.) : auto. & aud. adv. sig. & teacher's guide. $16.50 (Principles of electricity : $75.00) ji

    1. Electric batteries. 2. Electric generators. 3. Electric meters.

    The structure and principles of common electrical sources are depicted. Through simple experiments, students are introduced to the wet and dry cell battery, the electric generator, thermocouple and photocell, the ammeter and galvanometer. Some knowledge of basic electricity is necessary.-

621.31
    Current and pressure.
        prod. [Toronto] : M-L, 1973.- dist. Sch. Ser. or Vint. 41 fr. : col. : 35 mm. & cassette (8 min.) : auto. & aud. adv. sig. & teacher's guide. $16.50 (Principles of electricity : $75.00) ji

    1. Electric currents. 2. Electric circuits. 3. Electric lighting.

    The flow of electrons is explained using the analogy of water current. Demonstrates the use of a voltmeter and ammeter in measuring voltage and current. Demonstrates the principles of an electric light bulb and switch. Series and parallel circuits are explained.-

621.31
    Electrical energy.
        prod. [Toronto] : M-L, 1974.- dist. Sch. Ser. or Vint. 54 fr. : col. : 35 mm. & cassette (12 min.) : auto. & aud. adv. sig. & teacher's guide. $16.50 (Energy : crisis and resolution : $85.00) i

    1. Electric power.

    A detailed look at electricity, and the various ways in which it is generated. Uses photography and diagrams to examine the increasing demand for electricity, the scarcity of fossil fuels, and the danger to the environment caused by the present methods of production.-

621.310971
    Electrical energy in Canada.
        prod. [Montreal?] : NFB, 1974.- dist. Mcl. 50 fr. : b&w & col. : 35 mm. & captions. $9.00 ji

    1. Electric power.

    Sources of electrical energy in Canada and location of generating stations. Points out advantages and disadvantages of its use. Ranks use in Canada with use in other countries.-

621.319
    Domestic circuits.
        prod. [Toronto] : M-L, 1974.- dist. Sch. Ser. or Vint. 64 fr. : col. : 35 mm. & cassette (9 min.) : auto. & aud. adv. sig. & teacher's guide. $16.50 (Applications of electricity : $75.00) s

    1. Electric circuits. 2. Electric conductors.

    Discusses electrical conductors, receptacles, and fixture circuits. Close-up photography shows correct installation procedures. Includes two references to non-metric measurements.-

621.3815
    Application of the vacuum tube.
        prod. [Toronto] : M-L, 1974.- dist. Sch. Ser. or Vint. 63 fr. : col. : 35 mm. & cassette (8 min.) : auto. & aud. adv. sig. & teacher's guide. $16.50 (Electronics : $85.00) s

    1. Vacuum tubes.-

    Illustrations and photographs show practical applications of vacuum tubes. Demonstrates amplification using a triode tube circuit. Also includes multiple grid tubes and their functions.-

The Classified Catalogue

621.3815
    The Development of the vacuum tube.
        prod. [Toronto] : M-L, 41974.- dist. Sch. Ser. or Vint. 60 fr. : col. : 35 mm. & cassette (9 min.) : auto. & aud. adv. sig. & teacher's guide. $16.50 (Electronics : $85.00) s

        1. Vacuum tubes.

    Outlines the development of vacuum tubes from Edison's experiments to contemporary types. Discusses functions, using diode tube and twin diode circuits as examples. Explains diode, tetrode and pentode. Illustrated by photographs, diagrams.-

621.3815
    The Transistor.
        prod. [Toronto] : M-L, 1974.- dist. Sch. Ser. or Vint. 53 fr. : col. : 35 mm. & cassette (9 min.) : auto. & aud. adv. sig. & teacher's guide. $16.50 (Electronics : $85.00) s

        1. Transistors.

    Presents transistor as a smaller version of vacuum tube and discusses functions and advantages. Explains electronic principles behind operation, such as N & P type materials. Also includes transistor amplification, forward and reverse bias. Photographs, diagrams included.-

621.3815
    Transistor application.
        prod. [Toronto] : M-L, 1974.- dist. Sch. Ser. or Vint. 50 fr. : col. : 35 mm. & cassette (10 min.) : auto. & aud. adv. sig. & teacher's guide. $16.50 (Electronics : $85.00) s

        1. Transistors.

    Traces development and improvement of transistors and their application. Shows types of transistors and use in radio, television and stereo equipment. Discusses major functions, such as amplification, and defines terminology. Illustrated with photographs and drawings.-

621.3841
    Basic radio circuitry.
        prod. [Toronto] : M-L, 1974.- dist. Sch. Ser. or Vint. 67 fr. : col. : 35 mm. & cassette (8 min.) : auto. & aud. adv. sig. & teacher's guide. $16.50 (Electronics : $85.00) s

        1. Radio - Receivers and reception.
        2. Electronics.

    Examines the various circuits of radio receiver identifying five components of each. Follows a radio signal from the station to receiver, explaining how transmitted and received. Shows function of transformer, frequency and amplifier. Drawings and photographs illustrate.-

621.388
    The Television receiver.
        prod. [Toronto] : M-L, 1974.- dist. Sch. Ser. or Vint. 70 fr. : col. : 35 mm. & cassete (10 min.) : auto. & aud. adv. sig. & teacher's guide. $16.50 (Electronics : $85.00) s

        1. Television - Receivers and reception.
        2. Electronics.

    A clear explanation of television electronics. Coloured diagrams and photographs demonstrate a receiver dividing signals from a station into sound and picture for television viewing. Shows picture tube components and controlling horizontal and vertical deflection.-

621.48
    Nuclear energy.
        prod. [Toronto] : M-L, 1974.- dist. Sch. Ser. or Vint. 47 fr. : col. : 35 mm. & cassette (11 min.) : auto. & aud. adv. sig. & teacher's guide. $16.50 (Energy : crisis and resolution : $85.00) i

        1. Atomic energy.

    Examines the creation of nuclear energy and how man has learned to harness its power. Demonstrates, through photographs and diagrams, how the power can be put to use. Examines the advantages of nuclear energy as well as the dangers and how they can be controlled.-

621.9
Chuckwork on the lathe.
   prod. [Toronto] : M-L, 1973.- dist. Sch. Ser.
   or Vint. 42 fr. : col. : 35 mm. & cassette
   (11 min.) : auto. & aud. adv. sig. & teacher's
   guide. $16.50 (Metalwork : machine
   operations : $75.00) is

   1. Lathes.

   A concise step-by-step demonstration of an
   engine lathe and the lathe chuck. Identifies
   all parts of the machinery and how to use
   them, stressing necessary safety precautions.
   Using a metal toothpick holder as an
   example, it discusses how to plan a project,
   prepare the machine for it, concluding with
   polishing and filing.-

621.9
Drill presses and lathes.
   prod. [Toronto] : M-L, 1970.- dist. Sch. Ser.
   or Vint. 47 fr. : col. : 35 mm. & cassette
   (13 min.) : auto. & aud. adv. sig. & teacher's
   guide. $16.50 (Shop safety : $85.00) is

   1. Drill presses. 2. Lathes.

   Describes the safe use of the drill press
   and protective clothing required. Points out
   the use of correct bit sizes for the specific
   cutting speed and need for checking table
   adjustments. Explains correct way to set up
   a wood or metal lathe and how to make
   adjustments when the machine is stopped.
   French title available : FOREUSE SUR COLONNE
   ET TOUR.-

621.9
Foreuse sur colonne et tour.
   prod. [Toronto] : M-L, 1972.- dist. Sch. Ser.
   or Vint. 47 fr. : col. : 35 mm. & cassette
   (13 min.) : auto. & aud. adv. sig. & teacher's
   guide. $16.50 (Sécurité dans l'atelier :
   $85.00) is

   1. Drill presses. 2. Lathes.

   Describes the safe use of the drill press
   and protective clothing required. Points out
   the use of correct bit sizes for the specific
   cutting speed and need for checking table
   adjustments. Explains correct way to set up
   a wood or metal lathe and how to make
   adjustments when the machine is stopped.
   English title available : DRILL PRESSES AND
   LATHES.-

621.9
Forming metal by machine.
   prod. [Toronto] : M-L, 1973.- dist. Sch. Ser.
   or Vint. 43 fr. : col. : 35 mm. & cassette
   (7 min.) : auto. & aud. adv. sig. & teacher's
   guide. $16.50 (Metalwork : machine operation
   : $75.00) is

   1. Metalworking machinery. 2. Metalwork.

   Features forming machines used to bend
   metals into shape. Demonstrates use of
   adjustable bar folder, standard hand brake,
   box and hand brake, and slip roll former.
   Explains parts of each machine and functions
   by showing formation of a metal box. The
   photographs illustrate positioning work, making
   a hem, curving and rolling metal. Also
   discusses safety standards and metals to
   use on these machines.-

621.9
Grinders, routers, power saws & jointers.
   prod. [Toronto] : M-L, 1970.- dist. Sch. Ser.
   or Vint. 49 fr. : col. : 35 mm. & cassette
   (12 min.) : auto. & aud. adv. sig. & teacher's
   guide. $16.50 (Shop safety : $85.00) is

   1. Power tools - Safety measures.

   Examines the safe procedure for using power
   tools. Points out importance of being familiar
   with the tool, wearing protective clothing,
   and not overloading the tool with excessive
   pressure. Discusses details of using a
   grinder, router, jigsaw, bandsaw, circular saw,
   and jointer. French title available : MEULES,
   TOUPIES, SCIES ELECTRIQUES ET CORROYEURS.-

621.9
Hand saws, chisels and files.
   prod. [Toronto] : M-L, 1970.- dist. Sch. Ser.
   or Vint. 49 fr. : col. : 35 mm. & cassette
   (11 min.) : auto. & aud. adv. sig. & teacher's
   guide. $16.50 (Shop safety : $85.00) is

   1. Saws. 2. Chisels. 3. Files.

   Describes the safety rules for all sharp
   hand tools. Points out in detail how to keep
   one's hands behind the cutting edge, keeping
   edges sharp, and replacing broken handles,
   and replacing worn files. Stresses use of a
   vice and how to handle all tools with care.
   French title available : SCIES A MAIN, CISEAUX
   ET LIMES.-

The Classified Catalogue

621.9
    Meules, toupies, scies éléctriques, et corroyeurs.
        prod. [Toronto] : M-L, 1972.- dist. Sch. Ser. or Vint. 49 fr. : col. : 35 mm. & cassette (12 min.) : auto. & aud. adv. sig. & teacher's guide. $16.50 (Sécurité dans l'atelier : $85.00) is

        1. Power tools - Safety measures.

        Examines the safe procedure for using power tools. Points out importance of being familiar with the tool, wearing protective clothing, and not overloading the tool with excessive pressure. Discusse details of using a grinder, router, jigsaw, bandsaw, circlar saw, and jointer. English title available : GRINDERS, ROUTERS, POWER SAWS & JOINTERS.-

621.9
    Scies à main, ciseaux et limes.
        prod. [Toronto] : M-L, 1972.- dist. Sch. Ser. or Vint. 49 fr. : col. : 35 mm. & cassette (11 min.) : auto. & aud. adv. sig. & teacher's guide. $16.50 (Sécurité dans l'atelier : $85.00) is

        1. Saws. 2. Chisels. 3. Files.

        Describes the safety rules for all sharp hand tools. Points out in detail how to keep one's hands behind the cutting edge, keeping edges sharp, replacing broken handles, and replacing worn files. Stresses use of a vice and how to handle all tools with care. English title available : HAND SAWS, CHISELS AND FILES.-

621.9
    Scraping tools and abrasives.
        prod. [Toronto] : M-L, 1973.- dist. Sch. Ser. or Vint. 43 fr. : col. : 35 mm. & cassette (8 min.) : auto. & aud. adv. sig. & teacher's guide. $16.50 (Woodworking : hand tools (A) : $85.00) is

        1. Cabinet scrapers. 2. Hand scrapers. 3. Wood finishing.

        Detailed coverage of tools used to give a fine finish. Discusses the use of the cabinet scraper, the hand scraper, and sandpaper. Includes a demonstration of sharpening a scraper, and steaming a dent out of the wood.-

621.9
    Screwdrivers, wrenches, sheet metal, & welding.
        prod. [Toronto] : M-L, 1970.- dist. Sch. Ser. or Vint. 48 fr. : col. : 35 mm. & cassette (6 min.) : auto. & aud. adv. sig. & teacher's guide. $16.50 (Shop safety : $85.00) is

        1. Screwdrivers. 2. Wrenches.
        3. Sheet-metal work - Safety measures.

        Demonstrates the use of the correct screwdriver, stressing the importance of proper screw and wrench sizes. Examines safety rules for handling sheet metal, using vice grips, wearing gloves, and concentrating on the task. Points out the need for care when using flame and heat for welding. French title available : TOURNEVIS, CLEFS, TOLE ET SOUDURE.-

621.9
    Tournevis, clefs, tôle et soudure.
        prod. [Toronto] : M-L, 1972.- dist. Sch. Ser. or Vint. 48 fr. : col. : 35 mm. & cassette (11 min.) : auto. & aud. adv. sig. & teacher's guide. $16.50 (Sécurité dans l'atelier : $85.00) is

        1. Screwdrivers. 2. Wrenches.
        3. Sheet-metal work - Safety measures.

        Demonstrates the use of the correct screwdriver, stressing the importance of choosing proper screw and wrench sizes. Examines safety rules for handling sheet metal, using vice grips, wearing gloves, and concentrating on the task. Points out the need for care when using flame and heat for welding. English title available : SCREWDRIVERS, WRENCHES, SHEET METAL, & WELDING.-

621.9
    Using the drill press.
        prod. [Toronto] : M-L, 1973.- dist. Sch. Ser. or Vint. 49 fr. : col. : 35 mm. & cassette (10 min.) : auto. & aud. adv. sig. & teacher's guide. $16.50 (Metalwork : machine operation : $75.00) is

        1. Drill presses.

        An introduction to the basic parts and functions of the drill press, such as the belt and pulley system and various types of drill bits. Shows how to prepare work for layout, measuring and marking hole positions, adjusting and drilling blind holes. Also discusses safety precautions for operation of the drill press.-

The Classified Catalogue

621.9
    Working between centers on the lathe.
      prod. [Toronto] : M-L, 1973.- dist. Sch. Ser. or Vint. 54 fr. : col. : 35 mm. & cassette (10 min.) : auto. & aud. adv. sig. & teacher's guide. $16.50 (Metalwork : machine operation : $75.00) is

      1. Lathes. 2. Metalwork.

    Demonstrates the many results produced by working between centers on a machine lathe. Close-up photography accompanies clear explanations on setting up work on the lathe, centre drilling, turning, tapering, knurling, filing and polishing. Explains use of tools centre punch and drill press. Includes instructions on proper care of the lathe and tools.-

622
    Asbestos mining in Quebec.
      prod. [Stratford, Ont.] : Sch. Ch., 1974.- dist. Sch. Ch. 44 fr. : col. : 35 mm. & captions. $7.95 (Mining and processing in Canada : $39.75) ji

      1. Asbestos mines and mining.

    The process of asbestos mining, featuring photographs taken in Quebec mining towns. Aspects covered are: identification, uses, open pit mining, ore removal and processing. Also features a comparison of old mining methods with modern methods and machinery, using old photographs as illustrations.-

622
    Coal mining in Canada.
      prod. [Montreal?] : NFB, 1974.- dist. McI. 71 fr. : b&w & col. : 35 mm. & captions. $9.00 ji

      1. Coal mines and mining.

    A comprehensive treatment of coal in Canada. Traces factors influencing the growth of coal mining - expansion of railways and industry, need for power and a profitable export. Describes locations of coal mines, methods of mining, problems and solutions in transportation, and environment considerations. Includes maps, graphs, artwork, archival photographs.-

622
    Gold refining in Ontario.
      prod. [Stratford, Ont.] : Sch. Ch., 1974.- dist. Sch. Ch. 43 fr. : col. : 35 mm. & captions. $7.95 (Mining and processing in Canada : $39.75) ji

      1. Gold mines and mining.

    Explains the mining of gold, the preliminary processing stages to remove impurities, the final stages and the different procedures at the Royal Canadian Mint to achieve the ultimate perfect product.-

622
    Nickel mining in Manitoba.
      prod.]Winnipeg] : VCL, 1972.- dist. Sch. Ch. 47 fr. : col. : 35 mm. & captions. $7.95 (Mining and processing in Canada : $39.75) ji

      1. Nickel mines and mining.

    Photographs of an actual mine in Manitoba complement this presentation on mining and refining nickel. Discusses special clothing designed for miners, various sections of a mine, use of explosives, and refining of the metal where it is poured into moulds, cut, shaped, and boxed for shipping.-

622
    Uranium mining in Ontario.
      prod. [Stratford, Ont.] : Sch. Ch., 1977.- dist. Sch. Ch. 42 fr. : col. : 35 mm. & captions. $7.95 (Mining and processing in Canada : $39.75) ji

      1. Uranium mines and mining.

    Photographs taken at Denison Mines at Elliot Lake trace mining of uranium ore from when it is first located to its use as atomic energy fuel. Covers blasting, crushing and making slurry. Also shows machines and chemicals used to convert ore for fuel.-

The Classified Catalogue

629.132
    Aéronautique élémentaire.
        prod. [Montreal?] : NFB, made 1964 : 1966.- dist. SEC 29 fr. : col. : 35 mm. & captions. $9.00 ji

1. Aeronautics.

Uses drawings and diagrams to examine the basic principles of flight. Illustrates the relationship between the weight of the aircraft, the upward force of the air, and the speed of the aircraft. Discusses thrust versus drag and significance of aircraft shape. English title available : BASIC PRINCIPLES OF FLIGHT.-

629.132
    Basic principles of flight.
        prod. [Montreal?] : NFB, 1964.- dist. McI. 29 fr. : col. : 35 mm. & captions. $9.00 ji

1. Aeronautics.

Uses drawings and diagrams to examine the basic principles of flight. Illustrates the relationship between the weight of the aircraft, the upward force of the air, and the speed of the aircraft. Discusses thrust versus drag and significance of aircraft shape. French title available : AERONAUTIQUE ELEMENTAIRE.-

629.133
    Identifying airplanes.
        prod. [Scarborough, Ont.] : R.B.M., 1976.- dist. ETHOS 54 fr. : col. : 35 mm. & cassette (10 min.) : auto. & aud. adv. sig. & teacher's manual. $19.00 (Transportation in Canada) ji

1. Airplanes - Identification.

Outlines the details to watch for when trying to identify airplanes. Photographs of a variety of airplanes are shown, including a DC-8, DC-3, Otter, Cessna 206, and Piper "Cub".-

629.133074
    Airshows in Canada.
        prod. [Scarborough, Ont.] : R.B.M., 1976.- dist. ETHOS 46 fr. : col. : 35 mm. & cassette (9 min.) : auto. & aud. adv. sig. & teacher's manual. $19.00 (Transportation in Canada) ji

1. Airplanes - Exhibitions. 2. Canadian Warplane Heritage.

A visit to the Canadian Warplane Heritage airshow held in Hamilton, Ontario. Photographs show a variety of rare and historically valuable airplanes including a replica of the Nieuport 17, an AVRO CF-100, Grumman F3F "Wildcats", and a "Fairly Firefly".-

629.135
    Aircraft in motion.
        prod. [Montreal?] : NFB, made 1964 : 1975.- dist. McI. 24 fr. : col. : 35 mm. & captions. $9.00 j

1. Aeronautics.

Describes the parts of an aircraft that are used to control its movements in flight. Very specific teacher guidance is necessary for effective use..-

629.22
    Care of wheels and tires.
        prod. [Toronto] : M-L, 1973.- dist. Sch. Ser. or Wint. 63 fr. : col. : 35 mm. & cassette (11 min.) : auto. & aud. adv. sig. & teacher's guide. $16.50 (Auto mechanics : $75.00) is

1. Wheels - Care and treatment.

Construction, care and maintenance of tires, wheels, hubs and rims. Demonstrates removal and replacement of all parts. Covers tire rotation, lubrication and adjustment of front wheel bearings. Emphasizes safety precautions and care of tools.-

The Classified Catalogue

629.22
Driving mechanism.
    prod. [Toronto] : M-L, 1973.- dist. Sch. Ser. or Vint. 51 fr. : col. : 35mm & cassette (10 min.) : auto. & aud. adv. sig. & teacher's guide. $16.50 (Auto mechanics : $75.00) is

1. Automobiles - Transmission devices.

Easy to follow introduction to major units of drive train and operation of each. Thorough explanation of single plate dry disc clutch and standard manual and three speed transmission. Photographs of actual mechanism in car and diagrams accompany demonstrations of power transfer from engine to wheels.-

629.22
Pistons, oil and and fuel pumps.
    prod. [Toronto] : M-L, 1973.- dist. Sch. Ser. or Vint. 61 fr. : col. : 35 mm. & cassette (13 min.) : auto. & aud. adv. sig. & teacher's guide. $16.50 (Auto mechanics : $75.00) is

1. Automobiles - Engines.

Function and operation of fuel pump, rotor type oil and gear type oil pumps. Shows assembly and disassembly of oil pumps and piston removal and replacement. Parts are removed from car, photographed and discussed individually. Detailed explanation of how fuel and oil are pumped to engine.-

629.22074
Antique cars.
    prod. [Scarborough, Ont.] : R.B.M., 1976.- dist. ETHOS 49 fr. : b&w & col. : 35 mm. & reading script. $19.00 (Facts on Canada) pj

1. Automobiles - Exhibitions.

Uses photographs to present some of the many unusual models of the first "horseless carriages" including a Pierce-Arrow, a Cord, and a Model T. Concludes with a visit to a collectors' meet, illustrating the exhibits and activities of the competitors.-

629.45
Explorations lunaires.
    prod. [Toronto] : M-L, 1975.- dist. Sch. Ser. or Vint. 38 fr. : col. : 35 mm. & cassette (4 min.) : auto. & aud. adv. sig. & teacher's guide. $16.50 (Les Saisons, la terre, l'espace : $75.00) p

1. Moon - Exploration. 2. Astronomy - History.

Traces the history of astronomy and telescopes, and examines the space exploration programme. Illustrated with actual moon photographs, and drawings. English title available : MOON EXPLORATION.-

629.45
Moon exploration.
    prod. [Toronto] : M-L, 1973.- dist. Sch. Ser. or Vint. 38 fr. : col. : 35 mm. & cassette (7 min.) : auto. & aud. adv. sig. & teacher's guide. $16.50 (Learning about science : $75.00) p

1. Moon - Exploration. 2. Astronomy - History.

Traces the history of astronomy and telescopes, and examines the space exploration programme. Illustrated with actual moon photographs, and drawings. French title available : EXPLORATIONS LUNAIRES.-

630.1
Explorons la ferme.
    prod. [Montreal?] : NF.B, 1965.- dist. SEC 35 fr. : col. : 35 mm. & captions & teacher's manual. $9.00 p

1. Farm life.

Drawings illustrate many phases of farm life in all seasons of the year. Includes the work of a farm, the farm animals, and the wild animals. Machinery, plants and animals are identified in the notes. English title available : A VISIT TO A FARM.-

The Classified Catalogue

630.1
  A Visit to a farm.
   prod. [Montreal?] : NFB, 1965.- dist. McI. 30 fr. : col. : 35 mm. & captions & teacher's manual. $9.00 (Discovering life around us : $45.00) p

   1. Farm life.

   Drawings illustrate many phases of farm life in all the seasons of the year. Includes the work of a farm, the farm animals, and the wild animals. Machinery, plants, and animals are identified in the notes. French title available : EXPLORONS LA FERME.-

630.74
  The Canadian and World Plowing Match.
   prod. [Scarborough, Ont.] : R.B.M., 1975.- dist. ETHOS 50 fr. : col. : 35 mm. & cassette (8 min.) : auto. & aud. adv. sig. & teacher's manual. $19.00 (Special occasions and events) j

   1. Agriculture - Canada - Exhibitions.
   2. Canadian International Plowing Match.

   A glimpse of the variety of activities that take place during one of Canada's most important agricultural events. Shows old plowing techniques with draught animals, plus the latest in farm technology.-

630.74
  Royal Winter Fair.
   prod. [Scarborough, Ont.] : R.B.M., 1975.- dist. ETHOS 56 fr. : col. : 35 mm. & cassette (8 min.) : auto. & aud. adv. sig. & teacher's manual. $19.00 (Special occasions and events) j

   1. Agriculture - Canada - Exhibitions.
   2. Royal Agricultural Winter Fair.

   An overview of one of Canada's most important agricultural fairs held annually in Toronto. Includes photographs of opening nights, the live stock judging, and the Horse Show.-

630.74
  Royal Winter Fair.
   prod. [Stratford, Ont.] : Sch. Ch., 1975.- dist. Sch. Ch. 48 fr. : col. : 35 mm. & captions. $7.95 (Canadian studies) pj

   1. Royal Agricultural Winter Fair.
   2. Agriculture - Canada - Exhibitions.

   Presents animals, flower displays, and produce which make up the annual Royal Winter Fair in Toronto. Photographs of the livestock and animals judged during the Fair, show how they are displayed, bought and sold. Other parts of the Fair include the cars and farm machinery, and the Royal Horse Show.-

631
  Farm chores.
   prod. [Scarborough, Ont.] : FCC, 1976.- dist. FCC 10 fr. : col. : 35 mm. & cassette (7 min.) : auto. & aud. adv. sig. & reading script. $8.85 (Farm life : $35.40) p

   1. Farm life.

   A ten-frame filmstrip, with simple narration, points out such farm chores as collecting eggs, feeding farm animals, and gardening, with appropriate farmyard sounds as background. Flat filmstrip, cassette and printed material in clear vinyl 34 x 28 cm. envelope, designed for storage in filing cabinet.-

631.0951
  China 1 : food production.
   prod. [Don Mills, Ont.] : F&W, 1973.- dist. FW 25 fr. : col. : 35 mm. & captions & teacher's guide.- $7.20 (Man in his world) ji

   1. Agriculture - China.

   Highlights China's intensive system of land use, the meticulous care of the land, lack of mechanization, and the role of manual labour.-

The Classified Catalogue

631.0951
    Commune in the North.
        prod. [Kitchener, Ont.] : EDU, 1974.- dist. EDU 25 fr. : col. : 35 mm. & cassette (8 min.) : auto. & aud. adv. sig. & teacher's guide. $15.95 (China : $79.95) jis

        1. Agriculture - China. 2. Collective settlements - China.

        Describes the way of life in a Chinese commune, types of houses, and the primitive heating systems. Stresses importance of growing food for the large population. Discusses means of fertilization and irrigation, harvesting the crops both manually and mechanically, and the importance of the railway.-

631.0951
    Commune in the South.
        prod. [Kitchener, Ont.] : EDU, 1974.- dist. EDU 25 fr. : col. : 35 mm. & cassette (9 min.) : auto. & aud. adv. sig. & teacher's guide. $15.95 (China : $79.95) jis

        1. Agriculture - China. 2. Collective settlements - China.

        Explains methods for growing rice in rice paddies, and the use of the water buffalo and manual labour. Describe the effort taken in levelling the fields to grow and irrigate the crops. Discusses types of livestock raised and the shared activities of all members of the commune.-

631.0951
    Rural China.
        prod. [Toronto] : CFM, 1975.- dist. BAM 34 fr. : col. : 35 mm. & cassette (13 min.) : auto. & aud. adv. sig. & teacher's guide. $15.50 (China : $89.00) i

        1. Agriculture - China. 2. Collective settlements - China.

        A study of peasant life in rural China. Includes types of agriculture and life within a commune showing a school, hospital, typical home, styles of dress, and use of production teams. Illustrated with photographs taken on a fact-finding tour of China.-

631.0952
    Lowland agriculture in Japan.
        prod. [Hamilton, Ont.] : VCI, 1977.- dist. MHR 39 fr. : col. : 35 mm. & captions & teacher's guide. $12.85 (Japan : $72.00) j

        1. Agriculture - Japan.

        Describes the cultivation of food crops including rice, vegetables and small fruits on the few level Japanese plain sand valleys and illustrates the conflict between urban and rural land use typical of Japan today.-

631.0962
    Gifts of the Nile I : farming on the flood plains.
        prod. [Don Mills, Ont.] : F&V, 1973.- dist. FV 25 fr. : col. : 35 mm. & captions & teacher's guide.- $7.20 (Man in his world) ji

        1. Agriculture - Egypt. 2. Irrigation - Egypt. 3. Nile River.

        Explains how agriculture can survive in this barren land due to the existence of the Nile. The different irrigation methods used, the various kinds of crops, the people and their way of life are discussed. For classroom use.-

631.0971
    Farming in pioneer Canada.
        prod. [Stratford, Ont.] : Sch. Ch., 1977.- dist. Sch. Ch. 53 fr. : b&w & col. : 35 mm. & cassette (8 min.) : auto. & aud. adv. sig. $16.95 j

        1. Agriculture - Canada - History. 2. Farm life - Canada - History. 3. Frontier and pioneer life.

        A clear and detailed history of Canadian farming. Emphasizes how it has remained a family affair requiring team effort from the rural pioneer using primitive methods to what it is today-a-multi-faceted business enterprise with modern farm machinery. Authentic black and white and colour photographs are used with sound effects in the commentary.-

631.097127
    Mixed farming in Manitoba.
      prod. [Stratford, Ont.] : Sch. Ch., 1975.- dist. Sch. Ch.   42 fr. : b&w & col. : 35 mm. & captions. $7.95 (Agriculture in Canada : $55.65) ji

      1. Agriculture - Manitoba.

      The tradition of mixed farming in Manitoba by early Canadian pioneers to present day farming. Discusses raising of poultry, pigs, cattle, planting and harvesting of crops, and problems encountered in this type of farming.-

631.7
    Irrigated farming in Alberta.
      prod. [Stratford, Ont.] : Sch. Ch., 1975.- dist. Sch. Ch.   41 fr. : col. : 35 mm. & captions. $7.95 (Agriculture in Canada : $55.65) ji

      1. Agriculture - Alberta.   2. Irrigation - Alberta.

      Summarizes the how and why of irrigation farming in Southern Alberta. Explains how salty land is turned into fertile fields by means of dams, concrete canals, and ditch systems. Irrigation methods favoured by farmers are described, as well as types of crops produced and processed.-

633
    Tobacco farming in Ontario.
      prod. [Stratford, Ont.] : Sch. Ch., 1975.- dist. Sch. Ch.   42 fr. : col. : 35 mm. & captions. $7.95 (Agriculture in Canada : $55.65) ji

      1. Tobacco.

      Traces the tobacco industry from growing seedlings in greenhouses to the production of tobacco products. Describes the curing process and the tradition of auctioneering tobacco to buyers, as well as problems with crop irrigation, weed, and insect control.-

633.0951
    Rice growing in China.
      prod. [Stratford, Ont.] : Sch. Ch., 1974.- dist. Sch. Ch.   44 fr. : col. : 35 mm. & captions. $7.95 (China : $23.85) ji

      1. Agriculture - China.   2. Rice.

      Captioned presentation describes planting, growth and cultivation of China's most important crop. Shows rice growing areas and discusses conditions necessary for growing crops. Covers ploughing, planting, irrigation, harvesting, threshing and drying rice. Photographs illustrate simple tools and machines used, and need for improvements.-

633.0971
    Le blé canadien : une qualité rénommée.
      prod. [Montreal?] : NFB, 1967.- dist. SEC 46 fr. : b&w & col. : 35 mm. & captions & teacher's guide. $9.00 jis

      1. Wheat.

      An outline of the history of the wheat industry in Canada. Describes the development of hardy strains of wheat for changeable climate of the Canadian prairies. Discusses problems that wheat farmers face and ways in which they can increase the yield and quality of their crops. Uses drawings and photos. English title available : CANADIAN WHEAT : A REPUTATION FOR QUALITY.-

633.0971
    Canadian wheat : a reputation for quality.
      prod. [Montreal?] : NFB, 1967.- dist. McI. 46 fr. : b&w & col. : 35 mm. & captions & teacher's guide. $9.00 jis

      1. Wheat.

      An outline of the history of the wheat industry in Canada. Describes the development of hardy strains of wheat for the changeable climate of the Canadian prairies. Discusses problems that wheat farmers face and ways in which they can increase the yield and quality of their crops. Uses drawings and photos. French title available : LE BLE CANADIEN : UNE QUALITE RENOMMEE.-

The Classified Catalogue

633.0971
    Visit to a wheat farm.
        prod. [Montreal?] : NFB, 1961.- dist. McI. 36 fr. : col. : 35mm. & captions. $9.00 pj

        1. Wheat.

        A complete coverge of harvesting on a wheat farm in southern Saskatchewan, with photographs taken on location. Difficult words for a primary class are underlined.-

633.0971
    Wheat farming.
        prod. [Montreal?] : NFB, 1961.- dist. McI. 41 fr. : col. : 35 mm. & captions & teacher's guide. $9.00 ji

        1. Wheat.

        Traces wheat production in Western Canada from seed to harvest, pointing out reasons for excellent quality of Canadian wheat. Studies farm machinery, harvesting, storage and transportation methods. Measurements are not metric.-

634
    Berry farming in N.B.
        prod. [Stratford, Ont.] : Sch. Ch., 1975.- dist. Sch. Ch. 43 fr. : col. : 35 mm. & captions. $7.95 (Agriculture in Canada : $55.65) ji

        1. Fruit culture.

        Photographs show farming of strawberry and blueberries in New Brunswick. Describes the growth cycle of the strawberry from young plants, showing transplanting, thinning, and spraying, to harvesting in the second year. Explains blueberry cultivation on land where the fruit grows and treatment of that land to increase the crop.-

634
    Fruit farming in British Columbia.
        prod. [Stratford, Ont.] : Sch. Ch., 1974.- dist. Sch. Ch. 52 fr. : col. : 35 mm. & captions. $7.95 (Agriculture in Canada : $55.65) ji

        1. Fruit culture.

        Uses photographs to provide a general coverage of fruit farming in the Okanagan valley. Gives a map of major locations of farms in the valley, and discusses briefly the pruning, spraying, irrigating, harvesting, and transplanting of various fruits, as well as sorting and processing.-

634.9
    Le Bouclier canadien - industries forestières.
        prod. [Montreal?] : NFB, 1965.- dist. SEC 47 fr. : col. : 35 mm. & captions & teacher's manual. $9.00 jis

        1. Forests and forestry - Canada.

        Maps and photographs show the vegetation zones of the Canadian Shield and study a commercial forest in detail. Traces logging industry, the responsibility of the foresters, and the effect of a pulp and paper industry on the community. English title available : FORESTRY IN THE CANADIAN SHIELD.-

634.9
    Forest management and lumbering.
        prod. [Scarborough, Ont.] : R.B.M., 1975.- dist. ETHOS 47 fr. : col. : 35 mm. & cassette (11 min.) : auto. & aud. adv. sig. & teacher's manual. $19.00 (Follow your product : $34.50)

        1. Forests and forestry - Canada.

        In order to maintain forest as a valuable and renewable resource an intelligent program of harvesting and reforestation must be conducted. Discusses the concepts behind such a plan.-

634.9
    Forestry in the Canadian Shield.
        prod. [Montreal?] : NFB, 1965:c1966.- dist. McI. 43 fr. : col. : 35 mm. & captions & teacher's manual. $9.00 (Canadian Shield) jis

        1. Forests and forestry - Canada.

        Maps and photographs show the vegetation zones of the Canadian Shield and study a commercial forest in detail. Traces logging industry, the responsibility of the foresters, and the effect of a pulp and paper industry on the community. French title available : LE BOUCLIER CANADIEN INDUSTRIES FORESTIERES.-

634.9
  La Mécanisation dans l'expoitation forestière de l'est du Canada.
    prod. [Montreal?] : NFB, 1970.- dist. SEC 48 fr. : col. : 35 mm. & captions & teacher's manual. $9.00 is

  1. Lumber and lumbering.

  Mechanization has increased the efficiency of the logging harvest. Photos show the use of chain saws, skidders, mechanical slashers, and hydraulic loaders. Made with the assistance of Consolidated-Bathurst ltd. English title available : MECHANIZED LOGGING IN EASTERN CANADA.-

634.9
  Mechanized logging in eastern Canada.
    prod. [Montreal?] : NFB, 1970.- dist. McI. 48 fr. : col. : 35 mm. & captions & teacher's manual. $9.00 is

  1. Lumber and lumbering.

  Mechanization has increased the efficiency of the logging harvest. Photos show the use of chain saws, skidders, mechanical slashers, and hydraulic loaders. Made with the assistance of Consolidated-Bathurst ltd. French title available : LA MECANISATION DANS L'EXPLOITATION FORESTIERE DE L'EST DU CANADA.-

634.909711
  Forest industries in B.C. : part 1 :
    prod. [Stratford, Ont.] : Sch. Ch., 1975.- dist. Sch. Ch. 50 fr. : col. : 35 mm. & captions. $7.95 (Forest industries in Canada : $23.85) ji

  1. Lumber and lumbering.

  A comparison of different types of logging done in the interior and coastal regions of British Columbia. Photographs illustrate how modern machinery has facilitated the logging industry, by comparing the pioneer logging industry with present day logging methods. Concludes with planting of young trees to ensure re-growth of forests.-

635
  Explorons le jardin.
    prod. [Montreal?] : NFB, 1965.- dist. SEC 31 fr. : col. : 35 mm. & captions & teacher's guide. $9.00 p

  1. Gardening.

  Uses drawings to illustrate activities in a garden through the seasons. Includes preparing soil in Spring for planting, helpful and harmful insects, reasons for weeding, and different types of flowers and vegetables grown. Includes review section. Best for group viewing as an introduction or summary to garden and plant study. English title available : A VISIT TO A GARDEN.-

635
  A Visit to a garden.
    prod. [Montreal?] : NFB, 1965.- dist. McI. 29 fr. : col. : 35 mm. & captions & teacher's guide. $9.00 (Discovering life around us : $45.00) p

  1. Gardening.

  Uses drawings to illustrate activities in a garden through the seasons. Includes preparing soil in spring for planting, helpful and harmful insects, reasons for weeding, and different types of flowers and vegetables grown. Includes review section. Best for group viewing as an introduction or summary to garden and plant study. French title available : EXPLORONS LE JARDIN.-

636
  Animal pets.
    prod. [Toronto] : M-L, 1974.- dist. Sch. Ser. or Vint. 38 fr. : col. : 35 mm. & cassette (6 min.) : auto. & aud. adv. sig. & teacher's guide. $16.50 (Animal adventures with two endings : $49.50) p

  1. Pets - Care and treatment.

  Narrated study of pets to teach children responsibility for care of pets. Using photos of dogs, cats, birds, gerbils and goldfish as examples, it describes their growth processes, feeding, training and cleaning.-

The Classified Catalogue

636
    Big red barn.
        prod. [Toronto] : M-L, 1973.- dist. Sch. Ser. or Vint. 42 fr. : col. : 35 mm. & cassette (6 min.) : auto. & aud. adv. sig. & teaching guide. $16.50 (Reading motivation) pj

        1. Domestic animals. 2. Language arts - Study and teaching.

        A look at the animals which inhabit an old red barn. Uses simple, descriptive language to supplement the photographs. Useful for both science and language arts. French title available : LA GRANGE ROUGE.-

636
    La grange rouge.
        prod. [Toronto] : M-L, 1975.- dist. Sch. Ser. or Vint. 42 fr. : col. : 35 mm. & cassette (6 min.) : auto. & aud. adv. sig. & teacher's guide. $16.50 (Contes pour enfants) pj

        1. Domestic animals. 2. Language arts - Study and teaching.

        A look at the animals which inhabit an old red barn. Uses simple, descriptive language to supplement photographs. Useful for both science and language arts. English title available : BIG RED BARN.-

636
    Guinea pigs and their care.
        prod. [Toronto] : B & R, 1974.- dist. B & R 45 fr. : col. : 35 mm. & captions & teacher's manual. $10.00 (Pets and their care : $32.00) pj

        1. Guinea pigs - Care and treatment.

        Discusses the diet, care, and handling of guinea pigs. Includes a description of their physical characteristics, and shows several different breeds.-

636
    What pet for me.
        prod. [Toronto] : B & R, 1973 .- dist. B & R 47 fr. : col. : 35 mm. & teacher's manual. $10.00 (Pets and their care : $32.00) pj

        1. Pets.

        Illustrates a variety of pets suitable for children. Includes several breeds of dogs and cats, mice, birds, rabbits, guinea pigs, gerbils, raccoons, and a lizard.-

636.089
    A Visit with the vet.
        prod. [Toronto] : B & R, 1976.- dist. B & R 28 fr. : col. : 35 mm. & cassette (9 min.) : auto. & aud. adv. sig. & discussion guide. $16.00 (Pets and their care : $32.00) (Pets and their care : $32.00) pj

        1. Veterinarians. 2. Pets - Care and treatment.

        What to expect on a visit to the veterinarian is illustrated in this look at the daily routine and duties of a vet. His role in maintaining animal health is also discussed.-

636.2
    Cattle ranching in Alberta.
        prod. [Stratford, Ont.] : Sch. Ch., 1975.- dist. Sch. Ch. 44 fr. : col. : 35 mm. & captions. $7.95 (Agriculture in Canada : $55.65) ji

        1. Cattle. 2. Ranch life.

        A general summary outlining the types of cattle, ranch system, crops grown to feed the cows, and the role of the cowboy today. Describes the progress of cattle from ranch to feeder lots, stockyards, auction sales, meat-packing plants, and finally to supermarkets.-

636.3
    Sheep industry.
        prod. [Kitchener, Ont.] : EDU, 1974.- dist. EDU 25 fr. : col. : 35 mm. & cassette (9 min.) : auto. & aud. adv. sig. & teacher's manual. $15.95 (Australia : $79.95) jis

        1. Sheep. 2. Wool. 3. Agriculture - Australia.

        A detailed look at sheep farming in Australia. Follows wool production from the sheep to the harbour for export. Describes the regulation of the sheep farming industry, types of wool, and problems with roaming kangaroos.-

The Classified Catalogue

636.5
    The Chicken or the egg.
        prod. [Scarborough, Ont.] : FCC, 1976.- dist. FCC 10 fr. : col. : 35 mm. & cassette (6 min.) : auto. & aud. adv. sig. & reading script. $8.85 (Farm life : $35.40) p

        1. Poultry.

        A ten-frame filmstrip, with simple narration, describes the food eaten by a hen, how an egg is laid, and how a chick is hatched. Flat filmstrip, cassette and printed material in a clear vinyl envelope 34 x 28 cm. designed for storage in a filing cabinet.-

636.5
    Nova Scotia poultry farming.
        prod. [Stratford, Ont.] : Sch. Ch., 1972.- dist. Sch. Ch. 40 fr. : col. : 35 mm. & captions. $7.95 (Agriculture in Canada : $55.65) ji

        1. Poultry. 2. Eggs.

        The production of eggs and poultry in Nova Scotia's Annapolis Valley. Shows modern mass production of eggs in egg-producing plants, and procedure of raising broiler chickens in large factories, which are then processed, graded, and priced for market.-

637
    Milk and ice cream.
        prod. [Toronto] : Int. Cin., 1974.- dist. VEC 35 fr. : col. : 35 mm. & captions & teacher's guide. $24.00 (The story of food : $43.00) pj

        1. Milk. 2. Ice cream, pies, etc.

        A brief look at the automated milk pasteurization process showing how raw milk becomes either homogenized milk to be put into cartons or plastic bags, or a milk product, such as ice cream. Also shows how popsicles are made.-

637
    What's in a dairy barn.
        prod. [Scarborough, Ont.] : FCC, 1976.- dist. FCC 10 fr. : col. : 35 mm. & cassette (5 min.) : auto. & aud. adv. sig. & reading script. $8.85 (Farm life : $35.40) p

        1. Dairying.

        A ten-frame filmstrip, with simple narration, describes a modern milking machine and tank for collecting milk. Also shows how a farmer trains a calf to drink from a bucket. Flat filmstrip, cassette and printed material in a clear vinyl 34 x 28 cm. envelope, designed for storage in filing cabinet.-

639
    Le chalutage.
        prod. [Montreal?] : NFB, made 1967 : 1969.- dist. SEC 31 fr. : col. : 35 mm. & captions & teacher's manual. $9.00 ji

        1. Fisheries.

        Photographs and diagrams illustrate the use of otter boards or doors to hold open the mouth of the trawl in the water. The manual provides necessary detailed information. English title available :OTTER TRAWLING.-

639
    Electronic fish finding.
        prod. [Montreal?] : NFB, 1967.- dist. Mcl. 25 fr. : col. : 35 mm. & captions & teacher's manual. $9.00 is

        1. Fisheries.

        Captioned drawings and diagrams designed to be used with accompanying notes explain the technicalities of electronic fish finding based on the physics of sound. Describes the echo sounder and use of transducer. French title available : REPERAGE ELECTRONIQUE DU POISSON.-

639
    Engines de pêche (câbles et lignes pour la fabrication des fillets de pêch).
        prod. [Montreal?] : NFB, made 1967 : 1972.- dist. SEC 31 fr. : col. :$35 mm. & captions & teacher's guide. $9.00 is

        1. Rope. 2. Fisheries.

        Comprehensive coverage of the ropes and twines suitable for use as fishing nets. Discusses types of fibres, their properties, types of nets, and identification of ropes and twines. English title available : FISHING GEAR (ROPES AND TWINES FOR FISHING NETS).-

639

Fish processing in British Columbia.
prod. [Stratford, Ont.] : Sch. Ch., 1977.- dist. Sch. Ch. 45 fr. : b&w & col. : 35 mm. & captions. $7.95 (Fishing in Canada : $23.85) ji

1. Fisheries - British Columbia.

Black and white photos outline fish processing methods of long ago. The use of colour photos of today's methods emphasizes mechanization for faster processing and products. Although mainly about salmon processing, halibut, herring, and shellfish are mentioned.-

639

The Fish processing plant.
prod. [Scarborough, Ont.] : R.B.M., 1976.- dist. ETHOS 40 fr. : col. : 35 mm. & cassette (10 min.) : auto. & aud. adv. sig. & teacher's manual. $19.00 (Community studies : $69.00) i

1. Fisheries - Nova Scotia.

Follows a cargo containing a variety of fish as it is processed through a large, modern seafood plant. Shows each step of the processing from raw fish to finished product. Photographs taken at a plant located in Lunenberg, N.S.-

639

Fishing gear (ropes and twines for fishing nets).
prod. [Montreal?] : NFB, made 1967 : 1969.- dist. McI. 31 fr. : col. : 35 mm. & captions & teacher's guide. $9.00 is

1. Rope. 2. Fisheries.

Comprehensive coverage of the ropes and twines suitable for use as fishing nets. Discusses types of fibres, their properties, types of nets, and identification of ropes and twines. French title available : ENGINS DE PECHE : CABLES ET LIGNES POUR LA FABRICATION DES FILETS DE PECHE.-

639

Fishing methods.
prod. [Montreal?] : NFB, 1967.- dist. McI. 33 fr. : col. : 35 mm. & captions & teacher's guide. $9.00 is

1. Fisheries.

Diagrams and explanations of common fishing gear developed as a result of mechanization - including impaling gear, impounding gear, entangling gear, encircling gear. Manual essential. French title available : METHODS DE PECHE.-

639

Habitat : key to survival.
prod. [Georgetown, Ont.] : FMS, 1976.- dist. McI. 52 fr. : col. : 35 mm.& cassette (13 min.) : auto. & aud. adv. sig. & teacher's guide. $19.00 (Vanishing animals of North America : $38.00) ji

1. Wildlife - Conservation.

Illustrates the interdependence of wildlife species by examining specific endangered animals and the work of wildlife agencies to protect them from excessive killing, food scarcity, or modern oil spills.-

639

Habitat : key to survival.
prod. [Georgetown, Ont.] : FMS, 1976.- dist. McI. 52 fr. : col. : 35 mm. & cassette (13 min.) : auto. & aud. adv. sig. & teacher's guide. $19.00 (Vanishing animals of North America : $38.00) ji

1. Wildlife - Conservation.

Illustrates the interdependence of wildlife species by examining specific endangered animals and the work of wildlife agencies to protect them from excessive killing, food scarcity, or modern oil spills.-

639

Méthodes de pêche.
prod. [Montreal?] : NFB, made 1967 : 1969.- dist. SEC 33 fr. : col. : 35 mm. & captions & manual. $9.00 is

1. Fisheries.

Diagrams and explanations of common fishing gear developed as a result of mechanization - including impaling gear, impounding gear, entangling gear, encircling gear. Manual essential. English title available : FISHING METHODS.-

639
    Otter trawling.
        prod. [Montreal?] : NFB, 1967.- dist. McI. 31 fr. : col. : 35 mm. & captions & teacher's manual. $9.00 ji

        1. Fisheries.

    Photographs and diagrams illustrate the use of otter boards or doors to hold open the mouth of the trawl in the water. The manual provides necessary detailed information. French title available : LE CHALUTAGE.-

639
    La pêche à la Seine (Ecossaise et Danoise).
        prod. [Montreal?] : NFB, made 1967 : 1969.- dist. SEC 27 fr. : col. : 35 mm. & captions & teacher's manual. $9.00 is

        1. Fisheries.

    A technical description of two types of seine netting used for fishing cod, halibut, etc., with photographs and labelled diagrams. Manual essential for clarification. English title available : SEINE NETTING (SCOTTISH AND DANISH METHODS).-

639
    Le repérage électronique du poisson.
        prod. [Montreal?] : NFB, made 1967 : 1969.- dist. SEC 27 fr. : col. : 35 mm. & captions & teacher's manual. $9.00 is

        1. Fisheries.

    Captioned drawings and diagrams designed to be used with accompanying notes explain the technicalities of electronic fish finding based on the physics of sound. Describes the echo sounder and use of transducer. English title available : ELECTRONIC FISH FINDING.-

639
    Seine netting : Scottish and Danish methods.
        prod. [Montreal?] : FB, 1967.- dist. McI. 27 fr. : col. : 35 mm. & captions & teacher's manual. $9.00 is

        1. Fisheries.

    A technical description of two types of seine netting used for fishing cod, halibut, etc., with photographs and labelled diagrams. Manual essential for clarification. French title available : LA PECHE A LA SEINE : ECOSSAISE ET DANOISE.-

639
    Threatened and endangered wildlife.
        prod. [Georgetown, Ont.] : FMS, 1976.- dist. McI. 52 fr. : col. : 35 mm. & cassette (15 min.) : auto. & aud. adv. sig. & teacher's guide. $19.00 (Vanishing animals of North America : $38.00) ji

        1. Wildlife - Conservation.

    Examines problems threatening survival of some wildlife species in North America. Gives examples of man's efforts to save some birds and animals from extinction (waterfowl, bison, egret, alligator, cougar, grizzly bear, big horn sheep, falcon, osprey eagle, pelican, and racer snakes).

639
    Threatened and endangered wildlife.
        prod. [Georgetown, Ont.] : FMS, 1976.- 52 fr. : col. : 35 mm. & cassette (15 min.) : auto. & aud. adv. sig. & teacher's guide. $19.00 (Vanishing animals of North America : $38.00) ji

        1. Wildlife - Conservation.

    Examines problems threatening survival of some wildlife species in North America. Gives examples of man's efforts to save some birds and animals from extinction (waterfowl, bison, egret, alligator, cougar, grizzly bear, big horn sheep, falcon, osprey eagle, pelican, and racer snakes). -

639.09711
    Salmon fishing in B.C.
        prod. [Stratford, Ont.] : Sch. Ch., 1975.- dist. Sch. Ch. 44 fr. : b&w & col. : 35 mm. & captions. $7.95 (Fishing in Canada: $23.85) ji

        1. Salmon. 2. Fisheries - British Columbia.

    A history of salmon fishing in British Columbia comparing Indian fishing methods with modern fishing methods of today. Archival photographs and illustrations show salmon being caught by the Indians and the first white men. Photographs and drawings show how present-day fisherman in B.C. have adapted and improved upon the old methods. Gill-netting, trolling, and use of purse-seine are described. Included map of B.C. coastal waters showing the limits of pink, sockeye, and chum salmon.-

The Classified Catalogue

639.097127
    Trout farming in Manitoba.
        prod. [Stratford, Ont.] : Sch. Ch., 1975.- dist. Sch. Ch. 45 fr. : b&w & col. : 35 mm. & captions. $7.95 (Fishing in Canada : $23.85) ji

    1. Fisheries - Manitoba. 2. Trout.

Using photographs taken at trout farms located in Western Canada, describes preparation of the lakes for the trout, a provision for food, placing of fish in the lakes, and "harvesting" them in late October. Concludes with fish being weighed, cleaned, sorted and packed at the processing plant.-

639.09715
    Grand Manan Island : lobster fishing.
        prod. [Montreal?] : NFB, 1972.- dist. McI. 46 fr. : col. : 35 mm. & captions. $9.00 j

    1. Lobsters. 2. Fisheries - New Brunswick.

A clear description of lobster fishing methods off Grand Manan Island, showing the boats, the traps being weighted and lowered, the identifying marker buoys, measuring the lobsters, and packing for shipment. French title available : L'ILE GRAND MANAN : LA PECHE DU HOMARD.-

639.09715
    Grand Manan Island : weir fishing.
        prod. [Montreal?] : NFB, 1972.- dist. McI. 50 fr. : col. : 35 mm. & captions. $9.00 ji

    1. Fisheries - New Brunswick. 2. Herring.

Photographs, diagrams, and captions provide a clear description of weir fishing for herring off Grand Manan Island. Also shows fish being loaded, salted, and processed. Two frames give measurement in feet. French title available : L'ILE GRAND MANAN : LA PECHE A FASCINES.-

639.09715
    L'Ile Grand Manan : la pêche du homard.
        prod. [Montreal?] : NFB, 1972.- dist. SEC 46 fr. : col. : 35 mm. & captions. $9.00 j

    1. Fisheries - New Brunswick. 2. Lobsters.

A clear description of lobster fishing methods off Grand Manan Island, showing the boats, the traps being weighted and lowered, the identifying marker buoys, measuring the lobsters, and packing for shipment. English title available : GRAND MANAN ISLAND : LOBSTER FISHING.-

639.09715
    L'île Grand Manan : la pêche à fascines.
        prod. [Montreal?] : NFB, 1972.- dist. SEC 50 fr. : col. : 35 mm. & captions. $9.00 ji

    1. Fisheries - New Brunswick. 2. Herring.

Photographs, diagrams, and captions provide a clear description of weir fishing for herring off Grand Manan Island. Also shows fish being loaded, salted, and processed. Two frames give measurement in feet. English title available : GRAND MANAN ISLAND : WEIR FISHING.-

640
    La Cuisine : un atelier.
        prod. [Toronto] : M-L, 1975.- dist. Sch. Ser. or Vint. 52 fr. : col. : 35 mm. & cassette (9 min.) : auto. & aud. adv. sig. & teacher's guide. $16.50 (Cuisine et alimentation : $75.00) is

    1. Home economics.

Stresses the importance of organization of space, time, and equipment in the kitchen. Utensils are considered in relation to use, storage, and safety. Demonstrates table etiquette and choice of linen and tableware. Cleaning up after meals and dishwashing are analyzed for efficiency.-

640
    Principles of kitchen management.
        prod. [Toronto] : M-L, 1973.- dist. Sch. Ser. or Vint. 52 fr. : col. : 35 mm. & cassette (9 min.) : auto. & aud. adv. sig. & teacher's guide. $16.50 (Cooking and nutrition : $75.00) is

    1. Home economics.

Stresses the importance of organization of space, time, and equipment in the kitchen. Utensils are considered in relation to use, storage and safety. Demonstrates table etiquette and choice of linen and tableware. Cleaning up after meals and dishwashing are analyzed for efficiency. French title available : LA CUISINE : UN ATELIER.-

The Classified Catalogue

641.1
    Alimentation et bonne santé.
        prod. [Toronto] : M-L, 1975.- dist. Sch. Ser. or Vint. 43 fr. : col. : 35 mm. & cassette (8 min.) : auto. & aud. adv. sig. & teacher's guide. $16.50 (Cuisine et alimentation : $75.00) is

    1. Nutrition.

    Discusses the planning of meals for a balanced diet. Defines the main nutrients - protein, minerals, fats, and carbohydrates, outlining food sources for each and effects on the body. Explains calories and the importance of water to the diet. English title available : NUTRITION AND HEALTH.-

641.1
    Connaître les sortes d'aliments.
        prod. [Toronto] : M-L, 1975.- dist. Sch. Ser or Vint. 59 fr. : col. : 35 mm. & cassette (9 min.) : auto. & aud. adv. sig. & teacher's guide. $16.50 (Cuisine et alimentation : $75.00) is

    1. Nutrition.   2. Cookery.

    Discussion of the basic food groups. Recipes for foods from each group are provided and preparation is demonstrated. Includes recipes for custard, baked apples, banana sponge, meat loaf. Various methods of cooking and serving vegetables and fruit are shown. English title available : KNOWING YOUR FOOD GROUPS.-

641.1
    Help yourself to good cooking.
        prod. [Toronto] : M-L, 1973.- dist. Sch. Ser. or Vint. 44 fr. : col. : 35 mm. & cassette (7 min.) : auto. & aud. adv. sig. & teacher's guide. $16.50 (Cooking and nutrition : $75.00) is

    1. Nutrition.   2. Cookery.

    A summary of methods for the selection and preparation of food. Discusses the selection of fruits and vegetables according to quality and nutritional value, and how to store them properly. Also shows how to follow a recipe, measure ingredients, cream, mix, beat, blend, and fold. French title available : LES REPAS ET LE BUDGET.-

641.1
    Knowing your food groups.
        prod. [Toronto] : M-L, 1973.- dist. Sch. Ser. or Vint. 59 fr. : col. : 35 mm. & cassette (10 min.) : auto. & aud. adv. sig. & teacher's guide. $16.50 (Cooking and nutrition : $75.00) is

    1. Nutrition.   2. Cookery.

    Discussion of the basic food groups. Recipes for foods from each group are provided and preparation is demonstrated. Includes recipes for custard, baked apples, banana sponge, and meat loaf. Various methods of cooking and serving vegetables and fruit are shown. French title available : CONNAITRE LES SORTES D'ALIMENTS.-

641.1
    Nutrition - anew look.
        prod. [Toronto] : M-L, 1973.- dist. Sch. Ser. or Vint. 38 fr. : col. : 35 mm. & cassette (5 min.) : auto. & aud. adv. sig. & teacher's guide. $16.50 (Health - a new look : $65.00) kp

    1. Nutrition.

    Explains the importance of eating proper foods to provide the most energy and growth. Photographs show children gathering nutritious food from a market.-

641.1
    Nutrition and health.
        prod. [Toronto] : M-L, 1973.- dist. Sch. Ser. or Vint. 43 fr. : col. : 35 mm. & cassette (7 min.) : auto. & aud. adv. sig. & teacher's guide. $16.50 (Cooking and nutrition : $75.00) is

    1. Nutrition.

    Discusses the planning of meals for a balanced diet. Defines the main nutrients - protein, minerals, fats, and carbohydrates, outlining food sources for each and effects on the body. Explains calories and the importance of water to the diet. French title available : ALIMENTATION ET BONNE SANTE.-

The Classified Catalogue

641.1
    Qu'est-ce que l'hygiène alimentaire?
        prod. [Montreal?] : NFB, 1954.- dist. SEC 35 fr. : col. : 35 mm. & captions & teacher's manual. $9.00 p

    1. Nutrition.

    Drawings and captions explore nutrition, stressing the importance of good meals, rest, fresh air, exercise. Compares the body to a machine and the cells to workers on the machine who need proper food to function. English title available : WHAT IS NUTRITION?-

641.1
    Les Repas et le budget.
        prod. [Toronto] : M-L, 1975.- dist. Sch. Ser. or Wint. 44 fr. : col. : 35 mm. & cassette (7 min.) : auto. & aud. adv. sig. & teacher's guide. $16.50 (Cuisine et alimentation : $75.00) is

    1. Nutrition. 2. Cookery.

    A summary of methods for the selection and preparation of food. Discusses the selection of fruits and vegetables according to quality and nutritional value, and how to store them properly. Also shows how to follow a recipe, measure ingredients, cream, mix, beat, blend, and fold. English title available : HELP YOURSELF TO GOOD COOKING.-

641.1
    Sam Slice tells about snack foods.
        prod. [Toronto, Ont.] : McI., 1977.- dist. cI. 26 fr. : col. : 35 mm. & cassette (8 min.) : auto. & aud. adv. sig. & teacher's manual. $19.00 (Sam Slice tells the story of food : $95.00) pj

    1. Nutrition.

    Presentation of a list of "good" foods to eat between meals. As a follow-up activity it is suggested that the children might make a chart or booklet to tell about good snack foods.-

641.1
    The Story of how to eat to grow tall.
        prod. [Toronto, Ont.] : McI., 1977.- dist. McI. 32 fr. : col. : 35 mm. & cassette (12 min.) : auto. & aud. adv. sig. & teacher's manual. $19.00 (Sam Slice tells the story of food :$95.00) pj

    1. Nutrition.

    Sam Slice, an imaginary "tough guy" with a bread-slice head, teaches young children about proper nuitrition by introducing the various food groups necessary for a balanced diet. These include fresh fruits and vegetables, protein foods, dairy products and eggs, and grains and cereals.-

641.1
    What is nutrition?
        prod. [Montreal?] : NFB, made 1954 : 1975.- dist. McI. 35 fr. : col. : 35 mm. & captions & teacher's manual. $9.00 p

    1. Nutrition.

    Drawings and captions explore nutrition, stressing the importance of good meals, rest, fresh air, exercise. Compares the body to a machine and the cells to workers on the machine who need proper food to function. French title available : QU'EST CE QUE L'HYGIENE ALIMENTAIRE.-

641.3
    Get hooked on fish.
        prod. [Toronto] : Int. Cin., 1975.- dist. VEC 75 fr. : col. : 35 mm. & cassette (9 min.) : auto. & aud. adv. sig. & reading script & pamphlet. $24.00 s

    1. Seafood. 2. Cookery - Fish.

    A humourous approach to buying, preparing and cooking of fish found in Canada.
    Discusses cuts, packaging and purchasing of fresh and frozen fish. Shows methods of storing, freezing preparation and cooking. Illustrated with photographs of popular fish dishes. Included with filmstrip is reading script, plus a pamphlet with additional tips and recipes.-

The Classified Catalogue

641.3
  Learning about the fruits we eat.
    prod. [Toronto] : McI., 1977.- dist. McI. 29 fr. : col. : 35 mm. & cassette (10 min.) : auto. & aud. adv. sig. & teacher's manual. $19.00 (Sam Slice tells the story of food : $95.00) pj

    1. Fruit. 2. Nutrition.

    Re-enforces the definition that a fruit is the part of a plant containing the seed. Emphasizes the importance of fruit in our diet and teaches classification skills. Nine different classifications of fruit are shown.-

641.3
  Learning about the plants we eat.
    prod. [Toronto, Ont.] : McI., 1977.- dist. McI. 27 fr. : col. : 35 mm. & cassette (10 min.) : auto. & aud. adv. sig. & teacher's manual. $19.00 (Sam Slice tells the story of food : $95.00) pj

    1. Plants, Edible. 2. Food.

    "Sam Slice" discusses the edible parts of plants. Shows that our diets include some roots, leaves, stems, buds, flowers, fruits, and seeds.-

641.4
  Dressing fish.
    prod. [Toronto] : M-L, 1975.- dist. Sch. Ser. or Vint. 43 fr. : col. : 35 mm. & cassette (8 min.) : auto. & aud. adv. sig. & teaching guide. $16.50 (Outdoor education) is

    1. Fishes.

    Demonstrates in detail how to fillet two species of fresh water fish, the pickerel and the pike. Discusses the characteristics of a good filleting knife and stresses its careful use.-

641.5
  Fires and cooking.
    prod. [Montreal?] : NFB, 1964.- dist. McI. 33 fr. : col. : 35 mm. & captions. $9.00 is

    1. Cookery, Outdoor.

    Photographs show various methods of cooking outoors, as well as safety measures, helpful hints and diet ideas. Stoves vary from propane and gas to charcoal. Fires, such as the altar fire, the trench fire, the bean hole and teepee fire are shown.
    Directions for making a reflector oven are included. French title available : FEUX ET CUISINE.-

641.6
  Let's serve freshwater fish.
    prod. [Montreal?] : NFB, 1961.- dist. McI. 42 fr. : col. : 35 mm. &dcaptions & disc (33 1/3 rpm. 15 min.) : auto. & aud. adv. sig. & teacher's manual. $9.00 is

    1. Cookery - Fish.

    Presents many delicious ways to serve fish, and discusses proper care of fresh and frozen fish. Includes a chart of common varieties of freshwater fish.-

641.6
  Let's serve shellfish.
    prod. [Montreal?] : NFB, made 1956 : 1975.- dist. McI. 48 fr. : col. : 35 mm. & teacher's manual. $9.00 ji

    1. Cookery - Shellfish.

    Uses appetizing pictures of shellfish to show how they can be bought, how to remove from shells, methods of cooking and serving. Useful for home economics classes.-

641.6
  The Way to cook fish.
    prod. [Montreal?] : NFB, made 1953 : 1975.- dist. McI. 37 fr. : col. : 35 mm. & captions & teacher's manual. $9.00 is

    1. Cookery - Fish.

    An informative and concise description of step-by-step methods of cooking fish. Useful for home economics classes, along with the manual containing recipes.-

642
  Planning and preparing meals.
    prod. [Toronto] : M-L, 1973.- dist. Sch. Ser. or Vint. 53 fr. : col. : 35 mm. & cassette (10 min.) : auto. & aud. adv. sig. & teacher's guide. $16.50 (Cooking and nutrition : $75.00) is

    1. Menus.

    Demonstrates and discusses menu-planning and preparation. A sample breakfast, lunch, supper and snack are prepared using simple but nutritious ingredients. Stress is placed on careful planning of meals, avoiding food wastage. French title available : TROIS REPAS PAR JOUR.-

642
Trois repas par jour.
[Toronto] : M-L, 1975.- dist. Sch. Ser. or Wint. 53 fr. : col. : 35 mm. & cassette (11 min.) : auto. & aud. adv. sig. & teacher's guide. $16.50 (Cuisine et alimentation : $75.00) is

1. Menus.

Demonstrates and discusses menu-planning and preparation. A sample breakfast, lunch, supper and snack are prepared using simple but nutritious ingredients. Stress is placed on careful planning of meals, avoiding food wastage. English title available : PLANNING AND PREPARING MEALS.-

644
Electrical hazards.
prod. [Montreal?] : NFB, made 1958 : 1973. dist. McI. 52 fr. : col. : 35 mm. & captions & teacher's manual. $9.00 ji

1. Household appliances, Electric - Safety measures.

Drawings are used to illustrate the hazards and problems of inadequate wiring. Emphasizes the danger involved in overloading circuits, and suggests some safety rules to follow.-

646
Proper bush clothing.
prod. [Toronto] : M-L, 1975.- dist. Sch. Ser. or Wint. 50 fr. : col. : 35 mm. & cassette (10 min.) : auto. & aud. adv. sig. & teaching guide. $16.50 (Outdoor education) is

1. Clothing and dress. 2. Outdoor life.

Describes types of clothing for both summer and winter in the bush, and the protection each item provides. Useful for group discussion before preparation for bush travel.-

647
Hotel : city within a city.
prod. [Toronto] : Int. Cin., 1977.- dist. VEC 66 fr. : col. : 35 mm. & cassette (9 min.) : auto. & aud. adv. sig. & teacher's guide. $24.00 (Community close-ups : $192.00) pj

1. Hotels, motels, etc. - Canada.

While staying overnight with their parents in a large Canadian hotel, two children investigate various departments within the building and discover how a large hotel, with all its employees and responsibilities, functions as a city within a city.-

658.8
The Country store.
prod. [Oakville, Ont.] : Fasla, 1976.- dist. Fasla 31 fr. : col. : 35 mm. & cassette (8 min.) : auto. & aud. adv. sig. & teacher's guide. $18.00 (Let's go shopping : $66.00) pj

1. Retail trade. 2. Shopping.

A comprehensive presentation describing the variety of items in a general store. Examines the post office, the book exchange and old fixtures used for many years in the store.-

658.8
The Department store.
prod. [Oakville] : Fasla, 1976.- dist. Fasla 58 fr. : col. : 35 mm. & cassette (10 min.) : auto. & aud. adv. sig. & teacher's guide. $18.00 (Let's go shopping : $66.00) pj

1. Department stores. 2. Shopping.

Covers all aspects of a department store, encouraging discussion of the reasons for the many departments. Explores the manager's office, the checkout counter, snack bar, and discusses use of advertising.-

The Classified Catalogue

658.8
The shopping centre.
prod. [Toronto] : Int. Cin., 1975.- dist. VEC 81 fr. : col. : 35 mm. & cassette (8 min.) : auto. & aud. adv. sig. & teacher's guide. $24.00 (Community close-ups : $192.00) pj

1. Shopping centers and malls.

A description of the how and why of architectural design in a modern Canadian shopping centre. Using photos of actual shopping malls as examples, it also makes the comparison between the shopping centre of today and the old market places of yesterday as places for people to congregate.-

658.8
A Shopping centre.
prod. [Oakville, Ont.] : Fasla, 1976.- dist. Fasla 34 fr. : col. : 35 mm. & cassette (6 min.) : auto. & aud. adv. sig. & teacher's guide. $18.00 (Let's go shopping : $66.00) pj

1. Shopping centers and malls. 2. Shopping.

Explores a large shopping mall, pointing out services and types of stores available, including a bank, restaurant, grocery store, and service station. Also examines the use of industrial malls, street malls, and the building of a new mall. Encourages research on the need for malls and their advantage and disadvantages.-

658.8
The Supermarket.
prod. [Oakville, Ont.] : Fasla, 1976.- dist. Fasla 60 fr. : col. : 35 mm. & cassette (13 min.) : auto. & aud. adv. sig. & teacher's guide. $18.00 (Let's go shopping : $66.00) pj

1. Supermarkets. 2. Shopping.

Good coverage of the great variety of items in a supermarket and the value of wise shopping. Explains a shopping list and direction signs. Explores the warehouse, storage systems, and meat packing machines in a large supermarket.-

659.1
Getting down to basics about advertising.
prod. [Toronto] : B&R, 1976.- dist. B & R 2 filmstrips (10:11 fr.) : col. : 35 mm. & 2 cassettes (7:9 min.) : auto. & aud. adv. sig. & teacher's manual and idea piece & student materials & reading script. $36.00 is

1. Advertising.

Summarizes the role played by advertising in the overall marketing chain. Includes a number of excerpts from actual commercials for popular low-cost/high-volume goods and public services. Two-part set.-

664
Bread and pastry.
prod. [Toronto] : Int. Cin., 1974.- dist. VEC 35 fr. : col. : 35 mm. & captions & teacher's guide. $24.00 (The story of food : $43.00) pj

1. Bread. 2. Pastry.

Illustrates with captioned photographs the extent to which mass production of pies, fancy pastries and breads still relies on manual labour and dexterity.-

664
Chocolate.
prod. [Toronto] : Int. Cin., 1974.- dist. VEC 35 fr. : col. : 35 mm. & captions & teacher's guide. $24.00 (The story of food : $43.00) pj

1. Chocolate.

Roasted cocoa beans, sugar, milk and cocoa butter are shown being mixed, liquified and poured into various molds to form different kinds of chocolates and chocolate bars.-

664
Hot dogs.
prod. [Toronto] : Int. Cin., 1974.- dist. VEC 35 fr. : col. : 35 mm. & captions & teacher's guide. $24.00 (The story of food : $43.00) pj

1. Meat industry and trade.

Shows through photographs and simple captions the complete process of how hot dogs are automatically produced, starting with the raw meat and other ingredients.-

664
    Maple syrup.
        prod. [Toronto] : SHN, 1974.- dist. PHM 56 fr. : col. : 35 mm. & cassette (11 min.) : auto. & aud. adv. sig. $39.60 (The Little people) p

    1. Maple sugar.

    Combines sound effects and photographs to describe the production of maple syrup from the viewpoint of the participants. Designed to provide language experience and create an atmosphere for discussion, reading and writing.-

664
    Maple syrup.
        prod. [Montreal?] : NFB, made 1964 : 1975.- dist. McI. 32 fr. : col. : 35 mm. & captions. $9.00 pj

    1. Maple sugar.

    An examination of the gathering and production of maple syrup. Illustrates step-by-step methods of production in the original way and compares it to the modern method using plastic pipes, storage tanks, and controlled temperature. Includes a review section for group use. French title available : LES SUCRES.-

664
    Les sucres.
        prod. [Montreal?] : NFB, 1964.- dist. SEC 33 fr. : col. : 35 mm. & captions. $9.00 pj

    1. Maple sugar.

    An examination of the gathering and production of maple syrup. Illustrates step-by-step methods of production in the orginal way and compares it to the modern method using plastic pipes, storage tanks, and controlled temperature. Includes a review section for group use. English title available : MAPLE SYRUP.-

664
    Trip to the sugar bush.
        prod. [Toronto] : B&R, 1973.- dist. Lea. 54 fr. : col. : 35 mm. & teacher's manual & captions. $9.00 pji

    1. Maple sugar.

    Portrays the making of maple syrup in a sugar bush. Each step is shown in both the old and new methods of making the sap into syrup.-

664
    When the sap runs.
        prod. [Scarborough, Ont.] : R.B.M., 1975.- dist. ETHOS 58 fr. : col. : 35 mm. & cassette (8 min.) : auto. & aud. adv. sig. & teacher's manual.- $19.00 (Special occasions) pj

    1. Maple sugar.

    The old fashioned and modern methods of collecting maple sap and boiling it down to sweet syrup are presented in a visit to a maple bush camp which uses modern ways but keeps the old equipment for demonstration purposes.-

664
    Working in a bakery.
        prod. [Winnipeg] : WCL, 1972.- dist. Sch. Ch. 44 fr. : b&w & col. : 35 mm. & captions. $7.95 (Food processing in Canada : $15.90) ji

    1. Bread. 2. Pastry.

    The story of bread and baked goods from grain-harvesting to packaging for stores. Photographs from inside a bakery illustrate the machinery and techniques used to mix bread dough, bake, slice, and wrap it. Assembly line procedures for pastries, cakes, and pies are shown.-

664
    Working in a meat packing plant.
        prod. [Winnipeg] : WCL, 1974.- dist. Sch. Ch. 42 fr. : b&w & col. : 35 mm. & captions. $7.95 (Food processing in Canada : $15.90) ji

    1. Meat industry and trade.

    Depicts the production of meat, sausage, luncheon, packaged, and canned meat in a Canadian meat packing plant. Explains criteria used to decide upon location of plant, such as good transportation facilities. Photographs taken inside a meat packing plant cover such aspects as government inspection of meat, dividing meat into various cuts, and sorting, wrapping and packaging before shipping to stores across Canada.-

The Classified Catalogue

665
    Natural gas in Alberta.
        prod. [Winnipeg] : VCL, 1972.- dist. Sch. Ch. 44 fr. : col. : 35 mm. & captions. $7.95 (Energy in Canada : $23.85) ji

        1. Gas, Natural.

    Illustrates the procedure of piping natural gas from the ground to the refinery, to cities and towns in Eastern Canada. Includes photographs of a refining plant and laying pipelines, with an explanation of the problems involved. Shows the use of natural gas, and the types of industries that rely on it.-

665
    Oil in Alberta.
        prod. [Stratford, Ont.] : Sch. Ch., 1975.- dist. Sch. Ch. 44 fr. : col. : 35 mm. & captions. $7.95 (Energy in Canada : $23.85) ji

        1. Petroleum.

    An introduction to various aspects of petroleum industry, including how oil is discovered, pumped out, and refined. Shows actual photos of drilling rigs and oil refineries in operations, and discusses transportation and storage of petroleum products.-

669
    L'aluminum.
        prod. [Montreal?] : NFB, made 1969 : 1971.- dist. SEC 52 fr. : b&w & col. : 35 mm. & captions. $9.00 is

        1. Aluminum.

    A summary of aluminum production in Canada, including the characteristics of aluminum, its various uses, the importing of raw materials essential to the production, the different centres in Canada of aluminum manufacturing, and the vital role of electricity for the whole procedure. Uses maps, charts, diagrams, and photographs. English title available : ALUMINUM.-

669
    Aluminum.
        prod. [Montreal?] : NFB, 1969.- 52 fr. : b&w & col. : 35 mm. & captions. is

        1. Aluminum.

    A summary of aluminum production in Canada, including the characteristics of aluminum, its various uses, the importing of raw materials essential to the production, the different centres in Canada of aluminum manufacturing, and the vital role of electricity for the whole procedure. Uses maps, charts, diagrams and photographs. French title available : L'ALUMINIUM.-

669
    Aluminum processing in Quebec.
        prod. [Winnipeg] : VCL, 1972.- dist. Sch. Ch. 40 fr. : col. : 35 mm. & captions. $7.95 (Mining and processing in Canada :$39.75) ji

        1. Aluminum.

    A comprehensive treatment of aluminum production. Its origin in bauxite and the complex process involved are explained with photos. Also discusses the relationship between hydro-electric power plants and aluminum production, ending with a survey of the uses of aluminum.-

669
    Copper.
        prod. [Montreal?] : NFB, 1961.- dist. McI. 47 fr. : col. : 35 mm. & captions & teacher's manual. $9.00 jis

        1. Copper.

    Photographs, maps, and diagrams provide comprehensive coverage of the metal, from copper-producing areas in the world, prospecting for ore, types of mines, to filtering, smelting, refining, casting, fabrication and uses. French title available : CUIVRE.-

669
    Cuivre.
        prod. [Montreal?] : NFB, 1961.- dist. SEC 44 fr. : col. : 35 mm. & captions & teacher's manual. $9.00 jis

        1. Copper.

    Photographs, maps, and diagrams provide comprehensive coverage of the metal, from copper-producing areas in the world, prospecting for ore, types of mines, to filtering, smelting, refining, casting, fabrication and uses. English title available : COPPER.-

The Classified Catalogue

671.2
Parallel line development.
prod. [Toronto] : M-L, 1974.- dist. Sch. Ser. or Vint. 61 fr. : col. : 35 mm. & cassette (13 min.) : auto. & aud. adv. sig. & teacher's guide. $16.50 (Sheet metal) s

1. Sheet-metal work. 2. Pattern making. 3. Design, Industrial.

Patterning for objects with parallel sides using parallel line development. Photographs illustrate elevation, plan views and concept of three dimensional visualization. Explains transferring pattern onto object. Stresses precise measurements.-

671.2
Pattern development by triangulation.
prod. [Toronto] : M-L, 1974.- dist. Sch. Ser. or Vint. 69 fr. : col. : 35 mm. & cassette (6 min.) : auto. & aud. adv. sig. & teacher's guide. $16.50 (Sheet metal) s

1. Sheet-metal work. 2. Pattern making. 3. Design, Industrial.

A step-by-step pattern development by triangulation for an offset tapered duct. Stresses principles of triangulation, use and problems. Shows how to determine true length, height and width, precise calculation. Close-up photography aids concise instructions.-

671.2
Radial line development.
prod. [Toronto] : M-L, 1974.- dist. Sch. Ser. or Vint. 46 fr. : col. : 35 mm. & cassette (6 min.) : auto. & aud. adv. sig. & teacher's guide. $16.50 (Sheet metal) s

1. Sheet-metal work. 2. Pattern making. 3. Design, Industrial.

Radial line development as applied to patterns for conical shaped objects, ducts with centred round tapers, and ends cut at angles. Demonstrates pattern drawing stressing three dimensional visualization. Photographs accompany step-by-step instructions.-

671.3
Forging iron.
prod. [Toronto] : M-L, 1973.- dist. Sch. Ser. or Vint. 47 fr. : col. : 35 mm. & cassette (11 min.) : auto. & aud. adv. sig. & teacher's guide. $16.50 (Metalwork : hand tools) is

1. Forging.

The forging of a cold chisel demonstrates the tools and equipment used in the forging process. Explains use of a gas forge, anvil and tongs. Close-up photographs show heating of metal in forge, forging metal on anvil, squaring the edge, annealing, tapering and twisting. Stresses safety precautions with a gas forge. One reference to non-metric measurement does not interfere with presentation.-

671.5
Soldering methods.
prod. [Toronto] : M-L, 1973.- dist. Sch. Ser. or Vint. 50 fr. : col. : 35 mm. & cassettde (11 min.) : auto. & aud. adv. sig. & teacher's guide. $16.50 (Metalwork : hand tools) is

1. Solder and soldering.

Teaches the basic principles and techniques of soft and hard soldering with standard or electric solder. Describes a soldering iron, forms of solder, and use of fluxes. Outlines the soldering process, use of the blow torch, galvanizing iron with muriatic acid, pickling and cleaning. One reference to non-metric measurement does not interfere with presentation.-

671.5
Welding techniques.
prod. [Toronto] : M-L, 1973.- dist. Sch. Ser. or Vint. 54 fr. : col. : 35 mm. & cassette (11 min.) : auto. & aud. adv. sig. & teacher's guide. $16.50 (Metalwork : hand tools) is

1. Welding.

Introduces welding equipment and welding procedures. Discusses proper use of the blow torch, including the cylinders, regulators, parts of the flame and its adjustment. Provides step-by-step welding directions. Use of a welding rod, motion to use with torch, and polishing. Shows techniques of fusion welding, braising, "running a bead" and cutting.-

The Classified Catalogue

676
> Pulp and paper.
> prod. [Scarborough, Ont.] : RBM, 1975.- dist. ETHOS 44 fr. : col. : 35 mm. & cassette (9 min.) : auto. & aud. adv. sig. & teacher's manual. $19.00 (Follow your product : $34.50) ji
>
> 1. Paper making and trade.
>
> Illustrates and describes each step in the process of making a sheet of paper. Begins with the harvesting of trees in the forest, follows the timber through the milling process, and shows the drying and rolling step necessary in making paper. Concludes with an outline of the controversies surrounding the pulp and paper industry.-

676.09714
> Newsprint in Quebec.
> prod. [Winnipeg] : VCL, 1972.- dist. Sch. Ch. 42 fr. : col. : 35 mm. $7.95 (Forest industries in Canada : $23.85) ji
>
> 1. Paper making and trade.
>
> A clear sequential explanation of the production of paper for magazines and newspapers. Photographs and diagrams describe the progress from trees in the forest to the creating of pulp and paper. Shows the machinery used in the forest, as well as inside the mill.-

676.09718
> Pulp and paper manufacturing in Newfoundland.
> prod. [Stratford, Ont.] : Sch. Ch., 1974.- dist. Sch. Ch. 47 fr. : col. : 35 mm. $7.95 (Forest industries in Canada : $23.85) ji
>
> 1. Paper making and trade.
>
> A detailed description of pulp and paper manufacturing in Newfoundland. Shows the felling and stacking of trees to the actual making of paper. Concludes with examples of magazines and newspapers from Newfoundland paper. Uses photographs taken at Corner Brook.-

680
> Craft industries.
> prod. [Kitchener, Ont.] : EDU, 1974.- dist. EDU 25 fr. : col. : 35 mm. & cassette (8 min.) : auto. & aud. adv. sig. & teacher's manual. $15.95 (China : $79.95) jis
>
> 1. Art industries and trade - China.
>
> Describes the production of traditional craft work including jade and ivory carving, lacquer, landscapes, dough figurines, ceramics and porcelain. Great detail is given to carving and to cloisonné, a glass and copper craft.-

685
> Indian snowshoes.
> prod. [Montreal?] : NFB, 1963.- dist. McI 32 fr. : col. : 35 mm. & 1963.- $9.00 pj
>
> 1. Snowshoes and snowshoeing.
>
> Describes the detailed steps in producing Indian snowshoes by hand in Labrador. Close-up shots examine the tools used and the tasks of all the family members in helping to make the snowshoes. French title available : RAQUETTES INDIENNES.-

685
> Raquettes indiennes.
> prod. [Montreal?] : NFB, 1963.- dist. SEC 32 fr. : col. : 35 mm. & captions. $9.00 pj
>
> 1. Snowshoes and snowshoeing.
>
> Describes the detailed steps in producing Indian snowshoes by hand in Labrador. Close-up shots examine the tools used and the tasks of all the family members in helping to make the snowshoes. English title available : INDIAN SNOWSHOES.-

687
> Clothing design.
> prod. [Winnipeg] : VCL, 1972.- dist. Sch. Ch. 39 fr. : col. : 35 mm. & captions. $7.95 (Canadian clothing) ji
>
> 1. Clothing trade.
>
> An overview of the clothing industry, including a visit to a Montreal fashion house. Explains designers' ideas, sketching, selection of clothing, and the pattern and sample making. A few fashions are 1972 vintage, but do not detract.-

The Classified Catalogue

687
    Clothing manufacturing.
       prod. [Winnipeg] : VCL, 1972.- dist. Sch. Ch. 43 fr. : b&w & col. : 35 mm. & captions. $7.95 (Canadian clothing) ji

       1. Clothing trade.

       A large Montreal clothing manufacturer exemplifies how ready-made clothing is designed, sewn and sent to outlets across Canada. Depicts designers creating sketches, pattern makers, and the assembly line operation.-

690
    Bâtissons notre maison.
       prod. [Montreal?] : NFB, made 1964 : 1966.- dist. SEC 39 fr. : col. : 35 mm. & captions. $9.00 p

       1. Houses.

       Examines the steps in building a new house from the architect's plans and choice of lot to the moving day. Discusses the many skilled workers involved and their specialized tools. Includes a review section and vocabulary. English title available : BUILDING A HOUSE.-

690
    Build your own log house : part 2.
       prod. [Montreal?] : NFB, 1964.- dist. McI. 44 fr. : col. : 35 mm. & captions. $9.00 s

       1. Log cabins.

       Detailed diagrams and photographs illustrate the completion of the log house. This section deals with roof construction, windows, doors, partitions, and finishing. Types of windows are included. Suggestions are given for attractively completing the job.-

690
    Build your own log house : part 1.
       prod. [Montreal?] : NFB, 1964.- dist. McI. 45 fr. : col. : 35 mm. & captions. $9.00 s

       1. Log cabins.

       Photos and detailed diagrams describe how to build a log house in Canada's north. After consulting the Agency Superintendent on the Reserve, a plan and location are selected. Details are included for each heading, footings and foundations. Floor construction and wall construction continued in Part 2.-

690
    Building a house.
       prod. [Montreal?] : NFB, 1964.- dist. McI. 35 fr. : col. : 35 mm. & captions. $9.00 (Community helpers : $36.00) p

       1. Houses.

       Examines the steps in building a new house, from the architect's plans and choice of lot to the moving day. Discusses the many skilled workers involved and their specialized tools. Includes a review section and vocabulary. French title available : BATISSONS NOTRE MAISON.-

693.2
    Elements of brickwork.
       prod. [Toronto] : M-L. 1974.- dist. Sch. Ser. or Vint. dist. School Services or Vintergreen Communications 76 fr. : col. : 35 mm. & cassette (13 min.) : auto. & aud. adv. sig. & teacher's guide. $16.50 (Trades & technology : masonry) s

       1. Bricklaying.   2. Walls.

       An introduction to all bricklaying tools and the principles of brick-and-mortar construction. Step-by-step instructions show how to build a free-standing wall, covering the construction of a building line, dry bonding, mortar tempering and application, and making joints. Any reference to non-metric measurement does not interfere with presentation.-

693.2
    Walls and bonds.
       prod. [Toronto] : M-L. 1974.- dist. Sch. Ser. or Vint. 68 fr. : col. : 35 mm. & cassette (11 min.) : auto. & aud. adv. sig. & teacher's guide. $16.50 (Trades & technology : masonry) s

       1. Bricklaying.   2. Walls.

       Demonstrates the concepts of brick size and overlap for proper bonding in a brick wall. Detailed photos illustrate the construction of a variety of bonds, including Old English and English Cross, and the construction of a veneer wall showing the use of metal ties. Defines wythe, stretchers, headers.-

The Classified Catalogue

694
Five simple wood joints.
prod. [Toronto] : M-L, 1973.- dist. Sch. Ser. or Wint. 53 fr. : col. : 35 mm. & cassette (7 min.) : auto. & aud. adv. sig. & teacher's guide. $16.50 (Woodworking : hand tools (A) : $85.00) is

1. Woodwork. 2. Carpentry.

Demonstrates the making of five joints - the end butt, end rabbet, dado, groove, and lap. Details the use of glue and dowels to create stronger joints. Stresses the necessity for accuracy.-

698.3
Painting a panelled door.
prod. [Toronto] M-L, 1974.- dist. Sch. Ser. or Wint. 70 fr. : col. : 35 mm. & cassette (9 min.) : auto. & aud. adv. sig. & teacher's guide. $16.50 (Trades & technology : painting and decorating) s

1. Wood finishing.

A demonstration of proper preparation and application of paint to a wooden surface, using a panelled door. Shows sanding, shellacking and removing imperfections. Indicates the steps in painting, using primer, undercoat, and finishing paint. Discusses brush and paint selection and care of brushes.-

698.6
Paper hanging application.
prod. [Toronto] : M-L, 1974.- dist. Sch. Ser. or wint. 62 fr. : col. : 35 mm. & cassette (11 min.) : auto. & aud. adv. sig. & teacher's guide. $16.50 (Trades & technology : painting and decorating) s

1. Paper hanging. 2. Wallpaper.

A step-by-step guide to hanging both prepasted and unpasted wallpaper. Discusses and explains types of wallpaper, choosing paste, lapped seams, trimming edges and butt joints. Outlines equipment needed, and demonstrates measuring, matching and applying the paper to the wall.-

701
Where to find it.
prod. [Toronto] : B&R, 1974.- dist. B & R 34 fr. : b&w & col. : 35 mm. & teacher's manual. $10.00 (An Artist's notebook : $27.00) j

1. Art - Appreciation. 2. Art - Study and teaching.

Uses simple shapes to introduce basic art terms including "centre of interest", and to illustrate composing techniques used by an artist to achieve a balanced picture.
Separate scripts for primary and junior levels.-

708
The National Gallery of Canada.
prod. [Stratford, Ont.] : Sch. Ch., 1974.- dist. Sch. Ch. 55 fr. : b&w & col. : 35 mm. & captions. $7.95 (Our national capital : $39.75) ji

1. National Gallery of Canada.

Covers the role of the National Gallery in encouraging Canadian art, its collection, and programs. Features photographs of the gallery itself, and many paintings from European as well as Canadian collections. Includes information on art restoration.-

709.01
Haida art.
prod. [Toronto] : RQM, 1973.- dist. Lea 30 fr. : col. : 35 mm. & captions & teacher's guide. $9.00 is

1. Haida Indians - Art.

Original graphics demonstqrate the colourful, free flowing quality found in HHaida art. Explains Haida painting and carving, the media used, the purposes of the art, and the role of the different animals in the Indian art world.-

709.01
Indian arts and crafts.
prod. [Scarborough, Ont.] : R.B.M., 1974.- dist. ETHOS 44 fr. : col. : 35 mm. & cassette (19 min.) : auto. & aud. adv. sig. & reading script. $19.00 (Canadian Indian people) jis

1. Indians of North America - Canada - Art.

The story of native art in Canada, past and present, with a look at petroglyphs and petrographs, oral art, West Coast carvings, the use of a variety of media, and the art of the modern Indian.-

The Classified Catalogue

709.01
  The Symbol in Indian art.
   prod. [Scarborough, Ont.] : R.B.M., 1974.- dist. ETHOS 57 fr. : col. : 35 mm. & cassette (18 min.) : auto. & aud. adv. sig. & reading script. $19.00 (Indian culture in Canada : $69.00) jis

   1. Indians of North America - Canada - Art.

   Photographs of actual artwork and diagrams illustrate a discussion of symbols in Indian art. Covers symbolic animals, such as the buffalo and thunderbird, the eye and tongue, teepee and mountain, as well as the drum, but emphasizes the circle as the central symbol in Indian art.-

709.711
  Artistes de la côte canadienne du Pacifique.
   prod. [Montreal?] : NFB, 1971.- dist. SEC 57 fr. : col. : 35 mm. & captions. $9.00 (Les artistes canadiens [I]) is

   1. Artists, Canadian.

   Shows the works of many B.C. artists interspersed with comments on the factors that influenced their growth. Includes Binning, Shadbolt, Hughes, and Jarvis. English title available : ARTISTS OF PACIFIC CANADA.-

709.711
  Artists of Pacific Canada.
   prod. [Montreal?] : NFB, 1971.- dist. McI. 57 fr. : col. : 35 mm. & captions. $9.00 (Artists of Canada : series I) is

   1. Artists, Canadian.

   Shows the work of many B.C. artists interspersed with comments on the factors that influenced their growth. Includes Binning, Shadbolt, Hughes, and Jarvis. French title available : ARTISTS DE LA COTE CANADIENNE DU PACIFIQUE.-

720.944
  Paris.
   prod. [Oakville, Ont.] : SCO, 1970.- dist. SCO 75 fr. : col. : 35 mm. & teacher's manual and reading script. $10.50 is

   1. Architecture, French. 2. Paris, France.

   The many moods of Paris as revealed by its architecture. Uses aerial and close-up photography to show street scenes, churches, statues and such structures as Arc de Triomphe and the Eiffel Tower. Descriptions included in teacher's manual.-

722
  Athens ... Acropolis and Agora.
   prod. [Oakville, Ont.] : SCO 1970.- dist. SCO 40 fr. : col. : 35 mm. & teacher's manual and reading script. $7.50 is

   1. Architecture, Greek.

   The statues, temples and other structures of the Acropolis and Agora. Close-up and aerial photography provide unique views of exteriors and interiors, and types of architecture. Also includes models, drawings. Informative notes in manual.-

722
  Delphi, theatres and Olympia.
   prod. [Oakville, Ont.] : SCO 1970.- dist. SCO 40 fr. : col. : 35 mm. & teacher's manual and reading script. $7.50 is

   1. Architecture, Greek.

   Photographs taken from numerous angles show layout, detail and size of these Greek structures. Includes temples, theatres, stadiums and reconstructions of statue remains. There are descriptions in manual for each frame.-

722
  Roman provinces and Pompeii.
   prod. [Oakville, Ont.] : SCO, 1970.- dist. Scolaire Filmstrips. 42 fr. : col. : 35 mm. & teacher's manual and reading script. $7.50 is

   1. Architecture, Roman. 2. Excavations (Archeology) - Pompeii.

   Features examples of Roman architecture and remains of Pompeii. Photographs include Roman amphitheatres, aqueducts, baths and temples. Shows streets, homes, courtyards and buildings found during excavations in Pompeii. Manual discusses origins and functions of structures.-

726.0971
  Visiting early Canadian churches.
   prod. [Toronto] : B&R, 1976.- dist. &R 26 fr. : col. : 35 mm. & cassette (12 min.) : auto. & aud. adv. sig. & teacher's manual & reading script. $18.00 (Early day Canada : $96.00) ji

   1. Church architecture.

   Examines the primitive, classical, Gothic revival, and Romanesque revival styles of Canadian churches built during the period 1790-1890.-

The Classified Catalogue

728
Development of Canadian homes.
  prod. [Toronto] : B&R, 1976.- dist. B&R 27 fr. : col. : 35 mm. & cassette (11 min.) : auto. & aud. adv. sig. & script & teacher's manual. $16.00 (Homes in Canada and around the world : $84.00) pji

  1. Houses.

  Describes the three stages in the development of home construction: homes built by the family ("primitive"), homes requiring the labour of a number of people, ("traditional"), homes built by specialists, including architects and craftsmen ("modern"). Examples of each kind are shown.-

728
Factors influencing homes.
  prod. [Toronto] : B&R, 1976.- dist. B&R 27 fr. : col. : 35 mm. & cassette (12 min.) : auto. & aud. adv. sig. & script & teacher's manual. $16.00 (Homes in Canada and around the world : $84.00) pji

  1. Houses.

  Explores the factors which determine location, size and style of homes. Touches on the availability of land, resources, and transportation, as well as climate, culture and technology.-

728
Homes in cold climates.
  prod. [Toronto] : B&R, 1976.- dist. B&R 21 fr. : col. : 35 mm. & cassette (8 min.) : auto. & aud. adv. sig. & script & teacher's manual. $16.00 (Homes in Canada and around the world : $84.00) pji

  1. Houses.

  Outlines the ways in which homes are adapted for cold climates, such as small doors and windows, dark colours, insulation, peaked roofs, and common walls. Includes a photograph of an above-ground utility system used in the Canadian north.-

728
Homes in hot, dry climates.
  prod. [Toronto] : B&R, 1976.- dist. B&R 19 fr. : col. : 35 mm. & cassette (7 min.) : auto. & aud. adv. sig. & script & teacher's manual. $16.00 (Homes in Canada and around the world : $84.00) pji

  1. Houses.

  Uses examples taken from around the world to illustrate the ways homes are adapted to hot, dry climates. Includes the use of light colours, vegetation, close-spacing of buildings, and shaded windows and doors.-

728
Homes in hot, humid climates.
  prod. [Toronto] : B&R, 1976.- dist. B&R 21 fr. : col. : 35 mm. & cassette (8 min.) : auto. & aud. adv. sig. & script & teacher's manual. $16.00 (Homes in Canada and around the world : $84.00) pji

  1. Houses.

  The use of light colours, large and shaded windows and doors, high ceilings and raised floors are among the ways homes are adapted for hot, humid weather. Examples taken from around the world illustrate these adaptations.-

728
How homes are adapted to nature : wind and radiation.
  prod. [Toronto] : B&R, 1976.- dist. B&R 23 fr. : col. : 35 mm. & cassette (8 min.) : auto. & aud. adv. sig. & script & teacher's manual. $16.00 (Homes in Canada and around the world : $84.00) pji

  1. Houses.

  Considers ways homes may be protected from radiation (extreme light), including the use of recessed, narrow doors and windows, vegetation, shutters and awnings. Also discusses protecting homes from wind by using windbreaks or building close to the ground and in sheltered areas.-

The Classified Catalogue

728.0971
Homes of early day Canada.
prod. [Toronto] : B&R, 1976.- dist. B&R 29 fr. : col. : 35 mm. & cassette (14 min.) : auto. & aud. adv. sig. & teacher's manual & reading script. $18.00 (Early day Canada : $96.00) ji

1. Architecture, Domestic. 2. Frontier and pioneer life. 3. Canada - Historic buildings, etc.

Some of the styles used for Canadian homes during the period 1790-1890 are examined, including log cabins, stone houses, neo-classical homes, Gothic revival and Italianate. Includes photographs of the homes of Sir John A. Macdonald and Sir Wilfred Laurier.-

728.8
Versailles and Portugal.
prod. [Oakville, Ont.] : SCO, 1970.- dist. SCO 40 fr. : col. : 35 mm. & teacher's manual and reading script. $7.50 is

1. Palaces.

The architecture of French King Louis XIII's palace at Versailles and the Palace of Queluz near Lisbon, Portugal. Photographs feature interior of palaces, as well as cottages, gardens and fountains. Also shows carriages used by royalty. Descption for each frame included in manual.-

731
Masks.
prod. [Scarborough, Ont.] : R.B.M., 1974.- dist. ETHOS 64 fr. : col. : 35 mm. & cassette (13 min.) : auto. & aud. adv. sig. & teacher's manual. $19.00 (Theatre arts : "bare boards and a passion" : $69.00) is

1. Masks (for the face). 2. Costume.

Discusses the techniques of creating masks using such materials as latex rubber, plaster of paris and papier-mâché. Uses close-up photography to illustrate the methods.-

731
Wire sculpture with a twist.
prod. [Scarborough, Ont.] : R.B.M., 1975.- dist. ETHOS 35 fr. : col. : 35 mm. & cassette (7 min.) : auto. & aud. adv. sig. $19.00 (Art : $69.00) is

1. Wire sculpture. 2. Sculpture - Technique.

Discusses the tools necessary for wire sculpture, shaping, plastering and painting, and creating a patina.-

736
The Art of the totem pole.
prod. [Montreal?] : NFB, 1971.- dist. McI. 50 fr. : b&w & col. : 35 mm. & captions. $9.00 (Native arts : $35.00) ji

1. Indians of North America - Art.
2. Totems and totemism.

Photographs illustrate the history of different kinds of poles with their varying and ceremonial roles and the use and significance of symbolic animal figures. French title available : L'ART DU MAT TOTEMIQUE.-

736
L'art sculptural esquimau.
prod. [Montreal?] : NFB, 1962.- dist. SEC 50 fr. : col. : 35 mm. & captions & manual. $9.00 (L'art indigène) jis

1. Eskimos - Art. 2. Sculpture.

Portrays Eskimo carvings of three time periods, paying particular attention to characteristics of modern sculpture. Supplementary information is included in the manual. English title available : ESKIMO SCULPTURE.-

736
L'art totémique.
prod. [Montreal?] : NFB, 1971.- dist. SEC 46 fr. : b&w & col. : 35 mm. & captions. $9.00 ji

1. Indians of North America - Art.
2. Totems and totemism.

Photographs illustrate the history of different kinds of poles with their varying and ceremonial roles and the use and significance of symbolic animal figures. English title available : THE ART OF THE TOTEM POLE.-

736
    Eskimo carvings.
        prod. [Montreal?] : NFB, 1953.- dist. McI. 81 fr. : b&w : 35 mm. & captions. $9.00 jis

        1. Eskimos - Art. 2. Sculpture.

        A brief description precedes each black and white photograph of an Eskimo carving. Carvings are made of stone, ivory and bone, and depict the Eskimo way of life. French title available : SCULPTURE ESQUIMAU.-

736
    Eskimo sculpture.
        prod. [Montreal?] : NFB, made 1962 : 1973.- dist. McI. 50 fr. : col. : 35 mm. & captions & manual. $9.00 (Native arts) jis

        1. Eskimos - Art. 2. Sculpture.

        Portrays Eskimo carvings of three time periods, paying particular attention to characteristics of modern sculpture. Supplementary information is included in the manual. French title available : L'ART SCULPTURAL ESQUIMAU.-

736
    Haida argillite carvings.
        prod. [Montreal?] : NFB, 1958.- dist. McI. 36 fr. : b&w : 35 mm. & captions & printed notes. $9.00 (Native arts : $35.00) jis

        1. Haida Indians - Art.

        Illustrates a series of argillite carvings done by the Haida Indians of the Queen Charlotte Islands. French title available : LES SCULPTURES SUR ARGILITE DES HAIDAS.-

736
    Sculpture esquimau.
        prod. [Montreal?[: NFB, made 1953 : 1968.- dist. SEC 81 fr. : b&w : 35 mm. & captions. $9.00 jis

        1. Eskimos - Art. 2. Sculpture.

        A brief description precedes each black and white photograph of an Eskimo carving. Carvings are made of stone, ivory and bone, and depict the Eskimo way of life. English title available : ESKIMO CARVINGS.-

736
    Les scuptures sur argilite des Haïdas.
        prod. [Montreal?] : NFB, 1958.- dist. SEC 36 fr. : b&w: 35 mm. & captions & printed notes. $9.00 (L'art indigène) jis

        1. Haida Indians - Art.

        Illustrates a series of argillite carvings done by the Haida Indians of the Queen Charlotte Islands. English title available : HAIDA ARGILLITE CARVINGS.-

736
    Totem pole tales.
        prod. [Scarborough, Ont.] : R.B.M., 1974.- dist. ETHOS 69 fr. : col. : 35 mm. & cassette (19 min.) : auto. & aud. adv. sig. & reading script. $19.00 (Indian culture in Canada : $69.00) jis

        1. Indians of North America - Art.
        2. Totems and totemism.

        Describes totem poles as crest-bearing houseposts, the mythological creatures represented in the carving, and the stories the totems tell. Includes photographs of Alert Bay, B.C. and close-ups of, Indian carvings and paintings.-

736
    Totem poles.
        prod. [Stratford, Ont.] : Sch. Ch., 1977.- dist. Sch. Ch. 46 fr. : col. : 35 mm. & captions. $7.95 (Canadian mosaic : $39.75) ji

        1. Indians of North America - Art.
        2. Totems and totemism.

        Introduction to unique art form of West Coast Indians. Covers debarking, marking figures, carving and colouring. Discusses type of wood used and why, and significance of design. Numerous photographs indicate variety in size, artwork and use.-

The Classified Catalogue

737.4
Royal Canadian Mint.
    prod. [Winnipeg] : VCL, 1972.- dist. Sch. Ch. 45 fr. : b&w & col. : 35 mm. & captions. $7.95 (Our national capital : $39.75) ji

1. Royal Canadian Mint.

Illustrates the role of the Canadian federal government in manufacturing coins at the Royal Canadian Mint in Ottawa. Photographs taken inside the Mint show the procedure and the machinery used in making coins from molten ore to bagged coins ready for the banks. Explains creation of designs and how they are impressed on coins.-

738.1
Elements of pottery.
    prod. [Scarborough, Ont.] : R.B.M., 1975.- dist. ETHOS 41 fr. : col. : 35 mm. & cassette (8 min.) : auto. & aud. adv. sig. $19.00 (Art : $69.00) is

1. Pottery.

Uses close-up photos to demonstrate pottery techniques of air drying, glazing and firing.-

738.1
Pottery : hand building techniques.
    prod. [Scarborough, Ont] : R.B.M., 1975.- dist. ETHOS 48 fr. : col. : 35 mm. & cassette (9 min.) : auto. & aud. adv. sig. $19.00 (Art : $69.00) is

1. Pottery.

Close-up photography illustrates the techniques for shaping objects in clay by hand. Demonstrates the coil, slab and pinch methods.-

738.1
Using a potter's wheel.
    prod. [Scarborough, Ont.] : R.B.M., 1975.- dist. ETHOS 44 fr. : col. : 35 mm. & cassette (8 min.) : auto. & aud. adv. sig. $19.00 (Art : $69.00) is

1. Pottery - Technique.

Discusses and illustrates the preparation of clay for throwing. Also shows the techniques for throwing cylinders and shapes.-

741.2
The Shape of things : part 1.
    prod. [Toronto] : B&R, 1974.- dist. B&R 29 fr. : b&w & col. : 35 mm. & teacher's manual. $10.00 (An Artist's notebook : $27.00) j

1. Drawing.

Introduces geometric shapes, a variety of line types, and shading techniques. Shows how to assemble these components to create still life objects and landscape forms.-

741.2
The Shape of things : part 2.
    prod. [Toronto] : B&R, 1974.- dist. B&R 51 fr. : b&w & col. : 35 mm. & teacher's manual. $10.00 (An Artist's notebook : $27.00) j

1. Drawing.

Reviews basic shape identification and shading, and line techniques, applying this approach to the sketching of the human face (full and half profile) and figure.-

745.5
Beginnings.
    prod. [Toronto] : Int. Cin., 1973.- dist. VEC 49 fr. : col. : 35 mm. & cassette (6 min.) : auto. & aud. adv. sig. & teacher's guide. $24.00 (Tales from the treetops : $86.00) pji

1. Arts and crafts. 2. Seeds.

A series of seed pictures, made from the seeds of trees like the maple and elm. Children are shown how seeds may be combined to form pictures of running animals, cowboys, teepees, etc. French title available : COMMENCEMENT.-

745.5
Commencement.
    prod. [Toronto] : Int. Cin., 1974.- dist. VEC 49 fr. : col. : 35 mm. & cassette (7 min.) : auto. & aud. adv. sig. & teacher's guide. $24.00 (Les arbres m'ont raconté : $86.00) pji

1. Arts and crafts. 2. Seeds.

A series of seed pictures, made from the seeds of trees like the maple and elm. Children are shown how seeds may be combined to form pictures of running animals, cowboys, teepees, etc. English title available : BEGINNINGS.-

The Classified Catalogue

745.5
How would you use it?
prod. [Toronto] : Int. Cin., 1976.- dist. VEC 63 fr. : col. : 35 mm. & cassette (5 min.) : auto. & aud. adv. sig. & teacher's guide. $24.00 (Look, listen, discover! : $230.00) pj

1. Arts and crafts. 2. Thought and thinking - Problems, exercises, etc.

Teaches children how to transform common household objects, such as string, plastic containers, cardboard boxes, bottles and paper plates into something useful, decorative or playful. French title available : QU'EST-CE QU'ON PEUT FAIRE DE CA?-

745.5
Make something new.
prod. [Toronto] : Int. Cin., 1976.- dist. VEC 54 fr. : col. : 35 mm. & cassette (4 min.) : auto. & aud. adv. sig. & teacher's guide. $24.00 (Look, listen, discover! : $230.00) pj

1. Arts and crafts. 2. Thought and thinking - Problems, exercises, etc.

An artwork presentation of playthings that children can make from bleach bottles, pip cleaners, paper cups and felt pens. The objects shown are more complex than those in "How Would You Use It", requiring greater skill, patience and time. French title available : TROUVONS AUTRE CHOSE.-

745.5
Qu'est-ce qu'on peut faire de ca?
prod. [Toronto] : Int. Cin., 1976.- dist. VEC 63 fr. : col. : 35 mm. & cassette (5 min.) : auto. & aud. adv. sig. & teacher's guide. $24.00 (Ouvre l'oeil et le bon... : $230.00) pj

1. Arts and crafts. 2. Thought and thinking - Problems, exercises, etc.

Teaches children how to transform common household objects, such as string, plastic containers, cardboard boxes, bottles and paper plates into something useful, decorative or playful. English title available : HOW WOULD YOU USE IT?-

745.5
Trouvons autre chose.
prod. [Toronto] : Int. Cin., 1976.- dist. VEC 54 fr. : col. : 35 mm. & cassette (4 min.) : auto. & aud. adv. sig. & teacher's guide. $24.00 (Ouvre l'oeil et le bon... : $230.00) pj

1. Arts and crafts. 2. Thought and thinking - Problems, exercises, etc.

An artwork presentation of playthings that children can make from bleach bottles, pipe cleaners, paper cups, and felt pens. The objects shown are more complex than those in "How Would You Use It"., requiring greater skill, patience and time. English title available : MAKE SOMETHING NEW.-

746.3
Faire une bannière.
prod. [Montreal?] : NFB, 1972.- dist. SEC 47 fr. : col. : 35 mm. & captions. $9.00 jis

1. Collage. 2. Flags. 3. Tapestry.

Traces the history of banners from Roman battle insignia to the decorative fabric banners of today. Includes works by Norman Laliberté. Follows the construction of a banner including preparation of design, materials required and methods of application. English title available : MAKING BANNERS.-

746.3
Making banners.
prod. [Montreal?] : NFB, 1972.- dist. McI. 47 fr. : col. : 35 mm. & captions. $9.00 jis

1. Collage. 2. Flags. 3. Tapestry.

Traces the history of banners from Roman battle insignia to the decorative fabric banners of today. Includes works by Norman Laliberté. Follows the construction of a banner including preparation of design, materials required, and methods of application. French title available : FAIRE UNE BANNIERE.-

The Classified Catalogue

746.9
    Faire une cagoule.
        prod. [Montreal?] : NFB, 1972.- dist. SEC 27 fr. : col. : 35 mm. & captions. $9.00 jis

        1. Costume.

        Photographs and diagrams illustrate the method for making a body mask out of fabric. These can be used in plays, for Hallowe'en and for masquerades. Artist Norman Laliberté illustrates step-by-step procedure in decorating a body mask. English title available : MAKING A BODY MASK.-

746.9
    Making a body mask.
        prod. [Montreal?] : NFB, 1972.- dist. McI. 28 fr. : col. : 35 mm. & captions. $9.00 jis

        1. Costume.

        Photographs and diagrams illustrate the method for making a body mask out of fabric. These can be used in plays, for Hallowe'en and for masquerades. Artist Norman Laliberté illustrates step-by-step procedure in decorating a body mask. French title available : FAIRE UNE COGOULE.-

749
    Art work presentation : mat cutting.
        prod. [Oakville,Ont.] : SC, [1978].- 40 fr. : col. : 35 mm. & cassette (6 min.) : auto. adv. sig. only. $35.00 is

        1. Picture frames and framing.

        Illustrations and photographs are used to show preparation and cutting of mat. Gives tips on estimating mat size, ensuring a clean cut, and attaching mat to item.-

759.11
    Alfred Pellan.
        prod. [Montreal?] : NFB, c1961.- dist. SEC 31 fr. : col. : 35 mm. & captions & teacher's manual. $9.00 (Les artistes canadiens [I]) is

        1. Pellan, Alfred, 1906-

        Discusses the development of Alfred Pellan's style by studying examples of his work. Additional useful information is contained in the manual. English title available : ALFRED PELLAN.-

759.11
    Alfred Pellan.
        prod. [Montreal?] : NFB, 1961.- dist. McI. 31 fr. : col. : 35 mm. & captions & teacher's manaual. (Artists of Canada : series I) is

        1. Pellan, Alfred, 1906-

        Discusses the development of Alfred Pellan's style by studying examples of his work. Additional useful information is contained in the manual. French title available : ALFRED PELLAN.-

759.11
    Cornelius Krieghoff.
        prod. [Montreal?] : NFB, made 1957 : 1972.- dist. McI. 50 fr. : col. : 35 mm. & captions & reading script. $9.00 (Artists of Canada : series I) jis

        1. Krieghoff, Cornelius, 1812-1872.

        The paintings of Cornelius Krieghoff portray the history of Quebec life in the 1800's. Details of the artist and his work are included in the captions and the manual. French title available : CORNELIUS KRIEGHOFF.-

759.11
    David Milne.
        prod. [Montreal?] : NFB, 1961.- dist. SEC 52 fr. : col. : 35 mm. & captions & manual. $9.00 (Les artistes canadiens [I]) is

        1. Milne, David Brown, 1882-1953.

        Describes the development of Milne's career, focusing on his techniques and interests, and the forces that influenced him. Illustrated with captioned photos of his work. English title available : DAVID MILNE.-

759.11
    David Milne.
        prod. [Montreal?] : NFB, 1961.- dist. McI. 52 fr. : col. : 35 mm. & captions & manual. $9.00 (Artists of Canada : series I) is

        1. Milne, David Brown, 1882-1953.

        Describes the development of Milne's career, focussing on his techniques and interests, and the forces that influenced him. Illustrated with captioned photos of his work. French title available : DAVID MILNE.-

The Classified Catalogue

759.11
    Emily Carr.
        prod. [Montreal?] : NFB, made 1960 : 1972.- dist. McI. 58 fr. : col. : 35 mm. & captions & manual. $9.00 (Artists of Canada : series I) jis

        1. Carr, Emily, 1871-1945.

        A chronological presentation of the paintings of Emily Carr. Manual outlines background information about the artist and her work.-

759.11
    The Group of Seven.
        prod. [Montreal?] : NFB, 1963.- dist. McI. 52 fr. : col. : 35 mm. & captions & script. $9.00 (Artists of Canada : series I) is

        1. Group of Seven (Canadian painters). 2. Painters, Canadian.

        A good introduction to the Group of Seven, with examples of their paintings. Manual is necessary for biographical details and for titles of paintings. Includes Thomson, Carmichael, Casson, Fitzgerald, Harris, A.Y. Jackson, Johnston, MacDonald and Varley. French title available : LE GROUPE DES SEPT.-

759.11
    Le Groupe des Sept.
        prod. [Montreal?] : NFB, 1963.- dist. SEC 54 fr. : b&w & col. : 35 mm. & captions & manual. $9.00 (Les artistes canadiens [II]) is

        1. Painters, Canadian. 2. Group of Seven (Canadian painters).

        An introduction to the Group of Seven, with examples of their paintings. Manual is necessary for biographical details and for titles of paintings. Includes Thomson, Carmichael, Casson, Fitzgerald, Harris, A.Y. Jackson, Johnston, MacDonald and Varley. English title available : THE GROUP OF SEVEN.-

759.11
    Homer Watson.
        prod. [Montreal?] : NFB, made 1964 : 1966.- dist. SEC 49 fr. : col. : 35 mm. & captions & manual. $9.00 (Les artistes canadiens [I]) jis

        1. Watson, Homer Ransford, 1855-1936.

        The works of artist Homer Watson are examined chronologically to demonstrate the evolution of his style. Technical and symbolic aspects are discussed in the captions. English title available : HOMER WATSON.-

759.11
    James Wilson Morrice.
        prod. [Montreal?] : NFB, 1969.- dist. McI. 55 fr. : col. : 35 mm. & captions & notes. $9.00 (Artists of Canada : series II) is

        1. Morrice, James Wilson, 1865-1924

        Uses photographs of actual paintings to discuss the work of James Wilson Morrice. Compares the style of his earliest works with that of later paintings. Explains the effect on his work of several famous European artists. Covers various types of form, design, and texture. Useful for groups studying the history of art.-

759.11
    Jean-Paul Riopelle.
        prod. [Montreal?] : NFB, made 1963 : 1972.0 dist. SEC 42 fr. : col. : 35 mm. & captions & teacher's manual. $9.00 (Les artistes canadiens [II]) is

        1. Riopelle, Jean-Paul, 1923-

        Outlines the development of Riopelle's style and technique using captioned photos of the artist's works. English title available : JEAN-PAUL RIOPELLE.-

759.11
    Jean-Paul Riopelle.
        prod. [Montreal?] : NFB, 1963.- dist. McI. 38 fr. : col. : 35 mm. & captions. $9.00 (Artists of Canada : series II) is

        1. Riopelle, Jean-Paul, 1923-

        Outlines the development of Riopelle's style and technique using captioned photos of the artist's works. French title available : JEAN-PAUL RIOPELLE.-

759.11
    Lawren S. Harris.
        prod. [Montreal?] : NFB, made 1964 : 1967.- dist. SEC 56 fr. : col. :c35 mm. & captions & teacher's guide. $9.00 (Les artistes canadiens [II]) is

        1. Harris, Lawren Stewart, 1885-1970.

        Presents photographs of Harris' paintings from his earliest to latest works. The different periods with changing influences from Impressionism and Art Nouveau to mysticism and the use of abstract form are explained by the captions. English title available : LAWREN S. HARRIS.-

The Classified Catalogue

759.11
    Lawren S. Harris.
        prod. [Montreal?] : NFB, 1964.- dist. McI. 56 fr. : col. : 35 mm. & captions & manual $9.00 (Artists of Canada : series II) is

        1. Harris, Lawren Stewart, 1885-1970.

        Presents photographs of Harris' paintings from his earliest to his latest works. The different periods with changing influences from Impressionism and Art Nouveau to mysticism and the use of abstract form are explained by the captions. French title available : LAWREN S. HARRIS.-

759.11
    Paul-Emile Borduas.
        prod. [Montreal?] : NFB, made 1961 : 1965.- dist. SEC 37 fr. : col. : 35 mm. & teacher's manual. $9.00 (Les artistes canadiens [II]) is

        1. Borduas, Paul Emile, 1905-1960.

        Traces the development of Borduas' painting from his early days in Quebec through his studies in France and his latter days in New York and Paris. Illustrates the way his painting style was affected by Renoir, Morrice, Denis and LeDuc. Examines his period of expressionist painting. English title available : PAUL-EMILE BORDUAS.-

759.11
    Paul-Emile Borduas.
        prod. [Montreal?] : NFB, 1961.- dist. McI. 37 fr. : col. : 35 mm. & captions & teacher's manual. $9.00 (Artists of Canada : series II) is

        1. Borduas, Paul Emile, 1905-1960.

        Traces the development of Borduas' painting from his early days in Quebec through his studies in France and his latter days in New York and Paris. Illustrates the way his painting style was affected by Renoir, Morrice, Denis and LeDuc. Examines his period of expressionist painting. French title available : PAUL-EMILE BORDUAS.-

760.028
    Basic tools for graphic design.
        prod. [Oakville, Ont.] : SC, [197-].- dist. SC 79 fr. : col. : 35 mm. & cassette (15 min.) : auto. adv. sig. only. $35.00 is

        1. Graphic arts.

        Photographs and diagrams give a comprehensive introduction to the basic tools needed for graphic design. Discusses the correct use of tools such as the set square, the compass, French curve, brushes, pencils, pens and paste.-

760.028
    Creating your own visuals using a dry mount press.
        prod. [Oakville, Ont.] : SC, 1972.- dist. SC 61 fr. : col. : 35 mm. & cassette (10 min.) : auto. & aud. adv. sig. $35.00 is

        1. Dry mounting press.

        Uses photographs and drawings to describe in detail the method of using a dry mounting press. Examines various effects that can be achieved with it. Discusses mounting procedures, laminating, colour lifting and creating textures.-

769
    L'art graphique esquimau.
        prod. [Montreal?] : NFB, 1962.- dist. SEC 43 fr. : col. : 35 mm. & captions & teacher's manual. $9.00 (L'art indigène) jis

        1. Prints. 2. Eskimos - Art.

        Artwork and photos show how the Eskimo artist makes prints from inscribed stone blocks and sealskin pencils, providing many examples. English title available : ESKIMO PRINTS.-

769
Canada : people and environment.
   prod. [Toronto] : Int. Cin., 1973.- dist. VEC 68 fr. : col. : 35 mm. & cassette (14 min.) : auto. & aud. adv. sig. & teacher's guide. $24.00 (Postage stamps tell Canada's story : $86.00) ji

   1. Postage stamps. 2. Canada - History - Pictorial works.

   Discusses Canadian wildlife, sports, transportation, and famous people in the fields of art and medicine, using stamps. Shown are highlights of history, including Trans-Canada Highway, St. Lawrence Seaway, Group of Seven, and Dr. Norman Bethune. French title available : LE PEUPLE CANADIEN ET SON ENVIRONNEMENT.-

769
Canada and its provinces.
   prod. [Toronto] : Int. Cin., 1973.- dist. VEC 65 fr. : col. : 35 mm. & cassette (13 min.) : auto. & aud. adv. sig. & teacher's guide. $24.00 (Postage stamps tell Canada's story : $86.00) ji

   1. Postage stamps. 2. Canada - History - Pictorial works.

   Describes specific aspects of each province. Includes historical events and important landmarks, such as Charlottetown Conference, the Bluenose, Red River Settlement, the development of the West, and the Gold Rush. French title available : LES PROVINCES CANADIENNES.-

769
Eskimo prints.
   prod. [Montreal?] : NFB, 1962.- dist. McI. 45 fr. : col. : 35 mm. & captions & teacher's manual. $9.00 (Native arts) jis

   1. Prints. 2. Eskimos - Art.

   Artwork and photos show how the Eskimo artist makes prints from inscribed stone blocks and sealskin stencils, providing many examples. French title available : L'ART GRAPHIQUE ESQUIMAU.-

769
Introducing the postage stamp.
   prod. [Toronto] : Int. Cin., 1973.- dist. VEC 60 fr. : col. : 35 mm. & cassette (13 min.) : auto. & aud. adv. sig. & teacher's guide. $24.00 (Postage stamps tell Canada's story : $86.00) ji

   1. Postage stamps - History. 2. Postal service - Canada - History.

   Describes history of stamps and the development of our postal system. Emphasizes the historical significance of special issues, the various types of stamps and their uses, as well as the value of some rare examples. French title available : LA PRESENTATION DU TIMBRE POSTE.-

769
Le Peuple Canadien et son environnement.
   prod. [Toronto] : Int. Cin., 1973.- dist. VEC 68 fr. : col. : 35 mm. & cassette (13 min.) : auto. & aud. adv. sig. & teacher's guide. $24.00 (Les Timbres post raconte l'histoire du Canada : $86.00) ji

   1. Postage stamps. 2. Canada - History - Pictorial works.

   Discusses Canadian wildlife, sports, transportation, and famous people in the fields of art and medicine, using stamps. Shown are highlights of history, including Trans-Canada Highway, St. Lawrence Seaway, Group of Seven, and Dr. Norman Bethune. English title available : CANADA : PEOPLE AND ENVIRONMENT.-

769
Shaping the Canadian nation.
   prod. [Toronto] : Int. Cin., 1973.- dist. VEC 60 fr. : col. : 35 mm. & cassette (13 min.) : auto. & aud. adv. sig. & teacher's guide. $24.00 (Postage stamps tell Canada's story : $86.00) ji

   1. Canada - History - Pictorial works.
   2. Postage stamps.

   Traces Canada's history through historic and commemorative stamps. Includes Indians, explorers, famous battles, Confederation, well-known politicians, and people in the field of medicine. French title available : LA NAISSANCE D'UN PAYS.-

The Classified Catalogue

771
    Film and filters.
        prod. [Scarborough, Ont.] : R.B.M., 1976.- dist. ETHOS 66 fr. : col. : 35 mm. & cassette (9 min.) : auto. & aud. adv. sig. & teacher's manual. $19.00 (Basic photography : $69.00) ji

        1. Photography - Film.

    Presents the basics of filters and film, from choosing the film and the meaning of the ASA, to the use of coloured filters to create special effects.-

771.3
    The Camera.
        prod. [Scarborough, Ont.] : R.B.M., 1976.- dist. ETHOS 68 fr. : col. : 35 mm. & cassette (13 min.) : auto. & aud. adv. sig. & teacher's manual. $19.00 (Basic photography : $69.00) ji

        1. Cameras.

    Covers the basics of a simple camera and its capabilities. Useful for the beginning photographer of any age.-

778.2
    The 16mm film projector : part 3.
        prod. [Montreal?] : NFB, 1961.- dist. McI. 45 fr. : col. : 35 mm. & captions & teacher's manual. $9.00 is

        1. Projectors.

    Designed for training volunteer projectionists, this discusses the projectionist's job. Common troubles, including loss of picture, sound, and damaged film are mentioned, and remedies suggested. French title available : LE PROJECTEUR CINEMATOGRAPHIQUE DE 16 mm 3è partie.-

778.2
    Producing graphics for slides and filmstrips.
        prod. [Oakville, Ont.] : SC, 1972.- dist. SC 48 fr. : col. : 35 mm. & cassette (9 min.) : auto. adv. sig. only. $35.00 is

        1. Filmstrips. 2. Graphic arts. 3. Slides (Photography).

    Drawings, diagrams and photographs explain concept of graphics and how they can be used. Provides useful hints for effective slides or filmstrips including methods of lettering and titles. Examines uses and effects of graphics more than their actual production.-

778.2
    Le projecteur cinématographie de 16 mm : 3e partie.
        prod. [Montreal?] : NFB, 1961.- dist. SEC 45 fr. : col. : 35 mm. & captions & teacher's manual. $9.00 is

        1. Projectors.

    Designed for training volunteer projectionists, this discusses the projectionist's job. Common troubles including loss of picture, sound, and damaged film are mentioned, and remedies suggested. English title available : THE 16 mm FILM PROJECTOR : PART 3.-

778.2
    Le projecteur cinématographique de 16 mm. : 2e partie.
        prod. [Montreal?] : NFB, 1961.- dist. SEC 25 fr. : col. : 35 mm. & captions & teacher's manual. $9.00 is

        1. Projectors.

    Illustrates the movement of the film and gives threading diagrams. 35 mm, 16 mm and 8 mm are shown and diagrams explain each part of the projector involved in movement of the film. Includes threading diagrams for Ampro, Bell and Howell, Eastman Kodak, RCA and Victor projectors. Designed for training volunteer projectionists. English title available : THE 16 mm FILM PROJECTOR : PART 2.-

778.2
    Le projecteur cinématographique de 16 mm: 1ère partie.
        prod. [Montreal?] : NFB, 1961.- dist. SEC 18 fr. : col. : 35 mm. & captions & teacher's manual. $9.00 is

        1. Projectors.

    Illustrates the projection of the picture and the reproduction of the sound. Diagrams are labelled and the captions explain the function of each part. Designed for training volunteer projectionists. English title available : THE 16 mm FILM PROJECTOR : PART 1.-

The Classified Catalogue

778.2
    The 16 mm film projector : part 1.
        prod. [Montreal?] : NFB, 1961.- dist. McI. 18 fr. : col. : 35 mm. & captions & teacher's manual. $9.00 is

        1. Projectors.

        Illustrates the projection of the picture and the reproduction of the sound. Diagrams are labelled and the captions explain the function of each part. Designed for training volunteer projectionists. French title available : LE PROJECTEUR CINEMATOGRAPHIQUE DE 16 mm 1ère partie.-

784.40971
    Jack was every inch a sailor.
        prod. [Montreal?] : NFB, made 1956 : 1971.- dist. McI. 58 fr. : col. : 35 mm. & disc (33 1/3 rpm. mono. 8 min.) : auto. & aud. adv. sig. & teacher's guide. $18.00 pj

        1. Folk songs, Canadian.

        Teaches children the words and music to a popular Newfoundland ballad. Cartoons and music score accompany each line of song. Ballad sung using words, "la", and tonic sol-fa. To be used with teacher's manual that contains full music score.-

784.40971
    The Raftsmen.
        prod. [Montreal?] : NFB, made 1958 : 1968.- dist. McI. 93 fr. : col. : 35 mm. & disc (33 1/3 rpm. mono. 8 min.) : auto. & aud. adv. sig. & teacher's guide. $9.00 pj

        1. Folk songs, Canadian. 2. Lumber and lumbering - Songs and music.

        Captioned drawings by school children, with accompanying record and manual, teach a 19th century lumbermen's song, describing their seasonal activities at camp.-

784.709714
    Cadet Rousselle.
        prod. [Montreal?] : NFB, [1958] dist. SEC 96 fr. : col. : 35 mm. & captions & disc (33 1/3 rpm. 7 min.) & teacher's manual. $9.00 pj

        1. Folk songs, Canadian (French).

        Provides words and music, accompanied by record, to French folk song about eccentric man who does everything by threes. Music and verses are repeated in manual, which also contains brief history of ballad. English disc includes introduction in English and ballad in French.-

790
    Native games.
        prod. [Toronto] : RQM, 1973.- dist. Lea. 35 fr. : col. : 35 mm. & captions & teacher's guide. $9.00 (Our native people : customs and legends) is

        1. Indians of North America - Games.

        Authentic graphics portray objects used in Indian sport and show groups of natives involved in the specific games. No explanatory details are given.-

790.20971
    National Arts Centre.
        prod. [Winnipeg] : VCL, 1972.- dist. Sch. Ch. 37 fr. : b&w & col. : 35 mm. & captions. $7.95 (Our national capital :$39.75) ji

        1. National Arts Centre.

        Photographs of plays, ballets, and orchestras performed at the National Arts Centre in Ottawa illustrate the variety of entertainment provided. Also includes photographs of construction of the building, the finished interior, and the National Arts Centre Orchestra. Explains how the Centre makes citizens aware of the arts.-

791.5
    Telling stories with puppets and masks.
        prod. [Toronto] : Int. Cin., 1976.- dist. VEC 71 fr. : col. : 35 mm. & cassette (9 min.) : auto. & aud. adv. sig. & teacher's guide. $24.00 (Legends of the Micmac : $86.00) pji

        1. Puppets and puppet plays.

        Using characters from the Micmac legends, students are shown the basic principles of mask and puppet construction and how different kinds of puppets are operated.-

791.8
    Calgary stampede.
        prod. [Winnipeg] : VCL, 1972.- dist. Sch. Ch. 45 fr. : b&w & col. : 35 mm. & captions. $7.95 (Canadian mosaic) ji

        1. Calgary Stampede. 2. Rodeos.

        bBoth old photographs of the Calgary Stampede when it first began in 1912 and photographs taken today are used to show how the Stampede has retained many of the original competitions. Features roping of the steers, chuckwagon races, grandstand shows, parades, and Indian dance contests.-

The Classified Catalogue

792
    Basic makeup.
        prod. [Oakville, Ont.] : Fasla, 1975.- dist. Fasla 43 fr. : col. : 35 mm. & cassette (14 min.) : auto. & aud. adv. sig. & teacher's guide. $18.00 (Make-up for the stage : $66.00) is

        1. Makeup, Theatrical.

        A full coverage of all the types of make-up available to amateur and professional actors and how they should be applied. Close-up photographs show step-by-step presentation of make-up application. Study guide includes lists of supplies needed and where to buy them.-

792
    Basic set design and stages.
        prod. [Scarborough, Ont.] : R.B.M., 1974.- dist. ETHOS 45 fr. : col. : 35 mm. & cassette (12 min.) : auto. & aud. adv. sig. & teacher's manual. $19.00 (Theatre arts : "bare boards and a passion" : $69.00) is

        1. Theaters - Stage setting and scenery.

        Outlines the kinds of stages and scenery, the purposes for which they are used, and the effects they can create.-

792
    Beards.
        prod. [Oakville, Ont.] : Fasla, 1975.- dist. Fasla 38 fr. : col. : 35 mm. & cassette (10 min.) : auto. & aud. adv. sig. & guide. $18.00 (Make-up for the stage : $66.00) is

        1. Makeup, Theatrical.

        Close-up photography shows how to prepare theatrical crepe hair for beards and moustaches. Includes blending colours, applying liquid latex and mesh to the face to commence the building of the beard. Also deals with trimming and combing the hair to change its appearance.-

792
    Corrective makeup.
        prod. [Oakville, Ont.] : Fasla, 1975.- dist. Fasla 35 fr. : ocl. : 35 mm. & cassette (9 min.) : auto. & aud. adv. sig. & teacher's guide. $18.00 (Make-up for the stage : $66.00) is

        1. Makeup, Theatrical.

        Photographs and commentary demonstrate the methods used in applying corrective make-up which alters or accentuates features to suit the actor's role.-

792
    Fundamentals of make-up.
        prod. [Scarborough, Ont.] : R.B.M., 1974.- dist. ETHOS 89 fr. : col. : 35 mm. & cassette (13 min.) : auto. & aud. adv. sig. & teacher's manual. $19.00 (Theatre arts : "bare boards and a passion" : $69.00) is

        1. Makeup, Theatrical.

        Discusses character, expressionistic, and realistic forms of theatre make-up, outlining the techniques used to create each.-

792
    Old age makeup.
        prod. [Oakville, Ont.] : Fasla, 1975.- dist. Fasla 26 fr. : col. : 35 mm. & cassette (9 min.) : auto. & aud. adv. sig. & teacher's guide. $18.00 (Make-up for the stage : $66.00) is

        1. Makeup, Theatrical.

        Explores the application of old-age make-up, stressing changes in skin tones, hollower cheeks, loose skin under eyes, etc. Uses close-up photographs to illustrate step-by-step application of make-up.-

792
    Stage movement and directing.
        prod. [Scarborough, Ont.] : R.B.M., 1974.- dist. ETHOS 33 fr. : col. : 35 mm. & cassette (11 min.) : auto. & aud. adv. sig. & teacher's manual. $19.00 (narrator, Bert Devitt: editor, Geoffrey Sansom.-) is

        1. Theatre - Production and direction.

        Presents the basic of movement and positioning on the stage in order to give students necessary background for putting on their own performances.-

The Classified Catalogue

793.3
    Indian dances and masks.
        prod. [Scarborough, Ont.] : R.B.M., 1974.- dist. ETHOS 59 fr. : col. : 35 mm. & cassette (14 min.) : auto. & aud. adv. sig. & reading script. $19.00 (Indian culture in Canada : $69.00) jis

        1. Indians of North America - Dances.
        2. Indians of North America - Costume and adornment.

        Describes several native dances and the purposes they serve. Includes some commentary on the use of masks in the dances.-

796
    Un dimanche au parc.
        prod. [Montreal?] : NFB, 1975.- dist. SEC 53 fr. : col. : 35 mm. $9.00 p

        1. Outdoor recreation. 2. Parks.

        Photographs without captions illustrate children's activities in the park, - swings, games, model boats, picnic, feeding the squirrels. Provides a brief teacher's guide in first few frames of filmstrip, in English and French. Best for group viewing to develop language skills. English title available : SUNDAY IN THE PARK.-

796
    Sports and recreation.
        prod. [Willowdale, Ont.] : UEVA (Can), 1974.- dist. BAM 37 fr. : col. : 35 mm. & captions. $7.50 (Canadians : $27.95) pj

        1. Outdoor recreation. 2. Sports.

        Illustrates the variety of seasonal sports and activities enjoyed by Canadians across the country, from skiing and curling, to camping, swimming, and horseback riding. A brief introductory overview.-

796
    Sunday in the park.
        prod. [Montreal?] : NFB, 1975.- dist. McI. 53 fr. : col. : 35 mm. $9.00 p

        1. Outdoor recreation. 2. Parks.

        Photographs without captions illustrate children's activities in the park, - swings, games, model boats, picnic, feeding the squirrels. Provides a brief teacher's guide in first few frames of filmstrip, in English and French. Best for group viewing to develop language skills. French title available : UN DIMANCHE AU PARC.-

796.074
    Highland Games.
        prod. [Montreal?] : NFB, 1975.- dist. McI. 38 fr. : col. : 35 mm. & captions. $9.00 (Fieldtrips on filmstrips series) pj

        1. Sports - Exhibitions.

        A photographic essay illustrating the events at a highland games meet. Includes dancing, piping, tossing the caber and track and field. Suggests that filmstrip be used for language arts, art, or field trip preparation. Bilingual introduction.-

796.34
    La crosse canadienne.
        prod. [Montreal?] : NFB, 1964.- dist. SEC 39 fr. : b&w & col. : 35 mm. & captions & teacher's manual. $9.00 is

        1. Lacrosse.

        Photographs and artwork illustrate the basics of the game of lacrosse. Includes history, two types of game, equipment, stickhandling, shooting and passing, catching the ball, checking, intercepting, and the face-off. English title available : LACROSSE - THE CANADIAN GAME.-

796.34
    Lacrosse - the Canadian game.
        prod. [Montreal?] : NFB, 1964.- dist. McI. 39 fr. : b&w & col. : 35 mm. & captions & teacher's manual. $9.00 is

        1. Lacrosse.

        Photographs and artwork illustrate the basics of the game of lacrosse. Includes history, two types of game, equipment, stickhandling, shooting and passing, catching the ball, checking, intercepting, and the face-off. French title available : LA CROSSE CANADIENNE.-

The Classified Catalogue

796.5
> Orientation & compass.
>> prod. [Toronto] : RQM, 1975.- dist. Lea. 42 fr. : col. : 35 mm. & captions & teacher's guide. $9.00 (Survival & safety in the outdoors : $59.50) is

>> 1. Orienteering. 2. Compass. 3. Wilderness survival.

>> Defines orienteering and describes use of the sun, branches of mature pines and tree stumps in location directions, featuring use of the compass in orientation. Detailed diagrams of a compass and photos of students attempting to reach a specific destination are used.-

796.5
> Orienteering.
>> prod. [Willowdale, Ont.] : UEVA (Can), 1975.- dist. BAM 97 fr. : col. : 35 mm. & cassette (28 min.) : auto. & aud. adv. sig. & teacher's guide. $15.50 (Adventures with map and compass : $65.95) j

>> 1. Orienteering.

>> Shows how to combine the use of map and a compass with techniques of orienteering, such as step counting and aiming off in order to move effectively from one point to another. Concludes with a description of an actual orienteering meet. Convenient breaks in the narration for practice exercies would allow this to be useful for several lessons.-

796.5
> Rockhounding.
>> prod. [Toronto] : R.Q.M., 1973.- dist. Lea. 41 fr. : col. : 35 mm. & captions & teacher's guide. $9.00 (Survival & safety in the outdoors) ji

>> 1. Rockhounding. 2. Rocks - Collectors and collecting.

>> Of general interest to rock enthusiasts. It outlines the various places to look for rocks (mine shafts and dry creek beds), tools to use, emphasizing the elements of discovery, collecting and creating.-

796.54
> Le campement.
>> prod. [Montreal?] : NFB, 1964.- dist. SEC 38 fr. : col. : 35 mm. & captions. $9.00 is

>> 1. Camping.

>> Shows steps to follow when choosing a campsite. Discusses best location for comfort and safety, how to get clean drinking water, points out courtesy to other campers, and conservation of nature at all times. English title available : THE CAMPSITE.-

796.54
> The Camper and his equipment.
>> prod. [Montreal?] : NFB, 1964.- dist. McI. 36 fr. : col. : 35 mm. & captions. $9.00 jis

>> 1. Camping.

>> An explanation of necessary steps in planning a camping trip. Includes photos of the selection of a suitable tent and sleeping bags, proper safety equipment, and foods that carry well. Includes many small but important tips to make the camping trip more successful. French title available : LE CAMPEUR ET SON EQUIPEMENT.-

796.54
> Le campeur et son équipement.
>> prod. [Montreal?] : NFB, 1964.- dist. SEC 35 fr. : col. : 35 mm. & captions. $9.00 jis

>> 1. Camping.

>> An explanation of necessary steps in planning a camping trip. Incudes photos of the selection of a suitable tent and sleeping bags, proper safety equipment, and foods that carry well. Includes many small but important tips to make the camping trip more successful. English title available : THE CAMPER AND HIS EQUIPMENT.-

796.54
> The Campsite.
>> prod. [Montreal?] : NFB, 1964.- dist. McI. 38 fr. : col. : 35 mm. & captions. $9.00 is

>> 1. Camping.

>> Shows steps to follow when choosing a campsite. Discusses best location for comfort and safety, how to get clean drinking water, points out courtesy to other campers, and conservation of nature at all times. French title available : LE CAMPEMENT.-

The Classified Catalogue

796.54
>Elementary camping.
>>prod. [Toronto] : RQM, 1974.- dist. Lea. 51 fr. : col. : 35 mm. & captions. $9.00 (Living in the outdoors) jis
>
>>1. Camping.
>
>>A summary for the novice camper. Photos are used to outline the basic skills needed for camping, the types of tents available, essential items from axe to frying pan, the selection and packing of knapsacks, the setting up of camp and tent, and the starting of fires.-

796.54
>Wintering in the bush.
>>prod. [Toronto] : RQM, 1974.- dist. Lea. 42 fr. : col. : 35 mm. & captions. $9.00 (Living in the outdoors) jis
>
>>1. Camping. 2. Wilderness survival.
>
>>A good basic reference for students contemplating an overnight bush excursion. Photographs show necessary gear and their multi-uses. Extensive coverage given to the selection of various types of wood, their location, storage, and building of the fire. How to trap small animals in a dire emergency is also explained.-

796.9
>Goaltending.
>>prod. [Scarborough, Ont.] : R.B.M., 1975.- dist. ETHOS 45 fr. : col. : 35 mm. & reading script & captions. $19.00 (The Game of hockey : $72.00) pj
>
>>1. Ice hockey.
>
>>Explains what makes the goalie different from the other team members by looking at the special equipment used by the goal tender, strategies used during a game, and the particular demands of this position.-

796.9
>The History of hockey.
>>prod. [Scarborough, Ont.] : R.B.M., 1974.- dist. ETHOS 58 fr. : b&w & col. : 35 mm. & cassette (7 min.) : auto. & aud. sig. & teacher's manual. $19.00 (Hockey) j
>
>>1. Ice hockey - History.
>
>>Includes pictures of the early Canadian lacrosse and field hockey teams that preceded the contemporary game. The parts played by the Canadian Indians and settlers are outlined, and the story of the Stanley Cup is brought out.-

796.9
>The Hockey coach.
>>prod. [Scarborough, Ont.] : R.B.M., 1975.- dist. ETHOS 39 fr. : col. : 35 mm. & reading script & captions. $19.00 (The Game of hockey : $72.00) pj
>
>>1. Ice hockey coaching.
>
>>Examines the role played by the coach of a hockey team.-

796.9
>Hockey equipment.
>>prod. [Scarborough, Ont.] : R.B.M., 1975.- dist. ETHOS 50 fr. : col. : 35 mm. & reading script & captions. $19.00 (The Game of hockey : $72.00) pj
>
>>1. Ice hockey - Equipment and supplies.
>
>>Discusses the basic points for selecting proper hockey equipment.-

796.9
>Hockey I - getting ready.
>>prod. [Toronto] : Lea., 1972.- dist. Leamat ltd. 43 fr. : col. : 35 mm. & teacher's guide. $9.00 pji
>
>>1. Ice hockey. 2. Ice hockey - Equipment and supplies.
>
>>Brief comments on the purchase, preparation, and care of hockey equipment. Presents some of the basic "do's and don'ts" of the game.-

The Classified Catalogue

796.9
    Hockey II - the game -
        prod. [Toronto] : Lea., 1972 dist. Lea. 38 fr. : col. : 35 mm. & captions & teacher's manual. $9.00 pji

        1. Ice hockey.

        Offensive techniques, such as skillful skating, stickhandling, passing and receiving, and shooting are discussed.-

796.9
    Hockey III - the game -
        prod. [Toronto] : Lea, 1972.- dist. Lea. 29 fr. : col. : 35 mm. caption & teacher's guide. $9.00 pji

        1. Ice hockey

        Emphasizes checking of various kinds, skillful skating, and tactics for gaining control of the puck as techniques of defensive play.-

796.9
    Pin point passing.
        prod. [Scarborough, Ont.] : R.B.M., 1975.- dist. ETHOS 40 fr. : col : 35 mm. & captions & reading script. $19.00 (The Game of hockey : $72.00) pj

        1. Ice hockey.

        Outlines and illustrates the fundamental rules for stick handling and passing the puck.-

796.9
    Shoot to score.
        prod. [Scarborough, Ont.] : R.B.M., 1975.- dist. ETHOS 40 fr. : col. : 35 mm. & reading script & captions. $19.00 (The Game of hockey : $72.00) pj

        1. Ice hockey.

        Discusses and illustrates the basic steps in learning to shoot well when playing hockey.-

796.9
    Skating.
        prod. [Scarborough, Ont.] : R.B.M., 1975.- dist. ETHOS 39 fr. : col. : 35 mm. & reading script & captions. $19.00 (The Game of hockey : $72.00) pj

        1. Ice hockey. 2. Ice skating.

        Discusses the basic points to remember in order to develop a powerful and effective skating style suitable for playing hockey.-

796.9
    Le ski - mise en train pré-saisonnière.
        prod. [Montreal?] : NFB, 1964.- dist. SEC 38 fr. : b&w : 35 mm. & captions & teacher's manual. $9.00 is

        1. Skis and skiing.

        Describes a series of exercises - body bends and push-ups, suitable for ski conditioning. Stresses the importance of well-toned muscles and flexible joints. Use of manual with complete details is a necessity. English title available : SKIING : PRE-SEASON CONDITIONING.-

796.9
    Le ski - mouvements de base (1ère partie).
        prod. [Montreal?] : NFB, 1964.- dist. SEC 29 fr. : b&w : 35 mm. & captions & teacher's manual. $9.00 is

        1. Skis and skiing.

        Use photographs to show basic ski techniques, such as walking, step turns, and herringbone. The manual expands the captions, and is a necessity for proper instruction. English title available : SKIING : BASIC SKILLS : PART 1.-

796.9
    Le ski - mouvements de base (2e partie).
        prod. [Montreal?] : NFB, 1964.- dist. SEC 22 fr. : b&w : 35 mm. & captions & teacher's manual. $9.00 is

        1. Skis and skiing.

        Using sequence photos on one background, skills of skiing, such as hop christie, parallel christie are described. English title available : SKIING - BASIC SKILLS : PART 2.-

796.9
    Skiing - pre-season conditioning.
        prod. [Montreal?] : NFB, 1964.- dist. McI. 38 fr. : b&w. : 35 mm. & captions. $9.00 is

        1. Skis and skiing.

        pDescribes a series of exercises - body bends and pushups ,suitable for ski conditioning. Stresses the importance of well-toned muscles and flexible joints. Use of manual with complete details is a necessity. French title available : LE SKI MISE EN TRAIN PRE-SAISONNIERE.-

The Classified Catalogue

796.9
    Skiing : basic skills :
        prod. [Montreal?] : NFB, 1964.- dist. McI. 29 fr. : b&w : 35 mm. & captions & teacher's manual. $9.00 is

    1. Skis and skiing.

Uses photographs to show basic ski techniques, such as walking, step turns, and herringbone. The manual expands the captions, and is a necessity for proper instruction. French title available : LE SKI - MOUVEMENTS DE BASE - 1ère partie.-

796.9
    Skiing - basic skills :
        prod. [Montreal?] : NFB, 1964.- dist. McI. 22 fr. : b&w : 35 mm. & captions & teacher's manual. $9.00 is

    1. Skis and skiing.

Using sequence photos on one background, more skills of skiing, such as hop christie, parallel christie are described. French title available : LE SKI - MOUVEMENTS DE BASE : 2eme PARTIE.-

796.9
    Team play.
        prod. [Scarborough, Ont.] : R.B.M., 1975.- dist. ETHOS 40 fr. : col. : 35 mm. & reading script & captions. $19.00 (The Game of hockey : $72.00) pj

    1. Ice hockey.

Emphasizes that a team must play together, with each team member contributing fully to the overall effort. Particular tactics are discussed, among them face-offs, forechecking, and the role of the defenseman.-

797.1
    Canoeing : the strokes.
        prod. [Toronto] : R.Q.M., 1973.- dist. Lea. 40 fr. : col. : 35 mm. & captions. $9.00 (Survival & safety in the outdoors) ji

    1. Canoes and canoeing.

Emphasizes teamwork and safety in canoeing, and illustrates the various movements in canoe operation, such as drawing, sweeping, ruddering, and braking. The whys and wherefores of portaging are also described.-

797.1
    Canoeing : the basic.
        prod. [Toronto] : R.Q.M., 1973.- dist. Lea. 41 fr. : col. : 35 mm. & captions. $9.00 (Survival & safety in the outdoors) ji

    1. Canoes and canoeing.

A description of the role of the canoe in the past for exploration and its use for today. Diagram showing the basic shape of a canoe, safety tips for boarding, unboarding, and packing. Description and photographs of various types of paddles are presented.-

797.1
    Canoeing.
        prod. [Montreal?] : NFB, 1964.- dist. McI. 37 fr. : col. : 35 mm. & captions. $9.00 jis

    1. Canoes and canoeing.

Demonstrates the correct packing procedures for entering and packing a canoe. Discusses parts of a canoe, paddles, safety and care of a canvas canoe. French title available : LE CANOTAGE.-

797.1
    Canoeing skills and safety.
        prod. [Scarborough, Ont.] : R.B.M., 1975.- dist. ETHOS 65 fr. : col. : 35 mm. & cassette (14 min.) : auto. & aud. adv. sig. & reading script. $19.00 (Outdoor education) ji

    1. Canoes and canoeing - Safety measures.

Step-by-step instructions demonstrate canoeing safety. Identifies types of strokes and when to use them. Shows getting in and out of the canoe, and rescuing passengers from overturned canoe. Uses photographs to illustrate.-

797.1
    Le canotage.
        prod. [Montreal?] : NFB, 1964.- dist. SEC 40 fr. : col. : 35 mm. & captions. $9.00 jis

    1. Canoes and canoeing.

Demonstrates the correct procedure for entering and packing a canoe. Discusses parts of a canoe, paddles, safety and care of a canvas canoe. English title available : CANOEING.-

The Classified Catalogue

797.1
    Elementary canoeing.
        prod. [Toronto] : M-L, 1974.- dist. Sch. Ser. or Vint. 53 fr. : col. : 35 mm. & cassette (9 min.) : auto. & aud. adv. sig. & teacher's guide. $16.50 (Outdoor survival : $85.00) j

        1. Canoes and canoeing.

        Points out the flexibility, economy, dependability, speed and lightness of a canoe. Describes a canoe, its proper care, launching, portaging, plus choosing a paddle, and paddle strokes. Stresses the safety of canoe if properly used. French title available : PRINCIPES DE CANOTAGE.-

797.1
    Principes de canôtage.
        prod. [Toronto] : M-L, 1975.- dist. Sch. Ser. or Vint. 53 fr. : col. : 35 mm. & cassette (9 min.) : auto. & aud. adv. sig. & teacher's guide. $16.50 (Activités de plein air : survie : $85.00) i

        1. Canoes and canoeing.

        Points out the flexibility, economy, dependability, speed, and lightness of a canoe. Describes a canoe, its proper care, launching, portaging, plus choosing a paddle, and paddle strokes. Stresses the safety of canoe if properly used. English title available : ELEMENTARY CANOEING.-

797.1074
    Canoe Museum.
        prod. [Scarborough, Ont.] : R.B.M., 1975.- dist. ETHOS 80 fr. : col. : 35 mm. & cassette (15 min.) : auto. & aud. adv. sig. & reading script. $19.00 (Outdoor education) ji

        1. Canoes and canoeing - History.
        2. Museum of Historic Canoes and Kayaks.

        A photographic tour of the Museum of Historic Canoes and Kayaks at Camp Kandalare near Dorset, Ontario. Illustrates variety, materials used, and purpose of canoes once used by Canadian Indians and Eskimos.-

797.2
    Initiation à la plongée : tuba et scaphandre autonome.
        prod. [Montreal?] : NFB, made 1965 : 1967.- dist. SEC 44 fr. : col. : 35 mm. & captions. is

        1. Skin diving. 2. Scuba diving.

        Photographs and diagrams illustrate the correct equipment and basic skills needed for snorkel and scuba diving. Stresses safety in preparing for dives and what to do in an emergency. English title available : AN INTRODUCTION TO SNORKEL AND SCUBA DIVING.-

797.2
    An Introduction to snorkel and scuba diving.
        prod. [Montreal?] : NFB, made 1965 : 1966.- dist. McI. 44 fr. : col. : 35 mm. & captions. $9.00 is

        1. Skin diving. 2. Scuba diving.

        Photographs and diagrams illustrate the correct equipment and basic skills needed for snorkel and scuba diving. Stresses safety in preparying for dives and what to do in an emergency. French title av... ATION A LA PLONGEE TUBA ET SCHAPHANDRE AUTONOME.-

797.2
    Learning to swim and water safety.
        prod. [Scarborough, Ont.] : R.B.M., 1974.- dist. ETHOS 45 fr. : col. : 35 mm. & cassette (15 min.) : auto. & aud. adv. sig. & teacher's manual. $19.00 (Outdoor education : no. 910 : $76.00) s

        1. Swimming - Study and teaching.

        Aimed at the instructor, presentation covers some of the basics of learning to swim: floating, flutterkicking, drownproofing, and mouth-to-mouth resuscitation.-

797.2
    Swimming strokes.
        prod. [Scarborough, Ont.] : R.B.M., 1974.- dist. $19.00 61 fr. : col. : 35 mm. & cassette (10 min.) : auto. & aud. adv. sig. & teacher's manual. $19.00 (Outdoor education : no. 910 : $76.00) jis

        1. Swimming.

        Describes, step-by-step, the following swimming strokes: front crawl, back crawl, breast stroke, elementary back stroke, and side stroke.-

The Classified Catalogue

799.1
    Ice fishing.
        prod. [Toronto] : M-L, 1975.- dist. Sch. Ser. or Vint. 55 fr. : col. : 35 mm. & cassette (11 min.) : auto. & aud. adv. sig. & teacher's guide. $16.50 (Outdoor education) is

        1. Ice fishing.

    Helpful suggestions for choosing and preparing a fishing site. Describes materials necessary for successful ice fishing, and landing fish. Encourages research into habits and feeding grounds of different fish.-

799.3
    Riflery.
        prod. [Toronto] : R.Q.M., 1973.- dist. Lea. 44 fr. : col. : 35 mm. & captions & teacher's guide. $9.00 (Survival & safety in the outdoors) is

        1. Shooting - History. 2. Rifles.

    The history of riflery plus a general description of the sport. The idea of riflery as a serious undertaking is stressed through the detailed explanation of rifle parts, functions, and safety precaution.-

808.53
    Classroom debating in parliamentary style.
        prod. [Toronto, Ont.] : B & R, 1973.- dist. B & R 40 fr. : col. : 35 mm. & cassette (13 min.) : auto. & aud. adv. sig. & teacher's manual reading script & student's guide & debate marking sheets. $30.00 i

        1. Debates and debating.

    Describes each step necessary for a formal debate: initial planning, use of good sources and note-taking to prepare an argument, effective presentation of an argument, formalities of the debate itself, and final marking and voting.-

810.9
    Civil War and second thoughts.
        prod. [Scarborough] : SHN, 1974.- dist. PHM 101 fr. : b&w & col. : 35 mm. & cassette (23 min.) : auto. & aud. adv. sig. & teacher's guide. $39.60 (American literature : $158.40) s

        1. American literature - History and criticism.

    Discuss the effects of America's growth in the late 1800's as seen by Mark Twain, Emily Dickinson; and Upton Sinclair. Also considers Twenties' writers such as Dreiser, Lewis, and Fitzgerald whose writings reveal their disenchantment with the times.-

810.9
    A Declaration of faith.
        prod. [Scarborough[: SHN, 1974.- dist. PHM 97 fr. : b&w & col. : 35 mm. & cassette (23 min.) : auto. & aud. adv. sig. & teacher's guide. $39.60 (American literature : $158.40) s

        1. American literature - History and Criticism.

    Depicts the excitement of pre-Civil War America as revealed in its literature. Covers the authors Hawthorne, Poe, Thoreau, Emerson, and Whitman whose themes included equality of man and living with nature.-

810.9
    World War I and disillusionment.
        prod. [Scarborough] : SHN, 1974.- dist. PHM 102 fr. : b&w & col. : 35 mm. & cassette (27 min.) : auto. & aud. adv. sig. & teacher's guide. $39.60 (American literature : $158.40) s

        1. American literature - History and criticism.

    Describes the theories of various writers including Dos Passos, Hemingway, and Cummings. Includes descriptions of the Depression by Steinbeck, Faulkner, and Thomas Wolfe, and traces the development of theatre.-

The Classified Catalogue

810.9
World War II - an increasing conscience.
   prod. [Scarborough] : SHN, 1974.- dist. PHM
   109 fr. : b&w & col. : 35 mm. & cassette (25
   min.) : auto. & aud. adv. sig. & teacher's
   guide. $39.60 (American literature : $158.40)
   s

   1. American literature - History and criticism.

   Presents the age of protest and race
   consciousness as it is reflected in the works
   of Mailer, Miller, and Tennessee Williams.
   Examines the themes of violence, civil rights,
   and science fiction as handled by Kerovac,
   Spillane, Baldwin, and Asimov.-

820.9
The Elizabethan era.
   prod. [Scarborough, Ont.] : SHN, 1972.- dist.
   PHM 112 fr. : b&w & col. : 35 mm. &
   cassette (23 min.) : auto. & aud. adv. sig. &
   teacher's guide. $39.60 (British literature :
   $225.00) s

   1. English literature - History and criticism.

   An overview of English life in the changing
   times of Elizabeth's reign. Describes how new
   explorations, ideas in science and intellectual
   excitement brought about changes in
   literature giving rise to writers such as
   Marlowe, Jonson, Shakespeare, Sidney and
   others.-

820.9
From puritan to Augustan.
   prod. [Scarborough, Ont.] : SHN, 1974.- dist.
   PHM 122 fr. : b&w & col. : 35 mm. &
   cassette (27 min.) : auto. & aud. adv. sig. &
   teacher's guide. $39.60 (British literature :
   $255.00) s

   1. English literature - History and criticism.

   The Augustan era emphasized manners,
   decorum, and social propriety as found in
   the works of Milton and Bunyan. Satire
   became very popular. Highwaymen, pirates,
   manners, and the politics of the day were
   satirized. Major period writers discussed are
   Pope, Defoe, Swift, and Austen.-

820.9
From the beginnings to Elizabeth.
   prod. [Scarborough] : SHN, 1972.- dist. PHM
   108 fr. : b&w & col. : 35 mm. & cassette
   (22 min.) : auto. & aud. adv. sig. & teacher's
   guide. $39.60 (British literature : $255.00) s

   1. English literature - History and criticism.

   Traces English language and literature from
   the time of the Romans through the Dark
   Ages. Discusses the influence of monastaries
   and Christianity, the importance of chivalry,
   romance and morality, and their effects on
   literature. Includes the poem Mafdon, Beowulf,
   tales of King Arthur and his Knights of the
   Round Table, Sir Gawain and the Green
   Knight, and Canterbury Tales.-

820.9
The Romantic era.
   prod. [Scarborough, Ont.] : SHN, 1972.- dist.
   PHM 107 fr. : b&w & col. : 35 mm. &
   cassette (24 min.) : auto. & aud. adv. sig. &
   teacher's guide. $39.60 (British literature :
   $255.00) s

   1. English literature - History and criticism.

   Conveys the feeling of the era as it
   introduces major period poets and novelists.
   Among the writiers included are poets
   Shelley, Wordsworth, Blake, Byron, Keats, and
   novelists Scott, Austen and Mary Shelley.
   Illustrated with paintings and etchings.-

820.9
The Twentieth century : 1929 - present.
   prod. [Scarborough, Ont.] : SHN, 1973.- dist.
   PHM 104 fr. : b&w & col. : 35 mm. &
   cassette (24 min.) : auto. & aud. adv. sig. &
   teacher's guide. $39.60 (British literature :
   $255.00) s

   1. English literature - History and criticism.

   Describes the effects of the Depression and
   World War II on literature, taking examples
   from works by Orwell, Greene, Waugh, and
   Thomas. Traces the development of literature
   through the Fifties, discussing Osborne,
   Delaney, Jellicoe, and Sillitoe. Concludes with
   the revival of drama in works by Pinter,
   Beckett, Eliot, and Galsworthy.-

The Classified Catalogue

820.9
    The Twentieth century : 1900-1929.
        prod. [Scarborough, Ont.] : SHN, 1973.- dist. PHM 107 fr. : b&w & col. : 35 mm. & cassette (26 min.) : auto. & aud. adv. sig. & teacher's guide. $39.60 (British literature : $255.00) s

        1. English literature - History and criticism.

        An introduction to writers of the Edwardian era, World War I and the Twenties. Includes Shaw, Joyce, O'Casey, and Yeats.-

820.9
    The Victorian era.
        prod. [Scarborough] : SHN, 1972.- dist. PHM 103 fr. : b&w & col. : 35 mm. & cassette (27 min.) : auto. & aud. adv. sig. & teacher's guide. $39.60 (British literature : $255.00) s

        1. English literature - History and criticism.

        Introduces writers of the Victorian era and Industrial Revolution. The themes of death, injustice, and human suffering as handled by Dickens, Bronte, Darwin, Shaw, Tennyson, and Browning are discussed.-

822.3
    Shakespeare : the man, the times and the plays.
        prod. [Scarborough, Ont.] : SHN, 1972.- dist. PHM 107 fr. : b&w & col. : 35 mm. & cassette (28 min.) : auto. & aud. adv. sig. & teacher's guide. $39.60 (British literature : $255.00) s

        1. English literature - History and criticism. 2. Shakespeare, William, 1564-1616.

        Great detail is given to the theatre of Shakespeare's day, and the Elizabethan view of life. Many of Shakespeare's works are discussed, showing how they follow this theme. Compares Shakespeare's ideas of man with those of today.-

910
    Discoveries and disappointments.
        prod. [Toronto] : Int. Cin., 1974.- dist. Sch. Ch. 60 fr. : b&w & col. : 35 mm. & cassette (11 min.) : auto. & aud. adv. sig. & teacher's guide. $16.95 (Search for the Northwest Passage : $49.00) ji

        1. Northwest Passage.

        Features the voyages of captain Perry, Captain Franklin, and Captain Ross. Numerous sketches drawn during these voyages indicate the Eskimo lifestyle and the European's adoption of native methods for survival. Emphasizes the scientific aspects of each voyage, which provided increasing information of the Canadian Arctic, particularly where not to find the Northwest Passage.-

910
    Fact and fancy.
        prod. [Toronto] : Int. Cin., 1974.- dist. Sch. Ch. 67 fr. : b&w & col. : 35 mm. & cassette (12 min.) : auto. & aud. adv. sig. & teacher's guide. $16.95 (Search for the Northwest Passage : $49.00) ji

        1. Northwest Passage.

        A collection of drawings and maps sketched by the explorers who searched for the Northwest Passage in the 16th, 17th, and 18th centuries. Notable explorers from Frobisher to Franklin illustrate the Eskimo and Indian clothing and lifestyles, as well as the terrain and types of animals the Europeans encountered.-

910
    Land of gold : land of ice :
        prod. [Toronto] : G.H., [197-] dist. G.H. 32 fr. : b&w & col. : 35 mm. & 3 booklets. $8.90 (Concepts / a series in Canadian studies) pj

        1. Discoveries (in geography).

        Designed to help students develop an understanding of the concept of exploration. Prints, sketches, maps and photographs allow observation and interpretation of fifteenth century and modern exploration plus resources to use for further study. Source books contain excerpts from explorers' journals. Suitable for classroom instruction only.-

The Classified Catalogue

910
  Nomadic journey : three nomadic peoples.
    prod. [Don Mills, Ont.] : F & W, 1973.- dist. F & W 24 fr. : col. : 35 mm. & teacher's guide. $7.20 (Man in his world) ji

    1. Society, Nonliterate folk.

    Examines the lifestyles of three nomadic peoples : Arctic hunters and fishermen, desert herdsmen, and tundra herdsmen. Emphasizes the special characteristics of each group, and discusses the role played by environment in influencing each lifestyle. Designed for classroom use only.-

910
  Tragedy and triumph.
    prod. [Toronto] : Int. Cin., 1974.- dist. Sch. Ch. 67 fr. : b&w & col. : 35 mm. & cassette (12 min.) : auto. & aud. adv. sig. & teacher's guide. $16.95 (Search for the Northwest Passage : $49.00) ji

    A history of the search expeditions organized to find Captain Franklin and his crew who disappeared in 1845. Includes sketches drawn by members of the search parties depicting winter conditions and efforts to cope with the environment. Concludes with Captain Amundsen from Norway, first man to travel through the passage.-

912
  Cartes muettes du Canada.
    prod. [Montreal?] : NFB, 1953.- dist. SEC 30 fr. : b&w : 35 mm. $9.00 ji

    1. Canada - Maps.

    A collection of black and white physical maps of Canada and the ten provinces. They are designed to be projected onto a screen or chalkboard for teaching or tracing purposes. Some historical maps of Canada are included. English title available : OUTLINE MAPS OF CANADA.-

912
  Cartes muettes du monde : l'Amérique.
    prod. [Montreal?] : NFB, 1961.- dist. SEC 23 fr. : b&w : 35 mm. & captions. $9.00 ji

    1. North America - Maps. 2. South America - Maps.

    A collection of black and white physical maps of the world, North and South America and detailed areas of Canada, the United States and Mexico. Designed to be projected onto chalkboard or screen for teaching purposes or tracing. English title available : OUTLINE MAPS OF THE WORLD : PART 1 : THE AMERICAS.-

912
  Cartes muettes du monde : L'Europe et l'Afrique.
    prod. [Montreal?] : NFB, 1961.- dist. SEC 21 fr. : b&w : 35 mm. & captions. $9.00 ji

    1. Europe - Maps. 2. Africa - Maps. 3. Scandanavia - Maps.

    These black and white outline maps are designed to be projected onto a screen or chalkboard for teaching or tracing purposes. Portrays physical maps of the world, Europe, detailed areas of Europe, Africa and a map of Scandinavia. English title available : OUTLINE MAPS OF THE WORLD : PART 2 : EUROPE AND AFRICA.-

912
  Cartes muettes du monde : l'Asie et l'Océanie.
    prod. [Montreal?] : NFB, 1961.- dist. SEC 21 fr. : b&w 35 mm. & captions. $9.00 ji

    1. Australia - Maps. 2. Asia - Maps.

    A collection of black and white physical outline maps of areas of Asia, including Russia, Australia, New Zealand, and the Pacific Ocean. English title available : OUTLINE MAPS OF THE WORLD : PART 3 : ASIA AND AUSTRALIA.-

The Classified Catalogue

912
    Du plan á la carte.
        prod. [Montreal?] : NFB, made 1953 : 1976.- dist. SEC 30 fr. : b&w : 35 mm. & captions & manual $9.00 ji

        1. Maps. 2. Map drawing.

        Outlines the steps in drawing a simple map with symbols. Begins with a map of the school yard and progresses to maps of the surrounding areas. Relates the map of Canada to the map of North America and the World. Uses artwork and diagrams. English title available : INTRODUCTION TO MAPS.-

912
    Initiation à la carte topographique.
        prod. [Montreal?] : NFB, made 1956 : 1972.- dist. SEC 58 fr. : b&w & col. : 35 mm. & captions & manual. $9.00 ji

        1. Maps.

        Shows how to read the symbols representing the four main features on a topographical map - topography, drainage, forest and woodlands, and cultural features. English title available : INTRODUCING THE TOPOGRAPHICAL MAP.-

912
    Initiation à l'échelle de la carte.
        prod. [Montreal?] : NFB, made 1958 : 1972.- dist. SEC 36 fr. : col. : 35 mm. & captions & manual. $9.00 ji

        1. Maps.

        Uses artwork and diagrams to illustrate the concept of scale, explaining the advantages and disadvantages of larger and smaller scale maps. Includes an explanation of how to measure distance on a map by making use of its scale line. English title available : INTRODUCING MAP SCALE.-

912
    Introducing map scale.
        prod. [Montreal?] : NFB, 1977.- dist. McI. 36 fr. : col. : 35 mm. & captions & manual. $9.00 (Map skills : $36.00) ji

        1. Maps.

        Uses artwork and diagrams to illustrate the concept of scale explaining the advantages and disadvantages of larger and smaller scale maps. Includes an explanation of how to measure distance on a map by making use of its scale line. French title available : INITIATION A L'ECHELLE DE LA CARTE.-

912
    Introducing the topographical map.
        prod. [Montreal?] : NFB, 1956.- dist. McI. 58 fr. : col. : 35 mm. & captions & manual. $9.00 (Map skills) ji

        1. Maps.

        Shows how to read the symbols representing the four main features on a topographical map - topography, drainage, forests and woodlands, and cultural features. French title available : INITIATION A LA CARTE TOPOGRAPHIQUE.-

912
    Introduction to maps.
        prod. [Montreal?] : NFB, made 1953 : 1970.- dist. McI. 30 fr. : b&w : 35 mm. & captions & manual. $9.00 (Map skills : $36.00) ji

        1. Maps. 2. Map drawing.

        Outlines the steps in drawing a simple map with symbols. Begins with a map of the school yard and progresses to maps of the surrounding areas. Relates the map of Canada to the map of North America and the World. Uses artwork and diagrams. French title available : DU PLAN A LA CARTE.-

912
    The Map.
        prod. [Willowdale, Ont.] : UEVA (Can), 1975.- dist. BAM 58 fr. : col. : 35 mm. & cassette (30 min.) : auto. & adv. sig. & teacher's guide. $15.50 (Adventures with map and compass : $65.95) j

        1. Maps.

        A discussion of the basics of map use. Details include the relationship of each direction to the others, simple map symbols, contour lines and contour intervals, map scale, and how to orient a map. Breaks in the narration for practice exercises would allow this to be used for several lessons.-

912
    Map orientation.
        prod. [Montreal?] : NFB, 1969.- dist. McI. 36 fr. : col. : 35 mm. & captions & manual. $9.00 (Map skills : $36.00) ji

        1. Maps.

        Explains with artwork and diagrams how to orient or set a map by observation when one's location is known, by observation when it isn't, by a compass, by locating Polaris, and by using a watch and the sun. French title available : L'ORIENTATION DE LA CARTE.-

912
    L'orientation de la carte.
        prod. [Montreal?] : NFB, made 1958 : 1969.- dist. SEC 36 fr. : col. : 35 mm. & captions & manual.- $9.00

        1. Maps.

        Explains, with artwork and diagrams, how to orient or set a map by observation when one's location is known, by observation when it isn't, by a compass, by locating Polaris, and by using a watch and the sun. English title available : MAP ORIENTATION.-

912
    Outline maps of Canada.
        prod. [Montreal?] : NFB, made 1953 : 1968.- dist. McI. 35 fr. : b&w : 35 mm. $9.00 (Outline maps) ji

        1. Canada - Maps.

        A collection of black and white physical maps of Canada and the ten provinces. They are designed to be projected onto a screen or chalkboard for teaching or tracing purposes. Some historical maps of Canada are included. French title available : CARTES MUETTES DU CANADA.-

912
    Outline maps of the world : part 2 :
        prod. [Montreal?] : NFB, 1961.- dist. McI. 21 fr. : b&w : 35 mm. & captions. $9.00 (Outline maps) ji

        1. Europe - Maps. 2. Africa - Maps. 3. Scandinavia - Maps.

        These black and white outline maps are designed to be projected onto a screen or chalkboard for teaching or tracing purposes. Portrays physical maps of the world, Europe, detailed areas of Europe, Africa and a map of Scandinavia. French title available : CARTES MUETTES DU MONDE : L'EUROPE ET L'AFRIQUE.-

912
    Outline maps of the world : part 3 :
        prod. [Montreal?] : NFB, 1961.- 19 fr. : b&w : 35 mm. & captions. (Outline maps) ji

        1. Asia - Maps. 2. Australia - Maps.

        A collection of black and white physical outline maps of areas of Asia, including Russia, Australia, New Zealand, and the Pacific Ocean. French title available : CARTES MUETTES DU MONDE : L'ASIE ET L'OCENAIE.-

912
    Outline maps of the world : part 1 :
        prod. [Montreal?] : NFB, 1961.- 23 fr. : b&w : 35 mm. & captions. (Outline maps) ji

        1. North America - Maps. 2. South America - Maps.

        Outline maps of the world, North and South America, and detailed areas of Canada, the United States, and Mexico. Designed to be projected on the chalkboard or screen for teaching purposes or tracing. French title available : CARTES MUETTES DU MONDE : L'AMERIQUE.-

913
    Developing an Iroquoian village site.
        prod. [Scarborough, Ont.] : RBM, 1975.- dist. ETHOS 49 fr. : col. : 35 mm. & cassette (14 min.) : auto. & aud. adv. sig. & reading script. $19.00 (Archaelogy : $34.50) ji

        1. Iroquois Indians. 2. Archaeology.

        The archaeological techniques involved in the excavation, reconstruction, and interpretation of artifacts are explained within the context of the excavation of an Iroquoian village. Illustrated with photos of "digs" in the Great Lakes region.-

The Classified Catalogue

913
> The Iroquoian people.
> prod. [Scarborough, Ont.] : R.B.M., 1975.- dist. ETHOS 42 fr. : col. : 35 mm. & cassette (13 min.) : auto. & aud. adv. sig. & reading script. $19.00 (Archaelogy : $34.50) ij
>
> 1. Archaeology. 2. Iroquois Indians.
>
> An introduction to the science of archaeology, incorporating frequent references to its use as a means for learning the history of the Iroquoian people. Illustrated with photos of "digs" in the Great Lakes regions.-

913
> Stone Age man I : an archaeological dig.
> prod. [Don Mills, Ont.] : F & W, 1973.- dist. F & W 25 fr. : col. : 35 mm. & teacher's guide. $7.20 (Man in his world) ji
>
> 1. Excavations (Archeology) - Ontario.
> 2. Man, Prehistoric.
>
> A pictorial outline of how a grade 4 boy and two grade 6 boys were introduced to the fascinating world of archeology on the shore of a small lake in southern Ontario. Through their "dig" they discover much about past peoples and their habits.-

914.15
> Irish cultural heritage.
> prod. [Scarborough, Ont.] : R.B.M., 1978.- dist. ETHOS 53 fr. : b&w & col. : 35 mm. & cassette (17 min.) : auto. & aud. adv. sig. & reading script. $21.50 (Canadian folk culture : the Irish : $79.00) s
>
> 1. Irish - Social life and customs. 2. Irish in Canada - History.
>
> Examines effect of Ireland's history of religious, political and social persecution upon its cultural development. Gives examples of Irish culture found in Canada today in imported products, recreation and alcoholic beverages.-

914.7
> Easter greetings.
> prod. [Scarborough, Ont.] : R.B.M., 1977.- dist. ETHOS 57 fr. : col. : 35 mm. & cassette (12 min.) : auto. & aud. adv. sig. & teacher's manual. $19.00 (Ukranian Easter : $34.50) is
>
> 1. Ukranians - Social life and customs.
>
> Describes and illustrates the customs and rituals of a Ukrainian Easter . Discusses the importance of the pussy willow branch, the egg, the special Easter breads, blessing the Easter food, dance-songs, Wet Monday, and Seeing-off Sunday.-

914.7
> Pysanky.
> prod. [Scarborough, Ont.] : R.B.M., 1977.- dist. ETHOS 50 fr. : col. : 35 mm. & cassette (11 min.) : auto. & aud. adv. sig. & teacher's manual. $19.00 (Ukranian Easter : $34.50) is
>
> 1. Ukranians - Social life and customs.
> 2. Easter. 3. Arts and crafts.
>
> Detailed description of the ancient Ukrainian custom of egg colouring and painting, showing the meaning of each design.-

914.91
> Glaciers.
> prod. [Scarborough, Ont.] : R.B.M., 1974.- dist. ETHOS 55 fr. : col. : 35 mm. & cassette (10 min.) : auto. & aud. adv. sig. & reading script. $19.00 (Iceland : $69.00) ji
>
> 1. Glaciers. 2. Iceland.
>
> More than one square mile out of every ten of Icelandic soil is covered by glaciers. A group of students tours one such glacier, studying its structure and characeristics.-

914.91
> History and geography.
> prod. [Scarborough, Ont.] : R.B.M., 1974.- dist. ETHOS 60 fr. : col. : 35 mm. & cassette (13 min.) : auto. & aud. adv. sig. & reading script. $19.00 (Iceland : $69.00) ji
>
> 1. Iceland - Geography.
>
> An introductory overview of the geography and history of a remarkable country. Photos taken on a student field trip include scenes of volcanic landforms, vegetation, farms, and Thingvellir, site of the formation of the world's oldest continuous democracy.-

The Classified Catalogue

914.91
    The People and their work.
        prod. [Scarborough, Ont.] : R.B.M., 1974.- dist. ETHOS 74 fr. : col. : 35 mm. & cassette (11 min.) : auto. & aud. adv. sig. & reading script. $19.00 (Iceland : $69.00) ji

        1. Iceland - Description and travel.

        An introductory overview of the Icelandic way of life as seen through the eyes of a group of touring students. Includes photos of Reykjavik, the Vestmann Islands, the fishing and agriculture industries, and a whaling station.-

914.91
    Volcanoes.
        prod. [Scarborough, Ont.] : R.B.M., 1974.- dist. ETHOS 60 fr. : col. : 35 mm. & cassette (11 min.) : auto. & aud. adv. sig. & reading script. $19.00 (Iceland : $69.00) ji

        1. Volcanoes. 2. Iceland.

        A student field trip to Iceland provides the framework for a discussion of the island's Volcanic structure and a history of its volanic activity.-

914.95
    Children of Greece.
        prod. [Montreal?] : NFB, 1967.- dist. Mcl. 47 fr. : col. : 35 mm. & captions. $9.00 (Children of many lands : $54.00) pj

        1. Children in Greece. 2. Greece.

        Captioned photos of the mountains, plains, and cities cover various aspects of Greek life. Sheep grazing, road building industry, olive groves, fishing, schools, festivals and churches all portray the world of the Greek child. French title available : LES ENFANTS DE LA GRECE.-

914.95
    Les enfants de la Grèce.
        prod. [Montreal?] : NFB, 1967.- dist. SEC 51 fr. : col. : 35 mm. & captions. $9.00 (Les enfants du monde) pj

        1. Children in Greece. 2. Greece.

        Captioned photos of the mountains, plains, and cities cover various aspects of Greek life. Sheep grazing, road building industry, olive groves, fishing, schools, festivals and churches all portray the world of the Greek child. English title available : CHILDREN OF GREECE.-

915.1
    Agriculture, industry and transportation.
        prod. [Toronto] : CFM, 1975.- dist. BAM 40 fr. : col. : 35 mm. & cassette (15 min.) : auto. & aud. adv. sig. & teacher's guide. $15.50 (China : $89.00) i

        1. Agriculture - China. 2. Education - China. 3. China - Industries. 4. China - Transportation.

        An overview of present-day Chinese agricultural practices, industrial development, and modes of transportation. Highlights include the use of irrigation to control floods and improve agricultural productivity, and the combination of education with productive labour in the educational system.-

915.1
    Chinese cultural heritage.
        prod. [Scarborough, Ont] : R.B.M., 1978.- dist. ETHOS 54 fr. : b&w & col. : 35 mm. & cassette (16 min.) : auto. & aud. adv. sig. & reading script. $21.50 (Canadian folk culture :the Chinese : $79.00) s

        1. China - Civilization.

        Comprehensive coverage of the origins of Chinese civilization. Shows social structure, culture, educational system and civil service which governed feudal system. Relates impact of Confucianism, Taoism and Buddhism upon religious beliefs. Photographs, paintings and sketches portray aspects of this advanced society.-

915.1
    Cities of China.
        prod. [Toronto] : CFM, 1975.- dist. BAM 41 fr. : col. : 35 mm. & cassette (15 min.) : auto. & aud. adv. sig. & teacher's guide. $15.50 (China : $89.00) i

        1. Canton, China - Description. 2. Shanghai, China - Description. 3. Peking, China - Description

        Examines the cities of Canton, Shanghai, and Peking, illustrating architecture, age and lifestyle of each city. Illustrated with photographs taken on a fact-finding tour of China.-

The Classified Catalogue

915.1
    City life.
        prod. [Kitchener, Ont.] : EDU, 1974.- dist. EDU 25 fr. : col. : 35 mm. & cassette (9 min.) : auto. & aud. adv. sig. & teacher's guide. $15.95 (China : $79.95) jis

        1. Cities and towns - China. 2. China - Description and travel.

        Describes the way of life in cities like Shanghai and Peking, where pedicabs and bicycles are the important means of transportation. Stresses lack of crime, and devotion to Mao Tse-tung. Shows styles of homes and uses of communes, the importance of parks for leisure, fine dining facilities and excellent sports facilities.-

915.1
    Contemporary culture.
        prod. [Toronto] : CFM, 1975.- dist. BAM 41 fr. : col. : 35 mm. & cassette (15 min.) : aud. adv. sig. & manual. $15.50 (China) i

        1. Mao, Tse-tung, 1893-1976. 2. China - Civilization.

        A brief biography of Mao-Tse-tung followed by a look at his influence on the literature, theatre, arts and crafts, and recreation of contemporary China.-

915.1
    Hill and plain communes : North China.
        prod. [Hamilton, Ont.] : VCI, 1977.- dist. MHR 40 fr. : col. : 35 mm. & captions & teacher's guide. $35.00 (China : $38.50) ji

        1. Agriculture - China. 2. Collective settlements - China.

        Discusses life in the Chinese communes of the north including irrigation systems, general labour conditions, produce, flood-control and energy, housing and education. Detailed notes and discussion questions in teaching guide. Part of a series.-

915.1
    Life on a Chinese commune : part 2 :
        prod. [Stratford, Ont.] : Sch. Ch., 1974.- dist. Sch. Ch. 54 fr. : col. : 35 mm. & captions. $7.95 (China : $23.85) ji

        1. Collective settlements - China.

        Describes construction, manufacturing, transport, schools, and entertainment on a Chinese commune. Photographs of workers constructing a building show how local materials, simple hand tools and manual labour are used. Photos of the brick and tile and bottle-making factories emphasize how the young and old work together to create different products. Also includes a description of the educational system in which school lessons are combined with chores.-

915.1
    Life on a Chinese commune : homes and farming.
        prod. [Stratford, Ont.] : Sch. Ch., 1974.- dist. Sch. Ch. 48 fr. : col. : 35 mm. & captions. $7.95 (China : $23.85) ji

        1. Collective settlements - China. 2. Agriculture - China.

        Photographs taken inside a commune show several aspects of homes and farming in China. Shows one family's home - how it is heated, type of furniture used, their possessions, the food they eat, and what they do for recreation. Covers the organization of farming in a commune and how members work as a group to grow and produce food for their own consumption.-

915.1
    Monuments of the past.
        prod. [Toronto] : CFM, 1975.- dist. BAM 40 fr. : col. : 35 mm. & cassette (15 min.) : auto. & aud. adv. sig. & teacher's guide. $15.50 (China : $89.00) i

        1. China - Civilization.

        A glimpse of ancient Chinese culture as exemplified by the Great Wall, the Forbidden City, and the Valley of the Thirteen Tombs, as well as by its traditional painting, jade carvings, and embroidery.-

The Classified Catalogue

915.1
    Shanghai : city life in China.
        prod. [Hamilton, Ont.] : VCI, 1977.- dist. MHR 40 fr. : col. : 35 mm. & captions & teacher's guide. $12.85 (China : $38.50) ji

        1. Shanghai, China - Description.

        A comprehensive presentation showing Shanghai as an important harbour city. Discusses transportation, education, housing, the arts, and suburbia. Detailed notes and discussion questions in teaching guides. Part of a series.-

915.1
    A Yangtze rice commune.
        prod. [Hamilton, Ont.] : VCI, 1977.- dist. MHR 40 fr. : col. : 35 mm. & captions & teacher's guide. $12.85 (China : $38.50) ji

        1. Collective settlements - China.
        2. Agriculture - China.

        Describes life on a rice commune of Yangtze Delta near Shanghai, emphasizing importance of canals for travel and irrigation, and their contribution to village life in general. Rice growing described in detail. General description of peasant of today. Part of a series.-

915.2
    Children of Japan.
        prod. [Montreal?] : NFB, 1967.- dist. McI. 41 fr. : col. : 35 mm. & captions. $9.00 (Children of many lands : $54.00) pj

        1. Children in Japan. 2. Japan.

        Includes a map showing the location of Japan in the world, and photographs of the country, of family life, and of Japanese influences in our country. It encourages comparison between the lives of Japanese and Canadian children. The children are shown at play, at school, helping at home, eating, watching TV, and with their parents. Very few captions are used. Review questions included in the filmstrip. French title available : LES ENFANTS DU JAPON.-

915.2
    Les enfants du Japon.
        prod. [Montreal?] : NFB, 1967.- dist. SEC 46 fr. : col. : 35 mm. & captions. $9.00 (Les enfants du monde) pj

        1. Children in Japan. 2. Japan.

        Includes a map showing the location of Japan in the world, and photographs of the country, of family life, and of Japanese influences in our country. It encourages comparison between the lives of Japanese and Canadian children. The children are shown at play, at school, helping at home, eating, watching TV, and with their parents. Very few captions are used. Review questions included in the filmstrip. English title available : CHILDREN OF JAPAN.-

915.2
    Japan I : home life and food.
        prod. [Don Mills, Ont.] : F & V, 1976.- dist. F & V 25 fr. : col. : 35 mm. & teacher's guide. $7.20 (Man in his world) ji

        1. Japan - Social life and customs.

        Provides an intimate glimpse into the life of the average Japanese. The construction of houses, types of furniture found in the various rooms, the tradition of hospitality and serving of tea, typical meals favoured by the Japanese, and the colourful food markets are all included in the discussion. For classroom use.-

915.2
    Japanese cultural heritage.
        prod. [Scarborough, Ont.] : R.B.M., 1978.- dist. ETHOS 48 fr. : b&w & col. : 35 mm. & cassette (9 min.) : auto. & aud. adv. sig. & manual. $21.50 (Canadian folk culture : the Japanese : $79.00) s

        1. Japan - Civilization.

        Introduces all aspects of Japanese culture. Providing a brief history from 12th century to present, it covers religious beliefs, social structure, government, education and language. Shows how Japan's adaptation of western methodology has made the country an industrial leader. Illustrated with sketches, paintings and photographs.-

The Classified Catalogue

915.2
    Mountain environments of Japan.
        prod. [Hamilton, Ont.] : VCI, 1977.- dist. MHR 39 fr. : col. : 35 mm. & captions & teacher's guide. $12.85 (Japan : $72.00) j

        1. Japan - Geography.

        Describes mountainous areas of Japan characterized by volcanic mountains, waterfalls, parks, forests, valleys and terraced rice fields.-

915.2
    Seacoast environments of Japan.
        prod. [Hamilton, Ont.] : VCI, 1977.- dist. MHR 39 fr. : col. : 35 mm. & captions & teacher's guide. $12.85 (Japan : $72.00) j

        1. Japan - Geography.

        A comprehensive survey of the coastlines of Japan as they are used by fishing villages and related activities as well as serving the recreational needs of Japanese urban dwellers. Also discusses the necessary land reclamation along the seacoasts, the types of industry present (oil refineries chemical plants and shipbuilding) and the various harbour facilities.-

915.2
    Urban life in Japan (no. 1).
        prod. [Hamilton, Ont.] : VCI, 1977.- dist. MHR 39 fr. : col. : 35 mm. & captions & teacher's guide. $12.85 (Japan : $72.00) j

        1. Japan.

        Explains how urban exchange is made as efficient as possible in the densely populated areas of Japan.-

915.2
    Urban life in Japan (no. 2).
        prod. [Hamilton, Ont.] : VCI, 1977.- dist. MHR 39 fr. : col. : 35 mm. & captions & teacher's guide. $12.85 (Japan : $72.00) j

        1. Japan.

        Depicts life in the crowded central cities of Japan. Transportation, housing, industry, education, religion, recreation and pollution problems are some of the aspects covered.-

915.93
    Children of Thailand.
        prod. [Montreal] : NFB, made 1967 : 1972.- dist. McI. 49 fr. : col. : 35 mm. & captions. $9.00 (Children of many lands : $54.00) pj

        1. Children in Thailand. 2. Thailand.

        Portrays the world of the Thai child: household chores, rice farming, school, games for children, the market, temple, Buddhist religion, traditional customs and culture, and scenes of a visit to Bangkok. French title available : LES ENFANTS DE LA THAILANDE.-

915.93
    Les enfants de la Thailande.
        prod. [Montreal?] : NFB, 1967.- dist. SEC 50 fr. : col. : 35 mm. & captions. $9.00 (Les enfants du monde) pj

        1. Children in Thailand. 2. Thailand.

        Portrays the world of the Thai child : household chores, rice farming, school, games for children, the market, temple, Buddhist religion, traditional customs and culture, and scenes of a visit to Bangkok. English title available : CHILDREN OF THAILAND.-

915.95
    Malacca : gateway to Malaysia.
        prod. [Montreal?] : NFB, 1975.- dist. McI. 101 fr. : col. : 35 mm. & cassette (15 min.) : auto. & aud. adv. sig. & teacher's manual. $18.00 ji

        1. Malacca, Malaysia - Description.

        A young narrator provides a comprehensive description of life in Malaysia. Includes colourful details about rubber production, rice farming, sports, food, entertainment, religion, education, history, language, and the ethnic make-up of Malaysia. Part of a kit titled "Spotlight on Development". French title available : MALACCA : PORTE DE LA MALAYSIA.-

The Classified Catalogue

916.2
> Gifts of the Nile II : Cairo, the city.
> prod. [Don Mills, Ont.] : F & W, 1973.- dist. F & W 25 fr. : col. : 35 mm. & teacher's guide. $7.20 (Man in his world) ji
>
> 1. Cairo, Arab Republic of Egypt - Description.
>
> Illustrates many faces of Cairo - the blending of old and new, the numerous different ethnic groups, the gamut of transportation facilities and the role of the marketplace. Also stresses the role played by the Nile River in the life of the city.-

916.5
> Alger : un pas vers l'avenir un pas vers le passé.
> prod. [Montreal?] : NFB, 1975.- dist. SEC 108 fr. : b&w & col. : 35 mm. & cassette (14 min.) : auto. & aud. adv. sig. & teacher's manual. $18.00 ji
>
> 1. Algiers, Algeria - Description.
>
> A thorough examination of life in the capital city of a developing nation, narrated in part by a young Algerian university student. Contrasts between the ancient and modern, the French and Moslem cultures, the affluence of the city and poverty of rural Algeria, and a description of its history are all discussed. Part of a kit entitled "Spotlight on Development". English title available : ALGIERS : A STEP INTO THE FUTURE A STEP INTO THE PAST.-

916.5
> Algiers : a step into the future a step into the past.
> prod. [Montreal?] : NFB, 1975.- dist. McI. 108 fr. : b&w & col. : 35 mm. & cassette (14 min.) : auto. & aud. adv. sig. & teacher's manual. $18.00 ji
>
> 1. Algiers, Algeria - Description.
>
> A through examination of life in the capital city of a developing nation, narrated in part by a young Algerian university student. Contrasts between the ancient and modern, the French and Moslem cultures, the affluence of the city and poverty of rural Algeria, and a description of its history are all discussed. Part of a kit entitled "Spotlight on Development". French title available : ALGER : UN PAS VERS L'AVENIR UN PAS VERS LE PASSE.-

916.69
> Children of Northern Nigeria.
> prod. [Montreal?] : NFB, 1967.- dist. McI. 45 fr. : col. : 35 mm. & captions. $9.00 (Children of many lands : $54.00) pj
>
> 1. Children in Nigeria. 2. Nigeria.
>
> Portrays the life of the nomads, farmers, villagers, and city dwellers. Houses, climate, food, a market, a school and children are pictured and the famous blue dye of Nigeria is shown. Encourages viewers to notice similarities and differences between Nigeria and Canada. French title available : LES ENFANTS DE LA NIGERIA DU NORD.-

916.69
> Les enfants de la Nigéria du Nord.
> prod. [Montreal?] : NFB, 1967.- dist. SEC 48 fr. : col. : 35 mm. & captions. $9.00 (Les enfants du monde) pj
>
> 1. Children in Nigeria. 2. Nigeria.
>
> Portrays the life of the nomads, farmers, villagers, and city dwellers. House, climate, food, a market, a school and children are pictured, and the famous blue dye of Nigeria is shown. Encourages viewers to notice similarities and differences between Nigeria and Canada. English title available : CHILDREN OF NORTHERN NIGERIA.-

916.7
> Children of Gabon.
> prod. [Montreal?] : NFB, 1967.- dist. McI. 40 fr. : col. : 35 mm. & captions. $9.00 (Children of many lands : $54.00) pj
>
> 1. Children in Gabon. 2. Gabon.
>
> Photographs present the life of a child in the rain forest. Shows the jobs of many villagers, such as pounding flour, making basket containers, repairing houses, and a school where the children learn to hunt fish, build boats and houses. Review questions are included. French title available : LES ENFANTS DU GABON.-

The Classified Catalogue

916.7
    Les enfants du Gabon.
        prod. [Montreal?] : NFB, 1967.- dist. SEC 43 fr. : col. : 35 mm. & captions. $9.00 (Les enfants du monde) pj

        1. Children in Gabon.   2. Gabon.

    Photographs present the life of a child in the rain forest. Shows the jobs of many villagers, such as pounding flour, making basket containers, repairing houses, and a school where the children learn to hunt, fish, build boats and houses. Review questions are included. English title available : CHILDREN OF GABON.-

916.76
    Kandara : life in a Kenyan community.
        prod. [Montreal?] : NFB, 1974.- dist. McI. 105 fr. : col. : 35 mm. & cassette (16 min.) : auto. & aud. adv. sig. & teacher's guide. $18.00 ji

        1. Kandara, Kenya - Description.

    Describes life in Kandara, an isolated village in Kenya. Tribal customs, farming, division of labour, foods, social system, religion, house construction, sports, games, musical instruments, outdoor markets, and the importance of water are all discussed. Narrated by a young Canadian girl whose pen pal in Kandara provides information about the communtiy. Part of a multi-media kit titled "Spotlight on development" French available : KANDARA : LA VIE DANS UNE AGGLOMERATION KENYANE.-

917.1
    An Appetite for heritage.
        prod. [Toronto] : McI., 1977.- dist. McI. 30 fr. : col. : 35 mm. & cassette (13 min.) : auto. & aud. adv. sig. & teacher's manual. $19.00 (Canada's heritage today : $102.00) ji

        1. Canada - Civilization - Foreign influences.

    Defines the term heritage, showing examples of Canada's heritage in food through which the multicultural nature of our country can be seen.-

917.1
    Bouclier canadien : vue d'ensemble.
        prod. [Montreal?] : NFB, made 1964 : 1966.- dist. SEC 42 fr. : col. : 35 mm. & captions & teacher's guide. $9.00 ji

        1. Canadian Shield - Geography.

    Maps, photographs and diagrams portray the characteristics of the Shield : rocks and minerals, location, the effect of glaciation, climate, flora and fauna, and activities of the people. Measurements are not metric. English title available : INTRODUCING THE CANADIAN SHIELD.-

917.1
    Canada's forest regions.
        prod. [Montreal?] : NFB, made 1966 : 1971.- dist. McI.   46 fr. : col. : 35 mm. & captions. $9.00 is

        1. Forests and forestry - Canada.

    A discussion of the distribution of Canadian forests and how climate and geography affect their characteristics. Photographs examine the eight forest regions according to the history of the land surface, the ability of species to adapt and compete and the environment. Discusses man's role in the future of Canadian forests. Measurements not metric. Part of a multi-media kit titled "Canada's forests". French title available : LES REGIONS FORESTIERES DU CANADA.-

917.1
    Canada's seven regions.
        prod. [Montreal?] : NFB, 1966.- dist. McI.   48 fr. : col. : 35 mm. & teacher's guide. $9.00 ji

        1. Canada - Geography.

    Maps and photographs depict the seven regions of Canada: the Atlantic, the Great Lakes, St. Lawrence Lowlands, Canadian Shield, Hudson's Bay Lowlands, Great Plains, Western Mountains, and Arctic Archipelago. For each region resources and special features are shown, such as cities, occupations, industries and transportation. Manual explains each frame in detail. French title available : LES REGIONS NATURELLES DU CANADA.-

The Classified Catalogue

917.1
Changing identity.
prod. [Willowdale, Ont.] : UEVA (Can), 1974.- dist. BAM 35 fr. : col. : 35 mm. & captions. $7.50 (Canadians : $27.95) pj

1. Canadians.

A brief overview of the Canadian people emphasizing the diversity of their backgrounds, activities, beliefs, and occupations.-

917.1
Cities and towns.
prod. [Willowdale, Ont.] : UEVA, (Can), 1974.- dist. BAM 43 fr. : col. : 35 mm. & captions. $7.50 (Canadians : $27.95) pj

1. Cities and towns - Canada.

Illustrations of many of Canada's major cities and towns from east to west coast, from St. John's, Newfoundland to Dawson City, Yukon. A brief introductory overview of Canadian cities.-

917.1
Collecting my own heritage.
prod. [Toronto] : McI., 1977.- dist. McI. 30 fr. : col. : 35 mm. & cassette (9 min.) : auto. & aud. adv. sig. & teacher's manual. $19.00 (Canada's heritage today : $102.00) ji

1. Canada - Civilization.

Designed to show students that they have a responsibility for preserving their own heritage. Suggests activities by which they can accomplish this.-

917.1
Cultures in conflict.
prod. [Toronto] : M-L, 1976.- dist. Sch. Ser. or Vint. 74 fr. : b&w & col. : 35 mm. & cassette (16 min.) : auto. & aud. adv. sig. & teacher's guide. $16.50 (The Canadian mosaic : $105.00) is

1. Canada - Civilization - Foreign influences.
2. Canada - History.

Uses historical drawings and photographs to explore the development of Canada's national character in comparison to that of the United States. Covers the American Revolution, the War of 1812, the settlement of the West, and the growth of U.S. influence in Canada in the Twentieth Century.-

917.1
The Heritage puzzle.
prod. [Toronto] : McI., 1977.- dist. McI. 32 fr. : col. : 35 mm. & cassette (13 min.) : auto. & aud. adv. sig. & teacher's manual. $19.00 (Canada's heritage today : $102.00) ji

1. Canada - Civilization.

Provides many examples of Canada's heritage in order to encourage students to discuss the meaning of heritage and to create their own definition of the concept.-

917.1
Introducing the Canadian Shield.
prod. [Montreal] : McI. 1976.- dist. McI. 36 fr. : col. : 35 mm. & captions & teaching guide. $9.00 (Canadian Shield) ji

1. Canadian Shield - Geography.

Maps, photographs and diagrams portray the characteristics of the Shield : rocks and minerals, location, the effect of glaciation, climate, flora and fauna, and activities of the people. Measurements not metric.-

917.1
An Introduction to Canada's geography.
prod. [Montreal?] : NFB, 1964.- dist. McI. 48 fr. : col. : 35 mm. & captions & manual. $9.00 ji

1. Physical geography - Canada.

An overview of the major physical regions of Canada, including the Canadian Shield, the Interior Plains, the Southern Ontario and St. Lawrence lowlands, the Atlantic and the Western Mountain Regions. The manual provides additional detailed information for the classroom teacher. Comprehensive treatment compensates for somewhat inferior quality of colour.-

The Classified Catalogue

917.1
    Mosaic Canada.
        prod. [Toronto] : M-L, 1976.- dist. Sch. Ser. or Wint. 60 fr. : b&w & col. : 35 mm. & cassette (13 min.) : auto. & aud. adv. sig. & teacher's guide. $16.50 (The Canadian mosaic : $105.00) is

        1. Canada - Civilization - Foreign influences. 2. Canada - Immigration and emigration - History. 3. Canada - Foreign population.

        An introduction to the mosaic theory of Canadian culture comparing this theory to the "Melting Pot" theory in the U.S. Examines the cultural changes Canada has undergone throughout history, immigration patterns and the problems of prejudices.-

917.1
    Les régions forestières du Canada.
        prod. [Montreal?] : NFB, made 1966 : 1968.- dist. SEC 46 fr. : col. : 35 mm. & captions. $9.00 is

        1. Forests and forestry - Canada.

        Discussion of the distribution of Canadian forests and how climate and geography affect their characteristics. Photographs examine the eight forest regions according to the history of the land surface, the ability of species to adapt and compete and the environment. Discusses man's role in the future of Canadian forests. Measurements not metric. Part of a multi-media kit titled "Les forêts du Canada". English title available : CANADA'S FOREST REGIONS.-

917.1
    Scenic wonderland.
        prod. [Willowdale, Ont.] : UEVA (Can), 1974.- dist. BAM 37 fr. : col. : 35 mm. & captions. $7.50 (Canadians : $27.95) pj

        1. Canada - Geography.

        Scenery from all parts of Canada and in all seasons. Includes fishing villages of the Maritimes, the Laurentians, prairies, and seals on the rocky west coast. A brief introduction to Canada's geography.-

917.1
    Sharing heritage.
        prod. [Toronto] : McI., 1977.- dist. McI. 21 fr. : col. : 35 mm. & cassette (8 min.) : auto. & aud. adv. sig. & teacher's manual. $19.00 (Canada's heritage today : $102.00) ji

        1. Canada - Civilization - Foreign influences. 2. Canada - Foreign population.

        Canada's multicultural nature is explored, with an emphasis on developing a positive attitude toward a sharing of heritage.-

917.1
    The Canadian Shield.
        prod. [Montreal?] : NFB, 1964.- 40 fr. : col. : 35 mm. & captions & teacher's guide. ji

        1. Canadian Shield - Geography.

        Photographs and diagrams illustrate the landforms and climate of the Canadian Shield region of Canada. Discusses the primary industries of forestry and mining, transportation, and power developments.-

917.11
    L'archipel de la Reine-Charlotte.
        prod. [Montreal?] : NFB, 1970.- dist. SEC 64 fr. : col. : 35 mm. & manual. $10.00 is

        1. Queen Charlotte Islands, B.C. Geography.

        An introduction to the land, industry and people of these northern islands. Covers lumber, fishing and mining industries, the scenery and the daily life of its inhabitants, including the Haida Indian community. Comprehensive treatment compensates for somewhat inferior quality of colour. English title available : QUEEN CHARLOTTE ISLANDS.-

917.11
    British Columbia.
        prod. [Scarborough, Ont.] : R.B.M., 1976.- dist. ETHOS 45 fr. : col. : 35 mm. & reading script. $19.00 (Impressions : Canada) ji

        1. British Columbia - Description and travel.

        A general overview pointing out this coastal province's important features. Covers geography, industry, population, climate, and tourist attractions.-

The Classified Catalogue

917.11
    La Columbie Britannique.
        prod. [Toronto] : M-L, 1974.- dist. Sch. Ser. or Vint. 72 fr. : col. : 35 mm. & cassette (16 min.) : auto. & aud. adv. sig. & teacher's guide. $16.50 (Canada : "Il est né d'une race fiére" : $85.00) i

        1. British Columbia - Economic conditions.

        Describes favourable climate of British Columbia and benefits of its natural wealth and geography. Stresses dependence on the Pacific Ocean for fishing industries and trade with the Orient. Shows how British Columbia's economy is diversified with copper, lead and zinc mining, agriculture, and forest industries. Outlines B.C.'s economic and resource development in the past and for the future.

917.11
    Orchard City (Kelowna, B.C.).
        prod. [Montreal?] : NFB, 1971.- dist. McI. 54 fr. : col. : 35 mm. & manual $10.00 (Canadian communities) ji

        1. Fruit culture. 2. Kelowna, B.C. - Description. 3. British Columbia - Industries.

        Shows the growth and handling of fruit in the Okanagan Valley of British Columbia. Filmstrip focuses on orchard activity but also examines the surrounding community.
        Describes climate and geography of Kelowna and how the orchard, grape, wine and canning industries affect community life. Follows production, storage and transportation of fruit French title available : VILLE FRUITIERE.-

917.11
    Paul and Pauline visit British Columbia.
        prod. [Toronto] : Leamat Ltd., 1973.- dist. Lea. 41 fr. : col. : 35 mm. $9.00 (Canada : coast to coast with Paul and Pauline : $59.50) pj

        1. British Columbia - Description and travel.

        Photographic tour of British Columbia. Covers the mainland, Vancouver Island, and Victoria. Shows parliament buildings, city life and major industries, such as pulp mills, logging and mining. Numerous scenic photographs of mountains, Fraser River and Okanagan Valley. Suggests further research.-

917.11
    Queen Charlotte Islands.
        prod. [Montreal?] : NFB, made 1970 : 1971.- dist. McI. 64 fr. : col. : 35 mm. & manual. McI. is

        1. Queen Charlotte Islands, B.C. - Geography.

        An introduction to the land, industry and people of these northern islands. Covers lumber, fishing and mining industries, the scenery and the daily life of its inhabitants, including the Haida Indian community. Comprehensive treatment compensates for somewhat inferior quality of colour. French title available : L'ARCHIPEL DE LE REINE-CHARLOTTE.-

917.11
    Queen Charlotte Islands.
        prod. [Montreal?] : NFB, 1971.- dist. McI. 64 fr. : col. : 35 mm. & manual $10.00 is

        1. Queen Charlotte Islands, B.C. - Geography.

        An introduction to the land, industry and people of these northern islands. Covers lumber, fishing and mining industries, the scenery and the daily life of its inhabitants, including the Haida Indian community. Comprehensive treatment compensates for somewhat inferior quality of colour. French title available : L'ARCHIPEL DE LA REINE-CHARLOTTE.-

917.11
    The Rocky Mountains national parks.
        prod. [Georgetown, Ont.] : FMS, 1973.- dist. McI. 46 fr. : col. : 35 mm. & captions. $9.00 (National parks of Canada : $30.00) ji

        1. Rocky Mountains, Canadian - Description and travel.

        Views of Rocky Mountains national parks, comprising Jasper, Banff, Yoho, Glacier, Kootenay, and Vaterton show ice fields and glaciers, falls, rivers and lakes, as well as plants, birds and animals - sheep, goats, moose, rodents in their habitat.-

The Classified Catalogue

917.11
  Stanley Park.
    prod. [Winnipeg] : WCL, 1972.- dist. Sch. Ch. 46 fr. : col. : 35 mm. $7.95 (British Columbia : $15.90) ji

    1. Vancouver, B.C. - Parks.

    A look at one of Canada's largest city parks, illustrated with numerous photogaphs of the park in spring, summer and fall. Gives brief history of park from first opening in 1887 to present. Photographs and maps show park past and present-those who visit it, and the various activities including boating, bike riding, lawn bowling, etc.-

917.11
  Timber City : Vancouver.
    prod. [Montreal?] : NFB, 1964.- dist. McI. 37 fr. : col. : 35 mm. & manual. $10.00 (Canadian cities) ji

    1. Vancouver, B.C. - History.

    Photographs, drawings and graphs depict the history of Vancouver. Emphasizes the importance of the timber industry. Comprehensive background notes included in the manual. French title available : UNE VILLE DU BOIS D'OEUVRE.-

917.11
  Vancouver.
    prod. [Scarborough, Ont.] : R.B.M., 1975.- dist. ETHOS 62 fr. : col. : 35 mm. & cassette (13 min.) : auto. & aud. adv. sig. & teacher's manual. $19.00 (Cities of Canada) ji

    1. Vancouver, B.C. - Description.

    Shows the changing face of the west coast city from 1886 to the 1970's. Covers all aspects of Vancouver, including its harbours, fishing and lumbering industry, education, and residential growth. Illustrated with photographs from the past and present.-

917.11
  Vancouver Island.
    prod. [Stratford, Ont.] : Sch. Ch., 1974.- dist. Sch. Ch. 46 fr. : col. : 35 mm. $7.95 (British Columbia : $15.90) ji

    1. Vancouver Island, B.C. - Description and travel.

    Emphasizes various aspects of Vancouver Island-its native people, wildlife, fishing and pulp industries, and tourism. Archival photographs of early Indian villages alongvhe coast are contrasted with photographs shwing contemporary Indian lifestyles.-

917.11
  Victoria.
    prod. [Scarborough, Ont.] : R.B.M., 1975.- dist. ETHOS 51 fr. : b&w & col. : 35 mm. & cassette (10 min.) : auto. & aud. adv. sig. & teaching manual. $19.00 (Cities of Canada) ji

    1. Victoria, B.C. - Description.

    Drawings, maps and photographs are used to emphasize Victoria's past and present role as trading post and harbour. In addition to discussion on legislature and functions, mentions city's business section, its industry, housing, and famous tourist attractions.-

917.11
  Victoria, B.C.
    prod. [Winnipeg] : WCL, 1972.- dist. Sch. Ch. 45 fr. : b&w & col. : 35 mm. & captions. $7.95 (Provincial capitals) ji

    1. Victoria, B.C. - Description.

    Shows the growth of Victoria from a British fort to an industrial and residential centre. Old photographs and sketches show the fort complex, the city and the first parliament buildings. Modern photographs indicate changes in the city and harbour, and in the government's responsibilities to the citizens of British Columbia. Covers forest management, road maintenance in mountainous regions, fishing industry, and tourist attractions.-

The Classified Catalogue

917.11
    Victoria, B.C.
        prod. [Winnipeg, Man.] : VCL., 1972.- dist. Scholar's Choice Ltd. 45 fr. : col. : 35 mm. $7.95 (Provincial capitals) ji

        1. Victoria, B.C. - Description.

        The growth of Victoria from a British fort to an industrial and residential centre. Old photographs and sketches show fort complex, city and harbour, and the government's responsibilties to citizens. Also covers forest management, road maintenance fishing industry, and tourist attractions.-

917.11
    Une ville du bois d'oeuvre.
        prod. [Montreal?] : NFB, 1962.- dist. SEC 43 fr. : col. : 35 mm. & manual. $9.00 ji

        1. Vancouver, B.C. History.

        Photographs, drawings and graphs depict the history of Vancouver. Emphasizes the importance of the timber industry. Comprehensive background notes included in manual. English title available : TIMBER CITY : VANCOUVER.-

917.11
    Ville fruitière.
        prod. [Montreal?] : NFB, 1970.- dist. SEC 54 fr. : col. : 35 mm. & manual. $9.00 ji

        1. Fruit culture. 2. Kelowna, B.C. Description. 3. British Columbia - Industries.

        Shows growth and handling of fruit in the Okanagan Valley of British Columbia. Filmstrip focuses on orchard activity but also examines the surrounding community. Describes climate and geography of Kelowna and how the orchard, grape, wine, and canning industries affect community life. Follows production, storage, and transportation of fruit. English title available : ORCHARD CITY.-

917.12
    Arctic Delta town (Inuvik, N.W.T.).
        prod. [Montreal?] : NFB, 1972.- dist. McI. 61 fr. : b&w & col. : 35 mm. & captions & printed notes. $9.00 (Canadian communities) ji

        1. Inuvik, N.W.T. - Description.

        Describes life in the Mackenzie River delta town of Inuvik. Discusses problems caused by permafrost, the unusual way of life for school children who live in town hostels, and describes everyday activities common to most Canadians. Examines important industries of oil and natural gas production. French title available : UNE VILLE ARCTIQUE SU UN DELTA.-

917.12
    The Arctic today.
        prod. [Scarborough, Ont.] : R.B.M., 1974.- dist. ETHOS 74 fr. : col. : 35 mm. & cassette (10 min.) : auto. & aud. adv. sig. & reading script. $19.00 (The Canadian Arctic : $69.00) ji

        1. Eskimos - Social conditions. 2. Arctic regions.

        Photographs of modern-day Igloolik highlight both good and bad features of life in the north today. Scenes include modes of transportation, building, and services.-

917.12
    Eskimo 1 : Arctic village.
        prod. [Don Mills, Ont.] : F & V, 1973.- dist. F & V 20 fr. : col. : 35 mm. & teacher's guide. $7.20 (Man in his world) ji

        1. Eskimos.

        Views of life in the Arctic. Points out how the native people, plants and animals living here are affected by and adapt to the severe climate, and emphasizes the increasing influence of the white man's ways on Eskimo culture. For class use, since all information is in the accompanying guide.-

917.12
> Exploration de l'Arctique canadien.
> prod. [Montreal?] : NFB, made 1953 : 1974.- dist. SEC 42 fr. : b&w : 35 mm. & captions & teacher's guide. $9.00 j
>
> 1. Arctic regions.
>
> Traces the Arctic explorations of Frobisher, Hudson, Baffin, Hearne, Mackenzie, Franklin, Peary, Amundsen, Stefansson, and others, using black and white drawings and maps. English title available : EXPLORATION OF ARCTIC CANADA.-

917.12
> Exploration of Arctic Canada.
> prod. [Montreal?] : NFB, 1953.- dist. McI. 42 fr. : b&w : 35 mm. & captions & teacher's guide. $9.00 j
>
> 1. Arctic regions.
>
> Traces the Arctic explorations of Frobisher, Hudson, Baffin, Hearne, Mackenzie, Franklin, Peary, Amundsen, Stefansson, and others, using black and white drawings and maps. French title available : EXPLORATION DE L'ARCTIQUE CANADIEN.-

917.12
> Geography of the Arctic.
> prod. [Scarborough, Ont.] : R.B.M., 1974.- dist. ETHOS 67 fr. : col. : 35 mm. & cassette (9 min.) : auto. & aud. adv. sig. & reading script. $19.00 (The Canadian Arctic : $69.00) ji
>
> 1. Arctic regions - Geography.
>
> Photographs taken in June near Igloolik show the Arctic as it appears during the summer months and illustrate that it is not just a land of ice and snow. Illustrates the lemming snow bunting, lapland langspur as well as caribou moss and arctic flowers.

917.12
> The Interior Plains.
> prod. [Montreal?] : NFB, 1964.- dist. McIntyre Educational Media ltd. 45 fr. : col. : 35 mm. & manual $10.00 ji
>
> 1. Prairie Provinces - Geography.
>
> Illustrates the climate and geography of the Prairie provinces of Canada. Examines the vegetation of the region and the distribution of the types of farming. Describes the importance of oil and natural gas development, transportation and a variety of industries.-

917.12
> Introduction : the Western Plains.
> prod. [Montreal?] : NFB, made 1961 : 1977.- dist. McI. 41 fr. : col. : 35 mm. & captions. $9.00 ji
>
> 1. Prairie provinces - Geography.
>
> A photographic overview of the Western Plains region of Canada. Discusses physical geography, climate, economy, transportation systems and population. Points out the importance of wheat production, beef cattle, and the petroleum industry. Measurements are not metric. French title available : VUE D'ENSEMBLE (LES PLAINES DE L'OUEST).-

917.12
> The Northern territories.
> prod. [Toronto] : M-L, 1974.- dist. Sch. Ser. or Vint. 74 fr. : col. : 35 mm. & cassette (14 min.) : auto. & aud. adv. sig. & teacher's guide. $16.50 (Canada : the true north strong and free : $85.00) i
>
> 1. Northwest Territories - Economic conditions. 2. Northwest Territories - History.
>
> Illustrates the effects of the harsh Northern climate on the development of natural resources, such as oil and gold. Describes the changes in the lifestyle of the natives and harm caused by advanced technology. Traces the history of the North including the Gold Rush and formation of the Northwest Mounted Police. French title availabe : LES TERRITOIRES DU NORD-OUEST.-

917.12
> Paul and Pauline visit Manitoba and Saskatchewan.
> prod. [Toronto] : Lea., 1973.- dist. Leamat Ltd. 39 fr. : col. : 35 mm. $9.00 (Canada : coast to coast with Paul and Pauline : $59.50) pj
>
> 1. Manitoba - Description and travel. 2. Saskatchewan - Description and travel.
>
> General overview of industry and agriculture in these prairie provinces. Shows provincial capitals and legislative buildings.
> Photographs include farming and mining communities, national parks and tourist attractions such as Manitoba's Fort Garry.-

The Classified Catalogue

917.12
    Physical setting.
        prod. [Toronto] : Int. Cin., 1971.- dist. VEC 45 fr. : col. : 35 mm. & 4 pamphlets, 2 maps, 1 teacher's guide, 1 transparency & captions. $12.00 (The Living Arctic : $54.00) ji

        1. Eskimos. 2. Adaptation (Biology). 3. Arctic regions.

        A general introduction to the Arctic environment explaining its long summer days and winter nights. Also explains how plant and animal life have adapted to the harsh climate, and, in particular, how the Eskimo have developed a special way of life to ensure survival.-

917.12
    The Praire provinces.
        prod. [Toronto] : M-L, 1974.- dist. Sch. Ser. or Vint. 60 fr. : col. : 35 mm. & cassette (14 min.) : auto. & aud. adv. sig. & teacher's guide. $16.50 (Canada : the true north strong and free : $85.00) i

        1. Prairie Provinces - Economic conditions. 2. Prairie Provinces - History.

        Describes the geography of the Prairie provinces and importance of farming industries. Explains the development of other resources, such as lumbering, mining, and oil. Gives a brief history of the area including Red River Settlement, Riel Rebellion, World War I, and the Depression. French title available : LES PROVINCES DE PRAIRIES.-

917.12
    The Prairie region.
        prod. [Toronto] : Int. Cin., 1978.- dist. VEC 81 fr. : b&w & col. : 35 mm. & cassette (15 min.) : auto. & aud. adv. sig. & teacher's guide. $24.00 (Canada and its regions : the geography of a changing land : $155.00) ji

        1. Prairie Provinces - Economic conditions. 2. Prairie Provinces - Geography.

        Discusses traditional econoMic interests, success of area as grain growing centre, and re-emergence of Canadian West due to oil and petroleum industry. Provides a geographical description of region through use of maps and photographs.-

917.12
    Les Territoires du Nord-Ouest.
        prod. [Toronto] : M-L, 1974.- dist. Sch. Ser. or Vint. 74 fr. : col. : 35 mm. & cassette (14 min.) : auto. & aud. adv. sig. & teacher's guide. $16.50 (Canada : "Il est né d'une race fiée" : $85.00) i

        1. Northwest Territories - Economic conditions. 2. Northwest Territories - History.

        Illustrates the effects of the harsh Northern climate on the development of natural resources, such as oil and gold. Describes the changes in the lifestyle of the natives and harm caused by advanced technology. Traces the history of the North including the Gold Rush and formation of the Northwest Mounted Police. English title available : THE NORTHERN TERRITORIES.-

917.12
    The Way we live today.
        prod. [Toronto] : Int. Cin., 1975.- dist. VEC 69 fr. : col. : 35 mm. & cassette (9 min.) : auto. & aud. adv. sig. & teacher's guide. $24.00 (The Arctic through Eskimo eyes : $86.00) ji

        1. Eskimos. 2. Cape Dorset, N.W.T. - Description.

        Depicts Cape Dorset of today with authentic drawings and photographs. Shows modern homes and schools, the supermarket, snowmobile, and outboard canoe which have changed the Eskimo way of life. Making of Eskimo prints is well-illustrated.-

917.12
    The Yukon.
        prod. [Montreal?] : NFB, 1962.- dist. McI. 43 fr. : col. : 35 mm. & captions. & guide. $9.00 ji

        1. Yukon Territory - Description and travel.

        A general introduction to the terrain, cities, and industries of the Yukon. Shows major cities and industries, stressing the role of transportation in the region's development and expansion. Photographs convey the beauty of the area and the abundance of natural resources. French title available : LE YUKON.-

917.123
    Alberta.
        prod. [Scarborough, Ont.] : R.B.M., 1976.- dist. ETHOS 42 fr. : col. : 35 mm. & reading script. $19.00 (Impressions : Canada) ji

        1. Alberta - Description and travel.

        An introduction to Alberta covering its geography, resources, industries, history, and some special attractions, such as the Calgary Stampede and Edmonton Klondike Days.-

917.123
    Calgary.
        prod. [Scarborough, Ont.] : R.B.M., 1975.- dist. ETHOS 43 fr. : b&w & col. : 35 mm. & cassette (11 min.) : auto. & aud. adv. sig. & teacher's manual. $19.00 (Cities of Canada) ji

        1. Calgary, Alta. - Description.

        A chronological account of the city's social and economic development with emphasis on tourist attractions and recreational facilities. Includes major industries and products, public transportation, urbanization and education.-

917.123
    Edmonton.
        prod. [Scarborough, Ont.] : R.B.M., 1975.- dist. ETHOS 52 fr. : col. : 35 mm. & cassette (15 min.) : auto. & aud. adv. sig. & teacher's manual. $19.00 (Cities of Canada) ji

        1. Edmonton, Alta. - Description.

        General overview of Edmonton emphasizes dynamic growth as a result of the oil industry. Contrasts original Fort Edmonton with busy city of today. Photographs accompany discussion of natural resources, major industries, residential growth, and transportation.-

917.123
    Edmonton, Alberta.
        prod. [Stratford, Ont.] : Sch. Ch., 1977.- dist. Sch. Ch. 37 fr. : b&w & col. : 35 mm. & captions. $7.95 (Provincial capital) ji

        1. Edmonton Alta. - Description.

        Edmonton's past, present and future are featured in this imformative presentation. Begins with the city's early growth and how originally used by settlers, trappers and prospectors. Describes large and small industries including farming, ranching and oil. Concluded with comments on its future as Canada's "Gateway to the North".-

917.123
    Paul and Pauline Visit Alberta.
        prod. [Toronto] : Lea., 1973.- dist. Lea. 37 fr. : col. : 35 mm. $9.00 (Canada : coast to coast with Paul and Pauline $59.50) pj

        1. Alberta - Description and travel.

        A cursory overview of Alberta for primary grades. Photographs include Edmonton, Parliament buildings, farming, oil industry, Calgary Stampede and parks.-

917.124
    Regina.
        prod. [Scarborough, Ont.] : R.B.M., 1975.- dist. ETHOS 44 fr. : b&w & col. : 35 mm. & cassette (10 min.) : auto. & aud. adv. sig. & teacher's manual. $19.00 (Cities of Canada) ji

        1. Regina, Sask. - Description.

        A brief description of Regina touching on its growth and development, industries, recreational activities, and architecture. Includes photos of the original Diefenbaker homestead, the Legislature Building, and the R.C.M.P. training centre.-

917.124
    Regina, Sask.
        prod. [Stratford, Ont.] : Sch. Ch., 1974.- dist. Sch. Ch. 45 fr. : col. : 35 mm. $7.95 (Provincial capitals) ji

        1. Regina, Sask. - Description.

        Historic and current photographs of the province illustrate account of responsibilities of Saskatchewan's provincial government. Covers agricultural experimentation, forest protection and maintenance of publc thoroughfares. Also shows Saskatchewan's National Museum with life-like displays of provincial wildlife.-

917.124
    Saskatchewan.
        prod. [Scarborough, Ont.] : R.B.M., 1976.- dist. ETHOS 41 fr. : col. : 35 mm. & reading script. $19.00 (Impressions : Canada) ji

        1. Saskatchewan - Description and travel.

        An introductory overview of Saskatchewan. Discusses its history, resources, industries, people, and geography.-

The Classified Catalogue

917.127
    Flin Flon, Manitoba.
        prod. [Stratford, Ont.] : Sch. Ch., 1976.- dist. Sch. Ch. 54 fr. : col. : 35 mm. $7.95 (Canadian community studies) i

        1. Mines and minerals resources - Manitoba. 2. Flin Flon, Man.

        The interdependence between a mining company and the Manitoba town where it is situated. Photographs taken inside the mine illustrate mining, crushing and processing of ore. Also shows people working at various jobs in the mining company, as well as those employed to service the mining community in areas of health care, education, transportation and recreation.-

917.127
    Manitoba.
        prod. [Scarborough, Ont.] : R.B.M., 1976.- dist. ETHOS 46 fr. : col. : 35 mm. & reading script. $19.00 (Impressions : Canada) ji

        An introduction to Manitoba's varied attractions including its scenery, people, industries, and recreation.-

917.127
    Manitoba.
        prod. [Scarborough, Ont.] : R.B.M., 1976.- dist. ETHOS 46 fr. : col. : 35 mm. & reading script. $9.50 (Impressions : Canada) ji

        1. Manitoba - Description and travel.

        An overview of Manitoba's varied attractions including references to its natural beauty, brief description of agriculture, mining and manufacturing. Illustrates some of province's ethnic groups. Recreation, transportation and the arts are also mentioned.-

917.127
    Manitoba : a broader view.
        prod. [Montreal?] : NFB, 1969.- dist. McI. 76 fr. : col. : 35 mm. & printed notes. $10.00 (Geography of Manitoba : $27.00) js

        1. Manitoba - Geography.

        Provides an accurate and realistic impression of the province of Manitoba. Studies the various lifestyles found in the three main geographic regions: the Great Central Plains, the Canadian Shield, and the Hudson Bay Lowlands. Includes many natural resources, birds, animals and vegetation. For group viewing using the printed notes. French title available : LE MANITOBA : VUE D'ENSEMBLE.-

917.127
    Manitoba : the Shield.
        prod. [Montreal?] : NFB, 1969.- dist. McI. 37 fr. : col. : 35 mm. & manual. $9.00 (Geography of Manitoba : $27.00) ji

        1. Manitoba - Geography.

        Photographs and maps illustrate the harsh landscape of the Canadian Shield, plus development and potential of this area. Specially studies mining, water power, forestry and economic activities of the people. Includes Thompson and Flin Flon, and describes problems in developing the Shield. Measurements are not metric. French title available : LE MANITOBA : LE BOUCLIER.-

917.127
    Le Manitoba : vue d'ensemble.
        prod. [Montreal?] : NFB, 1969.- dist. SEC 80 fr. : col. : 35 mm. & captions & printed notes. $9.00 (La géographie du Manitoba) js

        1. Manitoba - Geography.

        Provides an accurate and realistic impression of the province of Mantioba. Studies the various lifestyles found in the three main geographic regions: the Great Central Plains, the Canadian Shield, and the Hudson Bay Lowlands. Includes many natural resources, birds, animals and vegetation. For group viewing using the printed notes. English title available : MANITOBA : A BROADER VIEW.-

The Classified Catalogue

917.127
    Le Manitoba : les Plaines.
      prod. [Montreal?] : NFB, 1969.- dist. SEC 43 fr. : col. : 35 mm. & captions & manual. $9.00 (La géographie du Manitoba) ji

      1. Manitoba - Geography.

      Photographs and maps are used to explain the landforms, soil, climatic regions, industry and people of Manitoba. English title available : MANITOBA : THE PLAINS.-

917.127
    Manitoba : the plains.
      prod. [Montreal?] : NFB, made 1969 : 1970.- dist. McI. 43 fr. : col. : 35 mm. & manual. $9.00 (Geography of Manitoba : $27.00) ji

      1. Manitoba - Geography.

      Photographs and maps are used to explain the landforms, soil, climatic regions, industry and people of Manitoba. French title available : LE MANITOBA : LES PLAINES.-

917.127
    Railway city : Winnipeg.
      prod. [Montreal?] : NFB, 1973.- dist. McI. 70 fr. : col. : 35 mm. & captions & teacher's guide. $9.00 (Canadian cities .) jis

      1. Winnipeg, Man. - History.

      Drawings, photographs and graphics describe the history of Winnipeg from the early days as the trading post known as Fort Rouge to its present position as an important rail and air centre, as well as a grain exchange. French title available : VILLE FERROVIAIRE.-

917.127
    Ville ferroviaire (Winnipeg).
      prod. [Montreal?] : NFB, 1973.- dist. SEC 70 fr. : b&w & col. : 35 mm. & captions. $9.00 jis

      1. Wnnipeg, Man. - History.

      Drawings, photographs and graphics describe the history of Winnipeg from early days as the trading post known as Fort Rouge to its present position as an important rail and air centre, as well as a grain exchange. English title available : RAILWAY CITY.-

917.127
    Winnipeg.
      prod. [Toronto] : R.B.M., 1975.- dist. ETHOS 53 fr. : col. : 35 mm. & cassette (11 min.) : auto. & aud. adv. sig. & teacher's manual. $18.50 (Cities of Canada) is

      1. Winnipeg, Man. - Description.

      Describes the largest city in the Prairie provinces with a brief history of its development.-

917.127
    Winnipeg, Man.
      prod. [Winnipeg] : VCL, 1972.- dist. Sch. Ch. 43 fr. : b&w & col. : 35 mm. & captions. $7.95 (Provincial capitals) ji

      1. Winnipeg, Man. - Description.

      Emphasizes Winnipeg's historical importance as a transportation centre, featuring photographs of the legislative buildings and other tourist attractions. Also illustrates the role Winnipeg government plays in hospital care, recreation, education, environmental protection, and farming.-

917.127
    Winnipeg, Man.
      prod. [Winnipeg] : VCL, 1972.- dist. Sch. Ch. 43 fr. : col. : 35 mm. $7.95 (Provincial capitals) ji

      1. Winnipeg, Man. - Description.

      Emphasizes Winnipeg's hospital care, historical importance as a transportation centre from its early beginnings to the present. Features colourful photographs of legislative buildings and other tourist attraction. Also illustrates role of Winnipeg government in hospital care, recreation, education, environmental protection, and farming.-

The Classified Catalogue

917.13
    Un contre d'industrie laitière.
        prod. [Montreal?] : NFB, 1971.- dist. SEC 58 fr. : col. : 35 mm. & captions. $9.00 ji

        1. Dairying. 2. Mennonites. 3. Elmira, Ont. - Description.

        Illustrates everyday life on a small Mennonite farm in Elmira, Ontario, and contrasts it with a large farm in the same area that uses modern farm technology. Follows milk production through all the processing stages. Discusses important community facilities in Elmira and takes a look at the Maple Syrup Festival, the Farmers' Market, and the Fall Fair. English title available : DAIRY FARMING COMMUNITY : (ELMIRA, ONT.).-

917.13
    Dairy farming community (Elmira, Ont.).
        prod. [Montreal?] : NFB, 1972.- dist. McI. 54 fr. : col. : 35 mm. & captions. $9.00 (Canadian communities) ji

        1. Dairying. 2. Mennonites. 3. Elmira, Ont. - Description.

        Illustrates everyday life on a small Mennonite farm in Elmira, Ontario, and contrasts it with a large farm in the same area that uses modern farm technology. Follows milk production through all the processing stages. Discusses important community facilities in Elmira and takes a look at the Maple Syrup Festival, the Farmers' Market, and the Fall Fair. French title available :UN CENTRE D'INDUSTRIE LAITIERE.-

917.13
    Images d'une ville minière.
        prod. [Montreal?] : NFB, 1964.- dist. SEC 44 fr. : col. : 35 mm. & captions & teacher's manual. $9.00 ji

        1. Mines and mineral resources - Ontario. 2. Manitouwadge, Ont. - Description.

        A description of the community of Manitouwadge, Ontario, and how it depends on the two copper-zinc mines in the area. Examines the method of mining with a cross-section diagram of a mine and many underground photographs. Detail is given to everyday life of the miners and their families, and community activities. Measurements are not metric. English title available : MINING TOWN (MANITOUWADGE, ONT).-

917.13
    The Industrial city.
        prod. [Scarborough, Ont.] : R.B.M., 1975.- dist. ETHOS 42 fr. : col. : 35 mm. & cassette (11 min.) : auto. & aud. adv. sig. & manual. $18.50 (Hamilton : $34.50) ji

        1. Hamilton, Ont. - Description.

        Reasons for Hamilton's development as Canada's number one iron and steel manufacturer and as a highly industrialized centre are discussed in a look at this modern Canadian city. The processes involved in manufacture of steel are described with references made to industries associated with steel manufacturing.-

917.13
    Introduction to the Niagara Fruit Belt.
        prod. [Scarborough, Ont.] : FCC, 1976.- dist. FCC 10 fr. : col. : 35 mm. & cassette (16 min.) : auto. & aud. adv. sig. & teacher's guide and reading script. $9.95 (Niagara Fruit Belt : $29.85) jis

        1. Fruit culture. 2. Niagara Peninsula, Ont.

        Describes areas of intensive vineyards and orchards in the Niagara fruit belt, outlining the factors that make the area excellent for growing grapes and tender fruit. Includes maps and photos. Repeats information given in "Overview of the Niagara Fruit Belt" but in greater detail. A condensed version of the narration is provided. Material packaged in clear vinyl envelope to fit a legal-size filing cabinet.-

917.13
    The Many Faces of Hamilton.
        prod. [Scarborough] : R.B.M., 1975.- dist. ETHOS 63 fr. : col. : 35mm. & cassette (14 min.) : auto. & aud. adv. sig. & manual. $18.50 (Hamilton) ji

        1. Hamilton, Ont. - Description.

        Describes the non-industrial aspects of Hamilton, Ontario. Business and commerce, the arts, recreation and urban development are discussed. Reference is made to the new Civic Square, Royal Botanical Gardens, Dundurn Castle, McMaster University and various transportation systems.-

The Classified Catalogue

917.13
    Marathon, Ontario.
        prod. [Stratford, Ont.] : Sch. Ch., 1976.- dist. Sch. Ch. 52 fr. : col. : 35 mm. & captions. $7.95 (Canadian community studies : $55.65) ji

        1. Marathon, Ont. - Description.

        A look at a Northern Ontario community where residents depend on one major industry for their livelihood. Photos show Marathon's pulp and paper industry, but stress how the schools, hospital, police, and recreational facilities meet the community's needs. Also deals with communication with other cities.-

917.13
    Mining town (Manitouwadge, Ont.).
        prod. [Montreal?] : NFB, 1964.- dist. McI. 44 fr. : col. : 35 mm. & captions & teacher's anual. $9.00 (Canadian communities) ji

        1. Manitouwadge, Ont. - Description.
        2. Mines and mineral resources - Ontario.

        A description of the community of Manitouwadge, Ontario and how it depends on the two copper-zinc mines in the area. Examines the method of mining with a cross-section diagram of a mine and many underground photographs. Detail is given to everyday life of the miners and their families, and community activities. Measurements are not metric. French title available : IMAGES D'UNE VILLE MINIERE.-

917.13
    The Natural environment.
        prod. [Scarborough, Ont.] : R.B.M., 1975.- dist. ETHOS 44 fr. : b&w & col. : 35 mm. & cassette (12 min.) : auto. & aud. adv. sig. & teacher's manual. $19.00 (Scarborough Bluffs : $34.50) ji

        1. Erosion. 2. Scarborough Bluffs region, Ont.

        Examines the effects of erosion on, and man's efforts to preserve, the spectacular Scarborough Bluffs in southern Ontario.-

917.13
    Ontario : the north, transportation and recreation.
        prod. [Scarborough, Ont.] : R.B.M., 1976.- dist. ETHOS 52 fr. : col. : 35 mm. & cassette (12 min.) : auto. & aud. adv. sig. & teacher's manual. $19.00 (Regional studies : $138.00) ji

        1. Ontario, Northern - Geography.
        2. Ontario, Northern - History.

        Although the main emphasis is on Northern Ontario's topography, history, and industry, the presentation includes a very brief comment on transportation and recreation from a provincial viewpoint.-

917.13
    Ontario.
        prod. [Scarborough, Ont.] : R.B.M., 1976.- dist. ETHOS 49 fr. : col. : 35 mm. & reading script. $19.00 (Impressions : Canada) ji

        1. Ontario - Description and travel.

        An overview of Ontario's history and geography, communities, transportation, recreation, major industries and resources.-

917.13
    L'Ontario.
        prod. [Toronto] : M-L, 1974.- dist. Sch. Ser. or Vint. 73 fr. : col. : 35 mm. & cassette (13 min.) : auto. & aud. adv. sig. & teacher's guide. $16.50 (Canada : "Il est né d'une race fiére" : $85.00) i

        1. Ontario - Economic conditions.

        Examines Ontario's location and the advantage of its proximity to large American centres. Discusses natural resources, including fresh water, hydro-electric power, nuclear power generators, solar energy, fertile farm land, mining, and pulp and paper, and the province's responsibility to the rest of Canada. English title available : ONTARIO.-

917.13
  Ontario.
    prod. [Toronto] : M-L, 1974.- dist. Sch. Ser. or Wint. 73 fr. : col. : 35 mm. & cassette (13 min.) : auto. & aud. adv. sig. & teacher's guide. $16.50 (Canada : the true north strong and free : $85.00) i

    1. Ontario - Economic conditions.

    Examines Ontario's location and the advantages of its proximity to large American centres. Discusses natural resources, including fresh water, hydro-electric power, nuclear power generators, solar energy, fertile farm land, mining, and pulp and paper, and the province's responsibility to the rest of Canada. French title available : L'ONTARIO.-

917.13
  Oshawa, Ontario.
    prod. [Stratford, Ont.] : Sch. Ch., 1976.- dist. Sch. Ch. 52 fr. : col. : 35 mm. $7.95 (Canadian community studies : $55.66) ji

    1. Automotive industry and trade.

    A clear approach showing the automotive industry in Oshawa, Ontario, and its influence upon the community in which it is located. Provides view of the industry itself, and the dependence of the automotive assembly line upon parts shipped from other locations in Canada. Shows how selling and servicing of vehicles create direct and indirect jobs in the community.-

917.13
  Ottawa - the urban community.
    prod. [Scarborough, Ont.] : R.B.M., 1976.- dist. ETHOS 49 fr. : b&w & col. : 35 mm. & cassette (11 min.) : auto. & aud. adv. sig. & teacher's manual. $19.00 (Cities of Canada) ji

    1. Ottawa, Ont. - Description.

    A look at today's Ottawa. Considers it as a major tourist centre, as a city of museums, monuments, and many recreational facilities, and as a quickly growing community whose development is closely monitored by the National Capital Commission.-

917.13
  Ottawa - Canada's capital.
    prod. [Scarborough, Ont.] : R.B.M., 1976.- dist. ETHOS 51 fr. : b&w & col. : 35 mm. & cassette (10 min.) : auto. & aud. adv. sig. & teaching guide. $19.00 (Cities of Canada) ji

    1. Ottawa, Ont. - Description.

    Both the old and the new are emphasized in this presentation on the major and historical points of interest in Canada's capital city, including the Parliament buildings and the National Arts Centre.-

917.13
  Paul and Pauline visit Ontario.
    prod. [Toronto] : Lea., 1973.- dist. Lea. 44 fr. : col. : 35 mm. & captions. $9.00 (Canada : coast to coast with Paul and Pauline : $59.50) pj

    1. Ontario - Description and travel.

    Briefly depicts governmental, cultural and recreational attractions found in Ontario. Includes most large and small cities in Ontario, and at least one major attraction of each.-

917.13
  Planning for future use.
    prod. [Scarborough, Ont.] : R.B.M., 1975.- dist. ETHOS 40 fr. : b&w & col. : 35 mm. & cassette (12 min.) : auto. & aud. adv. sig. & teacher's manual. $19.00 (Scarborough Bluffs : $34.50) ji

    1. Scarborough Bluffs region, Ont.

    Presents some of the history of the Scarborough Bluffs, and includes photographs showing activities and points of interest in the Bluffs area.-

The Classified Catalogue

917.13
    Point Pelee National Park.
        prod. [Georgetown, Ont.] : FMS, 1973.- dist. McI. 46 fr. : col. : 35 mm. & captions & teacher's guide. $10.00 (National parks of Canada : $30.00) ji

        1. Point Pelee National Park.

        An overview of the "living outdoor museum" at Point Pelee, Ontario, the southernmost tip of Canada's mainland. Shows the rare fresh-water marshes where migratory birds, such as whistling swans and egrets, visit. Discusses the almost original deciduous forest, the animals and birds that inhabit it, and the importance of the park as a site for birdwatchers.-

917.13
    Southern Ontario.
        prod. [Scarborough, Ont.] : R.B.M., 1976.- dist. ETHOS 52 fr. : col. : 35 mm. & cassette (11 min.) : auto. & aud. adv. sig. & teacher's manual. $19.00 (Regional studies : $138.00) ji

        1. Ontario, Southern - Geography.
        2. Ontario, Southern - History.

        An introductory overview of the geological background, early history, industry, and small communities of Southern Ontario.-

917.13
    Thunder Bay on tour.
        prod. [Thunder Bay, Ont.] : CP, 1975.- dist. CP 61 fr. : col. : 35 mm. & captions & reading script. $14.50 i

        1. Thunder Bay, Ont. - Description.

        A comprehensive guided tour of Thunder Bay and the surrounding district. Shown are the area's historical background, recreational facilities, parks, museums, major exhibitions and events, the university, the airport, industrial source of employment and natural phenomena (falls, canyons, mountains, lakes).-

917.13
    Toronto - growth, change & progress.
        prod. [Scarborough, Ont.] : R.B.M., 1976.- dist. ETHOS 48 fr. : col. : 35 mm. & cassette (10 min.) : auto. & aud. adv. sig. & teacher's manual. $19.00 (Cities of Canada) ji

        1. Toronto, Ont. - Description.

        Emphasizes the variety to be found in Toronto with photographs of architecture, recreational activities, services, and means of transportation.-

917.14
    Les Iles de la Madeleine.
        prod. [Montreal?] : NFB, 1973.- dist. SEC 48 fr. : col. : 35 mm. & captions. $9.00 (Image du Canada) ji

        1. Magdalen Islands, Que. - Description and travel.

        Photography depicts life on the Magadalen Islands. Includes history, geography, industry, culture, and many scenic views. English title available : MAGDALEN ISLANDS.-

917.14
    Magdalen Islands.
        prod. [Montreal?] : NFB, 1972.- dist. McI. 43 fr. : col. : 35 mm. & captions. $9.00 (Image Canada : $45.00) ji

        1. Magdalen Islands, Que. - Description and travel.

        Photography depicts life on the Magdalen Islands. Includes history, geography, industry, culture, and many scenic views. French title available : LES ILES DE LA MADELEINE.-

917.14
    Paul and Pauline visit Quebec.
        prod. [Toronto] : Lea., 1973.- dist. Lea. 37 fr. : col. : 35 mm. & captions. 9.00 (Canada : coast to coast with Paul and Pauline : $59.50) pj

        1. Quebec (Province) - Description and travel.

        Brief presentation of the many rural communities of Quebec, as well as its famous cities, Montreal, Quebec, Hull, and attractions such as Man and his World. Points out numerous farming regions and historic areas. Emphasizes contrast throughout province.-

917.14
The Province of Quebec : the Appalachian region.
prod. [Montreal?] : NFB, 1965.- dist. McI. 36 fr. : col. : 35 mm. & captions & teacher's manual. $9.00 (Province of Quebec : $27.00) jis

1. Quebec (Province) - Geography.
2. Appalachian region, Que.

Photographs and diagrams illustrate the geography of the Appalachian region under the headings of the Gaspé Peninsula, South of the Estuary, and the Eastern Townships. Detail is given to physical features and main activities of communities with important areas circled and identified on the photograph. French title available : LE QUEBEC : LES APPALACHES.-

917.14
The Province of Quebec : the Laurentian region.
prod. [Montreal?] : NFB, 1965.- dist. McI. 36 fr. : col. : 35 mm. & captions & teacher's guide. $9.00 (Province of Quebec : $27.00) jis

1. Quebec (Province) - Geography.

Uses photographs and diagrams to study the geography of the Laurentian region of Quebec under the headings of Laurentians, the Saguenay, Abitibi-Tamiskaming, New Quebec and the North Shore. Detail is given to physical features of industrial towns in each area and products and principal activities. French title available : LE QUEBEC : LE PLATEAU LAURENTIEN.-

917.14
The Province of Quebec : the St. Lawrence region.
prod. [Montreal?] : NFB, 1964.- dist. McI. 40 fr. : col. : 35 mm. & captions & teacher's manual. $9.00 (Province of Quebec : $27.00) jis

1. Quebec (Province) - Geography. 2. St. Lawrence Valley.

Photographs and diagrams examine the geography of the St. Lawrence region. Covers the landscape, and the history of the land, detailed studies of the cities in the region and their physical geography, and the development of small towns and farm communities in the area. French title available : LE QUEBEC : LA PLAINE DU SAINT-LAURENT.-

917.14
Quebec.
prod. [Toronto] : M-L, 1974.- dist. Sch. Ser. or Vint. 76 fr. : col. : 35 mm. & cassette (15 min.) : auto. & aud. adv. sig. & teacher's guide. $16.50 (Canada : the true north strong and free : $85.00) i

1. Quebec (Province) - Economic conditions.
2. Quebec (Province) - History.

Traces the history of Quebec including the first explorers and the settlement of the French. Examines the natural resources, such as electrical power, mining, farming, and forestry. Discusses the economic development of Quebec and growing feelings toward independance in politics. French title available : LE QUEBEC.-

917.14
Le Quebec : les Applaches.
prod. [Montreal?] : NFB, 1965.- dist. SEC 39 fr. : col. : 35 mm. & captions & teacher's manual. $9.00 jis

1. Quebec (Province) - Geography.
2. Appalachian region, Que.

Photographs and diagrams illustrate the geography of the Appalachian region under the headings of the Gaspé Peninsula, South of the Estuary, and the Eastern Townships. Detail is given to physical features and main activites of communities with important areas circled and identified on the photograph. English title available : THE PROVINCE OF QUEBEC : THE APPALACHIAN REGION.-

917.14
Le Quebec : la Plaine du Saint-Laurent.
prod. [Montreal?] : NFB, 1963.- dist. SEC 43 fr. : col. : 35 mm. & captions & teacher's manual. $9.00 (Le Quebec) jis

1. Quebec (Province) - Geography. 2. St. Lawrence Valley.

Photographs and diagrams examine the geography of the St. Lawrence region. Covers the landscape, the history of the land, detailed studies of the cities in the region and their physical geography, and the development of small towns and farm communities in the area. English title available : THE PROVINCE OF QUEBEC : THE ST LAWRENCE REGION.-

917.14
 Le Quebec : le Plateau laurentien.
  prod. [Montreal?] : NFB, 1964.- dist. SEC 40 fr. : col. : 35 mm. & captions & teacher's guide. $9.00 (Le Quebec) jis

  1. Quebec (Province) - Geography.
  2. Laurentides region, Que.

  Uses photographs and diagrams to study the geography of Laurentian region of Quebec under the headings of the Laurentians, the Saguenay, Abitibi - Tamiskaming, New Quebec and the North Shore. Detail is given to physical features of industrial towns in each area and products and principal activities. English title available : THE PROVINCE OF QUEBEC : THE LAURENTIAN REGION.-

917.14
 Quebec City, Quebec.
  prod. [Stratford, Ont.] : Sch. Ch., 1976.- dist. Sch. Ch. 49 fr. : b&w & col. : 35 mm. & captions. $7.95 (Provincial capitals) ji

  1. Quebec, Que. - Description.

  Shows how the same factors that made Quebec the centre of New France still make this city an important place for business and industry. Colourful photos show the old and new in Quebec City and how both aspects enhance the lifestyle.-

917.14
 River city : Montreal.
  prod. [Montreal?] : NFB, 1964.- dist. McI. 42fr. : col. : 35 mm. & captions & teacher's manual. $9.00 (Canadian cities) jis

  1. Montreal, Que. - Description.

  Maps, drawings, and photographs show the city of Montreal past and present, noting Champlain's settlement in 1603, its significance as a harbour for fur-traders, and as a port for steamships and ocean ships using the St. Lawrence Seaway. Discusses imports and exports, transportation and industries. French title available : VILLE FLUVIALE.-

917.14
 St. Jean, Port Joli, Quebec.
  prod. [Stratford, Ont.] : Sch. Ch., 1977.- dist. Sch. Ch. 53 fr. : col. : 35 mm. & captions. $7.95 (Canadian community studies : $55.65) pj

  1. Saint-Jean-Port-Joli, Que. - Description.

  A detailed look at St. Jean, Port Joli, located in Quebec near the St. Lawrence River, with photographs depicting different aspects of the town. Emphasizes the dependence of the town upon the wood carving industry, with several examples of wood sculpture and how it is done. Also covers other industries in the town which accomodate the tourist industry, such as hotels, types of services needed by the community, and historical town landmarks.-

917.14
 Three families of Montreal.
  prod. [Montreal?] : NFB, 1971.- dist. McI. 55 fr. : col. : 35 mm. & captions. $9.00 (Canadian communities) pj

  1. Children in Montreal, Que. 2. Montreal, Que. - Description.

  Describes the city of Montreal, pointing out some well- known landmarks. Compares the daily lives of three children and their families, explaining how each one is different. Examines apartment life, life in the suburbs, and a flat in downtown Montreal. Encourages discussion of city life with its advantages and disadvantages. French title available : TROIS FAMILLES MONTREALAISES.-

917.14
 Trois familles de Montréal.
  prod. [Montreal?] : NFB, 1971.- dist. SEC 55 fr. : col. : 35 mm. & captions. $9.00 pj

  1. Children in Montreal, Que. 2. Montreal, Que. - Description.

  Describes the city of Montreal, pointing out some well-known landmarks. Compares the daily lives of three children and their families, explaining how each one is different. Examines apartment life, life in the suburbs, and a flat in downtown Montreal. Encourages discussion of city life with its advantages and disadvantages. English title available : THREE FAMILIES OF MONTREAL.-

The Classified Catalogue

917.14
  Ville fluviale (Montreal).
    prod. [Montreal?] : NFB, 1964.- dist. SEC 42 fr. : b&w & col. : 35 mm. & captions & teacher's manual. $9.00 jis

    1. Montreal, Que. - Description.

    Maps, drawings, and photographs show the city of Montreal, past and present, noting Champlain's settlement in 1603, its significance as a harbour for fur traders, and as a port for steamships and ocean ships using the St. Lawrence Seaway. Discusses imports and exports, transportation, and industries. English title available : RIVER CITY.-

917.15
  Atlantic Canada : geography.
    prod. [Montreal?] : NFB, 1973.- dist. McI. 48 fr. : col. : 35 mm. & captions & teacher's guide. $9.00 (Atlantic Canada : $63.00) jis

    1. Atlantic Provinces - Geography.

    Attractive maps and charts are included to describe the two geographic areas of Atlantic Canada. Examines climate, vegetation, precipitation, and how these factors have influenced settlement patterns. Useful printed notes. French title available : LE CANADA ATLANTIQUE : GEOGRAPHIE.-

917.15
  The Atlantic provinces.
    dist. Sch. Ser. or Wint. dist. School Services or Wintergreen Communications 69 fr. : col. : 35 mm. & cassette (15 min.) : auto. & aud. adv. sig. & teacher's guide. $16.50 (Canada : the true north strong and free : $85.00) i

    1. Atlantic Provinces - Economic conditions.
    2. Atlantic Provinces - History.

    Examines the social and economic situation of the Maritimes and how they are affected by location. Stresses the important role of the sea including the fishing industry, deep harbours for shipping, off-shore oil deposits and container shipping by rail and sea. Includes a brief history of Atlantic provinces and their contributions to the development of Canada. French title available : LES PROVINCES MARITIME.-

917.15
  Le Canada atlantique : géographie.
    prod. [Montreal?] : NFB, 1973.- dist. SEC 53 fr. : col. : 35 mm. & notes, teacher's guide & captions. $9.00 (Le Canada Atlantique) jis

    1. Atlantic Provinces - Geography.

    Attractive maps and charts are included to describe the two geographic areas of Atlantic Canada. Examines climate, vegetation, precipitation, and how these factors have influenced settlement patterns. Useful printed notes. English title available : ATLANTIC CANADA : GEOGRAPHY.-

917.15
  Fredericton, New Brunswick.
    prod. [Stratford, Ont.] : Sch. Ch., 1970.- dist. Sch. Ch. 50 fr. : col. : 35 mm. & captions. $7.95 (Canadian community studies : $55.65) pj

    1. Fredericton, N.B. - Description.

    Features photographs of Fredericton's legislative buildings, and points out the various responsibilities of civil servants, such as education and the judicial system. Also discusses and shows Fredericton's City Hall and University, and the types of jobs provided by both. Concludes with photographs of the hospital and other types of jobs found in the city.-

917.15
  Grand Manan Island.
    prod. [Montreal?] : NFB, 1972.- dist. McI. 56 fr. : col. : 35 mm. & captions & notes. $9.00 (Image Canada : $45.00) ji

    1. Grand Manan, N.B. - Description and travel.

    A photographic guide to life on Grand Manan Island. Discusses its geographic position and geological make-up. Shows three important sea crops: herring, lobster, and dulse. French title available : L'ILE GRAND MANAN.-

917.15
L'Ile Grand Manan.
prod. [Montreal?] : NFB, 1972.- dist. SEC 61 fr. : col. : 35 mm.& captions & notes. $9.00 (Image du Canada) ji

1. Grand Manan, N.B. - Description and travel.

A photographic guide to life on Grand Manan Island. Discusses its geographic position and geological make-up. Shows three important sea crops: herring, lobster, and dulse. English title available : GRAND MANAN ISLAND.-

917.15
Paul and Pauline visit New Brunswick and Prince Edward Island.
prod. [Toronto] : Lea., 1973.- dist. Lea. 40 fr. : col. : 35 mm. & captions. $9.00 (Canada : coast to coast with Paul and Pauline : $59.50) pj

1. New Brunswick - Description and travel.
2. Prince Edward Island - Description and travel.

Depicts industry and major attractions of both provinces. Includes New Brunswick's major cities, agriculture, fishing, and tourist attractions. Briefly covers potato and fishing industry in P.E.I., and capital city Charlottetown.-

917.15
Les Provinces Maritimes.
prod. [Toronto] : M-L, 1974.- dist. Sch. Ser. or Wint. 69 fr. : col. : 35 mm. & cassette (15 min.) : auto. & aud. adv. sig. & teacher's guide. $16.50 (Canada : "Il est né d'une race fiére" : $85.00) i

1. Atlantic Provinces - Economic conditions.
2. Atlantic Provinces - History.

Examines the social and economic situation of the Maritime sand how they are affected by location. Stresses the important role of the sea including the fishing industry, deep harbours for shipping, off-shore oil deposits and container shipping by rail and sea. Includes a brief history of Atlantic provinces and their contributions to the development of Canada. English title available : THE ATLANTIC PROVINCES.-

917.15
Saint John - Canada's first city.
prod. [Scarborough, Ont.] : R.B.M., 1976.- dist. ETHOS 46 fr. : b&w & col. : 35 mm. & cassette (10 min.) : auto. & aud. adv. sig. & teacher's manual. $19.00 (Cities of Canada) ji

1. Saint John, N.B. - Description.

Shows how St. John has preserved its traditions amid expansion and change. Shows historic landmarks and tourist attractions, and compares the design or urban renewal programs with older homes. Indicates recent developments in commerce, industry and municipal services.-

917.16
Cape Breton Island : an overview.
prod. [Scarborough, Ont.] : R.B.M., 1976.- dist. ETHOS 45 fr. : b&w & col. : 35 mm. & cassette (9 min.) : auto. & aud. adv. sig. & teacher's manual. $19.00 (Regional studies : $138.00) ji

1. Cape Breton Island, N.S. - Description and travel.

An overview of the Island covering the farming, fishing and tourism industries. Notes Alexander Graham Bell's achievements at Baddeck and mentions the Fortress of Louisbourg.-

917.16
The City of Halifax.
prod. [Scarborough, Ont.] : R.B.M., .1976.- dist. ETHOS 45 fr. : b&w & col. : 35 mm. & cassette (9 min.) : auto. & aud. adv. sig. & teacher's manual. $19.00 (Cities of Canada) ji

1. Halifax, N.S. - Description.

A general introduction to Halifax as it is today. Emphasizes recreational facilities, transportation, services, and industry.-

917.16
    Fishing town (Port Bickerton, N.S.).
        prod. [Montreal?] : NFB, 1968.- dist. McI. 49 fr. : col. : 35 mm. & captions & reading script. $9.00 (Canadian communities) ji

        1. Fisheries - Nova Scotia. 2. Port Bickerton, N.S. - Description.

        Describes the growth and inhabitants of this Nova Scotia town. Also includes the fishing industry, showing the equipment and technology it requires. French title available : VILLAGE DE PECHE.-

917.16
    Halifax - historic seaport.
        prod. [Scarborough, Ont.] : R.B.M., 1976.- dist. ETHOS 45 fr. : b&w & col. : 35 mm. & cassette (11 min.) : auto. & aud. adv. sig. & teacher's manual. $19.00 (Cities of Canada) ji

        1. Halifax, N.S. - Description. 2. Halifax, N.S. - Harbor.

        While emphasizing the city's history as an important port, this overview also looks at other historically significant landmarks in Halifax, including the Citadel, the Old Town Clock and Province House.-

917.16
    Halifax, Nova Scotia.
        prod. [Stratford, Ont.] : Sch. Ch., 1974.- dist. Sch. Ch. 45 fr. : b&w & col. : 35 mm. & captions. $7.95 (Provincial capitals) ji

        1. Halifax, N.S. - Description.

        Early sketches and paintings illustrate the role of Halifax in the history of Nova Scotia. Photographs show not only restored historic landmarks, but the city as an important seaport, shipbuilding and fishing centre.-

917.16
    Nova Scotia.
        prod. [Scarborough, Ont.] : R.B.M., 1976.- dist. ETHOS 48 fr. : col. : 35 mm. & reading script. $19.00 (Impressions : Canada) ji

        1. Nova Scotia - Description and travel.

        A general introduction to Nova Scotia depicting the scenery, industries, towns and cities, and the people.-

917.16
    Paul and Pauline visit Nova Scotia and Newfoundland.
        prod. [Toronto] : Lea., 1973.- dist. Lea. 41 fr. : col. : 35 mm. & captions. $9.00 (Canada : coast to coast with Paul and Pauline : $59.50) pj

        1. Nova Scotia - Description and travel. 2. Newfoundland - Description and travel.

        A brief introduction to urban and rural areas of these two provinces. Shows Halifax and the Citadel, navy dock yards and farming regions. Includes tourist attractions, such as Peggy's Cove and Cabot Trail. Photographs of Newfoundland covers St. John's, harbours and fishing villages and parks, such as Terra Nova National Park.-

917.16
    Pictou, Nova Scotia.
        prod. [Stratford, Ont.] : Sch. Ch., 1977.- dist. Sch. Ch. 48 fr. : col. : 35 mm. & captions. $7.95 (Canadian community studies : $35.65) pj

        1. Fisheries - Nova Scotia. 2. Pictou, N.S. - Description.

        Photographs taken from inside a fish packing plant in Pictou, Nova Scotia, show the process of packaging fish for markets across Canada. Other photos illustrate the types of fishing boats used, and the ship building industry in Pictou. Also indicates the interdependence between the fishermen and other services provided by the town, such as recreation and education.-

917.16
    Village de pêche.
        prod. [Montreal?] : NFB, 1968.- dist. SEC 51 fr. : col. : 35 mm. & reading script. $9.00 ji

        1. Fisheries - Nova Scotia. 2. Port Bickerton, N.S. - Description.

        Describes the growth and inhabitants of this Nova Scotia town. Also includes the fishing industry, showing the equipment and technology it requires. English title available : FISHING TOWN (PORT BICKERTON, N.S.).-

The Classified Catalogue

917.17
    Charlottetown, P.E.I.
        prod. [Stratford, Ont.] : Sch. Ch., 1974.- dist. Sch. Ch.   43 fr. : b&w & col. : 35 mm. & captions. $7.95 (Provincial capitals) ji

        1. Charlottetown, P.E.I. - Description.

        Traces Charlottetown's historical importance as a meeting place for the Fathers of Confederation to the city as it is today and the role of the government regarding hospital care, education, research, farming, and tourism.-

917.17
    Prince Edward Island National Park.
        prod. [Georgetown, Ont.] : FMS, 1973.- dist. McI.   44 fr. : col. : 35 mm. & captions & teacher's guide. $10.00 (National parks of Canada : $30.00) ji

        1. Prince Edward Island National Park.

        An overview of this park with its varied landscapes of sand dunes, marshes, ponds, and woodland with plant and animal life. Ferns, gannets and blue herrons are seen in natural habitat,and wild fruit, flowers, mushrooms and lichens are also pictured.-

917.18
    St. John's, Newfoundland.
        prod. [Stratford, Ont.] : Sch. Ch., 1975.- dist. Sch. Ch.   48 fr. : b&w & col. : 35 mm. & captions. $7.95 (Provincial capitals) ji

        1. St. John's, Nfld. - Description.
        2. Newfoundland - History.

        Traces Newfoundland's history from Cabot's landing in 1497 to the present, using historic sketches, paintings, and photographs. Shows the services provided by the provincial government in St. John's, the importance of its harbour to the fishing and lumbering industry, as well as views of the city's people, homes, and recreation.-

917.19
    Churchill Falls.
        prod. [Winnipeg] : VCL, 1972.- dist. Sch. Ch.   48 fr. : b&w & col. : 35 mm. & captions. $7.95 (Energy in Canada : $23.85) ji

        1. Electric power plants. 2. Churchill Falls, Nfld.

        Describes the problems encountered in building the power plant at Churchill Falls. Photographs showing equipment being brought to the area indicate the difficulties caused by the terrain. Also features the building of a modern town designed to meet the educational and recreational needs of the workers and their families. Concludes with detailed photos of the the interior of the power site, and the machinery used to produce electricity.-

917.2
    Mexico I : across modern Mexico.
        prod. [Don Mills, Ont.] : F & W, 1973.- dist. F & W   25 fr. : col. : 35 mm. & teacher's guide. $7.20 (Man in his world) ji

        1. Mexico - Geography.

        Depicts the many contrasts to be found in Mexico-rugged mountains: wide, low plateaus: jungles and deserts: wet and dry seasons: simple villages and large industrialized cities. The total picture is of a quickly developing country.-

917.2
    Les pionniers des Prairies (1900-1912).
        prod. [Montreal?] : NFB, 1972.- dist. SEC   64 fr. : col. : 35 mm. & captions & notes. $9.00 (Les pionniers : $72.00) ji

        1. Frontier and pioneer life - Prairie Provinces. 2. Prairie provinces - History.

        Old photographs, maps, and quotations portray the development of agriculture on the prairies, the Homestead era, Doukhobors and Barr colonists. Filmstrip notes, providing all background information, must be consulted. English title available : PIONEER LIFE ON THE PRAIRIES (1900-1912).-

The Classified Catalogue

917.214
    Leroy, Saskatchewan.
        prod. [Stratford, Ont.] : Sch. Ch., 1976.- dist. Scholar's Choice Ltd. 52 fr. : col. : 35 mm. $7.95 (Canadian community studies : $55.65) ji

        1. Agriculture - Saskatchewan. 2. Leroy, Sask.

        Shows interdependence between a small town and its bordering farms. Photographs show type of farming characteristic of this area of Saskatchewan, and products used by townspeople. Includes variety of services provided by town for farming community, such as mail service, businesses, housing and clothing.-

917.95
    Greece 1 : life in a rural village.
        prod. [Don Mills, Ont.] : F&W, 1973.- dist. F & W 25 fr. : col. : 35 mm. & captions & teacher's guide.- $7.20 (Man in his world) ji

        1. Greece.

        Depicts the low standard of living and working for a Greek peasant. The poor soil, mountainous terrain, lack of vegetation, hot climate and archaic work methods are all discussed as they relate to the very hard life experienced by rural Greeks. For classroom use.-

918.1
    Rio de Janerio.
        prod. [Kitchener, Ont.] : EDU, 1974.- dist. EDU 31 fr. : col. : 35 mm. & cassette (10 min.) : auto. & aud. adv. sig. & teacher's manual. $15.95 (South America : $69.95) jis

        1. Rio de Janeiro, United States of Brazil - Description.

        Describes the people of Rio, the Cariocas, and the differences in social customs of the city. Compares the old city to the modern section, and shows Guanabara Bay, Copacabana Beach, and tunnels through the mountains connecting various communities.-

918.5
    Indian children of the Andes.
        prod. [Montreal?] : NFB, 1967.- dist. Mcl. 40 fr. : col. : 35 mm. & captions. $9.00 (Children of many lands : $54.00) pj

        1. Indians of South America - Peru. 2. Children in Peru.

        Photographs are used to examine life in the Andes mountains of Peru. Discusses problems of isolation, poor soil, and difficult transportation. Shows children who must work and live too far away to attend schools. Encourages discussion of the future for these children of Peru. For group viewing. French title available : LES JEUNES INDIENS DES ANDES.-

918.5
    Les jeunes Indiens de Andes.
        prod. [Montreal?] : NFB, 1967.- dist. SEC 45 fr. : col. : 35 mm. & captions. $9.00 (Les enfants du monde) pj

        1. Indians of South America - Peru. 2. Children in Peru.

        Photographs are used to examine life in the Andes mountains of Peru. Discusses problems of isolation, poor soil, and difficult transportation. Shows children who must work and live too far away to attend schools. Encourages discussion of the future for these children of Peru. For group viewing. English title available : INDIAN CHILDREN OF THE ANDES.-

918.5
    Peru 1 : life in the Andes.
        prod. [Don Mills, Ont.] : F & W, 1973.- dist. F & W 25 fr. : col. : 35 mm. & teacher's guide. $7.20 (Man in his world) ji

        1. Peru - Geography.

        Describes life in the Andes, giving details and statistics about the mountains, valleys, and the people. Terraced farming, cottage industries, mountain animals, native houses and clothing are described. Designed for instructional use, since the information must be read from the accompanying guide.-

The Classified Catalogue

919.4
    The Aborigine.
        prod. [Kitchener, Ont.] : EDU, 1974.- dist. EDU 26 fr. : col. : 35 mm. & cassette (10 min.) : auto. & aud. adv. sig. & teacher's manual. $15.95 (Australia : $79.95) jis

        1. Australian aborigines.

        Deals with the traditional picture of tribes of Aborigines and attempts to offer a view of the modern day native. Describes their life on reserves or stations, explaining traditional ceremonies, native art, food grown, hunting techniques and carving on boomerangs.-

919.4
    Frontier mining and grazing (the Outback).
        prod. [Kitchener, Ont.] : EDU, 1974.- dist. EDU 28 fr. : col. : 35 mm. & cassette (10 min.) : auto. & aud. adv. sig. & teacher's manual. $15.95 (Australia : $79.95) jis

        1. Australia - Geography.

        Compares the legends of the Outback pioneers to those of the American cowboy. Describes life on an Outback Station, focusing on children's education and transportation systems to the cities. Covers the Great Victoria Desert, the Flying Doctor Service and a tour of a gold mine at Kalgoorie.-

919.43
    Sugar and coral coast (Queensland).
        prod. [Kitchener, Ont.] : Edu-Media, 1974.- dist. EDU 25 fr. : col. : 35 mm. & cassette (8 min.) : auto. & aud. adv. sig. & teacher's manual. $15.95 (Australia : $79.95) jis

        1. Sugar cane. 2. Australia - Geography.

        Describes the climate and geography of this area near the Great Barrier Reef and its attraction for tourists. Discuisses the raising of sugar cane from newly-prepared beds, its production and shipment, and mentions the protection of Koala bears.-

919.44
    An Australian city : Sydney (no. II).
        prod. [Hamilton, Ont.] : VCI, 1977.- dist. MHR 38 fr. : col. : 35 mm. & captions & teacher's guide. $12.85 (Australia : $38.50) i

        1. Sydney, Australia - Description.

        Provides details about the various suburbs of Sydney, including the types of housing, the commuter ferries, railways and thoroughfares connecting them with the city's central business district. Includes the many different recreational activities available such as swimming, surfing, fishing, rugby and cricket.-

919.44
    An Australian city : Sydney (no. I).
        prod. [Hamilton, Ont] : VCI, 1977.- dist. MHR 35 fr. : col. : 35 mm. & captions & teacher's guide. $12.85 (Australia : $38.50) i

        1. Sydney, Australia - Description.

        A colourful introduction to Sydney, explaining how the city's economy and character have been shaped by its connection with the sea. The famous opera house, central business district, different residential areas as well as harbour functions and activities are also described.-

919.44
    Riverina (Murray-Darling Basin).
        prod. [Kitchener, Ont.] : EDU, 1974.- dist. EDU 25 fr. : col. : 35 mm. & cassette (9 min.) : auto. & aud. adv. sig. & teacher's manual. $15.95 (Australia : $79.95) jis

        1. Agriculture - Australia. 2. Australia - Geography.

        Describes the climate and geography of the area, outlining irrigation methods, and importance of the Burrinjuck Dam. Explains government regulation of fruit production as a disease-prevention measure and discusses important area crops including wheat, rice and citrus fruit.-

The Classified Catalogue

919.44
    Sydney.
        prod. [Kitchener, Ont.] : EDU, 1974.- dist. EDU 25 fr. : col. : 35 mm. & cassette (9 min.) : auto. & aud. adv. sig. & teacher's manual. $15.95 (Australia : $79.95) jis

        1. Sydney, Australia - Description.

        A tour of this sprawling city, looking at its excellent transportation system, high rise apartment buildings, and spectacular coastline. Shows the Snowy Power System, residential areas, the financial centre, and the harbour.-

919.47
    An Australian city : Canberra.
        prod. [Hamilton, Ont.] : VCI, 1977.- dist. MHR 39 fr. : col. : 35 mm. & captions & teacher's guide. $12.85 (Australia : $38.50) i

        1. Canberra, Australia - Description.

        Explains in detail the development of Canberra, the world's largest, completely planned city.-

920
    Adventuresome Marco Polo.
        prod. [Toronto] : M-L, 1974.- dist. Sch. Ser. or Vint. 68 fr. : col. : 35 mm. & cassette (11 min.) : auto. & aud. adv. sig. & teacher's guide. $16.50 (Famous stories of great courage : $85.00) i

        1. Polo, Marco, 1254-1323?

        A description of Marco Polo's overland trek to Cathay, and his seventeen year stay in the service of Kublai Khan before sailing home to Venice with his father and uncle. Includes maps. French title available : LES AVENTURES DE MARCO POLO.-

920
    Les aventures de Marco Polo.
        prod. [Toronto] : M-L, 1974.- dist. Sch. Ser. or Vint. 68 fr. : col. : 35 mm. & cassette (14 min.) : auto. & aud. adv. sig. & teacher's guide. $16.50 (Les Récits héroiques : $85.00) j

        1. Polo, Marco, 1254-1323?

        A description of Marco Polo's overland trek to Cathay, and his seventeen year stay in the service of Kublai Khan before sailing home to Venice with his father and uncle. Includes maps. English title available : ADVENTURESOME MARCO POLO.-

920
    Banting and Best : the discovery of insulin.
        prod. [Scarborough, Ont.] : R.B.M., 1976.- dist. ETHOS 40 fr. : col. : 35 mm. & cassette (10 min.) : auto. & aud. adv. sig. & reading script. $19.00 (Famous Canadians) ji

        1. Banting, Frederick Grant, Sir, 1891-1941. 2. Best, Charles Herbert, 1899-1978.

        Uses artwork and photos to tell of the successful efforts of Banting and Best to develop an extract to control sugar diabetes.-

920
    Billy Bishop.
        prod. [Scarborough, Ont.] : R.B.M., 1976.- 45 fr. : col. : 35 mm. & cassette (15 min.) : auto. & aud. adv. sig. & reading script. $19.00 (Famous Canadians) ij

        1. Bishop, William Avery, 1894-1956.

        Tells the story of the wartime career of William Avery Bishop, Canada's famous ace fighter pilot. Uses artwork and illustrations.-

920
    Cetewayo le magnifique.
        prod. [Toronto] : M-L, 1974.- dist. Sch. Ser. or Vint. 77 fr. : col. : 35 mm. & cassette (15 min.) : auto. & aud. adv. sig. & teacher's guide. $16.50 (Les Récits héroiques : $85.00) j

        1. Cettewayo, King of Zululand, 1826(ca.)-1884.

        Recounts the life of the last great Zulu chieftain and his incredible skills in ruling his people and commanding them in battle. Describes battle scenes with the British in which Zulu tribes defend their territory, the internment of Cetewayo, and his subsequent meeting with Queen Victoria. English title available : MAGNIFICENT CETEWAYO.-

The Classified Catalogue

920
    Commanding Joan of Arc.
        prod. [Toronto] : M-L, 1974.- dist. Sch. Ser. or Vint. 59 fr. : col. : 35 mm. & cassette (14 min.) : auto. & aud. adv. sig. & teacher's guide. $16.50 (Famous stories of great courage : $85.00) i

Uses art work to tell the story of a simple peasant girl, whose conviction that she is sent by God to drive the British out of France, provides her with the courage to lead her soldiers in the Battle of Orléans. Story does not deal with Joan's ultimate fate, but only her courage in battle. Has obvious and worthwhile feminist overtones. French title available: JEANNE D'ARC : HEROINE FRANCAISE.-

920
    David Thompson.
        prod. [Montreal?] : NFB, 1957.- dist. McI. 61 fr. : col. : 35 mm. & captions & reading script. $9.00 ji

1. Thompson, David, 1770-1857. 2. America - Discovery and exploration.

Uses excerpts from his own writings to describe David Thompson's career: his early schooling, his employment with the Hudson's Bay Company as fur trader and explorer, and with the Northwest Company as surveyor, his exploration of the Columbia River, and the making of his famous map. Illustrated with artist's sketches.-

920
    Dr. Norman Bethune.
        prod. [Scarborough, Ont.] : R.B.M., 1976.- dist. ETHOS 44 fr. : col. : 35 mm. & cassette (13 min.) : auto. & aud. adv. sig. & reading script. $19.00 (Famous Canadians) ij

1. Bethune, Norman, 1890-1939.

The story of Dr Bethune's troubled life is told, with emphasis on his medical achievements in war-torn China. Illustrated with artwork.-

920
    Dr. Wilder Penfield.
        prod. [Scarborough, Ont.] : R.B.M., 1976.- dist. ETHOS 44 fr. : col. : 35 mm. & cassette (13 min.) : auto. & aud. adv. sig. & reading script. $19.00 (Famous Canadians) ij

1. Penfield, Wilder Graves, 1891-1976.

Artwork and photos illustrate the career and achievements of the famous neuro-surgeon.-

920
    Grey Owl.
        prod. [Scarborough, Ont.] : R.B.M., 1976.- dist. ETHOS 47 fr. : col. : 35 mm. & cassette (12 min.) : auto. & aud. adv. sig. & reading script. $19.00 (Famous Canadians) ji

1. Grey Owl, 1888-1938.

Tells the story of a Canadian legend, the naturalist, guide and writer known as Grey Owl. Illustrated with photographs and artwork.-

920
    The Life of Mackenzie King : part II :
        prod. [Scarborough, Ont.] : SHN, 1977.- dist. PHM 89 fr. : b&w & col. : 35 mm. & cassette (21 min.) : auto. & aud. adv. sig. & teacher's guide. $39.60 (The Life of Mackenzie King : $65.00) is

1. King, William Lyon Mackenzie, 1874-1950.

Brings the King political years to a close as it discusses the Depression and the Second World War, ending with the Prime Minister's resignation in 1948 and his death in 1950.-

920
    The Life of Mackenzie King : part 1 :
        prod. [Scarborough, Ont.] : SHN, 1977.- dist. PHM 91 fr. : b&w & col. : 35 mm. & cassette (23 min.) : auto. & aud. adv. sig. & teacher's guide. $39.60 (The Life of Mackenzie King : $65.00) is

1. King, William Lyon Mackenzie, 1874-1950.

Examines both King's personal and public life and, featuring selections of his voice, relates his political growth in the Liberal Party.-

920
    The Life of Sir John A. MacDonald.
        prod. [Scarborough, Ont.] : SHN, 1972.- dist. PHM 80 fr. : b&w & col. : 35 mm. & cassette (29 min.) : auto. & aud. adv. sig. & teacher'sguide. $39.60 is

        1. Macdonald, John Alexander, Sir, 1815-1891.

        Uses a variety of materials including political cartoons , contemporary photos and prints to present a comprehensive view of Macdonald's life and career. Emphasizes his role in Confederation, the Charlottetown and Quebec conferences, the North-West Rebellion, and the Canadian Pacific Railway.-

920
    The Life of Sir Wilfrid Laurier.
        prod. [Scarborough] : SHN, 1972.- dist. PHM 127 fr. : col. : 35 mm. & cassette (25 min.) : auto. &aud. adv. sig. & teacher's guide. $39.60 is

        1. Laurier, Wilfrid Sir, 1841-1919.

        Surveys the events and issues of Laurier's life with particular emphasis on his political career. Illustrated with contemporary photos, prints, and poliical cartoons.-

920
    Lord Selkirk : the colonizer.
        prod. [Montreal?] : NFB, 1953.- dist. McI. 51 fr. : col. : 35 mm. & captions & manual. $9.00 ji

        1. Selkirk, Thomas Douglas, 5th Earl of, 1771-1820. 2. Red River Settlement, Man.

        Relates the lifelong attempts of Thomas Douglas, fifth Earl of Selkirk, to establish a settlement in the Red River Valley against the bitter opposition of the North West Company. Artist's sketches provide illustration.-

920
    Magnificent Cetewayo.
        prod. [Toronto] : M-L, 1974.- dist. Sch. Ser. or Vint. 77 fr. : col. : 35 mm. & cassette (16 min.) : auto. & aud. adv. sig. & teacher's guide. $16.50 (Famous stories of great courage : $85.00) i

        1. Cettiwayo, King of Zululand, 1826(ca.)-1884.

        Recounts the life of the lat great Zulu chieftain and his incredible skills in ruling his people and commanding them in battle. Describes battle scenes with the British in which Zulu tribes dafend their territory, the internment of Cetewayo, and his subsequent meeting with Queen Victoria. French title available : CETEVAYO LE MAGNIFIQUE.-

920
    Nurse of Newfoundland.
        prod. [Scarborough, Ont.] : R.B.M., 1976.- dist. ETHOS 41 fr. : col. : 35 mm. & cassette (9 min.) : auto. & aud. adv. sig. & reading script. $19.00 (Famous Canadians) ij

        1. Bennett, Myra Grimsley.

        Artwork illustrates the story of Myra Grimsley Bennett, a young nurse who, after World War 1, moved to Newfoundland from England and undertook the provision of medical care to remote coastal communities.-

920
    Painless Parker.
        prod. [Scarborough, Ont.] : R.B.M., 1976.- dist. ETHOS 40 fr. : col. : 35 mm. & cassette (7 min.) : auto. & aud. adv. sig. & reading script. $19.00 (Famous Canadians) ij

        1. Parker, Edgar Rudolph Randolph.

        Uses artwork to illustrate events in the colourful career of the early Canadian dentist credited with establishing the first dental clinic.-

The Classified Catalogue

920
   World of Jack Miner : the pioneer naturalist, 1865-1944.
      prod. [Toronto] : B&R, 1973.- dist. Lea. 41 fr. : col. : 35 mm. & teacher's manual & captions. pjis

   1. Miner, Jack, 1865-1944.

   Relates the life and works of Jack Miner who banded birds for study and identification at his bird sanctuary in Kingsville, Ontario. Describes how migration patterns were studied and how the viewer can help birds.-

929.90971
   Canadian flags and how they are used.
      prod. [Toronto] : Int. Cin., 1973.- dist. VEC 49 fr. : col. : 35 mm. & cassette (10 min.) : auto. & aud. adv. sig. & teacher's manual. $24.00 (The Canadian flag : $65.00) ji

   1. Flags - Canada.

   Describes uses of Canadian flag and rules of etiquette for flying it. Presents symbols and flags of the provinces and territories. Prime Minister Pearson's recorded speech at the first raising of the new flag at Parliament Hill, Ottawa, in March 1965 is included. French title available : LES DRAPEAUX CANADIENS ET LEUR USEAGE.-

929.90971
   Comment le Canada obtint son drapeau.
      prod. [Toronto] : Int. Cin., 1975.- dist. VEC 58 fr. : col. : 35 mm. & cassette (13 min.) : auto. & aud. adv. sig. & teacher's guide. $24.00 (Le Drapeau Canadien : $65.00) ji

   1. Flags - Canada - History.

   Explains the components of the new Canadian flag and presents the stages in the selection of our national flag. English title available : HOW CANADA GOT ITS FLAG.-

929.90971
   Les Drapeaux Canadiens d'autrefois.
      prod. [Toronto] : int. Cin., 1975.- dist. VEC 42 fr. : col. : 35 mm. & cassette (9 min.) : auto. & aud. adv. sig. & teacher's guide. $24.00 (Le Drapeau Canadien : $65.00) ji

   1. Flags - Canada - History.

   Discusses the origin of flags in general, and shows how the history of Canada affected the development of her national flag. English title available : THE FLAGS OF CANADA'S PAST.-

929.90971
   Les Drapeaux Canadiens et leur usage.
      prod. [Toronto] : Int. Cin., 1975.- dist. VEC 49 fr. : col. : 35 mm. & cassette (10 min.) : auto. & aud. adv. sig. & teacher's guide. $24.00 (Le Drapeau Canadien : $65.00) ji

   1. Flags - Canada.

   Describes uses of Canadian flag and rules of etiquette for flying it. Presents symbols and flags of the provinces and territories. English title available : CANADIAN FLAGS AND HOW THEY ARE USED.-

929.90971
   Les drapeaux canadiens et leur usage.
      prod. [Toronto] : Int. Cin., 1973.- dist. VEC 49 fr. : col. : 35 mm. & cassette (10 min.) : auto. & aud. adv. sig. & teacher's manual. $24.00 (Le drapeau canadien) ji

   1. Flags - Canada.

   Describes uses of Canadian flag and rules of etiquette for flying it. Presents symbols and flags of the provinces and territories.

   English title available : CANADIAN FLAGS AND HOW THEY ARE USED.-

929.90971
   Flags, coats of arms, and floral emblems of Canada.
      prod. [Winnipeg] : WCL, 1976.- dist. Sch. Ch. 45 fr. : b&w & col. : 35 mm. & captions. $7.95 (Canadian mosaic) ji

   1. Flags - Canada.

   Displays the flag, coat of arms, and floral emblem of each province moving from west to east. Includes the Territories and the flag and coat of arms of Canada.-

929.90971
   How Canada got its flag.
      prod. [Toronto] : Int. Cin., 1973.- dist. VEC 58 fr. : col. : 35 mm. & cassette (13 min.) : auto. & aud. adv. sig. & teacher's manual. $24.00 (The Canadian flag : $65.00) ji

   1. Flags - Canada - History.

   Explains the components of the new Canadian flag and presents the stages in the selection of our national flag. French title available : COMMENT LE CANADA OBTINT SON DRAPEAU.-

The Classified Catalogue

940
> Classic drama - hero vs. villain.
> prod. [Scarborough, Ont.] : RBM, 1975.- dist. ETHOS 40 fr. : b&w & col. : 35 mm. & cassette (9 min.) : auto. & aud. adv. sig. & reading script. $19.00 (First and Second World Wars : $138.00) ji
>
> 1. World War 1939-1945 - Campaigns and battles.
>
> A general overview of World War II up to bombing of Pearl Harbour. Covers German's invasion of Europe and Russia, and Battle of Britain. Photographs and artwork show prominent figures, battle scenes, with emphasis on London Blitz. Includes actual sound recordings of Hitler and Churchill.-

940.1
> Medieval community 1 : the knight.
> prod. [Don Mills, Ont.] : F & W, 1973.- dist. F & W 25 fr. : col. : 35 mm. & teacher's guide. $7.20 (Man in his world) ji
>
> 1. Knights and knighthood. 2. Chivalry.
>
> A detailed picture of the various aspects of a medieval knight's life. Illustrates and explains the importance of the castle, a knight's education, his mode of dress, weaponry, and the code of behaviour known as chivalry.-

940.4
> Canada and the First World War : that's how it was.
> prod. [Scarborough, Ont.] : SHN, 1972.- dist. PHM 103 fr. : col. : 35 mm. & cassette (29 min.) : auto. & aud. adv. sig. & study guide. $39.60 is
>
> 1. World War, 1914-1918 - Canada.
>
> Traces Canada's contribution to the Great War. Discusses Sir Sam Hughes, the Quebec conscription crisis, world food shortage, and the emancipation of women. Describes the battle of Ypres, Passchendaele, and Vimy Ridge.-

940.4
> First air aces : first women's liberators (1915).
> prod. [Scarborough, Ont.] : R.B.M., 1975.- dist. ETHOS 40 fr. : b&w & col. : 35 mm. & cassette (8 min.) : auto. & aud. adv. sig. & reading script. $19.00 (First and Second World Wars : $138.00) ji
>
> 1. World War, 1914-1918.
>
> A look at the events of 1915 highlighting the work of the first war aces and the role played by women on the home front. Illustrated with artwork and photographs.-

940.4
> The First convoys, and Armistice (1917).
> prod. [Scarborough, Ont.] : RBM, 1975.- dist. ETHOS 46 fr. : b&w & col. : 35 mm. & cassette (7 min.) : auto. & aud. adv. sig. & reading script. $19.00 (First and Second World Wars : $138.00) ji
>
> 1. World War, 1914-1918.
>
> Summarizes the concluding events of World War I, among them the battles of Vimy Ridge and Passchendaele, the use of convoys, the exploits of Billy Bishop and Baron Von Richthofen, and the American declaration of war on Germany. Illustrated with artwork and photographs.-

940.4
> The Terrible mud of Flanders (1916).
> prod. [Scarborough, Ont.] : R.B.M., 1975.- dist. ETHOS 40 fr. : b&w & col. : 35 mm. & cassette (6 min.) : auto. & aud. adv. sig. & reading script. $19.00 (First and Second World Wars : $138.00) ji
>
> 1. World War, 1914-1918.
>
> Recounts the events of 1916, the year of some of the costliest, most savage battles in man's history. Illustrated with artwork and photographs.-

940.4
> The War to end war (1914).
> prod. [Scarborough, Ont.] : R.B.M., 1975.- dist. ETHOS 40 fr. : b&w & col. : 35 mm. & cassette (9 min.) : auto. & aud. adv. sig. & reading script. $19.00 (First and Second World Wars : $138.00) ji
>
> 1. World War, 1914-1918.
>
> A summary of the first year of World War 1 documenting the events of 1914 and the progressive disillusionment with war. Illustrated with artwork and photographs.-

940.54
Battle of the North Atlantic.
prod. [Scarborough, Ont.] : R.B.M., 1975.- dist. ETHOS 40 fr. : b&w & col. : 35 mm. & cassette (10 min.) : auto. & aud. adv. sig. & reading script. $19.00 (First and Second World Wars : $138.00) ji

1. World War, 1939-1945 - Campaigns and battles. 2. North Atlantic, Battle of the, 1940-1943.

Describes the conflict between the Germans and the Allies in the North Atlantic. Illustrated with artwork and photographs.-

940.54
From mobilization to the battle of the Atlantic.
prod. [Scarborough, Ont.] : SHN, 1972.- dist. PHM 113 fr. : col. : 35 mm. & cassette (22 min.) : auto. & aud. adv. sig. & study guide. $39.60 (Canada and the Second World War : a nation comes of age : $63.25) is

1. World War, 1939-1945 - Canada.

Describes Canada's role in World War II from the declaration of war to the Battle of the Atlantic. Includes Canada's war effort at home, participation of Canadian pilots in the Battle of Britain and in bombing raids over Germany, and Canadian naval escorts in the North Atlantic.-

940.54
Hitler at bay (1942-43).
prod. [Scarborough, Ont.] : R.B.M., 1975.- dist. ETHOS 40 fr. : b&w & col. : 35 mm. & cassette (10 min.) : auto. & aud. adv. sig. & reading script. $19.00 (First and Second World Wars : $138.00) ji

1. World War, 1939-1945.

Uses artwork and photographs to illustrate the many conflicts of 1942-1943, among them Hong Kong, Stalingrad, North Africa, and Midway Island.-

940.54
Home front to victory.
prod. [Scarborough, Ont.] : SHN, 1972.- dist. PHM 98 fr. : col. : 35 mm. & cassette (17 min.) : auto. & aud. adv. sig. & teacher's guide. $39.60 (Canada and the Second World War : a nation comes of age : $82.00) is

1. World War, 1939-1945 - Canada.

An account of Canada's accomplishments and sacrifices in the war. Includes battles in Hong Kong, Dieppe, Ortona, and Normandy. Describes contributions of civilians in Canada.-

940.54
Surrender.
prod. [Scarborough, Ont.] : R.B.M., 1975.- dist. ETHOS 44 fr. : b&w & col. : 35 mm. & cassette (10 min.) : auto. & aud. adv. sig. & reading script. $19.00 (First and Second World Wars : $138.00) ji

1. World War, 1939-1945.

Describes the concluding events of World War II, in particular the invasion of France by the allies, the liberation of Holland, and the Battle of the Bulge. Illustrated with artwork and photographs.-

970
Commerce.
prod. [Toronto] : M-L, 1973.- dist. Sch. Ser. or Vint. 54 fr. : col. : 35 mm. & cassette (10 min.) : auto. & aud. adv. sig. & teacher's guide. $16.50 (Settlers of North America : $75.00) pji

1. Frontier and pioneer life.

Paintings, drawings, and photographs illustrate the development of commercial enterprise in pioneer times. Demonstrates the importance of the sawmill and gristmill, and goods and services provided by the blacksmith, cabinetmaker, weaver, and shoemaker. Barter and debt are explained in terms of village trade.-

970

Community life.
  prod. [Toronto] : M-L, 1973.- dist. Sch. Ser. or Vint. 55 fr. : col. : 35 mm. & cassette (12 min.) : auto. & aud. adv. sig. & teacher's guide. $16.50 (Settlers of North America : $75.00) pji

  1. Frontier and pioneer life.

  Describes the social and religious life of the pioneer community including such activities as land-clearing, barn raising, the quilting "bee", and "box social" gatherings. Shows the importance of religion in the community and the family unit, education in a one-room schoolhouse, and entertainments provided by travelling shows.-

970

Furniture and household goods.
  prod. [Toronto] : M-L, 1973.- dist. Sch. Ser. or Vint. 59 fr. : col. : 35 mm. & cassette (11 min.) : auto. & aud. adv. sig. & teacher's guide. $16.50 (Settlers of North America : $75.00) pji

  1. Frontier and pioneer life.

  Illustrates the homes and utensils built and used by the settlers in the 18th and 19th centuries. Discusses food preparation and other work activities performed in the home, including grinding wheat, churning, spinning, candle-making and soapmaking. Photographs of the interior of pioneer homes show furnishings.-

970

The Making of a farm.
  prod. [Toronto] : M-L, 1973.- dist. Sch. Ser. or Vint. 53 fr. : col. : 35 mm. & cassette (10 min.) : auto. & aud. adv. sig. & teacher's guide. $16.50 (Settlers of North America : $75.00) pji

  1. Frontier and pioneer life. 2. Agriculture - North America - History.

  General introduction to the process of settlement and land development used by the settlers. Step-by-step presentation of clearing the land, building log cabins, ploughing, and planting of crops. Farming implements and building techniques are demonstrated.-

970.05

The 1920's.
  prod. [Scarborough, Ont.] : R.B.M., 1975.- dist. ETHOS 40 fr. : b&w & col. : 35 mm. & cassette (9 min.) : auto. & aud. adv. sig. & reading script. $19.00 (Looking back) ji

  1. Twentieth century.

  A tour through the Twenties, illustrated with actual photos, artwork, and advertisements. Among the topics included: fashion, automobiles, and airplanes, the discovery of insulin, radio and movies, Charles Lindberg's transatlantic flight, and the 1929 stock market crash. A brief introductory overview to the era.-

970.05

The Edwardian era.
  prod. [Scarborough, Ont.] : R.B.M., 1975.- dist. ETHOS 40 fr. : b&w & col. : 35 mm. & cassette (10 min.) : auto. & aud. adv. sig. & reading script. $19.00 (Looking back) ji

  1. Twentieth century.

  Impressions of the Edwardian era conveyed through the use of actual photos, advertisements and artwork. The development of the automobile and airplane, the sinking of the Titanic, women's suffrage, fashions, and the literary scene are all covered. Provides a general introduction to the era.-

970.1

Les aborigènes du Canada.
  prod. [Montreal?] : NFB, 1969.- dist. SEC 54 fr. : col. : 35 mm. & captions & teacher's guide. $9.00 ji

  1. Indians of North America - History.

  Traces the history of the first inhabitants of North America and their possible migration patterns, describing how the lifestyles of various tribes changed to adapt to new environments. Also covers Indians of today and their contribution to society. Illustrated with drawings and photographs. Part of a multi-media kit titled "Les Indiens du Canada". English title available : CANADA' FIRST PEOPLE : THE INDIAN.-

The Classified Catalogue

970.1
    Canada's first people : the Indian.
        prod. [Montreal?] : NFB, 1969.- dist. McI. 54 fr. : col. : 35 mm. & captions & teacher's guide. $9.00 ji

        1. Indians of North America - History.

    Traces the history of the first inhabitants of North America and their possible migration patterns, describing how the lifestyles of various tribes changed to adapt to new environments. Also covers Indians of today and their contribution to society. Illustrated with drawings and photographs. Part of a multi-media kit titled "Indians of Canada". French title available : LES ABORIGENES DU CANADA

970.1
    Native and European in North America.
        prod. [Toronto] : M-L, 1977.- dist. Sch. Ser. or Wint. 64 fr. : col. : 35 mm. & cassette (9 min.) : auto. & aud. adv. sig. & teacher's guide. $16.50 (Indians and Inuit : the first people of North America : $105.00) ji

        1. Indians of North America - History.

    Early photographs, paintings, and sketches help illustrate the arrival of native people in North America, the effect of European technology on their natural way of life, and the loss of their lands through treaties. Concludes with a look at the efforts of native people today to cope with modern society.-

970.1
    Native Canadians.
        prod. [Toronto] : M-L, 1976.- dist. Sch. Ser. or Wint. 73 fr. : b&w & col. : 35 mm. & cassette (17 min.) : auto. & aud. adv. sig. & teacher's guide. $16.50 (The Canadian mosaic : $105.00) is

        1. Indians of North America - Canada.
        2. Eskimos.

    A detailed presentation describing traditional lifestyles of the Indians and Eskimos, and explaining changes wrought by the coming of Europeans to Canada. Outlines reasons for Indian dependence on the Canadian government and the steps being taken to preserve Indian and Inuit heritage and native land rights. Historical paintings and photographs.-

970.3
    The Algonkians : Eastern Woodland Indians.
        prod. [Montreal?] : NFB, 1970.- dist. McI. 46 fr. : col. : 35 mm. & captions & booklet. $9.00

        1. Algonquian Indians.

    Drawings illustrate the lives of the Algonkian Indians of the Eastern Woodlannds. Discusses social customs, the construction of a wigwam and birch bark canoe, hunting and fishing methods. Examines games and activities of the various tribes. Photographs illustrate Indian artifacts. Describes how Woodland Indians have contributed to our society today. Useful for group viewing as discussion is encouraged. Part of a multi-media kit titled "Indians of Canada". French title available : LES ALGONQUIENS DES FORETS DE L'EST.-

970.3
    Les Algonquins des forêts de l'Est.
        prod. [Montreal?] : NFB, made 1969 : 1975.- dist. SEC 52 fr. : col. : 35 mm. & captions & booklet. $9.00 ji

        1. Algonquian Indians.

    Drawings illustrate the lives of the Algonkian Indians of the Eastern Woodlands. Discusses social customs, the construction of a wigwam and birch bark canoe, hunting and fishing methods. Examines games and activities of the various tribes. Photographs illustrate Indian artifacts. Describes how Woodland Indians have contributed to our society today. Useful for group viewing as discussion is encouraged. Part of a multi-media kit titled "les Indiens du Canada." English title available : THE ALGONKIANS : EASTERN WOODLAND INDIANS.-

The Classified Catalogue

970.3
    Basket.
      prod. [Montreal?] : NFB, 1974.- dist. McI. 79 fr. : col. : 35 mm. & disc (33 1/3 rpm. 9 min.) : auto. & aud. adv. sig. & script. $18.00 pj

      1. L'ilawat Indians. 2. Basket making.

      Mathilda Jim, the oldest member of the tribe, is photographed in her own home as she explains her basketmaking, step-by-step. Shows how roots and saplings from the forest are boiled, dried, scraped, and woven. The narration is in Interior Salish, accompanied by an original recording of a 1912 Indian chant. Wording on filmstrip is in Salish, English, French. Part of a multi-media kit titled "L'ilawat" Salish title available : LHKW'ALUSH.-

970.3
    A Day in the life of an Indian boy.
      prod. [Montreal?] : NFB, 1964.- dist. McI. 37 fr. : col. : 35 mm.& captions. $9.00 pj

      1. Naskapi Indians.

      Photographs illustrate the life of Matoush, a Naskapi Indian boy of Labrador. Compares tools and weapons of the past with modern ones. Examines Indian hunting and fishing skills, the schools, and the games children play. Encourages comparison of Matoush's daily life with that of the viewer. French title available : LA VIE QUOTIDIENNE D'UN PETIT INDIEN.-

970.3
    A Day in the life of an Indian girl.
      prod. [Montreal?] : NFB, 1975.- dist. McI. 38 fr. : col. : 35 mm. & captions. $9.00 pj

      1. Naskapi Indians.

      A description of the daily life of Tenesh, a Naskapi Indian girl of Labrador. Examines the tasks she is learning in order to provide for her family when she is older. Studies many of the utensils and clothes used by Naskapi Indians. Encourages comparison of Tenesh's life with that of the viewer. French title available : LA VIE QUOTIDIENNE D'UNE PETITE INDIENNE.-

970.3
    Eléments de notre vie quotidienne.
      prod. [Montreal?] : NFB, 1975.- dist. SEC 37 fr. : col. : 35 mm. & reading script. $9.00 jis

      1. L'ilawat Indians.

      Close-up photographs of baskets, tools and utensils used in the past and still used today by the L'ilawat Indians of Canada. No captions, but printed notes describe the use of each basket or utensil illustrated. Both English and French are on same filmstrip. English title available : OBJECTS IN OUR LIVES.-

970.3
    La famille Huronne-Iroquoise (Indiens des forêts de l'Est).
      prod. [Montreal?] : NFB, 1969.- dist. McI. 57 fr. : col. : 35 mm. & captions & booklet. $9.00 jis

      1. Iroquois Indians. 2. Huron Indians.

      Uses photographs and drawings to explain the 13 moons calendar of the Iroquois Indians. Describes the way of life for the Iroquois and Huron Indians in their villages - their farming, hunting, cooking, and social customs. Compares the Iroquois of the past with those of today. Part of a multi-media kit titled "Les Indiens du Canada". English title available : THE IROQUOIS-HURON NATIONS (EASTERN WOODLAND INDIANS).-

970.3
    Gwúshum.
      prod. [Montreal?] : NFB, 1975.- dist. McI. 40 fr. : col. : 35 mm. & disc (33 1/3 rpm. 5 min.) : auto. & aud. adv. sig. & reading script. $18.00 jis

      1. L'ilawat Indians.

      An Indian woman makes "Indian ice cream" - a mousse-like dessert called gwushum.
Interior Salish dialogue, commentary and song accompany photographs showing how the soapberries are cooked, their juice strained and whipped with water and sugar using a whipping stick made from corn husks.
Available in Salish or English. Part of a multi-media kit titled "L'ilawat." Interior Salish available : GWUSHUM.-

970.3
    Huron Indian Village & Musem.
        prod. [Toronto] : Lea., 1975.- dist. Lea. 45 fr. : col. : 35 mm. & captions & teacher's manual. $9.00 (Huronia : $17.50) ji

        1. Huron Indians.

        A comprehensive view of the Huron's life style - food, tools, weapons, and clothing. Displays the skeletal remains of a Huron warrior, a model of the Huron's version of the birth of Christ and the Huron longhouse. Photographs are taken at the Huron Indian Village and the Huronia Museum.-

970.3
    Huron Indian Village (reconstructed).
        prod. [Toronto] : Lea., 1975.- dist. Lea. 44 fr. : col. : 35 mm. & captions & teacher's manual. $9.00 (Huronia : $17.50) ji

        1. Huron Indians.

        A photographic tour of an authentic Huron village at Midland, Ontario. Features maps of the Iroquois Indian area past and present, photographs of archeological "digs" and discoveries, as well as the reconstructed village. Includes some details of the Indian's daily life.-

970.3
    The Iroquois-Huron Nations (Eastern Woodland Indians).
        prod. [Montreal?] : NFB, 1969.- dist. McI. 51 fr. : col. : 35 mm. & captions & booklet. $9.00 jis

        1. Iroquois Indians. 2. Huron Indians.

        Uses photographs and drawings to explain the 13 moons calendar of the Iroquois Indians. Describes the way of life for the Iroquois and Huron Indians in their villages - their farming, hunting, cooking, and social customs. Compares the Iroquois Indians of the past with those of today. Part of a multi-media kit titled "Indians of Canada." French title available : LA FAMILLE HURONNE-IROQUOIS (INDIENS DES FORETS DE L'EST).-

The Classified Catalogue

970.3
    Mount Currie summer camp.
        prod. [Montreal?] : NFB, 1975.- dist. McI. 79 fr. : col. : 35 mm. & disc (33 1/3 rpm. 5 min.) : auto. & aud. adv. sig. & printed notes. $18.00 jis

        1. L'ilawat Indians.

        Provides a pictorial essay of the L'ilawat summer camp for children, built in the ancestral tradition, following the ancient designs for shelter. Examines the varied program and activities available, and the difficulty in obtaining financial support. Musical accompaniment by a L'ilawat Indian. Part of a multi-media kit titled "L'ilawat". Interior Salish title available : P'W'PANCHEK SWA7 ITI L'ILAWAT TA.-

970.3
    Objects in our lives.
        prod. [Montreal?] : NFB, 1975.- dist. McI. 37 fr. : col. : 35 mm. & reading script. $9.00 jis

        1. L'Ilawat Indians.

        Close-up photographs of baskets, tools and utensils used in the past and still used today by the L'ilawat Indians of Canada. No captions, but printed notes describe the use of each backet or utensil illustrated. Both English and French are on same filmstrip. French title : ELEMENTS DE NOTRE VIE QUOTIDIENNE.-

970.3
    Puberty : parts 1 & 2.
        prod. [Montreal?] : NFB, 1975.- dist. McI. 2 parts (35 : 45 fr.) : b&w & col. : 35 mm. & 2 discs (33 1/3 rpm. 5 : 7 min.) : auto. & aud. adv. sig. $18.00 jis

        1. L'ilawat Indians.

        Mary Leo, a Stalo Indian adopted as an infant by the l'ilawat tribe, tells of her childhood with ther adopted family. Includes details of the l'ilawat way of life, and describes the traditional customs of the tribe when a young girl reaches puberty. Produced in two parts for viewing convenience. Part of a multi-media kit titled "L'ilawat." Interior Salish title available : KW'AZANTSUT TI PAL7A 1 & 2.-

The Classified Catalogue

970.3
    Salmon.
        prod. [Montreal?] : NFB, 1974.- dist. McI. 36 fr. : col. : 35 mm. & cassette (5 min.) : auto. & aud. adv. sig. & reading script. $18.00 jis

        1. L'ílawat Indians. 2. Cookery - Salmon.

        Fresh sockeye salmon is cleaned, stretched out on a cedar stick, and placed near a fire to be cooked on both sides, according to traditional Indian methods. Included with the sound for the filmstrip are parts of an Indian song about fishing, sung by the people seen in the filmstrip. Part of a multi-media kit titled "L'ilawat". Interior Salish title available : SHTS'OZKWOZ.-

970.3
    La vie quotidienne d'un petit Indien.
        prod. [Montreal?] : NFB, 1964.- dist. SEC 37 fr. : col. : 35 mm. & captions. $9.00 pj

        1. Naskapi Indians.

        Photographs illustrate the life of Matoush, a Naskapi Indian boy of Labrador. Compares tools and weapons of the past with modern ones. Examines Indian hunting and fishing skills, the schools and the games children play. Encourages comparison of Matoush's daily life with that of the viewer. English title available : A DAY IN THE LIFE OF AN INDIAN BOY.-

970.3
    La vie quotidienne d'une petite Indienne.
        prod. [Montreal?] : NFB, 1964.- dist. SEC 38 fr. : col. : 35 mm. & captions. $9.00 pj

        1. Naskapi Indians.

        A description of the daily life of Tenesh, a Naskapi Indian girl of Labrador. Examines the tasks she is learning in order to provide for her family when she is older. Studies many of the utensils and clothes used by Naskapi Indians. Encourages comparison of Tenesh's life with that of the viewer. English title available : A DAY IN THE LIFE OF AN INDIAN GIRL.-

970.4
    Les amérindiens de la côte du pacifique : jusqu'à l'arrivée des européens.
        prod. [Toronto] : M-L, 1974.- dist. Sch. Ser. or Vint. 56 fr. : col. : 35 mm. & cassette (14 min.) : auto. & aud. adv. sig. & teacher's guide. $16.50 (Les amérindiens) is

        1. Indians of North America - Northwest, Pacific.

        An overview of the culture of the Pacific Northwest Indian tribes before the white man arrived. The changes which occurred with the meeting of the Indian and European cultures are well chronicled. Includes drawings, prints, maps, painting, and archival photographs of tribal events. English title available : THE NATIVE PEOPLE OF THE PACIFIC NORTHWEST : INITIAL EUROPEAN CONTACT.-

970.4
    Les amérindiens de la côte du pacifique : depuis l'arrivée des européens.
        prod. [Toronto] : M-L, 1974.- dist. Sch. Ser. or Vint. 60 fr. : col. : 35 mm. & cassette (12 min.) : auto. & aud. adv. sig. & teacher's guide. $16.50 (Les amérindiens : $85.00) is

        1. Indians of North America - Northwest, Pacific - History.

        Traces the cultural heritage of the Pacific Northwest Indian tribes from the advent of European civilization to the present. The tragic transition of the Indians from a highly developed cultural entity to a people dependent on the white man for survival is presented. Maps, drawings, paintings, and photographs. English title available : THE NATIVE PEOPLE OF THE PACIFIC NORTHWEST : EUROPEAN CONTACT TO THE PRESENT DAY.-

The Classified Catalogue

970.4
    Les amérindiens des forêts de l'est : jusqu' à l'arrivée des europeens.
        prod. [Toronto] : M-L, 1974.- dist. Sch. Ser. or Vint. 60 fr. : col. : 35 mm.& cassette (14 min.) : auto. & aud. adv. sig. & teacher's guide. $16.50 (Les amérindiens : $85.00) is

    1. Indians of North America - Northeastern States.

    An introduction to the culture of the Indians of the Northeastern Woodlands region. Drawings, paintings, photographs, and narration reveal their harmonious lifestyle before the arrival of the white settlers. English title available : THE NATIVE PEOPLES OF THE NORTHEASTERN WOODLANDS : INITIAL EUROPEAN CONTACT.-

970.4
    Les amérindiens des forêts de l'est : depuis l'arrivée des europeens.
        prod. [Toronto] : M-L, 1974.- dist. Sch. Ser. or Vint. 63 fr. : col. : 35 mm. & cassette (14 min.) : auto. & aud. adv. sig. & teacher's guide. $16.50 (Les amérindiens : $85.00) is

    1. Indians of North America - Northeastern States - History.

    Survey of the effect of advancing European civilization upon the Northeastern Woodlands tribes. Depicts the transition from self sufficiency to the poverty of reservation life. Also traces the Indian role in the fur trade, French-English relations, and the American Revolution plus their contribution to North American cultural heritage. Includes discussion of tribe politics and organization including the League of Six Nations. English title available : THE NATIVE PEOPLES OF THE NORTHEASTERN WOODLANDS : EUROPEAN CONTACT TO THE PRESENT DAY.-

970.4
    Les amérindiens des Grandes Plaines : jusqu'à l'arrivée des Europeens.
        prod. [Toronto] : M-L, 1974.- dist. Sch. Ser. or Vint. 53 fr. : col. : 35 mm. & cassette (11 min.) : auto. & aud. adv. sig. & teacher's guide. $16.50 (Les amérindiens : $85.00) is

    1. Indians of North America - Great Plains.

    Discusses the culture of the nomadic Plains tribes, using photographs, drawings, and paintings. Explains the dependence of the Indians on the buffalo for survival, the influence on native customs and religion, and the effects of the slaughter of buffalo herds. English title available : THE NATIVE PEOPLES OF THE GREAT PLAINS : INITIAL EUROPEAN CONTACT.-

970.4
    Les amérindiens des Grandes Plaines : depuis l'arrivée des europeens.
        prod. [Toronto] : M-L, 1974.- dist. Sch. Ser. or Vint. 61 fr. : col. : 35 mm. & cassette (14 min.) : auto. & aud. adv. sig. & teacher's guide. $16.50 (Les amérindiens : $85.00) is

    1. Indians of North America - Great Plains - History.

    An exploration of the struggle of the Plains Indian to preserve their cultural identity on the white civilization, beginning with the initial clash of the two cultures. Traces the relationship of the Indian and white man up to the present time, distinguishing between the Canadian and American treatment of the Indian. Includes paintings, drawings, and photographs of famous Indian leaders such as Sitting Bull and Crowfoot. English title available :THE NATIVE PEOPLES OF THE GREAT PLAINS : EUROPEAN CONTACT TO THE PRESENT DAY.-

970.4
    Autumn hunters.
        prod. [Montreal?] : NFB, 1975.- dist. Mcl. 36 fr. : col. : 35 mm. & captions. $9.00 (High Arctic heritage : $36.00) pji

    1. Eskimos.

    Examines the life of the Eskimo hunter and his family on Baffin Island. Describes preparations for winter including insulating houses with peat, taking in the big boats from the water. Illustrates hunting skills, the importance of the seal for food and clothing. Photos taken in the 1950's illustrate a vanishing way of life.-

The Classified Catalogue

970.4
The Caribou Eskimo.
prod. [Montreal?] : NFB, 1962.- dist. McI. 34 fr. : col. : 35 mm. & captions. $9.00 j

1. Eskimos.

A comprehensive study of the Caribou Eskimo, filmed in the Keewatin District. Emphasizes the importance of the caribou for food, clothing and shelter, as well as how civilization is affecting the old Eskimo life style. French title available : L'ESQUIMAU PRIMITIF.-

970.4
Days of the igloo.
prod. [Scarborough, Ont.] : R.B.M., 1974.- dist. ETHOS 61 fr. : col. : 35 mm. & cassette (11 min.) : auto. & aud. adv. sig. & reading script. $19.00 (The Canadian Arctic : $69.00) ji

1. Eskimos.

The old way of life of the Eskimo is illustrated with photographs of the land, boats, tools and hunting techniques of the past.-

970.4
The Eskimo and his work.
prod. Scarborough, Ont.] : R.B.M., 1974.- dist. ETHOS 91 fr. : col. : 35 mm. & cassette (10 min.) : auto. & aud. adv. sig. & reading script. $19.00 (The Canadian Arctic : $69.00) ji

1. Eskimos.

Photographs taken at Igloolik illustrate some of the occupations of the modern Eskimo. Emphasizes carving and print-making, but also mentions hunting, guiding, and jobs in transportation, government, and the oil industry.-

970.4
Eskimo heritage.
prod. [Toronto, Ont.] : Int. Cin., 1971.- dist. VEC 52 fr. : col. : 35 mm. & 4 pamphlets, 2 maps, 1 teacher's guide, 1 transparency & captions. $12.00 (The Living Arctic :$54.00) ji

1. Eskimos.

Briefly traces the Eskimo's heritage to his ancestors who crossed the wide land passage from Asia to the Arctic. Shows how they made total use of their environment for their clothing, food and shelter.-

970.4
Eskimo hunting.
prod. [Scarborough, Ont.] : RBM, 1974.- dist. ETHOS 58 fr. : col. : 35 mm. & cassette (11 min.) : auto. & aud. adv. sig. & teacher's manual. $19.00 (Eskimo stories) ji

1. Eskimos.

Uses artwork to illustrate the traditional Eskimo methods of hunting seal, caribou and bear. Discusses the different techniques required for each season of the year, and emphasizes the skill and endurance of the Eskimo hunter.-

970.4
Eskimos : part 2.
prod. [Toronto] : TBE, 1969.- dist. TBE 11 fr. : b&w : 35 mm. $2.00 (Canadian history pictures) jis

1. Eskimos.

Drawings of Eskimos, their dwellings and lifestyle, all by C.W. Jefferys. Shows traditional costumes of adults and children. Igloos, household articles, and hunting weapons illustrated.Also features watercraft and sleds.-

970.4
L'esquimau moderne.
prod. [Montreal?] : NFB, 1962.- dist. SEC 44 fr. : col. : 35 mm. & captions & reading script. $9.00 pji

1. Eskimos.

Illustrates the Eskimo's adaptation to a modern environment. Changes are shown in shelter, cooking, jobs, and education. English title available : THE MODERN ESKIMO.-

970.4
L'esquimau primitif.
prod. [Montreal?] : NFB, 1962.- dist. SEC 48 fr. : col. : 35 mm. & captions & reading script. $9.00 j

1. Eskimos.

A comprehensive study of the Caribou Eskimo, filmed in the Keewatin District. Emphasizes the importance of the caribou for food, clothing and shelter, as well as how civilization is affecting the old Eskimo life style. English title available : THE CARIBOU ESKIMO.-

The Classified Catalogue

970.4
    Hunters of the Arctic.
        prod. [Toronto] : Int. Cin., 1974.- dist. Sch. Ch. 53 fr. : col. : 35 mm. & cassette (10 min.) : auto. & aud. adv. sig. & teacher's manual. $16.95 (Arctic portrait : $49.00) ji

        1. Eskimos.

        Photographs of an actual hunt show traditional Eskimo hunting techniques. Describes and illustrates stalking, killing, and skinning caribou, walrus, polar bear, wolf and seal, emphasizing how each part of the animal is put to good use by the Eskimo. Also covers the Eskimo's way of life during the hunt, the responsibilities of the women, etc.-

970.4
    Indians : part II.
        prod. [Toronto] : TBE, 1974.- dist. TBE 11 fr. : b&w : 35 mm. & captions. $2.00 (Canadian history pictures) jis

        1. Indians of North America - Transportation. 2. Transportation - History.

        Illustrations by C.W. Jefferys show an assortment of articles used by Western and Eastern Canadian Indians for land and water transportation. Depicts difference between Eastern and Western snowshoes and canoes. Covers canoe construction and methods of land transportation including baggage packing and carrying.-

970.4
    Indians : part I.
        prod. [Toronto] : TBE, 1974.- dist. TBE 7 fr. : b&w : 35 mm. $2.00 jis

        1. Indians of North America - Canada.

        Dwellings of various Canadian Indian tribes. Shows Huron-Iroquois palisaded village, Ojibway birch bark lodge and Mohawk elm bark lodge. Compares exterior of Plains Indians' tipi with West Coast Indian dwellings. All drawings by C.W. Jefferys.-

970.4
    Indians I : life on the Plains.
        prod. [Don Mills, Ont.] : F & V, 1973.- dist. F & V 21 fr. : col. : 35 mm. & teacher's guide. $7.20 (Man in his world) ji

        1. Indians of North America - Great Plains.

        Photographs of modern Plains Indians at Calgary Stampede precede a presentation of past native life on the plains. Information is provided about their habitation, dependence on the buffalo, transportation, dance. Information is in the accompanying guide. No captions.-

970.4
    Indians leaders and centres of renewal.
        prod. [Scarborough, Ont.] : R.B.M., 1974.- dist. ETHOS 88 fr. : col. : 35 mm. & cassette (23 min.) : auto. & aud. adv. sig. & reading script. $19.00 (Canadian Indian people) jis

        1. Indians of North America - Canada.

        Photographs taken during a visit to reservations, cultural centres and provincial Indian headquarters from Ontario to British Columbia illustrate this description of the many programs of renewal and development now being conducted by Canadian Indian leaders.-

970.4
    Indians of the Great Plains.
        prod. [Toronto] : M-L, 1977.- dist. Sch. Ser. or Vint. 51 fr. : col. : 35 mm. & cassette (8 min.) : auto. & aud. adv. sig. & teacher's guide. $16.50 (Indians and Inuit : the first people of North America : $105.00) ji

        1. Indians of North America - Great Plains.

        Describes the traditional lifestyle of the Plains tribes (Blackfoot, Plains Cree, Cheyenne, Crow, and Sioux), emphasizing their almost total dependence on the bison for food, clothing, housing, weapons, and tools. Introduces and explains the terms pemmican, bison, shaman, sun dance, travois. Uses early photographs and drawings.-

970.4
Indians of the Northeastern Woodlands.
   prod. [Toronto] : M-L, 1977.- dist. Sch. Ser. or Vint. 51 fr. : col. : 35 mm. & cassette (8 min.) : auto. & aud. adv. sig. & teacher's guide. $16.50 (Indians and Inuit : the first people of North America : $105.00) ji

   1. Algonquian Indians. 2. Iroquois Indians.

   Using paintings and sketches, describes the traditional food, homes, clothing, spiritual beliefs, and lifestyles of the Algonkian and Iroquoian tribes. Introduces and explains the terms shaman, longhouse, and wigwam. Concludes by briefly mentioning the problem of native people in modern society.-

970.4
Indians of the Pacific Northwest.
   prod. [Toronto] : M-L, 1977.- dist. Sch. Ser. or Vint. 62 fr. : col. : 35 mm. & cassette (10 min.) : auto. & aud. adv. sig. & teacher's guide. $16.50 (Indians and Inuit : the first people of North America : $105.00) ji

   1. Haida Indians. 2. Nootka Indians. 3. Kwakuitl Indians.

   Using early photographs and drawings, describes the traditional, prosperous lifestyle of the Haida, Nootka, and Kwakuitl tribes, emphasizing the way the abundance of food from the land and sea allowed time for development of arts and crafts. Explains "potlatch". Concludes with their effort to function in modern society.-

970.4
Indians of the Southwest.
   prod. [Toronto] : M-L, 1977.- dist. Sch. Ser. or Vint. 64 fr. : col. : 35 mm. & cassette (10 min.) : auto. & aud. adv. sig. & teacher's guide. $16.50 (Indians and Inuit : the first people of North America : $105.00) ji

   1. Pueblo Indians. 2. Apache Indians. 3. Navajo Indians.

   Uses early photographs and drawings to describe the traditional food, homes, spiritual beliefs, and lifestyle of the Pueblo, Apache, and Navajo tribes, concluding with their efforts to fit in with modern society. Introduces the terms mesa, adobe, hogan, and wickiup.-

970.4
Indians yesterday and today.
   prod. [Scarborough, Ont.] : R.B.M., 1974.- dist. ETHOS 75 fr. : col. : 35 mm. & cassette (12 min.) : auto. & aud. adv. sig. & reading script. $19.00 (Canadian Indian people) jis

   1. Indians of North America - Canada.

   Uses photographs taken during a visit to reservations, cultural centres and provincial Indian headquarters from Ontario to British Columbia to present a brief history of the native people of Canada. Emphasizes their many difficulties, and their growing hope.-

970.4
Les Indiens des Plaines.
   prod. [Montreal?] : NFB, made, 1969 : 1977.- dist. SEC 53 fr. : col. : 35 mm. & captions & teacher's manual. $9.00 ji

   1. Indians of North America - Great Plains - History.

   Photographs and drawings describe the habitat of the Plains Indians in Canada before Europeans came to the New World. Discusses their tribes, way of life and the importance of the horse to their lifestyle. Examines the dependence on the roaming bison for food and clothing. Includes photographs of Plains Indian artifacts and how they were used. Describes Plain Indians of today and invites comparison with the past. Part of a multi-media kit titled "Les Indiens du Canada". English title available : PEOPLE OF THE PLAINS.-

970.4
Les Indiens des Régions subarctiques.
   prod. [Montreal?] : NFB, 1969.- dist. SEC 51 fr. : col. : 35 mm. & captions & teacher's manual. $9.00 j

   1. Indians of North America - Subarctic region.

   Provides a view of the Barren Ground Indian's past and present ways of life through photographs and drawings. Emphasizes the importance of the environment. Part of a multi-media kit titled "Les Indiens du Canada". English title available : PEOPLE OF THE SUB-ARCTIC.-

970.4
> The Inuit.
> prod. [Toronto] : M-L, 1977.- dist. Sch. Ser. or Vint. 60 fr. : col. : 35 mm. & cassette (9 min. : auto. & aud. adv. sig. & teacher's guide. $16.50 (Indians and Inuit : the first people of North America : $105.00) ji
>
> 1. Esimos.
>
> The Inuit's traditional way of life is described and then contrasted with their way of life today as they try to cope with modern society. Illustrated in part with drawings and early photographs.-

970.4
> The Modern Eskimo.
> prod. [Montreal?] : NFB, 1962.- dist. McI. 42 fr. : col. : 35 mm. & captions & reading script. $9.00 pji
>
> 1. Eskimos.
>
> Illustrates the Eskimo's adaptation to a modern environment. Changes are shown in shelter, cooking, jobs, and education. French title available : LE GRAND NORD CANADIEN : L'ESQUIMAU MODERNE.-

970.4
> My escape from death.
> prod. [Toronto] : Int. Cin., 1975.- dist. VEC 52 fr. : col. : 35 mm. & cassette (9 min.) : auto. & aud. adv. sig. & teacher's guide. $24.00 (The Arctic through Eskimo eyes : $86.00) ji
>
> 1. Eskimos.
>
> Uses authentic music, original drawings and text based on translated Eskimo accounts of Arctic life, to describe the Eskimo's everyday concern with hunting - in this case the hunt for walrus in a hostile environment which brings the narrator close to death.-

970.4
> The Native peoples of the Great Plains : initial European contact.
> prod. [Toronto] : M-L, 1974.- dist. Sch. Ser. or Vint. 53 fr. : col. : 35 mm. & cassette (11 min.) : auto. & aud. adv. sig. & teacher's guide. $16.50 (The Native peoples of North America : $85.00) is
>
> 1. Indians ofNorth America - Great Plains.
>
> Discusses the culture of the nomadic Plains tribes, using photographs, drawings, and paintings. Explains the dependence of the Indians on the buffalo for survival, the influence on native customs and religion, and the effects of the slaughter of buffalo herds. French title available : LES AMERINDIENS DES GRANDES PLAINES : JUSQU'A L'ARRIVEE DES EUROPEENS.-

970.4
> The Native peoples of the Great Plains : European contact to the present day.
> prod. [Toronto] : M-L, 1974.- dist. Sch. Ser. or Vint. 61 fr. : col. : 35 mm. & cassette (14 min.) : auto. & aud. adv. sig. & teacher's guide. $16.50 (The Native peoples of North America : $85.00) is
>
> 1. Indians of North America - Great Plains - History.
>
> An exploration of the struggle of the Plains Indian to preserve their cultural identity in the white civilization, beginning with the initial clash of the two cultures. Traces the relationship of the Indian and white man up to the present time, distinguishing between the Canadian and American treatment of the Indian. Includes paintings, drawings, and photographs of famous Indian leaders such as Sitting Bull and Crowfoot. French title available : LES AMERINDIENS DES GRANDES PLAINES : DEPUIS L'ARRIVEE DES EUROPEENS.-

The Classified Catalogue

970.4
    The Native peoples of the Northeastern Woodlands : European contact to the present day.
        prod. [Toronto] : M-L, 1974.- dist. Sch. Ser. or Vint. 63 fr. : col. : 35 mm. & cassette (14 min.) : auto. & aud. adv. sig. & teacher's guide. $16.50 (The Native peoples of North America : $85.00) is

        1. Indians of North America - Northeastern States - History.

        Survey of the effect of advancing European civilization upon the Northeastern Woodlands tribes Depicts the transition from self-sufficiency to the poverty of reservation life. Also traces the Indian role in the fur trade, French-English relations, and the American Revolution plus their contribution to North American cultural heritage. Includes discussion of tribal politics and organization including the League of Six Nations. French title available : LES AMERINDIENS DES FORETS DE L'EST : L'ARRIVEE DES EUROPEENS.-

970.4
    The Native peoples of the Northeastern Woodlands : initial European contact.
        prod. [Toronto] : M-L, 1974.- dist. Sch. Ser. or Vint. 60 fr. : col. : 35 mm. & cassette (14 min.) : auto. & aud. adv. sig. & teacher's guide. $16.50 (The Native peoples of North America : $85.00) is

        1. Indians of North America - Northeastern States.

        An introduction to the culture of the Indians of the Northeastern Woodlands region. Drawings, paintings, photographs, and narration reveal their harmonious lifestyle before the arrival of the white settlers. French title available : LES AMERINDIENS DES FORETS DE L'EST : JUSQU A L'ARRIVEE DES EUROPEENS.-

970.4
    The Native peoples of the Pacific Northwest : European contact to the present day.
        prod. [Toronto] : M-L, 1974.- dist. Sch. Ser. or Vint. 60 fr. : col. : 35 mm. & cassette (12 min.) : auto. & aud. adv. sig. & teacher's guide. $16.50 (The Native peoples of North America : $85.00) is

        1. Indians of North America - Northwest, Pacific - History.

        Traces the cultural heritage of the Pacific Northwest Indian tribes from the advent of European civilization to the present. The tragic transition of the Indians from a highly developed cultural entity to a people dependent on the white man for survival is presented. Maps, drawings, paintings, and photographs. French title available : LES AMERINDIENS DE LA COTE DU PACIFIQUE : DEPUIS L'ARRIVEE DES EUROPEENS.-

970.4
    The Native peoples of the Pacific Northwest : initial European contact.
        prod. [Toronto] : M-L, 1974.- dist. Sch. Ser. or Vint. 56 fr. : col. : 35 mm. & cassette (14 min.) : auto. & aud. adv. sig. & teacher's guide. $16.50 (The Native peoples of North America : $85.00) is

        1. Indians of North America - Northwest, Pacific.

        An overview of the Pacific Northwest Indian tribes before the white man arrived. The changes which occurred with the meeting of the Indian and European cultures are well chronicled. Includes drawings, prints, maps, paintings, and archival photographs of tribal events. French title available : LES AMERINDIENS DE LA COTE DU PACIFIQUE : JUSQU'A L'ARRIVEE DES EUROPEENS.-

970.4
    The New north.
        prod. [Toronto, Ont.] : Int. Cin., 1971.- dist. VEC 53 fr. : col. : 35 mm. & 4 pamphlets, 2 maps, 1 teacher's guide, 1 transparency & captions. $12.00 (The Living Arctic : $54.00) ji

        1. Eskimos.

        An examination of the role of the Eskimo in shaping the new North - their adaptation to the white man's way of life and their cultivation of old skills and art.-

970.4
  People of the North Pacific Coast.
    prod. [Montreal?] : NFB, 1969.- dist. McI.   47 fr. : col. : 35 mm. & captions. $9.00 jis

  1. Indians of North America - Northwest, Pacific.

  Drawings combine with photographs to illustrate the lifestyle of the early Indian tribes of the North Pacific coast of North America. Studies hunting and fishing methods, social customs, homes, and native art including totem poles. Compares Indian life today with the past. Part of a multi-media kit titled "Indians of Canada." French title available : LES PEUPLADES DE LA COTE NORD-OUEST.

970.4
  People of the Plains.
    prod. [Montreal?] : NFB, made 1969 : 1977.- dist. McI.   47 fr. : col. : 35 mm. & captions & teacher's manual. $9.00 j

  1. Indians of North America - Great Plains - History.

  Photographs and drawings describe the habitant of the Plains Indians in Canada before Europeans came to the New World. Discusses their tribes, way of life and the importance of the horse to their lifestyle. Examines the dependence on the roaming bison for food and clothing. Includes photographs of Plains Indian artifacts and how they were used. Describes Plains Indians of today and invites comparison with the past. Part of a multi-media kit titled "Indians of Canada." French title available : LES INDIENS DES PLAINES.-

970.4
  People of the sub-Arctic.
    prod. [Montreal?] : NFB, 1969.- dist. McI.   44 fr. : col. : 35 mm. & captions & teacher's manual. $9.00 j

  1. Indians of North America - Subarctic region.

  Provides a view of the Barren Ground Indian's past and present ways of life through photographs and drawings. Emphasizes the importance of the environment. Part of a multi-media kit titled "Indians of Canada." French title available : LES INDIENS DES REGIONS SUBARCTIQUES.-

970.4
  Les peuplades de la Côte Nord-Ouest.
    prod. [Montreal?] : NFB, 1969.- dist. SEC   53 fr. : col. : 35 mm. & captions & teacher's manual. $9.00 jis

  1. Indians of North America - Northwest, Pacific.

  Drawings combine with photographs to illustrate the lifestyle of the early Indian tribes of the North Pacific coast of North America. Studies hunting and fishing methods, social customs, homes, and native art including totem poles. Compares Indian life today with the past. Part of a multi-media kit titled "Les Indiens du Canada". English title available : PEOPLE OF THE NORTH PACIFIC COAST.-

970.4
  Spring journey.
    prod. [Montreal?] : NFB, 1975.- dist. McI.   33 fr. : col. : 35 mm. & captions. $9.00 (High Arctic heritage : $36.00) pji

  1. Eskimos.

  Describes spring activities in the long days of the Arctic. Examines packing up and moving camp, difficulties when crossing ice cracks and the spring camp at a beach. Discusses hunting and fishing methods. Pictures taken on Baffin Island in the 1959's illustrate a vanishing way of life.-

970.4
  Summer days.
    prod. [Montreal?] : NFB, 1975.- dist. McI.   36 fr. : col. : 35 mm. & captions. $9.00 (High Arctic heritage : $36.00) pji

  1. Eskimos.

  Depicts the life of an old Eskimo family on Baffin Island during the short Arctic summer. Examines whale hunting, bone carving, fishing and hunting for game. Discusses methods of fishing for the winter supply. Pictures taken in the 1950's illustrate a vanishing way of life.-

970.4
    Traditional Eskimo life.
        prod. [Scarborough, Ont.] : R.B.M., 1974.- dist. ETHOS 66 fr. : col. : 35 mm. & cassette (13 min.) : auto. & aud. adv. sig. & teacher's manual. $19.00 (Eskimo stories) ij

        1. Eskimos.

        Artwork is used to illustrate many aspects of traditional Eskimo daily life. Includes social customs, hunting skills, religious beliefs, transportation, tools and weapons, clothing, and recreation.-

970.4
    The way things used to be.
        prod. [Toronto] : Int. Cin., 1975.- dist. VEC 47 fr. : col. : 35 mm. & cassette (6 min.) : auto. & aud. adv. sig. & teacher's guide. $24.00 (The Arctic through Eskimo eyes : $86.00) ji

        1. Eskimos.

        Through authentic drawings, Cape Dorset Eskimos remind us of the old way of life, describing the building of igloos, making of warm clothes, use of native tools, and hunting of walrus, as well as describing their modes of transportation and the games children used to play.-

970.4
    Winter camp.
        prod. [Montreal?] : NFB, made 1975 : 1977.- dist. McI. 36 fr. : col. : 35 mm.& captions. $9.00 (High Arctic heritage : $36.00) pji

        1. Eskimos.

        Describes the way of life of an Eskimo family on Baffin Island during winter. Examines the social customs of a basically indoor life in the winter dusk. Discusses methods of preserving and cooking food, preparing for the winter hunt, using dog sleds and children's games. Pictures taken in the 1950's depict a vanishing way of life.-

970.5
    Cowichan : a question of survival.
        prod. [Vancouver] : TC, 1976.- dist. TC 95 fr. : col. : 35 mm. & cassette (19 min.) : auto. & aud. adv. sig. & teacher's guide. $20.00 (Native land claims in B.C. : $40.00) is

        1. Indians of North America - Canada - Claims. 2. Indians of North America - Canada - Government relations. 3. Indians of North America - Canada - Economic conditions.

        Examines the Cowichan reserves next to the city of Dugan. Interviews relate land claims to the future of the band's cultural and economic development. Joe Elliott, a tribal historian, discusses the Cowichan land claim. Simon Charlie, a master carver, explains his craft. Chief Ves Modeste discusses the economic and social importance of the native-owned farm co-op, fish hatchery and super-market.-

970.5
    L'histoire de Manowan : première partie.
        prod. [Montreal?] : NFB, 1972.- dist. SEC 112 fr. : b&w & col. : 35 mm. & disc (33 1/3 rpm. 17 min.) : auto. & aud. adv. sig. $18.00 (Manowan) is

        1. Indians of North America - Canada - Reservations.

        An account of how white men's civilization has invaded Indian lives, governed their hunting, trapping and fishing, confined them to a Reserve, and made them virtually helpless to pursue the "old life." English title available : HISTORY OF MANOWAN : PART 1.-

970.5
    L'histoire de Manowan : deuxième partie.
        prod. [Montreal?] : NFB, 1972.- dist. SEC 108 fr. : b&w & col. : 35 mm. & disc (33 1/3 rpm. 20 min.) : auto. & aud. adv. sig. $18.00 (Manowan) is

        1. Indians of North America - Canada - Reservations.

        A continuation of history of Manowan, Part 1. Discusses the death of Indian customs, independence and dignity, with the advent of the white man and his ways. English title available : A HISTORY OF MANOWAN : PART TWO.-

The Classified Catalogue

970.5
History of Manowan : part 1.
prod. [Montreal?] : NFB, 1972.- dist. McI. 112 fr. : b&w & col. : 35 mm. & disc (33 1/3 rpm. 17 min.) : auto. & aud. adv. sig. $18.00 (Manowan) is

1. Indians of North America - Canada - Reservations.

An account of how white man's civilization has invaded Indian lives, governed their hunting, trapping, and fishing, confined them to a Reserve, and made them virtually helpless to pursue the "old life." French title available : L'HISTOIRE DE MANOWAN : PREMIERE PARTIE.-

970.5
History of Manowan : part 2.
prod. [Montreal?] : NFB, 1972.- dist. McI. 108 fr. : b&w & col. : 35 mm. & disc (33 1/3 rpm. 20 min.) : auto. & aud. adv. sig. $18.00 (Manowan) is

1. Indians of North America - Canada - Reservations.

A continuation of History of Manowan Part 1. Discusses the death of Indian customs, independence and dignity, with the advent of the white man and his ways. French title available : L'HISTOIRE DE MANOWAN : DEUXIEME PARTIE.-

970.5
Native land claims in B.C. : an introduction (1850-1976).
prod. [Vancouver] : TC, 1976.- dist. TC 135 fr. : col. : 35 mm. & cassette (24 min.) : auto. & aud. adv. sig. & teacher's guide. $20.00 (Native land claims in B.C. : $40.00) is

1. Indians of North America - Canada - Claims. 2. Indians of North America - Canada - Government relations.

Highlights many complex themes including aboriginal rights, treaties, reserves and native petitions. Historical re-enactments and dramatic sequences are used.-

970.5
Northern development at what cost?
prod. [Toronto] : K.M., 1976.- dist. K.M. 80 fr. : col. : 35 mm. & cassette (17 min.) $35.00 is

1. Indians of North America - Canada - Claims. 2. Arctic regions - Economic conditions.

Describes the many ethical questions inherent in the search for new energy sources in the Canadian north and the problems raised by the Mackenzie Valley Pipeline proposal. Specifically discussed are the effects on the northern native peoples, and their desire to share in the shaping of their own destiny. Includes references to the Berger Inquiry and the Dene Declaration.-

971
A la découverte de notre patrimoine.
prod. [Toronto] : Int. Cin., 1975.- dist. VEC 50 fr. : b&w & col. : 35 mm. & cassette (11 min.) : auto. & aud. adv. sig. & teaching guide. $24.00 (Le Patrimoine vivant du Canada : $86.00) ij

1. Canada - History - Sources.

Using the actual reconstruction of historic Louisbourg and Dawson City as examples, explains how original documents, paintings, drawings, and artifacts are used to help us discover, preserve, and re-live Canada's past. English title available : DISCOVERING OUR HERITAGE.-

971
La Défense du Canada dans un monde en évolution.
prod. [Toronto] : Int. Cin., 1975.- dist. VEC 46 fr. : col. : 35 mm. & cassette (10 min.) : auto. & aud. adv. sig. & teacher's guide. $24.00 (Le Canada en guerre : l'histoire militaire d'un peuple pacifique : $86.00) i

1. Canada - History, Military.

Examines the present age of nuclear warfare, and the international role of Canada's armed forces during peace time, including our commitments to NATO and the UN. English title available : DEFENDING CANADA IN A CHANGING WORLD.-

The Classified Catalogue

971
    Discovering our heritage.
        prod. [Toronto] : Int. Cin., 1974.- dist. VEC 50 fr. : b&w & col. : 35 mm. & cassette (10 min.) : auto. & aud. adv. sig. & teaching guide. $24.00 (Canada's living heritage : $86.00) ji

    1. Canada - History - Sources.

    Using the actual reconstruction of historic Louisbourg and Dawson City as examples, explains how original documents, paintings, drawings, and artifacts are used to help us discover, preserve, and re-live Canada's past. French title available : A LA DECOUVERTE DE NOTRE PATRIMOINE.-

971
    D'une Guerre à l'autre.
        prod. [Toronto] : Int. Cin., 1975.- dist. VEC 57 fr. : col. : 35 mm. & cassette (14 min.) : auto. & aud. adv. sig. & teacher's guide. $24.00 (Le Canada en guerre : l'histoire militaire d'un peuple pacifique : $86.00) i

    1. World War, 1939-1945 - Canada. 2. Canada - History, Military.

    Discusses events in Canada and the world which led to Canada's involvement in the Second World War. English title available : FROM WAR TO WAR.-

971
    L'expansion du Canada.
        prod. [Montreal?] : NFB, 1958.- dist. SEC 29 fr. : col. : 35 mm. & captions. $9.00 j

    1. Canada - History.

    Maps and drawings with significant dates illustrate the geographical growth of Canada, from the New World of 1663 as French and British colonies to the addition of Newfoundland in 1949. English title available : THE GROWTH OF CANADA.-

971
    The Growth of Canada.
        prod. [Montreal?] : NFB, 1958.- dist. McI. 29 fr. : col. : 35 mm. & captions. $9.00 j

    1. Canada - History.

    Maps and drawings with significant dates illustrate the geographical growth of Canada, from the New World of 1663 as French and British colonies to the addition of Newfoundland in 1949. French title available : L'EXPANSION DU CANADA.-

971
    Life along the waterways.
        prod. [Toronto] : Int. Cin., 1975.- dist. VEC 58 fr. : col. : 35 mm. & cassette (9 min.) : auto. & aud. adv. sig. & teacher's guide. $24.00 (Journey through early Canada with W.H. Bartlett : $64.00) ji

    1. Shipping - Canada - History. 2. Canada - History - Pictorial works.

    W.H. Bartlett's sketches of Canada's natural beauty along the St. Lawrence show the various means of water transportation employed by Canadians in the early 1800's.-

971
    La Lutte pour une terre nouvelle.
        prod. [Toronto] : Int. Cin., 1975.- dist. VEC 50 fr. : col. : 35 mm. & cassette (13 min.) : auto. & aud. adv. sig. & teacher's guide. $24.00 (Le Canada en guerre : l'histoire militaire d'un peuple pacifique : $86.00) i

    1. Canada - History, Military. 2. Canada - History - To 1763 (New France). 3. Canada - History - 1763-1867.

    Brief military history of Canada up to Confederation showing the significance to Canadian history of conflict between the United States, France, and Britain. English title available : STRUGGLE FOR THE NEW LAND.-

971
    Pioneers : part 1.
        prod. [Toronto] : TBE, 1975.- dist. TBE 15 fr. : b&w : 35 mm. $2.00 (Canadian history pictures) jis

    1. Frontier and pioneer life.

    Selections from C.V. Jefferys' sketches on aspects of Canadian pioneer living. Depicts types of prairie homes, loghouse construction and shingle making. Illustrates farm tools and agricultural implements. Also includes British uniforms circa 1812.-

The Classified Catalogue

971
    Quebec and Ontario : old colony and new outpost.
      prod. [Toronto] : Int. Cin., 1975.- dist. VEC 71 fr. : col. : 35 mm. & cassette (11 min.) : auto. & aud. adv. sig. & teacher's guide. $24.00 (Journey through early Canada with W.H. Bartlett : $64.00) ji

    1. Canada - History - Pictorial works.

    Sketches of nineteenth century Quebec City, Montreal, Toronto, Brockville, and Queenston made by W. H. Bartlett on his travels through Upper and Lower Canada, point out the cultural differences between English and French communities.-

971
    Sketching the New World : Maritime scenes.
      prod. [Toronto] : Int. Cin., 1975.- dist. VEC 59 fr. : col. : 35 mm. & cassette (9 min.) : auto. & aud. adv. sig. & teacher's guide. $24.00 (Journey through early Canada with W.H. Bartlett : $64.00) ji

    1. Canada - History - Pictorial works.
    2. Bartlett,William H   , 1809-1854.

    Provides a general introduction to William Henry Bartlett's pencil sketches by using examples of his Maritime landscapes, and explains how his original drawings were later re-touched by European engravers to suit the European impression of Canada.-

971
    Struggle for the new land.
      prod. [Toronto] : Int. Cin., 1974.- dist. VEC 50 fr. : col. : 35 mm. & cassette (12 min.) : auto. & aud. adv. sig. & teaching guide. $24.00 (Canadians at war : the military story of a peaceful people : $86.00) i

    1. Canada - History, Military. 2. Canada - History - 1763-1867. 3. Canada - History - To 1763 (New France).

    Brief military history of Canada up to Confederation showing the significance to Canadian history of conflict between the United States, France, and Britain. French title available : LA LUTTE PUR UNE TERRE NOUVELLE.-

971
    A Trip through early day Canada.
      prod. [Toronto] : B&R, 1976.- dist. B&R 41 fr. : col. : 35 mm. & cassette (18 min.) : auto. & aud. adv. sig. & teacher's manual & reading script. $18.00 (Early day Canada : $96.00) ji

    1. Frontier and pioneer life.

    A tour across nineteenth-century Canada illustrates the contrasts to be found at that time in Canada-log cabins and stone mansions, small churches and great cathedrals.-

971.0074
    Places preseving our heritage.
      prod. [Toronto] : McI. 1977.- dist. McI. 37 fr. : col. : 35 mm. & cassette (11 min.) : auto. & aud. adv. sig. & teacher's guide. $19.00 (Canada's heritage today : $102.00) ji

    1. Canada - History - Collection and presevation.

    Viewers are taken on a photographic trip across Canada to visit places that are attempting to preserve our heritage. Examples of museums, libraries, parks, forts, schools, fairs are given.-

971.01
    The Discovery of Canada.
      prod. [Scarborough] : SHN. 1972.- dist. PHM 102 fr. : col. : 35 mm. & cassette (27 min.) : auto. & aud. adv. sig. & teacher's guide. $39.60 eng

    1. American - Exploration.

    A survey of the discovery of Canada from the earliest explorations to modern searches for oil and gas. Emphasis is placed on he difficulties of the early explorers and on their relationship with the native peoples. Illustrated with sketches and photographs.-

The Classified Catalogue

971.01
    The Era of royal government.
        prod. [Scarborough] : SHN, 1977.- dist. PHM 80 fr. : b&w & col. : 35 mm. & cassette (23 min.) : auto. & aud. adv. sig. & teacher's guide. $39.60 (Early Canada : $112.00) ji

        1. Canada - History - To 1763 (New France).

        A description of the French colony following establishment of Royal Rule. Discusses Talon's efforts to increase the population of New France and to encourage commerce. Includes events leading to the Seven Years' War. Illustrated with drawings and photographs.-

971.01
    France in the New World.
        prod. [Scarborough, Ont.] : HN, 1977.- dist. PHM 76 fr. : b&w & col. : 35 mm. & cassette (21 min.) : auto. & aud. adv. sig. & teacher's guide. $39.60 (Early Canada : $112.00) ji

        1. Canada - History - To 1763 (New France).

        Outlines the early history of Canada. Discussion includes explorations by Cabot and Cartier, Champlain's colony at Port Royal, the Treaty of Utrecht, the establishment of Quebec, and the Huron-Iroquois wars. Illustrated with drawings and photos.-

971.01
    From fleur-de-lis to Union Jack.
        prod. [Scarborough] : SHN, 1977.- dist. PHM 74 fr. : b&w & col. : 35mm. & cassette (19 min.) : auto. & aud. adv. sig. & teacher's guide. $39.60 (Early Canada : $112.00) ji

        1. Canada - History - To 1763 (New France). 2. Canada - History - (1763-1791.

        Traces the history of Canada to 1791, examining the events of the Seven Years' War in North America, and explaining the defeat of New France. Discusses French-British relations, and the effects of the American Revolution on Canada. Illustrated with drawings and photos.-

971.01
    Frontenac.
        prod. [Montreal?] : NFB, 1961.- dist. SEC 40 fr. : col. : 35 mm. & captions & manual. $9.00 pj

        1. Frontenac, Louis de Baude, comte de, 1620-1698. 2. Canada - History - To 1763 (New France).

        Depicts Frontenac's career as Governor of New France. Features La Salle's explorations of Louisiana, the English attacking Quebec in 1690, and the Iroquois expedition in 1696. English title available : FRONTENAC.-

971.01
    Frontenac.
        prod. [Montreal?] : NFB, 1961.- dist. McI. 40 fr. : col. : 35 mm. & captions & manual. $9.00 (New France : exploration and growth : $54.00) pj

        1. Frontenac, Louis de Baude, comte de, 1620-1698. 2. Canada - History - To 1763 (New France).

        Depicts Frontenac's career as Governor of New France. Features La Salle's exploration of Louisiana, the English attacking Quebec in 1690, and the Iroquois expedition in 1696. French title available : FRONTENAC.-

971.01
    Le Général James Wolfe.
        prod. [Montreal?] : NFB, 1953.- dist. SEC 46 fr. : col. : 35 mm. & captions & teacher's guide. $9.00 j

        1. Wolfe, James, 1727-1759. 2. Canada - History - To 1763 (New France).

        Traces General James Wolfe's military career in Europe and Canada. Covers European battles 1743-47 and events leading up to and including 1759 battle on the Plains of Abraham. Drawings and maps illustrate battle locations, uniforms, weapons and military strategy of English and French. To be used with manual. English title available : GENERAL JAMES WOLFE.-

The Classified Catalogue

971.01
    General James Wolfe.
        prod. [Montreal?] : NFB, made 1953 : 1970.- dist. McI. 46 fr. : col. : 35 mm. & captions & teacher's guide. $9.00 j

        1. Wolfe, James, 1727-1759. 2. Canada - History - To 1763 (New France).

        Traces General James Wolfe's military career in Europe and Canada. Covers European battles 1743-47 and events leading up to and including 1759 battle on the Plains of Abraham. Drawings and maps illustrate battle locations, uniforms, weapons and military strategy of English and French. To be used with manual. French title available : LE GENERAL JAMES WOLFE.-

971.01
    La guerre de Sept ans.
        prod. [Montreal?] : NFB, 1965.- dist. SEC 48 fr. : b&w & col. : 35 mm. & captions. $9.00 jis

        1. Seven Years' War, 1756-1763. 2. Canada - History - 1755-1763.

        Uses drawings to outline the incidents leading to the Seven Year's War between Britain and France. Examines the expulsion of the Acadians from Nova Scotia. Includes detail of the Seige of Quebec and the capture of Montreal. English title available : THE SEVEN YEARS' WAR.-

971.01
    Jacques Cartier.
        prod. [Montreal?] : NFB, made 1956 : 1967.- dist. SEC 62 fr. : col. : 35 mm. captions & teacher's guide. $9.00 ji

        1. Cartier, Jacques, 1491-1557. 2. America - Discovery and exploration. 3. Canada - History - To 1763 (New France).

        Uses drawings and maps to trace the three voyages of Jacques Cartier, the French navigator and explorer, to the region of the St. Lawrence River. Captions are written in the first person as though Cartier were narrator. Describes the relationship of the French with the Indians, and the way of life for the explorers. English title available : JACQUES CARTIER.-

971.01
    Jacques Cartier.
        prod. [Montreal?] : NFB, made 1956 : 1966.- dist. McI. 60 fr. : col. : 35 mm. & captions & teacher's guide. $9.00 (New France : exploration and growth : $54.00) ji

        1. Cartier, Jacques, 1491-1557. 2. America - Discovery and exploration. 3. Canada - History - To 1763 (New France).

        Uses drawings and maps to trace the three voyages of Jacques Cartier, the French navigator and explorer, to the region of the St. Lawrence River. Captions are written in the first person as though Cartier were narrator. Describes the relationship of the French with the Indians, and the way of life for the explorers. French title available : JACQUES CARTIER.-

971.01
    Jean Talon.
        prod. [Montreal?] : NFB, made 1960 : 1975.- dist. SEC 52 fr. : col. : 35 mm. & captions & manual. $9.00 j

        1. Talon, Jean, comte, d'Orsainville, 1625-1694. 2. Canada - History - To 1763 (New France).

        Drawings portray the work of Jean Talon in establishing a prosperous colony in New France. Describes expansion of population, industry and trade, as well as the establishment of seigneurial system. English title available : JEAN TALON.-

971.01
    Jean Talon.
        prod. [Montreal?] : NFB, made, 1960 : 1975.- dist. McI. 47 fr. : col. : 35 mm. & captions & manual. $9.00 (New France : exploration and growth : $54.00) j

        1. Talon, Jean, comte, d'Orsainville, 1625-1694. 2. Canada - History - To 1763 (New France).

        Drawings portray the work of Jean Talon in establishing a prosperous colony in New France. Describes expansion of population, industry and trade, as well as the establishment of seigneurial system. French title available : JEAN TALON.-

The Classified Catalogue

971.01
    Life in New France.
        prod. [Scarborough] : SHN, 1977.- dist. PHM 70 fr. : b&w & col. : 35 mm. & cassette (19 min.) : auto. & aud. adv. sig. & teacher's guide. $39.60 (Early Canada : $112.00) ji

        1. Canada - History - To 1763 (New France).

        An overview of the political, economic and social structures of New France. Describes habits, homes, and activities of the habitants compared to the wealthy merchants and seigneurs. Looks at the contributions of the Roman Catholic Church in the fields of education and health care. Illustrated with drawings and photos.-

971.01
    La Nouvelle-France.
        prod. [Montreal?] : NFB, 1963.- dist. SEC 51 fr. : col. : 35 mm. & captions & manual. $9.00 ji

        1. Canada - History - To 1763 (New France).

        Uses drawings to provide an overview of the history of New France from the time of Jacques Cartier in 1534 to the Treaty of Paris in 1763. Highlights the expansion of the French southward into Louisiana, and the development of settlements along the St. Lawrence River. English title available : THE STORY OF NEW FRANCE.-

971.01
    Samuel de Champlain.
        prod. [Montreal?] : NFB, 1963.- dist. SEC 53 fr. : col. : 35 mm. & captions & teacher's manual. $9.00 ji

        1. Champlain, Samuel de, 1567-1635.
        2. America - Discovery and travel.
        3. Canada - History - To 1763 (New France).

        Samuel de Champlain's life in New France, divided into three parts: travels along the St. Lawrence, exploration of Canada's interior, and establishment of New France. Frequent use of maps clearly plot routes taken during exploration. Illustrations show building of Port-Royal and Quebec, English - French relations, and wars against Iroquois. English title available : SAMUEL DE CHAMPLAIN.-

971.01
    Samuel de Champlain.
        prod. [Montreal?] : NFB, made 1963 : 1974.- dist. SEC 51 fr. : col. : 35 mm. & captions & teacher's manual. $9.00 (New France : exploration and growth : $54.00) ji

        1. Champlain, Samuel de, 1567-1635.
        2. Canada - History - To 1763 (New France).
        3. America - Discovery and exploration.

        Samuel de Champlain's life in New France, divided into three parts : travels along the St. Lawrence, exploration of Canada's interior, and establishment of New France. Frequent use of maps clearly plot routes taken during exploration. Illustrations show building of Port-Royal and Quebec, English-French relations, and wars against Iroquois. French title available : SAMUEL de CHAMPLAIN.-

971.01
    The Seven Years' War.
        prod. [Montreal?] : NFB, made 1965 : 1976.- dist. McI. 49 fr. : b&w & col. : 35 mm. & captions. $9.00 jis

        1. Seven Years' War, 1756-1763. 2. Canada - History - 1755-1763.

        Uses drawings to outline the incidents leading to the Seven Years' War between Britain and France. Examines the expulsion of the Acadians from Nova Scotia. Includes detail of the Siege of Quebec and the capture of Montreal. French title available : LA GUERRE DE SEPT ANS.-

971.01
    The Story of New France.
        prod. [Montreal?] : NFB, 1963.- dist. McI. 51 fr. : col. : 35 mm. & captions & manual. $9.00 (New France : seigneurial system : $45.00) ji

        1. Canada - History - To 1763 (New France)

        Uses drawings to provide an overview of the history of New France from the time of Jacques Cartier in 1534 to the Treaty of Paris in 1763. Highlights the expansion of the French southward into Louisiana, and the development of settlements along the St. Lawrence River. French title available : LE NOUVELLE-FRANCE.-

The Classified Catalogue

971.01
    La Vérendrye.
        prod. [Montreal?] : NFB, made 1957 : 1976.- dist. SEC 54 fr. : col. : 35 mm. & captions. $9.00 j

        1. La Verendrye, Pierre Gaultier de Varennes, sieur de, 1685-1749. 2. America - Discovery and exploration.

        Drawings and maps are used to illustrate the life and expeditions of the French explorer and fur trader whose quest for the Pacific contributed to the opening of the West. English title available : LA VERENDRYE.-

971.01
    La Vérendrye.
        prod. [Montreal?] : NFB, made 1957 : 1972.- dist. McI. 54 fr. : col. : 35 mm. & captions & teacher's manual. $9.00 (New France : exploration and growth : $54.00) j

        1. La Verendrye, Pierre Gaultier de Varennes, sieur de, 1685-1749. 2. America - Discovery and exploration.

        Drawings and maps are used to illustrate the life and expeditions of the French explorer and fur trader whose quest for the Pacific contributed to the opening of the West. French title available : LA VERENDRYE.-

971.03
    The 1837 Rebellion in Lower Canada.
        prod. [Toronto] : SHN, 1972.- dist. PHM 81 fr. : b&w & col. : 35 mm. & cassette (28 min.) : auto. & aud. adv. sig. & teacher's manual. $39.60 (1837 Rebellions : $54.05) is

        1. Papineau, Louis Joseph, 1786-1871. 2. Canada - History - Rebellion - 1837-1838. 3. Canada - Politics and government - 1791-1841

        Describes conflicts between French-Canadians and the British dominated government of Lower Canada. Traces the progress of Papineau and his followers prior to the Rebellion. Uses paintings, photographs of documents, and maps.-

971.03
    The 1837 Rebellion in Upper Canada.
        prod. [Toronto] : SHN, 1972.- dist. PHM 101 fr. : b&w & col. : 35 mm. & cassette (28 min.) : auto. & aud. adv. sig. & teacher's manual. $39.50 (1837 Rebellions : $54.05) is

        1. Mackenzie, William Lyon, 1795-1861. 2. Canada - History - Rebellion - 1837-1838. 3. Canada - Politics and government - 1791-1841.

        Discusses the causes of the Rebellion including grievances of settlers. Deals with William Lyon Mackenzie's role. Uses maps and documents to give details of the battles fought. Concludes with Durham Report.-

971.03
    La Guerre de 1812.
        prod. [Montreal?] : NFB, 1965.- dist. SEC 48 fr. : b&w & col. : 35 mm. & captions. $9.00 ji

        1. Canada - History - War of 1812.

        A summary of the circumstances leading to the war between Canada and U.S., the major events and battles at sea and on land, including Queenston Heights, York, and Lundy's Lane. Includes questions for discussion. English title available : THE WAR OF 1812.-

971.03
    Lord Durham's mission.
        prod. [Montreal?] : NFB, made, 1961 : 1972.- dist. McI. 42 fr. : col. & 35 mm. & captions & teacher's manual. $9.00 (Development of self-government : $45.00) cn

        1. Durham, John George Lambton, 1st Earl of, 1792-1840. 2. Canada - Politics and government 1791-1841.

        A presentation in two parts, - with Lord Durham's stay in Canada in 1838 and Lord Durham's report. Drawings with captions describe his accomplishments, recommendations for responsible government, and subsequent events leading to union of colonies. French title available : LA MISSION DE LORD DURHAM.-

971.03
 La mission de Lord Durham.
  prod. [Montreal?] : NFB, 1961.- dist. SEC 50 fr. : col. : 35 mm. & captions & teacher's manual. $9.00 (La conquête du gouvernement responsable : $45.00) is

  1. Durham, John George Lambton, 1st Earl of, 1792-1840. 2. Canada - Politics and government - 1791-1841.

  A presentation in two parts. - Lord Durham's stay in Canada in 1838 and Lord Durham's report. Drawings with captions describe his accomplishments, recommendations for responsible government, and subsequent events leading to union of colonies. English title available : LORD DURHAM'S MISSION.-

971.03
 Rébellion dans le Bas-Canada.
  prod. [Montreal?] : NFB, made 1960 : 1974.- dist. SEC 29 fr. : col. : 35 mm. & captions & teacher's manual. $9.00 (La conquête du gouvernement responsable : $45.00) is

  1. Papineau, Louis Joseph, 1786-1871.
  2. Canada - History - Rebellion, 1837-1838.
  3. Canada - Politics and governemnt - 1791-1841.

  Outlines the causes for the Rebellion, the role of Papineau in the French revolt, the three battles fought in 1837, and the significance of the Rebellion in terms of later government reform. Each drawing with caption is fully explained in the manual. English title available : REBELLION IN LOWER CANADA.-

971.03
 Rébellion dans le Haut-Canada.
  prod. [Montreal?] : NFB, 1960.- dist. SEC 39 fr. : col. : 35 mm. & captions & teacher's guide. $9.00 (La conquête du gouvernement responsable : $45.00) is

  1. Mackenzie, William Lyon, 1795-1861.-
  2. Canada - History - Rebellion, 1837-1838.
  3. Canada - Politics and government - 1791-1841.

  Uses drawings to trace the incidents leading to the Rebellion of 1837 - the Family Compact, Mackenzie's Reform Movement - the events of the Rebellion itself, and the consequences for later government. English title available : REBELLION IN UPPER CANADA.-

971.03
 Rebellion in Lower Canada.
  prod. [Montreal?] : NFB, made 1960 : 1973.- dist. McI. 25 fr. : col. : 35 mm. & captions & teacher's manual. $9.00 (Development of self-government : $45.00) is

  1. Canada - History - Rebellion, 1837-1838.
  2. Canada - Politics and government - 1791-1841. 3. Papineau, Louis Joseph, 1786-1871.

  Outlines the causes for the Rebellion, the role of Papineau in the French revolt, the three battles fought in 1837, and the significance of the Rebellion in terms of later government reform. Each drawing with caption is fully explained in the manual. French title available : REBELLION DANS LE BAS-CANADA.-

971.03
 Rebellion in Upper Canada.
  prod. [Montreal?] : NFB, made 1960 : 1972.- dist. McI. 37 fr. : col. : 35 mm. & captions & teacher's guide. $9.00 (Development of self-government : $45.00) is

  1. Mackenzie, William Lyon, 1795-1861.
  2. Canada - Politics and government - 1791-1841. 3. Canada - History - Rebellion, 1837-1838.

  Uses drawings to trace the incidents leading to Rebellion of 1837. - the Family Compact, Mackenzie's Reform Movement, - the events of the Rebellion itself, and the consequences for later government. French title available : REBELLION DANS LE HAUT-CANADA.-

971.03
 The War of 1812.
  prod. [Montreal?] : NFB, made 1965 : 1975.- dist. McI. 48 fr. : col. : 35mm. & captions. $9.00 ji

  1. Canada - History - War of 1812.

  A summary of the circumstances leading to the war between Canada and U.S., the major events and battles at sea and on land, including Queenston Heights, York, and Lundy's Lane. Includes questions for discussion. French title available : LA GUERRE DE 1812.-

The Classified Catalogue

971.03
    The War of 1812.
        prod. [Scarborough] : SHN, 1977.- dist. PHM 88 fr. : b&w & col. : 35 mm. & cassette (27 min.) : auto. & aud. adv. sig. & teacher's guide. $39.60 is

        1. Canada - History - War of 1812.
        2. United States - History - War of 1812.

        Discusses causes of the war and the role played by Tecumseh and the Indians.
        Includes the Declaration of War, the battles of Queeston Heights, Fort York., and Lundy's Lane. Follows with Treaty of Ghent. Uses drawings and art reprints of the period and sound effects in the commentary.-

971.04
    Confederation Canada.
        prod. [Scarborough, Ont.] : SHN, 1972.- dist. PHM 107 fr. : b&w & col. : 35 mm. & cassette (28 min.) : auto. & aud. adv. sig. teacher's guide. $39.60 is

        1. Canada - History - 1841-1867.

        Deals with the events leading to Confederation. Discusses U.S. interest in Canada, the Charlottetown, Quebec, and London Conferences, and the American Civil War. Includes roles of Macdonald, Cartier, and George Brown. Illustrated with photographs, paintings, drawings, portraits, as well as maps and diagrams.-

971.04
    La décision de Lord Elgin.
        prod. [Montreal?] : NFB, made 1961 : 1974.- dist. SEC 37 fr. : col. : 35 mm. & captions & teacher's manual. $9.00 (La conquête du gouvernement responsable : $45.00) is

        1. Elgin, James Bruce, 8th Earl of, 1811-1863.
        2. Canada - Politics and government - 1841-1867.

        Describes how governor-general Lord Elgin introduced responsible government to Canada after Britain allowed colonies free trade in 1840. Photos, drawings, newspaper cartoons explain improvements in judicial system, local government, railways and trade. Review questions included. English title available : LORD ELGIN'S DECISION.-

971.04
    Lord Elgin's decision.
        prod. [Montreal?] : NFB, made 1961 : 1974.- dist. McI. 31 fr. : col. : 35 mm. & captions & teacher's manual. $9.00 (Development of self-government : $45.00) is

        1. Elgin, James Bruce, 8th Earl of, 1811-1863.
        2. Canada - Politics and government - 1841-1867.

        Describes how governor-general Lord Elgin introduced responsible government to Canada after Britain allowed colonies free trade in 1840. Photos, drawings, newspaper cartoons explain improvements in judicial system, local government, railways and trade. Review questions included. French title available : LA DECISION DE LORD ELGIN.-

971.04
    Sir John A. Macdonald : part 1.
        prod. [Montreal?] : NFB, made 1959 : 1977.- dist. McI. 40 fr. : col. : 35 mm. & captions & teacher's manual. $9.00 (Early growth of Confederation : $36.00) ji

        1. Macdonald, John Alexander, Sir, 1815-1891.
        2. Politics and government 1841-1867.

        Traces the beginning of John A. Macdonald's career including the effect of the American Civil War on Canadian politics, Macdonald's role in Confederation, the Riel Rebellion, and the promise of a transcontinental railroad. Illustrated with drawings. French title available : SIR JOHN A. MACDONALD : PREMIER PARTIE.-

971.04
    Sir John A. Macdonald : part 2.
        prod.]Montreal?] : NFB, made 1959 : 1977.- dist. McI. 30 fr. : col. : 35 mm. & captions & teacher's manual. $9.00 (Early growth of Confederation : $36.00) ji

        1. Macdonald, John Alexander, Sir, 1815-1891.
        2. Canada - Politics and government - 1867-1896.

        Coloured drawings depict John A. Macdonald as a seasoned politician with his threefold National Policy and his success in completing the transcontinental railway to British Columbia. Includes the Northwest Rebellion, Riel's hanging and Macdonald's success in the election of 1891. Comprehensive when used with manual. French title available : SIR JOHN A. MACDONALD : DEUXIEME PARTIE.-

The Classified Catalogue

971.04

Sir John A. Macdonald (1ère partie).
prod. [Montreal?] : NFB, made 1965 : 1969.- dist. SEC 46 fr. : col. : 35 mm. & captions & teacher's manual. $9.00 (Les débuts de la Confederation : $36.00) ji

1. Macdonald, John Alexander, Sir, 1815-1891. 2. Canada - Politics and government, 1841-1867.

Traces the beginning of John A. Macdonald's career including the effect of American Civil War on Canadian politics, Macdonald's role in Confederation, the Riel Rebellion, and the promise of a transcontinental railroad. Illustrated with drawings. English title available : EARLY GROWTH OF CONFEDERATION.-

971.04

Sir John A. Macdonald (2e partie).
prod. [Montreal?] : NFB, made 1959 : 1965.- dist. SEC 24 fr. : col. : 35 mm. & captions & teacher's manual. $9.00 (Les débuts de la Confederation : $36.00) ji

1. Macdonald, John Alexander, Sir, 1815-1891. 2. Canada - Politics and government, - 1867-1896.

Coloured drawings depict John A. Macdonald as a seasoned politician with his threefold National Policy and his success in completing the transcontinental railway to British Columbia. Includes the Northwest Rebellion, Riel's hanging and Macdonald's success in the election of 1891. Comprehensive when used with manual. English title available : SIR JOHN A. MACDONALD : PART 2.-

971.05

1870 Rebellion.
prod. [Scarborough, Ont.] : SHN, 1977.- dist. PHM 94 fr. : b&w & col. : 35 mm. & cassette (23 min.) : auto. & aud. adv. sig. & teacher's guide. $39.60 (The Hard times of Louis Riel : $65.00) is

1. Red River Rebellion, 1869-1870. 2. Métis - History. 3. Riel, Louis David, 1844-1885.

Traces the history and problems of the Metis in Manitoba through the 1860's. Describes the events which led to the rise of Louis Riel and the Red River Rebellion. Contains details of Riel's background and education. Includes Riel's List of Rights and the Manitoba Act. Describes Riel's exile in America. Uses historical paintings and documents.-

971.05

1885 Rebellion.
prod. [Scarborough, Ont.] : SHN,#c1977.- dist. PHM 76 fr. : b&w & col. : 35 mm. & cassette (19 min.) : auto. & aud. adv. sig. & teacher's guide. $39.60 (The Hard times of Louis Riel : $65.00) is

1. Métis - History. 2. Riel, Louis David, 1844-1885. 3. Riel Rebellion, 1885.

Describes the hardships of the Metis settlement in Northern Saskatchewan and their trouble with land claims. Includes the support given by the Cree and Blackfoot tribes. Explains the military leadership of Gabriel Dumont and follows each event of the Rebellion until Riel's surrender, trial and execution. Contains many statements made by Riel and Sir John A. Macdonald. Uses historical documents and paintings.-

971.05

Big Bear, Poundmaker and Crowfoot.
prod. [Toronto] : NC, 1977.- dist. I.T.F. 98 fr. : b&w & col. : 35 mm. & cassette (28 min.) & 1 book, 5 assorted items & script. $25.00 (Métis and native uprisings and the land question) s

1. Riel Rebellion, 1885.

A description of the role played by these men during the Métis uprising and their subsequent trial, imprisonment and death. Discusses the effects of western settlement upon Indians, land problems, reserve question and representation in Canadian government. Illustrated with excellent photographs depicting Canadian Indian lifestyles of that time.-

971.05

Le Canada dans l'Empire Britannique.
prod. [Toronto] : Int. Cin., 1975.- dist. VEC 56 fr. : col. : 35 mm. & cassette (13 min.) : auto. & aud. adv. sig. & teacher's guide. $24.00 (Le Canada en guerre : l'histoire militaire d'un peuple pacifique : $86.00) i

1. World War, 1914-1918 - Canada. 2. Canada - History, Military. 3. Canada - History - 1867-1914.

Traces the growth and development of Canadian troops from the founding of the Northwest Mounted Police after Confederation to Canada's contrioution to both the South African and the First World Wars. Uses archival paintings, drawings, photos, and documents. English title available : CANADA IN THE BRITISH EMPIRE.-

The Classified Catalogue

971.05
    Canada in the British Empire.
        prod. [Toronto] : Int. Cin., 1974.- dist. VEC 56 fr. : col. : 35 mm. & cassette (12 min.) : auto. & aud. adv. sig. & teaching guide. $24.00 (Canadians at war : the military story of a peaceful people : $86.00) i

        1. World War, 1914-1918 - Canada.
        2. Canada - History, Military. 3. Canada - History - 1867-1914.

        Traces the growth and development of Canadian troops from the founding of the Northwest Mounted Police after Confederation to Canada's contribution to both the South African and the First World Wars. Uses archival paintings, drawings, photos, and documents. French title available : LE CANADA DANS L'EMPIRE BRITANNIQUE.-

971.05
    L'époque de Laurier (1ère partie).
        prod. [Montreal?] : NFB, made 1961 : 1973.- dist. SEC 41 fr. : b&w : 35 mm. & captions & teacher's manual. $9.00 (Les débuts de la Confederation : $36.00) ji

        1. Canada - History - 1867-1914. 2. The West, Canadian - History. 3. Laurier, Sir Wilfrid, 1841-1919.

        Authentic black and white photographs from the Public Archives portray the prosperity of the Laurier Era from 1896 to 1911. Describes the great migration to the West and the advancement in wheat production. English title available : THE LAURIER ERA : PART 1.-

971.05
    L'époque de Laurier (2e partie).
        prod. [Montreal?] : NFB, made 1961 : 1973.- dist. SEC 41 fr. : b&w : 35 mm. & captions. $9.00 (Les débuts de la Confederation : $36.00) ji

        1. Canada - History - 1867-1914. 2. Laurier, Sir Wilfrid, 1841-1919.

        Archival photographs illustrate the growth of industry in Canada during Sir Vilfrid Laurier's time. Discusses development of commercial activities, Maritime coal production, British Columbia fruit, fish and lumber and the advancement of communication and transportation. Examines Laurier's dedication to harmony between English and French-speaking Canadians. English title available : THE LAURIER ERA : PART 2. -

971.05
    The First Métis uprising, 1869-70.
        prod. [Toronto] : NC, 1977.- dist. I.T.F. 121 fr. : b&w & col. : 35 mm. & cassette (37 min.) & 1 book, 5 assorted items & script. $25.00 (Métis and native uprisings and the land question) s

        1. Red River Rebellion, 1869-1870. 2. Riel, Louis David, 1844-1885. 3. Métis - History.

        An account of the uprising, the people involved, and the consequences. Describes events leading up to rebellion, including hostilities between Métis and the Hudson's Bay Company, Canadian government, and settlers. Traces Louis Riel's life from childhood to years spent in Montana. Illustrated with maps, charts and numerous photographs.-

971.05
    The Laurier era : part 1.
        prod. [Montreal?] : NFB, 1961.- dist. McI. 35 fr. : b&w : 35 mm. & captions & teacher's manual. $9.00 (Early growth of Confederation : $36.00) ji

        1. The West, Canadian - History. 2. Laurier, Sir Wilfrid, 1841-1919. 3. Canada - History - 1867-1914.

        Authentic black and white photographs from the Public Archives portray the prosperity of the Laurier Era from 1896 to 1911. Describes the great migration to the West and the advancement in wheat production. French title available : L'EPOQUE DE LAURIER : PREMIERE PARTIE.-

971.05
    Macdonald to Borden.
        prod. [Scarborough, Ont.] : SHN, [1972] dist. PHM 106 fr. : b&w & col. : 35 mm. & cassette (30 min.) : auto. & aud. adv. sig. & teacher's guide. $39.60 (Canada's Prime Ministers : a matter of style : $75.90) is

        1. Prime Ministers - Canada. 2. Canada - Politics and government - 1867-1911.

        A broad overview of Canada's prime ministers Macdonald and Laurier. Uses an anecdotal approach and is illustrated with contemporary photographs, cartoons and headlines.-

The Classified Catalogue

971.05
    The Second Métis uprising, 1885.
        prod. [Toronto] : NC, 1977.- dist. I.T.F. 138 fr. : b&w & col. : 35 mm. & cassette (45 min.) & 1 book, 5 assorted items & script. $25.00 (Métis and native uprsisings and the land question) s

        1. Métis - History. 2. Riel, David Louis, 1844-1885. 3. Riel Rebellion, 1885.

        A thorough coverage of 1885 uprising, including reasons for second outbreak. Describes relations between settlers, Indians and Métis. Gives detailed account of battles, prominent figures involved, and capture and trial of Louis Riel. A unique presentation containing rare photograhs taken during the uprising.-

971.06
    Borden to St. Laurent.
        prod. [Scarborough, Ont.] : SHN, [1972] dist. PHM 80 fr. : b&w & col. : 35 mm. & cassette (28 min.) : auto. & aud. adv. sig. & teacher's guide. $39.60 (Canada's Prime Ministers : a matter of style : $75.90) is

        1. Prime Ministers - Canada. 2. Canada - Politics and government - 1911-1948.

        Surveys the governments of Meighen, Mackenzie King, and Bennett, describing the style and approach of each prime minister. Uses anecdotes, actual voice recordings, contemporary photos, cartoons and headlines.-

971.06
    Conscription crisis, 1917.
        prod. [Toronto] : NCM, 1977.- dist. ITF 2 filmstrips (88:82 fr.) : b&w & col. : 35 mm. & 2 cassettes (15:13 min.) : auto. & aud. adv. sig. & script. $57.50 s

        1. World War, 1914-1918 - Canada. 2. Military service, Compulsory.

        Describes and explains the conscription issue and its consequences. Discusses events that led to passing of Military Service Bill. Photographs depict contrast between Canada's romantic illusions of war and the actual horrors of trench warfare. Sound accompaniment recreates mood of era and includes excerpts from personal accounts. Production in two parts, for viewing convenience.-

971.06
    Defending Canada in a changing world.
        prod. [Toronto] : Int. Cin., 1974.- dist. VEC 46 fr. : col. : 35 mm. & cassette (10 min.) : auto. & aud. adv. sig. & teaching guide. $24.00 (Canadians at war : the military story of a peaceful people : $86.00) i

        1. Canada - History, Military.

        Examines the present age of nuclear warfare, and the international role of Canada's armed forces during peace time, including our commitments to NATO and the UN. French title available : LA DEFENSE DU CANADA DANS UN MONDE EN EVOLUTION.-

971.06
    The Diefenbaker-Pearson years : part II :
        prod. [Toronto] : SHN, 1973.- dist. PHM 92 fr. : b&w & col. : 35 mm. & cassette (28 min.) : auto. & aud. adv. sig. & guide. $39.60 (The Diefenbaker-Pearson years : $64.00) s

        1. Canada - Politics and government - 1957-1963. 2. Pearson, Lester Bowles, 1897-1972.

        Describes Pearson's education and background. Uses many actual voice recordings and compares Pearson with Diefenbaker. Discusses the National Flag debate and effects of scandals on the Liberal government.-

971.06
    The Diefenbaker-Pearson years : part 1 :
        prod. [Toronto] : SHN, 1973.- dist. PHM 104 fr. : b&w & col. : 35 mm. & cassette (26 min.) : auto. & aud. adv. sig. & study guide. $39.60 (The Diefenbaker-Pearson years : $64.35) s

        1. Canada - Politics and government - 1957-1963. 2. Diefenbaker, John G . 1895-

        Deals with workings of the parliamentary system, majority and minority government, and election issues. Traces Diefenbaker's background and important stages of his term as Prime Minister.-

The Classified Catalogue

971.06
    From war to war.
        prod. [Toronto] : Int. Cin., 1974.- dist. VEC 56 fr. : col. : 35 mm. & cassette (13 min.) : auto. & aud. adv. sig. & teaching guide. $24.00 (Canadians at war : the military story of a peaceful people : $86.00) i

        1. World War, 1939-1945 - Canada.
        2. Canada - History, Military.

        Discusses events in Canada and the world which led to Canada's involvement in the Second World War. French title available : D'UNE GUERRE A L'AUTRE.-

971.06
    The Great Depression.
        prod. [Scarborough, Ont.] : SHN, 1973.- dist. PHM 110 fr. : col. : 35 mm. & cassette (25 min.) : auto. & aud. adv. sig. & teacher's guide. $39.60 is

        1. Depressions, Economic.

        Explains reasons for the stock market crash in 1929. Describes unemployment, hunger, and riots of the thirties. Shows rise of unions.-

971.06
    St. Laurent to the present.
        prod. [Scarborough, Ont.] : SHN, [1972] dist. PHM 75 fr. : b&w & col. : 35 mm. & cassette (22 min.) : auto. & aud. adv. sig. & teacher's guide. $39.60 (Canada's Prime Ministers : a matter of style : $75.90) is

        1. Prime Ministers - Canada. 2. Canada - Politics and government - 1948- .

        Discusses the styles and contributions of St. Laurent, Diefenbaker, Pearson and Trudeau. Invites comparisons of leaders and their accomplishments. Uses actual voice recordings.-

971.1
    Le Fort Langley : carrefour de la côte ouest.
        prod. [Toronto] : Int. Cin., 1975.- dist. VEC 71 fr. : b&w & col. : 35 mm. & cassette (14 min.) : auto. & aud. adv. sig. & teacher's guide. $24.00 (La Traite des pelleteries : $45.00) jis

        1. Fur trade - History. 2. Fort Langley, B.C. - History.

        Describes the origin of Fort Langley and its importance to the Hudson's Bay Company in the early days of fur trade. Photos of the restored fort provide insight into life at the fort as it was in the past. English title available : FORT LANGLEY : GATEWAY TO THE WEST.-

971.1
    Fort Langley : gateway to the west.
        prod. [Toronto] : Int. Cin., 1975.- dist. VEC 71 fr. : col. : 35 mm. & cassette (14 min.) : auto. & aud. adv. sig. & teacher's manual. $24.00 (Fur-trade outposts : $45.00) jis

        1. Fur trade - History. 2. Fort Langley, B.C. - History.

        Describes the origin of Fort Langley and its importance to the Hudson's Bay Company in the early days of fur trade. Photos of the restored fort provide a glimpse of life at the fort in the past. French title available : LE FORT LANGLEY : CARREFOUR DE LA COTE OUEST.-

971.1
    Gold rush : pioneer mining in British Columbia.
        prod. [Montreal?] : NFB, 1967.- dist. McI. 46 fr. : b&w & col. : 35 mm. & captions & teacher's guide. $9.00 (Pioneer life : $72.00) jis

        1. Gold mines and mining - History.

        Describes the struggle of the prospectors on the journey to the British Columbia goldfields in 1858. Depicts the primitive means of transportation and the building of the Caribou Wagon Road from Yale, British Columbia, to Barkerville, British Columbia. Uses photographs of prospectors, local townspeople and the gold mines. French title available : LE COURSE A L'OR : LES PREMIERS MINEURS DE LA COLOMBIE-BRITANNIQUE.-

The Classified Catalogue

971.1
    The Town of Fort Steele.
        prod. [Montreal?] : NFB, 1971.- dist. McI. 40 fr. : b&w & col. : 35 mm. & captions & notes. $9.00 (Image Canada : $45.00) i

        1. Fort Steele, B.C. - History.

    Portrays the reconstruction of the town of Fort Steele, an abandoned western boom mining town at the turn of the century. Photos past and present are used. French title available : LA VILLE DE FORT STEELE.-

971.1
    La ville de Fort Steele.
        prod. [Montreal?] : NFB, 1970.- dist. SEC 45 fr. : b&w & col. : 35 mm. & captions & notes. $9.00 (Image du Canada) i

        1. Fort Steele, B.C. - History.

    Portrays the reconstruciton of the town of Fort Steele, an abandoned western boom mining town at the turn of the century. Photos past and present are used. English title available : THE TOWN OF FORT STEELE.-

971.14
    Saguenay-Lake St. Jean - the river.
        prod. [Scarborough, Ont.] : R.B.M., 1976.- dist. ETHOS 54 fr. : b&w & col. : 35 mm. & cassette (10 min.) : auto. & aud. adv. sig. & teacher's manual. $19.00 (Regional studies : $138.00) ji

        1. Saguenay-Lac Saint-Jean region, Que. - Description and travel.

    Describes aluminum making and forestry, the main industries of the region. Also mentions its transportation network, sports, recreation, and tourism.-

971.14
    Saguenay-Lake St. John - the Lake Region.
        prod. [Scarborough, Ont.] : R.B.M., 1976.- dist. ETHOS 50 fr. : b&w & col. : 35 mm. & cassette (8 min.) : auto. & aud. adv. sig. & teacher's manual. $19.00 (Regional studies : $138.00) ji

        1. Saguenay-Lac Saint-Jean region, Que. - Description and travel.

    A number of the communities found in the Lake St. John area, and the industries supporting them, are briefly described. Included are Roberval (agriculture and sawmilling), St. Prime (dairying), and Dolbeau (pulp annd paper). -

971.15
    Saint John River Valley - Edmunston to Kings Landing.
        prod. [Scarborough, Ont.] : R.B.M., 1976.- dist. ETHOS 45 fr. : b&w & col. : 35 mm. & cassette (8 min.) : auto. & aud. adv. sig. & teacher's manual. $19.00 (Regional studies : $138.00) ji

        1. New Brunswick - Description and travel.

    Examines the way of life, industries, and type of agriculture to be found along the shores of the St. John River between Edmunston and Kings Landing.-

971.15
    Saint John River Valley - Mactaquac to Saint John.
        prod. [Scarborough, Ont.] : R.B.M., 1976.- dist. ETHOS 44 fr. : b&w & col. : 35 mm. & cassette (9 min.) : auto. & aud. adv. sig. & teacher's manual. $19.00 (Regional studies : $138.00) ji

        1. New Brunswick - Description and travel.

    Follows the Saint John River from the Mactaquac Dam to Saint John, examining the variety of agricultural and industrial activities found along the way.-

971.2
    Discovering the land.
        prod. [Scarborough, Ont.] : SHN, 1972.- dist. PHM 92 fr. : b&w & col. : 35 mm. & cassette (24 min.) : auto. & aud. adv. sig. & teacher's guide. $39.60 (Canada's North : $59.40) i

        1. Arctic regions - History.

    Outlines the history of the Arctic including the Eskimos and Indians, Vikings, and explorers' attempts to find a northwest passage. Deals with Hudson's Bay Company, Mackenzie, Franklin, Frobisher, Davis, Hearne and Amundsen, with maps showing routes. Historic paintings, portraits and archival photos are used.-

The Classified Catalogue

971.2
Discovering the people.
prod. [Scarborough, Ont.] : SHN, 1972.- dist. PHM 1 filmstrip : b&w & col. : 35 mm. & cassette (24 min.) : auto. & aud. adv. sig. (Canada's North : $59.40) is

1. Arctic regions - History.

Discusses the changes in the North, following the arrival of the white man. Includes development of towns, discovery of gold and oil, weather stations, DEW-line. Deals with resources and ecology in the North.
Illustrated with early photos, maps and modern colour photos.-

971.2
Frontier heritage.
prod. [Toronto] : Int. Cin., 1974.- dist. VEC 59 fr. : b&w & col. : 35 mm. & cassette (14 min.) : auto. & aud. adv. sig. & teaching guide. $24.00 (Canada's living heritage : $86.00) ji

1. The West, Canadian - History.

A look at the early settlement of the Prairie Provinces and the west coast, including a brief history of the Yukon gold rush and the major early trading companies. Uses paintings, drawings, and photographs. French title available : LE PATRIMOINE DES PIONNIERS.-

971.2
Growing up.
prod. [Scarborough, Ont.] : SHN, 1972.- dist. PHM 85 fr. : col. : 35 mm. & cassette (17 min.) : auto. & aud. adv. sig. & teacher's guide. $39.60 (The Opening of the Canadian west : $67.00) is

1. The West, Canadian - History.

Describes the contribution of the West to the First World War, post-war strikes, effects of the Depression and development of the C.C.F. and Social Credit parties. Deals with the situation in the West today in terms of natural resources and growing communities. Includes many historical photos.-

971.2
Moving in.
prod. [Scarborough, Ont.] : SHN, 1972.- dist. PHM 64 fr. : col. : 35 mm. & cassette. (11 min.) : auto. & aud. adv. sig. & teacher's guide. $39.60 (The Opening of the Canadian west : $67.00) is

1. The West, Canadian - History.

Describes settlement of the West from 1885. Includes the Indians, Metis, and settlers from Montreal and Ontario. Deals with Laurier and the Sifton policy, the effect of the railroads, and the growth of the new cities of the West. Historical photographs and maps can be studied without the narration.-

971.2
Pioneer life on the Prairies (1812-1900).
prod. [Montreal?] : NFB, 1972.- dist. McI. 65 fr. : b&w & col. : 35 mm. & captions & notes. $9.00 (Pioneer life : $72.00) ji

1. Frontier and pioneer life - Prairie provinces. 2. Prairie provinces - History.

A chronological depiction of the growth of the prairies from the days of the Selkirk settlers. Uses maps, colourful drawings, old photographs, and quotations. Printed notes are necessary for viewing. French title available : LES PIONNIERS DES PRAIRIES (1812-1900).-

971.2
Pioneer life on the Prairies (1900-1912).
prod. [Montreal?] : NFB, 1972.- dist. McI. 61 fr. : b&w & col. : 35 mm. & captions & notes. $9.00 (Pioneer life : $72.00) ji

1. Frontier and pioneer life - Prairie Provinces.

Old photographs, maps, and quotations portray the development of agriculture on the prairies, the Homestead era, Doukhobors and Barr colonists. Filmstrip notes, providing all background information, must be consulted. French title available : LES PIONNIERS DES PRAIRIES (1900-1912).-

971.2
    Les pioneers des Prairies (1812-1900).
        prod. [Montreal?] : NFB, 1972.- dist. SEC 71 fr. : col. : 35 mm. & captions & notes. $9.00 (Les pionniers : $72.00) ji

        1. Frontier and pioneer life - Prairie provinces. 2. Prairie provinces - History.

        A chronological depiction of the growth of the prairies from the days of the Selkirk settlers. Uses maps, colourful drawings, old photographs, and quotations. Printed notes are necessary for viewing. English title available : PIONEER LIFE ON THE PRAIRIES (1812-1900).-

971.2
    Staking a claim.
        prod. [Scarborough, Ont.] : SHN, 1972.- dist. PHM 72 fr. : col. : 35 mm. & cassette (18 min.) : auto. & aud. adv. sig. & teacher's guide. $39.60 (The Opening of the Canadian West : $67.00) is

        1. The West, Canadian - History.

        Deals with early exploration of the West. Includes Hudson's Bay Company, the 49th Parallel, Oregon territory, Confederation and the C.P.R., using historical photographs and maps.-

971.2
    White men in the Arctic.
        prod. [Toronto] : Int. Cin., 1971.- dist. VEC 51 fr. : col. : 35 mm. & 4 pamphlets, 2 maps, 1 teacher's guide, 1 transparency & captions. $12.00 (The Living Arctic : $54.00) ji

        1. Natural resources - Arctic regions. 2. Arctic regions - History.

        Covers the white man's exploitation of the North for its natural resources by early European explorers, fur traders, gold miners, as well as the present day search for fuel resources.-

971.24
    Le Fort Walsh dans les collines Cyprès.
        prod. [Montreal?] : NFB, 1970.- dist. SEC 46 fr. : b&w & col. : 35 mm. & captions & teacher's guide. $9.00 (Image du Canada) ji

        Recounts the history of Fort Walsh, established by N.W.M.P., and describes the Cypress Hills region located on the Saskatchewan-Alberta border, with photos, old and new. English title available : FORT WALSH IN THE CYPRESS HILLS.-

971.24
    Fort Walsh in the Cypress Hills.
        prod. [Montreal?] : NFB, 1970.- dist. McI. 46 fr. : col. : 35 mm. & captions & teacher's guide. $9.00 (Image Canada : $45.00)

        1. Fort Walsh, Sask. - History. 2. Cypress Hills region, Sask.

        Recounts the history of Fort Walsh, established by N.W.M.P., and describes the Cypress Hills region located on the Sasktchewan-Alberta border, with photos, old and new. French title available : LE FORT WALSH DANS LES COLLINES CYPRES.-

971.27
    Lower Fort Garry : legacy of the fur trade.
        prod. [Toronto] : Int. Cin., 1975.- dist. VEC &79 fr. : b&w & col. : 35 mm. & cassette (14 min.) : auto. & aud. adv. sig. & teacher's manual. $24.00 (Fur-trade outposts : $45.00) jis

        1. Fur trade - History. 2. Lower Fort Garry, Man. - History. 3. Manitoba - History.

        Traces Lower Fort Garry from early days of fur trading through the periods of the Riel Rebellion, the Northwest Mounted Police and the creation of the province of Manitoba. Shows many scenes of the fort today as it is for tourists and students. French title available : LE PETIT FORT GARRY : L'HERITAGE DE LA TRAITE DES PELLETERIES.-

971.3
   Activities in pioneer days.
   prod. [Toronto] : & R, 1976.- dist. B & R 40 fr. : col. : 35 mm. & cassette (15 min.) : auto. & aud. adv. sig. & teacher's manual & script. $18.00 (Canadian pioneer days : $128.00) pji

   1. Frontier and pioneer life - Ontario.

   Examines some of the services in a pioneer community, including the village store, boot and shoe shop, printer, saddlery, and local blacksmith. Also looks at some agricultural products activities, such as tending cattle and raising chickens. Uses photographs of Black Creek Pioneer Village.-

971.3
   The Cabinet maker.
   prod. [Rexdale, Ont.] : McI. 1978.- dist. McI. 30 fr. : col. : 35 mm. & cassette (8 min.) : auto. & aud. adv. sig. & teacher's manual. $19.00 (The Pioneer community at work : $114.00) ji

   1. Frontier and pioneer life - Ontario.
   2. Cabinet work.

   The village cabinet maker describes the role of his trade in the pioneer community. Stresses skills and knowledge necessary to operate tools and machinery. Shown are toys and furniture indicative of period.
   Photographed at Black Creek Pioneer Village.-

971.3
   Canada's pioneer life & customs.
   prod. [Weston, Ont.] : B & R Products, 1975.- dist. Lea. 39 fr. : col. : 35 mm. & captions & teacher's guide. $9.00 ji

   1. Frontier and pioneer life - Ontario.

   Photographs of buildings, furniture, tools and clothing from Black Creek Pioneer Village in Toronto portray life in 19th century Canada. Questions inserted to stimulate discussion suggests classroom viewing with a teacher.-

971.3
   Canadian Christmas : Christmas decorations.
   prod. [Toronto] : B & R, 1973.- dist. B & R 21 fr. : col. : 35 mm. & cassette (5 min.) : auto. & aud. adv. sig. & script & teacher's manual. $16.00 (Canadian holidays : $180.00) pj

   1. Frontier and pioneer life - Ontario.
   2. Christmas decorations. 3. Christmas - Canada - History.

   Photographs taken at Black Creek Pioneer Village show Christmas decorations with which an early Canadian home might be decorated. Emphasizes making the decorations by hand with available materials. Includes directions for making a pomander.-

971.3
   Canadian christmas : festive foods.
   prod. [Toronto] : B & R, 1973.- dist. B & R 20 fr. : col. : 35 mm. & cassette (5 min.) : auto. & aud. adv. sig. & script & teacher's manual. $16.00 (Canadian holidays : $180.00) pj

   1. Frontier and pioneer life - Ontario.
   2. Christmas - Canada - History.

   Describes the foods a Canadian pioneer family would be likely to enjoy on Christmas day, with emphasis on the use of local produce. Illustrated with photographs taken at Black Creek Pioneer Village.-

971.3
   Country life.
   prod. [Toronto] : B & R, 1976.- dist. B & R 25 fr. : col. : 35 mm. & cassette (10 min.) : auto. & aud. adv. sig. & teacher's manual & script. $18.00 (Canadian pioneer days : $128.00) pji

   1. Frontier and pioneer life - Ontario.

   A visit to the home of a well-to-do landowner of the 1840's helps to show the style of living and way of life of wealthier Eastern Canadians at that time. Illustrated with photographs taken at Black Creek Pioneer Village.-

The Classified Catalogue

971.3
    Crafts.
        prod. [Toronto] : M-L, 1970.- dist. Sch. Ser. or Vint. 46 fr. : col. : 35 mm. & cassette (11 min.) : auto. & aud. adv. sig. & teacher's guide. $16.50 (Pioneer community : $85.00) ji

        1. Frontier and pioneer life - Ontario.

        Shows pioneer women practising crafts, such as spinning wool, weaving cloth, and quilting. Rug making and candle making are also demonstrated in an attempt to show how these crafts contributed to the comfort and welfare of the pioneers. French title available : LES METIERS.-

971.3
    Early pioneer life in Upper Canada.
        prod. [Montreal?] : NFB, 1967.- dist. McI. 45 fr. : col. : 35 mm. & captions & notes. $9.00 (Pioneer life : $72.00) j

        1. Frontier and pioneer life - Ontario.

        Drawings examine the origins of the pioneers in Upper Canada, and the hard life they endured. Describes how homes were built, land was cleared, food was gathered and stored, and the method of making the family's clothing. Includes recreational activities. French title available : LES PIONNIERS DU HAUT-CANADA.-

971.3
    La Famille.
        prod. [Toronto] : M-L, 1972.- dist. Sch. Ser. or Vint. 47 fr. : col. : 35 mm. & cassette (13 min.) : auto. & aud. adv. sig. & teacher's guide. $16.50 (La Vie quotidienne des pioneers du Haut-Canada : $85.00) ji

        1. Frontier and pioneer life. - Ontario.

        Photos taken at Upper Canada Village, Ontario, show a pioneer family establishing a new home. Narration describes what the home was like, the cooking and sewing, and how the pioneers entertained themselves. English title available : FAMILY LIFE.-

971.3
    Family life.
        prod. [Toronto] : M-L, 1970.- dist. Sch. Ser. or Vint. 47 fr. : col. : 35 mm. & cassette (13 min.) : auto. & aud. adv. sig. & teacher's guide. $16.50 (Pioneer community : $85.00) ji

        1. Frontier and pioneer life - Ontario.

        Photos taken at Upper Canada Village, Ontario, show a pioneer family establishing a new home. Narration describes what the home was like, the cooking and sewing, and how pioneers entertained themselves. French title available : LA FAMILLE.-

971.3
    Farm life.
        prod. [Toronto] : M-L, 1970.- dist. Sch. Ser. or Vint. 47 fr. : col. : 35 mm. & cassette (12 min.) : auto. & aud. adv. sig. & teacher's guide. $16.50 (Pioneer community : $85.00) ji

        1. Frontier and pioneer life - Ontario.

        Emphasizes the importance of farming to the pioneers as each step from preparing the soil for planting to the final harvest is shown. Photos taken at Upper Canada Village include scenes of grinding wheat into flour and the making of linens from flax. French title available : LA FERME.-

971.3
    Foods.
        prod. [Toronto] : M-L, 1970.- dist. Sch. Ser. or Vint. 46 fr. : col. : 35 mm. & cassette (11 min.) : auto. & aud. adv. sig. & teacher's guide. $16.50 (Pioneer community : $85.00) ji

        1. Frontier and pioneer life - Ontario.

        Photos taken at Upper Canada Village, Ontario illustrate pioneer cooking methods of preserving food, and the cutting of meat. Bread making and butter making are discussed in detail. French title available : LE FOYER.-

The Classified Catalogue

971.3
Going to Canada : in the backwoods.
prod. [Toronto] : NCM, 1977.- dist. I.T.F. 150 fr. : b&w & col. : 35 mm. & cassette (25 min.) : auto. & aud. adv. sig. & script. $47.50 (Victorians : $95.00) s

1. Frontier and pioneer life - Ontario.

A photographic essay depicting the harsh realities of Ontario homesteading in the 1880's. Narration in form of a woman's diary gives insight to personal impressions and hardships. Archival Victorian drawings and photographs cover all aspects of pioneer life in Ontario.-

971.3
The Growth, the decline.
prod. [Thunder Bay, Ont.] : CP, 1975.- dist. CP 50 fr. : col. : 35 mm. & captions & reading script. $14.50 (Thunder Bay's historic old Fort William) i

1. Fort William, Ont. - History.

A detailed account of the growth of Fort William from 1679 to 1881. Discusses importance of beaver, pelts, and structural materials required for construction of the fort. Includes specific background information on several buildings in the fort, and describes the importance of the Red River Settlement.-

971.3
L'Histoire de Sainte-Marie-des-Hurons : part2
prod. [Toronto] : RQM, 1975.- dist. Lea. 41 fr. : col. : 35 mm. & captions & teacher's guide. $9.00 (L'Histoire de Sainte-Marie-des-Hurons : $17.50) ji

1. Jesuits - Missions. 2. Ste. Marie among the Hurons, Ont. - Description.

Provides general coverage of Ste.-Marie-Among-the-Hurons as it is today, including buildings and aritsans. For use in conjunction with Part I, or as a prelude to a visit to Ste.-Marie. English title available : SAINTE-MARIE AMONG THE HURONS.-

971.3
L'Histoire de Sainte-Marie-des-Hurons : part I.
prod. [Toronto] : RQM, 1975.- dist. Lea. 44 fr. : col. : 35 mm. & captions & teacher's guide. $9.00 (L'Histoire de Sainte-Marie-des-Hurons : $17.50) ji

1. Jesuits - Missions. 2. Ste. Marie among the Hurons, Ont. - Description.

A basic outline of what Ste.-Marie-Among-the-Hurons is, and how it came to be. The pictures are clear and authentic looking: captions are to the point, emphatic but not always easily legible. Includes maps. English title available : SAINTE-MARIE AMONG THE HURONS.-

971.3
Life in the old Fort.
prod. [Thunder Bay, Ont.] : CP, 1975.- dist. CP 54 fr. : col. : 35 mm. & captions & reading script. $14.50 (Thunder Bay's historic old Fort William) i

1. Fort William, Ont. - History.

Provides a pictorial study of the day-to-day activities that were characteristic of life in Fort William, during the existence of the North West Company.-

971.3
Life in Upper Canada in the 1860's.
prod. [Montreal?] : NFB, 1967.- dist. McI. 36 fr. : col. : 35 mm. & captions & printed notes. $9.00 (Pioneer life $72.00) pj

1. Frontier and pioneer life - Ontario.

Uses photographs to illustrate everyday life in a pioneer village. Includes family life, school life, the farmer's work, tradespeople, such as the blacksmith, carpenter and miller, and community life. Photographed at Upper Canada Village, Morrisburg, Ontario. French title available : LA VIE DANS LE HAUT-CANADA 1860.-

The Classified Catalogue

971.3
   "Mary Davidson's home".
      prod. [Toronto] : B&R, 1976.- dist. B&R 24 fr. : col. : 35 mm. & cassette (7 min.) : auto & aud. adv. sig. & teacher's manual & guide sheet. $18.00 (Our living pioneer ancestors) pji

      1. Frontier and pioneer life - Ontario. 2. Lighting - History.

      Describes heating and lighting methods in early Canadian home. Candles of tallow and paraffin, candle holders, rush lamps, kerosene and gas lamps, fireplaces, and iron stoves are all mentioned. Illustrated with photos taken at a model pioneer village.-

971.3
   Les Métiers.
      prod. [Toronto] : M-L, 1972.- dist. Sch. Ser. or Vint. 46 fr. : col. : 35 mm. & cassette (11 min.) : auto. & aud. adv. sig. & teacher's guide. $16.50 (La vie quotidienne des pioneers du Haut-Canada : $85.00) ji

      1. Frontier and pioneer life - Ontario.

      Shows pioneer women practising crafts, such as spinning wool, weaving cloth, and quilting. Rug making and candle making are also demonstrated in an attempt to show how these crafts contributed to the comfort and welfare of the pioneers. English title available : CRAFTS.-

971.3
   The Mill.
      prod. [Rexdale, Ont.] : McI. 1978.- dist. cI. 37 fr. : col. : 35 mm. & cassette (8 min.) : auto. & aud. adv. sig. & teacher's manual. $19.00 (The Pioneer community at work : $114.00) ji

      1. Frontier and pioneer life - Ontario. 2. Flour mills.

      Close-up photos show how numerous mechanisms inside a mill work to grind wheat into flour. Indicates importance of location, use of water and horse power, and role of miller in community.-

971.3
   The Newspaper business.
      prod. [Rexdale, Ont.] : McI. 1978.- dist. McI. 38 fr. : col. : 35 mm. & cassette (8 min.) : auto. & aud. adv. sig. & teacher's manual. $19.00 (The Pioneer community at work : $114.00) ji

      1. Newspapers. 2. Firearms. 3. Leather work. 4. Frontier and pioneer life - Ontario.

      Emphasis here is on the printer's role as soliciter of potential advertisers in community, with only brief coverage of printing process. Included are visits to the gunsmith and saddle-harness maker, showing gun construction and tooling in leather. Photographed at Black Creek Pioneer Village.-

971.3
   Ontario's heritage.
      prod. [Toronto] : Int. Cin., 1974.- dist. VEC 55 fr. : b&w & col. : 35 mm. & cassette (13 min.) : auto. & aud. adv. sig. & teaching guide. $24.00 (Canada's living heritage : $86.00) ji

      1. Ontario - History.

      Briefly describes the early history of Upper Canada with the use of paintings, drawings and photographs of historic Ontario figures, homes, and forts. French title available : LE PATRIMOINE ONTARIEN.-

971.3
   Ontario's heritage.
      prod. [Toronto] : Int. Cin. 1974.- dist. VEC 55 fr. : b&w & col. : 35 mm. & cassette (13 min.) : auto. & aud. adv. sig. & teacher's guide. $24.00 (Canada's living heritage : $86.00) ji

      1. Ontario - History.

      Briefly describes the early history of Upper Canada with the use of paintings, drawings and photographs of historic Ontario figures, homes, and forts. French title available : LE PATRIMOINE ONTARIEN.-

The Classified Catalogue

971.3
Pioneer Christmas.
prod. [Toronto] : B & R, 1976.- dist. B & R 31 fr. : col. : 35 mm. & cassette (16 min.) : auto. & aud. adv. sig. & reading script. $18.00 (Canadian pioneer days : $128.00) pji

1. Frontier and pioneer life - Ontario.
2. Christmas - Canada - History.

The celebration of Christmas in pioneer days is discussed with emphasis on the way available resources, technology, popular fads, and religious beliefs influenced the food, decorations, and activities of the time.-

971.3
The Pioneer community.
prod. [Rexdale, Ont.] : McI., 1978.- dist. McI. 33 fr. : col. : 35 mm. & cassette (8 min.) : auto. & aud. adv. sig. & teacher's manual. $19.00 (The Pioneer community at work : $114.00) ji

1. Frontier and pioneer life - Ontario.

A general overview of the people, buildings and industries typical of an early Canadian pioneering community. Emphasizes interdependence among settlers and effects of social and technological change upon industries. Photographed entirely at Black Creek Pioneer Village.-

971.3
The Pioneer community.
prod. [Montreal?] : NFB, made 1966 : 1976.- dist. McI. 37 fr. : col. : 35 mm. & captions & teacher's manual. $9.00 (Pioneer life) ji

1. Frontier and pioneer life - Ontario.

A description of the development of a pioneer community from the first farm and log house, to the mill, sawmill, and the small shops that were established near the mill. Examines the tradesmen in the community, the education system, and the social activities of the people, using photos with authentic costumes. Compares a pioneer community with a modern one. French title available : UN VILLAGE DU HAUT CANADA.-

971.3
Pioneer entertainment.
prod. [Toronto] : B & R, 1976.- dist. B & R 23 fr. : col. : 35 mm. & cassette (9 min.) : auto. & aud. adv. sig. & teacher's manual & script. $18.00 (Canadian pioneer days : $128.00) pji

1. Frontier and pioneer life - Ontario.

A tour through the village inn, centre of entertainment for the pioneer community, highlights the factors that affected early nineteenth century social life in Eastern Canada, including climate, transportation, and community attitudes. Uses photographs of restored inn.-

971.3
Pioneer family life.
prod. [Toronto] : B & R, 1976.- dist. B & R 36 fr. : col. : 35 mm. & cassette (12 min.) : auto. & aud. adv. sig. & teacher's manual & script. $18.00 (Canadian pioneer days : $128.00) pji

1. Frontier and pioneer life - Ontario.

Highlights many of the factors affecting family life in the early nineteenth century in this tour of a restored early 19th century home in Eastern Canada.-

971.3
Pioneer homes and schools in Eastern Canada.
prod. [Toronto] : RP, 1957.- dist. McI. 55 fr. : b&w : 35 mm. & captions & teacher's manual. $9.00 ji

1. Frontier and pioneer life - Ontario.

Black and white drawings depict scenes from the 1830's to the 1850's. Home scenes show building a log cabin, the bake-oven, making maple syrup, candles and soap, weaving and quilting. School scenes include a flogging and a spelling match.-

The Classified Catalogue

971.3
Pioneer inventions.
prod. [Toronto] : B & R, 1976.- dist. B & R 25 fr. : col. : 35 mm. & cassette (14 min.) : auto. & aud. adv. sig. & teacher's manual & reading script. $18.00 (Canadian pioneer days : $128.00) pji

1. Frontier and pioneer life - Ontario.

Emphasis is placed on technology and its effects on community life in this look at some common items found at Black Creek Pioneer Village-a fireplace with its implements, an iron, candles, and a broom-making machine. Also shows the sawmill, woollen mill, and the different types of transportation.-

971.3
Les pionniers du Haut-Canada.
prod. [Montreal?] : NFB, 1967.- dist. SEC 47 fr. : col. : 35 mm. & captions & notes. $9.00 (Les pionniers : $72.00) pj

1. Frontier and pioneer life - Ontario.

Drawings examine the origins of the pioneers in Upper Canada, and the hard life they endured. Describes how homes were built, land was cleared, food was gathered and stored, and the method of making the family's clothing. Includes recreational activities. English title available : EARLY PIONEER LIFE IN UPPER CANADA.-

971.3
Sainte-Marie-among-the-Hurons : part I.
prod. [Toronto] : RQM., 1975.- dist. Lea. 44 fr. : col. : 35 mm. & captions & teacher's guide. $9.00 (Sainte Marie among the Hurons : $17.50) ji

1. Jesuits - Missions. 2. Ste. Marie among the Hurons, Ont. - Description.

A basic outline of what Ste.-Marie-Among-the-Hurons is, and how it came to be. The pictures are clear and authentic looking; captions are to the point, emphatic but not always easily legible. Includes maps. French title available : L'HISTOIRE DE SAINTE-MARIE-DES-HURONS : PART 1.-

971.3
Sainte-Marie-among-the-Hurons.
prod. [Montreal?] : NFB, 1969.- dist. McI. 45 fr. : col. : 35 mm. & captions & teacher's manual. $9.00 (New France : exploration and growth : $54.00) pjis

1. Jesuits - Missions. 2. Huron Indians. 3. Ste. Marie-among-the-Hurons, Ont. - Description.

Maps and photographs of the reconstruction at Midland, Ontario illustrate the Jesuit settlement of Sainte-Marie, including the chapel, residence and cook-house. Describes the first waterway with locks built by the Jesuits. Examines the Indian compound with its church, hospital, and houses. French title available : SAINTE-MARIE-AUX-HURONS.-

971.3
Sainte-Marie-aux-Hurons.
prod. [Montreal?] : NFB, 1969.- dist. SEC 49 fr. : col. : 35 mm. & captions & teacher's manual. $9.00 pjis

1. Jesuits - Missions. 2. Huron Indians. 3. Ste. Marie-among-the-Hurons, Ont. - Desicrption.

Maps and photographs of the reconstruction at Midland, Ontario illustrate the Jesuit settlement of Sainte-Marie, including the chapel, residence and cookhouse. Describes the first waterway with locks built by the Jesuits. Examines the Indian compound with its church, hospital, and houses. English title available : SAINTE-MARIE-AMONG-THE-HURONS.-

971.3
School and recreation.
prod. [Toronto] : M-L, 1970.- dist. Sch. Ser. or Vint. 46 fr. : col. : 35 mm. & cassette (11 min.) : auto. & aud. adv. sig. & teacher's guide. $16.50 (Pioneer community : $85.00) ji

1. Frontier and pioneer life - Ontario.

Photos taken at Upper Canada Village depict learning in a one-room school. A quilting bee and a wedding are shown as forms of entertainment for the pioneers. French title available : L'ECOLE ET LES LOISIRS.-

The Classified Catalogue

971.3
- Thanksgiving foods.
  prod. [Toronto] : B & R, 1973.- dist. B & R 17 fr. : col. : 35 mm. & cassette (5 min.) : auto. & aud. adv. sig. & teacher's manual. $16.00 (Canadian holidays : $180.00) pj

  1. Frontier and pioneer life - Ontario.
  2. Thanksgiving Day.

  A look at both the Thanksgiving and everyday foods of pioneer families, using photographs of Black Creek Pioneer Village. Pumpkins, apples, cabbages, onions, turnips, poultry, cookies and cakes are the foods discussed.-

971.3
- Thanksgiving in pioneer Canada.
  prod. [Toronto] : B & R, 1976.- dist. B & R 29 fr. : col. : 35 mm. & cassette (13 min.) : auto. & aud. adv. sig. & reading script. $18.00 (Canadian pioneer days : $ 128.00) pji

  1. Frontier and pioneer life - Ontario.
  2. Thanksgiving day.

  The Canadian Thanksgiving tradition unfolds as pioneer activities typical of the season are discussed. These include candle-dipping, the preparation of dyes, flower-drying, harvesting, cider-making, and weaving.-

971.3
- La vie dans le Haut-Canada vers 1860.
  prod. [Montreal?] : NFB, 1967.- dist. SEC 39 fr. : col. : 35 mm. & captions & printed notes. $9.00 (Les pionniers : $72.00) pj

  1. Frontier and pioneer life - Ontario.

  Uses photographs to illustrate everyday life in a pioneer village. Includes family life, school life, the farmer's work, tradespeople, such as the blacksmith, carpenter and miller, and community life. Photographed at Upper Canada Village, Morrisburg, Ontario. English title available : LIFE IN UPPER CANADA IN THE 1860's.-

971.3
- Le Village.
  prod. [Toronto] : M-L, 1972.- dist. Sch. Ser. or Vint. 48 fr. : col. : 35 mm. & cassette (12 min.) : auto. & aud. adv. sig. & teacher's guide. $16.50 (La Vie quotidienne des pioneers du Haut-Canada : $85.00) ji

  1. Frontier and pioneer life - Ontario.

  Describes and explains various methods of livelihood, a blacksmith, and a furniture maker as examples. Helps provide insight into village life. English title available :WORK AND TRADE.-

971.3
- The Village broom shop.
  prod. [Rexdale, Ont.] : McI. 1978.- dist. McI. 24 fr. : col. : 35 mm. & cassette (5 min.) : auto. & aud. adv. sig. & teacher's manual. $19.00 (The Pioneer community at work : $114.00) ji

  1. Frontier and pioneer life - Ontario.

971.3
- Un village du Haut-Canada.
  prod. [Montreal?] : NFB, made 1966 : 1976.- dist. SEC 42 fr. : col. : 35 mm. & captions & teacher's manual. $9.00 (Les pionniers : $72.00) ji

  1. Frontier and pioneer life - Ontario.

  A description of the development of a pioneer community from the first farm and log house, to the mill, sawmill, and the small shops that were established near the mill. Examines the tradesmen in the community, the education system and the social activities of the people, using photos with authentic costumes. Compares a pioneer community with a modern one. English title available : THE PIONEER COMMUNITY.-

The Classified Catalogue

971.3
Visiting a pioneer cemetery.
prod. [Toronto] : B&R, 1976.- dist. B&R 25 fr. : col. : 35 mm. & cassette (11 min.) : auto. & aud. adv. sig. & teacher's manual & reading script. $18.00 (Early day Canada : $96.00) ji

1. Frontier and pioneer life - Ontario.
2. Cemeteries.

Shows how the interpretation of data gathered inn a churchyard, such as symbols used, birth and death dates, causes of death, and names, can provide insight into the life of the pioneers.-

971.3
Visiting an early day Canadian town house.
prod. [Toronto] : B&R, 1976.- dist. B&R 25 fr. : col. : 35 mm. & cassette (14 min.) : auto. & aud. adv. sig. & teacher's manual & reading script. $18.00 (Early day Canada : $96.00) ji

1. Houses.   2. Frontier and pioneer life.
3. Canada - Historic buildings, etc.

A tour through the home of William L. Mackenzie highlights factors such as family activities, storage requirements, and the needs of particular family members which influence the way a home is planned and used.-

971.3
Visiting pioneer Canada.
prod. [Toronto] : B & R, 1976.- dist. B & R 27 fr. : col. : 35 mm. & cassette (11 min.) : auto. & aud. adv. sig. & teacher's manual & script. $18.00 (Canadian pioneer days : $128.00) pji

1. Frontier and pioneer life - Ontario.

Uses photographs of Black Creek Pioneer Village, to consider factors such as technology, culture, and geography which influnced life in pre-Confederation communities of Eastern Canada.-

971.3
The Weaver.
prod. [Rexdale, Ont.] : McI. 1978.- dist. McI. 32 fr. : col. : 35 mm. & cassette (6 min.) : auto. & aud. adv. sig. & teacher's manual. $19.00 (The Pioneer community at work : $114.00) ji

1. Frontier and pioneer life - Ontario.
2. Weaving.

The weaving shop at Black Creek Pioneer Village serves as an example of the adaptation of an industrialized craft to rural environments. Covers wool dyeing, spinning and weaving processes. Also indicates weaver's social status in community.-

971.3
Work and trade.
prod. [Toronto] : M-L, 1970.- dist. Sch. Ser. or Vint. 48 fr. : col. : 35 mm. & cassette (12 min.) : auto. & aud. adv. sig. & teacher's guide. $16.50 (Pioneer community : $85.00) ji

1. Frontier and pioneer life - Ontario.

Describes and explains various methods of livelihood practised in pioneer times using merchants, a sawyer, a blacksmith, and a furniture maker as examples. Helps provide insight into village life. French title available : LE VILLAGE.-

971.4
Going to Canada : Government House.
prod. [Toronto] : NCM, 1977.- dist. I.T.F. 130 fr. : b&w & col. : 35 mm. & cassette (24 min.) : auto. & aud. adv. sig. & reading script. $47.50 (Victorians : $95.00) s

1. Frontier and pioneer life - Quebec - Personal narratives.   2. Frontier and pioneer life - Ontario - Personal narratives.

Life in Upper and Lower Canada is depicted using passages from an Englishwoman's personal diary. Contrasts deplorable conditions while sailing across Atlantic with social atmosphere of Quebec's Government House. Descriptive accounts of towns and environs and of prominent politicians and politics offer insights into social growth of Pre-Confederation Canada.-

971.4
The Habitant and his home [in the 18th century].
prod. [Montreal?] : NFB, made 1965 : 1975.- dist. McI. 48 fr. : col. : 35 mm. & captions & teacher's guide. $9.00 (New France : seigneurial system : $45.00) ji

1. Frontier and pioneer life - Quebec.

Drawings, as well as photographs depict typical habitant homes of the eighteenth century and compare regional styles. Illustrated are individual rooms, costumes, furniture and social activities of the period. French title available : L'HABITANT ET SA MAISON AU XVIIe SIECLE.-

971.4
The Habitant and his land [in the 18th century].
prod. [Montreal?] : NFB, made 1965 : 1973.- dist. McI. 43 fr. : col. : 35 mm. & captions & manual. $9.00 (New France : seigneurial system : $45.00) ji

1. Frontier and pioneer life - Quebec.

Uses drawings and photographs to illustrate the life of the habitant farmer in Quebec in the eighteenth century. Explains the types of tools and utensils used and compares winter activities with those of summer. Traces early transportation methods and describes the responsibilites of all the family members. French title available : L'HABITANT ET SA TERRE AU XVIIIe SIECLE.-

971.4
L'habitant et sa maison au XVIIIe siècle.
prod. [Montreal?] : NFB, 1965.- dist. SEC 53 fr. : col. : 35 mm. & captions& teacher's guide. $9.00 ji

1. Frontier and pioneer life - Québec.

Drawings, as well as photographs depict typical habitant homes of the eighteenth century and compare regional styles. Illustrated are individual rooms, costumes, furniture and social activities of the period. English title available : THE HABITANT AND HIS HOME.-

971.4
L'habitant et sa terre au XVIIIe siècle.
prod. [Montreal?] : NFB, made 1965 : 1970.- dist. SEC 43 fr. : col. : 35 mm. & captions & manual. $9.00 ji

1. Frontier and pioneer life - Quebec.

Uses drawings and photographs to illustrate the life of the habitant farmer in Quebec in the eighteenth century. Explains the types of tools and utensils used and compares winter activities with those of summer. Traces early transportation methods and describes the responsibilities of all the family members. English title available : THE HABITANT AND HIS LAND.-

971.5
La Dualité de notre patrimoine.
prod. [Toronto] : Int. Cin., 1975.- dist. VEC 57 fr. : col. : 35 mm. & cassette (15 min.) : auto. & aud. adv. sig. & teacher's guide. $24.00 (Le Patrimoine vivant du Canada : $86.00) ji

1. Frontier and pioneer life - Quebec. 2. Acadians - History. 3. Atlantic Provinces - History. 4. Quebec - History.

Photography and original paintings bring to life the people and places of Canada's past in Quebec and the Eastern region of Canada. English title available : OUR DUAL HERITAGE.-

971.5
Our dual heritage.
prod. [Toronto] : Int. Cin., 1974.- dist. VEC 57 fr. : b&w & col. : 35 mm. & cassette (15 min.) : auto. & aud. adv. sig. & teacher's guide. $24.00 (Canada's living heritage : $86.00) ji

1. Acadians - History. 2. Frontier and pioneer life - Ontario. 3. Quebec - History. 4. Atlantic Provinces - History.

Photography and original paintings bring to life the people and places of Canada's past in Quebec and the Eastern region of Canada. French title available : LA DUALITE DE NOTRE PARTIMOINE.-

The Classified Catalogue

971.5
    Pioneer life in the Maritimes : part 1.
        prod. [Montreal?] : NFB, 1972.- dist. McI. 36 fr. : col. : 35 mm. & captions. $9.00 (Pioneer life : $72.00) ji

        1. Frontier and pioneer life - Maritime Provinces. 2. Maritime Provinces - History.

        Drawings depict the early life of the Acadian settlers who came to the Maritimes from France. Explains ways the Indians helped the early settlers to hunt and fish. Examines Scottish settlements at Port Royal and on Cape Breton Island. An appendix of photographs of authentic Maritime pioneer artifacts is included. French title available : LES PIONNIERS DES MARITIMES : Pt. 1.-

971.5
    Pioneer life in the Maritimes. part 2.
        prod. [Montreal?] : NFB, 1972.- dist. McI. 41 fr. : col. : 35 mm. & captions. $9.00 (Pioneer life : $72.00) ji

        1. Frontier and pioneer life - Maritime Provinces. 2. Maritime Provinces - History.

        Describes the settling of the Maritimes, beginning in 1749 with the arrival of 2,500 English immigrants. Includes photographs of authentic artifacts of the pioneers of the Atlantic provinces. French title available : LES PIONNIERS DES MARITIMES : Pt. 2.-

971.5
    Les pionniers des Maritimes : 1ère partie.
        prod. [Montreal?] : NFB, 1972.- dist. SEC $9.00 (Les pionniers : $72.00) ji

        1. Frontier and pioneer life - Maritime Provinces. 2. Maritime Provinces - History.

        Drawings depict the early life of the Acadian settlers who come to the Maritimes from France. Explains ways the Indians helped the early settlers to hunt and fish. Examines Scottish settlements at Port Royal and on Cape Breton Island. An appendix of photographs of authentic Maritime pioneer artifacts is included. English title available : PIONEER LIFE IN THE MARITIMES : PART 1.-

971.5
    Les pionniers des Maritimes : 2e partie.
        prod. [Montreal?] : NFB, 1972.- dist. SEC $44 fr. : col. : 35 mm. & captions. $9.00 (Les pionniers : $72.00) ji

        1. Frontier and pioneer life - Maritime Provinces. 2. Maritime Provinces - History.

        Describes the settling of the Maritimes, beginning in 1749 with the arrival of 2,500 English immigrants. Includes photographs of authentic artifacts of the pioneers of the Atlantic provinces. English title available : PIONEER LIFE IN THE MARITIMES : PART 2.-

971.5
    Reform in the Atlantic colonies.
        prod. [Montreal?] : NFB, made 1961 : 1970.- dist. McI. 38 fr. : b&w & col. : 35 mm. & captions & teacher's manual. $9.00 (Development of self-government : $45.00) is

        1. Howe, Joseph, 1804-1873. 2. Atlantic Provinces - Politics and government.

        A survey of the development of self government in Nova Scotia, New Brunswick, Prince Edward Island, and Newfoundland, showing how each Atlantic colony wanted reform but for different reasons, and how they got it. Uses drawings, photos, map, and includes review questions for group discussion. French title available : LES REFORMISTES DES COLONIES DE L'ATLANTIQUE.-

971.5
    Les réformistes des colonies de l'Atlantique.
        prod. [Montreal?] : NFB, 1961.- dist. SEC 34 fr. : b&w & col. : 35 mm. & captions & teacher's manual. $9.00 (La conquête du gouvernement responsable : $45.00) is

        1. Howe, Joseph, 1804-1873. 2. Atlantic Provinces - Politics and government.

        A survey of the development of self government in Nova Scotia, New Brunswick, Prince Edward Island, and Newfoundland, showing how each Atlantic colony wanted reform but for different reasons, and how they got it. Uses drawings, photos, map, and includes review questions for group discussion. English title available : REFORM IN THE ATLANTIC COLONIES.-

971.8
L'histoire de Terre-Neuve (1000-1824).
prod. [Montreal?] : NFB, 1967.- dist. SEC 51 fr. : b&w & col. : 35 mm. & captions. & teacher's guide. $9.00 ji

1. Newfoundland - History.

A good overview of the island's history using drawings, maps, archival documents, and photographs. Manual is necessary for answers to questions asked on filmstrip. English title available : THE HISTORY OF NEWFOUNDLAND (1000-1824). -

971.8
The History of Newfoundland (1000-1824).
prod. [Montreal?] : NFB, 1967.- dist. McI. 51 fr. : b&w & col. : 35 mm. & captions & teacher's guide. $9.00 ji

1. Newfoundland - History.

A good overview of the island's history using drawings, maps, archival documents, and photographs. Manual is necessary for answers to questions asked on filmstrip. French title available : L'HISTOIRE DE TERRE-NEUVE (1000-1824).-

973.6
Growth and conflict.
prod. [Toronto] : M-L, 1976.- dist. Sch. Ser. or Vint. 76 fr. : col. : 35 mm. & cassette (15 min.) : auto. & aud. adv. sig. & teacher's guide.- $16.50 (The United States : "From sea to shining sea" : $65.00) is

1. United States - History - 1815-1861.
2. United States - History - Civil War - Causes.

Uses historical drawings and diagrams to trace the separate political and economic growth of the North and the South in the early nineteenth century. Explains the events leading to the American Civil War.-

C810.9
The Beginnings (1867-1929).
prod. [Scarborough, Ont.] SHN, 1974.- dist. PHM 107 fr. : b&w & col. : 35 mm. & cassette (25 min.) : auto. & aud. adv. sig. & teacher's guide. $39.60 (Canadian literature : $140.00) s

1. Canadian literature (English) - History and criticism.

Uses a variety of Canadian paintings, photographs, and music to describe early Canada and its literature. Discusses the changes brought about by industrialization. Includes T.C. Haliburton, Pauline Johnson, Mazo de la Roche, and Stephen Leacock.-

C810.9
A Coming of age (1950-present).
prod. [Scarborough, Ont.] : SHN, 1975.- dist. PHM 121 fr. : b&w & col. : 35 mm. & cassette (24 min.) : auto. & aud. adv. sig. & teacher's guide. $39.60 (Canadian literature : $140.00) s

1. Canadian literature (English) - History and criticism.

Describes increasing interest in Canadian culture in the fifties. Discusses development of theatre, music, poetry, and television in the sixties. Includes Northrop Frye, Robertson Davies, Gabrielle Roy, Margaret Atwood and others.-

C810.9
The Emergence (1929-1950).
prod. [Scarborough, Ont.] : SHN, 1976.- dist. PHM 112 fr. : b&w & col. : 35 mm. & cassette (29 min.) : auto. & aud. adv. sig. & teacher's guide. $39.60 (Canadian literature : $140.00) s

1. Canadian literature (English) - History and criticism.

Discusses the change in Canadian culture through the 1930's and its effect on literature. Includes works of Morley Callaghan and Dorothy Livesay, Irving Layton, Raymond Souster and Paul Hiebert Comment on the post-second World War literary scene.-

The Classified Catalogue

C810.9
    Prologue (1759-1867).
        prod. [Scarborough, Ont.] : SHN, 1974.- dist. PHM 112 fr. : b&w & col. : 35 mm. & cassette (26 min.) : auto. & aud. adv. sig. & teacher's guide. $39.60 (Canadian literature : $140.00) s

        1. Canadian literature (English) - History and criticism.

        Traces development of Canadian literature from the accounts of voyageurs, explorers, and missionaries to 19th century novels of Susanna Moodie, R.M. Ballantyne, John Richardson and others.-

F
    The Birds' Christmas carol.
        prod. [Toronto] : M-L, 1973.- dist. Sch. Ser. or Vint. 52 fr. : col. : 35 mm. & cassette (9 min.) : auto. & aud. adv. sig. & teacher's guide. $16.50 (The Christmas classics : $75.00) pj

        1. Christmas stories.

        Wiggins' touching Christmas story of the child who plans a Christmas for the poor children next door is illustrated with art work and accompanied by music. French title available : LA NOEL DE LA FAMILLE MARTIN.-

F
    Charlie Squash goes to town.
        prod. [Montreal?] : NFB, 1970.- dist. McI. 35 fr. : col. : 35 mm. & captions. $9.00 pj

        1. Indians of North America - Fiction.

        The wryly humourous story of Charlie Squash, an Indian who finally achieves a happy compromise between the Indian and white man's way of life. Written and illustrated by Duke Redbird, a Chipewyan Indian. Useful as an introduction to a study of native people and their difficulties. French title avaialble : CHARLIE SQUASH SE REND A SA VILLE.-

F
    Charlie Squash se rend à la ville.
        prod. [Montreal?] : NFB, 1970.- dist. SEC 35 fr. : col. : 35 mm. & captions. $9.00 pj

        1. Indians of North America - Fiction.

        The wryly humourous story of Charlie Squash, an Indian who finally achieves a happy compromise between the Indian and white man's way of life. Written and illustrated by Duke Redbird, a Chipewyan Indian. Useful as an introduction to a study of native people and their difficulties. English title available : CHARLIE SQUASH GOES TO TOWN.-

F
    Le Conte de Noël de Dickens.
        prod. [Toronto] : M-L, 1974.- dist. Sch. Ser. or Vint. 59 fr. : col. : 35 mm. & cassette (8 min.) : auto. & aud. adv. sig. & teacher's guide. $16.50 (Les Contes de Noël : $75.00) pj

        1. Christmas stories.

        Artwork is used to illustrate Charles Dickens' classic tale. English title available : DICKENS' CHRISTMAS CAROL.-

F
    Dickens' Christmas carol.
        prod. [Toronto] : M-L, 1973.- dist. Sch. Ser. or Vint. 59 fr. : col. : 35 mm. & cassette (13 min.) : auto. & aud. adv. sig. & teaching guide. $16.50 (The Christmas classics : $75.00) pj

        1. Christmas stories.

        Artwork is used to illustrate Charles Dickens' classic tale. French title available : LE CONTE DE NOEL DE DICKENS.-

F
    The Legend of the Christmas tree.
        prod. [Toronto] : M-L, 1973.- dist. Sch. Ser. or Vint. 42 fr. : col. : 35 mm. & cassette (8 min.) : auto. & aud. adv. sig. & teacher's guide. (The Christmas classics : $75.00) pj

        1. Christmas stories.

        Recounts this famous story using simple coloured illustrations, and background music. French title available : LA LEGENDE DE L'ARBRE DE NOEL.-

The Classified Catalogue

F La Legende de l'arbre de Noël.
    prod. [Toronto] : M-L, 1974.- dist. Sch. Ser. or Vint. 42 fr. : col. : 35 mm. & cassette (13 min.) : auto. & aud. adv. sig. & teacher's guide. $16.50 (Les Contes de Noël : $75.00) pj

    1. Christmas stories.

    Recounts this famous story using simple coloured illustrations, and background music. English title available : THE LEGEND OF THE CHRISTMAS TREE.-

F The Little match girl.
    prod. [Toronto] : M-L, 1973.- dist. Sch. Ser. or Vint. 48 fr. : col. : 35 mm. & cassette (7 min.) : auto. & aud. adv. sig. & teacher's guide. $16.50 (The Christmas classics : $75.00) pj

    1. Christmas stories.

    Retells the story of a young girl trying to sell matches while others celebrate New Year's Eve. Simple coloured drawings, narration and music. French title available : LA PETITE MARCHANDE AUX ALLUMETTES.-

F The Night before Christmas.
    prod. [Toronto] : M-L, 1973.- dist. Sch. Ser. or Vint. 39 fr. : col. : 35 mm. & cassette (5 min.) : auto. & aud. adv. sig. & teacher's guide. $16.50 (The Christmas classics : $75.00) pj

    1. Christmas stories.

    Clement Moore's poem is portrayed in simply drawn illustrations accompanied by appropriate music. French title available : LA VEILLE DE NOEL.-

F Le Noël de la famille Martin.
    prod. [Toronto] : M-L, 1974.- dist. Sch. Ser. or Vint. 52 fr. : col. : 35 mm. & cassette (9 min.) : auto. & aud. adv. sig. & teacher's guide. $16.50 (Les Contes de Noël : $75.00) pj

    1. Christmas stories.

    Wiggins' touching Christmas story of the child who plans a Christmas for the poor children next door is illustrated with artwork and accompanied by music. English title available : THE BIRDS' CHRISTMAS CAROL.-

F One kitten for Kim.
    prod. [Toronto] : M-L, 1973.- dist. Sch. Ser. or Vint. 58 fr. : col. : 35 mm. & cassette (11 min.) : auto. & aud. adv. sig. & teaching guide. $16.50 (Reading motivation) pj

    1. Pets - Fiction.

    Photographs illustrate this story of a boy who must give away his cat's kittens, but is given a rooster, parrot, alligator and goldfish in return. His parents' reactions when he arrives home provide a humourous ending. French title available : UN SEUL CHATON.-

F Pepper's Christmas.
    prod. [Scarborough, Ont.] : R.B.M., 1975.- dist. ETHOS 63 fr. : col. : 35 mm. & cassette (8 min.) : auto. & aud. adv. si& teacher's manual.- $19.00 (Special occasions) p

    1. Christmas stories.

    Pepper, a lonely apartment cat, discovers the wonder of Christmas with the arrival of Sparky, the mischievous kitten. Illustrated with photographs of actual cats.-

F La Petite marchande aux allumettes.
    prod. [Toronto] : M-L, 1974.- dist. Sch. Ser. or Vint. 48 fr. : col. : 35 mm. & cassette (7 min.) : auto. & aud. adv. sig. & teacher's guide. $16.50 (Les Contes de Noël : $75.00) pj

    1. Christmas stories.

    Retells the story of a young girl trying to sell matches while others celebrate New Year's Eve. Simple coloured drawings, narration and music. English title available : THE LITTLE MATCH GIRL.-

F Scarecrow and pumpkin.
    prod. [Toronto] : SHN, [197-] dist. PHM 76 fr. : col. : 35 mm. & captions. $39.60 (The Little people) p

    1. Halloween stories.

    A Hallowe'en story about a scarecrow who comes to life to find his friend, Pumpkin, carved into a jack-o-lantern. Includes carving the pumpkin, stressing safety with knife and matches, reading Hallowe'en stories, and "trick or treat".-

F
    The Secret in the barn.
        prod. [Scarborough, Ont.] : R.B.M., 1975.- dist. ETHOS 50 fr. : col. : 35 mm. & cassette (9 min.) : auto. & aud. adv. sig. & teacher's manual.- $19.00 (Special occasions) pj

        1. Christmas stories.

    The story of a little girl, told in verse and illustrated with drawings, who wishes for a horse for Christmas. Narrated by a child.-

F
    Un seul chaton.
        prod. [Toronto] : M-L, 1975.- dist. Sch. Ser. or Vint. 58 fr. : col. : 35 mm. & cassette (11 min.) : auto. & aud. adv. sig. & teacher's guide. $16.50 (Contes pour enfants) pj

        1. Pets - Fiction.

    Photographs illustrate this story of a boy who must give away his cat's kittens, but is given a rooster, parrot, alligator, and goldfish in return. His parents' reaction when he arrives home provides a humourous ending. English title available : ONE KITTEN FOR KIM.-

F
    La Veille de Noël.
        prod. [Toronto] : M-L, 1974.- dist. Sch. Ser. or Vint. 39 fr. : col. : 35 mm. & cassette (5 min.) : auto. & aud. adv. sig. & teacher's guide. $16.50 (Les Contes de Noël : $75.00) pj

        1. Christmas stories.

    Clement Moore's poem is portrayed in simply drawn illustrations accompanied by appropriate music. English title available : THE NIGHT BEFORE CHRISTMAS.-

Part Two

Precis Subject Index

PRECIS SUBJECT INDEX

ABORIGINES. Australia
   Social life -- J,I,S
       919.4   The Aborigine.

ACCOMMODATION BUILDINGS
   See also
       HOTELS
       RESIDENCES

ADAPTATION. Animals
   To environment -- J
       591.5   L'Habitat.

ADAPTATION. Animals
   To environment in winter -- J,I
       591.5   Discovering animals in winter.

ADAPTATION. Animals. Arctic North America
   To environment -- J,I
       591.9712 Animals of the Arctic.

ADAPTATION. Animals. Grasslands. Africa
   To environment -- J,I
       591.96   Grassland 1 : animals of the African Grasslands.

ADAPTATION. Birds
   To environment -- J,I
       598.2   Comment les oiseaux s'adaptent pour survivre.
       598.2   How birds adapt to survive.
       598.2   Birds and their environment.

ADAPTATION. Mammals. Arctic North America
   To environment -- P,J
       599.09712 The Arctic.

ADAPTATION. Mammals. Forests. North America
   To environment -- J,I
       599.097 Life in the boreal forest.

ADAPTATION. Mammals. Forests. North America
   To environment -- P,J
       599.097 The Eastern forest.

ADAPTATION. Mammals. North America
   To environment -- J,I
       599   The Story of mammals.

ADAPTATION. Mammals. Prairies. North America
   To environment -- J,I
       591.5   Life on the Prairies.

ADAPTATION. Mammals. Prairies. North America
   To environment -- P,J
       599.097 The Grasslands.

ADAPTATION. Mammals. Rocky Mountains. North America
   To environment -- P,J
       599.097 The Rocky Mountains.

ADAPTATION. Mammals. Tundra. Arctic North America
   To environment -- J,I
       574.509712 Life on the Barren Lands.

ADAPTATION. Organisms
   To environment -- J
       574.5   Les Organismes et le milieu.

ADAPTATION. Organisms. Cities
   To environment -- J,I
       574.5   Nature in the neighbourhood.
       574.5   Nature adapts to the city.
       574.5   City habitats.

ADAPTATION. Plants
   To environment in winter -- J,I
       581.5   Discovering plants in winter.

ADJUSTMENT
   See also
       PERSONAL ADJUSTMENT

ADJUSTMENT. Native peoples. North America
   To contemporary society -- J,I
       970.1   Native and European in North America.

ADMINISTRATION
   See also
       MANAGEMENT

ADOLESCENCE
   See also
       PUBERTY

PRECIS SUBJECT INDEX

ADOLESCENTS
  Marriage -- I,S
    362.8   Love and marriage.

ADOLESCENTS
  Pregnancy -- I,S
    301.41   Teenage father.
    301.41   Teenage mother.

ADOLESCENTS
  Sex relations -- I,S
    176   Growing up.

ADULTHOOD
  Personal adjustment of children -- P,J
    152.4   Je ne peux pas.
    152.4   But I don't know how.

ADULTS
  Responsibilities -- P,J
    152.4   Quand je serai grand.
    152.4   When I grow up.

ADVERTISING
  -- J,I
    659.1   Getting down to basics about advertising.

AERODROMES
  See also
    AIRPORTS

AFRICA
  -- Maps -- J,I
    912   Cartes muettes du monde :
                 L'Europe et l'Afrique.
    912   Outline maps of the world : part 2

AFRICA
  Animals -- J
    591.96   Large animals of Africa.

AFRICA
  Animals. Social behaviour -- J
    591.96   Animals together.

AFRICA
  Carnivores -- J
    591.96   African meat-eaters.

AFRICA
  Grasslands. Environment. Adaptation of animals -- I
    591.96   Grassland 1 : animals of the African Grasslands.

AFRICAN FOLKLORE
  -- Stories -- P,J
    398.2096   Why the spider has a narrow wai
    398.2096   How the leopard got its spots.

AGRICULTURAL INDUSTRIES
  See also
    WHEAT INDUSTRY

AGRICULTURAL INDUSTRIES. China
  -- I
    915.1   Agriculture, industry and transportation.

AGRICULTURAL INDUSTRIES. China
  Role of communes -- J,I,S
    631.0951   Commune in the South.
    631.0951   Commune in the North.

AGRICULTURAL INDUSTRIES. Leroy. Saskatchewan
  -- J,I
    917.214   Leroy, Saskatchewan.

AGRICULTURAL INDUSTRIES. Riverina. New South Wales. Australia
  -- J,I,S
    919.44   Riverina (Murray-Darling Basin)

AGRICULTURAL LAND. Niagara Peninsula. Ontario
  Development. Effects of regional planning -- J,I,S
    333.7   Fruit Belt preservation and regional planning.

AGRICULTURAL SHOWS. Canada
  Canadian & World Plowing Match -- J
    630.74   The Canadian and World Plowing Match.

AGRICULTURAL SHOWS. Toronto
  Royal Winter Fair -- J
    630.74   Royal Winter Fair.

PRECIS SUBJECT INDEX

AGRICULTURAL SHOWS. Toronto
Royal Winter Fair -- P,J
    630.74   Royal Winter Fair.

AGRICULTURE
See also
    FARMING
    RICE GROWING
    WHEAT PRODUCTION

AGRICULTURE. China
-- J,I
    631.0951   China 1 : food production.

AGRICULTURE. Flood plains. Nile. Egypt
-- J,I
    631.0962   Gifts of the Nile I : farming on the flood plains.

AGRICULTURE. Lowlands. Japan
-- J
    631.0952   Lowland agriculture in Japan.

AIR CAMPAIGNS. World War 1
Royal Canadian Air Force. Bishop, Billy -- J,I
    920   Billy Bishop.

AIR FORCES
See also
    ROYAL CANADIAN AIR FORCE

AIR SERVICES
See also
    AIRPORTS
    AVIATION

AIR SERVICES. Canada
1903-1977 -- J,I
    387.70971   Wings over Canada.

AIRCRAFT
Flight -- J,I
    629.132   Aéronautique élémentaire.
    629.132   Basic principles of flight.
    629.135   Aircraft in motion.

AIRCRAFT
Identification -- Field guides -- J,I
    629.133   Identifying airplanes.

AIRPORTS
-- P,J
    387.7   Une visite à l'aéroport.
    387.7   A Visit to the airport.

AIRPORTS. Toronto
Toronto International Airport -- P,J
    387.7   International airport.

AIRSHOWS
Canadian Warplane Heritage -- J,I
    629.133074   Airshows in Canada.

ALBERTA
Calgary. Description & travel -- J,I
    917.123   Calgary.

ALBERTA
Calgary. Rodeos: Calgary Stampede -- J,I
    791.8   Calgary stampede.

ALBERTA
Cattle farming -- J,I
    636.2   Cattle ranching in Alberta.

ALBERTA
Cypress Hills. Geological features -- J,I
    971.24   Fort Walsh in the Cypress Hills.
    971.24   Le Fort Walsh dans les collines Cyprès.

ALBERTA
Description & travel -- J,I
    917.123   Alberta.

ALBERTA
Description & travel -- P,J
    917.123   Paul and Pauline Visit Alberta.

ALBERTA
Edmonton, to 1976 -- J,I
    917.123   Edmonton.

ALBERTA
Edmonton. Description & travel -- J,I
    917.123   Edmonton, Alberta.

PRECIS SUBJECT INDEX

ALBERTA
  Fort Walsh. Description & travel -- J,I
      971.24   Fort Walsh in the Cypress Hills.
      971.24   Le Fort Walsh dans les collines Cyprès.

ALBERTA
  Hutterites. Social life -- P,J
      301.450971   The Hutterite ways.

ALBERTA
  Irrigated farming -- J,I
      631.7   Irrigated farming in Alberta.

ALBERTA
  Natural gas industry -- J,I
      665   Natural gas in Alberta.

ALBERTA
  Petroleum industry -- J,I
      665   Oil in Alberta.

ALBERTA
  Rocky Mountains. National parks -- J,I
      917.11   The Rocky Mountains national parks

ALCEDINIDAE See KINGFISHERS

ALCOHOL
  -- I,S
      613.8   L'alcool.
      613.8   Alcohol.

ALCOHOLISM
  -- I,S
      613.8   The Trouble with alcohol.

ALGAE
  See also
    SEAWEED

ALGERIA
  Algiers. Description & travel -- J,I
      916.5   Alger : un pas vers l'avenir un pas vers le passé.
      916.5   Algiers : a step into the future a step into the past.

ALGIERS. Algeria
  Description & travel -- J,I
      916.5   Alger : un pas vers l'avenir un pas vers le passé.
      916.5   Algiers : a step into the futur a step into the past.

ALGONQUIAN INDIANS. Canada
  Social life -- J,I
      970.3   Les Algonquins des forêts de l'
      970.3   The Algonkians : Eastern Woodla Indians.

ALPHABET. Cree language
  -- I,S
      411.09701   Cree syllabary.

ALUMINUM INDUSTRIES. Canada
  -- I,S
      669   L'aluminum.
      669   Aluminum.

ALUMINUM INDUSTRIES. Quebec Province
  -- J,I
      669   Aluminum processing in Quebec.

AMERICA
  -- Maps -- J,I
      912   Cartes muettes du monde : l'Amérique.
      912   Outline maps of the world : par

AMERICA
  Native peoples. Religions. Use of drugs -- S
      299   Drugs and religious ritual.

AMERICAN LITERATURE
to 1861 -- S
      810.9   A Declaration of faith.

AMERICAN LITERATURE
1861-1917 -- S
      810.9   Civil War and second thoughts.

AMERICAN LITERATURE
1917-1941 -- S
      810.9   World War I and disillusionment

PRECIS SUBJECT INDEX

AMERICAN LITERATURE
  1941-1974 -- S
      810.9   World War II - an increasing conscience.

AMPHETAMINES
  -- I,S
      615   Amphetamines and barbiturates.
      615   Les amphétamines et les barbituriques.

AMPHIBIANS
  See also
    FROGS
    TOADS

ANCIENT GREECE
  Athens. Architecture -- I,S
      722   Athens ... Acropolis and Agora.

ANCIENT GREECE
  Delphi. Architecture -- I,S
      722   Delphi, theatres and Olympia.

ANCIENT MIDDLE EAST
  Cities -- I,S
      301.34   The Urban revolution : the first cities.

ANCIENT ROME
  Pompeii. Architecture -- I,S
      722   Roman provinces and Pompeii.

ANDES. Peru
  Geography -- J,I
      918.5   Peru 1 : life in the Andes.

ANGER
  -- J
      152.4   Je me mets en colère.
      152.4   Your anger.

ANGER
  -- P,J
      152.4   Rrrrr.
      152.4   Gr-r-r-r.

ANGIOSPERMAE See FLOWERING PLANTS

ANIMALS
  See also
    BIRDS
    CHICKENS
    COWS
    CRUSTACEANS
    ECHINODERMS
    FISH
    FROGS
    INSECTS
    MAMMALS
    MARINE COELENTERATES
    MARINE MOLLUSCS
    PETS
    SPIDERS
    SPONGES. Marine invertebrates
    TOADS
    VETERINARY MEDICINE
    WILDLIFE

ANIMALS
  -- Stories -- P
      372.6   The Adventures of puppy dog.

ANIMALS
  Adaptation to environment -- J
      591.5   L'Habitat.
      591.5   Habitat and adaptation.

ANIMALS
  Adaptation to environment in winter -- J,I
      591.5   Discovering animals in winter.

ANIMALS
  Population -- Surveys -- J
      591.5   Les populations.
      591.5   Populations.

ANIMALS. Africa
  -- J
      591.96   Large animals of Africa.

ANIMALS. Africa
  Social behaviour -- J
      591.96   Animals together.

ANIMALS. Arctic Canada
  -- J,I
      591.9712 The Arctic animals.

PRECIS SUBJECT INDEX

ANIMALS. Arctic North America
  Adaptation to environment -- J,I
        591.9712   Animals of the Arctic.

ANIMALS. Arctic North America
  Hunting by Innuit -- J,I
        970.4   My escape from death.
        970.4   Eskimo hunting.
        970.4   Hunters of the Arctic.

ANIMALS. Baffin Island. Northwest Territories
  Hunting by Innuit -- P,J,I
        970.4   Autumn hunters.

ANIMALS. Canada
  Tracks -- Field guides -- P,J
        591   Animal tracks.

ANIMALS. Grasslands. Africa
  Adaptation to environment -- J,I
        591.96   Grassland 1 : animals of the
                   African Grasslands.

ANTIQUITIES
  Excavation -- J,I
        913   Stone Age man I : an
                   archaeological dig.

ANTIQUITIES. China
  -- I
        915.1   Monuments of the past.

ANTIQUITIES. North America
  Iroquois antiquities. Excavation -- J,I
        913   The Iroquoian people.
        913   Developing an Iroquoian village
                   site.

ANURA
  See also
     FROGS
     TOADS

APIS See HONEYBEES

APOSTROPHES. Punctuation. English language
  -- J
        421   Quotation marks and the apostrophe

APPALACHIAN REGION. Quebec Province
  Geography -- J,I,S
        917.14   Le Quebec : les Applaches.
        917.14   The Province of Quebec : the
                   Appalachian region.

AQUATIC SPORTS See WATER SPORTS

ARACHNIDA
  See also
     SPIDERS

ARCHAEOLOGY
  See also
     ANTIQUITIES

ARCHITECTURAL DESIGN. Houses
  Environmental factors -- P,J,I
        728   Factors influencing homes.

ARCHITECTURAL DESIGN. Houses. Canada
  -- P,J,I
        728   Development of Canadian homes.

ARCHITECTURAL DESIGN. Houses in cold climates
  -- P,J,I
        728   Homes in cold climates.

ARCHITECTURAL DESIGN. Houses in hot dry climates
  -- P,J,I
        728   Homes in hot, dry climates.

ARCHITECTURAL DESIGN. Houses in hot humid climates
  -- P,J,I
        728   Homes in hot, humid climates.

ARCHITECTURAL DESIGN. Houses in sunny or windy climate
  -- P,J,I
        728   How homes are adapted to nature
                   wind and radiation.

ARCHITECTURAL FEATURES. Churches. 1790-1890. Canada
  -- J,I
        726.0971   Visiting early Canadian churches

ARCHITECTURAL FEATURES. Houses. 1790-1890. Canada
  -- J,I
        728.0971   Homes of early day Canada.

PRECIS SUBJECT INDEX

ARCHITECTURAL FEATURES. Houses, 1790-1890. Canada -- Study examples: Mackenzie home -- J,I
    971.3   Visiting an early day Canadian town house.

ARCHITECTURE
  See also
    BUILDINGS

ARCHITECTURE. Athens. Ancient Greece -- I,S
    722   Athens ... Acropolis and Agora.

ARCHITECTURE. Canada 1790-1890 -- J,I
    971   A Trip through early day Canada.

ARCHITECTURE. Cities -- P,J,I,S
    301.34   City patterns.

ARCHITECTURE. Delphi. Ancient Greece -- I,S
    722   Delphi, theatres and Olympia.

ARCHITECTURE. Palace of Queluz. Lisbon -- I,S
    728.8   Versailles and Portugal.

ARCHITECTURE. Palace of Versailles. France -- I,S
    728.8   Versailles and Portugal.

ARCHITECTURE. Paris -- I,S
    720.944   Paris.

ARCHITECTURE. Pompeii. Ancient Rome -- I,S
    722   Roman provinces and Pompeii.

ARCTIC
  Nomadic communities -- J,I
    910   Nomadic journey : three nomadic peoples.

ARCTIC
  Northwest Passage. Exploration, 1576-1822 -- J,I
    910   Fact and fancy.

ARCTIC
  Northwest Passage. Exploration, 1576-1906 -- I,S
    971.2   Discovering the land.

ARCTIC
  Northwest Passage. Exploration, 1819-1845 -- J,I
    910   Discoveries and disappointments.

ARCTIC
  Northwest Passage. Exploration, 1845-1906 -- J,I
    910   Tragedy and triumph.

ARCTIC CANADA 1898-1972 -- I,S
    971.2   Discovering the people.

ARCTIC CANADA
  Animals -- J,I
    591.9712   The Arctic animals.

ARCTIC CANADA
  Birds -- J,I
    598.2   The Arctic birds.

ARCTIC CANADA
  Ecology -- J,I
    574.509712 Ecology of the Arctic.

ARCTIC CANADA
  Environment. Conservation -- J,I
    574.509712 Patterns of life.

ARCTIC CANADA
  Exploration -- J
    917.12   Exploration of Arctic Canada.
    917.12   Exploration de l'Arctique canadien

ARCTIC CANADA
  Geography -- J,I
    917.12   Geography of the Arctic.
    917.12   Physical setting.

ARCTIC CANADA
  Natural resources. Exploitation, to 1971 -- J,I
    971.2   White men in the Arctic.

ARCTIC CANADA
  Wildflowers -- Field guides -- P,J,I,S
    582.09712 Fleurs sauvages de l'Arctique.
    582.09712 Arctic wildflowers.

PRECIS SUBJECT INDEX

ARCTIC NORTH AMERICA
    Animals. Hunting by Innuit -- J,I
        970.4   My escape from death.
        970.4   Eskimo hunting.
        970.4   Hunters of the Arctic.

ARCTIC NORTH AMERICA
    Environment. Adaptation of animals -- J,I
        591.9712   Animals of the Arctic.

ARCTIC NORTH AMERICA
    Environment. Adaptation of mammals -- P,J
        599.09712   The Arctic.

ARCTIC NORTH AMERICA
    Plants -- J,I
        581.9712   Plants of the Arctic.

ARCTIC NORTH AMERICA
    Tundra. Environment. Adaptation of mammals -- J,I
        574.509712 Life on the Barren Lands.

AREA
    Measurement. Metric system -- I
        389   Unité de surface.
        389   Area units.

AREA
    Measurement. Metric system -- J,I
        389   Square stories.

AREA
    Measurement. Metric system -- J,I,S
        389   Linear - area.

AREA
    Measurement. Metric system -- P,J
        389   Area.

AREA
    Measurement. S.I. -- J
        389   Une Ligne - une surface.
        389   Measuring length and area.

ARMED FORCES
    See also
        ROYAL CANADIAN AIR FORCE

ARMED FORCES
    Canadian armed forces, 1873-1918 -- I
        971.05   La Canada dans l'Empire
                        Britannique.
        971.05   Canada in the British Empire.

ARMED FORCES
    Canadian armed forces, 1919-1945 -- I
        971   D'une Guerre à l'autre.
        971.06   From war to war.

ARMED FORCES
    Canadian armed forces, 1945-1974 -- I
        971   La Défense du Canada dans un
                       monde en évolution.
        971.06   Defending Canada in a changing
                       world.

ARMED FORCES. World War 1
    Canadian armed forces. Conscription, 1917 -- S
        971.06   Conscription crisis, 1917.

ART GALLERIES. Ottawa
    National Gallery of Canada -- J,I
        708   The National Gallery of Canada

ART INDUSTRIES See VISUAL ARTS INDUSTRIES

ARTHROPODA
    See also
        INSECTS
        SPIDERS

ARTHUR, King. Legends
    -- J
        398.2   Good King Arthur.

ARTIFICIAL RESPIRATION. Wilderness survival
    Techniques -- I
        614.8   Techniques antinoyade.
        614.8   Water rescue.

ARTS
    See also
        LITERATURE
        PERFORMING ARTS
        VISUAL ARTS

PRECIS SUBJECT INDEX

ARTS
  Canadian Indian arts -- J,I,S
        709.01   Indian arts and crafts.

ASBESTOS. Quebec Province
  Mining -- J,I
        622   Asbestos mining in Quebec.

ASIA
  -- Maps -- J,I
        912   Cartes muettes du monde : l'Asie et l'Océanie.
        912   Outline maps of the world : part 3

ASIA
  Exploration. Polo, Marco -- J
        920   Adventuresome Marco Polo.
        920   Les aventures de Marco Polo.

ASTRONOMICAL BODIES
  See also
      MOON
      STARS

ASTRONOMY
  See also
      SOLAR SYSTEM

ASTRONOMY
  to 1977 -- J,I,S
        523.1   Our discovery of the universe.

ATHENS. Ancient Greece
  Architecture -- I,S
        722   Athens ... Acropolis and Agora.

ATLANTIC
  See also
      BATTLE OF THE ATLANTIC

ATLANTIC PROVINCES See MARITIME PROVINCES

ATLANTIC SALMON
  -- P,J,I
        597   Le saumon atlantique.
        597   The Story of Atlantic salmon.

ATMOSPHERE
  See also
      WEATHER

ATOMIC ENERGY See NUCLEAR POWER

ATTITUDES
  To sexual roles, 1950-1976 -- I,S
        301.41   It isn't easy.
        301.41   C'est pas facile!

ATTITUDES. British Columbians
  To Chinese immigrants, 1858-1904 -- S
        301.450971 Difficulties of Chinese immigrants

ATTITUDES. Canadian Indians
  To earth -- J,I,S
        299   Mother Earth : an Indian view.

ATTITUDES. Canadians
  To Japanese immigrants, to 1939 -- S
        301.450971 The Japanese come to Canada.

ATTITUDES. Canadians
  To sex relations -- S
        176   To be together.
        176   Vivre ensemble.

ATTITUDES. Children. Canada
  To Third world -- J,I
        330.9   I was asked to draw this picture : children's views on world development.

ATTITUDES. Single people
  To loneliness -- S
        152.4   To be alone.
        152.4   Vivre seule.

AUDIOVISUAL AIDS
  Projectors -- S
        778.2   Le projecteur cinématographique de 16 mm. : 2e partie.
        778.2   Le projecteur cinématographie de 16 mm : 3e partie.
        778.2   Le projecteur cinématographique de 16 mm: 1ère partie.
        778.2   The 16 mm film projector : part 1.
        778.2   The 16mm film projector : part 3.

PRECIS SUBJECT INDEX

AUDIOVISUAL MATERIALS
See also
    FILMSTRIPS
    SLIDE PROGRAMMES

AUDIOVISUAL MATERIALS
Production -- I,S
    371.33   Producing your own instructional audio-visual programme.

AUSTRALASIA
-- Maps -- J,I
    912   Cartes muettes du monde : l'Asie et l'Océanie.
    912   Outline maps of the world : part 3

AUSTRALIA
Aborigines. Social life -- J,I,S
    919.4   The Aborigine.

AUSTRALIA
Canberra. Urban planning -- I
    919.47   An Australian city : Canberra.

AUSTRALIA
New South Wales. Riverina. Agricultural industries -- J,I,S
    919.44   Riverina (Murray-Darling Basin)

AUSTRALIA
New South Wales. Sydney. Description & travel -- I
    919.44   An Australian city : Sydney (no. I)

AUSTRALIA
New South Wales. Sydney. Description & travel -- J,I,S
    919.44   Sydney.

AUSTRALIA
New South Wales. Sydney. Suburbs. Description & travel -- I
    919.44   An Australian city : Sydney (no. II)

AUSTRALIA
Outback. Description & travel -- J,I,S
    919.4   Frontier mining and grazing (the Outback)

AUSTRALIA
Queensland. Eastern coastal region. Description & travel -- J,I,S
    919.43   Sugar and coral coast (Queensland)

AUSTRALIA
Sheep farming -- J,I,S
    636.3   Sheep industry.

AUTHOR CATALOGUES. Libraries
-- Users' guides -- P,J
    028.7   Have you a book by?

AUTOMOBILES See CARS

AUTOMOTIVE INDUSTRY. Oshawa. Ontario
-- J,I
    917.13   Oshawa, Ontario.

AUTUMN See FALL

AVES See BIRDS

AVIATION. Canada
-- I,S
    387.70971   Aviation in Canada.

AVIATION. Canada
-- J,I
    387.70971   Aviation in Canada - today.

AVIATION. Canada
1908-1937 -- J,I
    387.70971   Aviation in Canada : the early days.

AVIATION. Canada
to 1972 -- J,I
    387.70971   Histoire de l'aviation au Canada
    387.70971   History of flight in Canada.

BAFFIN ISLAND. Northwest Territories
Animals. Hunting by Inuit -- P,J,I
    970.4   Autumn hunters.

BAFFIN ISLAND. Northwest Territories
Inuit. Spring activities -- P,J,I
    970.4   Spring journey.

PRECIS SSBJECT INDEX

BAFFIN ISLAND. Northwest Territories
  Innuit. Summer activities -- P,J,I
        970.4   Summer days.

BAFFIN ISLAND. Northwest Territories
  Innuit. Winter activities -- P,J,I
        970.4   Winter camp.

BANKING
  -- S
        332.1   Creation of money by the banking system.

BANNERS
  Design techniques -- J,I,S
        746.3   Faire une bannière.
        746.3   Making banners.

BANTING, Sir FREDERICK GRANT
  Discovery of insulin -- J,I
        920   Banting and Best : the discovery of insulin.

BARBITURATES
  -- I,S
        615   Amphetamines and barbiturates.
        615   Les amphétamines et les barbituriques.

BARREN GROUNDS. Northwest Territories
  Canadian Indians -- J
        970.4   People of the sub-Arctic.
        970.4   Les Indiens des Régions subarctiques.

BARTLETT, WILLIAM HENRY. Drawings
  Special subjects: Canada. Water transport -- J,I
        971   Life along the waterways.

BARTLETT, WILLIAM HENRY. Drawings
  Special subjects: Ontario & Quebec Province -- J,I
        971   Quebec and Ontario : old colony and new outpost.

BARTLETT, WILLIAM HENRY. Landscape drawings
  Special subjects: Maritime Provinces -- J,I
        971   Sketching the New World : Maritime scenes.

BASKET MAKING
  By L'ilawat Indians -- P,J
        970.3   Basket.

BATS. Canada
  -- J
        599   Insectivores and bats.

BATTLE OF THE ATLANTIC. World War 2
  -- J,I
        940.54   Battle of the North Atlantic.

BAUXITE INDUSTRY. Study examples
  Guyana. Natural resources. Nationalisation -- Study examples: Bauxite industry -- I,S
        338.988   I can see clearly now.

BEARDS. Make-up. Theatre
  Techniques -- I,S
        792   Beards.

BEARS
  See also
    BLACK BEARS
    POLAR BEARS

BEAVERS
  -- P,J
        599   The Beaver.

BEEF CATTLE. Rocky Mountains. North America
  -- P,J,I
        599   Les Bestiaux de l'ouest.

BEES
  See also
    HONEYBEES

BEETLES
  Life cycle -- P
        595.7   Les coléoptères.

BEHAVIOUR
  See also
    PSYCHOLOGY

BEHAVIOUR
  Concealment of emotions -- P,J
        152.4   Inside outside.
        152.4   Les Masques.

PRECIS SUBJECT INDEX

BEHAVIOUR. Animals. Africa
  Social behaviour -- J
      591.96   Animals together.

BEHAVIOUR. Birds
  -- J,I
      598.2   Comment les oiseaux élèvent leur petits.
      598.2   How birds raise their young.

BELANEY, ARCHIBALD See GREY OWL

BELL, ALEXANDER GRAHAM
  Invention of telephones -- P,J
      384.6   Allô, Monsieur Bell!

BENNETT, MYRA GRIMSLEY. Nursing. Newfoundland
  -- J,I
      920   Nurse of Newfoundland.

BERRY FARMING. New Brunswick
  -- J,I
      634   Berry farming in N.B.

BEST, CHARLES HERBERT
  Discovery of insulin -- J,I
      920   Banting and Best : the discovery of insulin.

BETHUNE, NORMAN. Medicine
  -- J,I
      920   Dr. Norman Bethune.

BICYCLES
  See also
      CYCLING

BIOLOGY
  See also
      BOTANY
      GENETICS
      ORNITHOLOGY
      ZOOLOGY

BIOMES
  See also
      DESERTS
      FORESTS
      GRASSLANDS
      TUNDRA

BIRDS
  See also
      BIRDS OF PREY
      CANADA GEESE
      CHICKENS
      FOWL-LIKE BIRDS
      KINGFISHERS
      ORNITHOLOGY
      PERCHING BIRDS
      SHORE BIRDS
      WATERFOWL
      WHOOPING CRANES

BIRDS
  Adaptation to environment -- J,I
      598.2   Comment les oiseaux s'adaptent pour survivre.
      598.2   How birds adapt to survive.
      598.2   Birds and their environment.

BIRDS
  Behaviour -- J,I
      598.2   Comment les oiseaux élèvent leur petits.
      598.2   How birds raise their young.

BIRDS
  Food -- J,I
      598.2   How birds find food.

BIRDS
  Reproduction -- J,I
      598.2   Comment les oiseaux élèvent leur petits.
      598.2   How birds raise their young.

BIRDS. Study examples
  Sexual reproduction -- Study examples: Birds -- P,J
      591.1   Le Mâle - la femelle.
      591.1   Male and female.

BIRDS. Arctic Canada
  -- J,I
      598.2   The Arctic birds.

BIRDS. Canada
  -- P,J
      598.2   Common birds of Canada.

BIRDS. Everglades. Florida
  -- J,I
      598.2   Birds of the Everglades.

PRECIS SUBJECT INDEX

BIRDS. North America
  -- J,I
    598.2   Birds, their upland homes and habits.

BIRDS. Urban regions. Canada
  -- P,J
    598.2   Birds of the city.
    598.2   Les oiseaux des villes.

BIRDS OF PREY
  See also
    HAWKS
    OWLS

BIRDS OF PREY. Canada
  -- P,J,I
    598.2   The Predators.

BIRDS OF PREY. North America
  -- J,I
    598.2   Predators.

BIRTH
  See also
    CHILDBIRTH

BIRTH. Mammals
  -- P,J
    591.1   La Naissance.
    591.1   Birth.

BIRTH CONTROL
  See also
    CONTRACEPTION

BISHOP, BILLY. Royal Canadian Air Force. World War 1
  -- J,I
    920   Billy Bishop.

BISON
  See also
    BUFFALO

BLACK BEARS
  -- P,J
    599   L'ours noir.
    599   The Black bear.

BLACK CREEK PIONEER VILLAGE
  Canada. Christmas food, 1800-1860 -- Re-enactments at Black Creek Pioneer Village -- P,J
    971.3   Canadian christmas : festive foods

BLACK CREEK PIONEER VILLAGE
  Canada. Houses. Heating, 1800-1860 -- Re-enactments at Black Creek Pioneer Village -- P,J,I
    971.3   "Mary Davidson's home"

BLACK CREEK PIONEER VILLAGE
  Canada. Houses. Lighting, 1800-1860 -- Re-enactments at Black Creek Pioneer Village -- P,J,I
    971.3   "Mary Davidson's home"

BLACK CREEK PIONEER VILLAGE
  Canada. Thanksgiving food, 1800-1860 -- Re-enactments at Black Creek Pioneer Village -- P,J
    971.3   Thanksgiving foods.

BLACK CREEK PIONEER VILLAGE
  Christmas. Canadian social customs, 1800-1860: Decorations -- Re-enactments at Black Creek Pioneer Village -- P,J
    971.3   Canadian Christmas : Christmas decorations.

BLACK CREEK PIONEER VILLAGE
  Christmas. Canadian social customs, 1820-1867 -- Re-enactments at Black Creek Pioneer Village -- P,J,I
    971.3   Pioneer Christmas.

BLACK CREEK PIONEER VILLAGE
  Eastern Canada. Entertainments, 1820-1867 -- Re-enactments at Black Creek Pioneer Village -- P,J,I
    971.3   Pioneer entertainment.

BLACK CREEK PIONEER VILLAGE
  Eastern Canada. Family life, 1820-1867 -- Re-enactments at Black Creek Pioneer Village -- P,J,I
    971.3   Pioneer family life.

BLACK CREEK PIONEER VILLAGE
  Eastern Canada. Holidays: Thanksgiving. Social customs, 1820-1867 -- Re-enactments at Black Creek Pioneer Village -- P,J,I
    971.3   Thanksgiving in pioneer Canada.

BLACK CREEK PIONEER VILLAGE
  Eastern Canada. Pioneer life, 1820-1867 -- Re-enactments at Black Creek Pioneer Village -- P,J,I
    971.3   Activities in pioneer days.
    971.3   Country life.

PRECIS SUBJECT INDEX

    971.3   Visiting pioneer Canada.

BLACK CREEK PIONEER VILLAGE
  Eastern Canada. Technology, 1820-1867 -- Re-
  enactments at Black Creek Pioneer Village -- P,J,I
    971.3   Pioneer inventions.

BLACK CREEK PIONEER VILLAGE
  Ontario. Broom making, 1800-1850 -- Re-enactments at
  Black Creek Pioneer Village -- J,I
    971.3   The Village broom shop.

BLACK CREEK PIONEER VILLAGE
  Ontario. Cabinet making, 1800-1850 -- Re-enactments
  at Black Creek Pioneer Village -- J,I
    971.3   The Cabinet maker.

BLACK CREEK PIONEER VILLAGE
  Ontario. Flour milling, 1800-1850 -- Re-enactments
  at Black Creek Pioneer Village -- J,I
    971.3   The Mill.

BLACK CREEK PIONEER VILLAGE
  Ontario. Newspapers, 1800-1850 -- Re-enactments at
  Black Creek Pioneer Village -- J,I
    971.3   The Newspaper business.

BLACK CREEK PIONEER VILLAGE
  Ontario. Pioneer life -- Re-enactments at Black
  Creek Pioneer Village -- J,I
    971.3   The Pioneer community.
    971.3   Canada's pioneer life & customs.

BLACK CREEK PIONEER VILLAGE
  Ontario. Weaving, 1800-1850 -- Re-enactments at
  Black Creek Pioneer Village -- J,I
    971.3   The Weaver.

BLACKS. Ethnic groups. Canada
  -- I,S
    301.450971 Black Canadians.

BLOCK PARENTS. Welfare services for children
  -- P,J
    362.7   June's narrow escape.
    362.7   Jimmie to the rescue.
    362.7   Short cut to trouble.

BOATING
  Safety measures -- P,J
    614.8   Small boat safety.

BOATS
  See also
    CANOES

BODY See HUMAN BODY

BODY MASKS
  Design techniques -- J,I,S
    746.9   Faire une cagoule.
    746.9   Making a body mask.

BONDING. Walls
  -- S
    693.2   Walls and bonds.

BOOKS
  See also
    TELEPHONE DIRECTORIES

BOOKS
  -- K,P
    001.54   A Book is a friend.

BORDUAS, PAUL EMILE. Paintings
  -- I,S
    759.11   Paul-Emile Borduas.
    759.11   Paul-Emile Borduas.

BOREAL FORESTS. Canada
  compared with deciduous forests -- I,S
    581.5   La forêt feuille et la forêt
                boréale : une comparaison.
    581.5   Deciduous and boreal forests :
                comparison.

BOTANY
  See also
    PLANTS

BOVINES
  See also
    BUFFALO
    CATTLE

PRECIS SUBJECT INDEX

BRAVERY See COURAGE

BRAZIL
  Rio de Janeiro. Description & travel -- J,I,S
      918.1   Rio de Janerio.

BREAD
  Manufacture -- J,I
      664   Working in a bakery.

BREAD
  Manufacture -- P,J
      664   Bread and pastry.

BREATHING See RESPIRATION

BRICKLAYING
  -- S
      693.2   Elements of brickwork.

BRICKLAYING. Walls
  Bonding -- S
      693.2   Walls and bonds.

BRITISH CANADIANS
  -- I,S
      301.450971 British Canadians.

BRITISH COLUMBIA
  Chinese immigrants. Attitudes of society, 1858-1904 -
  - S
      301.450971 Difficulties of Chinese immigrants

BRITISH COLUMBIA
  Chinese immigrants. Social life, 1858-1885 -- S
      301.450971 The First Chinese communities in
                  British Columbia.

BRITISH COLUMBIA
  Commercial fishing -- J,I
      639.09711 Salmon fishing in B.C.

BRITISH COLUMBIA
  Cowichan Indians. Reservation life -- I,S
      970.5   Cowichan : a question of survival.

BRITISH COLUMBIA
  Description & travel -- I
      917.11   La Columbie Britannique.

BRITISH COLUMBIA
  Description & travel -- J,I
      917.11   British Columbia.

BRITISH COLUMBIA
  Description & travel -- P,J
      917.11   Paul and Pauline visit British
                Columbia.

BRITISH COLUMBIA
  Doukhobors, 1908-1978 -- S
      301.4509711 A Time of migration and troubles

BRITISH COLUMBIA
  Fish processing -- J,I
      639   Fish processing in British
                Columbia.

BRITISH COLUMBIA
  Fort Steele. Description & travel -- I
      971.1   The Town of Fort Steele.
      971.1   La ville de Fort Steele.

BRITISH COLUMBIA
  Fur trade. Trading posts: Fort Langley -- J,I,S
      971.1   Le Fort Langley : carrefour de la
               côte ouest.
      971.1   Fort Langley : gateway to the west

BRITISH COLUMBIA
  Gold rush, 1858 -- J,I,S
      971.1   Gold rush : pioneer mining in
               British Columbia.

BRITISH COLUMBIA
  Land tenure. Claims of Canadian Indians -- I,S
      970.5   Native land claims in B.C. : an
               introduction (1850-1976)

BRITISH COLUMBIA
  Logging -- J,I
      634.909711 Forest industries in B.C. : part 1

BRITISH COLUMBIA
  Okanagan Valley. Fruit farming -- J,I
      634   Fruit farming in British Columbia.
      917.11   Ville fruitière.
      917.11   Orchard City (Kelowna, B.C.)

PRECIS SUBJECT INDEX

BRITISH COLUMBIA
   Port of Vancouver -- J,I
       387.109711   The Port of Vancouver.

BRITISH COLUMBIA
   Queen Charlotte Islands. Description & travel -- J,I,S
       917.11   L'archipel de la Reine-Charlotte.
       917.11   Queen Charlotte Islands.
       917.11   Queen Charlotte Islands.

BRITISH COLUMBIA
   Rocky Mountains. National parks -- J,I
       917.11   The Rocky Mountains national parks

BRITISH COLUMBIA
   Spring wildflowers -- Field guides -- P,J,I,S
       582.09711   Fleurs sauvages printanières : Colombie-Britannique.
       582.09711   Spring wildflowers : British Columbia.

BRITISH COLUMBIA
   Totem poles -- J,I
       736   Totem poles.

BRITISH COLUMBIA
   Totem poles -- J,I,S
       736   Totem pole tales.

BRITISH COLUMBIA
   Vancouver. Description & travel -- J,I
       917.11   Vancouver.

BRITISH COLUMBIA
   Vancouver. Parks: Stanley Park -- J,I
       917.11   Stanley Park.

BRITISH COLUMBIA
   Vancouver. Timber industry -- J,I
       917.11   Timber City : Vancouver.
       917.11   Une ville du bois d'oeuvre.

BRITISH COLUMBIA
   Vancouver Island. Description & travel -- J,I
       917.11   Vancouver Island.

BRITISH COLUMBIA
   Victoria, to 1972 -- J,I
       917.11   Victoria, B.C.
       917.11   Victoria, B.C.

BRITISH COLUMBIA
   Victoria. Description & travel -- J,I
       917.11   Victoria.

BRITISH COLUMBIAN VISUAL ARTS
   -- I,S
       709.711   Artistes de la côte canadienne du Pacifique.
       709.711   Artists of Pacific Canada.

BRITISH GUIANA See GUYANA

BROADCASTING
   See also
      TELEVISION

BROOM MAKING. Ontario
   1800-1850 -- Re-enactments at Black Creek Pioneer Village -- J,I
       971.3   The Village broom shop.

BUFFALO. North America
   -- P,J
       599   Le bison d'Amérique.
       599   The North American buffalo.

BUFFALO. North America
   -- P,J,I
       599   Les Bisons des plaines.
       599   Buffalo, buffalo, buffalo.

BUILDING
   See also
      BRICKLAYING
      PAINTING
      WALLPAPER
      Hanging

BUILDING. Houses
   -- P
       690   Bâtissons notre maison.

BUILDING. Log houses. Northern Canada
   -- Do it yourself guides -- S,A
       690   Build your own log house : part
       690   Build your own log house : part

BUILDINGS
   See also
      ARCHITECTURE

PRECIS SUBJECT INDEX

BUILDINGS
  See also
    CHURCHES
    FORT LANGLEY
    FORT STEELE
    FORT WALSH
    FORT WILLIAM
    HOTELS
    LOWER FORT GARRY
    RESIDENCES

BUILDINGS. Parliament. Canada
  -- J
    328.71   Une visite au Palais du Parlement.

BUILDINGS. Parliament. Canada
  -- J,I
    328.71   Parliament buildings.

BUSES
  School buses. Safety measures -- P,J
    614.8   School bus safety.

BUSINESS MANAGEMENT See MANAGEMENT

BUTTERFLIES
  Monarch butterflies. Life cycle -- P,J,I
    595.7   Le papillon monarque.
    595.7   The Monarch butterfly.

BUYING. Goods
  -- Consumers' guides -- P,J
    332.024   Money : how to spend it.

CABINET MAKING. Ontario
  1800-1850 -- Re-enactments at Black Creek Pioneer
  Village -- J,I
    971.3   The Cabinet maker.

CAIRO
  Description & travel -- J,I
    916.2   Gifts of the Nile II : Cairo, the city.

CALGARY. Alberta
  Description & travel -- J,I
    917.123   Calgary.

CALGARY. Alberta
  Rodeos: Calgary Stampede -- J,I
    791.8   Calgary stampede.

CALGARY STAMPEDE
  -- J,I
    791.8   Calgary stampede.

CAMERAS. Photography
  -- J,I
    771.3   The Camera.

CAMPAIGNS. World War 1
  1914 -- J,I
    940.4   The War to end war (1914)

CAMPAIGNS. World War 1
  1915 -- J,I
    940.4   First air aces : first women's liberators (1915)

CAMPAIGNS. World War 1
  1916 -- J,I
    940.4   The Terrible mud of Flanders (1916)

CAMPAIGNS. World War 1
  1917-1918 -- J,I
    940.4   The First convoys, and Armistice (1917)

CAMPAIGNS. World War 2
  -- J,I
    940   Classic drama - hero vs. villain.

CAMPAIGNS. World War 2
  1942-1943 -- J,I
    940.54   Hitler at bay (1942-43)

CAMPAIGNS. World War 2
  1944-1945 -- J,I
    940.54   Surrender.

CAMPING
  See also
    CAMPSITES

PRECIS SUBJECT INDEX

CAMPING
   -- J,I,S
       796.54   Elementary camping.

CAMPING
   Preparations & equipment -- I,S
       796.54   Le campeur et son équipement.
       796.54   The Camper and his equipment.

CAMPING
   Winter camping -- J,I,S
       796.54   Vintering in the bush.

CAMPSITES
   -- I,S
       796.54   Le campement.
       796.54   The Campsite.

CANADA
   See also
      Names of individual Provinces & Territories & of
         groups thereof
   NEW FRANCE

CANADA
   -- Maps -- J,I
       912   Cartes muettes du Canada.
       912   Outline maps of Canada.

CANADA
   1896-1911 -- J,I
       971.05   L'époque de Laurier (1ère partie)
       971.05   The Laurier era : part 1.
       971.05   L'époque de Laurier (2e partie)

CANADA
   1957-1968 -- S
       971.06   The Diefenbaker-Pearson years :
                   part II.
       971.06   The Diefenbaker-Pearson years :
                   part 1.

CANADA
   to 1973. Information sources: Postage stamps -- J,I
       769   Shaping the Canadian nation.

CANADA
   Algonquian Indians. Social life -- J,I
       970.3   Les Algonquins des forêts de l'Est
       970.3   The Algonkians : Eastern Woodland
                  Indians.

CANADA
   Arctic Canada. 1898-1972 -- I,S
       971.2   Discovering the people.

CANADA
   Arctic Canada. Environment. Conservation -- J,I
       574.509712 Patterns of life.

CANADA
   Arctic Canada. Exploration -- J
       917.12   Exploration of Arctic Canada.
       917.12   Exploration de l'Arctique canad

CANADA
   Arctic Canada. Geography -- J,I
       917.12   Geography of the Arctic.
       917.12   Physical setting.

CANADA
   Civil rights -- I
       323.40971 Le Canada, pays de liberté.

CANADA
   Communities -- I
       301.340971 Kinds of Canadian communities.

CANADA
   Confederation -- I,S
       971.04   Confederation Canada.

CANADA
   Constitution -- I,S
       342.4   L'Evolution constitutionelle.
       342.4   Constitutional development.

CANADA
   Culture. Historical aspects -- J,I
       917.1   The Heritage puzzle.

CANADA
   Culture. Historical aspects. Preservation -- J,I
       971   A la découverte de notre
                   patrimoine.
       971   Discovering our heritage.
       971.0074   Places preseving our heritage.

CANADA
   Culture. Preservation -- J,I
       917.1   Collecting my own heritage.

PRECIS SUBJECT INDEX

CANADA
    Doukhobors. Social life -- S
        301.4509711 Doukhobor way of life.
        301.4509711 Doukhobor contribution to Canadian society.

CANADA
    Durham, John George Lambton, Earl of -- I,S
        971.03 Lord Durham's mission.
        971.03 La mission de Lord Durham.

CANADA
    Eastern Canada, to 1867 -- J,I
        971.5 La Dualité de notre patrimoine.
        971.5 Our dual heritage.

CANADA
    Economic conditions. Depression, 1929 -- I,S
        971.06 The Great Depression.

CANADA
    Economic conditions. Policies of federal government -- S
        339.5 Economic policy in perspective.

CANADA
    Elgin, James Bruce, Earl of -- I,S
        971.04 Lord Elgin's decision.
        971.04 La décision de Lord Elgin.

CANADA
    Ethnic groups -- I,S
        917.1 Mosaic Canada.

CANADA
    Ethnic groups: Blacks -- I,S
        301.450971 Black Canadians.

CANADA
    Ethnic groups: Chinese -- I,S
        301.450971 Chinese and Japanese Canadians.

CANADA
    Ethnic groups: Chinese -- P,J
        301.450971 My family is Chinese.

CANADA
    Ethnic groups: Chinese -- S
        301.450971 Chinese contribution to Canadian life.

CANADA
    Ethnic groups: Europeans -- I,S
        325.71 European Canadians.

CANADA
    Ethnic groups: Indians -- P,J
        301.450971 My birthplace was India.

CANADA
    Ethnic groups: Irish -- S
        301.450971 Irish contributions to Canadian life.

CANADA
    Ethnic groups: Italians -- P,J
        301.450971 My Italian heritage.

CANADA
    Ethnic groups: Jamaicans -- P,J
        301.450971 I come from Jamaica.

CANADA
    Ethnic groups: Japanese -- I,S
        301.450971 Chinese and Japanese Canadians.

CANADA
    Ethnic groups: Japanese -- S
        301.450971 Japanese contribution to Canadian society.

CANADA
    Ethnic groups: Japanese. Internment, 1939-1945 -- S
        301.450971 The Japanese during World War II.

CANADA
    Ethnic groups: Portuguese -- P,J
        301.450971 I was born in Portugal.

CANADA
    Expansion, 1663-1949 -- J
        971 L'expansion du Canada.
        971 The Growth of Canada.

CANADA
    Exploration -- I,S
        971.01 The Discovery of Canada.

PRECIS SUBJECT INDEX

CANADA
   Exploration. Cartier, Jacques -- J,I
      971.01   Jacques Cartier.
      971.01   Jacques Cartier.

CANADA
   Exploration. Champlain, Samuel de -- J,I
      971.01   Samuel de Champlain.
      971.01   Samuel de Champlain.

CANADA
   Exploration. La Verendrye, Pierre Gualtier de
     Varennes, sieur de -- J
      971.01   La Vérendrye.
      971.01   La Vérendrye.

CANADA
   Federal government -- I,S
      328.71   Le gouvernement fédéral.
      328.71   Federal government.

CANADA
   Federal government. Elections -- J
      324.71   Voting in Canada.
      324.71   Le vote au Canada.

CANADA
   Federal government. Elections -- J,I
      324.71   Get out and vote! election
                  campaigns and issues.

CANADA
   Federal government. Relations with provincial
     government -- J,I
      342.4   Ottawa and the provinces : issues,
                 choices and values.

CANADA
   Foreign aid to Third world -- S
      338.91   What is international development
                assistance?
      338.91   Qu'est-ce que l'aide au
                developpement international?

CANADA
   Foreign relations with United States, 1775-1914 -- S
      327.71   Canadian-American relations :
                part 1.

CANADA
   Foreign relations with United States, 1914-1963 -- S
      327.71   Canadian-American relations :
                part 2.

CANADA
   Foreign relations with United States, 1963-1977 -- S
      327.71   Canadian-American relations :
                part 3.

CANADA
   French colonisation, 1534-1713 -- J,I
      971.01   France in the New World.

CANADA
   Geography -- J,I
      330.971   Introduction : the people and the
                land.
      917.1   Canada's seven regions.

CANADA
   Geography -- P,J
      917.1   Scenic wonderland.

CANADA
   Government -- J,I
      342   Why governments?

CANADA
   Hutterites, 1917-1978 -- I,S
      301.450971 Hutterites in Canada : 1917 -
                present.

CANADA
   Immigration, 1896-1914. Social aspects -- S
      325.71   The Fourth wave.

CANADA
   Immigration, to 1945 -- I,S
      325.71   Two cultures.

CANADA
   Immigration, 1945-1975. Social aspects -- I,S
      325.71   Changing profile.

CANADA
   Immigration from Ireland, to 1910 -- S
      325.71   Irish immigration.

PRECIS SUBJENT INDEX

CANADA
  Innuit -- I,S
    970.1   Native Canadians.

CANADA
  Innuit. Culture -- J,I
    917.12   Eskimo 1 : Arctic village.
    970.4   The Inuit.
    970.4   Days of the igloo.
    970.4   The New north.
    970.4   Eskimo heritage.

CANADA
  Japanese immigrants. Attitudes of society, to 1939 -- S
    301.450971 The Japanese come to Canada.

CANADA
  King, Mackenzie -- I,S
    920   The Life of Mackenzie King : part II.
    920   The Life of Mackenzie King : part 1.

CANADA
  Landforms. Effects of glaciers -- I,S
    551.3   Glacier water deposits.
    551.3   Glacier land deposits.

CANADA
  Laurier, Sir Wilfrid -- I,S
    920   The Life of Sir Wilfrid Laurier.

CANADA
  Law -- I
    340   What are laws?
    340   Too many laws... or too few?
    342   How do we make laws?

CANADA
  Local government -- I,S
    352.071   Local government.
    352.071   Le gouvernement local.

CANADA
  Macdonald, Sir John A. -- I,S
    920   The Life of Sir John A. MacDonald.

CANADA
  Macdonald, Sir John A. -- J,I
    971.04   Sir John A. Macdonald (2e partie)
    971.04   Sir John A. Macdonald (1ère partie)

    971.04   Sir John A. Macdonald : part 1.
    971.04   Sir John A. Macdonald : part 2.

CANADA
  Multiculturalism -- I,S
    917.1   Cultures in conflict.

CANADA
  Multiculturalism -- J,I
    917.1   Sharing heritage.

CANADA
  Municipal government -- J,I
    352.071   Go fight City Hall! local decision making.

CANADA
  Municipal government -- Study regions: Ontario. Toronto -- J,I
    352.071   Urban government.

CANADA
  Municipal government. Elections -- Study regions: Ontario. Toronto -- J,I
    324.71   The Municipal election.

CANADA
  Native peoples. Effects of economic development of northern Canadian energy resources -- I,S
    970.5   Northern development at what cost?

CANADA
  Native peoples. Languages. Picture writing -- I,S
    411.09701 Native picture writing.

CANADA
  Northern Canada. Geography -- J,I
    330.9712   The Northland.

CANADA
  Parliament -- J
    328.71   Le régime parlementaire.
    328.71   Parliamentary government.

CANADA
  Parliament -- J,I
    328.71   Parliament : making and changing laws.

PRECIS SUBJECT INDEX

CANADA
   Parliament. Buildings -- J
      328.71   Une visite au Palais du Parlement.

CANADA
   Parliament. Buildings -- J,I
      328.71   Parliament buildings.

CANADA
   Physical geography -- J,I
      917.1   An Introduction to Canada's geography.

CANADA
   Political parties -- J
      329.971   Parties and elections.
      329.971   Partis et elections.

CANADA
   Politics. Effects of television -- I,S
      329   Electronic politics.
      329   L'Electronique en politique.

CANADA
   Prairies. Social life, 1812-1900 -- J,I
      971.2   Pioneer life on the Prairies (1812-1900)
      971.2   Les pioneers des Prairies (1812-1900)

CANADA
   Prairies. Social life, 1900-1912 -- J,I
      917.2   Les pionniers des Prairies (1900-1912)
      971.2   Pioneer life on the Prairies (1900-1912)

CANADA
   Prime Ministers, 1867-1911 -- I,S
      971.05   Macdonald to Borden.

CANADA
   Prime Ministers, 1911-1957 -- I,S
      971.06   Borden to St. Laurent.

CANADA
   Prime Ministers, 1948-1970 -- I,S
      971.06   St. Laurent to the present.

CANADA
   Provinces. Information sources: Postage stamps -- I
      769   Canada and its provinces.

CANADA
   Provincial government -- I,S
      354.71   Le gouvernement provincial.
      354.71   Provincial government.

CANADA
   Public service -- J,I
      350.971   The Role of the Public Service.

CANADA
   Rebellion, 1837 -- I,S
      971.03   The 1837 Rebellion in Lower Canada
      971.03   The 1837 Rebellion in Upper Canada
      971.03   Rebellion in Lower Canada.
      971.03   Rebellion in Upper Canada.
      971.03   Rébellion dans le Bas-Canada.
      971.03   Rébellion dans le Haut-Canada.

CANADA
   Role in wars, to 1867 -- I
      971   La Lutte pour une terre nouvelle
      971   Struggle for the new land.

CANADA
   Role in World War 1 -- I,S
      940.4   Canada and the First World War that's how it was.

CANADA
   Role in World War 2 -- I,S
      940.54   Home front to victory.
      940.54   From mobilization to the battle of the Atlantic.

CANADA
   Seven Years' War -- J,I,S
      971.01   The Seven Years' War.
      971.01   La guerre de Sept ans.

CANADA
   Social life, 1837-1867 -- S
      971.4   Going to Canada : Government House

CANADA
   Social life. Information sources: Postage stamps -- J,I
      769   Le Peuple Canadien et son environnement.

PRECIS SUBJECT INDEX

769   Canada : people and environment.

CANADA
Trade, to 1969 -- J
    382.0971   A Survey.

CANADA
Ukrainian immigrants, 1885-1920 -- I,S
    301.450971   Strangers to Canada.

CANADA
Ukrainian immigrants, 1890-1910 -- I,S
    301.450971   Prairie homestead.

CANADA
War of 1812 -- I,S
    971.03   The War of 1812.

CANADA
War of 1812 -- J,I
    971.03   The War of 1812.
    971.03   La Guerre de 1812.

CANADA
Western Canada, to 1885 -- I,S
    971.2   Staking a claim.

CANADA
Western Canada, 1886-1914 -- I,S
    971.2   Moving in.

CANADA
Western Canada, to 1900 -- J,I
    971.2   Frontier heritage.

CANADA
Western Canada, 1914-1972 -- I,S
    971.2   Growing up.

CANADA
Western Canada. Geography -- J,I
    330.9711   The Mountainous West.

CANADA
Western Plains. Geography -- J,I
    917.12   Introduction : the Western Plains.

CANADA
Wolfe, James -- J
    971.01   Le Général James Wolfe.
    971.01   General James Wolfe.

CANADA. Special subjects. Drawings by W.H.Bartlett
Water transport -- J,I
    971   Life along the waterways.

CANADA GEESE
-- P,J
    598.2   The Canada goose.
    598.2   La bernache canadienne.

CANADIAN & WORLD PLOWING MATCH
-- J
    630.74   The Canadian and World Plowing Match.

CANADIAN ARMED FORCES
1873-1918 -- I
    971.05   Le Canada dans l'Empire Britannique.
    971.05   Canada in the British Empire.

CANADIAN ARMED FORCES
1919-1945 -- I
    971   D'une Guerre à l'autre.
    971.06   From war to war.

CANADIAN ARMED FORCES
1945-1974 -- I
    971   La Défense du Canada dans un monde en évolution.
    971.06   Defending Canada in a changing world.

CANADIAN ARMED FORCES. World War 1
Conscription, 1917 -- S
    971.06   Conscription crisis, 1917.

CANADIAN CLOTHING
c.1800-c.1860 -- J,I,S
    391.0971   Historic costumes : part 1.
    971   Pioneers : part 1.

CANADIAN COINS
Minting. Royal Canadian Mint -- J,I
    737.4   Royal Canadian Mint.

PRECIS SUBJECT INDEX

CANADIAN CUISINE
  Multicultural factors -- J,I
      917.1   An Appetite for heritage.

CANADIAN FLAG
  1965- -- J.I
      929.90971 Comment le Canada obtint son drapeau.
      929.90971 Les Drapeaux Canadiens et leur usage.
      929.90971 How Canada got its flag.
      929.90971 Canadian flags and how they are used.
      929.90971 Les drapeaux canadiens et leur usage.

CANADIAN FLAG
  to 1965. Historical aspects -- J.I
      929.90971 Les Drapeaux Canadiens d'autrefois

CANADIAN FOLKLORE
  -- Stories -- P
      398.20971 La mouette et la baleine.

CANADIAN FOLKLORE
  French Canadian folklore -- Stories -- P
      398.2   Ti-Jean and the lumberjacks.
      398.2   Ti-Jean saves the harvest.
      440.7   Ti-Jean et les bûcherons.
      440.7   Les exploits de Ti-Jean dans l'Ouest.

CANADIAN FOLKLORE
  French Canadian folklore -- Stories -- P,J
      398.2   The Legend of the flying canoe.

CANADIAN FOLKSONGS
  -- Film interpretations -- P,J
      784.40971 The Raftsmen.
      784.40971 Jack was every inch a sailor.

CANADIAN FOLKSONGS
  French Canadian folksongs -- Film interpretations -- P,J
      784.709714 Cadet Rousselle.

CANADIAN INDIAN ARTS
  -- J,I,S
      709.01   Indian arts and crafts.

CANADIAN INDIAN GAMES
  -- I,S
      790   Native games.

CANADIAN INDIAN TRANSPORT
  -- J,I,S
      970.4   Indians : part II.

CANADIAN INDIAN VISUAL ARTS
  Symbolism -- J,I,S
      709.01   The Symbol in Indian art.

CANADIAN INDIANS
  See also
    COWICHAN INDIANS
    L'ILAWAT INDIANS
    MANOWAN INDIANS
    NASKAPI CHILDREN

CANADIAN INDIANS
  -- I,S
      970.1   Native Canadians.

CANADIAN INDIANS
  -- J,I
      970.1   Les aborigènes du Canada.
      970.1   Canada's first people : the Indian.

CANADIAN INDIANS
  -- J,I,S
      970.4   Indians leaders and centres of renewal.
      970.4   Indians yesterday and today.

CANADIAN INDIANS
  Attitudes to earth -- J,I,S
      299   Mother Earth : an Indian view.

CANADIAN INDIANS
  Dwellings -- J,I,S
      970.4   Indians : part I.

CANADIAN INDIANS. Barren Grounds. Northwest Territories
  -- J
      970.4   People of the sub-Arctic.
      970.4   Les Indiens des Régions subarctiques.

PRECIS SUBJECT INDEX

CANADIAN INDIANS. British Columbia
   Claims to land tenure -- I,S
       970.5   Native land claims in B.C. : an
                 introduction (1850-1976)

CANADIAN INDIANS. Labrador. Newfoundland
   Snowshoe making -- P,J
       685   Raquettes indiennes.
       685   Indian snowshoes.

CANADIAN INDIANS. Saskatchewan
   Role in Riel rebellion, 1885 -- S
       971.05   Big Bear, Poundmaker and Crowfoot.

CANADIAN LITERATURE
   1759-1867 -- S
       C810.9   Prologue (1759-1867)

CANADIAN LITERATURE
   1867-1929 -- S
       C810.9   The Beginnings (1867-1929)

CANADIAN LITERATURE
   1929-1950 -- S
       C810.9   The Emergence (1929-1950)

CANADIAN LITERATURE
   1950-1973 -- S
       C810.9   A Coming of age (1950-present)

CANADIAN NATIONAL
   Trains: Turbo train -- P,J
       385.0971 Inter-city train.

CANADIAN PAVILIONS. Expo '70
   -- P,J,I
       607.4   Canada at Osaka '70.
       607.4   Le Canada à Osaka '70.

CANADIAN POSTAGE STAMPS
   -- J,I
       769   Introducing the postage stamp.

CANADIAN SHIELD
   Forest products industries -- J,I,S
       634.9   Le Bouclier canadien - industries
                 forestières.
       634.9   Forestry in the Canadian Shield.

CANADIAN SHIELD
   Geography -- J,I
       917.1   Bouclier canadien : vue d'ensemble
       917.1   Introducing the Canadian Shield.
       917.1   The Canadian Shield.

CANADIAN SHIELD
   Transport -- J,I,S
       380.5   Transportation in the Canadian
                 Shield.
       380.5   Le Bouclier canadien - moyens de
                 transport.

CANADIAN SHIELD. Manitoba
   Geography -- J,I,S
       917.127 Manitoba : the Shield.

CANADIAN SHIELD. Special subjects. Photographs
   -- P,J,I
       407   Of the land.

CANADIAN SOCIAL CUSTOMS. Christmas
   -- P,J
       394.2   Christmas today.

CANADIAN SOCIAL CUSTOMS. Christmas
   1800-1860: Decorations -- Re-enactments at Black
   Creek Pioneer Village -- P,J
       971.3   Canadian Christmas : Christmas
                 decorations.

CANADIAN SOCIAL CUSTOMS. Christmas
   1820-1867 -- Re-enactments at Black Creek Pioneer
   Village -- P,J,I
       971.3   Pioneer Christmas.

CANADIAN SOCIAL CUSTOMS. Christmas
   Historical aspects -- P,J
       394.2   Canadian Christmas : traditions
                 of Christmas.

CANADIAN SOCIAL CUSTOMS. Easter
   Historical aspects -- P,J
       394.2   Easter in Canada.

CANADIAN SOCIAL CUSTOMS. Halloween
   -- P,J
       394.2   Hallowe'en in Canada.

PRECIS SUBJECT INDEX

CANADIAN SOCIAL CUSTOMS. St. Valentine's Day
   Historical aspects -- P,J
        394.2   St. Valentine's Day.

CANADIAN WARPLANE HERITAGE
   -- J,I
        629.133074 Airshows in Canada.

CANADIANS
   -- P,J
        917.1   Changing identity.

CANADIANS
   Attitudes to sex relations -- S
        176   To be together.
        176   Vivre ensemble.

CANADIANS
   British Canadians -- I,S
        301.450971 British Canadians.

CANADIANS
   French Canadians -- I,S
        301.450971 French Canadians.

CANALS
   See also
      RIDEAU CANAL
      WELLAND CANAL

CANBERRA. Australia
   Urban planning -- I
        919.47   An Australian city : Canberra.

CANNABIS See POT

CANOEING
   -- I
        797.1   Elementary canoeing.

CANOEING
   -- J,I
        797.1   Canoeing : the strokes.
        797.1   Canoeing : the basic.[Filmstrip].
                --

CANOEING
   -- J,I,S
        797.1   Le canotage.
        797.1   Canoeing.

CANOEING
   Safety measures -- J,I
        797.1   Canoeing skills and safety.

CANOES
   1800-1974 -- J,I
        797.1074   Canoe Museum.

CANTON. China
   Description & travel -- I
        915.1   Cities of China.

CAPACITY
   Measurement. Metric system -- J,I
        389   Capacity counts.

CAPACITY
   Measurement. Metric system -- J,I,S
        389   Volume - capacity.

CAPACITY
   Measurement. Metric system -- P,J
        389   Volume and capacity.

CAPE BRETON ISLAND. Nova Scotia
   Economic conditions -- J,I
        330.9716 Cape Breton Island : industrial regions.

CAPE BRETON ISLAND. Nova Scotia
   Geography -- J,I
        917.16   Cape Breton Island : an overv

CAPITAL LETTERS. Punctuation. English language
   -- J
        421   Using capital letters.

CARE. Teeth
   -- J,I,S
        617.6   Summary and conclusion.
        617.6   Dental aids and trends in dentistry.

CARIBOU ESKIMO. Keewatin District. Northwest Territories
   -- J
        970.4   The Caribou Eskimo.
        970.4   L'esquimau primitif.

PRECIS SUBJECT INDEX

CARNIVORES
  See also
    BLACK BEARS
    FELINES
    POLAR BEARS
    RACCOONS

CARNIVORES. Africa
  -- J
    591.96   African meat-eaters.

CARNIVORES. Canada
  -- J,I
    599.0971   Carnivores : the flesh eaters.

CARR, EMILY. Paintings
  -- I,S
    759.11   Emily Carr.

CARS
  to 1947 -- P,J
    629.22074   Antique cars.

CARTIER, JACQUES
  Exploration of Canada -- J,I
    971.01   Jacques Cartier.
    971.01   Jacques Cartier.

CARTOGRAPHY
  See also
    MAPS

CARTOGRAPHY
  -- J,I
    912   Du plan á la carte.
    912   Introduction to maps.

CARVINGS
  See also
    TOTEM POLES

CARVINGS
  Haida carvings -- J,I,S
    736   Les scuptures sur argilite des Haïdas.
    736   Haida argillite carvings.

CARVINGS
  Innuit carvings -- J,I,S
    736   Sculpture esquimau.
    736   Eskimo carvings.

CASTORIDAE See BEAVERS

CATALOGUES. Libraries
  Author catalogues -- Users' guides -- P,J
    028.7   Have you a book by?

CATALOGUES. Libraries
  Subject catalogues -- Users' guides -- P,J
    028.7   Have you a book about?

CATALOGUES. Libraries
  Title catalogues -- Users' guides -- P,J
    028.7   Have you a book called?

CATS See FELINES

CATTLE
  See also
    COWS

CATTLE. Rocky Mountains. North America
  Beef cattle -- P,J,I
    599   Les Bestiaux de l'ouest.

CATTLE FARMING. Alberta
  -- J,I
    636.2   Cattle ranching in Alberta.

CAVIES
  See also
    GUINEA PIGS

CECROPIA MOTHS
  Life cycle -- J,I,S
    595.7   Le paon de nuit.
    595.7   The Cecropia moth.

CELSIUS. Temperature measuring scales
  -- J,I
    389   Celsius scenes.

CELSIUS. Temperature measuring scales
  -- J,I,S
    389   Temperature.

CELSIUS. Temperature measuring scales
  -- P,J
    389   Temperature and mass.

PRECIS SUBJECT INDEX

CETACEANS
  See also
    WHALES

CETEWAYO, King
  -- J
    920   Magnificent Cetewayo.
    920   Cetewayo le magnifique.

CHAMPLAIN, SAMUEL DE
  Exploration of Canada -- J,I
    971.01   Samuel de Champlain.
    971.01   Samuel de Champlain.

CHARLOTTETOWN. Prince Edward Island
  to 1974 -- J,I
    917.17   Charlottetown, P.E.I.

CHARTS
  See also
    MAPS

CHICKENS
  -- K
    636.5   The Chicken or the egg.

CHILDBIRTH
  -- I,S
    612.6   Conception and birth.

CHILDBIRTH
  -- J
    612.6   La Naissance d'un être humain.

CHILDREN
  See also
    HOSPITALS FOR CHILDREN
    WELFARE SERVICES FOR CHILDREN

CHILDREN
  Cognition. Development -- Teaching materials -- P,J
    160.76   Les Objets disparus.
    160.76   Qu'est-ce qui manque?
    160.76   Trouvons les ressemblance.
    160.76   Classons, classons!
    160.76   Ecoute bien.
    160.76   Qu'est-ce qui ne va pas?
    160.76   Je me suis trompé de groupe : que suis-je?
    160.76   A quoi cela ressemble-t-il?
    160.76   Which group will they go to?
    160.76   Mets-toi à ma place!
    160.76   Pick the picture.

    160.76   What do they have in common.
    160.76   Listen for the clues.
    160.76   What's missing?
    160.76   Put them in order.
    160.76   Can you find them?
    160.76   Does it belong?
    160.76   What's wrong here?
    160.76   How will it look?
    745.5   Make something new.
    745.5   How would you use it?
    745.5   Qu'est-ce qu'on peut faire de c
    745.5   Trouvons autre chose.

CHILDREN
  Development -- P,J
    612.6   Le développement et l'apprentissage.
    612.6   Growing and learning.

CHILDREN
  L'ilawat children. Summer camp -- J,I,S
    970.3   Mount Currie summer camp.

CHILDREN
  Personal adjustment to adulthood -- P,J
    152.4   Je ne peux pas.
    152.4   But I don't know how.

CHILDREN. Canada
  Attitudes to Third world -- J,I
    330.9   I was asked to draw this pictu children's views on world development.

CHILDREN. Gabon
  -- P,J
    916.7   Children of Gabon.
    916.7   Les enfants du Gabon.

CHILDREN. Greece
  -- P,J
    914.95   Children of Greece.
    914.95   Les enfants de la Grèce.

CHILDREN. Japan
  -- P,J
    915.2   Children of Japan.
    915.2   Les enfants du Japon.

CHILDREN. Labrador. Newfoundland
  Naskapi children. Social life -- P,J
    970.3   La vie quotidienne d'un petit Indien.
    970.3   La vie quotidienne d'une petit Indienne.

PRECIS SUBJECT INDEX

| | 970.3 | A Day in the life of an Indian boy |
| | 970.3 | A Day in the life of an Indian girl. |

CHILDREN. Nigeria
-- P,J
    916.69   Children of Northern Nigeria.
    916.69   Les enfants de la Nigéria du Nord.

CHILDREN. Peru
-- P,J
    918.5   Indian children of the Andes.
    918.5   Les jeunes Indiens de Andes.

CHILDREN. Thailand
-- P,J
    915.93   Children of Thailand.
    915.93   Les enfants de la Thailande.

CHINA
  Agricultural industries -- I
    915.1   Agriculture, industry and transportation.

CHINA
  Agricultural industries. Role of communes -- J,I,S
    631.0951   Commune in the South.
    631.0951   Commune in the North.

CHINA
  Agriculture -- J,I
    631.0951   China 1 : food production.

CHINA
  Antiquities -- I
    915.1   Monuments of the past.

CHINA
  Canton. Description & travel -- I
    915.1   Cities of China.

CHINA
  Civilisation -- S
    915.1   Chinese cultural heritage.

CHINA
  Communes -- J,I
    915.1   Hill and plain communes : North China.
    915.1   Life on a Chinese commune : part 2
    915.1   Life on a Chinese commune : homes and farming.

CHINA
  Culture -- I
    915.1   Contemporary culture.

CHINA
  Education -- I
    379.51   Education and health.

CHINA
  Education -- J,I,S
    379.51   Education.

CHINA
  Industries -- I
    915.1   Agriculture, industry and transportation.

CHINA
  Medicine -- I
    379.51   Education and health.

CHINA
  Peking. Description & travel -- I
    915.1   Cities of China.

CHINA
  Politics -- J,I,S
    320.951   Political life.

CHINA
  Rice growing -- J,I
    633.0951   Rice growing in China.

CHINA
  Rice growing. Role of communes -- J,I
    915.1   A Yangtze rice commune.

CHINA
  Rural life -- I
    631.0951   Rural China.

CHINA
  Shanghai. Description & travel -- I
    915.1   Cities of China.

CHINA
  Shanghai. Description & travel -- J,I
    915.1   Shanghai : city life in China.

PRECIS SUBJECT INDEX

CHINA
  Transport -- I
      915.1   Agriculture, industry and
                  transportation.

CHINA
  Transport -- J,I
      380.5   China II - transportation.

CHINA
  Urban life -- J,I,S
      915.1   City life.

CHINA
  Visual arts industries -- J,I,S
      680   Craft industries.

CHINESE. Ethnic groups. Canada
  -- I,S
      301.450971 Chinese and Japanese Canadians.

CHINESE. Ethnic groups. Canada
  -- P,J
      301.450971 My family is Chinese.

CHINESE. Ethnic groups. Canada
  -- S
      301.450971 Chinese contribution to Canadian
               life.

CHINESE FOLKLORE
  -- Stories -- J
      398.20951 The Wishing bowl (China)

CHINESE FOLKLORE
  -- Stories -- P,J
      398.20951 The Superlative horse.
      398.20951 The Mandarin and the butterflies.

CHINESE IMMIGRANTS. British Columbia
  Attitudes of society, 1858-1904 -- S
      301.450971 Difficulties of Chinese immigrants

CHINESE IMMIGRANTS. British Columbia
  Social life, 1858-1885 -- S
      301.450971 The First Chinese communities in
               British Columbia.

CHIROPTERA See BATS

CHOCOLATE
  Manufacture -- P,J
      664   Chocolate.

CHRIST See JESUS CHRIST

CHRISTIANS
  See also
    DOUKHOBORS
    HUTTERITES
    JOAN OF ARC, Saint
    MENNONITES

CHRISTMAS
  -- Stories -- P
      F   Pepper's Christmas.

CHRISTMAS
  -- Stories -- P,J
      F   Le Noël de la famille Martin.
      F   La Petite marchande aux allumet
      F   La Legende de l'arbre de Noël.
      F   The Secret in the barn.
      F   Le Conte de Noël de Dickens.
      F   The Legend of the Christmas tre
       F   Dickens' Christmas carol.
      F   The Little match girl.
      F   The Birds' Christmas carol.
      F   The Night before Christmas.
      F   La Veille de Noël.

CHRISTMAS
  Canadian social customs, 1800-1860: Decorations --
  Re-enactments at Black Creek Pioneer Village -- P
      971.3   Canadian Christmas : Christmas
                  decorations.

CHRISTMAS
  Canadian social customs, 1820-1867 -- Re-enactments
  at Black Creek Pioneer Village -- P,J,I
      971.3   Pioneer Christmas.

CHRISTMAS
  Canadian social customs -- P,J
      394.2   Christmas today.

CHRISTMAS
  Canadian social customs. Historical aspects -- P,
      394.2   Canadian Christmas : tradition
                 of Christmas.

PRECIS SUBJECT INDEX

CHRISTMAS. Special subjects. German folklore
-- Stories -- P,J
    398.20943   Germany : the nutcracker's happy Christmas.

CHRISTMAS. Special subjects. Irish folklore
-- Stories -- P,J
    398.209415 Ireland : O'Reilly's Christmas cap

CHRISTMAS. Special subjects. Italian folklore
-- Stories -- P,J
    398.20945   L'Italie : la legende de Dame la Befana.

CHRISTMAS. Special subjects. Mexican folklore
-- Stories -- P,J
    398.20972   Le Mexique : l'humble présent.
    398.20972   Mexico : the humblest gift.

CHRISTMAS. Special subjects. Syrian folklore
-- Stories -- P,J
    398.2095691 Syria : the little camel.

CHRISTMAS FOOD. Canada
1800-1860 -- Re-enactments at Black Creek Pioneer Village -- P,J
    971.3   Canadian christmas : festive foods

CHRISTMAS PARADES. Toronto
-- P
    394.09713   The Day Santa came to town.

CHRISTMAS PARADES. Toronto
-- P,J
    394.09713   La Parade du Père Noël à Toronto.

CHURCHES. Canada
1790-1890. Architectural features -- J,I
    726.0971   Visiting early Canadian churches.

CHURCHILL FALLS. Newfoundland
Hydroelectric power stations -- J,I
    917.19   Churchill Falls.

CHURCHYARDS. Information sources. Pioneer life, 1790-1890. Canada
Monumental inscriptions -- J,I
    971.3   Visiting a pioneer cemetery.

CIRCUITS. Electricity supply equipment
-- J,I
    621.31   Current and pressure.

CIRCUITS. Electricity supply equipment. Residences Hazards -- J,I
    644   Electrical hazards.

CIRCUITS. Radio receivers
-- S
    621.3841   Basic radio circuitry.

CITIES
-- P,J,I,S
    301.34   City moods.

CITIES
Architecture -- P,J,I,S
    301.34   City patterns.

CITIES
Environment. Adaptation of organisms -- J,I
    574.5   Nature in the neighbourhood.
    574.5   Nature adapts to the city.
    574.5   City habitats.

CITIES
Historical aspects -- J,I
    301.31   The City : laboratory of history.

CITIES
Transport -- Study regions: Ontario. Toronto -- J,I
    388.409713 Transportation.

CITIES. Ancient Middle East
-- I,S
    301.34   The Urban revolution : the first cities.

CITIES. Canada
Housing -- J,I
    301.5   Housing : the Canadian city.

CITIES. Canada
Public transport -- Study regions: Ontario. Toronto -- P,J,I
    388.409713 Public transportation in the city.

PRECIS SUBJECT INDEX

CITIES. Canada
   Recreations -- J,I
       301.34   Recreation : the Canadian city.

CIVIL RIGHTS. Canada
   -- I
       323.40971 Le Canada, pays de liberté.

CIVIL SERVICE See PUBLIC SERVICE

CIVILISATION
   See also
       CULTURE

CIVILISATION. China
   -- S
       915.1   Chinese cultural heritage.

CIVILISATION. Ireland
   -- S
       914.15   Irish cultural heritage.

CIVILISATION. Japan
   -- S
       915.2   Japanese cultural heritage.

CLEANING. Teeth
   -- J,I,S
       617.6   Details of brushing, disclosing &
                   flossing.

CLIFFS. Ontario
   Scarborough Bluffs -- J,I
       917.13   Planning for future use.

CLIFFS. Ontario
   Scarborough Bluffs. Erosion. Counter-measures -- J,I
       917.13   The Natural environment.

CLIMATE
   See also
       WEATHER

CLOTHING
   Canadian clothing, c.1800-c.1860 -- J,I,S
       391.0971   Historic costumes : part 1.
       971   Pioneers : part 1.

CLOTHING
   Innuit clothing -- J,I,S
       970.4   Eskimos : part 2.

CLOTHING
   North American Indian clothing -- I,S
       391.09701 Native clothing.

CLOTHING
   Outdoor clothing -- I,S
       646   Proper bush clothing.

CLOTHING INDUSTRY. Canada
   -- J,I
       687   Clothing manufacturing.
       687   Clothing design.

CN See CANADIAN NATIONAL

COACHING. Hockey
   -- J,I
       796.9   The Hockey coach.

COAL MINING INDUSTRY. Canada
   -- J,I
       622   Coal mining in Canada.

COAL MINING INDUSTRY. Canada
   to 1974 -- I
       333.8   Fossil fuels : coal.

COASTAL FORESTS. Canada
   compared with montane forests -- I,S
       581.5   Coast and montane forest : a
                  comparison.
       581.6   La forêt des montagnes et la
                  forêt côtière : une comparai

COASTAL REGION. Queensland. Australia
   Eastern coastal region. Description & travel -- J
       919.43   Sugar and coral coast (Queensl

COASTAL WATERS. Canada
   Seals -- J,I
       599   Marine mammals of Canada.
       599   Les mammifères marins du Canad

COASTAL WATERS. Canada
  Whales -- J,I
    599   Marine mammals of Canada.
    599   Les mammifères marins du Canada.

COASTS. Japan
  Geography -- J
    915.2   Seacoast environments of Japan.

COATS OF ARMS
  Provincial coats of arms -- J,I
    929.90971 Flags, coats of arms, and floral
               emblems of Canada.

COATS OF ARMS
  Territorial coats of arms -- J,I
    929.90971 Flags, coats of arms, and floral
               emblems of Canada.

COELENTERATES
  See also
    MARINE COELENTERATES

COGNITION
  See also
    PERCEPTION

COGNITION. Children
  Development -- Teaching materials -- P,J
    160.76   Les Objets disparus.
    160.76   Qu'est-ce qui manque?
    160.76   Trouvons les ressemblance.
    160.76   Classons, classons!
    160.76   Ecoute bien.
    160.76   Qu'est-ce qui ne va pas?
    160.76   Je me suis trompé de groupe : que
               suis-je?
    160.76   A quoi cela ressemble-t-il?
    160.76   Which group will they go to?
    160.76   Mets-toi à ma place!
    160.76   Pick the picture.
    160.76   What do they have in common.
    160.76   Listen for the clues.
    160.76   What's missing?
    160.76   Put them in order.
    160.76   Can you find them?
    160.76   Does it belong?
    160.76   What's wrong here?
    160.76   How will it look?
    745.5   Make something new.
    745.5   How would you use it?
    745.5   Qu'est-ce qu'on peut faire de ca?
    745.5   Trouvons autre chose.

COINS
  Canadian coins. Minting. Royal Canadian Mint -- J,I
    737.4   Royal Canadian Mint.

COLD CLIMATES
  Houses. Architectural design -- P,J,I
    728   Homes in cold climates.

COLEOPTERA See BEETLES

COLLAGES
  Seed collages -- P,J,I
    745.5   Beginnings.
    745.5   Commencement.

COLLECTORS' GUIDES
  Rocks -- Collectors' guides -- J,I
    796.5   Rockhounding.

COLONISATION. Canada
  French colonisation, 1534-1713 -- J,I
    971.01   France in the New World.

COLOUR. Visual arts
  -- S
    152.1   Colour sets.

COLOURS
  -- K,P
    152.1   Observing by seeing : colours
               purple, orange, green.
    152.1   Observing by seeing : colours
               black, white, brown.

COMMAS. Punctuation. English language
  -- J
    421   Commas.

COMMERCE
  See also
    TRADE

COMMERCIAL FISHING
  See also
    HERRING FISHING
    LOBSTER FISHING

PRECIS SUBJECT INDEX

COMMERCIAL FISHING
   Nets. Materials -- I,S
      639   Engines de pêche (câbles et lignes pour la fabrication des fillets de pêch)
      639   Fishing gear (ropes and twines for fishing nets)

COMMERCIAL FISHING
   Otter trawling -- I,S
      639   Le chalutage.
      639   Otter trawling.

COMMERCIAL FISHING
   Seine netting -- I,S
      639   Seine netting : Scottish and Danish methods.
      639   La pêche à la Seine (Ecossaise et Danoise)

COMMERCIAL FISHING
   Techniques -- I,S
      639   Fishing methods.
      639   Méthodes de pêche.

COMMERCIAL FISHING. British Columbia -- J,I
      639.09711 Salmon fishing in B.C.

COMMON LOONS. Canada -- P,J
      598.2   The Common loon.
      598.2   Le plongeon à collier.

COMMUNES
   See also
      KIBBUTZIM

COMMUNES. China -- J,I
      915.1   Hill and plain communes : North China.
      915.1   Life on a Chinese commune : part 2
      915.1   Life on a Chinese commune : homes and farming.

COMMUNES. China
   Role in agricultural industries -- J,I,S
      631.0951 Commune in the South.
      631.0951 Commune in the North.

COMMUNES. China
   Role in rice growing -- J,I
      915.1   A Yangtze rice commune.

COMMUNES. Western Canada
   Hutterite communes -- I,S
      301.450971 Hutterite contribution to Canadian society.
      301.450971 Hutterite way of life.

COMMUNICATION SERVICES
   See also
      POSTAL SERVICES

COMMUNICATION SYSTEMS
   See also
      AUDIOVISUAL MATERIALS
      BOOKS
      DOCUMENTS
      GRAPHIC MEDIA
      NEWSPAPERS
      TELECOMMUNICATION SYSTEMS
      TELEVISION
      WRITING

COMMUNICATION SYSTEMS
   to 1967 -- J,I
      380   Our shrinking world.

COMMUNITIES
   See also
      NOMADIC COMMUNITIES

COMMUNITIES -- J,I
      301.34   What is a community?

COMMUNITIES
   Industrial communities. Growth -- J,I
      301.34   Industrial community 1 : patter of growth.

COMMUNITIES
   Telephone systems -- P,J,I
      384.6   Et maintenant, tous ensemble.

COMMUNITIES. Canada -- I
      301.340971 Kinds of Canadian communities.

PRECIS SUBJECT INDEX

COMPASSES. Navigation
-- J,I,S,A
    538.028   The Compass.

COMPASSES. Wilderness survival
  Use in orientation -- I,S
    796.5   Orientation & compass.

CONCEIT See VANITY

CONCEPTION
  See also
    CONTRACEPTION

CONCEPTION. Man
-- I,S
    612.6   Conception and birth.

CONDOMS
-- I,S,A
    613.9   Vaginal spermicides and the condom

CONFECTIONERY
  Manufacture -- J,I
    664   Working in a bakery.

CONFECTIONERY
  Manufacture -- P,J
    664   Bread and pastry.

CONFEDERATION. Canada
-- I,S
    971.04   Confederation Canada.

CONSCRIPTION. Canadian armed forces. World War 1
  1917 -- S
    971.06   Conscription crisis, 1917.

CONSERVATION. Endangered species. North America
-- J,I
    639   Threatened and endangered wildlife
    639   Habitat : key to survival.
    639   Threatened and endangered wildlife
        McI.
    639   Habitat : key to survival.

CONSERVATION. Environment
-- I,S
    333.9   La protection de l'environnement.
    333.9   Environment protection.

CONSERVATION. Environment. Arctic Canada
-- J,I
    574.509712 Patterns of life.

CONSERVATION. Wildlife
-- Stories -- P,J,I
    398.209701 The Story of Greedy Pan.
    398.209701 L'histoire de Pan de Glouton.

CONSIDERATION FOR OTHERS
  See also
    UNSELFISHNESS

CONSIDERATION FOR OTHERS
-- K,P,J
    177   The Living room and clothes.
    177   The Grocery cart and noise.

CONSTITUTION. Canada
-- I,S
    342.4   L'Evolution constitutionelle.
    342.4   Constitutional development.

CONSUMERS' GUIDES
  Canada. Food. Grading -- Consumers' guides -- J,I,S
    614.3   Aliments classés du Canada.
    614.3   Canada's graded foods.

CONSUMERS' GUIDES
  Food: Fish -- Consumers' guides -- S
    641.3   Get hooked on fish.

CONSUMERS' GUIDES
  Goods. Buying -- Consumers' guides -- P,J
    332.024   Money : how to spend it.

CONSUMERS' GUIDES
  Personal finance. Credit -- Consumers' guides -- P,J
    332.024   Money : how much do you need?

CONTRACEPTION
-- I,S
    613.9   Contraception.

CONTRACEPTION
  to 1977 -- S
    613.9   A history of contraception.
    613.9   Un historique de la contraception.

PRECIS SUBJECT INDEX

CONTRACEPTION
   Condoms -- I,S,A
      613.9   Vaginal spermicides and the condom

CONTRACEPTION
   Intrauterine devices -- I,S,A
      613.9   The Intrauterine device.

CONTRACEPTION
   Oral contraceptives -- I,S,A
      613.9   The Pill.

CONTRACEPTION
   Rhythm method -- I,S,A
      613.9   The Rhythm and sympto-thermal methods.

CONTRACEPTION
   Spermicides -- I,S,A
      613.9   Vaginal spermicides and the condom

CONTRACEPTION
   Sympto-thermal method -- I,S,A
      613.9   The Rhythm and sympto-thermal methods.

CONTRACEPTION
   Tubal ligation -- I,S,A
      613.9   Tubal ligation and vasectomy.

CONTRACEPTION
   Vasectomy -- I,S,A
      613.9   Tubal ligation and vasectomy.

COOKERY
   See also
      CUISINE

COOKERY
   -- I,S
      641.1   Les Repas et le budget.
      641.1   Help yourself to good cooking.

COOKERY
   Kitchen management -- I,S
      640   La Cuisine : un atelier.
      640   Principles of kitchen management.

COOKERY
   Outdoor cookery -- I,S
      641.5   Fires and cooking.

COOKERY. Fish. Food
   -- J,I
      641.6   The Way to cook fish.

COOKERY. Freshwater fish. Food
   -- I,S
      641.6   Let's serve freshwater fish.

COOKERY. Ontario
   1800-1850 -- Re-enactments at Upper Canada Village -- J,I
      971.3   Foods.

COOKERY. Salmon
   L'ilawat methods -- P,J
      970.3   Salmon.

COOKERY. Shellfish
   -- J,I
      641.6   Let's serve shellfish.

COOKERY. Wilderness survival
   -- Techniques -- I
      613.6   Outdoor cooking.

COPPER
   -- J,I,S
      669   Copper.
      669   Cuivre.

COPPER MINING INDUSTRY. Manitouwadge. Ontario
   -- J,I
      917.13   Images d'une ville minière.
      917.13   Mining town (Manitouwadge. Ont.

COSMETICS
   See also
      MAKE-UP

COSTUME
   See also
      CLOTHING
      MASKS

PRECIS SUBJECT INDEX

COURAGE
-- I,S
    179   Courage.

COURTS
  See also
    TRIALS

COWICHAN INDIANS. British Columbia
  Reservation life -- I,S
    970.5   Cowichan : a question of survival.

COWS
  Milking -- K
    637   What's in a dairy barn.

CRAFTS
  See also
    BASKET MAKING
    BROOM MAKING
    METALWORKING
    POTTERY
    SNOWSHOE MAKING
    WEAVING
    WOODWORKING

CRAFTS. Ontario
  1800-1850 -- Re-enactments at Upper Canada Village -- J,I
    971.3   Les Métiers.
    971.3   Crafts.

CRANES. Birds
  See also
    WHOOPING CRANES

CREATIVE WRITING. English language
  -- Teaching materials -- J
    372.6   Three in a haunted house.
    372.6   The Absent-minded Mr. Willoughby.
    372.6   Moving day mix-up.
    372.6   Surprise adventure.
    372.6   The Old map mystery.

CREATIVE WRITING. English language
  -- Teaching materials -- P,J
    372.6   The Great horse contest.
    372.6   The Rescue of Julius the donkey.
    372.6   The Sparkling imagination.
    372.6   The Runaway.

CREATIVE WRITING. French language
  -- Teaching materials -- J
    372.6   L'aventure de Robert.
    372.6   La chasse aux trésors.
    372.6   La maison aux fantômes.
    372.6   Le déménagement.
    372.6   Le sac de M. Danlune.

CREDIT. Personal finance
  -- Consumers' guides -- P,J
    332.024   Money : how much do you need?

CREE LANGUAGE
  Alphabet -- I,S
    411.09701   Cree syllabary.

CRUSTACEANS
  See also
    LOBSTERS

CRUSTACEANS
  -- I,S
    594   Crustaceans, molluscs.

CRYSTALLOGRAPHY
  Experiments -- J,I
    548   How to grow crystals.
    548   Croissance de cristaux.

CUISINE
  Canadian cuisine. Multicultural factors -- J,I
    917.1   An Appetite for heritage.

CULTURAL ASPECTS. Urban regions. Canada
  -- J,I
    301.34   Urban culture.

CULTURE
  See also
    HUMANITIES
    MULTICULTURALISM

CULTURE. Canada
  Historical aspects -- J,I
    917.1   The Heritage puzzle.

CULTURE. Canada
  Historical aspects. Preservation -- J,I
    971   A la découverte de notre patrimoine.
    971   Discovering our heritage.
    971.0074   Places preseving our heritage.

PRECIS SUBJECT INDEX

CULTURE. Canada
 Preservation -- J,I
  917.1 Collecting my own heritage.

CULTURE. China
 -- I
  915.1 Contemporary culture.

CULTURE. Huron Indians
 -- J,I
  970.3 Huron Indian Village & Musem.

CULTURE. Huron Indians
 -- J,I,S
  970.3 The Iroquois-Huron Nations (Eastern Woodland Indians)
  970.3 La famille Huronne-Iroquoise (Indiens des forêts de l'Est)

CULTURE. Innuit. Canada
 -- J,I
  917.12 Eskimo 1 : Arctic village.
  970.4 The Inuit.
  970.4 Days of the igloo.
  970.4 The New north.
  970.4 Eskimo heritage.

CULTURE. Iroquois
 -- J,I,S
  970.3 The Iroquois-Huron Nations (Eastern Woodland Indians)
  970.3 La famille Huronne-Iroquoise (Indiens des forêts de l'Est)

CULTURE. North American Indians. North-eastern North America
 -- J,I
  970.4 Indians of the Northeastern Woodlands.

CULTURE. North American Indians. North-eastern North America
 to c.1600 -- I,S
  970.4 The Native peoples of the Northeastern Woodlands : initial European contact.
  970.4 Les amérindiens des forêts de l'est : jusqu' á l'arrivée des europeens.

CULTURE. North American Indians. Pacific coast
 -- J,I
  970.4 Indians of the Pacific Northwest

CULTURE. North American Indians. Pacific coast
 -- J,I,S
  970.4 People of the North Pacific Coast
  970.4 Les peuplades de la Côte Nord-Ouest.

CULTURE. North American Indians. Pacific coast to c.1600 -- I,S
  970.4 The Native peoples of the Pacif Northwest : initial European contact.
  970.4 Les amérindiens de la côte du pacifique : jusqu'à l'arrivée des europeens.

CULTURE. North American Indians. South-western United States
 -- J,I
  970.4 Indians of the Southwest.

CULTURE. Plains Indians
 -- J,I
  970.4 Indians of the Great Plains.

CULTURE. Plains Indians to c.1600 -- I,S
  970.4 The Native peoples of the Great Plains : initial European contact.
  970.4 Les amérindiens des Grandes Plaines : jusqu'à l'arrivée des Europeens.

CULTURE. Plains Indians to c.1600 -- J,I
  970.4 People of the Plains.
  970.4 Les Indiens des Plaines.

CURRENCY See MONEY

CURRENT. Electricity
 -- J,I
  621.31 Current and pressure.

CUSTOMS
 See also
  SOCIAL CUSTOMS

PRECIS SUBJECT INDEX

CYCLING
  Road safety -- P,J
        614.8   Bicycle safety.

CYPRESS HILLS. Alberta & Saskatchewan
  Geological features -- J,I
        971.24   Fort Walsh in the Cypress Hills.
        971.24   Le Fort Walsh dans les collines
                      Cyprès.

DAIRY FARMING. Elmira. Ontario
  By Mennonites -- J,I
        917.13   Dairy farming community (Elmira,
                      Ont.)
        917.13   Un centre d'industrie laitière.

DAMSELFLIES
  -- P,J
        595.7   Libellules et demoiselles.
        595.7   Dragonflies and damselflies.

DANCES
  North American Indian dances -- J,I,S
        793.3   Indian dances and masks.

DANGEROUS MATERIALS
  See also
     POISONS

DANGERS See HAZARDS

DEBATING
  -- I
        808.53   Classroom debating in
                      parliamentary style.

DECAY. Teeth
  -- J,I,S
        617.6   Awareness of dental problems.

DECAY. Teeth
  Prevention -- K,P
        617.6   Teeth : a new look.

DECEIT
  See also
     HONESTY
     LYING

DECIDUOUS FORESTS. Canada
  compared with boreal forests -- I,S
        581.5   La forêt feuille et la forêt
                      boréale : une comparaison.
        581.5   Deciduous and boreal forests : a
                      comparison.

DECIDUOUS TREES
  -- Field guides -- I,S
        582   Deciduous trees.

DECORATING
  See also
     PAINTING
     WALLPAPER
     Hanging

DECORATIONS. Christmas customs. 1800-1860
  -- Re-enactments at Black Creek Pioneer Village -- P,J
        971.3   Canadian Christmas : Christmas
                      decorations.

DEFENSIVE PLAY. Hockey
  Techniques -- P,J,I
        796.9   Hockey III - the game -

DELPHI. Ancient Greece
  Architecture -- I,S
        722   Delphi, theatres and Olympia.

DENTISTRY
  See also
     TEETH

DENTISTRY
  Parker, Edgar Rudolph Randolph -- J,I
        920   Painless Parker.

DEPARTMENT STORES
  -- P,J
        658.8   The Department store.

DEPRESSION. Economic conditions. Canada
  1929 -- I,S
        971.06   The Great Depression.

DESERTS
  Nomadic communities -- J,I
        910   Nomadic journey : three nomadic
                      peoples.

PRECIS SUBJECT INDEX

DEVELOPED COUNTRIES
   Economic relations with Third world -- S
        382.1   Toward a new international
                  economic order.

DEVELOPING COUNTRIES See THIRD WORLD

DEVELOPMENT
   See also
       ECONOMIC DEVELOPMENT

DEVELOPMENT. Agricultural land. Niagara Peninsula. Ontario
   Effects of regional planning -- J,I,S
        333.7   Fruit Belt preservation and
                  regional planning.

DEVELOPMENT. Children
   -- P,J
        612.6   Le développement et
                  l'apprentissage.
        612.6   Growing and learning.

DEVELOPMENT. Embryos. Man
   -- J
        591.1   Ovulation - mammifères.

DIABETES
   Control by drugs: Insulin. Discovery by Banting, Sir Frederick Grant & Best, Charles Herbert -- J,I
        920   Banting and Best : the discovery
                  of insulin.

DIAZO PROCESS. Overhead transparencies
   -- S
        371.33   The Diazo process.

DIRECTION. Theatre
   -- I,S
        792   Stage movement and directing.

DIRECTORIES
   See also
       TELEPHONE DIRECTORIES

DISEASES
   See also
       DIABETES
       VENEREAL DISEASES

DISPERSAL. Seeds. Plants
   -- P,J
        582   La dissémination des graines.
        582   How seeds are spread.

DISTRESS SIGNALS. Wilderness survival
   -- I
        384   Principaux signaux de détresse.

DO IT YOURSELF GUIDES
   Northern Canada. Log houses. Building -- Do it yourself guides -- S,A
        690   Build your own log house : part
        690   Build your own log house : part

DOCUMENTS
   See also
       BOOKS
       LIBRARIES
       NEWSPAPERS

DOMESTIC ANIMALS
   See also
       CHICKENS
       COWS
       PETS

DOMINION DAY
   Historical aspects -- P,J
        394.2   Dominion Day.
        394.2   Dominion Day.

DONKEYS
   -- P,J,I
        599   Les Anes domestiques.
        599   Donkeys, donkeys, donkeys.

DOORS. Houses
   Panelled doors. Painting -- S
        698.3   Painting a panelled door.

DOUKHOBORS. British Columbia
   1908-1978 -- S
        301.4509711 A Time of migration and troub

DOUKHOBORS. Canada
   Social life -- S
        301.4509711 Doukhobor way of life.
        301.4509711 Doukhobor contribution to
                         Canadian society.

PRECIS SUBJECT INDEX

DOUKHOBORS. Saskatchewan
  1899-1908 -- S
      301.4509711   Doukhobor immigrants in the West

DRAGONFLIES
  -- P,J
      595.7   Libellules et demoiselles.
      595.7   Dragonflies and damselflies.

DRAMA
  See also
      THEATRE

DRAMA IN ENGLISH
  Shakespeare, William -- S
      822.3   Shakespeare : the man, the times and the plays.

DRAWINGS
  Bartlett, William Henry. Special subjects: Canada. Water transport -- J,I
      971   Life along the waterways.

DRAWINGS
  Bartlett, William Henry. Special subjects: Ontario & Quebec Province -- J,I
      971   Quebec and Ontario : old colony and new outpost.

DRAWINGS
  Landscape drawings. Bartlett, William Henry. Special subjects: Maritime Provinces -- J,I
      971   Sketching the New World : Maritime scenes.

DRAWINGS
  Techniques -- P,J
      741.2   The Shape of things : part 1.
      741.2   The Shape of things : part 2.

DRESS See CLOTHING

DRILL PRESSES. Metalworking
  -- I,S
      621.9   Using the drill press.

DROWNPROOFING. Wilderness survival
  Techniques -- I
      614.8   Techniques antinoyade.
      614.8   Water rescue.

DRUG ABUSE
  -- J
      613.8   Effects of misuse.
      615   How people misuse them.

DRUG ABUSE
  Psychological aspects -- J,I
      613.8   Why do people take drugs?
      613.8   Pourquoi prend-on de la drogue?

DRUG ADDICTION
  See also
      ALCOHOLISM
      SMOKING

DRUGS
  See also
      DRUG ABUSE
      OPIATES
      PSYCHOTROPIC DRUGS

DRUGS
  Effects -- J
      615   What they do.

DRUGS
  Insulin. Control of diabetes. Discovery by Banting, Sir Frederick Grant & Best, Charles Herbert -- J,I
      920   Banting and Best : the discovery of insulin.

DRUGS
  Sources -- J
      615   Where they come from.

DRUGS
  Use. Safety measures -- J
      615   Using them safely.

DRUGS
  Use in native religions of America -- S
      299   Drugs and religious ritual.

DRY CLIMATES
  Hot dry climates. Houses. Architectural design -- P,J,I
      728   Homes in hot, dry climates.

PRECIS SUBJECT INDEX

DRY MOUNTING. Graphic media
-- I,S
    760.028   Creating your own visuals using a dry mount press.

DURHAM, JOHN GEORGE LAMBTON, Earl of. Canada
-- I,S
    971.03   Lord Durham's mission.
    971.03   La mission de Lord Durham.

DWELLINGS. Canadian Indians
-- J,I,S
    970.4   Indians : part I.

EARTH
  See also
    GEODESY
    GEOGRAPHY
    GEOLOGICAL FEATURES

EARTH
  Attitudes of Canadian Indians -- J,I,S
    299   Mother Earth : an Indian view.

EARTH. Planets
-- J,I
    525   Notre planète : la terre.
    525   The Planet we live on.

EARTH. Planets
-- J,I,S
    523.1   Our place in the universe.

EARTH. Planets
-- K,P
    525   La Forme de la terre.
    525   The Shape of the earth.

EARTH. Planets
  Effects of sunlight -- J,I
    523.7   La Lumière du soleil.
    523.7   Light from the sun.

EARTH SCIENCES
  See also
    GEOMORPHOLOGY
    PETROLOGY
    TOPOGRAPHY

EASTER
  Canadian social customs. Historical aspects -- P,J
    394.2   Easter in Canada.

EASTER
  Ukrainian social customs -- I,S
    914.7   Easter greetings.

EASTER
  Ukrainian social customs: Egg-painting -- I,S
    914.7   Pysanky.

EASTERN CANADA
  to 1867 -- J,I
    971.5   La Dualité de notre patrimoine.
    971.5   Our dual heritage.

EASTERN CANADA
  Entertainments, 1820-1867 -- Re-enactments at Black Creek Pioneer Village -- P,J,I
    971.3   Pioneer entertainment.

EASTERN CANADA
  Family life, 1820-1867 -- Re-enactments at Black Creek Pioneer Village -- P,J,I
    971.3   Pioneer family life.

EASTERN CANADA
  Frogs & toads -- P,J,I
    597   Toads and frogs of Eastern Canada.

EASTERN CANADA
  Holidays: Thanksgiving. Social customs, 1820-1867 Re-enactments at Black Creek Pioneer Village -- P,J,I
    971.3   Thanksgiving in pioneer Canada.

EASTERN CANADA
  Pioneer life, 1820-1867 -- Re-enactments at Black Creek Pioneer Village -- P,J,I
    971.3   Activities in pioneer days.
    971.3   Country life.
    971.3   Visiting pioneer Canada.

EASTERN CANADA
  Pioneer life, 1830-1850 -- J,I
    971.3   Pioneer homes and schools in Eastern Canada.

PRECIS SUBJECT INDEX

EASTERN CANADA
Technology, 1820-1867 -- Re-enactments at Black Creek Pioneer Village -- P,J,I
    971.3   Pioneer inventions.

EASTERN CANADA
Wildflowers -- Field guides -- P,J,I,S
    582.0971   Fleurs sauvages diverses : l'est du Canada.
    582.0971   Selected wildflowers : eastern Canada.

EASTERN COASTAL REGION. Queensland. Australia
Description & travel -- J,I,S
    919.43   Sugar and coral coast (Queensland)

EASTERN NORTH AMERICA
Spring wildflowers -- Field guides -- J,I
    582.097   Spring wildflowers of eastern North America.

EASTERN NORTH AMERICA
Summer wildflowers -- Field guides -- J,I
    582.097   Summer wildflowers of eastern North America.

EASTERN NORTH AMERICA
Wild orchids -- Field guides -- J,I
    584   Orchids of Eastern North America.

ECHINODERMS
-- I,S
    593   Echinoderms.
    593   Echinoderms.

ECOLOGY
See also
    BIOMES
    ECOSYSTEMS
    ENVIRONMENT

ECOLOGY
-- I,S
    333.9   Environment : biosphere.
    333.9   L'environnement et la biosphère.

ECOLOGY. Arctic Canada
-- J,I
    574.509712 Ecology of the Arctic.

ECOLOGY. Everglades. Florida
-- J,I
    574.509759 Ecology of the Everglades.

ECOLOGY. Spiders
-- J,I
    595   Spider ecology.

ECONOMIC ASPECTS. Urban regions. Canada
-- J,I
    330.12   Urban economy.

ECONOMIC CONDITIONS. Canada
Depression, 1929 -- I,S
    971.06   The Great Depression.

ECONOMIC CONDITIONS. Canada
Policies of federal government -- S
    339.5   Economic policy in perspective.

ECONOMIC CONDITIONS. Cape Breton Island. Nova Scotia
-- J,I
    330.9716   Cape Breton Island : industrial regions.

ECONOMIC CONDITIONS. Labrador. Newfoundland
-- J,I,S
    330.9719   Le Canada atlantique : le Labrador
    330.9719   Atlantic Canada : Labrador.

ECONOMIC CONDITIONS. Maritime Provinces
-- J,I,S
    330.9715   Le Canada atlantique : économie.
    330.9715   Atlantic Canada : economy.

ECONOMIC CONDITIONS. New Brunswick
-- J,I,S
    330.9715   Le Canada atlantique : le Nouveau-Brunswick.
    330.9715   Atlantic Canada : New Brunswick.

ECONOMIC CONDITIONS. Newfoundland
-- J,I,S
    330.9718   Le Canada atlantique : L'Ile de Terre-Neuve.
    330.9718   Atlantic Canada : Island of Newfoundland.

PRECIS SUBJECT INDEX

ECONOMIC CONDITIONS. Nova Scotia
-- J,I,S
    330.9716   Le Canada atlantique : la Nouvelle Ecosse.
    330.9716   Atlantic Canada : Nova Scotia.

ECONOMIC CONDITIONS. Prince Edward island
-- J,I,S
    330.9717   Le Canada atlantique : l'Ile du Prince-Edouard.
    330.9717   Atlantic Canada : Prince Edward Island.

ECONOMIC DEVELOPMENT. Energy resources. Northern Canada
Effects on native peoples -- I,S
    970.5   Northern development at what cost?

ECONOMIC RELATIONS
See also
    FOREIGN AID

ECONOMIC RELATIONS
-- S
    338.91   Let's talk about it.
    338.91   Un nouvel ordre economique international : "parlons-en"

ECONOMIC RELATIONS. Developed countries
With Third world -- S
    382.1   Toward a new international economic order.

ECONOMIC RELATIONS. Third world
With developed countries -- S
    382.1   Toward a new international economic order.

ECONOMICS
See also
    COMMERCE
    FINANCE
    GROSS NATIONAL PRODUCT
    INDUSTRIES
    REVENUE
    SOCIALISM

ECOSYSTEMS
-- J
    574.5   Les ecosystèmes.

ECOSYSTEMS
Food chains -- J
    574.5   Les cycles de nourriture.

ECOSYSTEMS
Forest ecosystems. Forms of life -- P
    574.5   A Visit to the woods.
    574.5   Explorons la forêt.

ECOSYSTEMS
Forest ecosystems. Symbiosis -- J
    574.5   Les communantés végétales et animales.

ECOSYSTEMS
Pond ecosystems. Forms of life -- P
    574.92   A Visit to a pond.
    574.92   Explorons l'etang.

ECOSYSTEMS
Seashore ecosystems. Forms of life -- P
    574.92   Explorons le bord de la mer.
    574.92   A Visit to the seashore.

EDIBLE FRUITS
-- P,J
    641.3   Learning about the fruits we eat

EDIBLE PLANTS
-- Field guides -- J,I,S
    581.6   Eating out II.
    581.6   Eating out I.

EDIBLE PLANTS
-- P,J
    641.3   Learning about the plants we eat

EDMONTON
to 1976 -- J,I
    917.123   Edmonton.

EDMONTON
Description & travel -- J,I
    917.123   Edmonton, Alberta.

EDUCATION
See also
    SCHOOLS

PRECIS SUBJECT INDEX

EDUCATION. China
-- I
    379.51   Education and health.

EDUCATION. China
-- J,I,S
    379.51   Education.

EGG-PAINTING. Ukrainian social customs. Easter
-- I,S
    914.7   Pysanky.

EGYPT
  Cairo. Description & travel -- J,I
    916.2   Gifts of the Nile II : Cairo, the city.

EGYPT
  Nile. Flood plains. Agriculture -- J,I
    631.0962   Gifts of the Nile I : farming on the flood plains.

ELECTIONS. Federal government. Canada
-- J
    324.71   Voting in Canada.
    324.71   Le vote au Canada.

ELECTIONS. Federal government. Canada
-- J,I
    324.71   Get out and vote! election campaigns and issues.

ELECTIONS. Municipal government. Canada
-- Study regions: Ontario. Toronto -- J,I
    324.71   The Municipal election.

ELECTRIC POWER
-- I
    621.31   Electrical energy.

ELECTRIC POWER. Canada
-- J,I
    621.310971   Electrical energy in Canada.

ELECTRICAL ENGINEERING
  See also
    ELECTRIC POWER
    ELECTRICITY SUPPLY

ELECTRICAL EQUIPMENT
  See also
    ELECTRONIC EQUIPMRENT

ELECTRICITY
-- J,I
    537.2   Fundamentals of electricity.

ELECTRICITY
  Current -- J,I
    621.31   Current and pressure.

ELECTRICITY
  Generation -- J,I
    621.3   Sources of electricity.

ELECTRICITY
  Voltage -- J,I
    621.31   Current and pressure.

ELECTRICITY SUPPLY
  See also
    ELECTRICITY SUPPLY EQUIPMENT
    POWER STATIONS

ELECTRICITY SUPPLY EQUIPMENT
  Circuits -- J,I
    621.31   Current and pressure.

ELECTRICITY SUPPLY EQUIPMENT. Residences
-- S
    621.319   Domestic circuits.

ELECTRICITY SUPPLY EQUIPMENT. Residences
  Circuits. Hazards -- J,I
    644   Electrical hazards.

ELECTRONIC EQUIPMENT
-- J,I
    537.5   General electronics.

ELECTRONIC EQUIPMENT
  Location of shoals of fish -- S
    639   Le repérage électronique du poisson.
    639   Electronic fish finding.

PRECIS SUBJECT INDEX

ELECTRONIC EQUIPMENT
   Transistors -- S
       621.3815   The Transistor.

ELECTRONIC EQUIPMENT
   Transistors. Applications -- S
       621.3815   Transistor application.

ELECTRONIC EQUIPMENT
   Vacuum tubes -- S
       621.3815   The Development of the vacuum tube

ELECTRONIC EQUIPMENT
   Vacuum tubes. Applications -- S
       621.3815   Application of the vacuum tube.

ELECTRONIC EQUIPMRENT
   See also
       RADIO EQUIPMENT
       TELEPHONES
       TELEVISION EQUIPMENT

ELGIN, JAMES BRUCE, Earl of. Canada
   -- I,S
       971.04   Lord Elgin's decision.
       971.04   La décision de Lord Elgin.

ELLIOT LAKE. Ontario
   Uranium. Mining -- J,I
       622   Uranium mining in Ontario.

ELMIRA. Ontario
   Dairy farming by Mennonites -- J,I
       917.13   Dairy farming community (Elmira, Ont.)
       917.13   Un contre d'industrie laitière.

EMBRYOS. Man
   Development -- J
       591.1   Ovulation - mammifères.
       612.6   L'Embryon se développe.
       612.6   Développement pré-natal.
       612.6   Pre-natal development.
       612.6   Pattern of embryo development.

EMERGENCY SERVICES
   See also
       FIREFIGHTERS

EMIGRATION
   See also
       IMMIGRATION

EMIGRATION. Ireland
   To Canada, to 1910 -- S
       325.71   Irish immigration.

EMOTIONS
   See also
       ANGER
       ENVY
       FEAR
       FRUSTRATION
       JEALOUSY
       VANITY

EMOTIONS
   -- P,J
       152.4   Ce n'est pas juste.
       152.4   Cesse de faire le bébé.
       152.4   Stop acting like a baby.
       152.4   That's not fair.

EMOTIONS
   Concealment by behaviour -- P,J
       152.4   Inside outside.
       152.4   Les Masques.

EMPLOYMENT. Innuit. Canada
   -- J,I
       970.4   The Eskimo and his work.

ENDANGERED SPECIES
   See also
       WHOOPING CRANES

ENDANGERED SPECIES. North America
   Conservation -- J,I
       639   Threatened and endangered wildl
       639   Habitat : key to survival.
       639   Threatened and endangered wildli McI.
       639   Habitat : key to survival.

ENERGY
   See also
       ELECTRIC POWER
       ELECTRICITY
       LIGHT
       NUCLEAR POWER

PRECIS SUBJECT INDEX

ENERGY INDUSTRIES
   See also
      COAL MINING INDUSTRY
      NATURAL GAS INDUSTRY
      PETROLEUM INDUSTRY

ENERGY RESOURCES
  -- Forecasts -- I
     333.7   Alternatives for the future.

ENERGY RESOURCES
  -- I
     333.7   Introduction to energy.

ENERGY RESOURCES
  -- J,I
     333.7   Sources of power.

ENERGY RESOURCES. Canada
  -- J,I
     333.7   The Energy crisis?

ENERGY RESOURCES. Northern Canada
  Economic development. Effects on native peoples -- I, S
     970.5   Northern development at what cost?

ENGINEERING
   See also
      ELECTRIC POWER
      ELECTRICITY SUPPLY
      HEATING
      LIGHTING
      MACHINERY
      MILITARY ENGINEERING
      WORKSHOP PRACTICE

ENGINES. Motor vehicles
  Fuel pumps. Maintenance & repair -- I,S
     629.22   Pistons, oil and and fuel pumps.

ENGINES. Motor vehicles
  Oil pumps. Maintenance & repair -- I,S
     629.22   Pistons, oil and and fuel pumps.

ENGLISH LANGUAGE
   See also
      LITERATURE IN ENGLISH

ENGLISH LANGUAGE
  to 1400 -- I,S
     420.9   Origins and early history of English.

ENGLISH LANGUAGE
  Creative writing -- Teaching materials -- J
     372.6   Three in a haunted house.
     372.6   The Absent-minded Mr. Willoughby.
     372.6   Moving day mix-up.
     372.6   Surprise adventure.
     372.6   The Old map mystery.

ENGLISH LANGUAGE
  Creative writing -- Teaching materials -- P,J
     372.6   The Great horse contest.
     372.6   The Rescue of Julius the donkey.
     372.6   The Sparkling imagination.
     372.6   The Runaway.

ENGLISH LANGUAGE
  Pronunciation. Pitch -- J
     421   Pitch, stress and juncture.

ENGLISH LANGUAGE
  Pronunciation. Stress -- J
     421   Pitch, stress and juncture.

ENGLISH LANGUAGE
  Punctuation -- J
     421   Using punctuation marks.

ENGLISH LANGUAGE
  Punctuation: Apostrophes -- J
     421   Quotation marks and the apostrophe

ENGLISH LANGUAGE
  Punctuation: Capital letters -- J
     421   Using capital letters.

ENGLISH LANGUAGE
  Punctuation: Commas -- J
     421   Commas.

ENGLISH LANGUAGE
  Punctuation: Exclamation marks -- J
     421   Periods, question marks, and exclamation marks.

PRECIS SUBJECT INDEX

ENGLISH LANGUAGE
   Punctuation: Periods -- J
      421   Periods, question marks, and exclamation marks.

ENGLISH LANGUAGE
   Punctuation: Quotation marks -- J
      421   Quotation marks and the apostrophe

ENGLISH LANGUAGE
   Reading -- Teaching materials -- P
      411   The Gobbler.
      411   The Ticker.
      411   The Doodler.
      411   The Puffer.
      411   The Cowboy.
      411   The Bungler.

ENGLISH LANGUAGE
   Reading -- Teaching materials -- P,J
      F   One kitten for Kim.
      636   Big red barn.

ENGLISH LITERATURE
   to 1558 -- S
      820.9   From the beginnings to Elizabeth.

ENGLISH LITERATURE
   1558-1625 -- S
      820.9   The Elizabethan era.

ENGLISH LITERATURE
   1625-1798 -- S
      820.9   From puritan to Augustan.

ENGLISH LITERATURE
   1798-1837 -- S
      820.9   The Romantic era.

ENGLISH LITERATURE
   1837-1901 -- S
      820.9   The Victorian era.

ENGLISH LITERATURE
   1901-1929 -- S
      820.9   The Twentieth century : 1900-1929.

ENGLISH LITERATURE
   1929-1974 -- S
      820.9   The Twentieth century : 1929 - present.

ENTERTAINMENTS
   See also
      AIRSHOWS
      FAIRS
      PARADES
      PERFORMING ARTS
      RECREATIONS
      RODEOS

ENTERTAINMENTS. Eastern Canada
   1820-1867 -- Re-enactments at Black Creek Pioneer Village -- P,J,I
      971.3   Pioneer entertainment.

ENVIRONMENT
   See also
      ATMOSPHERE
      ECOLOGY

ENVIRONMENT
   Adaptation of animals -- J
      591.5   L'Habitat.

ENVIRONMENT
   Adaptation of birds -- J,I
      598.2   Comment les oiseaux s'adaptent pour survivre.
      598.2   How birds adapt to survive.
      598.2   Birds and their environment.

ENVIRONMENT
   Adaptation of organisms -- J
      574.5   Les Organismes et le milieu.

ENVIRONMENT
   Conservation -- I,S
      333.9   La protection de l'environnement
      333.9   Environment protection.

ENVIRONMENT
   Effects on personality -- J,I
      155.2   Vous et votre personnalité.
      155.2   You and your personality.

ENVIRONMENT
   Pollution -- I,S
      333.9   La crise de l'environnement.
      333.9   Environment crisis.

PRECIS SUBJECT INDEX

ENVIRONMENT. Arctic Canada
  Conservation -- J,I
        574.509712 Patterns of life.

ENVIRONMENT. Arctic North America
  Adaptation of animals -- J,I
        591.9712   Animals of the Arctic.

ENVIRONMENT. Arctic North America
  Adaptation of mammals -- P,J
        599.09712   The Arctic.

ENVIRONMENT. Cities
  Adaptation of organisms -- J,I
        574.5   Nature in the neighbourhood.
        574.5   Nature adapts to the city.
        574.5   City habitats.

ENVIRONMENT. Forests. North America
  Adaptation of mammals -- J,I
        599.097   Life in the boreal forest.

ENVIRONMENT. Forests. North America
  Adaptation of mammals -- P,J
        599.097   The Eastern forest.

ENVIRONMENT. Grasslands. Africa
  Adaptation of animals -- J,I
        591.96   Grassland 1 : animals of the African Grasslands.

ENVIRONMENT. North America
  Adaptation of mammals -- J,I
        599   The Story of mammals.

ENVIRONMENT. Prairies. North America
  Adaptation of mammals -- J,I
        591.5   Life on the Prairies.

ENVIRONMENT. Prairies. North America
  Adaptation of mammals -- P,J
        599.097   The Grasslands.

ENVIRONMENT. Rocky Mountains. North America
  Adaptation of mammals -- P,J
        599.097   The Rocky Mountains.

ENVIRONMENT. Tundra. Arctic North America
  Adaptation of mammals -- J,I
        574.509712 Life on the Barren Lands.

ENVIRONMENT. Urban regions
  Pollution -- J,I
        301.34   Problems of urban environment.

ENVIRONMENT. Winter
  Adaptation of animals -- J,I
        591.5   Discovering animals in winter.

ENVIRONMENT. Winter
  Adaptation of plants -- J,I
        581.5   Discovering plants in winter.

ENVIRONMENTAL ENGINEERING
  See also
    HEATING
    LIGHTING

ENVIRONMENTAL FACTORS. Architectural design. Houses
  -- P,J,I
        728   Factors influencing homes.

ENVIRONMENTAL PLANNING
  See also
    URBAN PLANNING

ENVY
  See also
    JEALOUSY

ENVY
  -- J
        152.4   Je l'envie.

EROSION. Scarborough Bluffs. Ontario
  Counter-measures -- J,I
        917.13   The Natural environment.

ESKIMOS See INNUIT

ETHICS
  See also
    MORAL DECISIONS

PRECIS SUBJECT INDEX

ETHNIC GROUPS
  See also
    IMMIGRANTS
    MULTICULTURALISM

ETHNIC GROUPS. Canada
  -- I,S
      917.1   Mosaic Canada.

ETHNIC GROUPS. Canada
  Blacks -- I,S
      301.450971 Black Canadians.

ETHNIC GROUPS. Canada
  Chinese -- I,S
      301.450971 Chinese and Japanese Canadians.

ETHNIC GROUPS. Canada
  Chinese -- P,J
      301.450971 My family is Chinese.

ETHNIC GROUPS. Canada
  Chinese -- S
      301.450971 Chinese contribution to Canadian
              life.

ETHNIC GROUPS. Canada
  Europeans -- I,S
      325.71   European Canadians.

ETHNIC GROUPS. Canada
  Indians -- P,J
      301.450971 My birthplace was India.

ETHNIC GROUPS. Canada
  Irish -- S
      301.450971 Irish contributions to Canadian
              life.

ETHNIC GROUPS. Canada
  Italians -- P,J
      301.450971 My Italian heritage.

ETHNIC GROUPS. Canada
  Jamaicans -- P,J
      301.450971 I come from Jamaica.

ETHNIC GROUPS. Canada
  Japanese -- I,S
      301.450971 Chinese and Japanese Canadians

ETHNIC GROUPS. Canada
  Japanese -- S
      301.450971 Japanese contribution to Canad
              society.

ETHNIC GROUPS. Canada
  Japanese. Internment, 1939-1945 -- S
      301.450971 The Japanese during World War

ETHNIC GROUPS. Canada
  Portuguese -- P,J
      301.450971 I was born in Portugal.

EURACTOS See BLACK BEARS

EUROPE
  -- Maps -- J,I
      912   Cartes muettes du monde :
                L'Europe et l'Afrique.
      912   Outline maps of the world : pa

EUROPEANS. Ethnic groups. Canada
  -- I,S
      325.71   European Canadians.

EVERGLADES. Florida
  Birds -- J,I
      598.2   Birds of the Everglades.

EVERGLADES. Florida
  Ecology -- J,I
      574.509759 Ecology of the Everglades.

EVERGREEN TREES
  -- Field guides -- I,S
      585   Evergreen trees.

EXCAVATION. Antiquities
  -- J,I
      913   Stone Age man I : an
                archaeological dig.

EXCAVATION. Iroquois antiquities. North America
  -- J,I
      913   The Iroquoian people.
      913   Developing an Iroquoian villag
                site.

PRECIS SUBJECT INDEX

EXCLAMATION MARKS. Punctuation. English language
  -- J
        421   Periods, question marks, and exclamation marks.

EXERCISE See PHYSICAL EXERCISE

EXPERIMENTS. Crystallography
  -- J,I
        548   How to grow crystals.
        548   Croissance de cristaux.

EXPERIMENTS. Science
  -- P,J
        507   5 sens + mésures = observation.
        507   5 senses + measurement = observation.

EXPLORATION
  -- P,J
        910   Land of gold : land of ice.

EXPLORATION. Arctic Canada
  -- J
        917.12   Exploration of Arctic Canada.
        917.12   Exploration de l'Arctique canadien

EXPLORATION. Asia
Polo, Marco -- J
        920   Adventuresome Marco Polo.

EXPLORATION. Canada
  -- I,S
        971.01   The Discovery of Canada.

EXPLORATION. Canada
Cartier, Jacques -- J,I
        971.01   Jacques Cartier.
        971.01   Jacques Cartier.

EXPLORATION. Canada
Champlain, Samuel de -- J,I
        971.01   Samuel de Champlain.
        971.01   Samuel de Champlain.

EXPLORATION. Canada
La Verendrye, Pierre Gualtier de Varennes, sieur de -- J
        971.01   La Vérendrye.

EXPLORATION. Moon
  -- P,J
        629.45   Explorations lunaires.
        629.45   Moon exploration.

EXPLORATION. North America
Thompson, David -- J,I
        920   David Thompson.

EXPLORATION. Northwest Passage
1576-1822 -- J,I
        910   Fact and fancy.

EXPLORATION. Northwest Passage
1576-1906 -- I,S
        971.2   Discovering the land.

EXPLORATION. Northwest Passage
1819-1845 -- J,I
        910   Discoveries and disappointments.

EXPLORATION. Northwest Passage
1845-1906 -- J,I
        910   Tragedy and triumph.

EXPLORATION. Solar system
  -- J,I,S
        523.4   Our journey into space.

EXPO '67
  -- J,I,S
        607.4   Expo 67 : Montreal, Canada.
        607.4   Expo '67 : [Montreal, (Canada)]

EXPO '70
Canadian pavilions -- P,J,I
        607.4   Canada at Osaka '70.
        607.4   Le Canada à Osaka '70.

FAIRS
  -- P,J
        607.4   Let's go to the fair.

FALL. Seasons
  -- J
        525   Autumn.

PRECIS SUBJECT INDEX

FALL. Seasons
 -- K,P
  525   L'Automne et l'hiver : ce qu'ils sont.
  525   Autumn and winter : what they mean

FALL FLOWERING PLANTS. Canada
 -- Gardening guides -- I,S
  582   Garden flowers of summer and autumn.

FALL WILDFLOWERS. Canada
 -- Field guides -- I,S
  582   Wild flowers of summer & autumn.

FALL WILDFLOWERS. North America
 -- Field guides -- J,I
  582.097 Autumn wildflowers of eastern North America.

FAMILIES
 See also
  MARRIAGE

FAMILIES
 -- P
  301.42 Backwards is forwards in reverse.
  301.42 Derriere est evant sens devant derriere.

FAMILY LIFE
 See also
  PARENTHOOD

FAMILY LIFE. Eastern Canada
 1820-1867 -- Re-enactments at Black Creek Pioneer Village -- P,J,I
  971.3   Pioneer family life.

FAMILY LIFE. Montreal
 -- Comparative studies -- P,J
  917.14 Trois familles de Montréal.
  917.14 Three families of Montreal.

FAMILY LIFE. Ontario
 1800-1850 -- Re-enactments at Upper Canada Village -- J,I
  971.3   La Famille.
  971.3   Family life.

FAMILY PLANNING
 See also
  CONTRACEPTION

FARM CHORES
 -- K
  631   Farm chores.

FARMING
 See also
  CATTLE FARMING
  DAIRY FARMING
  FRUIT FARMING
  MILKING
  POULTRY FARMING
  SHEEP FARMING

FARMING
 -- P
  630.1   A Visit to a farm.

FARMING. Alberta
 Irrigated farming -- J,I
  631.7   Irrigated farming in Alberta.

FARMING. Canada
 to 1977 -- J
  631.0971 Farming in pioneer Canada.

FARMING. Manitoba
 Mixed farming -- J,I
  631.097127 Mixed farming in Manitoba.

FARMING. North America
 1800-1850 -- P,J,I
  970   The Making of a farm.

FARMING. Ontario
 1800-1850 -- Re-enactments at Upper Canada Village J,I
  971.3   Farm life.

FARMS. Special subjects. Photographs
 -- P,J,I
  407   Of the farm.

FEAR
 -- J
  152.4   J'ai peur.
  152.4   Your fear.

PRECIS SUBJECT INDEX

FEAR
  -- P,J
      152.4   Tout le monde a peur de quelque chose.
      152.4   Everybody's afraid of something.

FEDERAL GOVERNMENT. Canada
  -- I,S
      328.71   Le gouvernement fédéral.
      328.71   Federal government.

FEDERAL GOVERNMENT. Canada
  Elections -- J
      324.71   Voting in Canada.
      324.71   Le vote au Canada.

FEDERAL GOVERNMENT. Canada
  Elections -- J,I
      324.71   Get out and vote! election campaigns and issues.

FEDERAL GOVERNMENT. Canada
  Policies on economic conditions -- S
      339.5   Economic policy in perspective.

FEDERAL GOVERNMENT. Canada
  Relations with provincial government -- J,I
      342.4   Ottawa and the provinces : issues, choices and values.

FEDERAL PARLIAMENT. Canada See PARLIAMENT. Canada

FEELINGS See EMOTIONS

FELINES. Canada
  -- P,J
      599   Félins du Canada.
      599   The Cat family.

FESTIVALS
  See also
    CHRISTMAS
    EASTER
    HALLOWEEN
    PASSOVER
    ST. VALENTINE'S DAY

FETUSES
  See also
    EMBRYOS

FILLETING. Fish
  -- I,S
      641.4   Dressing fish.

FILMS. Photography
  -- J,I
      771   Film and filters.

FILMSTRIPS
  Graphic design -- I,S
      778.2   Producing graphics for slides and filmstrips.

FILTERS. Photography
  -- J,I
      771   Film and filters.

FINANCE
  See also
    BANKING
    MONEY
    PERSONAL FINANCE

FIRE
  Safety measures -- P
      614.8   "Flashy" the fire bug.

FIRE MAKING. Wilderness survival
  -- I
      613.6   Faire un feu et construire un abri
      613.6   How to make a fire and shelter.

FIREFIGHTERS
  -- K
      363.3   The Firefighter.

FIREFIGHTERS
  -- P
      363.3   My father the fireman.

FIRST AID
  See also
    ARTIFICIAL RESPIRATION

FIRST AID. Wilderness survival
  -- I
      614.8   Premiers soins en forêt.
      614.8   First aid in the bush.

PRECIS SUBJECT INDEX

FISH
   See also
      SALMON

FISH
   Filleting -- I,S
      641.4   Dressing fish.

FISH
   Shoals. Location. Electronic equipment -- S
      639   Le repérage électronique du poisson.
      639   Electronic fish finding.

FISH. Food
   See also
      SHELLFISH

FISH. Food
   -- Consumers' guides -- S
      641.3   Get hooked on fish.

FISH. Food
   Cookery -- J,I
      641.6   The Way to cook fish.

FISH. Food
   Freshwater fish. Cookery -- I,S
      641.6   Let's serve freshwater fish.

FISH PROCESSING. British Columbia
   -- J,I
      639   Fish processing in British Columbia.

FISH PROCESSING. Lunenberg. Nova Scotia
   -- I
      639   The Fish processing plant.

FISHING
   See also
      COMMERCIAL FISHING

FISHING. Sports
   Ice fishing -- I,S
      799.1   Ice fishing.

FISHING INDUSTRIES
   See also
      COMMERCIAL FISHING
      TROUT FARMING

FISHING INDUSTRIES. Canada
   to 1969 -- J
      338.30971   Fish.

FISHING INDUSTRIES. Pictou. Nova Scotia
   -- J
      917.16   Pictou, Nova Scotia.

FLAGS
   Canadian flag. 1965- -- J,I
      929.90971   Comment le Canada obtint son drapeau.
      929.90971   Les Drapeaux Canadiens et leur usage.
      929.90971   How Canada got its flag.
      929.90971   Canadian flags and how they are used.
      929.90971   Les drapeaux canadiens et leur usage.

FLAGS
   Canadian flag. to 1965. Historical aspects -- J,I
      929.90971   Les Drapeaux Canadiens d'autrefois

FLAGS
   Canadian Provincial flags -- J,I
      929.90971   Flags, coats of arms, and floral emblems of Canada.
      929.90971   Les Drapeaux Canadiens et leur usage.
      929.90971   Canadian flags and how they are used.
      929.90971   Les drapeaux canadiens et leur usage.

FLAGS
   Canadian Territorial flags -- J,I
      929.90971   Flags, coats of arms, and floral emblems of Canada.
      929.90971   Les Drapeaux Canadiens et leur usage.
      929.90971   Canadian flags and how they are used.
      929.90971   Les drapeaux canadiens et leur usage.

PRECIS SUBJECT INDEX

FLIGHT. Aircraft
-- J,I
    629.132   Aéronautique élémentaire.
    629.132   Basic principles of flight.
    629.135   Aircraft in motion.

FLIN FLON. Manitoba
Mining industries -- I
    917.127   Flin Flon, Manitoba.

FLOOD PLAINS. Nile. Egypt
Agriculture -- J,I
    631.0962   Gifts of the Nile I : farming on the flood plains.

FLORAL EMBLEMS
Provincial floral emblems -- J,I
    929.90971   Flags, coats of arms, and floral emblems of Canada.

FLORAL EMBLEMS
Territorial floral emblems -- J,I
    929.90971   Flags, coats of arms, and floral emblems of Canada.

FLORIDA
Everglades. Birds -- J,I
    598.2   Birds of the Everglades.

FLORIDA
Everglades. Ecology -- J,I
    574.509759   Ecology of the Everglades.

FLOSSING. Teeth
-- J,I,S
    617.6   Flossing vs. gum disease.

FLOUR MILLING. Ontario
1800-1850 -- Re-enactments at Black Creek Pioneer Village -- J,I
    971.3   The Mill.

FLOWERING PLANTS
See also
    ORCHIDS
    WILDFLOWERS

FLOWERING PLANTS. Canada
Fall flowering plants -- Gardening guides -- I,S
    582   Garden flowers of summer and autumn.

FLOWERING PLANTS. Canada
Spring flowering plants -- Gardening guides -- I,S
    582   Garden flowers of spring.

FLOWERING PLANTS. Canada
Summer flowering plants -- Gardening guides -- I,S
    582   Garden flowers of summer and autumn.

FOETUSES See FETUSES

FOLKLORE
African folklore -- Stories -- P,J
    398.2096   Why the spider has a narrow waist.
    398.2096   How the leopard got its spots.

FOLKLORE
Canadian folklore -- Stories -- P
    398.20971   La mouette et la baleine.

FOLKLORE
Chinese folklore -- Stories -- J
    398.20951   The Wishing bowl (China)

FOLKLORE
Chinese folklore -- Stories -- P,J
    398.20951   The Superlative horse.
    398.20951   The Mandarin and the butterflies.

FOLKLORE
French Canadian folklore -- Stories -- P
    398.2   Ti-Jean and the lumberjacks.
    398.2   Ti-Jean saves the harvest.
    440.7   Ti-Jean et les bûcherons.
    440.7   Les exploits de Ti-Jean dans l'Ouest.

FOLKLORE
French Canadian folklore -- Stories -- P,J
    398.2   The Legend of the flying canoe.

FOLKLORE
French folklore -- Stories -- P,J
    398.20944   Sleeping Beauty : a French legend.
    398.20944   Puss 'n Boots.

FOLKLORE
German folklore -- Stories -- J
    398.20943   Baron Münchhausen in a whale of a tale : a German legend.

PRECIS SSBJECT INDEX

FOLKLORE
    German folklore. Special subjects: Christmas --
    Stories -- P,J
        398.20943   Germany : the nutcracker's happy
                    Christmas.

FOLKLORE
    Haida folklore -- Stories -- P,J
        398.209701 Le premier saumon.
        398.209701 The First salmon.

FOLKLORE
    Hungarian folklore -- Stories -- P,J
        398.209439 The Miraculous hind : a hungarian
                    legend.
        398.209439 La biche miraculeuse : une
                    légende hongroise.

FOLKLORE
    Indian folklore -- Stories -- J
        398.20954   The Rajah's garden.

FOLKLORE
    Innuit folklore -- Stories -- J
        398.2   The Festival of the seals.
        398.2   Le Festival des phoques.

FOLKLORE
    Innuit folklore -- Stories -- P
        398.2   Le hibou et le lemming : une
                    légende eskimo.
        398.2   The Owl and the lemming : Eskimo
                    legend.

FOLKLORE
    Innuit folklore -- Stories -- P,J
        398.2   The Shaman goes to the moon.
        398.2   Attituk and the caribou.
        398.2   The Legend of the raven who flew
                    backwards.
        398.2   The Angekkok of Thule.

FOLKLORE
    Innuit folklore -- Stories -- P,J,I
        398.2   The Hunter who went away.
        398.2   Le chasseur qui partit.

FOLKLORE
    Irish folklore. Special subjects: Christmas --
    Stories -- P,J
        398.209415 Ireland : O'Reilly's Christmas cap

FOLKLORE
    Italian folklore -- Stories -- P,J
        398.20945   The Silliest man in Italy.

FOLKLORE
    Italian folklore. Special subjects: Christmas --
    Stories -- P,J
        398.20945   L'Italie : la legende de Dame
                    Befana.

FOLKLORE
    Japanese folklore -- Stories -- P
        398.20952   The Two frogs : a Japanese lege

FOLKLORE
    Japanese folklore -- Stories -- P,J
        398.20952   Urashima Taro the fisherlad.

FOLKLORE
    Jewish folklore -- Stories -- J
        398.2095694 The Lost wisdom (Israel)

FOLKLORE
    Jewish folklore -- Stories -- P,J
        398.2095694 The Value of a boiled egg.

FOLKLORE
    Mexican folklore. Special subjects: Christmas --
    Stories -- P,J
        398.20972   La Mexique : l'humble présent.
        398.20972   Mexico : the humblest gift.

FOLKLORE
    Micmac folklore -- Stories -- P,J,I
        398.209701 How summer came to our land.
        398.209701 The Legend of the loon.

FOLKLORE
    North American Indian folklore -- Stories -- J
        398.209701 Glooskap brings summer.
        398.209701 The Medicine that restores life
        398.209701 How it all began.
        398.209701 Le Bouc à une corne.
        398.209701 The Sun dance of the Plains
                    Indians.
        398.209701 The One-horned mountain goat.
        398.209701 Le remède de la vie.
        398.209701 Au tout début.
        398.209701 La danse du soleil des
                    Amérindiens de Plaines.

PRECIS SUBJECT INDEX

FOLKLORE
    North American Indian folklore -- Stories -- P
        398.209701 Naba-Cha and the Rocky Mountains.
        398.209701 Why a porcupine has quills.
        398.209701 Glooscap and the four wishes.
        398.209701 Les piquants du Porc-Epic.
        398.209701 Glooscap et les quatre voeux :
          [légende indienne]

FOLKLORE
    North American Indian folklore -- Stories -- P,J
        398.209701 How the deer got fire.

FOLKLORE
    North American Indian folklore -- Stories -- P,J,I
        398.209701 Pourquoi les pieds-noirs ne font jamais de mal aux souris.

FOLKLORE
    Polish folklore -- Stories -- P
        398.209438 Foolish Bartek : (a Polish tale)
        398.209438 Bartek l'étourdi : un conte polinais.

FOLKLORE
    Puerto Rican folklore -- Stories -- P,J
        398.2097295 The Tiger and the rabbit.

FOLKLORE
    Russian folklore -- Stories -- P,J
        398.20947 The Firebird and the magic horse.
        398.20947 Peter and the wolf.

FOLKLORE
    Syrian folklore. Special subjects: Christmas -- Stories -- P,J
        398.2095691 Syria : the little camel.

FOLKLORE
    Turkish folklore -- Stories -- J
        398.209561 Foolish friends : Turkey.

FOLKLORE
    Ukrainian folklore -- Stories -- P,J
        398.20947 Ilia the mighty : a Ukrainian legend.
        398.20947 Ilia le Grans : une légende Ukrainienne.

FOLKSONGS
    Canadian folksongs -- Film interpretations -- P,J
        784.40971 The Raftsmen.
        784.40971 Jack was every inch a sailor.

FOLKSONGS
    French Canadian folksongs -- Film interpretations -- P,J
        784.709714 Cadet Rousselle.

FOOD
    See also
        BREAD
        CHOCOLATE
        CUISINE
        EDIBLE FRUITS
        EDIBLE PLANTS
        FISH. Food
        GVUSHUM
        HOT DOGS
        MAPLE SYRUP
        MEALS
        MILK
        NUTRITION
        SNACKS

FOOD
    -- I,S
        641.1   Connaître les sortes d'aliments.
        641.1   Knowing your food groups.

FOOD. Birds
    -- J,I
        598.2   How birds find food.

FOOD. Canada
    Christmas food, 1800-1860 -- Re-enactments at Black Creek Pioneer Village -- P,J
        971.3   Canadian christmas : festive foods

FOOD. Canada
    Grading -- Consumers' guides -- J,I,S
        614.3   Aliments classés du Canada.
        614.3   Canada's graded foods.

FOOD. Canada
    Thanksgiving food. 1800-1860 -- Re-enactments at Black Creek Pioneer Village -- P,J
        971.3   Thanksgiving foods.

PRECIS SUBJECT INDEX

FOOD CHAINS. Ecosystems
-- J
    574.5   Les cycles de nourriture.
    574.5   Food chains.

FOOD PRESERVATION. Wilderness survival
-- Techniques -- I
    613.6   Outdoor cooking.

FOOD PROCESSING
See also
    FISH PROCESSING
    MEAT PACKING

FOOD PRODUCTION
See also
    AGRICULTURE
    SHOOTING

FOOD PRODUCTION INDUSTRIES
See also
    AGRICULTURAL INDUSTRIES
    FISHING INDUSTRIES

FOREIGN AID. Third world
From Canada -- S
    338.91   What is international development assistance?

FOREIGN RELATIONS. Canada
With United States, 1775-1914 -- S
    327.71   Canadian-American relations : part 1.

FOREIGN RELATIONS. Canada
With United States, 1914-1963 -- S
    327.71   Canadian-American relations : part 2.

FOREIGN RELATIONS. Canada
With United States, 1963-1977 -- S
    327.71   Canadian-American relations : part 3.

FOREIGN RELATIONS. United States
With Canada, 1775-1914 -- S
    327.71   Canadian-American relations : part 1.

FOREIGN RELATIONS. United States
With Canada, 1914-1963 -- S
    327.71   Canadian-American relations : part 2.

FOREIGN RELATIONS. United States
With Canada, 1963-1977 -- S
    327.71   Canadian-American relations : part 3.

FOREST ECOSYSTEMS
Forms of life -- P
    574.5   A Visit to the woods.
    574.5   Explorons la forêt.

FOREST ECOSYSTEMS
Symbiosis -- J
    574.5   Les communantés végétales et animales.

FOREST PRODUCTS INDUSTRIES
See also
    PULP & PAPER INDUSTRIES
    TIMBER INDUSTRY

FOREST PRODUCTS INDUSTRIES
Resources management -- J,I
    634.9   Forest management and lumberir

FOREST PRODUCTS INDUSTRIES. Canada
-- J,I,S
    338.10971   The Forest economy.
    338.10971   L'economie forestière.

FOREST PRODUCTS INDUSTRIES. Canada
to 1969 -- J
    338.10971   Timber.

FOREST PRODUCTS INDUSTRIES. Canadian Shield
-- J,I,S
    634.9   Le Bouclier canadien - indus forestières.
    634.9   Forestry in the Canadian Shie

FORESTRY
See also
    LOGGING

FORESTS. Canada
Boreal forests compared with deciduous forests -- I,S
    581.5   La forêt feuille et la forêt
                boréale : une comparaison.
    581.5   Deciduous and boreal forests : a
                comparison.

FORESTS. Canada
Coastal forests compared with montane forests -- I,S
    581.5   Coast and montane forest : a
                comparison.
    581.6   La forêt des montagnes et la
                forêt côtière : une comparaison.

FORESTS. Canada
Distribution -- I,S
    917.1   Canada's forest regions.
    917.1   Les régions forestières du Canada.

FORESTS. North America
Environment. Adaptation of mammals -- J,I
    599.097 Life in the boreal forest.

FORESTS. North America
Environment. Adaptation of mammals -- P,J
    599.097 The Eastern forest.

FORGING. Metalworking
-- I,S
    671.3   Forging iron.

FORMING. Metalworking
-- I,S
    621.9   Forming metal by machine.

FORT LANGLEY. Trading posts. Fur trade. British Columbia
-- J,I,S
    971.1   Le Fort Langley : carrefour de la
                côte ouest.
    971.1   Fort Langley : gateway to the west

FORT STEELE. British Columbia
Description & travel -- I
    971.1   The Town of Fort Steele.
    971.1   La ville de Fort Steele.

FORT WALSH. Alberta
Description & travel -- J,I
    971.24   Fort Walsh in the Cypress Hills.
    971.24   Le Fort Walsh dans les collines
                 Cyprès.

FORT WILLIAM. Trading posts. Fur trade. Ontario
-- I
    971.3   Life in the old Fort.
    971.3   The Growth, the decline.

FORTS
See also
    FORT LANGLEY
    FORT STEELE
    FORT WALSH
    FORT WILLIAM
    LOWER FORT GARRY

FOWL-LIKE BIRDS. North America
-- J,I
    598.2   Fowl-like birds.

FRANCE
Joan of Arc, Saint -- J
    920   Commanding Joan of Arc.

FRANCE
Palace of Versailles. Architecture -- I,S
    728.8   Versailles and Portugal.

FRANCE
Paris. Architecture -- I,S
    720.944 Paris.

FRANCE
Seven Years' War -- J,I,S
    971.01   The Seven Years' War.
    971.01   La guerre de Sept ans.

FREDERICTON. New Brunswick
Description & travel -- P,J
    917.15   Fredericton, New Brunswick.

FRENCH CANADIAN FOLKLORE
-- Stories -- P
    398.2   Ti-Jean and the lumberjacks.
    398.2   Ti-Jean saves the harvest.
    440.7   Ti-Jean et les bûcherons.
    440.7   Les exploits de Ti-Jean dans
                l'Ouest.

FRENCH CANADIAN FOLKLORE
-- Stories -- P,J
    398.2   The Legend of the flying canoe.

PRECIS SUBJECT INDEX

FRENCH CANADIAN FOLKSONGS
-- Film interpretations -- P,J
    784.709714 Cadet Rousselle.

FRENCH CANADIANS
-- I,S
    301.450971 French Canadians.

FRENCH COLONISATION. Canada
1534-1713 -- J,I
    971.01   France in the New World.

FRENCH FOLKLORE
-- Stories -- P,J
    398.20944 Sleeping Beauty : a French legend.
    398.20944 Puss 'n Boots.

FRENCH LANGUAGE
-- Teaching materials -- J,I
    440.7   Le corbeau et le renard.
    440.7   Conseil tenu par les rats.
    440.7   Le rat de ville et le rat des champs.
    440.7   Le renard et la cigogne.
    440.7   Le lion et le rat.
    440.7   L'ours et les deux compagnons.
    440.7   Le cordonnier et le banquier.
    440.7   Les deux chevres.
    440.7   La cigale et la fourmi.
    440.7   Le renard et le bouc.

FRENCH LANGUAGE
Creative writing -- Teaching materials -- J
    372.6   L'aventure de Robert.
    372.6   La chasse aux trésors.
    372.6   La maison aux fantômes.
    372.6   Le déménagement.
    372.6   Le sac de M. Danlune.

FRENCH LANGUAGE
Reading -- Teaching materials -- P,J
    F   Un seul chaton.
    440.7   Les aventures de Léo à la ferme.
    636   La grange rouge.

FRENCH LETTERS See CONDOMS

FRESHWATER FISH. Food
Cookery -- I,S
    641.6   Let's serve freshwater fish.

FRIGHT See FEAR

FROGS
Life cycle -- J
    597   La Vie commence - grenouilles.

FROGS
Reproduction -- J
    597   La Vie commence - grenouilles.

FROGS. Canada
Life cycle -- P,J,I
    597   The Frog.
    597   La grenouille.

FROGS. Eastern Canada
-- P,J,I
    597   Toads and frogs of Eastern Canada

FRONTENAC, LOUIS DE BAUDE, comte de. New France
-- P,J
    971.01   Frontenac.
    971.01   Frontenac.

FRUIT FARMING
See also
    BERRY FARMING

FRUIT FARMING. Niagara Peninsula. Ontario
-- I,S
    333.7   An Overview of the Niagara Fruit Belt.
    917.13   Introduction to the Niagara Fruit Belt.

FRUIT FARMING. Okanagan Valley. British Columbia
-- J,I
    634   Fruit farming in British Columbia
    917.11   Ville fruitière.
    917.11   Orchard City (Kelowna, B.C.)

FRUITS
See also
    EDIBLE FRUITS

FRUSTRATION
-- J
    152.4   C'est frustrant.
    152.4   Your frustration.

PRECIS SUBJECT INDEX

FUEL PUMPS. Engines. Motor vehicles
  Maintenance & repair -- I,S
       629.22   Pistons, oil and and fuel pumps.

FUR TRADE. British Columbia
  Trading posts: Fort Langley -- J,I,S
       971.1   Le Fort Langley : carrefour de la
                      côte ouest.
       971.1   Fort Langley : gateway to the west

FUR TRADE. Canada
  to 1969 -- J
       338.30971 Fur.

FUR TRADE. Manitoba
  Trading posts: Lower Fort Garry -- J,I,S
       971.27   Lower Fort Garry : legacy of the
                     fur trade.

FUR TRADE. Ontario
  Trading posts: Fort William -- I
       971.3   Life in the old Fort.
       971.3   The Growth, the decline.

G.N.P. See GROSS NATIONAL PRODUCT

GABON
  Children -- P,J
       916.7   Children of Gabon.
       916.7   Les enfants du Gabon.

GALLANTRY See COURAGE

GALLIFORMES See FOWL-LIKE BIRDS

GAMES
  See also
      HOCKEY
      LACROSSE
      SPORTS

GAMES
  Canadian Indian games -- I,S
       790   Native games.

GARDENING
  -- P
       635   A Visit to a garden.

GARDENING GUIDES
  Canada. Fall flowering plants -- Gardening guides --
   I,S
       582   Garden flowers of summer and
                 autumn.

GARDENING GUIDES
  Canada. Spring flowering plants -- Gardening guides -
  - I,S
       582   Garden flowers of spring.

GARDENING GUIDES
  Canada. Summer flowering plants -- Gardening guides -
  - I,S
       582   Garden flowers of summer and
                 autumn.

GAVIIFORMES See LOONS

GEESE
  See also
      CANADA GEESE

GENERAL STORES
  -- P,J
       658.8   The Country store.

GENERAL STRIKE. Winnipeg
  1919 -- S
       331.890971 Winnipeg General Strike, 1919.

GENERATION. Electricity
  -- J,I
       621.3   Sources of electricity.

GENETICS
  See also
      HEREDITY

GEODESY
  See also
      LATITUDE
      LONGITUDE

GEOGRAPHY
  See also
      PHYSICAL GEOGRAPHY

PRECIS SUBJECT INDEX

GEOGRAPHY. Andes. Peru
-- J,I
    918.5   Peru 1 : life in the Andes.

GEOGRAPHY. Appalachian region. Quebec Province
-- J,I,S
    917.14   Le Quebec : les Applaches.
    917.14   The Province of Quebec : the Appalachian region.

GEOGRAPHY. Arctic Canada
-- J,I
    917.12   Geography of the Arctic.
    917.12   Physical setting.

GEOGRAPHY. Canada
-- J,I
    330.971   Introduction : the people and the land.
    917.1   Canada's seven regions.

GEOGRAPHY. Canada
-- P,J
    917.1   Scenic wonderland.

GEOGRAPHY. Canadian Shield
-- J,I
    917.1   Bouclier canadien : vue d'ensemble
    917.1   Introducing the Canadian Shield.
    917.1   The Canadian Shield.

GEOGRAPHY. Canadian Shield. Manitoba
-- J,I,S
    917.127   Manitoba : the Shield.

GEOGRAPHY. Cape Breton Island. Nova Scotia
-- J,I
    917.16   Cape Breton Island : an overview.

GEOGRAPHY. Coasts. Japan
-- J
    915.2   Seacoast environments of Japan.

GEOGRAPHY. Laurentian region. Quebec Province
-- J,I,S
    917.14   Le Quebec : le Plateau laurentien.
    917.14   The Province of Quebec : the Laurentian region.

GEOGRAPHY. Manitoba
-- I,S
    917.127   Le Manitoba : les Plaines.
    917.127   Manitoba : the plains.

GEOGRAPHY. Manitoba
-- J,I,S
    917.127   Manitoba : a broader view.
    917.127   Le Manitoba : vue d'ensemble.

GEOGRAPHY. Maritime Provinces
-- J,I
    330.9715 Atlantic Canada.

GEOGRAPHY. Maritime Provinces
-- J,I,S
    917.15   Le Canada atlantique : géograph
    917.15   Atlantic Canada : geography.

GEOGRAPHY. Mountains. Japan
-- J
    915.2   Mountain environments of Japan.

GEOGRAPHY. Northern Canada
-- J,I
    330.9712 The Northland.

GEOGRAPHY. Northern Ontario
-- J,I
    917.13   Ontario : the north, transportation and recreatio

GEOGRAPHY. Nova Scotia
-- J,I
    917.16   Nova Scotia.

GEOGRAPHY. Ontario
-- J,I
    330.9713 Central Canada : the people.
    330.9713 Central Canada : the place.
    917.13   Ontario.

GEOGRAPHY. Prairie Provinces
-- J,I
    917.12   The Prairie region.
    917.12   The Interior Plains.

GEOGRAPHY. Quebec Province
-- J,I
    330.9713 Central Canada : the people.
    330.9713 Central Canada : the place.

PRECIS SUBJECT INDEX

GEOGRAPHY. St. Lawrence region. Quebec Province
-- J,I,S
    917.14   Le Quebec : la Plaine du Saint-Laurent.
    917.14   The Province of Quebec : the St. Lawrence region.

GEOGRAPHY. Southern Ontario
-- J,I
    917.13   Southern Ontario.

GEOGRAPHY. Western Canada
-- J,I
    330.9711   The Mountainous West.

GEOGRAPHY. Western Plains. Canada
-- J,I
    917.12   Introduction : the Western Plains.

GEOGRAPHY. Yukon Territory
-- J,I
    917.12   The Yukon.

GEOLOGICAL FEATURES
See also
    MINERALS

GEOLOGICAL FEATURES. Cypress Hills. Alberta & Saskatchewan
-- J,I
    971.24   Fort Walsh in the Cypress Hills.
    971.24   Le Fort Walsh dans les collines Cyprès.

GEOLOGY
See also
    PETROLOGY

GEOMETRIC SHAPES
-- J,I
    516   Shapes designed by man.

GEOMETRIC SHAPES
-- P
    516   Observing by seeing : shapes and sizes.

GEOMETRIC SHAPES
Occurrence in nature -- J,I
    516   Shapes in nature.

GEOMORPHOLOGY
See also
    LANDFORMS

GERMAN FOLKLORE
-- Stories -- J
    398.20943   Baron Münchhausen in a whale of a tale : a German legend.

GERMAN FOLKLORE
Special subjects: Christmas -- Stories -- P,J
    398.20943   Germany : the nutcracker's happy Christmas.

GESTATION See PREGNANCY

GLACIERS
-- J,I,S
    551.3   Les glaciers.
    551.3   Glaciers.

GLACIERS
Effects on landforms -- J,I
    551.3   Les formes de relief glaciaire.
    551.3   Glacial landforms.

GLACIERS. Canada
Effects on landforms -- I,S
    551.3   Glacier water deposits.
    551.3   Glacier land deposits.

GLACIERS. Iceland
-- J,I
    914.91   Glaciers.

GOALTENDING. Hockey
-- P,J
    796.9   Goaltending.

GOATS
-- P,J,I
    599   Les Chèvres en vedette.
    599   Goats, goats, goats.

GOLD. Ontario
Refining -- J,I
    622   Gold refining in Ontario.

PRECIS SUBJECT INDEX

GOLD RUSH. British Columbia
  1858 -- J,I,S
        971.1   Gold rush : pioneer mining in British Columbia.

GOLD RUSH. Klondike. Yukon Territory
  1896. Role of Royal Canadian Mounted Police -- J,I,S
       363.20971   North West Mounted Police : the Klondike Gold Rush.

GONORRHEA
  -- I,S
       616.9   About V.D. - gonorrhea.

GOODS
  Buying -- Consumers' guides -- P,J
       332.024   Money : how to spend it.

GOOSE See GEESE

GOPHERS. Canada
  Pocket gophers -- P,J
       599   Le gaufre á poches.
       599   The Pocket gophers.

GOVERNMENT
  See also
    FEDERAL GOVERNMENT
    LOCAL GOVERNMENT
    PARLIAMENT
    PRIME MINISTERS
    PROVINCIAL GOVERNMENT
    SELF-GOVERNMENT

GOVERNMENT. Canada
  -- J,I
       342   Why governments?

GOVERNMENT. Northwest Territories
  -- J,I
       354.712   The Structure of government.

GRADING. Food. Canada
  -- Consumers' guides -- J,I,S
       614.3   Aliments classés du Canada.
       614.3   Canada's graded foods.

GRAMMAR
  See also
    PUNCTUATION

GRAND MANAN ISLAND. New Brunswick
  Description & travel -- J,I
       917.15   L'Ile Grand Manan.
       917.15   Grand Manan Island.

GRAND MANAN ISLAND. New Brunswick
  Herring fishing -- J,I
       639.09715   L'Ile Grand Manan : la pêche à fascines.
       639.09715   Grand Manan Island : weir fishing

GRAND MANAN ISLAND. New Brunswick
  Lobster fishing -- J
       639.09715   L'Ile Grand Manan : la pêche du homard.
       639.09715   Grand Manan Island : lobster fishing.

GRAPHIC ARTS
  See also
    DRAWINGS
    PAINTINGS
    PHOTOGRAPHY
    PRINTS

GRAPHIC ARTS
  Equipment -- I,S
       760.028   Basic tools for graphic design

GRAPHIC ARTS
  Techniques -- P,J
       701   Where to find it.

GRAPHIC DESIGN. Filmstrips
  -- I,S
       778.2   Producing graphics for slides filmstrips.

GRAPHIC DESIGN. Slide programmes
  -- I,S
       778.2   Producing graphics for slides filmstrips.

GRAPHIC MEDIA
  See also
    MAPS
    PHOTOGRAPHS
    TRANSPARENCIES

PRECIS SUBJECT INDEX

GRAPHIC MEDIA
   Dry mounting -- I,S
      760.028   Creating your own visuals using a dry mount press.

GRAPHIC MEDIA
   Mounting. Mat cutting -- I,S
      749   Art work presentation : mat cutting.

GRASSHOPPERS
   Life cycle -- P,J
      595.7   Le criquet (sauterrelle)
      595.7   The Grasshopper.

GRASSLANDS
   See also
      PRAIRIES

GRASSLANDS. Africa
   Environment. Adaptation of animals -- J,I
      591.96   Grassland 1 : animals of the African Grasslands.

GREAT BRITAIN
   Seven Years' War -- J,I,S
      971.01   The Seven Years' War.
      971.01   La guerre de Sept ans.

GREAT BRITAIN
   War of 1812 -- I,S
      971.03   The War of 1812.

GREAT BRITAIN
   War of 1812 -- J,I
      971.03   The War of 1812.
      971.03   La Guerre de 1812.

GREAT WAR See WORLD WAR 1

GREECE
   See also
      ANCIENT GREECE

GREECE
   Children -- P,J
      914.95   Children of Greece.
      914.95   Les enfants de la Grèce.

GREECE
   Rural life -- J,I
      917.95   Greece 1 : life in a rural village

GREEK MYTHS
   Heracles -- J
      292   Nobel Hercules.

GREY OWL
   -- J,I
      920   Grey Owl.

GROSS NATIONAL PRODUCT
   -- S
      339.3   National output and its measurement.
      339.4   The Determination of the levels of gross national product and incomes.

GROUP OF SEVEN. Paintings
   -- I,S
      759.11   Le Groupe des Sept.
      759.11   The Group of Seven.

GROUPS. Society See SOCIAL GROUPS

GROWTH. Industrial communities
   -- J,I
      301.34   Industrial community 1 : patterns of growth.

GROWTH. Lobsters
   -- P,J,I
      595   How lobsters grow.
      595   La croissance du homard.

GROWTH. Organisms
   -- P,J
      574.3   Comes from ... grows to.
      574.3   Vient de - devient.

GROWTH. Trees
   -- P,J,I
      581.3   Nutrition et croissance de l'arbre
      581.3   Why do trees grow?

GROWTH. Urban regions
   -- J,I
      301.34   Aging of the urban site.

PRECIS SUBJECT INDEX

GRUIDAE See CRANES. Birds

GUINEA PIGS. Pets
  -- P,J
    636   Guinea pigs and their care.

GUNS
  See also
    RIFLES

GUYANA
  Natural resources. Nationalisation -- Study examples:
    Bauxite industry -- I,S
    338.988   I can see clearly now.

GWUSHUM
  Preparation: L'ilawat methods -- P,J
    970.3   Gwúshum.

HAIDA CARVINGS
  -- J,I,S
    736   Les scuptures sur argilite des
                 Haîdas.
    736   Haida argillite carvings.

HAIDA FOLKLORE
  -- Stories -- P,J
    398.209701 Le premier saumon.
    398.209701 The First salmon.

HAIDA VISUAL ARTS
  -- I,S
    709.01   Haida art.

HALIFAX
  See also
    PORT OF HALIFAX

HALIFAX. Nova Scotia
  to 1972 -- J,I,S
    387.109716 Port city : Halifax.
    387.109716 Ville portuaire (Halifax)

HALIFAX. Nova Scotia
  to 1974 -- J,I
    917.16   Halifax, Nova Scotia.

HALIFAX. Nova Scotia
  to 1976 -- J,I
    917.16   Halifax - historic seaport.

HALIFAX. Nova Scotia
  Description & travel -- J,I
    917.16   The City of Halifax.

HALLOWEEN
  -- Stories -- P
    F   Scarecrow and pumpkin.

HALLOWEEN
  Canadian social customs -- P,J
    394.2   Hallowe'en in Canada.

HALLUCINOGENIC DRUGS
  See also
    LSD
    POT

HAMILTON. Ontario
  Description & travel -- J,I
    917.13   The Many Faces of Hamilton.

HAMILTON. Ontario
  Industries -- J,I
    917.13   The Industrial city.

HAND TOOLS
  Safety measures -- I,S
    621.9   Scies à main, ciseaux et limes.
    621.9   Hand saws, chisels and files.

HAND TOOLS. Woodworking
  Scrapers -- I,S
    621.9   Scraping tools and abrasives.

HARES
  Rabbits & hares compared with rodents -- P,J
    599   Rodents, rabbits and hares.
    599   Rongeurs, lapins et lièvres.

HARRIS, LAWREN STEWART. Paintings
  -- I,S
    759.11   Lawren S. Harris.
    759.11   Lawren S. Harris.

PRECIS SUBJECT INDEX

HARVESTING. Wheat production. Saskatchewan
-- P,J
    633.0971   Visit to a wheat farm.

HAWKS. Canada
-- P,J
    598.2   Hawks.
    598.2   Les faucons.

HAZARDS
  See also
    POISONS
    SAFETY MEASURES

HAZARDS. Circuits. Electricity supply equipment. Residences
-- J,I
    644   Electrical hazards.

HAZARDS. Residences
-- P,J
    614.8   Home safety.
    614.8   Home safety.

HAZARDS. Schools
-- P,J
    614.8   School safety.

HEALTH ASPECTS. Smoke
-- J,I,S
    614.7   Qu'est-ce que la fumée?
    614.7   What is smoke? (Filmstrip)

HEALTH ASPECTS. Smoking
-- J,I,S
    613.8   The Smoking epidemic.
    613.8   Le fumeur est une victime.

HEARING
-- P,J
    152.1   Listen to my world.

HEARING
  Physiology -- J
    612   Hearing.

HEATING. Houses. Canada
  1800-1860 -- Re-enactments at Black Creek Pioneer Village -- P,J,I
    971.3   "Mary Davidson's home"

HERACLES. Greek myths
-- J
    292   Nobel Hercules.

HERALDRY
  See also
    COATS OF ARMS

HEREDITY
  Effects on personality -- J,I
    155.2   Vous et votre personnalité.
    155.2   You and your personality.

HERRING FISHING. Grand Manan Island. New Brunswick
-- J,I
    639.09715   L'île Grand Manan : la pêche à fascines.
    639.09715   Grand Manan Island : weir fishing.

HIGHLAND GAMES
-- P
    796.074   Highland Games.

HISTORICAL ASPECTS. Canadian culture
-- J,I
    917.1   The Heritage puzzle.

HISTORICAL ASPECTS. Canadian culture
  Preservation -- J,I
    971   A la découverte de notre patrimoine.
    971   Discovering our heritage.
    971.0074   Places preseving our heritage.

HISTORICAL ASPECTS. Canadian flag, to 1965
-- J,I
    929.90971   Les Drapeaux Canadiens d'autrefois

HISTORICAL ASPECTS. Canadian social customs. Christmas
-- P,J
    394.2   Canadian Christmas : traditions of Christmas.

HISTORICAL ASPECTS. Canadian social customs. Easter
-- P,J
    394.2   Easter in Canada.

HISTORICAL ASPECTS. Canadian social customs. St. Valentine's Day
-- P,J
    394.2   St. Valentine's Day.

PRECIS SUBJECT INDEX

HISTORICAL ASPECTS. Cities
-- J,I
    301.31   The City : laboratory of history.

HISTORICAL ASPECTS. Dominion Day
-- P,J
    394.2   Dominion Day.
    394.2   Dominion Day.

HISTORICAL ASPECTS. Holidays. Canada
-- J,I
    394.2   Inventing a heritage.

HISTORICAL ASPECTS. Remembrance Day
-- P,J
    394.2   Remembrance Day.

HISTORICAL ASPECTS. Thanksgiving. Canada
-- P,J
    394.2   The Story of Thanksgiving.

HISTORICAL ASPECTS. Victoria Day
-- P,J
    394.2   Victoria Day.

HOCKEY
Coaching -- J,I
    796.9   The Hockey coach.

HOCKEY
Defensive play. Techniques -- P,J,I
    796.9   Hockey III - the game -

HOCKEY
Equipment -- P,J
    796.9   Hockey equipment.

HOCKEY
Equipment -- P,J,I
    796.9   Hockey I - getting ready.

HOCKEY
Goaltending -- P,J
    796.9   Goaltending.

HOCKEY
Offensive play. Techniques -- P,J,I
    796.9   Hockey II - the game -

HOCKEY
Passing -- P,J
    796.9   Pin point passing.

HOCKEY
Shooting -- P,J
    796.9   Shoot to score.

HOCKEY
Skating -- P,J
    796.9   Skating.

HOCKEY
Team play -- P,J
    796.9   Team play.

HOCKEY. Canada
to 1974 -- J
    796.9   The History of hockey.

HOLIDAYS. Canada
Dominion Day. Historical aspects -- P,J
    394.2   Dominion Day.
    394.2   Dominion Day.

HOLIDAYS. Canada
Historical aspects -- J,I
    394.2   Inventing a heritage.

HOLIDAYS. Canada
Remembrance Day. Historical aspects -- P,J
    394.2   Remembrance Day.

HOLIDAYS. Canada
Thanksgiving. Historical aspects -- P,J
    394.2   The Story of Thanksgiving.

HOLIDAYS. Canada
Thanksgiving. Social customs -- P,J
    394.2   Thanksgiving today.

HOLIDAYS. Canada
Victoria Day. Historical aspects -- P,J
    394.2   Victoria Day.

HOLIDAYS. Eastern Canada
Thanksgiving. Social customs, 1820-1867 -- Re-enactments at Black Creek Pioneer Village -- P,J
    971.3   Thanksgiving in pioneer Canada

PRECIS SUBJECT INDEX

HOMO SAPIENS See MAN

HONESTY
  See also
    DECEIT
    INTEGRITY

HONESTY
  -- I,S
    174   Values : yours and theirs.

HONESTY
  -- K,P,J
    179   Wet cement and the radio.
    179   The Test and bottles.
    179   The Chocolate bar and the bicycle.

HONESTY
  -- P,J
    179   L'honnêteté.

HONEYBEES
  -- J,I,S
    595.7   La vie dans la ruche.
    595.7   Life in a beehive.

HONEYBEES
  Life cycle -- P,J
    595.7   L'abeille.
    595.7   The Honeybee.

HORSES
  See also
    PONIES

HORSES. Special subjects. Photographs
  -- P,J,I
    407   Of the horse.

HOSPITALS FOR CHILDREN
  -- P,J
    362.7   Un Hôpital pour enfants : examen et urgences.
    362.7   Un Hôpital pour enfants : patient hospitalisé.
    362.7   Children's hospital : in-patient.
    362.7   Children's hospital : check-ups and emergencies.

HOT CLIMATES
  Hot dry climates. Houses. Architectural design -- P,J,I
    728   Homes in hot, dry climates.

HOT CLIMATES
  Hot humid climates. Houses. Architectural design -- P,J,I
    728   Homes in hot, humid climates.

HOT DOGS
  Manufacture -- P,J
    664   Hot dogs.

HOTELS. Canada
  -- P,J
    647   Hotel : city within a city.

HOUSES
  Architectural design. Environmental factors -- P,J,I
    728   Factors influencing homes.

HOUSES
  Building -- P
    690   Bâtissons notre maison.
    690   Building a house.

HOUSES
  Panelled doors. Painting -- S
    698.3   Painting a panelled door.

HOUSES. Canada
  1790-1890. Architectural features -- J,I
    728.0971   Homes of early day Canada.

HOUSES. Canada
  1790-1890. Architectural features -- Study examples: Mackenzie home -- J,I
    971.3   Visiting an early day Canadian town house.

HOUSES. Canada
  Architectural design -- P,J,I
    728   Development of Canadian homes.

HOUSES. Canada
  Heating, 1800-1860 -- Re-enactments at Black Creek Pioneer Village -- P,J,I
    971.3   "Mary Davidson's home"

PRECIS SUBJECT INDEX

HOUSES. Canada
   Lighting, 1800-1860 -- Re-enactments at Black Creek
   Pioneer Village -- P,J,I
      971.3   "Mary Davidson's home"

HOUSES. Cold climates
   Architectural design -- P,J,I
      728   Homes in cold climates.

HOUSES. Hot dry climates
   Architectural design -- P,J,I
      728   Homes in hot, dry climates.

HOUSES. Hot humid climates
   Architectural design -- P,J,I
      728   Homes in hot, humid climates.

HOUSES. Northern Canada
   Log houses. Building -- Do it yourself guides -- S,A
      690   Build your own log house : part 2.
      690   Build your own log house : part 1.

HOUSES. Sunny or windy climates
   Architectural design -- P,J,I
      728   How homes are adapted to nature :
                  wind and radiation.

HOUSING. Cities. Canada
   -- J,I
      301.5   Housing : the Canadian city.

HUMAN BODY
   See also
      Names of specific parts & functions of the human
      body

HUMAN SETTLEMENTS
   See also
      URBAN REGIONS
      VILLAGES

HUMAN SETTLEMENTS. Red River Valley. Manitoba
   Role of Selkirk, Thomas Douglas, Earl of -- J,I
      920   Lord Selkirk : the colonizer.

HUMANITIES
   See also
      ARTS

HUMID CLIMATES
   Hot humid climates. Houses. Architectural design
   P,J,I
      728   Homes in hot, humid climates.

HUNGARIAN FOLKLORE
   -- Stories -- P,J
      398.209439 The Miraculous hind : a hungarian
                  legend.
      398.209439 La biche miraculeuse : une
                  légende hongroise.

HUNTING
   See also
      SHOOTING

HUNTING. Animals. Arctic North America
   By Inuit -- J,I
      970.4   My escape from death.
      970.4   Eskimo hunting.
      970.4   Hunters of the Arctic.

HUNTING. Animals. Baffin Island. Northwest
   Territories
   By Inuit -- P,J,I
      970.4   Autumn hunters.

HURON INDIAN VILLAGES. Midland. Ontario
   -- J,I
      970.3   Huron Indian Village
               (reconstructed)

HURON INDIANS
   Culture -- J,I
      970.3   Huron Indian Village & Museum.

HURON INDIANS
   Culture -- J,I,S
      970.3   The Iroquois-Huron Nations
               (Eastern Woodland Indians)
      970.3   La famille Huronne-Iroquoise
               (Indiens des forêts de l'Est)

HUTTERITE COMMUNES. Western Canada
   -- I,S
      301.450971 Hutterite contribution to
                  Canadian society.
      301.450971 Hutterite way of life.

PRECIS SUBJECT INDEX

HUTTERITES
   1526-1917 -- I,S
       289.9   Hutterite persecution : 1526-1917.

HUTTERITES. Alberta
   Social life -- P,J
       301.450971 The Hutterite ways.

HUTTERITES. Canada
   1917-1978 -- I,S
       301.450971 Hutterites in Canada : 1917 -
                present.

HYDROELECTRIC POWER STATIONS. Churchill Falls.
   Newfoundland
    -- J,I
       917.19   Churchill Falls.

HYGIENE
   Personal hygiene -- K,P
       613   Cleanliness - anew look.

HYMENOPTERA
   See also
      HONEYBEES

ICE
   See also
      GLACIERS

ICE FISHING
   -- I,S
       799.1   Ice fishing.

ICELAND
   -- J,I
       914.91   History and geography.

ICELAND
   Glaciers -- J,I
       914.91   Glaciers.

ICELAND
   Social life -- J,I
       914.91   The People and their work.

ICELAND
   Volcanoes -- J,I
       914.91   Volcanoes.

IDENTIFICATION. Aircraft
   -- Field guides -- J,I
       629.133   Identifying airplanes.

ILLUMINATION See LIGHTING

IMMIGRANTS. British Columbia
   Chinese immigrants. Attitudes of society, 1858-1904 -
    -- S
       301.450971 Difficulties of Chinese immigrants

IMMIGRANTS. British Columbia
   Chinese immigrants. Social life, 1858-1885 -- S
       301.450971 The First Chinese communities in
                British Columbia.

IMMIGRANTS. Canada
   Japanese immigrants. Attitudes of society, to 1939 --
   S
       301.450971 The Japanese come to Canada.

IMMIGRANTS. Canada
   Ukrainian immigrants, 1885-1920 -- I,S
       301.450971 Strangers to Canada.

IMMIGRANTS. Canada
   Ukrainian immigrants, 1890-1910 -- I,S
       301.450971 Prairie homestead.

IMMIGRANTS. Ontario
   Irish immigrants. Role in politics -- S
       301.4509713 Irish feuds and quarrels.

IMMIGRATION
   See also
      EMIGRATION

IMMIGRATION. Canada
   1896-1914. Social aspects -- S
       325.71   The Fourth wave.

IMMIGRATION. Canada
   to 1945 -- I,S
       325.71   Two cultures.

IMMIGRATION. Canada
   1945-1975. Social aspects -- I,S
       325.71   Changing profile.

PRECIS SUBJECT INDEX

IMMIGRATION. Canada
  From Ireland, to 1910 -- S
        325.71   Irish immigration.

IMPERIAL SYSTEM. Weights & measures
  -- J,I,S
        389   The Metric system : how?

IMPERIAL SYSTEM. Weights & measures
  compared with S.I. -- J
        389   Standardizing measurement.

INCOME TAX. Canada
  1650-1972 -- I,S
        336.20971   The History of income tax in Canada.

INDEPENDENCE
  See also
      SELF-GOVERNMENT

INDIAN FOLKLORE
  -- Stories -- J
        398.20954   The Rajah's garden.

INDIANS. Ethnic groups. Canada
  -- P,J
        301.450971 My birthplace was India.

INDIANS OF NORTH AMERICA See NORTH AMERICAN INDIANS

INDUSTRIAL COMMUNITIES
  Growth -- J,I
        301.34   Industrial community 1 : patterns of growth.

INDUSTRIES
  See also
      AGRICULTURAL INDUSTRIES
      ALUMINUM INDUSTRIES
      AUTOMOTIVE INDUSTRY
      CLOTHING INDUSTRY
      COAL MINING INDUSTRY
      FISHING INDUSTRIES
      FOREST PRODUCTS INDUSTRIES
      IRON INDUSTRIES
      MINING INDUSTRIES
      NATURAL GAS INDUSTRY
      PETROLEUM INDUSTRY
      STEEL INDUSTRIES
      TOBACCO INDUSTRY

INDUSTRIES
  See also
      TRADE
      VISUAL ARTS INDUSTRIES

INDUSTRIES. China
  -- I
        915.1   Agriculture, industry and transportation.

INDUSTRIES. Hamilton, Ontario
  -- J,I
        917.13   The Industrial city.

INDUSTRIES. Lac Saint-Jean region. Quebec province
  -- J,I
        971.14   Saguenay-Lake St. John - the La Region.

INDUSTRIES. Saguenay River region. Quebec Province
  -- J,I
        971.14   Saguenay-Lake St. Jean - the ri

INDUSTRIES. St. John River valley. New Brunswick
  -- J,I
        971.15   Saint John River Valley - Edmunston to Kings Landing.
        971.15   Saint John River Valley - Mactaquac to Saint John.

INDUSTRIES. Thunder Bay. Ontario
  -- I
        386.09713 Thunder Bay's industrial harbou

INFORMATION CENTRES
  See also
      LIBRARIES

INFORMATION SOURCES
  See also
      AUDIOVISUAL MATERIALS
      BOOKS
      DOCUMENTS
      NEWSPAPERS

INFORMATION SOURCES
  Use in projects -- Researchers' guides -- J
        028.7   Doing a project.

PRECIS SUBJECT INDEX

INFORMATION SOURCES. Canada, to 1973
  Postage stamps -- J,I
      769   Shaping the Canadian nation.

INFORMATION SOURCES. Pioneer life, 1790-1890. Canada
  Churchyards. Monumental inscriptions -- J,I
      971.3   Visiting a pioneer cemetery.

INFORMATION SOURCES. Provinces. Canada
  Postage stamps -- J,I
      769   Canada and its provinces.

INFORMATION SOURCES. Social life. Canada
  Postage stamps -- J,I
      769   Le Peuple Canadien et son
                environnement.
      769   Canada : people and environment.

INNUIT
  Personal adjustment to contemporary society -- J,I
      917.12   The Way we live today.

INNUIT
  Social life -- J,I
      970.4   The way things used to be.

INNUIT. Arctic North America
  Hunting of animals -- J,I
      970.4   My escape from death.
      970.4   Eskimo hunting.
      970.4   Hunters of the Arctic.

INNUIT. Baffin Island. Northwest Territories
  Hunting of animals -- P,J,I
      970.4   Autumn hunters.

INNUIT. Baffin Island. Northwest Territories
  Spring activities -- P,J,I
      970.4   Spring journey.

INNUIT. Baffin Island. Northwest Territories
  Summer activities -- P,J,I
      970.4   Summer days.

INNUIT. Baffin Island. Northwest Territories
  Winter activities -- P,J,I
      970.4   Winter camp.

INNUIT. Canada
  See also
    CARIBOU ESKIMO

INNUIT. Canada
  -- I,S
      970.1   Native Canadians.

INNUIT. Canada
  Culture -- J,I
      917.12   Eskimo 1 : Arctic village.
      970.4   The Inuit.
      970.4   Days of the igloo.
      970.4   The New north.
      970.4   Eskimo heritage.

INNUIT. Canada
  Employment -- J,I
      970.4   The Eskimo and his work.

INNUIT. Canada
  Social life -- J,I
      917.12   The Arctic today.
      970.4   Traditional Eskimo life.

INNUIT. Canada
  Social life -- P,J,I
      970.4   L'esquimau moderne.
      970.4   The Modern Eskimo.

INNUIT CARVINGS
  -- J,I,S
      736   Sculpture esquimau.
      736   Eskimo carvings.

INNUIT CLOTHING
  -- J,I,S
      970.4   Eskimos : part 2.

INNUIT FOLKLORE
  -- Stories -- J
      398.2   The Festival of the seals.
      398.2   Le Festival des phoques.

INNUIT FOLKLORE
  -- Stories -- P
      398.2   Le hibou et le lemming : une
                légende eskimo.
      398.2   The Owl and the lemming : Eskimo
                legend.

PRECIS SUBJECT INDEX

INNUIT FOLKLORE
  -- Stories -- P,J
    398.2   The Shaman goes to the moon.
    398.2   Attituk and the caribou.
    398.2   The Legend of the raven who flew backwards.
    398.2   The Angekkok of Thule.

INNUIT FOLKLORE
  -- Stories -- P,J,I
    398.2   The Hunter who went away.
    398.2   Le chasseur qui partit.

INNUIT PRINTS
  -- J,I,S
    769   L'art graphique esquimau.
    769   Eskimo prints.

INNUIT RELIGION
  -- J,I
    299   Spirits and monsters.

INNUIT SCULPTURES
  -- J,I,S
    736   L'art sculptural esquimau.
    736   Eskimo sculpture.

INSCRIPTIONS. Churchyards. Information sources. Pioneer life, 1790-1890. Canada
Monumental inscriptions -- J,I
    971.3   Visiting a pioneer cemetery.

INSECTIVORES
  See also
    MOLES
    SHREWS

INSECTS
  See also
    BEETLES
    BUTTERFLIES
    DAMSELFLIES
    DRAGONFLIES
    GRASSHOPPERS
    HONEYBEES
    MOTHS

INSECTS
  -- J,I
    595.7   The Fantastic world of insects (B)
    595.7   The Fantastic world of insects (A)

INSULIN. Drugs
Control of diabetes. Discovery by Banting, Sir Frederick Grant & Best, Charles Herbert -- J,I
    920   Banting and Best : the discovery of insulin.

INTEGRITY
  See also
    HONESTY

INTEGRITY
  -- P,J
    179   L'integrité.
    179   Integrity.

INTERIOR DECORATING
  See also
    WALLPAPER
    Hanging

INTERNATIONAL RELATIONS
  See also
    ECONOMIC RELATIONS
    FOREIGN RELATIONS
    WAR

INTERNATIONAL SYSTEM OF UNITS See S.I.

INTERNMENT. Japanese. Ethnic groups. Canada 1939-1945 -- S
    301.450971   The Japanese during World War I

INTERPERSONAL RELATIONSHIPS
  See also
    SEX RELATIONS

INTERPERSONAL RELATIONSHIPS
  -- J,I
    158   Le Comportement humain.
    158   Human behaviour.

INTRAUTERINE DEVICES
  -- I,S,A
    613.9   The Intrauterine device.

INUIT See INNUIT

PRECIS SUBJECT INDEX

INUVIK. Northwest Territories
  Description & travel -- J,I
        917.12   Arctic Delta town (Inuvik, N.W.T.)

INVENTION. Telephones
  Bell, Alexander Graham -- P,J
        384.6   Allô, Monsieur Bell!

INVERTEBRATES
  See also
        CRUSTACEANS
        ECHINODERMS
        INSECTS
        MARINE COELENTERATES
        MARINE MOLLUSCS
        SPIDERS
        SPONGES. Marine invertebrates

INVERTED COMMAS See QUOTATION MARKS

IRELAND
  Civilisation -- S
        914.15   Irish cultural heritage.

IRELAND
  Emigration to Canada, to 1910 -- S
        325.71   Irish immigration.

IRISH. Ethnic groups. Canada
  -- S
        301.450971 Irish contributions to Canadian
                    life.

IRISH FOLKLORE
  Special subjects: Christmas -- Stories -- P,J
        398.209415 Ireland : O'Reilly's Christmas cap

IRISH IMMIGRANTS. Ontario
  Role in politics -- S
        301.4509713 Irish feuds and quarrels.

IRON INDUSTRIES. Canada
  Iron & steel industries -- J,I
        338.40971 L'industrie du fer et de l'acier
                   au Canada.
        338.40971 Iron and steel industry in Canada.

IROQUOIS
  Culture -- J,I,S
        970.3   The Iroquois-Huron Nations
                  (Eastern Woodland Indians)
        970.3   La famille Huronne-Iroquoise
                  (Indiens des forêts de l'Est)

IROQUOIS ANTIQUITIES. North America
  Excavation -- J,I
        913   The Iroquoian people.
        913   Developing an Iroquoian village
                  site.

IRRIGATED FARMING. Alberta
  -- J,I
        631.7   Irrigated farming in Alberta.

ISRAEL
  Kibbutz Yavneh -- P,J
        335   A Kibbutz in Israel.

ITALIAN FOLKLORE
  -- Stories -- P,J
        398.20945 The Silliest man in Italy.

ITALIAN FOLKLORE
  Special subjects: Christmas -- Stories -- P,J
        398.20945 L'Italie : la legende de Dame la
                   Befana.

ITALIANS. Ethnic groups. Canada
  -- P,J
        301.450971 My Italian heritage.

JAMAICANS. Ethnic groups. Canada
  -- P,J
        301.450971 I come from Jamaica.

JAPAN
  Children -- P,J
        915.2   Children of Japan.
        915.2   Les enfants du Japon.

JAPAN
  Civilisation -- S
        915.2   Japanese cultural heritage.

JAPAN
  Coasts. Geography -- J
        915.2   Seacoast environments of Japan.

JAPAN
  Lowlands. Agriculture -- J
        631.0952 Lowland agriculture in Japan.

PRECIS SUBJECT INDEX

JAPAN
  Mountains. Geography -- J
      915.2   Mountain environments of Japan.

JAPAN
  Social life -- J,I
      915.2   Japan I : home life and food.

JAPAN
  Telecommunication systems -- J
      380   Transportation and communication in Japan.

JAPAN
  Transport -- J
      380   Transportation and communication in Japan.

JAPAN
  Transport -- J,I
      380.5   Japan II : transportation and communication.

JAPAN
  Urban life -- J
      915.2   Urban life in Japan (no. 1)
      915.2   Urban life in Japan (no. 2)

JAPANESE. Ethnic groups. Canada
  -- I,S
      301.450971 Chinese and Japanese Canadians.

JAPANESE. Ethnic groups. Canada
  -- S
      301.450971 Japanese contribution to Canadian society.

JAPANESE. Ethnic groups. Canada
  Internment, 1939-1945 -- S
      301.450971 The Japanese during World War II.

JAPANESE FOLKLORE
  -- Stories -- P
      398.20952   The Two frogs : a Japanese legend.

JAPANESE FOLKLORE
  -- Stories -- P,J
      398.20952   Urashima Taro the fisherlad.

JAPANESE IMMIGRANTS. Canada
  Attitudes of society, to 1939 -- S
      301.450971 The Japanese come to Canada.

JEALOUSY
  See also
    ENVY

JEALOUSY
  -- I,S
      179   Jealousy.

JEANNE D'ARC, Saint See JOAN OF ARC, Saint

JESUS CHRIST
  -- J
      232.9   Super Jesus.

JEWISH FOLKLORE
  -- Stories -- J
      398.2095694 The Lost wisdom (Israel)

JEWISH FOLKLORE
  -- Stories -- P,J
      398.2095694 The Value of a boiled egg.

JOAN OF ARC, Saint
  -- J
      920   Commanding Joan of Arc.

JOINING. Woodworking
  -- I,S
      694   Five simple wood joints.

JOURNALISM
  See also
    NEWSPAPERS

JUDAISM
  -- P,J
      296.4   The Jewish people.

KANDARA, Kenya
  Social life -- J,I
      916.76   Kandara : life in a Kenyan community.

PRECIS SUBJECT INDEX

KEEWATIN DISTRICT. Northwest Territories
  Caribou Eskimo -- J
      970.4   The Caribou Eskimo.
      970.4   L'esquimau primitif.

KENYA
  Kandara. Social life -- J,I
      916.76   Kandara : life in a Kenyan
                   community.

KIBBUTZ YAVNEH. Israel
  -- P,J
      335   A Kibbutz in Israel.

KING, MACKENZIE
  -- I,S
      920   The Life of Mackenzie King : part
                  II.
      920   The Life of Mackenzie King : part
                  1.

KINGFISHERS. Canada
  -- P,J
      598.2   The Kingfisher.

KITCHEN MANAGEMENT. Cookery
  -- I,S
      640   La Cuisine : un atelier.
      640   Principles of kitchen management.

KLONDIKE. Yukon Territory
  Gold rush, 1896. Role of Royal Canadian Mounted
    Police -- J,I,S
      363.20971 North West Mounted Police : the
                   Klondike Gold Rush.

KNIGHTS
  -- J,I
      940.1   Medieval community 1 : the knight.

KRIEGHOFF, CORNELIUS. Paintings
  -- I,S
      759.11   Cornelius Krieghoff.

LA VERENDRYE, PIERRE GUALTIER DE VARENNES, sieur de
  Exploration of Canada -- J
      971.01   La Vérendrye.
      971.01   La Vérendrye.

LABOR See LABOUR

LABOUR MOVEMENT
  See also
    TRADE UNIONS

LABOUR UNIONS See TRADE UNIONS

LABRADOR. Newfoundland
  Economic conditions -- J,I,S
      330.9719   Le Canada atlantique : le Labrador
      330.9719   Atlantic Canada : Labrador.

LABRADOR. Newfoundland
  Naskapi children. Social life -- P,J
      970.3   La vie quotidienne d'un petit
                  Indien.
      970.3   La vie quotidienne d'une petite
                  Indienne.
      970.3   A Day in the life of an Indian boy
      970.3   A Day in the life of an Indian
                  girl.

LABRADOR. Newfoundland
  Snowshoe making by Canadian Indians -- P,J
      685   Raquettes indiennes.
      685   Indian snowshoes.

LAC SAINT-JEAN REGION. Quebec province
  Industries -- J,I
      971.14   Saguenay-Lake St. John - the Lake
                 Region.

LACROSSE
  -- I,S
      796.34   La crosse canadienne.
      796.34   Lacrosse - the Canadian game.

LAGOMORPHA
  See also
    HARES
    RABBITS

LAND. Niagara Peninsula. Ontario
  Agricultural land. Development. Effects of regional
    planning -- J,I,S
      333.7   Fruit Belt preservation and
                  regional planning.

PRECIS SUBJECT INDEX

LAND TENURE. British Columbia
Claims of Canadian Indians -- I,S
    970.5   Native land claims in B.C. : an introduction (1850-1976)

LAND TENURE. New France
Seigneurial system -- J,I
    333.3   Seigneurs et seigneuries.
    333.3   Seigneurs and seigneuries.
    333.3   The Habitants.
    333.3   Les censitaires.

LAND TRANSPORT
See also
    RAILWAYS

LAND TRANSPORT. Canada
-- J,I
    388   Transportation today : by land.

LAND TRANSPORT. Canada
to 1974 -- J,I
    380.5   De la traction animal à la vapeur.

LAND TRANSPORT. Canada
to 1977 -- J,I
    388.30971   On Canadian roads.

LAND USE. Niagara Peninsula. Ontario
-- J,I,S
    333.7   Problems of land use in urban fringe - urban shadow areas.

LANDFORMS
See also
    CLIFFS
    MOUNTAINS
    PRAIRIES

LANDFORMS
-- J,I,S
    551   Our ever-changing earth.

LANDFORMS
Effects of glaciers -- J,I
    551.3   Les formes de relief glaciaire.
    551.3   Glacial landforms.

LANDFORMS
Effects of volcanoes -- J,I
    551.2   Geomorphologie volcanique.
    551.2   Volcanic landforms.

LANDFORMS. Canada
Effects of glaciers -- I,S
    551.3   Glacier water deposits.
    551.3   Glacier land deposits.

LANDSCAPE DRAWINGS
Bartlett, William Henry. Special subjects: Maritime Provinces -- J,I
    971   Sketching the New World : Maritime scenes.

LANGUAGES
See also
    CREE LANGUAGE
    ENGLISH LANGUAGE
    FRENCH LANGUAGE
    PUNCTUATION

LANGUAGES
-- I,S
    401   Introduction to language study.

LANGUAGES. Native peoples. Canada
Picture writing -- I,S
    411.09701   Native picture writing.

LATHES. Metalworking
-- I,S
    621.9   Working between centers on the lathe.
    621.9   Chuckwork on the lathe.

LATITUDE
-- P,J,I
    526   The Earth grid.
    526   Latitude.

LAURENTIAN REGION. Quebec Province
Geography -- J,I,S
    917.14   Le Quebec : le Plateau laurentien
    917.14   The Province of Quebec : the Laurentian region.

LAURENTIAN REGION. Quebec Province
Winter activities -- P,J,I,S
    525   Laurentian winter.

PRECIS SUBJECT INDEX

LAURIER, Sir WILFRID
-- I,S
    920   The Life of Sir Wilfrid Laurier.

LAW
  See also
      CIVIL RIGHTS
      CONSTITUTION
      COURTS
      PENAL SYSTEM

LAW. Canada
-- I
    340   What are laws?
    340   Too many laws... or too few?
    342   How do we make laws?

LAW & ORDER See PUBLIC ORDER

LAW ENFORCEMENT SERVICES
  See also
      POLICE

LEARNING RESOURCE CENTRES See RESOURCE CENTRES

LEGENDS
  See also
      MYTHS

LEGENDS
  Arthur, King -- J
    398.2   Good King Arthur.

LEGISLATURES
  See also
      PARLIAMENT

LEISURE ACTIVITIES
  See also
      RECREATIONS

LEPIDOPTERA
  See also
      BUTTERFLIES
      MOTHS

LEROY. Saskatchewan
  Agricultural industries -- J,I
    917.214   Leroy, Saskatchewan.

LETTER CARRIERS. Canada
  Duties -- J,I
    383   A Day in the life of a letter carrier.

LIBRARIES
-- Users' guides -- J,I
    028.7   The Library. (Or, how I learned to love Melvil Dewey)

LIBRARIES
  Author catalogues -- Users' guides -- P,J
    028.7   Have you a book by?

LIBRARIES
  Subject catalogues -- Users' guides -- P,J
    028.7   Have you a book about?

LIBRARIES
  Title catalogues -- Users' guides -- P,J
    028.7   Have you a book called?

LIBRARIES. Schools
-- Users' guides -- J
    024   How do you share your library?
    024   Discovering your library.

LIFE CYCLE. Beetles
-- P
    595.7   Les coléoptères.

LIFE CYCLE. Cecropia moths
-- J,I,S
    595.7   Le paon de nuit.
    595.7   The Cecropia moth.

LIFE CYCLE. Frogs
-- J
    597   La Vie commence - grenoiulles.

LIFE CYCLE. Frogs. Canada
-- P,J,I
    597   The Frog.
    597   La grenouille.

LIFE CYCLE. Grasshoppers
-- P,J
    595.7   Le criquet (sauterrelle)
    595.7   The Grasshopper.

PRECIS SUBJECT INDEX

LIFE CYCLE. Honeybees
-- P,J
    595.7   L'abeille.
    595.7   The Honeybee.

LIFE CYCLE. Monarch butterflies
-- P,J,I
    595.7   Le papillon monarque.
    595.7   The Monarch butterfly.

LIFE SCIENCES
  See also
    AGRICULTURE
    BOTANY
    ECOLOGY
    GENETICS
    MEDICINE
    ORNITHOLOGY
    ZOOLOGY

LIGHT. Sun
  Effects on earth -- J,I
    523.7   La Lumière du soleil.
    523.7   Light from the sun.

LIGHTING. Houses. Canada
  1800-1860 -- Re-enactments at Black Creek Pioneer
  Village -- P,J,I
    971.3   "Mary Davidson's home"

L'ILAWAT CHILDREN
  Summer camp -- J,I,S
    970.3   Mount Currie summer camp.

L'ILAWAT INDIANS
  Basket making -- P,J
    970.3   Basket.

L'ILAWAT INDIANS
  Social customs: Puberty rites -- J,I,S
    970.3   Puberty : parts 1 & 2.

L'ILAWAT METHODS. Cookery. Salmon
-- P,J
    970.3   Salmon.

L'ILAWAT METHODS. Preparation of gwushum
-- P,J
    970.3   Gwushum.

L'ILAVAT UTENSILS
-- J,I,S
    970.3   Objects in our lives.
    970.3   Eléments de notre vie quotidienne

LINEAR MEASUREMENT
  Metric system -- I
    389   Linear units.

LINEAR MEASUREMENT
  Metric system -- J,I
    389   Lengthy tales.

LINEAR MEASUREMENT
  Metric system -- J,I,S
    389   Linear - area.

LINEAR MEASUREMENT
  Metric system -- P,J
    389   Linear measurement.

LINEAR MEASUREMENT
  S.I. -- J
    389   Une Ligne - une surface.
    389   Measuring length and area.

LINGUISTICS
  See also
    LANGUAGES

LISBON
  Palace of Queluz. Architecture -- I,S
    728.8   Versailles and Portugal.

LITERATURE IN ENGLISH
  See also
    AMERICAN LITERATURE
    CANADIAN LITERATURE
    DRAMA IN ENGLISH
    ENGLISH LITERATURE

LIVING SYSTEMS See ORGANISMS

LOBSTER FISHING. Grand Manan Island. New Brunswick
-- J
    639.09715   L'Ile Grand Manan : la pêche du homard.
    639.09715   Grand Manan Island : lobster fishing.

PRECIS SUBJECT INDEX

LOBSTERS
  Growth -- P,J,I
      595   How lobsters grow.
      595   La croissance du homard.

LOCAL GOVERNMENT
  See also
    MUNICIPAL GOVERNMENT

LOCAL GOVERNMENT. Canada
  -- I,S
      352.071 Local government.
      352.071 Le gouvernement local.

LOCATION. Shoals of fish
  Electronic equipment -- S
      639   Le repérage électronique du poisson.
      639   Electronic fish finding.

LOG HOUSES. Northern Canada
  Building -- Do it yourself guides -- S,A
      690   Build your own log house : part 2.
      690   Build your own log house : part 1.

LOGGING
  Mechanised logging -- I,S
      634.9   La Mécanisation dans l'expolitation forestière de l'est du Canada.
      634.9   Mechanized logging in eastern Canada.

LOGGING. British Columbia
  -- J,I
      634.909711 Forest industries in B.C. : part 1

LONELINESS
  Attitudes of single people -- S
      152.4   To be alone.
      152.4   Vivre seule.

LONGITUDE
  -- P,J,I
      526   The Earth grid.
      526   Longitude.

LOONS. Canada
  Common loons -- P,J
      598.2   The Common loon.
      598.2   Le plongeon à collier.

LOWER FORT GARRY. Trading posts. Fur trade. Manitoba
  -- J,I,S
      971.27   Lower Fort Garry : legacy of the fur trade.

LOWLANDS. Japan
  Agriculture -- J
      631.0952 Lowland agriculture in Japan.

LOYALTY
  -- I,S
      179   Loyalty.

LSD
  -- I,S
      615   LSD.
      615   LSD.

LUNENBERG. Nova Scotia
  Fish processing -- I
      639   The Fish processing plant.

LYING
  -- I,S
      177   Deceit.

LYSERGIC ACID DIETHYLAMIDE See LSD

MACDONALD, Sir JOHN A.
  -- I,S
      920   The Life of Sir John A. MacDonald.

MACDONALD, Sir JOHN A.
  -- J,I
      971.04   Sir John A. Macdonald (2e partie)
      971.04   Sir John A. Macdonald (1ère partie)
      971.04   Sir John A. Macdonald : part 1.
      971.04   Sir John A. Macdonald : part 2.

MACHINERY
  See also
    ENGINES

MACKENZIE HOME. Study examples
  Canada. Houses, 1790-1890. Architectural features -- Study examples: Mackenzie home -- J,I
      971.3   Visiting an early day Canadian town house.

MAGDALEN ISLANDS. Quebec Province
    Description & travel -- J,I
        917.14   Magdalen Islands.
        917.14   Les Iles de la Madeleine.

MAGNETISM
    -- J,I
        538.01   Principles of magnetism.

MAIL DELIVERY. Canada
    -- J,I
        383   How a letter travels.

MAINTENANCE & REPAIR. Fuel pumps. Engines. Motor
        vehicles
    -- I,S
        629.22   Pistons, oil and and fuel pumps.

MAINTENANCE & REPAIR. Oil pumps. Engines. Motor
        vehicles
    -- I,S
        629.22   Pistons, oil and and fuel pumps.

MAINTENANCE & REPAIR. Tires. Motor vehicles
    -- I,S
        629.22   Care of wheels and tires.

MAINTENANCE & REPAIR. Transmission systems. Motor
        vehicles
    -- I,S
        629.22   Driving mechanism.

MAINTENANCE & REPAIR. Wheels. Motor vehicles
    -- I,S
        629.22   Care of wheels and tires.

MAKE-UP. Theatre
    Beards & moustaches. Techniques -- I,S
        792   Beards.

MAKE-UP. Theatre
    Old age make-up. Techniques -- I,S
        792   Old age makeup.

MAKE-UP. Theatre
    Techniques -- I,S
        792   Fundamentals of make-up.
        792   Basic makeup.
        792   Corrective makeup.

MALACCA. Malaysia
    Description & travel -- J,I
        915.95   Malacca : gateway to Malaysia.

MALAYSIA
    Malacca. Description & travel -- J,I
        915.95   Malacca : gateway to Malaysia.

MAMMALS
    See also
        BATS
        CARNIVORES
        HARES
        MAN
        MOLES
        RABBITS
        RODENTS
        SEALS. Mammals
        SHREWS
        UNGULATES
        WHALES

MAMMALS
    Birth -- P,J
        591.1   La Naissance.
        591.1   Birth.

MAMMALS
    Ovulation -- J
        591.1   Ovulation - mammifères.

MAMMALS
    Reproduction -- J,I
        591.1   Les Cellules reproductives.
        591.1   Le Processus de reproduction.
        591.1   The Process of reproduction.

MAMMALS
    Reproduction -- P,J
        591.1   Un de deux.
        591.1   From two to one.

MAMMALS. Arctic North America
    Adaptation to environment -- P,J
        599.09712   The Arctic.

MAMMALS. Forests. North America
    Adaptation to environment -- J,I
        599.097   Life in the boreal forest.

PRECIS SUBJECT INDEX

MAMMALS. Forests. North America
  Adaptation to environment -- P,J
      599.097   The Eastern forest.

MAMMALS. North America
  Adaptation to environment -- J,I
      599   The Story of mammals.

MAMMALS. Prairies. North America
  Adaptation to environment -- J,I
      591.5   Life on the Prairies.

MAMMALS. Prairies. North America
  Adaptation to environment -- P,J
      599.097   The Grasslands.

MAMMALS. Rocky Mountains. North America
  Adaptation to environment -- P,J
      599.097   The Rocky Mountains.

MAMMALS. Tundra. Arctic North America
  Adaptation to environment -- J,I
      574.509712 Life on the Barren Lands.

MAN
  See also
     HUMAN BODY

MAN
  Conception -- I,S
      612.6   Conception and birth.

MANAGEMENT
  See also
     MARKETING

MANITOBA
  Canadian Shield. Geography -- J,I,S
      917.127   Manitoba : the Shield.

MANITOBA
  Description & travel -- J,I
      917.127   Manitoba.
      917.127   Manitoba.

MANITOBA
  Description & travel -- P,J
      917.12   Paul and Pauline visit Manitoba
                     and Saskatchewan.

MANITOBA
  Flin Flon. Mining industries -- I
      917.127   Flin Flon, Manitoba.

MANITOBA
  Fur trade. Trading posts: Lower Fort Garry -- J,I,S
      971.27   Lower Fort Garry : legacy of the
                     fur trade.

MANITOBA
  Geography -- I,S
      917.127   Le Manitoba : les Plaines.
      917.127   Manitoba : the plains.

MANITOBA
  Geography -- J,I,S
      917.127   Manitoba : a broader view.
      917.127   Le Manitoba : vue d'ensemble.

MANITOBA
  Mixed farming -- J,I
      631.097127 Mixed farming in Manitoba.

MANITOBA
  Nickel. Mining -- J,I
      622   Nickel mining in Manitoba.

MANITOBA
  Red River Valley. Human settlements. Role of
  Selkirk, Thomas Douglas, Earl of -- J,I
      920   Lord Selkirk : the colonizer.

MANITOBA
  Riel rebellion, 1870 -- I,S
      971.05   1870 Rebellion.

MANITOBA
  Riel rebellion, 1870 -- S
      971.05   The First Métis uprising, 1869-70.

MANITOBA
  Trout farming -- J,I
      639.097127 Trout farming in Manitoba.

MANITOBA
  Winnipeg, to 1959 -- J,I,S
      917.127   Ville ferroviaire (Winnipeg)
      917.127   Railway city : Winnipeg.

PRECIS SUBJECT INDEX

MANITOBA
   Winnipeg. Description & travel -- I,S
        917.127   Winnipeg.

MANITOBA
   Winnipeg. Description & travel -- J,I
        917.127   Winnipeg, Man.
        917.127   Winnipeg, Man.

MANITOBA
   Winnipeg: General strike, 1919 -- S
        331.890971 Winnipeg General Strike, 1919.

MANITOUWADGE. Ontario
   Copper mining industry & zinc mining industry -- J,I
        917.13   Images d'une ville minière.
        917.13   Mining town (Manitouwadge, Ont.).

MANOWAN INDIANS. Quebec Province
   Reservation life -- I,S
        970.5   L'histoire de Manowan : première partie.
        970.5   History of Manowan : part 1.
        970.5   L'histoire de Manowan : deuxième partie.
        970.5   History of Manowan : part 2.

MANUFACTURE. Bread & confectionery
   -- J,I
        664   Working in a bakery.

MANUFACTURE. Bread & confectionery
   -- P,J
        664   Bread and pastry.

MANUFACTURE. Chocolate
   -- P,J
        664   Chocolate.

MANUFACTURE. Hot dogs
   -- P,J
        664   Hot dogs.

MANUFACTURE. Milk products
   -- P,J
        637   Milk and ice cream.

MAPLE SYRUP
   Production -- J,I,S
        664   Trip to the sugar bush.

MAPLE SYRUP
   Production -- P
        664   Maple syrup.

MAPLE SYRUP
   Production -- P,J
        664   When the sap runs.
        664   Maple syrup.
        664   Les sucres.

MAPS
   See also
        CARTOGRAPHY

MAPS
   -- J,I
        912   Introducing the topographical map
        912   Initiation à la carte topographique.

MAPS
   -- J,I,S,A
        912   The Map.

MAPS
   Africa -- Maps -- J,I
        912   Cartes muettes du monde : L'Europe et l'Afrique.
        912   Outline maps of the world : part

MAPS
   America -- Maps -- J,I
        912   Cartes muettes du monde : l'Amérique.
        912   Outline maps of the world : part

MAPS
   Asia -- Maps -- J,I
        912   Cartes muettes du monde : l'Asie et l'Océanie.
        912   Outline maps of the world : part

MAPS
   Australasia -- Maps -- J,I
        912   Cartes muettes du monde : l'Asie et l'Océanie.
        912   Outline maps of the world : part

MAPS
   Canada -- Maps -- J,I
        912   Cartes muettes du Canada.
        912   Outline maps of Canada.

PRECIS SUBJECT INDEX

MAPS
  Europe -- Maps -- J,I
    912   Cartes muettes du monde :
            L'Europe et l'Afrique.
    912   Outline maps of the world : part 2

MAPS
  Orientation -- J,I
    912   L'orientation de la carte.
    912   Map orientation.

MAPS
  Scale -- J,I
    912   Introducing map scale.
    912   Initiation à l'échelle de la carte

MARATHON, Ontario
  Pulp & paper industries -- J,I
    917.13   Marathon, Ontario.

MARIJUANA See POT

MARINE ALGAE See SEAWEED

MARINE COELENTERATES
  -- I,S
    574.92   Plants, sponges, coelenterates.
    574.92   Plants, sponges, coelenterates.

MARINE INVERTEBRATES
  See also
    CRUSTACEANS
    ECHINODERMS
    SPONGES. Marine invertebrates

MARINE MOLLUSCS
  -- I,S
    594   Crustaceans, molluscs.

MARITIME PROVINCES
  -- I
    917.15   Les Provinces Maritimes.

MARITIME PROVINCES
  Economic conditions -- J,I,S
    330.9715   Le Canada atlantique : économie.
    330.9715   Atlantic Canada : economy.

MARITIME PROVINCES
  Geography -- J,I
    330.9715   Atlantic Canada.

MARITIME PROVINCES
  Geography -- J,I,S
    917.15   Le Canada atlantique : géographie.
    917.15   Atlantic Canada : geography.

MARITIME PROVINCES
  Pioneer life -- J,I
    971.5   Pioneer life in the Maritimes :
            part 1.
    971.5   Pioneer life in the Maritimes.
            part 2.
    971.5   Les pionniers des Maritimes :
            1ère partie.
    971.5   Les pionniers des Maritimes : 2e
            partie.

MARITIME PROVINCES
  Self-government. Development, to 1873 -- I,S
    971.5   Reform in the Atlantic colonies.
    971.5   Les réformistes des colonies de
            l'Atlantique.

MARITIME PROVINCES
  Spring wildflowers -- Field guides -- P,J,I,S
    582.09715   Spring wildflowers : the Maritimes
    582.09715   Fleurs sauvages printanières :
            les Maritimes.

MARITIME PROVINCES. Special subjects. Landscape
  drawings by W.H.Bartlett
  -- J,I
    971   Sketching the New World :
            Maritime scenes.

MARKETING
  See also
    ADVERTISING

MARRIAGE. Adolescents
  -- I,S
    362.8   Love and marriage.

MASKS
  Body masks. Design techniques -- J,I,S
    746.9   Faire une cagoule.
    746.9   Making a body mask.

PRECIS SUBJECT INDEX

MASKS
   Design techniques -- I,S
        731   Masks.

MASKS
   North American Indian masks -- J,I,S
        391.09701 Masques des Indiens de
                     l'Amérique du Nord.
        391.09701 Masks of the North American
                     Indians.

MASS
   Measurement. Metric system -- J,I
        389   Mass matters.

MASS
   Measurement. Metric system -- J,I,S
        389   Mass.

MASS
   Measurement. Metric system -- P,J
        389   Temperature and mass.

MASS
   Measurement. SI -- J
        389   Un Poids - une masse.
        389   Measuring mass.

MASS MEDIA
   See also
      NEWSPAPERS
      TELEVISION

MAT CUTTING. Mounting. Graphic media
   -- I,S
        749   Art work presentation : mat
                  cutting.

MATERIALS
   See also
      POISONS

MATERIALS. Nets. Commercial fishing
   -- I,S
        639   Engines de pêche (câbles et
                  lignes pour la fabrication des
                  fillets de pêch)
        639   Fishing gear (ropes and twines
                  for fishing nets)

MEALS
   Planning -- I,S
        642   Trois repas par jour.
        642   Planning and preparing meals.

MEASUREMENT
   See also
      LINEAR MEASUREMENT
      TEMPERATURE MEASURING SCALES

MEASUREMENT
   -- J,I,S
        389   The Metric system : why?

MEASUREMENT. Area
   Metric system -- I
        389   Unité de surface.

MEASUREMENT. Area
   Metric system -- J,I
        389   Square stories.

MEASUREMENT. Area
   Metric system -- J,I,S
        389   Linear - area.

MEASUREMENT. Area
   Metric system -- P,J
        389   Area.

MEASUREMENT. Area
   S.I. -- J
        389   Une Ligne - une surface.
        389   Measuring length and area.

MEASUREMENT. Capacity
   Metric system -- J,I
        389   Capacity counts.

MEASUREMENT. Capacity
   Metric system -- J,I,S
        389   Volume - capacity.

MEASUREMENT. Capacity
   Metric system -- P,J
        389   Volume and capacity.

MEASUREMENT. Mass
  Metric system -- J,I
      389   Mass matters.

MEASUREMENT. Mass
  Metric system -- J,I,S
      389   Mass.

MEASUREMENT. Mass
  Metric system -- P,J
      389   Temperature and mass.

MEASUREMENT. Mass
  SI -- J
      389   Un Poids - une masse.
      389   Measuring mass.

MEASUREMENT. Volume
  -- P,J
      389   Mesure de volumes.
      389   To measure volume.

MEASUREMENT. Volume
  Metric system -- I
      389   Les Unités de volume.
      389   Volume units.

MEASUREMENT. Volume
  Metric system -- J,I
      389   Cubic concepts.

MEASUREMENT. Volume
  Metric system -- J,I,S
      389   Volume - capacity.

MEASUREMENT. Volume
  SI -- J
      389   Un Volume - une capacité.
      389   Measuring volume.

MEASURES
  See also
    WEIGHTS & MEASURES

MEAT
  See also
    HOT DOGS

MEAT PACKING
  -- J,I
      664   Working in a meat packing plant.

MECHANISED LOGGING
  -- I,S
      634.9   La Mécanisation dans
                  l'expolitation forestière de
                  l'est du Canada.
      634.9   Mechanized logging in eastern
                  Canada.

MEDIA
  See also
    AUDIOVISUAL MATERIALS
    BOOKS
    DOCUMENTS
    GRAPHIC MEDIA
    NEWSPAPERS
    TELEVISION

MEDICINE
  See also
    DENTISTRY
    DISEASES
    FIRST AID
    GENETICS
    HOSPITALS
    HYGIENE
    NEUROSURGERY
    NURSING
    OBSTETRICS
    PHARMACOLOGY
    PHYSIOLOGY
    TOXICOLOGY
    VETERINARY MEDICINE

MEDICINE
  Bethune, Norman -- J,I
      920   Dr. Norman Bethune.

MEDICINE. China
  -- I
      379.51   Education and health.

MENNONITES. Elmira. Ontario
  Dairy farming -- J,I
      917.13   Dairy farming community (Elmira,
                  Ont.)
      917.13   Un contre d'industrie laitière.

PRECIS SUBJECT INDEX

MENTAL PROCESSES
  See also
    COGNITION

METALS
  See also
    COPPER
    GOLD
    NICKEL
    URANIUM

METALWORKING
  Forging -- I,S
    671.3   Forging iron.

METALWORKING
  Forming -- I,S
    621.9   Forming metal by machine.

METALWORKING
  Power tools: Drill presses -- I,S
    621.9   Using the drill press.

METALWORKING
  Power tools: Lathes -- I,S
    621.9   Working between centers on the lathe.
    621.9   Chuckwork on the lathe.

METALWORKING
  Sheet metal working. Patterns. Development -- S
    671.2   Pattern development by triangulation.
    671.2   Parallel line development.
    671.2   Radial line development.

METALWORKING
  Soldering -- I,S
    671.5   Soldering methods.

METALWORKING
  Welding -- I,S
    671.5   Welding techniques.

METEOROLOGY
  See also
    WEATHER

METRIC SYSTEM
  See also
    S.I.

METRIC SYSTEM
  -- J,I,S
    389   The Metric system : a better way ... for all!
    389   The Metric system : a better way .. for some.

METRIC SYSTEM. Linear measurement
  -- I
    389   Linear units.

METRIC SYSTEM. Linear measurement
  -- J,I
    389   Lengthy tales.

METRIC SYSTEM. Linear measurement
  -- J,I,S
    389   Linear - area.

METRIC SYSTEM. Linear measurement
  -- P,J
    389   Linear measurement.

METRIC SYSTEM. Measurement. Area
  -- I
    389   Unité de surface.
    389   Area units.

METRIC SYSTEM. Measurement. Area
  -- J,I
    389   Square stories.

METRIC SYSTEM. Measurement. Area
  -- J,I,S
    389   Linear - area.

METRIC SYSTEM. Measurement. Area
  -- P,J
    389   Area.

METRIC SYSTEM. Measurement. Capacity
  -- J,I
    389   Capacity counts.

PRECIS SUBJECT INDEX

METRIC SYSTEM. Measurement. Capacity
-- J,I,S
    389   Volume - capacity.

METRIC SYSTEM. Measurement. Capacity
-- P,J
    389   Volume and capacity.

METRIC SYSTEM. Measurement. Mass
-- J,I
    389   Mass matters.

METRIC SYSTEM. Measurement. Mass
-- J,I,S
    389   Mass.

METRIC SYSTEM. Measurement. Mass
-- P,J
    389   Temperature and mass.

METRIC SYSTEM. Measurement. Volume
-- I
    389   Les Unités de volume.
    389   Volume units.

METRIC SYSTEM. Measurement. Volume
-- J,I
    389   Cubic concepts.

METRIC SYSTEM. Measurement. Volume
-- J,I,S
    389   Volume - capacity.

MEXICAN FOLKLORE
  Special subjects: Christmas -- Stories -- P,J
        398.20972 La Mexique : l'humble présent.
        398.20972 Mexico : the humblest gift.

MEXICO
  Description & travel -- J,I
        917.2   Mexico I : across modern Mexico.

MICMAC FOLKLORE
  -- Stories -- P,J,I
        398.209701 How summer came to our land.
        398.209701 The Legend of the loon.

MICROSCOPY
-- J,I
    535   The Microscope - a delicate tool.
    535   The Microscope - its operation.
    578   The World of microscopy.

MICROSCOPY
  Slide preparation -- J,I
    578   Making your own microscopic slides

MIDDLE EAST
  Ancient Middle East. Cities -- I,S
    301.34   The Urban revolution : the first cities.

MIDLAND. Ontario
  Huron Indian villages -- J,I
    970.3   Huron Indian Village (reconstructed)

MIGRATION
  See also
    EMIGRATION
    IMMIGRATION

MILITARY ENGINEERING
  See also
    FORTS

MILITARY FORCES See ARMED FORCES

MILK
  Pasteurisation -- P,J
    637   Milk and ice cream.

MILK PRODUCTS
  Manufacture -- P,J
    637   Milk and ice cream.

MILKING. Cows
-- K
    637   What's in a dairy barn.

MILLING
  See also
    FLOUR MILLING

PRECIS SUBJECT INDEX

MILNE, DAVID. Paintings
-- I,S
    759.11   David Milne.
    759.11   David Milne.

MIND
  See also
    PSYCHOLOGY

MINER, JACK. Ornithology
-- P,J,I,S
    920   World of Jack Miner : the pioneer naturalist, 1965-1944.

MINERAL RESOURCES
  See also
    COPPER
    GOLD
    NICKEL
    URANIUM

MINERALS
  See also
    ROCKS

MINERALS
-- J,I
    549   Les roches et les minéraux.
    549   Learning about rocks and minerals.

MINING. Asbestos. Quebec Province
-- J,I
    622   Asbestos mining in Quebec.

MINING. Nickel. Manitoba
-- J,I
    622   Nickel mining in Manitoba.

MINING. Uranium. Elliot Lake. Ontario
-- J,I
    622   Uranium mining in Ontario.

MINING INDUSTRIES
  See also
    BAUXITE INDUSTRY
    COAL MINING INDUSTRY
    COPPER MINING INDUSTRY
    ZINC MINING INDUSTRY

MINING INDUSTRIES. Canada
-- I,S
    338.20971   Minerals for Canadians.
    338.20971   Les Canadiens et leurs minéraux.

MINING INDUSTRIES. Canada
to 1969 -- J
    338.20971   Minerals.

MINING INDUSTRIES. Flin Flon. Manitoba
-- I
    917.127   Flin Flon, Manitoba.

MINTING. Canadian coins
Royal Canadian Mint -- J,I
    737.4   Royal Canadian Mint.

MIXED FARMING. Manitoba
-- J,I
    631.097127   Mixed farming in Manitoba.

MOLES. Canada
-- J
    599   Insectivores and bats.

MOLLUSCS
  See also
    MARINE MOLLUSCS

MONARCH BUTTERFLIES
Life cycle -- P,J,I
    595.7   Le papillon monarque.
    595.7   The Monarch butterfly.

MONEY
  See also
    COINS

MONEY
-- I,S
    332.4   What is money?

MONTANE FORESTS. Canada
compared with coastal forests -- I,S
    581.5   Coast and montane forest : a comparison.
    581.6   La forêt des montagnes et la forêt côtière : une comparai

MONTREAL
    to 1965 -- J,I,S
        917.14   Ville fluviale (Montreal)
        917.14   River city : Montreal.

MONTREAL
    Family life -- Comparative studies -- P,J
        917.14   Trois familles de Montréal.
        917.14   Three families of Montreal.

MONUMENTAL INSCRIPTIONS. Churchyards. Information sources. Pioneer life. 1790-1890. Canada -- J,I
        971.3   Visiting a pioneer cemetery.

MOON
    -- J,I
        523.3   La position de la lune.
        523.3   The Moon's position in space.

MOON
    Exploration -- P,J
        629.45   Explorations lunaires.
        629.45   Moon exploration.

MOON
    Phases -- J,I
        523.3   La Lune : ses phases.
        523.3   Phases of the moon.

MORAL DECISIONS
    -- P,J
        179   L'Hostilité.
        179   Hostility.
        179   La culpabilité.
        179   Guilt.

MORRICE, JAMES WILSON. Paintings
    -- I,S
        759.11   James Wilson Morrice.

MOTHS
    Cecropia moths. Life cycle -- J,I,S
        595.7   Le paon de nuit.
        595.7   The Cecropia moth.

MOTOR VEHICLES
    See also
        BUSES
        CARS
        TRUCKS. Motor vehicles

MOTOR VEHICLES
    Engines: Fuel pumps. Maintenance & repair -- I,S
        629.22   Pistons, oil and and fuel pumps.

MOTOR VEHICLES
    Engines: Oil pumps. Maintenance & repair -- I,S
        629.22   Pistons, oil and and fuel pumps.

MOTOR VEHICLES
    Tires. Maintenance & repair -- I,S
        629.22   Care of wheels and tires.

MOTOR VEHICLES
    Transmission systems. Maintenance & repair -- I,S
        629.22   Driving mechanism.

MOTOR VEHICLES
    Wheels. Maintenance & repair -- I,S
        629.22   Care of wheels and tires.

MOUNTAINS
    See also
        ANDES
        ROCKY MOUNTAINS

MOUNTAINS. Japan
    Geography -- J
        915.2   Mountain environments of Japan.

MOUNTIES See ROYAL CANADIAN MOUNTED POLICE

MOUNTING. Graphic media
    Dry mounting -- I,S
        760.028   Creating your own visuals using a dry mount press.

MOUNTING. Graphic media
    Mat cutting -- I,S
        749   Art work presentation : mat cutting.

MOUSTACHES. Make-up. Theatre
    Techniques -- I,S
        792   Beards.

MULTICULTURAL FACTORS. Canadian cuisine
    -- J,I
        917.1   An Appetite for heritage.

PRECIS SUBJECT INDEX

MULTICULTURALISM. Canada
-- I,S
    917.1   Cultures in conflict.

MULTICULTURALISM. Canada
-- J,I
    917.1   Sharing heritage.

MUNICIPAL GOVERNMENT. Canada
-- J,I
    352.071   Go fight City Hall! local decision making.

MUNICIPAL GOVERNMENT. Canada
-- Study regions: Ontario. Toronto -- J,I
    352.071   Urban government.

MUNICIPAL GOVERNMENT. Canada
Elections -- Study regions: Ontario. Toronto -- J,I
    324.71   The Municipal election.

MUSIC
  See also
    FOLKSONGS

MYTHS
  See also
    LEGENDS

MYTHS
  Greek myths: Heracles -- J
    292   Nobel Hercules.

NARCOTICS
  See also
    OPIATES

NASKAPI CHILDREN. Labrador. Newfoundland
  Social life -- P,J
    970.3   La vie quotidienne d'un petit Indien.
    970.3   La vie quotidienne d'une petite Indienne.
    970.3   A Day in the life of an Indian boy
    970.3   A Day in the life of an Indian girl.

NATIONAL ARTS CENTRE
-- J,I
    790.20971   National Arts Centre.

NATIONAL GALLERY OF CANADA
-- J,I
    708   The National Gallery of Canada.

NATIONAL PARKS. Ontario
Point Pelee National Park -- J,I
    917.13   Point Pelee National Park.

NATIONAL PARKS. Prince Edward Island
Prince Edward Island National Park -- J,I
    917.17   Prince Edward Island National Pa

NATIONAL PARKS. Rocky Mountains. Alberta & British Columbia
-- J,I
    917.11   The Rocky Mountains national par

NATIONAL RESEARCH COUNCIL OF CANADA
-- J,I
    607   National Research Council.

NATIONALISATION. Natural resources. Guyana
-- Study examples: Bauxite industry -- I,S
    338.988   I can see clearly now.

NATIVE PEOPLES. America
Religions. Use of drugs -- S
    299   Drugs and religious ritual.

NATIVE PEOPLES. Canada
  See also
    CANADIAN INDIANS
    INNUIT. Canada

NATIVE PEOPLES. Canada
Effects of economic development of northern Canadi
energy resources -- I,S
    970.5   Northern development at what co

NATIVE PEOPLES. Canada
Languages. Picture writing -- I,S
    411.09701   Native picture writing.

NATIVE PEOPLES. North America
  See also
    INNUIT
    NORTH AMERICAN INDIANS

PRECIS SUBJECT INDEX

NATIVE PEOPLES. North America
   Adjustment to contemporary society -- J,I
      970.1   Native and European in North America.

NATURAL GAS INDUSTRY. Alberta
  -- J,I
      665   Natural gas in Alberta.

NATURAL GAS INDUSTRY. Canada
   to 1974 -- I
      333.8   Fossil fuels : oil and natural gas

NATURAL RESOURCES
   See also
      ENERGY RESOURCES
      FORESTS

NATURAL RESOURCES. Arctic Canada
   Exploitation, to 1971 -- J,I
      971.2   White men in the Arctic.

NATURAL RESOURCES. Guyana
   Nationalisation -- Study examples: Bauxite industry -
   -- I,S
      338.988   I can see clearly now.

NAVIGATION
   Compasses -- J,I,S,A
      538.028   The Compass.

NEGROES See BLACKS

NETS. Commercial fishing
   Materials -- I,S
      639   Engines de pêche (câbles et lignes pour la fabrication des fillets de pêch)
      639   Fishing gear (ropes and twines for fishing nets)

NEUROSURGERY
   Penfield, Wilder Graves -- J,I
      920   Dr. Wilder Penfield.

NEW BRUNSWICK
   Berry farming -- J,I
      634   Berry farming in N.B.

NEW BRUNSWICK
   Description & travel -- P,J
      917.15   Paul and Pauline visit New Brunswick and Prince Edward Island.

NEW BRUNSWICK
   Economic conditions -- J,I,S
      330.9715   Le Canada atlantique : le Nouveau-Brunswick.
      330.9715   Atlantic Canada : New Brunswick.

NEW BRUNSWICK
   Fredericton. Description & travel -- P,J
      917.15   Fredericton, New Brunswick.

NEW BRUNSWICK
   Grand Manan Island. Description & travel -- J,I
      917.15   L'Ile Grand Manan.
      917.15   Grand Manan Island.

NEW BRUNSWICK
   Grand Manan Island. Herring fishing -- J,I
      639.09715 L'Ile Grand Manan : la pêche à fascines.
      639.09715 Grand Manan Island : weir fishing.

NEW BRUNSWICK
   Grand Manan Island. Lobster fishing -- J
      639.09715 L'Ile Grand Manan : la pêche du homard.
      639.09715 Grand Manan Island : lobster fishing.

NEW BRUNSWICK
   Port of Saint John -- J,I
      387.109715 The Port of St. John.

NEW BRUNSWICK
   Saint John, to 1976 -- J,I
      917.15   Saint John - Canada's first city.

NEW BRUNSWICK
   St. John River valley. Industries -- J,I
      971.15   Saint John River Valley - Edmunston to Kings Landing.
      971.15   Saint John River Valley - Mactaquac to Saint John.

PRECIS SUBJECT INDEX

NEW FRANCE
   1534-1763 -- J,I
      971.01   The Story of New France.
      971.01   La Nouvelle-France.

NEW FRANCE
   1660-1763 -- J,I
      971.01   The Era of royal government.

NEW FRANCE
   Frontenac, Louis de Baude, comte de -- P,J
      971.01   Frontenac.
      971.01   Frontenac.

NEW FRANCE
   Land tenure: Seigneurial system -- J,I
      333.3   Seigneurs et seigneuries.
      333.3   Seigneurs and seigneuries.
      333.3   The Habitants.
      333.3   Les censitaires.

NEW FRANCE
   Social life -- J,I
      971.01   Life in New France.

NEW FRANCE
   Talon, Jean, Comte d'Orsainville -- J
      971.01   Jean Talon.
      971.01   Jean Talon.

NEW SOUTH WALES. Australia
   Riverina. Agricultural industries -- J,I,S
      919.44   Riverina (Murray-Darling Basin)

NEW SOUTH WALES. Australia
   Sydney. Description & travel -- I
      919.44   An Australian city : Sydney (no. I)

NEW SOUTH WALES. Australia
   Sydney. Description & travel -- J,I,S
      919.44   Sydney.

NEW SOUTH WALES. Australia
   Sydney. Suburbs. Description & travel -- I
      919.44   An Australian city : Sydney (no. II)

NEWFOUNDLAND
   1000-1824 -- J,I
      971.8   L'histoire de Terre-Neuve (1000-1824)
      971.8   The History of Newfoundland (1000-1824)

NEWFOUNDLAND
   Churchill Falls. Hydroelectric power stations -- J
      917.19   Churchill Falls.

NEWFOUNDLAND
   Description & travel -- P,J
      917.16   Paul and Pauline visit Nova Scotia and Newfoundland.

NEWFOUNDLAND
   Economic conditions -- J,I,S
      330.9718   Le Canada atlantique : L'Ile de Terre-Neuve.
      330.9718   Atlantic Canada : Island of Newfoundland.

NEWFOUNDLAND
   Labrador. Economic conditions -- J,I,S
      330.9719   Le Canada atlantique : le Labrador
      330.9719   Atlantic Canada : Labrador.

NEWFOUNDLAND
   Labrador. Naskapi children. Social life -- P,J
      970.3   La vie quotidienne d'un petit Indien.
      970.3   La vie quotidienne d'une petite Indienne.
      970.3   A Day in the life of an Indian
      970.3   A Day in the life of an Indian girl.

NEWFOUNDLAND
   Labrador. Snowshoe making by Canadian Indians --
      685   Raquettes indiennes.
      685   Indian snowshoes.

NEWFOUNDLAND
   Nursing. Bennett, Myra Grimsley -- J,I
      920   Nurse of Newfoundland.

NEWFOUNDLAND
   Pulp & paper industries -- J,I
      676.09718 Pulp and paper manufacturing in Newfoundland.

PRECIS SUBJECT INDEX

NEWFOUNDLAND
    St. John's, to 1975 -- J,I
        917.18   St. John's, Newfoundland.

NEWFOUNDLAND
    Spring wildflowers -- Field guides -- P,J,I,S
        582.09718   Spring wildflowers : Newfoundland.
        582.09718   Fleurs sauvages printanières :
                        Terre-Neuve.

NEWSPAPERS
    Production -- P,J
        070   The Newspaper : part 2.
        070   The Newspaper : part 1.

NEWSPAPERS. Ontario
    1800-1850 -- Re-enactments at Black Creek Pioneer
    Village -- J,I
        971.3   The Newspaper business.

NIAGARA PENINSULA. Ontario
    Agricultural land. Development. Effects of regional
    planning -- J,I,S
        333.7   Fruit Belt preservation and
                    regional planning.

NIAGARA PENINSULA. Ontario
    Fruit farming -- I,S
        333.7   An Overview of the Niagara Fruit
                    Belt.
        917.13   Introduction to the Niagara Fruit
                    Belt.

NIAGARA PENINSULA. Ontario
    Land use -- J,I,S
        333.7   Problems of land use in urban
                    fringe - urban shadow areas.

NICKEL. Manitoba
    Mining -- J,I
        622   Nickel mining in Manitoba.

NIGERIA
    Children -- P,J
        916.69   Children of Northern Nigeria.
        916.69   Les enfants de la Nigéria du Nord.

NILE. Egypt
    Flood plains. Agriculture -- J,I
        631.0962   Gifts of the Nile 1 : farming on
                        the flood plains.

NOMADIC COMMUNITIES. Arctic
    -- J,I
        910   Nomadic journey : three nomadic
                    peoples.

NOMADIC COMMUNITIES. Deserts
    -- J,I
        910   Nomadic journey : three nomadic
                    peoples.

NOMADIC COMMUNITIES. Tundra
    -- J,I
        910   Nomadic journey : three nomadic
                    peoples.

NONBOOK MATERIALS
    See also
        AUDIOVISUAL MATERIALS

NORTH AMERICA
    Arctic North America. Environment. Adaptation of
    animals -- J,I
        591.9712   Animals of the Arctic.

NORTH AMERICA
    Arctic North America. Environment. Adaptation of
    mammals -- P,J
        599.09712   The Arctic.

NORTH AMERICA
    Arctic North America. Tundra. Environment.
    Adaptation of mammals -- J,I
        574.509712 Life on the Barren Lands.

NORTH AMERICA
    Environment. Adaptation of mammals -- J,I
        599   The Story of mammals.

NORTH AMERICA
    Exploration. Thompson, David -- J,I
        920   David Thompson.

NORTH AMERICA
    Forests. Environment. Adaptation of mammals -- J,I
        599.097   Life in the boreal forest.

NORTH AMERICA
    Forests. Environment. Adaptation of mammals -- P,J
        599.097   The Eastern forest.

PRECIS SUBJECT INDEX

NORTH AMERICA
   Native peoples. Adjustment to contemporary society -- J,I
      970.1   Native and European in North America.

NORTH AMERICA
   North-eastern North America. North American Indians, c.1600-1974 -- I,S
      970.4   The Native peoples of the Northeastern Woodlands : European contact to the present day.
      970.4   Les amérindiens des forêts de l'est : depuis l'arrivée des européens.

NORTH AMERICA
   North-eastern North America. North American Indians. Culture, to c.1600 -- I.S
      970.4   The Native peoples of the Northeastern Woodlands : initial European contact.
      970.4   Les amérindiens des forêts de l'est : jusqu' à l'arrivée des européens.

NORTH AMERICA
   North-eastern North America. North American Indians. Culture -- J,I
      970.4   Indians of the Northeastern Woodlands.

NORTH AMERICA
   Pioneer life, 1800-1850 -- P,J,I
      970   Community life.
      970   Furniture and household goods.

NORTH AMERICA
   Prairies. Environment. Adaptation of mammals -- J,I
      591.5   Life on the Prairies.

NORTH AMERICA
   Prairies. Environment. Adaptation of mammals -- P,J
      599.097   The Grasslands.

NORTH AMERICA
   Rocky Mountains. Environment. Adaptation of mammals -- P,J
      599.097   The Rocky Mountains.

NORTH AMERICA
   Trade, 1800-1850 -- P,J,I
      970   Commerce.

NORTH AMERICAN INDIAN CLOTHING
   -- I,S
      391.09701 Native clothing.

NORTH AMERICAN INDIAN DANCES
   -- J,I,S
      793.3   Indian dances and masks.

NORTH AMERICAN INDIAN FOLKLORE
   -- Stories -- J
      398.209701 Glooskap brings summer.
      398.209701 The Medicine that restores life.
      398.209701 How it all began.
      398.209701 Le Bouc à une corne.
      398.209701 The Sun dance of the Plains Indians.
      398.209701 The One-horned mountain goat.
      398.209701 Le remède de la vie.
      398.209701 Au tout début.
      398.209701 La danse du soleil des Amérindiens de Plaines.

NORTH AMERICAN INDIAN FOLKLORE
   -- Stories -- P
      398.209701 Naba-Cha and the Rocky Mountain
      398.209701 Why a porcupine has quills.
      398.209701 Glooscap and the four wishes.
      398.209701 Les piquants du Porc-Epic.
      398.209701 Glooscap et les quatre voeux : (légende indienne)

NORTH AMERICAN INDIAN FOLKLORE
   -- Stories -- P,J
      398.209701 How the deer got fire.

NORTH AMERICAN INDIAN FOLKLORE
   -- Stories -- P,J,I
      398.209701 Pourquoi les pieds-noirs ne for jamais de mal aux souris.

NORTH AMERICAN INDIAN LANGUAGES
   See also
      CREE LANGUAGE

NORTH AMERICAN INDIAN MASKS
   -- J,I,S
      391.09701 Masques des Indiens de l'Amérique du Nord.
      391.09701 Masks of the North American Indians.

PRECIS SUBJECT INDEX

NORTH AMERICAN INDIANS
  See also
    ALGONQUIAN INDIANS
    CANADIAN INDIANS
    HURON INDIANS
    IROQUOIS
    MICMAC
    PLAINS INDIANS

NORTH AMERICAN INDIANS
  Personal adjustment to contemporary society -- P,J
    F   Charlie Squash goes to town.
    F   Charlie Squash se rend à la ville.

NORTH AMERICAN INDIANS. North-eastern North America
  c.1600-1974 -- I,S
    970.4   The Native peoples of the
              Northeastern Woodlands :
              European contact to the present
              day.
    970.4   Les amérindiens des forêts de
              l'est : depuis l'arrivée des
              europeens.

NORTH AMERICAN INDIANS. North-eastern North America
  Culture, to c.1600 -- I,S
    970.4   The Native peoples of the
              Northeastern Woodlands :
              initial European contact.
    970.4   Les amérindiens des forêts de
              l'est : jusqu' à l'arrivée des
              europeens.

NORTH AMERICAN INDIANS. North-eastern North America
  Culture -- J,I
    970.4   Indians of the Northeastern
              Woodlands.

NORTH AMERICAN INDIANS. Pacific coast
  c.1600-1974 -- I,S
    970.4   The Native peoples of the Pacific
              Northwest : European contact to
              the present day.
    970.4   Les amérindiens de la côte du
              pacifique : depuis l'arrivée
              des europeens.

NORTH AMERICAN INDIANS. Pacific coast
  Culture, to c.1600 -- I,S
    970.4   The Native peoples of the Pacific
              Northwest : initial European
              contact.
    970.4   Les amérindiens de la côte du
              pacifique : jusqu'à l'arrivée
              des europeens.

NORTH AMERICAN INDIANS. Pacific coast
  Culture -- J,I
    970.4   Indians of the Pacific Northwest.

NORTH AMERICAN INDIANS. Pacific coast
  Culture -- J,I,S
    970.4   People of the North Pacific Coast.
    970.4   Les peuplades de la Côte Nord-
              Ouest.

NORTH AMERICAN INDIANS. South-western United States
  Culture -- J,I
    970.4   Indians of the Southwest.

NORTH-EASTERN NORTH AMERICA
  North American Indians, c.1600-1974 -- I,S
    970.4   The Native peoples of the
              Northeastern Woodlands :
              European contact to the present
              day.
    970.4   Les amérindiens des forêts de
              l'est : depuis l'arrivée des
              europeens.

NORTH-EASTERN NORTH AMERICA
  North American Indians. Culture, to c.1600 -- I,S
    970.4   The Native peoples of the
              Northeastern Woodlands :
              initial European contact.
    970.4   Les amérindiens des forêts de
              l'est : jusqu' à l'arrivée des
              europeens.

NORTH-EASTERN NORTH AMERICA
  North American Indians. Culture -- J,I
    970.4   Indians of the Northeastern
              Woodlands.

NORTH WEST MOUNTED POLICE See ROYAL CANADIAN MOUNTED
POLICE

NORTHERN CANADA
  Energy resources. Economic development. Effects on
  native peoples -- I,S
    970.5   Northern development at what cost?

NORTHERN CANADA
  Geography -- J,I
    330.9712 The Northland.

PRECIS SUBJECT INDEX

NORTHERN CANADA
    Log houses. Building -- Do it yourself guides -- S,A
        690   Build your own log house : part 2.
        690   Build your own log house : part 1.

NORTHERN ONTARIO
    Geography -- J,I
        917.13   Ontario : the north,
                     transportation and recreation.

NORTHERN ONTARIO
    Spring wildflowers -- Field guides -- P,J,I,S
        582.09713 Spring wildflowers : Northern
                     Ontario and Quebec.
        582.09713 Fleurs sauvages printanières :
                     nord de l'Ontario et du Québec.

NORTHERN PRAIRIE PROVINCES
    Spring wildflowers -- Field guides -- P,J,I,S
        582.09712 Spring wildflowers : northern
                     Prairie provinces.
        582.09712 Fleurs sauvages printanières :
                     nord des provinces des Prairies.

NORTHWEST PASSAGE
    Exploration, 1576-1822 -- J,I
        910   Fact and fancy.

NORTHWEST PASSAGE
    Exploration, 1576-1906 -- I,S
        971.2   Discovering the land.

NORTHWEST PASSAGE
    Exploration, 1819-1845 -- J,I
        910   Discoveries and disappointments.

NORTHWEST PASSAGE
    Exploration, 1845-1906 -- J,I
        910   Tragedy and triumph.

NORTHWEST TERRITORIES
    -- I
        917.12   Les Territoires du Nord-Ouest.
        917.12   The Northern territories.

NORTHWEST TERRITORIES
    Baffin Island. Animals. Hunting by Inuit -- P,J,I
        970.4   Autumn hunters.

NORTHWEST TERRITORIES
    Baffin Island. Inuit. Spring activities -- P,J,I
        970.4   Spring journey.

NORTHWEST TERRITORIES
    Baffin Island. Inuit. Summer activities -- P,J,I
        970.4   Summer days.

NORTHWEST TERRITORIES
    Baffin Island. Inuit. Winter activities -- P,J,I
        970.4   Winter camp.

NORTHWEST TERRITORIES
    Barren Grounds. Canadian Indians -- J
        970.4   People of the sub-Arctic.
        970.4   Les Indiens des Régions
                    subarctiques.

NORTHWEST TERRITORIES
    Government -- J,I
        354.712   The Structure of government.

NORTHWEST TERRITORIES
    Inuvik. Description & travel -- J,I
        917.12   Arctic Delta town (Inuvik, N.W.T

NORTHWEST TERRITORIES
    Keewatin District. Caribou Eskimo -- J
        970.4   The Caribou Eskimo.
        970.4   L'esquimau primitif.

NOVA SCOTIA
    Cape Breton Island. Economic conditions -- J,I
        330.9716   Cape Breton Island : industrial
                     regions.

NOVA SCOTIA
    Cape Breton Island. Geography -- J,I
        917.16   Cape Breton Island : an overvie

NOVA SCOTIA
    Description & travel -- P,J
        917.16   Paul and Pauline visit Nova
                     Scotia and Newfoundland.

NOVA SCOTIA
    Economic conditions -- J,I,S
        330.9716   Le Canada atlantique : la
                     Nouvelle Ecosse.
        330.9716   Atlantic Canada : Nova Scotia.

PRECIS SUBJECT INDEX

NOVA SCOTIA
   Geography -- J,I
      917.16   Nova Scotia.

NOVA SCOTIA
   Halifax, to 1972 -- J,I,S
      387.109716 Port city : Halifax.
      387.109716 Ville portuaire (Halifax)

NOVA SCOTIA
   Halifax, to 1974 -- J,I
      917.16   Halifax, Nova Scotia.

NOVA SCOTIA
   Halifax, to 1976 -- J,I
      917.16   Halifax - historic seaport.

NOVA SCOTIA
   Halifax. Description & travel -- J,I
      917.16   The City of Halifax.

NOVA SCOTIA
   Lunenberg. Fish processing -- I
      639   The Fish processing plant.

NOVA SCOTIA
   Pictou. Fishing industries -- J
      917.16   Pictou, Nova Scotia.

NOVA SCOTIA
   Port Bickerton. Description & travel -- J,I
      917.16   Village de pêche.
      917.16   Fishing town (Port Bickerton, N.S.

NOVA SCOTIA
   Port of Halifax -- J,I
      387.109716 Port of Halifax.

NOVA SCOTIA
   Poultry farming -- J,I
      636.5   Nova Scotia poultry farming.

NUCLEAR POWER
   -- I
      621.48   Nuclear energy.

NURSING. Newfoundland
   Bennett, Myra Grimsley -- J,I
      920   Nurse of Newfoundland.

NURSING. Professions. Canada
   -- I,S
      610.73   Nursing : the challenge of caring.

NUTRITION
   -- I,S
      641.1   Alimentation et bonne santé.
      641.1   Nutrition and health.

NUTRITION
   -- K,P
      641.1   Nutrition - anew look.

NUTRITION
   -- P
      641.1   What is nutrition?
      641.1   Qu'est-ce que l'hygiène alimentaire?

NUTRITION
   -- P,J
      641.1   The Story of how to eat to grow tall.

OBSTETRICS
   See also
      CHILDBIRTH

OCCUPATIONS
   See also
      LETTER CARRIERS
      PROFESSIONS

OCEANS
   See also
      ATLANTIC

ODONATA
   See also
      DAMSELFLIES
      DRAGONFLIES

OFFENSIVE PLAY. Hockey
   Techniques -- P,J,I
      796.9   Hockey II - the game -

PRECIS SUBJECT INDEX

OGOKI. Ontario
  Ojibway students. Visits to Toronto -- I,S
      370.19   Ogoki native people visit the city

OGOKI. Ontario
  Visits by students from Toronto -- I,S
      370.19   City students visit Ogoki.

OIL INDUSTRY. Canada
  to 1974 -- I
      333.8   Fossil fuels : oil and natural gas

OIL PUMPS. Engines. Motor vehicles
  Maintenance & repair -- I,S
      629.22   Pistons, oil and and fuel pumps.

OJIBWAY STUDENTS. Ogoki. Ontario
  Visits to Toronto -- I,S
      370.19   Ogoki native people visit the city

OKANAGAN VALLEY. British Columbia
  Fruit farming -- J,I
      634   Fruit farming in British Columbia.
      917.11   Ville fruitière.
      917.11   Orchard City (Kelowna, B.C.)

OLD AGE MAKE-UP. Theatre
  Techniques -- I,S
      792   Old age makeup.

ONTARIO
  -- I
      917.13   L'Ontario.
      917.13   Ontario.

ONTARIO
  to 1867 -- J,I
      971.3   Ontario's heritage.
      971.3   Ontario's heritage.

ONTARIO
  Broom making, 1800-1850 -- Re-enactments at Black Creek Pioneer Village -- J,I
      971.3   The Village broom shop.

ONTARIO
  Cabinet making, 1800-1850 -- Re-enactments at Black Creek Pioneer Village -- J,I
      971.3   The Cabinet maker.

ONTARIO
  Cliffs: Scarborough Bluffs -- J,I
      917.13   Planning for future use.

ONTARIO
  Cliffs: Scarborough Bluffs. Erosion. Countermeasures -- J,I
      917.13   The Natural environment.

ONTARIO
  Cookery, 1800-1850 -- Re-enactments at Upper Canada Village -- J,I
      971.3   Foods.

ONTARIO
  Crafts, 1800-1850 -- Re-enactments at Upper Canada Village -- J,I
      971.3   Les Métiers.
      971.3   Crafts.

ONTARIO
  Description & travel -- P,J
      917.13   Paul and Pauline visit Ontario.

ONTARIO
  Elliot Lake. Uranium. Mining -- J,I
      622   Uranium mining in Ontario.

ONTARIO
  Elmira. Dairy farming by Mennonites -- J,I
      917.13   Dairy farming community (Elmira Ont.)
      917.13   Un contre d'industrie laitìere

ONTARIO
  Family life, 1800-1850 -- Re-enactments at Upper Canada Village -- J,I
      971.3   La Famille.
      971.3   Family life.

ONTARIO
  Farming, 1800-1850 -- Re-enactments at Upper Canada Village -- J,I
      971.3   Farm life.

ONTARIO
  Flour milling, 1800-1850 -- Re-enactments at Black Creek Pioneer Village -- J,I
      971.3   The Mill.

PRECIS SUBJECT INDEX

ONTARIO
   Fur trade. Trading posts: Fort William -- I
      971.3   Life in the old Fort.
      971.3   The Growth, the decline.

ONTARIO
   Geography -- J,I
      330.9713   Central Canada : the people.
      330.9713   Central Canada : the place.
      917.13   Ontario.

ONTARIO
   Gold. Refining -- J,I
      622   Gold refining in Ontario.

ONTARIO
   Hamilton. Description & travel -- J,I
      917.13   The Many Faces of Hamilton.

ONTARIO
   Hamilton. Industries -- J,I
      917.13   The Industrial city.

ONTARIO
   Manitouwadge. Copper mining industry & zinc mining industry -- J,I
      917.13   Images d'une ville minière.
      917.13   Mining town (Manitouwadge, Ont.)

ONTARIO
   Marathon. Pulp & paper industries -- J,I
      917.13   Marathon, Ontario.

ONTARIO
   Midland. Huron Indian villages -- J,I
      970.3   Huron Indian Village (reconstructed)

ONTARIO
   National parks: Point Pelee National Park -- J,I
      917.13   Point Pelee National Park.

ONTARIO
   Newspapers, 1800-1850 -- Re-enactments at Black Creek Pioneer Village -- J,I
      971.3   The Newspaper business.

ONTARIO
   Niagara Peninsula. Agricultural land. Development. Effects of regional planning -- J,I,S
      333.7   Fruit Belt preservation and regional planning.

ONTARIO
   Niagara Peninsula. Fruit farming -- I,S
      333.7   An Overview of the Niagara Fruit Belt.
      917.13   Introduction to the Niagara Fruit Belt.

ONTARIO
   Niagara Peninsula. Land use -- J,I,S
      333.7   Problems of land use in urban fringe - urban shadow areas.

ONTARIO
   Northern Ontario. Geography -- J,I
      917.13   Ontario : the north, transportation and recreation.

ONTARIO
   Northern Ontario. Spring wildflowers -- Field guides -- P,J,I,S
      582.09713 Spring wildflowers : Northern Ontario and Quebec.
      582.09713 Fleurs sauvages printanières : nord de l'Ontario et du Québec.

ONTARIO
   Ogoki. Ojibway students. Visits to Toronto -- I,S
      370.19   Ogoki native people visit the city

ONTARIO
   Ogoki. Visits by students from Toronto -- I,S
      370.19   City students visit Ogoki.

ONTARIO
   Oshawa. Automotive industry -- J,I
      917.13   Oshawa, Ontario.

ONTARIO
   Ottawa. Art galleries: National Gallery of Canada -- J,I
      708   The National Gallery of Canada.

ONTARIO
   Ottawa. Description & travel -- J,I
      917.13   Ottawa - the urban community.
      917.13   Ottawa - Canada's capital.

ONTARIO
   Ottawa. Rideau Canal -- J,I
      386.09713 Le Canal Rideau.
      386.09713 Rideau Canal.

PRECIS SUBJECT INDEX

ONTARIO
   Pioneer life, 1800-1850 -- J,I
      971.3   The Pioneer community.
      971.3   Un village du Haut-Canada.

ONTARIO
   Pioneer life, c.1880 -- S
      971.3   Going to Canada : in the backwoods

ONTARIO
   Pioneer life -- P,J
      971.3   Les pionniers du Haut-Canada.
      971.3   Early pioneer life in Upper Canada

ONTARIO
   Pioneer life -- Re-enactments at Black Creek Pioneer Village -- J,I
      971.3   The Pioneer community.
      971.3   Canada's pioneer life & customs.

ONTARIO
   Politics. Role of Irish immigrants -- S
      301.4509713 Irish feuds and quarrels.

ONTARIO
   Port of Thunder Bay -- J,I
      386.09713 Port of Thunder Bay.

ONTARIO
   Port of Toronto -- J,I
      386.09713 The Port of Toronto.
      386.09713 A Seaway port.

ONTARIO
   Port of Toronto -- J,I,S
      386.09713 Port of Toronto.

ONTARIO
   Recreations, 1800-1850 -- Re-enactments at Upper Canada Village -- J,I
      971.3   School and recreation.

ONTARIO
   Sainte Marie among the Hurons -- J,I
      971.3   L'Histoire de Sainte-Marie-des-Hurons : part2.
      971.3   L'Histoire de Sainte-Marie-des-Hurons : part I.
      971.3.   Sainte-Marie-among-the-Hurons : part I.

ONTARIO
   Sainte Marie among the Hurons -- P,J,I,S
      971.3   Sainte-Marie-among-the-Hurons.
      971.3   Sainte-Marie-aux-Hurons.

ONTARIO
   Schools, 1800-1850 -- Re-enactments at Upper Canada Village -- J,I
      971.3   School and recreation.

ONTARIO
   Social life, 1860-1870 -- Re-enactments at Upper Canada Village -- P,J
      971.3   La vie dans le Haut-Canada vers 1860.
      971.3   Life in Upper Canada in the 1860

ONTARIO
   Southern Ontario. Geography -- J,I
      917.13   Southern Ontario.

ONTARIO
   Southern Ontario. Spring wildflowers -- Field guide -- P,J,I,S
      528.09713 Spring wildflowers : southern Ontario and Quebec.
      582.09713 Fleurs sauvages printanières : sud de l'Ontario et du Québec.

ONTARIO
   Thunder Bay. Description & travel -- I
      917.13   Thunder Bay on tour.

ONTARIO
   Thunder Bay. Industries -- I
      386.09713 Thunder Bay's industrial harbour

ONTARIO
   Tobacco industry -- J,I
      633   Tobacco farming in Ontario.

ONTARIO
   Toronto. Agricultural shows: Royal Winter Fair --
      630.74   Royal Winter Fair.

ONTARIO
   Toronto. Agricultural shows: Royal Winter Fair -- J
      630.74   Royal Winter Fair.

PRECIS SUBJECT INDEX

ONTARIO
   Toronto. Airports: Toronto International Airport -- P,J
      387.7   International airport.

ONTARIO
   Toronto. Christmas parades -- P
      394.09713 The Day Santa came to town.

ONTARIO
   Toronto. Christmas parades -- P,J
      394.09713 La Parade du Père Noël à Toronto.

ONTARIO
   Toronto. Description & travel -- J,I
      917.13   Toronto - growth, change & progress.

ONTARIO
   Toronto. Students. Visits to Ogoki -- I,S
      370.19   City students visit Ogoki.

ONTARIO
   Toronto. Transport, 1849-1972 -- J,I
      388.409713 Transportation in Toronto.

ONTARIO
   Toronto. Visits by Ojibway students from Ogoki -- I,S
      370.19   Ogoki native people visit the city

ONTARIO
   Trade, 1800-1850 -- Re-enactments at Upper Canada Village -- J,I
      971.3   Le Village.
      971.3   Work and trade.

ONTARIO
   Weaving, 1800-1850 -- Re-enactments at Black Creek Pioneer Village -- J,I
      971.3   The Weaver.

ONTARIO
   Welland Canal, 1829-1932 -- J,I,S
      386.09713 The Welland Canal (historical)

ONTARIO
   Welland Canal, 1932-1978 -- J,I,S
      386.09713 The Welland Canal (today)

ONTARIO. Study regions
   Canada. Cities. Public transport -- Study regions: Ontario. Toronto -- P,J,I
      388.409713 Public transportation in the city.

ONTARIO. Study regions
   Canada. Municipal government -- Study regions: Ontario. Toronto -- J,I
      352.071   Urban government.

ONTARIO. Study regions
   Canada. Municipal government. Elections -- Study regions: Ontario. Toronto -- J,I
      324.71   The Municipal election.

ONTARIO. Study regions
   Cities. Transport -- Study regions: Ontario. Toronto -- J,I
      388.409713 Transportation.

ONTARIO. Special subjects. Drawings by V.H.Bartlett -- J,I
      971   Quebec and Ontario : old colony and new outpost.

ONTARIO SCIENCE CENTRE
   -- J,I
      507.4   The Science Centre.

OPIATES
   -- I,S
      615   Opiates.
      615   Les stupéfiants opiacés.

OPTICS
   See also
      LIGHT

ORAL CONTRACEPTIVES
   -- I,S,A
      613.9   The Pill.

ORCHIDS. Eastern North America
   Wild orchids -- Field guides -- J,I
      584   Orchids of Eastern North America.

ORGANISATION
   See also
      MANAGEMENT

PRECIS SUBJECT INDEX

ORGANISMS
  See also
    ANIMALS
    ECOSYSTEMS
    PLANTS

ORGANISMS
  Adaptation to environment -- J
    574.5   Les Organismes et le milieu.

ORGANISMS
  Growth -- P,J
    574.3   Comes from ... grows to.
    574.3   Vient de - devient.

ORGANISMS
  Reproduction -- P,J
    574.1   La Vie commence - plantes et poissons.
    574.1   The Beginning of life : plants and fish.

ORGANISMS. Cities
  Adaptation to environment -- J,I
    574.5   Nature in the neighbourhood.
    574.5   Nature adapts to the city.
    574.5   City habitats.

ORIENTATION. Maps
  -- J,I
    912   L'orientation de la carte.
    912   Map orientation.

ORIENTATION. Wilderness survival
  Use of compasses -- I,S
    796.5   Orientation & compass.

ORIENTEERING
  -- I,S,A
    796.5   Orienteering.

ORNITHOLOGY
  See also
    BIRDS

ORNITHOLOGY
  Miner, Jack -- P,J,I,S
    920   World of Jack Miner : the pioneer naturalist, 1965-1944.

OSHAWA. Ontario
  Automotive industry -- J,I
    917.13   Oshawa, Ontario.

OTTAWA
  Art galleries: National Gallery of Canada -- J,I
    708   The National Gallery of Canada.

OTTAWA
  Description & travel -- J,I
    917.13   Ottawa - the urban community.
    917.13   Ottawa - Canada's capital.

OTTAWA
  Rideau Canal -- J,I
    386.09713   Le Canal Rideau.
    386.09713   Rideau Canal.

OTTER TRAWLING. Commercial fishing
  -- I,S
    639   Le chalutage.
    639   Otter trawling.

OUTBACK. Australia
  Description & travel -- J,I,S
    919.4   Frontier mining and grazing (the Outback)

OUTDOOR CLOTHING
  -- I,S
    646   Proper bush clothing.

OUTDOOR COOKERY
  -- I,S
    641.5   Fires and cooking.

OVERHEAD TRANSPARENCIES
  -- I,S
    371.33   Handmade overhead transparencies and their use.

OVERHEAD TRANSPARENCIES
  Diazo process -- S
    371.33   The Diazo process.

OVULATION. Mammals
  -- J
    591.1   Ovulation - mammifères.

PRECIS SUBJECT INDEX

OWLS. Canada
-- P,J
    598.2   Les hiboux.

PACIFIC COAST. North America
  North American Indians, c.1600-1974 -- I,S
    970.4   The Native peoples of the Pacific Northwest : European contact to the present day.
    970.4   Les amérindiens de la côte du pacifique : depuis l'arrivée des europeens.

PACIFIC COAST. North America
  North American Indians. Culture, to c.1600 -- I,S
    970.4   The Native peoples of the Pacific Northwest : initial European contact.
    970.4   Les amérindiens de la côte du pacifique : jusqu'à l'arrivée des europeens.

PACIFIC COAST. North America
  North American Indians. Culture -- J,I
    970.4   Indians of the Pacific Northwest.

PACIFIC COAST. North America
  North American Indians. Culture -- J,I,S
    970.4   People of the North Pacific Coast.
    970.4   Les peuplades de la Côte Nord-Ouest.

PACIFIC SALMON
-- P,J,I
    597   The Story of Pacific salmon.
    597   Le saumon du Pacifique.

PAINTING. Panelled doors. Houses
-- S
    698.3   Painting a panelled door.

PAINTINGS
  Borduas, Paul Emile -- I,S
    759.11   Paul-Emile Borduas.
    759.11   Paul-Emile Borduas.

PAINTINGS
  Carr, Emily -- I,S
    759.11   Emily Carr.

PAINTINGS
  Group of Seven -- I,S
    759.11   Le Groupe des Sept.
    759.11   The Group of Seven.

PAINTINGS
  Harris, Lawren Stewart -- I,S
    759.11   Lawren S. Harris.
    759.11   Lawren S. Harris.

PAINTINGS
  Krieghoff, Cornelius -- I,S
    759.11   Cornelius Krieghoff.

PAINTINGS
  Milne, David -- I,S
    759.11   David Milne.
    759.11   David Milne.

PAINTINGS
  Morrice, James Wilson -- I,S
    759.11   James Wilson Morrice.

PAINTINGS
  Pellan, Alfred -- I,S
    759.11   Alfred Pellan.
    759.11   Alfred Pellan.

PAINTINGS
  Riopelle, Jean Paul -- I,S
    759.11   Jean-Paul Riopelle.
    759.11   Jean-Paul Riopelle.

PAINTINGS
  Watson, Homer -- I,S
    759.11   Homer Watson.

PALACE OF QUELUZ. Lisbon
  Architecture -- I,S
    728.8   Versailles and Portugal.

PALACE OF VERSAILLES. France
  Architecture -- I,S
    728.8   Versailles and Portugal.

PANELLED DOORS. Houses
  Painting -- S
    698.3   Painting a panelled door.

PRECIS SUBJECT INDEX

PAPER INDUSTRIES See PULP & PAPER INDUSTRIES

PAPERHANGING
  See WALLPAPER
    Hanging

PARADES. Toronto
  Christmas parades -- P
    394.09713   The Day Santa came to town.

PARADES. Toronto
  Christmas parades -- P,J
    394.09713   La Parade du Père Noël à Toronto.

PARENTHOOD
  -- J,I
    173   Ce qu'est la maturite.
    173   The Meaning of maturity.

PARIS
  Architecture -- I,S
    720.944   Paris.

PARKER, EDGAR RUDOLPH RANDOLPH. Dentistry
  -- J,I
    920   Painless Parker.

PARKS
  See also
    NATIONAL PARKS

PARKS
  Recreations -- P
    796   Sunday in the park.
    796   Un dimanche au parc.

PARKS. Vancouver
  Stanley Park -- J,I
    917.11   Stanley Park.

PARLIAMENT. Canada
  -- J
    328.71   Le régime parlementaire.
    328.71   Parliamentary government.

PARLIAMENT. Canada
  -- J,I
    328.71   Parliament : making and changing laws.

PARLIAMENT. Canada
  Buildings -- J
    328.71   Une visite au Palais du Parlement

PARLIAMENT. Canada
  Buildings -- J,I
    328.71   Parliament buildings.

PASSENGER TRANSPORT
  See also
    PUBLIC TRANSPORT

PASSERIFORMES See PERCHING BIRDS

PASSING. Hockey
  -- P,J
    796.9   Pin point passing.

PASSOVER
  -- P,J,I,S,A
    296.4   Passover.

PASTEURISATION. Milk
  -- P,J
    637   Milk and ice cream.

PATTERNS. Sheet metal working
  Development -- S
    671.2   Pattern development by triangulation.
    671.2   Parallel line development.
    671.2   Radial line development.

PEKING. China
  Description & travel -- I
    915.1   Cities of China.

PELLAN, ALFRED. Paintings
  -- I,S
    759.11   Alfred Pellan.
    759.11   Alfred Pellan.

PENAL SYSTEM
  See also
    PRISONS

PENFIELD, WILDER GRAVES. Neurosurgery
  -- J,I
    920   Dr. Wilder Penfield.

PRECIS SUBJECT INDEX

PERCEPTION
  See also
    SENSORY PERCEPTION

PERCEPTION. Personality
  By others -- P,J
    152.4   Many different me-s.
    152.4   Moi et mes diverses personalités.

PERCHING BIRDS. North America
  -- J,I
    598.2   Perching birds.

PERFORMING ARTS
  See also
    DANCES
    MUSIC
    THEATRE

PERFORMING ARTS. Canada
  National Arts Centre -- J,I
    790.20971   National Arts Centre.

PERIODS. Punctuation. English language
  -- J
    421   Periods, question marks, and
           exclamation marks.

PERSEVERANCE
  -- I,S
    179   Perseverance.

PERSONAL ADJUSTMENT. Children
  To adulthood -- P,J
    152.4   Je ne peux pas.
    152.4   But I don't know how.

PERSONAL ADJUSTMENT. Innuit
  To contemporary society -- J,I
    917.12   The Way we live today.

PERSONAL ADJUSTMENT. North American Indians
  To contemporary society -- P,J
    F   Charlie Squash goes to town.
    F   Charlie Squash se rend à la ville.

PERSONAL FINANCE
  -- P,J
    332.024   Money : planning a budget.

PERSONAL FINANCE
  Credit -- Consumers' guides -- P,J
    332.024   Money : how much do you need?

PERSONAL HYGIENE
  -- K,P
    613   Cleanliness - a new look.

PERSONAL RELATIONSHIPS See INTERPERSONAL RELATIONSHIPS

PERSONALITY
  Effects of environment -- J,I
    155.2   Vous et votre personnalité.
    155.2   You and your personality.

PERSONALITY
  Effects of heredity -- J,I
    155.2   Vous et votre personnalité.
    155.2   You and your personality.

PERSONALITY
  Perception by others -- P,J
    152.4   Many different me-s.
    152.4   Moi et mes diverses personalités.

PERU
  Andes. Geography -- J,I
    918.5   Peru 1 : life in the Andes.

PERU
  Children -- P,J
    918.5   Indian children of the Andes.
    918.5   Les jeunes Indiens de Andes.

PET OWNERS' GUIDES
  Veterinary medicine -- Pet owners' guides -- P,J
    636.089   A Visit with the vet.

PETROLEUM INDUSTRY
  See also
    OIL INDUSTRY

PETROLEUM INDUSTRY. Alberta
  -- J,I
    665   Oil in Alberta.

PETROLOGY
  See also
    ROCKS

PRECIS SUBJECT INDEX

PETS
-- P
    636   Animal pets.

PETS
-- P,J
    636   What pet for me.

PETS
  Guinea pigs -- P,J
    636   Guinea pigs and their care.

PHARMACOLOGY
  See also
    DRUGS

PHASES. Moon
-- J,I
    523.3   La Lune : ses phases.
    523.3   Phases of the moon.

PHILOSOPHY
  See also
    MORAL DECISIONS

PHOTOGRAPHS
  Special subjects: Canadian Shield -- P,J,I
    407   Of the land.

PHOTOGRAPHS
  Special subjects: Farms -- P,J,I
    407   Of the farm.

PHOTOGRAPHS
  Special subjects: Horses -- P,J,I
    407   Of the horse.

PHOTOGRAPHY
  Cameras -- J,I
    771.3   The Camera.

PHOTOGRAPHY
  Films & filters -- J,I
    771   Film and filters.

PHYSICAL EXERCISE
-- For skiing -- I,S
    796.9   Skiing - pre-season conditioning.
    796.9   Le ski - mise en train pré-saisonnière.

PHYSICAL EXERCISE
-- K,P
    612   Exercise - a new look.

PHYSICAL GEOGRAPHY
  See also
    DESERTS
    FORESTS
    GRASSLANDS
    RIVERS
    TUNDRA

PHYSICAL GEOGRAPHY. Canada
-- J,I
    917.1   An Introduction to Canada's geography.

PHYSICAL PROPERTIES
  See also
    MASS
    VOLUME

PHYSICS
  See also
    ENERGY
    MAGNETISM
    OPTICS

PHYSIOGRAPHY See GEOMORPHOLOGY

PHYSIOLOGY. Hearing
-- J
    612   Hearing.

PHYSIOLOGY. Smell
-- J
    612   Smell, taste and touch.

PHYSIOLOGY. Smell
-- J,I
    612   The Biology of taste and smell.

PHYSIOLOGY. Spiders
-- J,I
    595   What is a spider?

PHYSIOLOGY. Taste
-- J
    612   Smell, taste and touch.

PRECIS SUBJECT INDEX

PHYSIOLOGY. Taste
-- J,I
    612   The Biology of taste and smell.

PHYSIOLOGY. Touch
-- J
    612   Smell, taste and touch.

PHYSIOLOGY. Touch
-- J,I
    612   Our five senses of touch.

PHYSIOLOGY. Vision
-- J
    612   Vision.

PICTOU. Nova Scotia
Fishing industries -- J
    917.16   Pictou, Nova Scotia.

PICTURE WRITING. Languages. Native peoples. Canada
-- I,S
    411.09701 Native picture writing.

PIONEER LIFE. Canada
1790-1890. Information sources: Churchyards. Monumental inscriptions -- J,I
    971.3   Visiting a pioneer cemetery.

PIONEER LIFE. Eastern Canada
1820-1867 -- Re-enactments at Black Creek Pioneer Village -- P,J,I
    971.3   Activities in pioneer days.
    971.3   Country life.
    971.3   Visiting pioneer Canada.

PIONEER LIFE. Eastern Canada
1830-1850 -- J,I
    971.3   Pioneer homes and schools in Eastern Canada.

PIONEER LIFE. Maritime Provinces
-- J,I
    971.5   Pioneer life in the Maritimes : part 1.
    971.5   Pioneer life in the Maritimes. part 2.
    971.5   Les pionniers des Maritimes : 1ère partie.
    971.5   Les pionniers des Maritimes : 2e partie.

PIONEER LIFE. North America
1800-1850 -- P,J,I
    970   Community life.
    970   Furniture and household goods.

PIONEER LIFE. Ontario
-- P,J
    971.3   Les pionniers du Haut-Canada.
    971.3   Early pioneer life in Upper Canada

PIONEER LIFE. Ontario
-- Re-enactments at Black Creek Pioneer Village -- J,I
    971.3   The Pioneer community.
    971.3   Canada's pioneer life & customs.

PIONEER LIFE. Ontario
1800-1850 -- J,I
    971.3   The Pioneer community.
    971.3   Un village du Haut-Canada.

PIONEER LIFE. Ontario
c.1880 -- S
    971.3   Going to Canada : in the backwoods

PIONEER LIFE. Quebec Province
1700-1800 -- J,I
    971.4   The Habitant and his home [in the 18th century]
    971.4   L'habitant et sa terre au XVIIIe siècle.
    971.4   L'habitant et sa maison au XVIIIe siècle.
    971.4   The Habitant and his land [in the 18th century]

PISCES See FISH

PITCH. Pronunciation. English language
-- J
    421   Pitch, stress and juncture.

PLAINS INDIANS
c.1600-1974 -- I,S
    970.4   The Native peoples of the Great Plains : European contact to the present day.
    970.4   Les amérindiens des Grandes Plaines : depuis l'arrivée des européens.

PRECIS SUBJECT INDEX

PLAINS INDIANS
   Culture, to c.1600 -- I,S
      970.4   The Native peoples of the Great
               Plains : initial European
               contact.
      970.4   Les amérindiens des Grandes
               Plaines : jusqu'à l'arrivée des
               Europeens.

PLAINS INDIANS
   Culture, to c.1600 -- J,I
      970.4   People of the Plains.
      970.4   Les Indiens des Plaines.

PLAINS INDIANS
   Culture -- J,I
      970.4   Indians of the Great Plains.

PLAINS INDIANS. Canada
   -- J,I
      970.4   Indians I : life on the Plains.

PLANNING
   See also
      REGIONAL PLANNING
      URBAN PLANNING

PLANTS
   See also
      EDIBLE FRUITS
      EDIBLE PLANTS
      FLOWERING PLANTS
      SEAWEED
      TREES

PLANTS
   Adaptation to environment in winter -- J,I
      581.5   Discovering plants in winter.

PLANTS
   Seeds. Dispersal -- P,J
      582   La dissémination des graines.
      582   How seeds are spread.

PLANTS. Arctic North America
   -- J,I
      581.9712 Plants of the Arctic.

PLANTS. Canada
   -- P,J
      581.971   Canadian wildlife - flora.

PLANTS. North America
   -- J,I
      581.97   What on earth! : a look at plants

PLAYS See DRAMA

POCKET GOPHERS. Canada
   -- P,J
      599   Le gaufre à poches.
      599   The Pocket gophers.

POINT PELEE NATIONAL PARK. Ontario
   -- J,I
      917.13   Point Pelee National Park.

POISONS
   -- P,J
      614.8   Things dangerous to eat.

POLAR BEARS. Canada
   -- P,J
      599   L'ours polaire.
      599   The Polar bear.

POLAR REGIONS
   See also
      ARCTIC

POLICE
   See also
      ROYAL CANADIAN MOUNTED POLICE

POLICE. Canada
   -- P,J
      363.2   The Police force : part of the
               community.

POLICE WORK
   -- J
      363.2   The Police force : behind the
               scenes.

POLICE WORK
   -- K
      363.2   The Police officer.

POLISH FOLKLORE
   -- Stories -- P
      398.209438 Foolish Bartek : (a Polish tale)

PRECIS SUBJECT INDEX

POLITICAL PARTIES. Canada
-- J
    329.971   Parties and elections.

POLITICO-ECONOMIC SYSTEMS
See also
    SOCIALISM

POLITICS
See also
    CONSTITUTION
    ELECTIONS
    FOREIGN RELATIONS
    GOVERNMENT

POLITICS. Canada
Effects of television -- I,S
    329   Electronic politics.
    329   L'Electronique en politique.

POLITICS. China
-- J,I,S
    320.951   Political life.

POLITICS. Ontario
Role of Irish immigrants -- S
    301.4509713   Irish feuds and quarrels.

POLLUTION. Environment
-- I,S
    333.9   La crise de l'environnement.
    333.9   Environment crisis.

POLLUTION. Environment. Urban regions
-- J,I
    301.34   Problems of urban environment.

POLO, MARCO
Exploration of Asia -- J
    920   Adventuresome Marco Polo.
    920   Les aventures de Marco Polo.

POMPEII. Ancient Rome
Architecture -- I,S
    722   Roman provinces and Pompeii.

POND ECOSYSTEMS
Forms of life -- P
    574.92   A Visit to a pond.
    574.92   Explorons l'etang.

PONIES
Welsh ponies -- P,J,I
    599   Les poneys : petits et grands.

POPULATION
See also
    MIGRATION

POPULATION. Animals
-- Surveys -- J
    591.5   Les populations.
    591.5   Populations.

PORIFERA See SPONGES. Marine invertebrates

PORT BICKERTON. Nova Scotia
Description & travel -- J,I
    917.16   Village de pêche.
    917.16   Fishing town (Port Bickerton, N.S.

PORT OF HALIFAX
-- J,I
    387.109716 Port of Halifax.

PORT OF SAINT JOHN
-- J,I
    387.109715 The Port of St. John.

PORT OF THUNDER BAY
-- J,I
    386.09713 Port of Thunder Bay.

PORT OF TORONTO
-- J,I
    386.09713   The Port of Toronto.
    386.09713   A Seaway port.

PORT OF TORONTO
-- J,I,S
    386.09713 Port of Toronto.

PORT OF VANCOUVER
-- J,I
    387.109711 The Port of Vancouver.

PORTS
See also
    PORT OF HALIFAX

PRECIS SUBJECT INDEX

PORTS
  See also
    PORT OF SAINT JOHN
    PORT OF THUNDER BAY
    PORT OF TORONTO
    PORT OF VANCOUVER

PORTUGAL
  Lisbon. Palace of Queluz. Architecture -- I,S
    728.8   Versailles and Portugal.

PORTUGUESE. Ethnic groups. Canada
  -- P,J
    301.450971 I was born in Portugal.

POSTAGE STAMPS
  Canadian postage stamps -- J,I
    769   Introducing the postage stamp.

POSTAGE STAMPS. Information sources. Canada, to 1973
  -- J,I
    769   Shaping the Canadian nation.

POSTAGE STAMPS. Information sources. Provinces. Canada
  -- J,I
    769   Canada and its provinces.

POSTAGE STAMPS. Information sources. Social life. Canada
  -- J,I
    769   Le Peuple Canadien et son environnement.
    769   Canada : people and environment.

POSTAL CODES. Canada
  Use in postal services -- P,J
    383   Anna sends a letter.

POSTAL SERVICES. Canada
  Mail delivery -- J,I
    383   How a letter travels.

POSTAL SERVICES. Canada
  Use of postal codes -- P,J
    383   Anna sends a letter.

POSTAL WORKERS
  See also
    LETTER CARRIERS

POT
  -- I,S
    615   La marijuana : quelques vérités

POTTERY
  Techniques -- I,S
    738.1   Using a potter's wheel.
    738.1   Elements of pottery.
    738.1   Pottery : hand building techniq

POULTRY FARMING. Nova Scotia
  -- J,I
    636.5   Nova Scotia poultry farming.

POWER RESOURCES See ENERGY RESOURCES

POWER STATIONS. Churchill Falls. Newfoundland
  Hydroelectric power stations -- J,I
    917.19   Churchill Falls.

POWER TOOLS
  Safety measures -- I,S
    621.9   Foreuse sur colonne et tour.
    621.9   Meules, toupies, scies électriques, et corroyeurs.
    621.9   Drill presses and lathes.
    621.9   Grinders, routers, power saws & jointers.

POWER TOOLS. Metalworking
  Drill presses -- I,S
    621.9   Using the drill press.

POWER TOOLS. Metalworking
  Lathes -- I,S
    621.9   Working between centers on the lathe.
    621.9   Chuckwork on the lathe.

PRAIRIE PROVINCES
  -- I
    917.12   The Praire provinces.

PRAIRIE PROVINCES
  Geography -- J,I
    917.12   The Prairie region.
    917.12   The Interior Plains.

PRECIS SUBJECT INDEX

PRAIRIE PROVINCES
Northern Prairie Provinces. Spring wildflowers --
Field guides -- P,J,I,S
    582.09712   Spring wildflowers : northern Prairie provinces.
    582.09712   Fleurs sauvages printanières : nord des provinces des Prairies.

PRAIRIE PROVINCES
Southern Prairie Provinces. Spring wildflowers --
Field guides -- P,J,I,S
    582.0971   Fleurs sauvages printanières : sud des provinces des Prairies.
    582.09712   Spring wildflowers : southern Prairie provinces.

PRAIRIE PROVINCES
Wheat production -- J,I
    633.0971   Wheat farming.

PRAIRIE PROVINCES
Wheat production -- J,I,S
    338.10971   Canadian wheat : from farm to market.
    338.10971   Le blé canadien : de la ferme au marché.

PRAIRIE PROVINCES
Wheat trade, to 1969 -- J
    338.10971   Wheat.

PRAIRIES. Canada
Social life, 1812-1900 -- J,I
    971.2   Pioneer life on the Prairies (1812-1900)
    971.2   Les pioneers des Prairies (1812-1900)

PRAIRIES. Canada
Social life, 1900-1912 -- J,I
    917.2   Les pionniers des Prairies (1900-1912)
    971.2   Pioneer life on the Prairies (1900-1912)

PRAIRIES. North America
Environment. Adaptation of mammals -- J,I
    591.5   Life on the Prairies.

PRAIRIES. North America
Environment. Adaptation of mammals -- P,J
    599.097   The Grasslands.

PRECIOUS METALS
See also
    GOLD

PREDATORS
See also
    BIRDS OF PREY
    CARNIVORES

PREGNANCY
See also
    BIRTH

PREGNANCY
-- P,J
    612.6   Being born.
    612.6   Il etait une fois un oeuf.

PREGNANCY. Adolescents
-- I,S
    301.41   Teenage father.
    301.41   Teenage mother.

PRESS
See also
    NEWSPAPERS

PRESSES. Metalworking
Drill presses -- I,S
    621.9   Using the drill press.

PRIMATES
See also
    MAN

PRIME MINISTERS. Canada
1867-1911 -- I,S
    971.05   Macdonald to Borden.

PRIME MINISTERS. Canada
1911-1957 -- I,S
    971.06   Borden to St. Laurent.

PRIME MINISTERS. Canada
1948-1970 -- I,S
    971.06   St. Laurent to the present.

PRECIS SUBJECT INDEX

PRIME MOVERS
　　See also
　　　　ENGINES

PRINCE EDWARD ISLAND
　　Charlottetown, to 1974 -- J,I
　　　　917.17　　　Charlottetown, P.E.I.

PRINCE EDWARD ISLAND
　　Description & travel -- P,J
　　　　917.15　　　Paul and Pauline visit New
　　　　　　　　　　Brunswick and Prince Edward
　　　　　　　　　　Island.

PRINCE EDWARD ISLAND
　　Economic conditions -- J,I,S
　　　　330.9717　　Le Canada atlantique : l'Ile du
　　　　　　　　　　Prince-Edouard.
　　　　330.9717　　Atlantic Canada : Prince Edward
　　　　　　　　　　Island.

PRINCE EDWARD ISLAND
　　National parks: Prince Edward Island National Park --
　　J,I
　　　　917.17　　　Prince Edward Island National Park

PRINCE EDWARD ISLAND NATIONAL PARK
　　-- J,I
　　　　917.17　　　Prince Edward Island National Park

PRINTS
　　Innuit prints -- J,I,S
　　　　769　　　　L'art graphique esquimau.
　　　　769　　　　Eskimo prints.

PRISONS. Canada
　　-- I,S
　　　　365　　　　Un monde fermés.
　　　　365　　　　A Captive society.

PROCYONINAE See RACCOONS

PRODUCTION. Audiovisual materials
　　-- I,S
　　　　371.33　　　Producing your own instructional
　　　　　　　　　　audio-visual programme.

PRODUCTION. Maple syrup
　　-- J,I,S
　　　　664　　　　Trip to the sugar bush.

PRODUCTION. Maple syrup
　　-- P
　　　　664　　　　Maple syrup.

PRODUCTION. Maple syrup
　　-- P,J
　　　　664　　　　When the sap runs.
　　　　664　　　　Maple syrup.
　　　　664　　　　Les sucres.

PRODUCTION. Slide programmes
　　-- S
　　　　371.33　　　Producing your own slide prog

PROFESSIONS. Canada
　　Nursing -- I,S
　　　　610.73　　　Nursing : the challenge of ca

PROJECTORS. Audiovisual aids
　　-- S
　　　　778.2　　　Le projecteur cinématographiq
　　　　　　　　　　de 16 mm. : 2e partie.

PROJECTS
　　Use of information sources -- Researchers' guides
　　J
　　　　028.7　　　Doing a project.

PRONUNCIATION. English language
　　Pitch -- J
　　　　421　　　　Pitch, stress and juncture.

PRONUNCIATION. English language
　　Stress -- J
　　　　421　　　　Pitch, stress and juncture.

PROVINCES. Canada
　　Information sources: Postage stamps -- J,I
　　　　769　　　　Canada and its provinces.

PROVINCIAL COATS OF ARMS
　　-- J,I
　　　　929.90971　Flags, coats of arms, and flor
　　　　　　　　　　emblems of Canada.

PROVINCIAL FLAGS
　　Canadian Provincial flags -- J,I
　　　　929.90971　Flags, coats of arms, and flor
　　　　　　　　　　emblems of Canada.
　　　　929.90971　Les Drapeaux Canadiens et leur
　　　　　　　　　　usage.
　　　　929.90971　Canadian flags and how they ar
　　　　　　　　　　used.

PRECIS SUBJECT INDEX

    929.90971   Les drapeaux canadiens et leur usage.

PROVINCIAL FLORAL EMBLEMS
-- J,I
    929.90971   Flags, coats of arms, and floral emblems of Canada.

PROVINCIAL GOVERNMENT. Canada
-- I,S
    354.71   Le gouvernement provincial.
    354.71   Provincial government.

PROVINCIAL GOVERNMENT. Canada
Relations with federal government -- J,I
    342.4   Ottawa and the provinces : issues, choices and values.

PSYCHOLOGICAL ASPECTS. Drug abuse
-- J,I
    613.8   Why do people take drugs?
    613.8   Pourquoi prend-on de la drogue?

PSYCHOLOGY
See also
    BEHAVIOUR
    EMOTIONS
    MENTAL PROCESSES
    PERSONALITY
    SOCIAL PSYCHOLOGY

PSYCHOTROPIC DRUGS
See also
    ALCOHOL
    AMPHETAMINES
    BARBITURATES
    LSD
    POT

PSYCHOTROPIC DRUGS
Solvents -- I,S
    613.8   Les solvants.
    613.8   Solvents.

PUBERTY
-- J
    612.6   Puberty.

PUBERTY
-- J,I
    612.6   Etre pubère.
    612.6   The Meaning of puberty.

PUBERTY RITES. L'ilawat Indians
-- J,I,S
    970.3   Puberty : parts 1 & 2.

PUBLIC ORDER SERVICES
See also
    POLICE

PUBLIC SERVICE. Canada
-- J,I
    350.971   The Role of the Public Service.

PUBLIC TRANSPORT
Safety measures -- P,J
    614.8   Transit safety.

PUBLIC TRANSPORT. Cities. Canada
-- Study regions: Ontario. Toronto -- P,J,I
    388.409713   Public transportation in the city.

PUERTO RICAN FOLKLORE
-- Stories -- P,J
    398.2097295   The Tiger and the rabbit.

PULP & PAPER INDUSTRIES
-- J,I
    676   Pulp and paper.

PULP & PAPER INDUSTRIES. Marathon. Ontario
-- J,I
    917.13   Marathon, Ontario.

PULP & PAPER INDUSTRIES. Newfoundland
-- J,I
    676.09718   Pulp and paper manufacturing in Newfoundland.

PULP & PAPER INDUSTRIES. Quebec Province
-- J,I
    676.09714   Newsprint in Quebec.

PUMPS. Engines. Motor vehicles
Fuel pumps. Maintenance & repair -- I,S
    629.22   Pistons, oil and and fuel pumps.

PUMPS. Engines. Motor vehicles
Oil pumps. Maintenance & repair -- I,S
    629.22   Pistons, oil and and fuel pumps.

PRECIS SUBJECT INDEX

PUNCTUATION. English language
  -- J
    421   Using punctuation marks.

PUNCTUATION. English language
  Apostrophes -- J
    421   Quotation marks and the apostrophe

PUNCTUATION. English language
  Capital letters -- J
    421   Using capital letters.

PUNCTUATION. English language
  Commas -- J
    421   Commas.

PUNCTUATION. English language
  Exclamation marks -- J
    421   Periods, question marks, and
                  exclamation marks.

PUNCTUATION. English language
  Periods -- J
    421   Periods, question marks, and
                  exclamation marks.

PUNCTUATION. English language
  Quotation marks -- J
    421   Quotation marks and the apostrophe

PUNISHMENT
  See also
    PENAL SYSTEM

PUPPETRY
  -- P,J,I
    791.5   Telling stories with puppets and
                  masks.

QUEBEC CITY
  to 1976 -- J,I
    917.14   Quebec City, Quebec.

QUEBEC PROVINCE
  -- I
    917.14   Quebec.

QUEBEC PROVINCE
  1756-1791 -- J,I
    971.01   From fleur-de-lis to Union Jack

QUEBEC PROVINCE
  Aluminum industries -- J,I
    669   Aluminum processing in Quebec.

QUEBEC PROVINCE
  Appalachian region. Geography -- J,I,S
    917.14   Le Quebec : les Appalaches.
    917.14   The Province of Quebec : the
                 Appalachian region.

QUEBEC PROVINCE
  Asbestos. Mining -- J,I
    622   Asbestos mining in Quebec.

QUEBEC PROVINCE
  Description & travel -- P,J
    917.14   Paul and Pauline visit Quebec.

QUEBEC PROVINCE
  Geography -- J,I
    330.9713   Central Canada : the people.
    330.9713   Central Canada : the place.

QUEBEC PROVINCE
  Lac Saint-Jean region. Industries -- J,I
    971.14   Saguenay-Lake St. John - the L
                 Region.

QUEBEC PROVINCE
  Laurentian region. Geography -- J,I,S
    917.14   Le Quebec : le Plateau laurent
    917.14   The Province of Quebec : the
                 Laurentian region.

QUEBEC PROVINCE
  Laurentian region. Winter activities -- P,J,I,S
    525   Laurentian winter.

QUEBEC PROVINCE
  Magdalen Islands. Description & travel -- J,I
    917.14   Magdalen Islands.
    917.14   Les Iles de la Madeleine.

QUEBEC PROVINCE
  Manowan Indians. Reservation life -- I,S
    970.5   L'histoire de Manowan : premièr
                 partie.
    970.5   History of Manowan : part 1.

PRECIS SUBJECT INDEX

970.5		L'histoire de Manowan : deuxième partie.
970.5		History of Manowan : part 2.

QUEBEC PROVINCE
Montreal, to 1965 -- J,I,S
- 917.14 Ville fluviale (Montreal)
- 917.14 River city : Montreal.

QUEBEC PROVINCE
Montreal. Family life -- Comparative studies -- P,J
- 917.14 Trois familles de Montréal.
- 917.14 Three families of Montreal.

QUEBEC PROVINCE
Pioneer life, 1700-1800 -- J,I
- 971.4 The Habitant and his home [in the 18th century]
- 971.4 L'habitant et sa terre au XVIIIe siècle.
- 971.4 L'habitant et sa maison au XVIIIe siècle.
- 971.4 The Habitant and his land [in the 18th century]

QUEBEC PROVINCE
Pulp & paper industries -- J,I
- 676.09714 Newsprint in Quebec.

QUEBEC PROVINCE
Quebec City, to 1976 -- J,I
- 917.14 Quebec City, Quebec.

QUEBEC PROVINCE
Saguenay River region. Industries -- J,I
- 971.14 Saguenay-Lake St. Jean - the river

QUEBEC PROVINCE
St. Jean Port Joli. Description & travel -- P,J
- 917.14 St. Jean, Port Joli, Quebec.

QUEBEC PROVINCE
St. Lawrence region. Geography -- J,I,S
- 917.14 Le Quebec : la Plaine du Saint-Laurent.
- 917.14 The Province of Quebec : the St. Lawrence region.

QUEBEC PROVINCE
Spring wildflowers -- Field guides -- P,J,I,S
- 528.09713 Spring wildflowers : southern Ontario and Quebec.
- 582.09713 Spring wildflowers : Northern Ontario and Quebec.
- 582.09713 Fleurs sauvages printanières : sud de l'Ontario et du Québec.
- 582.09713 Fleurs sauvages printanières : nord de l'Ontario et du Québec.

QUEBEC PROVINCE. Special subjects. Drawings by W.H. Bartlett
-- J,I
- 971 Quebec and Ontario : old colony and new outpost.

QUEEN CHARLOTTE ISLANDS. British Columbia
Description & travel -- J,I,S
- 917.11 L'archipel de la Reine-Charlotte.
- 917.11 Queen Charlotte Islands.
- 917.11 Queen Charlotte Islands.

QUEENSLAND. Australia
Eastern coastal region. Description & travel -- J,I,S
- 919.43 Sugar and coral coast (Queensland)

QUOTATION MARKS. Punctuation. English language
-- J
- 421 Quotation marks and the apostrophe

R.C.M.P. See ROYAL CANADIAN MOUNTED POLICE

RABBITS
-- K
- 599 Wiggle nose and long ears.

RABBITS
Rabbits & hares compared with rodents -- P,J
- 599 Rodents, rabbits and hares.
- 599 Rongeurs, lapins et lièvres.

RACCOONS. Canada
-- P,J
- 599 The Raccoon.

RADIATION
See also
   LIGHT

RADIO EQUIPMENT
Receivers. Circuits -- S
- 621.3841 Basic radio circuitry.

PRECIS SUBJECT INDEX

RAGE See ANGER

RAILWAYS
  See also
      TRAINS

RAILWAYS. Canada
  -- J,I
      385   Rail transportation in Canada :
                    today.

RAILWAYS. Canada
  1836-1976 -- J,I
      385.0971   Rail transportation in Canada :
                    the early days.

RAILWAYS. Canada
  to 1977 -- J,I
      385.0971   Rails across Canada.

RAILWAYS. Canada
  Canadian National. Trains: Turbo train -- P,J
      385.0971   Inter-city train.

READING. English language
  -- Teaching materials -- P
      411   The Gobbler.
      411   The Ticker.
      411   The Doodler.
      411   The Puffer.
      411   The Cowboy.
      411   The Bungler.

READING. English language
  -- Teaching materials -- P,J
      F   One kitten for Kim.
      636   Big red barn.

READING. French language
  -- Teaching materials -- P,J
      F   Un seul chaton.
      440.7   Les aventures de Léo à la ferme.
      636   La grange rouge.

REBELLION. Canada
  1837 -- I,S
      971.03   The 1837 Rebellion in Lower Canada
      971.03   The 1837 Rebellion in Upper Canada
      971.03   Rebellion in Lower Canada.
      971.03   Rebellion in Upper Canada.
      971.03   Rébellion dans le Bas-Canada.
      971.03   Rébellion dans le Haut-Canada.

REBELLION. Manitoba
  Riel rebellion, 1870 -- I,S
      971.05   1870 Rebellion.

REBELLION. Manitoba
  Riel rebellion, 1870 -- S
      971.05   The First Métis uprising, 1869-

REBELLION. Saskatchewan
  Riel rebellion, 1885 -- I,S
      971.05   1885 Rebellion.

REBELLION. Saskatchewan
  Riel rebellion, 1885 -- S
      971.05   The Second Métis uprising, 188

REBELLION. Saskatchewan
  Riel rebellion, 1885. Role of Canadian Indians --
      971.05   Big Bear, Poundmaker and Crowf

REBELLION. Saskatchewan
  Riel rebellion, 1885. Role of Royal Canadian Moun
  Police -- J,I
      363.20971   La Gendarmerie du Nord-Ouest :
                     rébellion de 1885.
      363.20971   The North West Mounted Police
                     the Rebellion of 1885.

RECEIVERS. Radio equipment
  Circuits -- S
      621.3841   Basic radio circuitry.

RECEIVERS. Television equipment
  -- S
      621.388   The Television receiver.

RECORDS
  See also
      AUDIOVISUAL MATERIALS
      BOOKS
      DOCUMENTS
      NEWSPAPERS

RECREATIONS
  See also
      BOATING
      CAMPING
      CANOEING
      CYCLING
      FISHING. Sports
      GAMES

PRECIS SUBJECT INDEX

RECREATIONS
　See also
　　HIGHLAND GAMES
　　ORIENTEERING
　　SCUBA DIVING
　　SKIING
　　SNORKEL DIVING
　　SWIMMING

RECREATIONS. Canada
　-- P,J
　　796　　　Sports and recreation.

RECREATIONS. Cities. Canada
　-- J,I
　　301.34　　Recreation : the Canadian city.

RECREATIONS. Ontario
　1800-1850 -- Re-enactments at Upper Canada Village -- J,I
　　971.3　　School and recreation.

RECREATIONS. Parks
　-- P
　　796　　　Sunday in the park.
　　796　　　Un dimanche au parc.

RED RIVER VALLEY. Manitoba
　Human settlements. Role of Selkirk, Thomas Douglas, Earl of -- J,I
　　920　　　Lord Selkirk : the colonizer.

REFERENCE BOOKS
　See also
　　TELEPHONE DIRECTORIES

REFINING. Gold. Ontario
　-- J,I
　　622　　　Gold refining in Ontario.

REGINA
　to 1975 -- J,I
　　917.124　Regina.

REGINA
　Description & travel -- J,I
　　917.124　Regina, Sask.

REGIONAL PLANNING. Niagara Peninsula. Ontario
　Effects on development of agricultural land -- J,I,S
　　333.7　　Fruit Belt preservation and regional planning.

RELATIONSHIPS
　See also
　　INTERPERSONAL RELATIONSHIPS

RELIGIONS
　See also
　　INNUIT RELIGION
　　JUDAISM
　　MYTHS

RELIGIONS. Native peoples. America
　Use of drugs -- S
　　299　　　Drugs and religious ritual.

RELIGIOUS BUILDINGS
　See also
　　CHURCHES

RELIGIOUS CATEGORIES
　See also
　　CHRISTIANS

RELIGIOUS FESTIVALS
　See also
　　CHRISTMAS
　　EASTER
　　PASSOVER

REMEMBRANCE DAY
　Historical aspects -- P,J
　　394.2　　Remembrance Day.

REPRODUCTION
　See also
　　SEXUAL REPRODUCTION

REPRODUCTION. Birds
　-- J,I
　　598.2　　Comment les oiseaux élèvent leur petits.
　　598.2　　How birds raise their young.

REPRODUCTION. Frogs
　-- J
　　597　　　La Vie commence - grenoiulles.

REPRODUCTION. Mammals
-- J,I
    591.1   Les Cellules reproductives.
    591.1   Le Processus de reproduction.
    591.1   The Process of reproduction.

REPRODUCTION. Mammals
-- P,J
    591.1   Un de deux.
    591.1   From two to one.

REPRODUCTION. Organisms
-- P,J
    574.1   La Vie commence - plantes et poissons.
    574.1   The Beginning of life : plants and fish.

RESEARCH. Science. Canada
National Research Council of Canada -- J,I
    607   National Research Council.

RESEARCH & DEVELOPMENT
See also
    INVENTION

RESERVATION LIFE. Cowichan Indians. British Columbia
-- I,S
    970.5   Cowichan : a question of survival.

RESERVATION LIFE. Manowan Indians. Quebec Province
-- I,S
    970.5   L'histoire de Manowan : première partie.
    970.5   History of Manowan : part 1.
    970.5   L'histoire de Manowan : deuxième partie.
    970.5   History of Manowan : part 2.

RESIDENCES
See also
    DWELLINGS
    HOUSES

RESIDENCES
Electricity supply equipment -- S
    621.319   Domestic circuits.

RESIDENCES
Electricity supply equipment. Circuits. Hazards -- J,I
    644   Electrical hazards.

RESIDENCES
Hazards -- P,J
    614.8   Home safety.
    614.8   Home safety.

RESOURCE CENTRES
See also
    LIBRARIES

RESOURCES
See also
    COPPER
    GOLD
    NATURAL RESOURCES
    NICKEL
    URANIUM

RESOURCES MANAGEMENT. Forest products industries
-- J,I
    634.9   Forest management and lumbering

RESPIRATION
See also
    ARTIFICIAL RESPIRATION

RESPONSIBILITIES. Adults
-- P,J
    152.4   Quand je serai grand.
    152.4   When I grow up.

RESUSCITATION
See also
    ARTIFICIAL RESPIRATION

REVENUE
See also
    INCOME TAX

RHYTHM METHOD. Contraception
-- I,S,A
    613.9   The Rhythm and sympto-thermal methods.

RICE GROWING. China
-- J,I
    633.0951   Rice growing in China.

RICE GROWING. China
Role of communes -- J,I
    915.1   A Yangtze rice commune.

PRECIS SUBJECT INDEX

RIDEAU CANAL. Ottawa
-- J,I
    386.09713   Le Canal Rideau.
    386.09713   Rideau Canal.

RIEL REBELLION. Manitoba
1870 -- I,S
    971.05   1870 Rebellion.

RIEL REBELLION. Manitoba
1870 -- S
    971.05   The First Métis uprising, 1869-70.

RIEL REBELLION. Saskatchewan
1885 -- I,S
    971.05   1885 Rebellion.

RIEL REBELLION. Saskatchewan
1885 -- S
    971.05   The Second Métis uprising, 1885.

RIEL REBELLION. Saskatchewan
1885. Role of Canadian Indians -- S
    971.05   Big Bear, Poundmaker and Crowfoot.

RIEL REBELLION. Saskatchewan
1885. Role of Royal Canadian Mounted Police -- J,I
    363.20971   La Gendarmerie du Nord-Ouest : la rébellion de 1885.
    363.20971   The North West Mounted Police - the Rebellion of 1885.

RIFLES
Use in shooting -- I,S
    799.3   Riflery.

RIGHTS
See also
    CIVIL RIGHTS

RIO DE JANEIRO. Brazil
Description & travel -- J,I,S
    918.1   Rio de Janerio.

RIOPELLE, JEAN PAUL. Paintings
-- I,S
    759.11   Jean-Paul Riopelle.
    759.11   Jean-Paul Riopelle.

RIVERINA. New South Wales. Australia
Agricultural industries -- J,I,S
    919.44   Riverina (Murray-Darling Basin)

RIVERS
See also
    NILE

ROAD SAFETY
-- P,J
    614.8   Safety on the street.
    614.8   Traffic safety.
    614.8   Ride safely to school.

ROAD SAFETY. Cycling
-- P,J
    614.8   Bicycle safety.

ROAD VEHICLES
See also
    BICYCLES
    MOTOR VEHICLES

ROCKS
-- Collectors' guides -- J,I
    796.5   Rockhounding.

ROCKS
-- J,I
    549   Les roches et les minéraux.
    549   Learning about rocks and minerals.

ROCKY MOUNTAINS. Alberta & British Columbia
National parks -- J,I
    917.11   The Rocky Mountains national parks

ROCKY MOUNTAINS. North America
Beef cattle -- P,J,I
    599   Les Bestiaux de l'ouest.

ROCKY MOUNTAINS. North America
Environment. Adaptation of mammals -- P,J
    599.097   The Rocky Mountains.

RODENTS
See also
    BEAVERS
    GOPHERS
    GUINEA PIGS
    SQUIRRELS

PRECIS SUBJECT INDEX

RODENTS
    compared with rabbits & hares -- P,J
        599   Rodents, rabbits and hares.
        599   Rongeurs, lapins et lièvres.

RODEOS. Calgary, Alberta
    Calgary Stampede -- J,I
        791.8   Calgary stampede.

ROLLING STOCK
    See also
        TRAINS

ROME
    See also
        ANCIENT ROME

ROYAL CANADIAN AIR FORCE. World War 1
    Bishop, Billy -- J,I
        920   Billy Bishop.

ROYAL CANADIAN MINT
    -- J,I
        737.4   Royal Canadian Mint.

ROYAL CANADIAN MOUNTED POLICE
    1873-1875 -- J,I,S
        363.20971 North West Mounted Police : the
                       long march west.
        363.20971 La Gendarmerie du Nord-Ouest : la
                       longue marche vers l'Ouest.

ROYAL CANADIAN MOUNTED POLICE
    1873-1898 -- J,I
        363.20971 The Northwest Mounted Police.
        363.20971 The Force keeps the peace.
        363.20971 The Force rides west.

ROYAL CANADIAN MOUNTED POLICE
    1898-1937 -- J,I
        363.20971 The Beginning of a new era.

ROYAL CANADIAN MOUNTED POLICE
    to 1972 -- I,S
        363.20971 History of the Royal Canadian
                       Mounted Police.

ROYAL CANADIAN MOUNTED POLICE
    Role in Klondike Gold Rush, 1896 -- J,I,S
        363.20971 North West Mounted Police : the
                     Klondike Gold Rush.

ROYAL CANADIAN MOUNTED POLICE
    Role in Riel rebellion, 1885 -- J,I
        363.20971 La Gendarmerie du Nord-Ouest :
                     rébellion de 1885.
        363.20971 The North West Mounted Police :
                     the Rebellion of 1885.

ROYAL WINTER FAIR. Toronto
    -- J
        630.74   Royal Winter Fair.

ROYAL WINTER FAIR. Toronto
    -- P,J
        630.74   Royal Winter Fair.

RUMINANTS
    See also
        BUFFALO
        CATTLE
        GOATS

RURAL LIFE
    See also
        PIONEER LIFE

RURAL LIFE. China
    -- I
        631.0951   Rural China.

RURAL LIFE. Greece
    -- J,I
        917.95   Greece 1 : life in a rural vi

RUSSIAN FOLKLORE
    -- Stories -- P,J
        398.20947 The Firebird and the magic hor
        398.20947 Peter and the wolf.

S.I.
    See also
        METRIC SYSTEM

S.I.
    -- I
        389   Le Monde à l'heure du système
                   international.

S.I.
    compared with Imperial System -- J
        389   Standardizing measurement.
        389   Un Système de mesure.

PRECIS SUBJECT INDEX

S.I. Linear measurement
-- J
    389   Une Ligne - une surface.
    389   Measuring length and area.

S.I. Measurement. Area
-- J
    389   Une Ligne - une surface.
    389   Measuring length and area.

SAFETY MEASURES
  See also
      ROAD SAFETY

SAFETY MEASURES. Boating
-- P,J
    614.8   Small boat safety.

SAFETY MEASURES. Canoeing
-- J,I
    797.1   Canoeing skills and safety.

SAFETY MEASURES. Fire
-- P
    614.8   "Flashy" the fire bug.

SAFETY MEASURES. Hand tools
-- I,S
    621.9   Scies à main, ciseaux et limes.
    621.9   Hand saws, chisels and files.

SAFETY MEASURES. Power tools
-- I,S
    621.9   Foreuse sur colonne et tour.
    621.9   Meules, toupies, scies
                 éléctriques, et corroyeurs.
    621.9   Drill presses and lathes.
    621.9   Grinders, routers, power saws &
                 jointers.

SAFETY MEASURES. Public transport
-- P,J
    614.8   Transit safety.

SAFETY MEASURES. School buses
-- P,J
    614.8   School bus safety.

SAFETY MEASURES. Skiing
-- J,I
    614.8   Safety on the slopes.

SAFETY MEASURES. Swimming
-- P,J
    614.8   Swimming safety.
    614.8   Water safety.

SAFETY MEASURES. Use of drugs
-- J
    615   Using them safely.

SAFETY MEASURES. Winter activities
-- P,J
    614.8   Winter safety.
    614.8   Sécurité en hiver.

SAFETY MEASURES. Workshop practice
-- I,S
    614.8   Pensez "sécurité"
    614.8   Dangers fréquents en atelier.
    614.8   General shop hazards.
    614.8   Think safety.
    621.9   Tournevis, clefs, tôle et soudure.
    621.9   Screwdrivers, wrenches, sheet
                 metal, & welding.

SAGUENAY RIVER REGION. Quebec Province
  Industries -- J,I
    971.14   Saguenay-Lake St. Jean - the river

ST. JEAN PORT JOLI. Quebec Province
  Description & travel -- P,J
    917.14   St. Jean, Port Joli, Quebec.

SAINT JOHN
  See also
      PORT OF SAINT JOHN

SAINT JOHN. New Brunswick
  to 1976 -- J,I
    917.15   Saint John - Canada's first city.

ST. JOHN RIVER VALLEY. New Brunswick
  Industries -- J,I
    971.15   Saint John River Valley -
                  Edmunston to Kings Landing.
    971.15   Saint John River Valley -
                  Mactaquac to Saint John.

PRECIS SUBJECT INDEX

ST. JOHN'S. Newfoundland
  to 1975 -- J,I
      917.18   St. John's, Newfoundland.

ST. LAWRENCE REGION. Quebec Province
  Geography -- J,I,S
      917.14   Le Quebec : la Plaine du Saint-Laurent.
      917.14   The Province of Quebec : the St. Lawrence region.

ST. LAWRENCE SEAWAY
  -- J,I
      386.0971   The Great Lakes - St. Lawrence Seaway.
      386.0971   Ships and power.

ST. LAWRENCE SEAWAY
  -- J,I,S
      386.0971   The Seaway and its ships.

ST. LAWRENCE SEAWAY
  to 1959 -- J,I
      386.0971   The Seaway.

ST. VALENTINE'S DAY
  Canadian social customs. Historical aspects -- P,J
      394.2   St. Valentine's Day.

SAINTE MARIE AMONG THE HURONS. Ontario
  -- J,I
      971.3   L'Histoire de Sainte-Marie-des-Hurons : part2.
      971.3   L'Histoire de Sainte-Marie-des-Hurons : part I.
      971.3   Sainte-Marie-among-the-Hurons : part I.

SAINTE MARIE AMONG THE HURONS. Ontario
  -- P,J,I,S
      971.3   Sainte-Marie-among-the-Hurons.
      971.3   Sainte-Marie-aux-Hurons.

SAINTS
  See also
    JOAN OF ARC, Saint

SALIENTIA See ANURA

SALMON
  Atlantic salmon -- P,J,I
      597   Le saumon atlantique.
      597   The Story of Atlantic salmon.

SALMON
  Cookery: L'ilawat methods -- P,J
      970.3   Salmon.

SALMON
  Pacific salmon -- P,J,I
      597   The Story of Pacific salmon.
      597   Le saumon du Pacifique.

SASKATCHEWAN
  Cypress Hills. Geological features -- J,I
      971.24   Fort Walsh in the Cypress Hills
      971.24   Le Fort Walsh dans les collines Cyprès.

SASKATCHEWAN
  Description & travel -- J,I
      917.124   Saskatchewan.

SASKATCHEWAN
  Description & travel -- P,J
      917.12   Paul and Pauline visit Manitoba and Saskatchewan.

SASKATCHEWAN
  Doukhobors, 1899-1908 -- S
      301.4509711 Doukhobor immigrants in the W

SASKATCHEWAN
  Leroy. Agricultural industries -- J,I
      917.214   Leroy, Saskatchewan.

SASKATCHEWAN
  Regina, to 1975 -- J,I
      917.124   Regina.

SASKATCHEWAN
  Regina. Description & travel -- J,I
      917.124   Regina, Sask.

SASKATCHEWAN
  Riel rebellion, 1885 -- I,S
      971.05   1885 Rebellion.

PRECIS SUBJECT INDEX

SASKATCHEWAN
    Riel rebellion, 1885 -- S
        971.05   The Second Métis uprising, 1885.

SASKATCHEWAN
    Riel rebellion, 1885. Role of Canadian Indians -- S
        971.05   Big Bear, Poundmaker and Crowfoot.

SASKATCHEWAN
    Riel rebellion, 1885. Role of Royal Canadian Mounted Police -- J,I
        363.20971   La Gendarmerie du Nord-Ouest : la rébellion de 1885.
        363.20971   The North West Mounted Police - the Rebellion of 1885.

SASKATCHEWAN
    Wheat production. Harvesting -- P,J
        633.0971   Visit to a wheat farm.

SATELLITES
    See also
        MOON

SCALE. Maps
    -- J,I
        912   Introducing map scale.
        912   Initiation à l'échelle de la carte

SCARBOROUGH BLUFFS. Ontario
    -- J,I
        917.13   Planning for future use.

SCARBOROUGH BLUFFS. Ontario
    Erosion. Counter-measures -- J,I
        917.13   The Natural environment.

SCHOOL BUSES
    Safety measures -- P,J
        614.8   School bus safety.

SCHOOLS
    Hazards -- P,J
        614.8   School safety.

SCHOOLS
    Libraries -- Users' guides -- J
        024   How do you share your library?
        024   Discovering your library.

SCHOOLS. Ontario
    1800-1850 -- Re-enactments at Upper Canada Village -- J,I
        971.3   School and recreation.

SCIENCE
    See also
        AGRICULTURE
        ASTRONOMY
        AVIATION
        BOTANY
        CRYSTALLOGRAPHY
        ECOLOGY
        GENETICS
        GEOMORPHOLOGY
        MEDICINE
        METEOROLOGY
        ORNITHOLOGY
        PETROLOGY
        PHYSICS
        TOPOGRAPHY
        ZOOLOGY

SCIENCE
    Experiments -- P,J
        507   5 sens + mésures = observation.
        507   5 senses + measurement = observation.

SCIENCE
    Ontario Science Centre -- J,I
        507.4   The Science Centre.

SCIENCE. Canada
    Research. National Research Council of Canada -- J,I
        607   National Research Council.

SCRAPERS. Woodworking
    -- I,S
        621.9   Scraping tools and abrasives.

SCUBA DIVING
    -- I,S
        797.2   An Introduction to snorkel and scuba diving.
        797.2   Initiation à la plongée : tuba et scaphandre autonome.

SCULPTURES
    See also
        CARVINGS

PRECIS SUBJECT INDEX

SCULPTURES
   Innuit sculptures -- J,I,S
        736   L'art sculptural esquimau.
        736   Eskimo sculpture.

SCULPTURES
   Wire sculptures. Techniques -- I,S
        731   Wire sculpture with a twist.

SEALS. Mammals. Coastal waters. Canada
  -- J,I
        599   Marine mammals of Canada.
        599   Les mammifères marins du Canada.

SEAS See OCEANS

SEASHORE ECOSYSTEMS
   Forms of life -- P
        574.92 Explorons le bord de la mer.
        574.92 A Visit to the seashore.

SEASONS
   Fall -- J
        525   Autumn.

SEASONS
   Fall -- K,P
        525   L'Automne et l'hiver : ce qu'ils
                  sont.
        525   Autumn and winter : what they mean

SEASONS
   Spring -- J
        525   Spring.

SEASONS
   Spring -- K,P
        525   Le Printemps et l'été : ce qu'ils
                  sont.
        525   Spring and summer : what they mean

SEASONS
   Spring -- P
        525   Spring is coming.

SEASONS
   Summer -- J
        525   Summer.

SEASONS
   Summer -- K,P
        525   Le Printemps et l'été : ce qu'i
                  sont.
        525   Spring and summer : what they m

SEASONS
   Summer -- P,J
        525   Summer - reflections on Lake B
                  Water.

SEASONS
   Winter -- J
        525   Winter.

SEASONS
   Winter -- K,P
        525   L'Automne et l'hiver : ce qu'i
                  sont.
        525   Autumn and winter : what they m

SEASONS
   Winter -- P,J
        525   Winter - ice fire lights.

SEASONS
   Winter. Environment. Adaptation of animals -- J,
        591.5   Discovering animals in winter.

SEASONS
   Winter. Environment. Adaptation of plants -- J,I
        581.5   Discovering plants in winter.

SEAWEED
  -- I,S
        574.92 Plants, sponges, coelenterates
        574.92 Plants, sponges, coelenterates

SEED COLLAGES
  -- P,J,I
        745.5   Beginnings.
        745.5   Commencement.

SEEDS. Plants
   Dispersal -- P,J
        582   La dissémination des graines.
        582   How seeds are spread.

PRECIS SUBJECT INDEX

SEEING See VISION

SEIGNEURIAL SYSTEM. Land tenure. New France
  -- J,I
    333.3   Seigneurs et seigneuries.
    333.3   Seigneurs and seigneuries.
    333.3   The Habitants.
    333.3   Les censitaires.

SEINE NETTING. Commercial fishing
  -- I,S
    639   Seine netting : Scottish and
               Danish methods.
    639   La pêche à la Seine (Ecossaise
               et Danoise)

SELF-GOVERNMENT. Maritime Provinces
  Development, to 1873 -- I,S
    971.5   Reform in the Atlantic colonies.
    971.5   Les réformistes des colonies de
               l'Atlantique.

SELFISHNESS
  See also
    UNSELFISHNESS

SELKIRK, THOMAS DOUGLAS, Earl of
  Role in settlement of Red River Valley -- J,I
    920   Lord Selkirk : the colonizer.

SENSES
  See also
    HEARING
    SMELL
    TASTE
    TOUCH
    VISION

SENSORY PERCEPTION
  See also
    SENSES

SENSORY PERCEPTION
  -- K,P
    152.1   Observing by hearing, tasting,
               smelling, touching.

SERVICES
  See also
    ARMED FORCES

SETS. Theatre
  -- I,S
    792   Basic set design and stages.

SETTLEMENTS See HUMAN SETTLEMENTS

SEVEN YEARS' WAR
  -- J,I,S
    971.01   The Seven Years' War.
    971.01   La guerre de Sept ans.

SEX RELATIONS
  Attitudes of Canadians -- S
    176   To be together.

SEX RELATIONS. Adolescents
  -- I,S
    176   Growing up.

SEXUAL REPRODUCTION
  See also
    CONCEPTION
    OVULATION
    PREGNANCY

SEXUAL REPRODUCTION
  -- Study examples: Birds -- P,J
    591.1   Le Mâle - la femelle.
    591.1   Male and female.

SEXUAL ROLES
  Attitudes of society, 1950-1976 -- I,S
    301.41   It isn't easy.
    301.41   C'est pas facile!

SHAKESPEARE, WILLIAM. Drama in English
  -- S
    822.3   Shakespeare : the man, the times
               and the plays.

SHANGHAI. China
  Description & travel -- I
    915.1   Cities of China.

SHANGHAI. China
  Description & travel -- J,I
    915.1   Shanghai : city life in China.

PRECIS SUBJECT INDEX

SHEEP FARMING. Australia
  -- J,I,S
        636.3   Sheep industry.

SHEET METAL WORKING
  Patterns. Development -- S
        671.2   Pattern development by triangulation.
        671.2   Parallel line development.
        671.2   Radial line development.

SHELLFISH
  Cookery -- J,I
        641.6   Let's serve shellfish.

SHELTER BUILDING. Wilderness survival
  -- I
        613.6   Faire un feu et construire un abri
        613.6   How to make a fire and shelter.

SHIPPING
  See also
    PORTS
    ST. LAWRENCE SEAWAY

SHOOTING
  Use of rifles -- I,S
        799.3   Riflery.

SHOOTING. Hockey
  -- P,J
        796.9   Shoot to score.

SHOPPING
  See also
    STORES

SHOPPING CENTRES
  -- P,J
        658.8   The shopping centre.
        658.8   A Shopping centre.

SHORE
  See also
    SEASHORE

SHORE BIRDS. North America
  -- J,I
        598.2   Shorebirds.

SHREWS. Canada
  -- J
        599   Insectivores and bats.

SI. Measurement. Mass
  -- J
        389   Un Poids - une masse.

SI. Measurement. Volume
  -- J
        389   Un Volume - une capacité.

SIAM See THAILAND

SIGHT See VISION

SINGLE PEOPLE
  Attitudes to loneliness -- S
        152.4   To be alone.
        152.4   Vivre seule.

SKATING. Hockey
  -- P,J
        796.9   Skating.

SKIING
  -- I,S
        796.9   Skiing : basic skills.
        796.9   Skiing - basic skills.
        796.9   Le ski - mouvements de base (1ère partie)
        796.9   Le ski - mouvements de base (2 partie)

SKIING
  Physical exercise -- For skiing -- I,S
        796.9   Skiing - pre-season conditioning
        796.9   Le ski - mise en train pré-saisonnière.

SKIING
  Safety measures -- J,I
        614.8   Safety on the slopes.

SLIDE PREPARATION. Microscopy
  -- J,I
        578   Making your own microscopic sl

PRECIS SUBJECT INDEX

SLIDE PROGRAMMES
   Graphic design -- I,S
      778.2   Producing graphics for slides and filmstrips.

SLIDE PROGRAMMES
   Production -- S
      371.33   Producing your own slide program.

SMELL
   Physiology -- J
      612   Smell, taste and touch.

SMELL
   Physiology -- J,I
      612   The Biology of taste and smell.

SMOKE
   Health aspects -- J,I,S
      614.7   Qu'est-ce que la fumée?
      614.7   What is smoke? (Filmstrip)

SMOKING
   Health aspects -- J,I,S
      613.8   The Smoking epidemic.
      613.8   Le fumeur est une victime.

SNACKS
   -- P,J
      641.1   Sam Slice tells about snack foods.

SNORKEL DIVING
   -- I,S
      797.2   An Introduction to snorkel and scuba diving.
      797.2   Initiation á la plongée : tuba et scaphandre autonome.

SNOWSHOE MAKING. Labrador. Newfoundland
   By Canadian Indians -- P,J
      685   Raquettes indiennes.
      685   Indian snowshoes.

SOCIAL ASPECTS. Immigration, 1896-1914. Canada
   -- S
      325.71   The Fourth wave.

SOCIAL ASPECTS. Immigration, 1945-1975. Canada
   -- I,S
      325.71   Changing profile.

SOCIAL BEHAVIOUR. Animals. Africa
   -- J
      591.96   Animals together.

SOCIAL CUSTOMS
   See also
      SMOKING

SOCIAL CUSTOMS. Christmas
   Canadian social customs, 1800-1860: Decorations -- Re-enactments at Black Creek Pioneer Village -- P,J
      971.3   Canadian Christmas : Christmas decorations.

SOCIAL CUSTOMS. Christmas
   Canadian social customs, 1820-1867 -- Re-enactments at Black Creek Pioneer Village -- P,J,I
      971.3   Pioneer Christmas.

SOCIAL CUSTOMS. Christmas
   Canadian social customs -- P,J
      394.2   Christmas today.

SOCIAL CUSTOMS. Christmas
   Canadian social customs. Historical aspects -- P,J
      394.2   Canadian Christmas : traditions of Christmas.

SOCIAL CUSTOMS. Easter
   Canadian social customs. Historical aspects -- P,J
      394.2   Easter in Canada.

SOCIAL CUSTOMS. Easter
   Ukrainian social customs -- I,S
      914.7   Easter greetings.

SOCIAL CUSTOMS. Easter
   Ukrainian social customs: Egg-painting -- I,S
      914.7   Pysanky.

SOCIAL CUSTOMS. Halloween
   Canadian social customs -- P,J
      394.2   Hallowe'en in Canada.

SOCIAL CUSTOMS. L'Ilawat Indians
   Puberty rites -- J,I,S
      970.3   Puberty : parts 1 & 2.

PRECIS SUBJECT INDEX

SOCIAL CUSTOMS. St. Valentine's Day
  Canadian social customs. Historical aspects -- P,J
    394.2   St. Valentine's Day.

SOCIAL CUSTOMS. Thanksgiving. Canada
  -- P,J
    394.2   Thanksgiving today.

SOCIAL CUSTOMS. Thanksgiving. Eastern Canada
  1820-1867 -- Re-enactments at Black Creek Pioneer
  Village -- P,J,I
    971.3   Thanksgiving in pioneer Canada.

SOCIAL GROUPS
  See also
    COMMUNES
    ETHNIC GROUPS
    KNIGHTS
    RELIGIOUS CATEGORIES

SOCIAL INSTITUTIONS
  See also
    FAMILIES

SOCIAL LIFE
  See also
    FAMILY LIFE
    RESERVATION LIFE
    RURAL LIFE
    URBAN LIFE

SOCIAL LIFE. Aborigines. Australia
  -- J,I,S
    919.4   The Aborigine.

SOCIAL LIFE. Algonquian Indians. Canada
  -- J,I
    970.3   Les Algonquins des forêts de l'Est
    970.3   The Algonkians : Eastern Woodland
               Indians.

SOCIAL LIFE. Canada
  1837-1867 -- S
    971.4   Going to Canada : Government House

SOCIAL LIFE. Canada
  Information sources: Postage stamps -- J,I
    769   Le Peuple Canadien et son
               environnement.
    769   Canada : people and environment.

SOCIAL LIFE. Chinese immigrants. British Columbia
  1858-1885 -- S
    301.450971 The First Chinese communities in
               British Columbia.

SOCIAL LIFE. Doukhobors. Canada
  -- S
    301.4509711 Doukhobor way of life.
    301.4509711 Doukhobor contribution to
                Canadian society.

SOCIAL LIFE. Hutterites. Alberta
  -- P,J
    301.450971 The Hutterite ways.

SOCIAL LIFE. Iceland
  -- J,I
    914.91   The People and their work.

SOCIAL LIFE. Inuit
  -- J,I
    970.4   The way things used to be.

SOCIAL LIFE. Inuit. Canada
  -- J,I
    917.12   The Arctic today.
    970.4   Traditional Eskimo life.

SOCIAL LIFE. Inuit. Canada
  -- P,J,I
    970.4   L'esquimau moderne.
    970.4   The Modern Eskimo.

SOCIAL LIFE. Japan
  -- J,I
    915.2   Japan I : home life and food.

SOCIAL LIFE. Kandara. Kenya
  -- J,I
    916.76   Kandara : life in a Kenyan
               community.

SOCIAL LIFE. Naskapi children. Labrador. Newfoundl
  -- P,J
    970.3   La vie quotidienne d'un petit
               Indien.
    970.3   La vie quotidienne d'une petite
               Indienne.
    970.3   A Day in the life of an Indian
    970.3   A Day in the life of an Indian
               girl.

PRECIS SUBJECT INDEX

SOCIAL LIFE. New France
-- J,I
    971.01   Life in New France.

SOCIAL LIFE. Ontario
1860-1870 -- Re-enactments at Upper Canada Village -- P,J
    971.3   La vie dans le Haut-Canada vers 1860.
    971.3   Life in Upper Canada in the 1860's

SOCIAL LIFE. Prairies. Canada
1812-1900 -- J,I
    971.2   Pioneer life on the Prairies (1812-1900)
    971.2   Les pioneers des Prairies (1812-1900)

SOCIAL LIFE. Prairies. Canada
1900-1912 -- J,I
    917.2   Les pionniers des Prairies (1900-1912)
    971.2   Pioneer life on the Prairies (1900-1912)

SOCIAL PSYCHOLOGY
See also
    ATTITUDES
    INTERPERSONAL RELATIONSHIPS

SOCIAL SERVICES
See also
    FIREFIGHTERS
    POLICE
    WELFARE SERVICES

SOCIALISM. Canada
1800-1975 -- S
    320.50971   The Rise of Socialism in Canada.

SOCIETY
See also
    COMMUNITIES

SOLAR SYSTEM
See also
    EARTH. Planets
    MOON
    SUN

SOLAR SYSTEM
Exploration -- J,I,S
    523.4   Our journey into space.

SOLDERING. Metalworking
-- I,S
    671.5   Soldering methods.

SOLVENTS. Psychotropic drugs
-- I,S
    613.8   Les solvants.
    613.8   Solvents.

SONGS
See also
    FOLKSONGS

SOURCES OF INFORMATION See INFORMATION SOURCES

SOUTH-WESTERN UNITED STATES
North American Indians. Culture -- J,I
    970.4   Indians of the Southwest.

SOUTHERN ONTARIO
Geography -- J,I
    917.13   Southern Ontario.

SOUTHERN ONTARIO
Spring wildflowers -- Field guides -- P,J,I,S
    528.09713   Spring wildflowers : southern Ontario and Quebec.
    582.09713   Fleurs sauvages printanières : sud de l'Ontario et du Québec.

SOUTHERN PRAIRIE PROVINCES
Spring wildflowers -- Field guides -- P,J,I,S
    582.0971   Fleurs sauvages printanières : sud des provinces des Prairies.
    582.09712   Spring wildflowers : southern Prairie provinces.

SPACE SCIENCES
See also
    ASTRONOMY
    AVIATION

SPERMICIDES
-- I,S,A
    613.9   Vaginal spermicides and the condom

PRECIS SUBJECT INDEX

SPIDERS
-- P,J,I
  595 Les araignées.
  595 Spiders.

SPIDERS
 Ecology -- J,I
  595 Spider ecology.

SPIDERS
 Physiology -- J,I
  595 What is a spider?

SPONGES. Marine invertebrates
-- I,S
  574.92 Plants, sponges, coelenterates.
  574.92 Plants, sponges, coelenterates.

SPORTS
 See also
  BOATING
  CANOEING
  CYCLING
  FISHING. Sports
  GAMES
  HIGHLAND GAMES
  ORIENTEERING
  SCUBA DIVING
  SKIING
  SNORKEL DIVING
  SWIMMING

SPRING. Seasons
-- J
  525 Spring.

SPRING. Seasons
-- K,P
  525 Le Printemps et l'été : ce qu'ils sont.
  525 Spring and summer : what they mean

SPRING. Seasons
-- P
  525 Spring is coming.

SPRING ACTIVITIES. Innuit. Baffin Island. Northwest Territories
-- P,J,I
  970.4 Spring journey.

SPRING FLOWERING PLANTS. Canada
-- Gardening guides -- I,S
  582 Garden flowers of spring.

SPRING WILDFLOWERS. British Columbia
-- Field guides -- P,J,I,S
  582.09711 Fleurs sauvages printanières : Colombie-Britannique.
  582.09711 Spring wildflowers : British Columbia.

SPRING WILDFLOWERS. Canada
-- Field guides -- I,S
  582 Wild flowers of spring.

SPRING WILDFLOWERS. Eastern North America
-- Field guides -- J,I
  582.097 Spring wildflowers of eastern North America.

SPRING WILDFLOWERS. Maritime Provinces
-- Field guides -- P,J,I,S
  582.09715 Spring wildflowers : the Marit
  582.09715 Fleurs sauvages printanières : les Maritimes.

SPRING WILDFLOWERS. Newfoundland
-- Field guides -- P,J,I,S
  582.09718 Spring wildflowers : Newfoundl
  582.09718 Fleurs sauvages printanières : Terre-Neuve.

SPRING WILDFLOWERS. Northern Ontario & Quebec Provi
-- Field guides -- P,J,I,S
  582.09713 Spring wildflowers : Northern Ontario and Quebec.
  582.09713 Fleurs sauvages printanières : nord de l'Ontario et du Québ

SPRING WILDFLOWERS. Northern Prairie Provinces
-- Field guides -- P,J,I,S
  582.09712 Spring wildflowers : northern Prairie provinces.
  582.09712 Fleurs sauvages printanières : nord des provinces des Prair

SPRING WILDFLOWERS. Southern Ontario & Quebec Provi
-- Field guides -- P,J,I,S
  528.09713 Spring wildflowers : southern Ontario and Quebec.
  582.09713 Fleurs sauvages printanières : sud de l'Ontario et du Québec

PRECIS SUBJECT INDEX

SPRING WILDFLOWERS. Southern Prairie Provinces
  -- Field guides -- P,J,I,S
      582.0971   Fleurs sauvages printanières :
                     sud des provinces des Prairies.
      582.09712   Spring wildflowers : southern
                     Prairie provinces.

SQUIRRELS. Canada
  -- P,J
      599   Squirrels.

STAMPS. Printed materials See POSTAGE STAMPS

STANLEY PARK. Vancouver
  -- J,I
      917.11   Stanley Park.

STARS
  See also
     SUN

STARS
  -- J,I
      523.8   Les Millions d'etoiles.

STARS
  -- P,J
      523.8   Regardent les étoiles.
      523.8   Looking at the stars.

STEEL INDUSTRIES. Canada
  Iron & steel industries -- J,I
      338.40971   L'industrie du fer et de l'acier
                     au Canada.
      338.40971   Iron and steel industry in Canada.

STORES
  See also
     SUPERMARKETS

STORES
  Department stores -- P,J
      658.8   The Department store.

STORES
  General stores -- P,J
      658.8   The Country store.

STRESS. Pronunciation. English language
  -- J
      421   Pitch, stress and juncture.

STRIGIFORMES See OWLS

STRIKES. Winnipeg
  General strike, 1919 -- S
      331.890971 Winnipeg General Strike, 1919.

STRUCTURE
  See also
     GRAMMAR

STRUCTURES
  See also
     BUILDINGS
     RIDEAU CANAL
     WALLS
     WELLAND CANAL

STUDENTS. Ogoki. Ontario
  Ojibway students. Visits to Toronto -- I,S
      370.19   Ogoki native people visit the city

STUDENTS. Toronto
  Visits to Ogoki -- I,S
      370.19   City students visit Ogoki.

SUBJECT CATALOGUES. Libraries
  -- Users' guides -- P,J
      028.7   Have you a book about?

SUBURBS
  -- J,I
      301.34   Suburban site.

SUBURBS. Sydney. New South Wales. Australia
  Description & travel -- I
      919.44   An Australian city : Sydney (no.
                  II)

SUMMER. Seasons
  -- J
      525   Summer.

SUMMER. Seasons
  -- K,P
      525   Le Printemps et l'été : ce qu'ils
                sont.
      525   Spring and summer : what they mean

PRECIS SUBJECT INDEX

SUMMER. Seasons
-- P,J
    525   Summer - reflections on Lake Blue Water.

SUMMER ACTIVITIES. Innuit. Baffin Island. Northwest Territories
-- P,J,I
    970.4   Summer days.

SUMMER CAMP. L'ilawat children
-- J,I,S
    970.3   Mount Currie summer camp.

SUMMER FLOWERING PLANTS. Canada
-- Gardening guides -- I,S
    582   Garden flowers of summer and autumn.

SUMMER WILDERNESS SURVIVAL
-- I,S
    613.6   Summer survival.

SUMMER WILDFLOWERS. Canada
-- Field guides -- I,S
    582   Wild flowers of summer & autumn.

SUMMER WILDFLOWERS. Eastern North America
-- Field guides -- J,I
    582.097   Summer wildflowers of eastern North America.

SUN
-- J,I
    523.7   Influence du soleil sur la terre.
    523.7   What the sun means to the earth.

SUN
Light. Effects on earth -- J,I
    523.7   La Lumière du soleil.
    523.7   Light from the sun.

SUNNY CLIMATES
Houses. Architectural design -- P,J,I
    728   How homes are adapted to nature : wind and radiation.

SUPERMARKETS
-- P,J
    658.8   The Supermarket.

SURGERY
See also
    NEUROSURGERY

SURVIVAL
Summer wilderness survival -- I,S
    613.6   Summer survival.

SURVIVAL
Wilderness survival -- J,I,S
    613.6   Survival in the bush.

SURVIVAL
Wilderness survival. Artificial respiration. Techniques -- I
    614.8   Techniques antinoyade.
    614.8   Water rescue.

SURVIVAL
Wilderness survival. Cookery -- Techniques -- I
    613.6   Outdoor cooking.

SURVIVAL
Wilderness survival. Distress signals -- I
    384   Principaux signaux de détresse.

SURVIVAL
Wilderness survival. Drownproofing. Techniques --
    614.8   Techniques antinoyade.
    614.8   Water rescue.

SURVIVAL
Wilderness survival. Equipment -- I
    613.6   Trousse de survie.
    613.6   Outdoor survival kit.

SURVIVAL
Wilderness survival. Fire making -- I
    613.6   Faire un feu et construire un a
    613.6   How to make a fire and shelter.

SURVIVAL
Wilderness survival. First aid -- I
    614.8   Premiers soins en forêt.
    614.8   First aid in the bush.

SURVIVAL
Wilderness survival. Food preservation -- Techniqu
-- I
    613.6   Outdoor cooking.

PRECIS SUBJECT INDEX

SURVIVAL
   Wilderness survival. Orientation. Use of compasses -- I,S
        796.5   Orientation & compass.

SURVIVAL
   Wilderness survival. Shelter building -- I
        613.6   Faire un feu et construire un abri
        613.6   How to make a fire and shelter.

SURVIVAL
   Winter wilderness survival -- I,S
        613.6   Winter survival.

SWIMMING
   See also
       DROWNPROOFING

SWIMMING
   -- S
        797.2   Learning to swim and water safety.

SWIMMING
   Safety measures -- P,J
        614.8   Swimming safety.
        614.8   Water safety.

SWIMMING
   Strokes -- J,I,S
        797.2   Swimming strokes.

SYDNEY. New South Wales. Australia
   Description & travel -- I
        919.44   An Australian city : Sydney (no. I)

SYDNEY. New South Wales. Australia
   Description & travel -- J,I,S
        919.44   Sydney.

SYDNEY. New South Wales. Australia
   Suburbs. Description & travel -- I
        919.44   An Australian city : Sydney (no. II)

SYMBIOSIS. Forest ecosystems
   -- J
        574.5   Les communantés végétales et animales.

SYMBOLISM. Canadian Indian visual arts
   -- J,I,S
        709.01   The Symbol in Indian art.

SYMPTO-THERMAL METHOD. Contraception
   -- I,S,A
        613.9   The Rhythm and sympto-thermal methods.

SYPHILIS
   -- I,S
        616.9   About V.D. - syphilis.

SYRIAN FOLKLORE
   Special subjects: Christmas -- Stories -- P,J
        398.2095691 Syria : the little camel.

SYSTEME INTERNATIONALE D'UNITES See S.I.

TALON, JEAN, Comte d'Orsainville. New France
   -- J
        971.01   Jean Talon.
        971.01   Jean Talon.

TASTE
   Physiology -- J
        612   Smell, taste and touch.

TASTE
   Physiology -- J,I
        612   The Biology of taste and smell.

TAXATION
   See also
       INCOME TAX

TEACHING MATERIALS
   Children. Cognition. Development -- Teaching materials -- P,J
        160.76   Les Objets disparus.
        160.76   Qu'est-ce qui manque?
        160.76   Trouvons les ressemblance.
        160.76   Classons, classons!
        160.76   Ecoute bien.
        160.76   Qu'est-ce qui ne va pas?
        160.76   Je me suis trompé de groupe : que suis-je?
        160.76   A quoi cela ressemble-t-il?
        160.76   Which group will they go to?
        160.76   Mets-toi à ma place!
        160.76   Pick the picture.
        160.76   What do they have in common.
        160.76   Listen for the clues.

PRECIS SUBJECT INDEX

160.76	What's missing?
160.76	Put them in order.
160.76	Can you find them?
160.76	Does it belong?
160.76	What's wrong here?
160.76	How will it look?
745.5	Make something new.
745.5	How would you use it?
745.5	Qu'est-ce qu'on peut faire de ca?
745.5	Trouvons autre chose.

TEACHING MATERIALS
English language. Creative writing -- Teaching materials -- J

372.6	Three in a haunted house.
372.6	The Absent-minded Mr. Willoughby.
372.6	Moving day mix-up.
372.6	Surprise adventure.
372.6	The Old map mystery.

TEACHING MATERIALS
English language. Creative writing -- Teaching materials -- P,J

372.6	The Great horse contest.
372.6	The Rescue of Julius the donkey.
372.6	The Sparkling imagination.
372.6	The Runaway.

TEACHING MATERIALS
English language. Reading -- Teaching materials -- P

411	The Gobbler.
411	The Ticker.
411	The Doodler.
411	The Puffer.
411	The Cowboy.
411	The Bungler.

TEACHING MATERIALS
English language. Reading -- Teaching materials -- P,J

F	One kitten for Kim.
636	Big red barn.

TEACHING MATERIALS
French language -- Teaching materials -- J,I

440.7	Le corbeau et le renard.
440.7	Conseil tenu par les rats.
440.7	Le rat de ville et le rat des champs.
440.7	Le renard et la cigogne.
440.7	Le lion et le rat.
440.7	L'ours et les deux compagnons.
440.7	Le cordonnier et le banquier.
440.7	Les deux chevres.
440.7	La cigale et la fourmi.
440.7	Le renard et le bouc.

TEACHING MATERIALS
French language. Creative writing -- Teaching materials -- J

372.6	L'aventure de Robert.
372.6	La chasse aux trésors.
372.6	La maison aux fantômes.
372.6	Le déménagement.
372.6	Le sac de M. Danlune.

TEACHING MATERIALS
French language. Reading -- Teaching materials -- F

	Un seul chaton.
440.7	Les aventures de Léo à la ferme
636	La grange rouge.

TEAM PLAY. Hockey -- P,J

796.9	Team play.

TECHNOLOGY
See also
ELECTRIC POWER
ELECTRICITY SUPPLY
ENGINEERING
HEATING
LIGHTING
MILITARY ENGINEERING
WORKSHOP PRACTICE

TECHNOLOGY. Eastern Canada 1820-1867 -- Re-enactments at Black Creek Pioneer Village -- P,J,I

971.3	Pioneer inventions.

TEENAGERS See ADOLESCENTS

TEETH
See also
DENTISTRY

TEETH
Care -- J,I,S

617.6	Summary and conclusion.
617.6	Dental aids and trends in dentistry.

TEETH
Cleaning -- J,I,S

617.6	Details of brushing, disclosing flossing.

PRECIS SUBJECT INDEX

TEETH
   Decay -- J,I,S
      617.6   Awareness of dental problems.

TEETH
   Decay. Prevention -- K,P
      617.6   Teeth : a new look.

TEETH
   Flossing -- J,I,S
      617.6   Flossing vs. gum disease.

TELECOMMUNICATION EQUIPMENT
   See also
      RADIO EQUIPMENT
      TELEPHONES
      TELEVISION EQUIPMENT

TELECOMMUNICATION SYSTEMS
   See also
      TELEPHONE SYSTEMS
      TELEVISION

TELECOMMUNICATION SYSTEMS. Japan
   -- J
      380   Transportation and communication in Japan.

TELEPHONE DIRECTORIES
   -- P,J
      025   What's white and yellow and read all over?
      384.6025 Qu'est-ce qui est blanc ou jaune, et qui fait marcher les doigts?

TELEPHONE SYSTEMS. Communities
   -- P,J,I
      384.6   Et maintenant, tous ensemble.

TELEPHONES
   to 1976 -- P,J
      384.6   Allô, Monsieur Bell!

TELEPHONES
   Invention. Bell, Alexander Graham -- P,J
      384.6   Allô, Monsieur Bell!

TELEPHONES
   Use -- P,J
      384.6   Les Experts en téléphonie.

TELEVISION. Canada
   Effects on politics -- I,S
      329   Electronic politics.
      329   L'Electronique en politique.

TELEVISION EQUIPMENT
   Receivers -- S
      621.388   The Television receiver.

TEMPERATURE MEASURING SCALES
   Celsius -- J,I
      389   Celsius scenes.

TEMPERATURE MEASURING SCALES
   Celsius -- J,I,S
      389   Temperature.

TEMPERATURE MEASURING SCALES
   Celsius -- P,J
      389   Temperature and mass.

TERRITORIAL COATS OF ARMS
   -- J,I
      929.90971 Flags, coats of arms, and floral emblems of Canada.

TERRITORIAL FLAGS
   Canadian Territorial flags -- J,I
      929.90971 Flags, coats of arms, and floral emblems of Canada.
      929.90971 Les Drapeaux Canadiens et leur usage.
      929.90971 Canadian flags and how they are used.
      929.90971 Les drapeaux canadiens et leur usage.

TERRITORIAL FLORAL EMBLEMS
   -- J,I
      929.90971 Flags, coats of arms, and floral emblems of Canada.

THAILAND
   Children -- P,J
      915.93   Children of Thailand.
      915.93   Les enfants de la Thaïlande.

THALARCTOS See POLAR BEARS

PRECIS SUBJECT INDEX

THANKSGIVING. Canada
  Historical aspects -- P,J
      394.2   The Story of Thanksgiving.

THANKSGIVING. Canada
  Social customs -- P,J
      394.2   Thanksgiving today.

THANKSGIVING. Eastern Canada
  Social customs, 1820-1867 -- Re-enactments at Black Creek Pioneer Village -- P,J,I
      971.3   Thanksgiving in pioneer Canada.

THANKSGIVING FOOD. Canada
  1800-1860 -- Re-enactments at Black Creek Pioneer Village -- P,J
      971.3   Thanksgiving foods.

THEATRE
  See also
    DRAMA
    PUPPETRY

THEATRE
  Direction -- I,S
      792   Stage movement and directing.

THEATRE
  Make-up: Beards & moustaches. Techniques -- I,S
      792   Beards.

THEATRE
  Make-up. Techniques -- I,S
      792   Fundamentals of make-up.
      792   Basic makeup.
      792   Corrective makeup.

THEATRE
  Old age make-up. Techniques -- I,S
      792   Old age makeup.

THEATRE
  Sets -- I,S
      792   Basic set design and stages.

THIRD WORLD
  Attitudes of Canadian children -- J,I
      330.9   I was asked to draw this picture : children's views on world development.

THIRD WORLD
  Economic relations with developed countries -- S
      382.1   Toward a new international economic order.

THIRD WORLD
  Foreign aid from Canada -- S
      338.91   What is international development assistance?
      338.91   Qu'est-ce que l'aide au developpement international?

THOMPSON, DAVID
  Exploration of North America -- J,I
      920   David Thompson.

THUNDER BAY
  See also
    PORT OF THUNDER BAY

THUNDER BAY. Ontario
  Description & travel -- I
      917.13   Thunder Bay on tour.

THUNDER BAY. Ontario
  Industries -- I
      386.09713 Thunder Bay's industrial harbour

TIMBER INDUSTRY. Vancouver -- J,I
      917.11   Timber City : Vancouver.
      917.11   Une ville du bois d'oeuvre.

TIRES. Motor vehicles
  Maintenance & repair -- I,S
      629.22   Care of wheels and tires.

TITLE CATALOGUES. Libraries -- Users' guides -- P,J
      028.7   Have you a book called?

TOADS. Eastern Canada -- P,J,I
      597   Toads and frogs of Eastern Canada

TOBACCO INDUSTRY. Ontario -- J,I
      633   Tobacco farming in Ontario.

PRECIS SUBJECT INDEX

TOOLS
　See also
　　　HAND TOOLS
　　　POWER TOOLS

TOOTH See TEETH

TOPOGRAPHY
　See also
　　　LANDFORMS

TORONTO
　See also
　　　PORT OF TORONTO

TORONTO
　Agricultural shows: Royal Winter Fair -- J
　　　630.74　　Royal Winter Fair.

TORONTO
　Agricultural shows: Royal Winter Fair -- P,J
　　　630.74　　Royal Winter Fair.

TORONTO
　Airports: Toronto International Airport -- P,J
　　　387.7　　International airport.

TORONTO
　Christmas parades -- P
　　　394.09713　The Day Santa came to town.

TORONTO
　Christmas parades -- P,J
　　　394.09713　La Parade du Père Noël à Toronto.

TORONTO
　Description & travel -- J,I
　　　917.13　　Toronto - growth, change & progress.

TORONTO
　Students. Visits to Ogoki -- I,S
　　　370.19　　City students visit Ogoki.

TORONTO
　Transport, 1849-1972 -- J,I
　　　388.409713 Transportation in Toronto.

TORONTO
　Visits by Ojibway students from Ogoki -- I,S
　　　370.19　　Ogoki native people visit the city

TORONTO. Study regions
　Canada. Cities. Public transport -- Study regions:
　Ontario. Toronto -- P,J,I
　　　388.409713 Public transportation in the city.

TORONTO. Study regions
　Canada. Municipal government -- Study regions:
　Ontario. Toronto -- J,I
　　　352.071　　Urban government.

TORONTO. Study regions
　Canada. Municipal government. Elections -- Study
　regions: Ontario. Toronto -- J,I
　　　324.71　　The Municipal election.

TORONTO. Study regions
　Cities. Transport -- Study regions: Ontario.
　Toronto -- J,I
　　　388.409713 Transportation.

TORONTO INTERNATIONAL AIRPORT
　-- P,J
　　　387.7　　International airport.

TOTEM POLES
　-- J,I
　　　736　　L'art totémique.
　　　736　　The Art of the totem pole.

TOTEM POLES. British Columbia
　-- J,I
　　　736　　Totem poles.

TOTEM POLES. British Columbia
　-- J,I,S
　　　736　　Totem pole tales.

TOUCH
　-- P,J
　　　152.1　　Touch my world.

TOUCH
　Physiology -- J
　　　612　　Smell, taste and touch.

PRECIS SUBJECT INDEX

TOUCH
   Physiology -- J,I
       612   Our five senses of touch.

TOWN PLANNING See URBAN PLANNING

TOWNS
   See also
      CITIES

TOXICOLOGY
   See also
      POISONS

TRACKS. Animals. Canada
  -- Field guides -- P,J
       591   Animal tracks.

TRADE
   See also
      FUR TRADE
      INDUSTRIES
      WHEAT TRADE

TRADE. Canada
   to 1969 -- J
      382.0971   A Survey.

TRADE. North America
   1800-1850 -- P,J,I
      970   Commerce.

TRADE. Ontario
   1800-1850 -- Re-enactments at Upper Canada Village --
   J,I
      971.3   Le Village.
      971.3   Work and trade.

TRADE EXHIBITIONS
   See also
      AGRICULTURAL SHOWS
      EXPO '67
      EXPO '70

TRADE UNIONS. Canada
   1800-1919 -- S
      331.880971 Beginnings.

TRADE UNIONS. Canada
   1872-1975 -- S
      331.880971 Development.

TRADING POSTS. Fur trade. British Columbia
   Fort Langley -- J,I,S
      971.1   Le Fort Langley : carrefour de
                     côte ouest.
      971.1   Fort Langley : gateway to the w

TRADING POSTS. Fur trade. Manitoba
   Lower Fort Garry -- J,I,S
      971.27   Lower Fort Garry : legacy of th
                    fur trade.

TRADING POSTS. Fur trade. Ontario
   Fort William -- I
      971.3   Life in the old Fort.
      971.3   The Growth, the decline.

TRADITIONS
   See also
      CUSTOMS

TRAINS. Canadian National
   Turbo train -- P,J
      385.0971   Inter-city train.

TRANSISTORS. Electronic equipment
   -- S
      621.3815   The Transistor.

TRANSISTORS. Electronic equipment
   Applications -- S
      621.3815   Transistor application.

TRANSMISSION SYSTEMS. Motor vehicles
   Maintenance & repair -- I,S
      629.22   Driving mechanism.

TRANSPARENCIES
   Overhead transparencies -- I,S
      371.33   Handmade overhead transparencie
                    and their use.

TRANSPARENCIES
   Overhead transparencies. Diazo process -- S
      371.33   The Diazo process.

PRECIS SUBJECT INDEX

TRANSPORT
  See also
    AIR SERVICES
    LAND TRANSPORT
    PUBLIC TRANSPORT
    VEHICLES
    WATER TRANSPORT

TRANSPORT
  to 1967 -- J,I
      380   Our shrinking world.

TRANSPORT
  Canadian Indian transport -- J,I,S
      970.4   Indians : part II.

TRANSPORT. Canada
  -- Forecasts -- J,I
      380.5   Today and tomorrow.

TRANSPORT. Canada
  -- J,I
      380.5   Transportation today : by air and water.

TRANSPORT. Canada
  1850-1930 -- J,I
      380.5   Age of steam and the automobile.

TRANSPORT. Canada
  1900-1974 -- J,I
      380.5   De la terre à l'air.
      380.5   Wheels and wings.

TRANSPORT. Canadian Shield
  -- J,I,S
      380.5   Transportation in the Canadian Shield.
      380.5   Le Bouclier canadien - moyens de transport.

TRANSPORT. China
  -- I
      915.1   Agriculture, industry and transportation.

TRANSPORT. China
  -- J,I
      380.5   China II - transportation.

TRANSPORT. Cities
  -- Study regions: Ontario. Toronto -- J,I
      388.409713 Transportation.

TRANSPORT. Japan
  -- J
      380   Transportation and communication in Japan.

TRANSPORT. Japan
  -- J,I
      380.5   Japan II : transportation and communication.

TRANSPORT. North America
  1800-1850 -- P,J,I
      380.5   Transportation.

TRANSPORT. Toronto
  1849-1972 -- J,I
      388.409713 Transportation in Toronto.

TRAWLING. Commercial fishing
  Otter trawling -- I,S
      639   Le chalutage.
      639   Otter trawling.

TREES
  See also
    FORESTS

TREES
  Deciduous trees -- Field guides -- I,S
      582   Deciduous trees.

TREES
  Evergreen trees -- Field guides -- I,S
      585   Evergreen trees.

TREES
  Growth -- P,J,I
      581.3   Nutrition et croissance de l'arbre
      581.3   Why do trees grow?

TRIALS. Canada
  Procedure -- I
      340   How does the law work?

PRECIS SUBJECT INDEX

TROUT FARMING. Manitoba
 -- J,I
    639.097127 Trout farming in Manitoba.

TRUCKS. Motor vehicles. Canada
 -- P,J
    388.34   Trucks in Canada.

TUBAL LIGATION. Contraception
 -- I,S,A
    613.9   Tubal ligation and vasectomy.

TUNDRA
 Nomadic communities -- J,I
    910   Nomadic journey : three nomadic peoples.

TUNDRA. Arctic North America
 Environment. Adaptation of mammals -- J,I
    574.509712 Life on the Barren Lands.

TURBO TRAIN. Canadian National
 -- P,J
    385.0971   Inter-city train.

TURKISH FOLKLORE
 -- Stories -- J
    398.209561 Foolish friends : Turkey.

UKRAINIAN FOLKLORE
 -- Stories -- P,J
    398.20947   Ilia the mighty : a Ukrainian legend.
    398.20947   Ilia le Grans : une légende Ukrainienne.

UKRAINIAN IMMIGRANTS. Canada
 1885-1920 -- I,S
    301.450971 Strangers to Canada.

UKRAINIAN IMMIGRANTS. Canada
 1890-1910 -- I,S
    301.450971 Prairie homestead.

UKRAINIAN SOCIAL CUSTOMS. Easter
 -- I,S
    914.7   Easter greetings.

UKRAINIAN SOCIAL CUSTOMS. Easter
 Egg-painting -- I,S
    914.7   Pysanky.

UNDERDEVELOPED COUNTRIES See THIRD WORLD

UNGULATES
 See also
    BUFFALO
    CATTLE
    DONKEYS
    GOATS
    HORSES

UNGULATES. Canada
 -- J,I
    599   Hoofed mammals of Canada.

UNICEF
 -- P,J,I
    362.706   What is UNICEF?
    362.706   Qu'est-ce qu'UNICEF?

UNIONS. Employment See TRADE UNIONS

UNITED NATIONS INTERNATIONAL CHILDREN'S EMERGENCY FUND
    See UNICEF

UNITED STATES
 See also
    Names of individual states

UNITED STATES
 1783-1865 -- I,S
    973.6   Growth and conflict.

UNITED STATES
 Foreign relations with Canada, 1775-1914 -- S
    327.71   Canadian-American relations : part 1.

UNITED STATES
 Foreign relations with Canada, 1914-1963 -- S
    327.71   Canadian-American relations : part 2.

UNITED STATES
 Foreign relations with Canada, 1963-1977 -- S
    327.71   Canadian-American relations : part 3.

PRECIS SUBJECT INDEX

UNITED STATES
   South-western United States. North American Indians.
     Culture -- J,I
       970.4   Indians of the Southwest.

UNITED STATES
   War of 1812 -- I,S
      971.03   The War of 1812.

UNITED STATES
   War of 1812 -- J,I
      971.03   The War of 1812.
      971.03   La Guerre de 1812.

UNSELFISHNESS
   See also
     CONSIDERATION FOR OTHERS

UNSELFISHNESS
   -- P,J
      177   La générosité.

UPPER CANADA VILLAGE
   Ontario. Cookery, 1800-1850 -- Re-enactments at
     Upper Canada Village -- J,I
      971.3   Foods.

UPPER CANADA VILLAGE
   Ontario. Crafts, 1800-1850 -- Re-enactments at Upper
     Canada Village -- J,I
      971.3   Les Métiers.
      971.3   Crafts.

UPPER CANADA VILLAGE
   Ontario. Family life, 1800-1850 -- Re-enactments at
     Upper Canada Village -- J,I
      971.3   La Famille.
      971.3   Family life.

UPPER CANADA VILLAGE
   Ontario. Farming, 1800-1850 -- Re-enactments at
     Upper Canada Village -- J,I
      971.3   Farm life.

UPPER CANADA VILLAGE
   Ontario. Recreations, 1800-1850 -- Re-enactments at
     Upper Canada Village -- J,I
      971.3   School and recreation.

UPPER CANADA VILLAGE
   Ontario. Schools, 1800-1850 -- Re-enactments at
     Upper Canada Village -- J,I
      971.3   School and recreation.

UPPER CANADA VILLAGE
   Ontario. Social life, 1860-1870 -- Re-enactments at
     Upper Canada Village -- P,J
      971.3   La vie dans le Haut-Canada vers
                    1860.
      971.3   Life in Upper Canada in the 1860's

UPPER CANADA VILLAGE
   Ontario. Trade, 1800-1850 -- Re-enactments at Upper
     Canada Village -- J,I
      971.3   Le Village.
      971.3   Work and trade.

URANIUM. Elliot Lake. Ontario
   Mining -- J,I
      622   Uranium mining in Ontario.

URBAN CENTRES
   -- J,I
      301.340971 Kinds of urban centres.

URBAN LIFE
   -- P,J,I,S
      301.34   City life.

URBAN LIFE. China
   -- J,I,S
      915.1   City life.

URBAN LIFE. Japan
   -- J
      915.2   Urban life in Japan (no. 1)
      915.2   Urban life in Japan (no. 2)

URBAN PLANNING. Canberra. Australia
   -- I
      919.47   An Australian city : Canberra.

URBAN REGIONS
   See also
     CITIES
     SUBURBS
     URBAN CENTRES

PRECIS SUBJECT INDEX

URBAN REGIONS
  Environment. Pollution -- J,I
        301.34   Problems of urban environment.

URBAN REGIONS
  Growth -- J,I
        301.34   Aging of the urban site.

URBAN REGIONS. Canada
  -- J,I
        301.34   Urbanization : the new accent on cities.

URBAN REGIONS. Canada
  -- P,J
        917.1   Cities and towns.

URBAN REGIONS. Canada
  Birds -- P,J
        598.2   Birds of the city.
        598.2   Les oiseaux des villes.

URBAN REGIONS. Canada
  Cultural aspects -- J,I
        301.34   Urban culture.

URBAN REGIONS. Canada
  Economic aspects -- J,I
        330.12   Urban economy.

URSINES See BEARS

UTENSILS
  L'llawat utensils -- J,I,S
        970.3   Objects in our lives.
        970.3   Elements de notre vie quotidienne.

V.D. See VENEREAL DISEASES

VACUUM TUBES. Electronic equipment
  -- S
        621.3815   The Development of the vacuum tube

VACUUM TUBES. Electronic equipment
  Applications -- S
        621.3815   Application of the vacuum tube.

VALENTINE'S DAY See ST. VALENTINE'S DAY

VALOUR See COURAGE

VANCOUVER
  See also
    PORT OF VANCOUVER

VANCOUVER
  Description & travel -- J,I
        917.11   Vancouver.

VANCOUVER
  Parks: Stanley Park -- J,I
        917.11   Stanley Park.

VANCOUVER
  Timber industry -- J,I
        917.11   Timber City : Vancouver.
        917.11   Une ville du bois d'oeuvre.

VANCOUVER ISLAND
  Description & travel -- J,I
        917.11   Vancouver Island.

VANITY
  -- I,S
        179   Vanity.

VASECTOMY
  -- I,S,A
        613.9   Tubal ligation and vasectomy.

VEGETATION ZONES See BIOMES

VEHICLES
  See also
    AIRCRAFT
    BICYCLES
    CANOES
    MOTOR VEHICLES
    TRAINS

VENEREAL DISEASES
  See also
    GONORRHEA
    SYPHILIS

PRECIS SUBJECT INDEX

VENEREAL DISEASES
-- History -- I,S,A
      616.9   The History of venereal disease.

VENEREAL DISEASES
-- I,S
      616.9   The Facts about venereal disease.

VERENDRYE, PIERRE GUALTIER DE VARENNES, sieur de la See
   LA VERENDRYE, PIERRE GUALTIER DE VARENNES,
   sieur de

VERSAILLES. France
  Palace of Versailles. Architecture -- I,S
      728.8   Versailles and Portugal.

VERTEBRATES
  See also
    BIRDS
    FISH
    FROGS
    MAMMALS
    TOADS

VETERINARY MEDICINE
  See also
    ANIMALS

VETERINARY MEDICINE
-- Pet owners' guides -- P,J
      636.089   A Visit with the vet.

VICTORIA. British Columbia
  to 1972 -- J,I
      917.11   Victoria, B.C.
      917.11   Victoria, B.C.

VICTORIA. British Columbia
  Description & travel -- J,I
      917.11   Victoria.

VICTORIA DAY
  Historical aspects -- P,J
      394.2   Victoria Day.

VILLAGES. Midland. Ontario
  Huron Indian villages -- J,I
      970.3   Huron Indian Village
                   (reconstructed)

VISION
-- P,J
      152.1   Look at my world.

VISION
Physiology -- J
      612   Vision.

VISUAL ARTS
  See also
    ARCHITECTURE
    BANNERS
    COLLAGES
    COSTUME
    GRAPHIC ARTS
    SCULPTURES

VISUAL ARTS
  British Columbian visual arts -- I,S
      709.711   Artistes de la côte canadienne du
                     Pacifique.
      709.711   Artists of Pacific Canada.

VISUAL ARTS
  Canadian Indian visual arts. Symbolism -- J,I,S
      709.01   The Symbol in Indian art.

VISUAL ARTS
  Colour -- S
      152.1   Colour sets.

VISUAL ARTS
  Haida visual arts -- I,S
      709.01   Haida art.

VISUAL ARTS INDUSTRIES. China
-- J,I,S
      680   Craft industries.

VISUAL MEDIA
  See also
    GRAPHIC MEDIA

VOLCANOES
  Effects on landforms -- J,I
      551.2   Geomorphologie volcanique.
      551.2   Volcanic landforms.

PRECIS SUBJECT INDEX

VOLCANOES. Iceland
-- J,I
    914.91   Volcanoes.

VOLTAGE. Electricity
-- J,I
    621.31   Current and pressure.

VOLUME
Measurement -- P,J
    389   Mesure de volumes.
    389   To measure volume.

VOLUME
Measurement. Metric system -- I
    389   Les Unités de volume.
    389   Volume units.

VOLUME
Measurement. Metric system -- J,I
    389   Cubic concepts.

VOLUME
Measurement. Metric system -- J,I,S
    389   Volume - capacity.

VOLUME
Measurement. SI -- J
    389   Un Volume - une capacité.
    389   Measuring volume.

WALLPAPER
Hanging -- S
    698.6   Paper hanging application.

WALLS
Bricklaying. Bonding -- S
    693.2   Walls and bonds.

WAR
See also
    MILITARY ENGINEERING

WAR OF 1812
-- I,S
    971.03   The War of 1812.

WAR OF 1812
-- J,I
    971.03   The War of 1812.
    971.03   La Guerre de 1812.

WARS
See also
    SEVEN YEARS' WAR
    WAR OF 1812
    WORLD WAR 1
    WORLD WAR 2

WARS
Role of Canada, to 1867 -- I
    971   La Lutte pour une terre nouvelle
    971   Struggle for the new land.

WATER
See also
    ICE

WATER
-- J,I
    574.5   The Natural ecology of water.

WATER SPORTS
See also
    BOATING
    CANOEING
    SCUBA DIVING
    SNORKEL DIVING
    SWIMMING

WATER TRANSPORT
See also
    CANALS
    SHIPPING

WATER TRANSPORT. Canada
to 1830 -- J,I
    386.0971   New ways in a new land.
    386.0971   Un Monde nouveau, des méthodes nouvelles.

WATER TRANSPORT. Canada
to 1977 -- J,I
    386.0971   On Canadian waters.

WATER TRANSPORT. Canada. Special subjects. Drawings by W.H.Bartlett
-- J,I
    971   Life along the waterways.

PRECIS SUBJECT INDEX

WATERFOWL
See also
    CANADA GEESE
    LOONS

WATERFOWL. North America
-- J,I
    598.2   Birds, in wetlands.
    598.2   Waterfowl.

WATSON, HOMER. Paintings
-- I,S
    759.11   Homer Watson.

WEAPONS
See also
    RIFLES

WEATHER FORECASTING
Equipment & techniques -- J
    551.6   Starting your own weather station.

WEAVING. Ontario
1800-1850 -- Re-enactments at Black Creek Pioneer Village -- J,I
    971.3   The Weaver.

WEIGHT
See also
    MASS

WEIGHTS & MEASURES
Imperial System -- J,I,S
    389   The Metric system : how?

WEIGHTS & MEASURES
Imperial System compared with S.I. -- J
    389   Standardizing measurement.
    389   Un Système de mesure.

WELDING. Metalworking
-- I,S
    671.5   Welding techniques.

WELFARE SERVICES
See also
    FIREFIGHTERS

WELFARE SERVICES FOR CHILDREN
Block parents -- P,J
    362.7   June's narrow escape.
    362.7   Jimmie to the rescue.
    362.7   Short cut to trouble.

WELFARE SERVICES FOR CHILDREN
UNICEF -- P,J,I
    362.706   What is UNICEF?
    362.706   Qu'est-ce qu'UNICEF?

WELLAND CANAL. Ontario
1829-1932 -- J,I,S
    386.09713   The Welland Canal (historical)

WELLAND CANAL. Ontario
1932-1978 -- J,I,S
    386.09713   The Welland Canal (today)

WELSH PONIES
-- P,J,I
    599   Les poneys : petits et grands.

WESTERN CANADA
to 1885 -- I,S
    971.2   Staking a claim.

WESTERN CANADA
1886-1914 -- I,S
    971.2   Moving in.

WESTERN CANADA
to 1900 -- J,I
    971.2   Frontier heritage.

WESTERN CANADA
1914-1972 -- I,S
    971.2   Growing up.

WESTERN CANADA
Geography -- J,I
    330.9711   The Mountainous West.

WESTERN CANADA
Hutterite communes -- I,S
    301.450971   Hutterite contribution to Canadian society.
    301.450971   Hutterite way of life.

PRECIS SUBJECT INDEX

WESTERN CANADA
  Wildflowers -- Field guides -- P,J,I,S
      582.09712   Selected wildflowers : Western Canada.
      582.09712   Fleurs sauvages diverses : l'ouest du Canada.

WESTERN PLAINS. Canada
  Geography -- J,I
      917.12   Introduction : the Western Plains.

WHALES. Coastal waters. Canada
  -- J,I
      599   Marine mammals of Canada.
      599   Les mammifères marins du Canada.

WHEAT INDUSTRY. Canada
  -- J,I,S
      633.0971   Le blé canadien : une qualité renommée.
      633.0971   Canadian wheat : a reputation for quality.

WHEAT PRODUCTION. Prairie Provinces
  -- J,I
      633.0971   Wheat farming.

WHEAT PRODUCTION. Prairie Provinces
  -- J,I,S
      338.10971   Canadian wheat : from farm to market.
      338.10971   Le blé canadien : de la ferme au marché.

WHEAT PRODUCTION. Saskatchewan
  Harvesting -- P,J
      633.0971   Visit to a wheat farm.

WHEAT TRADE. Prairie Provinces
  to 1969 -- J
      338.10971   Wheat.

WHEELS. Motor vehicles
  Maintenance & repair -- I,S
      629.22   Care of wheels and tires.

WHOOPING CRANES. Canada
  -- P,J
      598.2   The Whooping crane : [a study of a vanishing species]
      598.2   La grue blanche d'Amérique.

WILD ORCHIDS. Eastern North America
  -- Field guides -- J,I
      584   Orchids of Eastern North America

WILDERNESS SURVIVAL
  -- J,I,S
      613.6   Survival in the bush.

WILDERNESS SURVIVAL
  Artificial respiration. Techniques -- I
      614.8   Techniques antinoyade.
      614.8   Water rescue.

WILDERNESS SURVIVAL
  Cookery -- Techniques -- I
      613.6   Outdoor cooking.

WILDERNESS SURVIVAL
  Distress signals -- I
      384   Principaux signaux de détresse.

WILDERNESS SURVIVAL
  Drownproofing. Techniques -- I
      614.8   Techniques antinoyade.
      614.8   Water rescue.

WILDERNESS SURVIVAL
  Equipment -- I
      613.6   Trousse de survie.
      613.6   Outdoor survival kit.

WILDERNESS SURVIVAL
  Fire making -- I
      613.6   Faire un feu et construire un ab
      613.6   How to make a fire and shelter.

WILDERNESS SURVIVAL
  First aid -- I
      614.8   Premiers soins en forêt.
      614.8   First aid in the bush.

WILDERNESS SURVIVAL
  Food preservation -- Techniques -- I
      613.6   Outdoor cooking.

WILDERNESS SURVIVAL
  Orientation. Use of compasses -- I,S
      796.5   Orientation & compass.

PRECIS SUBJECT INDEX

WILDERNESS SURVIVAL
   Shelter building -- I
      613.6   Faire un feu et construire un abri
      613.6   How to make a fire and shelter.

WILDERNESS SURVIVAL
   Summer wilderness survival -- I,S
      613.6   Summer survival.

WILDERNESS SURVIVAL
   Winter wilderness survival -- I,S
      613.6   Winter survival.

WILDFLOWERS. Arctic Canada
  -- Field guides -- P,J,I,S
      582.09712 Fleurs sauvages de l'Arctique.
      582.09712 Arctic wildflowers.

WILDFLOWERS. British Columbia
   Spring wildflowers -- Field guides -- P,J,I,S
      582.09711 Fleurs sauvages printanières :
                   Colombie-Britannique.
      582.09711 Spring wildflowers : British
                   Columbia.

WILDFLOWERS. Canada
  -- Field guides -- J,I
      581.971   Plant communities, woodlot and
                 wetlands.
      582   Plant communities, wasteland
                 wildflowers.

WILDFLOWERS. Canada
   Fall wildflowers -- Field guides -- I,S
      582   Wild flowers of summer & autumn.

WILDFLOWERS. Canada
   Spring wildflowers -- Field guides -- I,S
      582   Wild flowers of spring.

WILDFLOWERS. Canada
   Summer wildflowers -- Field guides -- I,S
      582   Wild flowers of summer & autumn.

WILDFLOWERS. Eastern Canada
  -- Field guides -- P,J,I,S
      582.0971   Fleurs sauvages diverses : l'est
                 du Canada.
      582.0971   Selected wildflowers : eastern
                 Canada.

WILDFLOWERS. Eastern North America
   Spring wildflowers -- Field guides -- J,I
      582.097   Spring wildflowers of eastern
                North America.

WILDFLOWERS. Eastern North America
   Summer wildflowers -- Field guides -- J,I
      582.097   Summer wildflowers of eastern
                North America.

WILDFLOWERS. Maritime Provinces
   Spring wildflowers -- Field guides -- P,J,I,S
      582.09715 Spring wildflowers : the Maritimes
      582.09715 Fleurs sauvages printanières :
                les Maritimes.

WILDFLOWERS. Newfoundland
   Spring wildflowers -- Field guides -- P,J,I,S
      582.09718 Spring wildflowers : Newfoundland.
      582.09718 Fleurs sauvages printanières :
                Terre-Neuve.

WILDFLOWERS. North America
   Fall wildflowers -- Field guides -- J,I
      582.097   Autumn wildflowers of eastern
                North America.

WILDFLOWERS. Northern Ontario & Quebec Province
   Spring wildflowers -- Field guides -- P,J,I,S
      582.09713 Spring wildflowers : Northern
                Ontario and Quebec.
      582.09713 Fleurs sauvages printanières :
                nord de l'Ontario et du Québec.

WILDFLOWERS. Northern Prairie Provinces
   Spring wildflowers -- Field guides -- P,J,I,S
      582.09712 Spring wildflowers : northern
                Prairie provinces.
      582.09712 Fleurs sauvages printanières :
                nord des provinces des Prairies.

WILDFLOWERS. Southern Ontario & Quebec Province
   Spring wildflowers -- Field guides -- P,J,I,S
      528.09713 Spring wildflowers : southern
                Ontario and Quebec.
      582.09713 Fleurs sauvages printanières :
                sud de l'Ontario et du Québec.

WILDFLOWERS. Southern Prairie Provinces
   Spring wildflowers -- Field guides -- P,J,I,S
      582.0971   Fleurs sauvages printanières :
                sud des provinces des Prairies.
      582.09712 Spring wildflowers : southern
                Prairie provinces.

PRECIS SUBJECT INDEX

WILDFLOWERS. Western Canada
-- Field guides -- P,J,I,S
    582.09712 Selected wildflowers : Western Canada.
    582.09712 Fleurs sauvages diverses : l'ouest du Canada.

WILDLIFE
See also
    ENDANGERED SPECIES

WILDLIFE
Conservation -- Stories -- P,J,I
    398.209701 The Story of Greedy Pan.
    398.209701 L'histoire de Pan de Glouton.

WINDY CLIMATES
Houses. Architectural design -- P,J,I
    728   How homes are adapted to nature : wind and radiation.

WINNIPEG
to 1959 -- J,I,S
    917.127 Ville ferroviaire (Winnipeg)
    917.127 Railway city : Winnipeg.

WINNIPEG
Description & travel -- I,S
    917.127 Winnipeg.

WINNIPEG
Description & travel -- J,I
    917.127 Winnipeg, Man.
    917.127 Winnipeg, Man.

WINNIPEG
General strike, 1919 -- S
    331.890971 Winnipeg General Strike, 1919.

WINTER. Seasons
-- J
    525   Winter.

WINTER. Seasons
-- K,P
    525   L'Automne et l'hiver : ce qu'ils sont.
    525   Autumn and winter : what they mean

WINTER. Seasons
-- P,J
    525   Winter - ice fire lights.

WINTER. Seasons
Environment. Adaptation of animals -- J,I
    591.5   Discovering animals in winter.

WINTER. Seasons
Environment. Adaptation of plants -- J,I
    581.5   Discovering plants in winter.

WINTER ACTIVITIES
-- P
    372.6   Une promenade en traineau.
    407   Sleigh ride.

WINTER ACTIVITIES
Safety measures -- P,J
    614.8   Winter safety.
    614.8   Sécurité en hiver.

WINTER ACTIVITIES. Innuit. Baffin Island. Northwest Territories
-- P,J,I
    970.4   Winter camp.

WINTER ACTIVITIES. Laurentian region. Quebec Province
-- P,J,I,S
    525   Laurentian winter.

WINTER CAMPING
-- J,I,S
    796.54   Wintering in the bush.

WINTER SPORTS
See also
    SKIING

WINTER WILDERNESS SURVIVAL
-- I,S
    613.6   Winter survival.

WIRE SCULPTURES
Techniques -- I,S
    731   Wire sculpture with a twist.

PRECIS SUBJECT INDEX

WOLFE, JAMES. Canada
-- J
    971.01   Le Général James Wolfe.
    971.01   General James Wolfe.

WOMEN. Canada
  to 1973 -- S
    301.410971 From Europe to Parliament Hill.
    301.410971 From franchise to freedom.

WOODWORKING
  See also
    CABINET MAKING

WOODWORKING
  Hand tools: Scrapers -- I,S
    621.9   Scraping tools and abrasives.

WOODWORKING
  Joining -- I,S
    694   Five simple wood joints.

WORK
  See also
    EMPLOYMENT

WORKSHOP PRACTICE
  Safety measures -- I,S
    614.8   Pensez "sécurité"
    614.8   Dangers fréquents en atelier.
    614.8   General shop hazards.
    614.8   Think safety.
    621.9   Tournevis, clefs, tôle et soudure.
    621.9   Screwdrivers, wrenches, sheet metal, & welding.

WORLD EVENTS
  1901-1912 -- Collections of contemporary materials -- J,I
    970.05   The Edwardian era.

WORLD EVENTS
  1920-1929 -- Collections of contemporary materials -- J,I
    970.05   The 1920's.

WORLD WAR 1
  Air campaigns. Royal Canadian Air Force. Bishop, Billy -- J,I
    920   Billy Bishop.

WORLD WAR 1
  Campaigns, 1914 -- J,I
    940.4   The War to end war (1914)

WORLD WAR 1
  Campaigns, 1915 -- J,I
    940.4   First air aces : first women's liberators (1915)

WORLD WAR 1
  Campaigns, 1916 -- J,I
    940.4   The Terrible mud of Flanders (1916)

WORLD WAR 1
  Campaigns, 1917-1918 -- J,I
    940.4   The First convoys, and Armistice (1917)

WORLD WAR 1
  Canadian armed forces. Conscription, 1917 -- S
    971.06   Conscription crisis, 1917.

WORLD WAR 1
  Role of Canada -- I,S
    940.4   Canada and the First World War : that's how it was.

WORLD WAR 2
  Battle of the Atlantic -- J,I
    940.54   Battle of the North Atlantic.

WORLD WAR 2
  Campaigns, 1942-1943 -- J,I
    940.54   Hitler at bay (1942-43)

WORLD WAR 2
  Campaigns, 1944-1945 -- J,I
    940.54   Surrender.

WORLD WAR 2
  Campaigns -- J,I
    940   Classic drama - hero vs. villain.

WORLD WAR 2
  Role of Canada -- I,S
    940.54   Home front to victory.
    940.54   From mobilization to the battle of the Atlantic.

PRECIS SUBJECT INDEX

WRITING
  -- I,S
        411   Writing systems.

WRITING. Languages. Native peoples. Canada
  Picture writing -- I,S
        411.09701 Native picture writing.

YOUNG PEOPLE
  See also
      ADOLESCENTS
      CHILDREN

YUKON TERRITORY
  -- I
        917.12   Les Territoires du Nord-Ouest.
        917.12   The Northern territories.

YUKON TERRITORY
  Geography -- J,I
        917.12   The Yukon.

YUKON TERRITORY
  Klondike. Gold rush, 1896. Role of Royal Canadian
    Mounted Police -- J,I,S
        363.20971 North West Mounted Police : the
                   Klondike Gold Rush.

ZINC MINING INDUSTRY. Manitouwadge. Ontario
  -- J,I
        917.13   Images d'une ville minière.
        917.13   Mining town (Manitouwadge, Ont.)

ZOOLOGY
  See also
      ANIMALS
      ORNITHOLOGY

ZOOS
  -- K,P
        590.74   At the zoo.
        590.74   Au zoo.

ZULULAND
  Cetewayo, King -- J
        920   Magnificent Cetewayo.
        920   Cetewayo le magnifique.

Part Three

Title Index

Title Index

5 sens + mésures = observation. 507

5 senses + measurement = observation. 507

The 16mm film projector : part 3. 778.2

The 1837 Rebellion in Lower Canada. 971.03

The 1837 Rebellion in Upper Canada. 971.03

1870 Rebellion. 971.05

1885 Rebellion. 971.05

The 1920's. 970.05

A la découverte de notre patrimoine. 971

A quoi cela ressemble-t-il? 160.76

L'abeille. 595.7

Les aborigènes du Canada. 970.1

The Aborigine. 919.4

About V.D. - gonorrhea. 616.9

About V.D. - syphilis. 616.9

The Absent-minded Mr. Willoughby. 372.6

Activities in pioneer days. 971.3

The Adventures of bunny rabbit. 372.6

The Adventures of kitty cat. 372.6

The Adventures of puppy dog. 372.6

Adventuresome Marco Polo. 920

Aéronautique élémentaire. 629.132

African meat-eaters. 591.96

Age of steam and the automobile. 380.5

Aging of the urban site. 301.34

Agriculture, industry and transportation. 915.1

Aircraft in motion. 629.135

Airshows in Canada. 629.133074

Alberta. 917.123

Alcohol. 613.8

L'alcool. 613.8

Alfred Pellan. 759.11

Alfred Pellan. 759.11

Alger : un pas vers l'avenir un pas vers le passé. 916.5

Algiers : a step into the future a step into the past. 916.5

The Algonkians : Eastern Woodland Indians. 970.3

Les Algonquins des forêts de l'Est. 970.3

Alimentation et bonne santé. 641.1

Aliments classés du Canada. 614.3

Allô, Monsieur Bell! 384.6

Alternatives for the future. 333.7

L'aluminum. 669

Aluminum. 669

Aluminum processing in Quebec. 669

Les amérindiens de la côte du pacifique : jusqu'à l'arrivée des europeens. 970.4

Les amérindiens de la côte du pacifique : depuis l'arrivée des europeens. 970.4

Les amérindiens des forêts de l'est : jusqu' à l'arrivée des europeens. 970.4

Les amérindiens des forêts de l'est : depuis l'arrivée des europeens. 970.4

Les amérindiens des Grandes Plaines : jusqu'à l'arrivée des Europeens. 970.4

Les amérindiens des Grandes Plaines : depuis l'arrivée des europeens. 970.4

Amphetamines and barbiturates. 615

Les amphétamines et les barbituriques. 615

Les Anes domestiques. 599

The Angekkok of Thule. 398.2

Animal pets. 636

Animal tracks. 591

Title Index

Animals of the Arctic. 591.9712

Animals together. 591.96

Anna sends a letter. 383

Antique cars. 629.22074

An Appetite for heritage. 917.1

Application of the vacuum tube. 621.3815

Les araignées. 595

L'archipel de la Reine-Charlotte. 917.11

The Arctic. 599.09712

The Arctic animals. 591.9712

The Arctic birds. 598.2

Arctic Delta town (Inuvik, N.W.T.). 917.12

The Arctic today. 917.12

Arctic wildflowers. 582.09712

Area. 389

Area units. 389

L'art graphique esquimau. 769

The Art of the totem pole. 736

L'art sculptural esquimau. 736

L'art totémique. 736

Art work presentation : mat cutting. 749

Artistes de la côte canadienne du Pacifique. 709.711

Artists of Pacific Canada. 709.711

Asbestos mining in Quebec. 622

At the zoo. 590.74

Athens ... Acropolis and Agora. 722

Atlantic Canada. 330.9715

Atlantic Canada : New Brunswick. 330.9715

Atlantic Canada : Nova Scotia. 330.9716

Atlantic Canada : Prince Edward Island. 330.9717

Atlantic Canada : geography. 917.15

Atlantic Canada : Island of Newfoundland. 330.9718

Atlantic Canada : Labrador. 330.9719

Atlantic Canada : economy. 330.9715

The Atlantic provinces. 917.15

Attituk and the caribou. 398.2

Au tout début. 398.209701

Au zoo. 590.74

An Australian city : Sydney (no. II). 919.44

An Australian city : Canberra. 919.47

An Australian city : Sydney (no. I). 919.44

L'Automne et l'hiver : ce qu'ils sont. 525

Autumn. 525

Autumn and winter : what they mean. 525

Autumn hunters. 970.4

Autumn wildflowers of eastern North America. 582.097

L'aventure de Robert. 372.6

Les aventures de Léo à la ferme. 440.7

Les aventures de Marco Polo. 920

Aviation in Canada. 387.70971

Aviation in Canada : the early days. 387.70971

Aviation in Canada - today. 387.70971

Awareness of dental problems. 617.6

Backwards is forwards in reverse. 301.42

Banting and Best : the discovery of insulin. 920

Baron Münchhausen in a whale of a tale : a German legend. 398.20943

Bartek l'étourdi : un conte polinais. 398.209438

Basic makeup. 792

Basic principles of flight. 629.132

Basic radio circuitry. 621.3841

Basic set design and stages. 792

Basic tools for graphic design. 760.028

Title Index

Basket. 970.3

Bâtissons notre maison. 690

Battle of the North Atlantic. 940.54

Beards. 792

The Beaver. 599

The Beginning of a new era. 363.20971

The Beginning of life : plants and fish. 574.1

Beginnings. 331.880971

Beginnings. 745.5

The Beginnings (1867-1929). C810.9

Being born. 612.6

La belle au bois dormant. 398.20944

La bernache canadienne. 598.2

Berry farming in N.B. 634

Les Bestiaux de l'ouest. 599

La biche miraculeuse : une légende hongroise. 398.209439

Bicycle safety. 614.8

Big Bear, Poundmaker and Crowfoot. 971.05

Big red barn. 636

Billy Bishop. 920

The Biology of taste and smell. 612

Birds and their environment. 598.2

The Birds' Christmas carol. F

Birds, in wetlands. 598.2

Birds of the city. 598.2

Birds of the Everglades. 598.2

Birds, their upland homes and habits. 598.2

Birth. 591.1

Le bison d'Amérique. 599

Les Bisons des plaines. 599

The Black bear. 599

Black Canadians. 301.450971

Le blé canadien : une qualité rénommée. 633.0971

Le blé canadien : de la ferme au marché. 338.10971

A Book is a friend. 001.54

Borden to St. Laurent. 971.06

Le Bouc à une corne. 398.209701

Le Bouclier canadien - industries forestières. 634.9

Bouclier canadien : vue d'ensemble. 917.1

Le Bouclier canadien - moyens de transport. 380.5

Bread and pastry. 664

Bread and roses : the struggle of the Canadian working women. 331.40971

British Canadians. 301.450971

British Columbia. 917.11

Buffalo, buffalo, buffalo. 599

Build your own log house : part 2. 690

Build your own log house : part 1. 690

Building a house. 690

The Bungler. 411

But I don't know how. 152.4

The Cabinet maker. 971.3

Cadet Rousselle. 784.709714

Calgary. 917.123

Calgary stampede. 791.8

The Camera. 771.3

Le campement. 796.54

The Camper and his equipment. 796.54

Le campeur et son équipement. 796.54

The Campsite. 796.54

Can you find them? 160.76

Canada : people and environment. 769

Le Canada à Osaka '70. 607.4

Title Index

Canada and its provinces. 769

Canada and the First World War : that's how it was. 940.4

Canada at Osaka '70. 607.4

Le Canada atlantique : L'Ile de Terre-Neuve. 330.9718

Le Canada atlantique : le Nouveau-Brunswick. 330.9715

Le Canada atlantique : le Labrador. 330.9719

Le Canada atlantique : économie. 330.9715

Le Canada atlantique : géographie. 917.15

Le Canada atlantique : l'Ile du Prince-Edouard. 330.9717

Le Canada atlantique : la Nouvelle Ecosse. 330.9716

La Canada dans l'Empire Britannique. 971.05

The Canada goose. 598.2

Canada in the British Empire. 971.05

Le Canada, pays de liberté. 323.40971

Canada's first people : the Indian. 970.1

Canada's forest regions. 917.1

Canada's graded foods. 614.3

Canada's pioneer life & customs. 971.3

Canada's seven regions. 917.1

Canadian-American relations : part 2 : 1914-1963. 327.71

Canadian-American relations : part 1 : 1775-1914. 327.71

Canadian-American relations : part 3 : 1963 to the present. 327.71

The Canadian and World Plowing Match. 630.74

Canadian Christmas : Christmas decorations. 971.3

Canadian christmas : festive foods. 971.3

Canadian Christmas : traditions of Christmas. 394.2

Canadian flags and how they are used. 929.90971

The Canadian Shield. 917.1

Canadian wheat : from farm to market. 338.10971

Canadian wheat : a reputation for quality. 633.0971

Canadian wildlife - flora. 591.971

Les Canadiens et leurs minéraux. 338.20971

Le Canal Rideau. 386.09713

Canoe Museum. 797.1074

Canoeing : the strokes. 797.1

Canoeing : the basic. -- 797.1

Canoeing. 797.1

Canoeing skills and safety. 797.1

Le canotage. 797.1

Capacity counts. 389

Cape Breton Island : an overview. 917.16

Cape Breton Island : industrial regions. 330.9716

A Captive society. 365

Care of wheels and tires. 629.22

The Caribou Eskimo. 970.4

Carnivores : the flesh eaters. 599.0971

Cartes muettes du Canada. 912

Cartes muettes du monde : l'Amérique. 912

Cartes muettes du monde : L'Europe et l'Afrique. 912

Cartes muettes du monde : l'Asie et l'Océanie. 912

The Cat family. 599

Cattle ranching in Alberta. 636.2

Ce n'est pas juste. 152.4

Ce qu'est la maturite. 173

The Cecropia moth. 595.7

Les Cellules reproductives. 591.1

Celsius scenes. 389

Les censitaires. 333.3

Central Canada : the people. 330.9713

Central Canada : the place. 330.9713

430

Title Index

Cesse de taire le bébé. 152.4

C'est frustrant. 152.4

C'est pas facile! 301.41

Cetewayo le magnifique. 920

Le chalutage. 639

Changing identity. 917.1

Changing profile. 325.71

Charlie Squash goes to town. F

Charlie Squash se rend à la ville. F

Charlottetown, P.E.I. 917.17

La chasse aux trésors. 372.6

Le chasseur qui partit. 398.2

Les Chèvres en vedette. 599

The Chicken or the egg. 636.5

Children of Gabon. 916.7

Children of Greece. 914.95

Children of Japan. 915.2

Children of Northern Nigeria. 916.69

Children of Thailand. 915.93

Children's hospital : in-patient. 362.7

Children's hospital : check-ups and emergencies. 362.7

China 1 : food production. 631.0951

China II - transportation. 380.5

Chinese and Japanese Canadians. 301.450971

Chinese contribution to Canadian life. 301.450971

Chinese cultural heritage. 915.1

Chocolate. 664

The Chocolate bar and the bicycle. 179

Christmas today. 394.2

Chuckwork on the lathe. 621.9

Churchill Falls. 917.19

La cigale et la fourmi. 440.7

Cities and towns. 917.1

Cities of China. 915.1

The City : laboratory of history. 301.31

City habitats. 574.5

City life. 915.1

City life. 301.34

City moods. 301.34

The City of Halifax. 917.16

City patterns. 301.34

City students visit Ogoki. 370.19

Civil War and second thoughts. 810.9

Classic drama - hero vs. villain. 940

Classons, classons! 160.76

Classroom debating in parliamentary style. 808.53

Cleanliness - a new look. 613

Clothing design. 687

Clothing manufacturing. 687

Coal mining in Canada. 622

Coast and montane forest : a comparison. 581.5

Les coléoptères. 595.7

Collecting my own heritage. 917.1

Colour sets. 152.1

La Columbie Britannique. 917.11

Comes from ... grows to. 574.3

A Coming of age (1950-present). C810.9

Commanding Joan of Arc. 920

Commas. 421

Commencement. 745.5

Comment le Canada obtint son drapeau. 929.90971

Comment les oiseaux élèvent leur petits. 598.2

Title Index

Comment les oiseaux s'adaptent pour survivre. 598.2

Commerce. 970

Common birds of Canada. 598.2

The Common loon. 598.2

Les communantés végétales et animales. 574.5

Commune in the North. 631.0951

Commune in the South. 631.0951

Community life. 970

The Compass. 538.028

Le Comportement humain. 158

Conception and birth. 612.6

Confederation Canada. 971.04

Connaître les sortes d'aliments. 641.1

Conscription crisis, 1917. 971.06

Conseil tenu par les rats. 440.7

Constitutional development. 342.4

Le Conte de Noël de Dickens. F

Contemporary culture. 915.1

Contraception. 613.9

Un contre d'industrie laitière. 917.13

Copper. 669

Le corbeau et le renard. 440.7

Le cordonnier et le banquier 440.7

Cornelius Krieghoff. 759.11

Cornelius Krieghoff. 759.11

Corrective makeup. 792

Country life. 971.3

The Country store. 658.8

Courage. 179

The Cowboy. 411

Cowichan : a question of survival. 970.5

Craft industries. 680

Crafts. 971.3

Creating your own visuals using a dry mount press. 760.028

Creation of money by the banking system. 332.1

Cree syllabary. 411.09701

Le criquet (sauterrelle). 595.7

La crise de l'environnement. 333.9

Croissance de cristaux. 548

La croissance du homard. 595

La crosse canadienne. 796.34

Crustaceans, molluscs. 594

Cubic concepts. 389

La Cuisine : un atelier. 640

Cuivre. 669

La culpabilité. 179

Cultures in conflict. 917.1

Current and pressure. 621.31

Les cycles de nourriture. 574.5

Dairy farming community (Elmira, Ont.). 917.13

Dangers fréquents en atelier. 614.8

La danse du soleil des Amérindiens de Plaines. 398.209701

David Milne. 759.11

David Milne. 759.11

David Thompson. 920

A Day in the life of a letter carrier. 383

A Day in the life of an Indian boy. 970.3

A Day in the life of an Indian girl. 970.3

The Day Santa came to town. 394.09713

Days of the igloo. 970.4

De la terre à l'air. 380.5

Title Index

De la traction animal à la vapeur. 380.5

Deceit. 177

Deciduous and boreal forests : a comparison. 581.5

Deciduous trees. 582

La décision de Lord Elgin. 971.04

A Declaration of faith. 810.9

Defending Canada in a changing world. 971.06

La Défense du Canada dans un monde en évolution. 971

Delphi, theatres and Olympia. 722

Le déménagement. 372.6

Dental aids and trends in dentistry. 617.6

The Department store. 658.8

Derriere est devant sens devant derriere. 301.42

Details of brushing, disclosing & flossing. 617.6

The Determination of the levels of gross national product and incomes. 339.4

Les deux chevres. 440.7

Developing an Iroquoian village site. 913

Development. 331.880971

Development of Canadian homes. 728

The Development of the vacuum tube. 621.3815

Le développement et l'apprentissage. 612.6

Développement pré-natal. 612.6

The Diaphragm. 613.9

The Diazo process. 371.33

Dickens' Christmas carol. F

The Diefenbaker-Pearson years : part II : 1963-1968. 971.06

The Diefenbaker-Pearson years : part 1 : 971.06

Difficulties of Chinese immigrants. 301.450971

Un dimanche au parc. 796

Discoveries and disappointments. 910

Discovering animals in winter. 591.5

Discovering our heritage. 971

Discovering plants in winter. 581.5

Discovering the land. 971.2

Discovering the people. 971.2

Discovering your library. 024

The Discovery of Canada. 971.01

La dissémination des graines. 582

Does it belong? 160.76

Doing a project. 028.1

Domestic circuits. 621.319

Dominion Day. 394.2

Dominion Day. 394.2

Donkeys, donkeys, donkeys. 599

The Doodler. 411

Doukhobor contribution to Canadian society. 301.4509711

Doukhobor immigrants in the West. 301.4509711

Doukhobor way of life. 301.4509711

Dr. Norman Bethune. 920

Dr. Wilder Penfield. 920

Dragonflies and damselflies. 595.7

Les Drapeaux Canadiens d'autrefois. 929.90971

Les Drapeaux Canadiens et leur usage. 929.90971

Les drapeaux canadiens et leur usage. 929.90971

Dressing fish. 641.4

Drill presses and lathes. 621.9

Driving mechanism. 629.22

Drugs and religious ritual. 299

Du plan á la carte. 912

La Dualité de notre patrimoine. 971.5

D'une Guerre à l'autre. 971

Title Index

Early pioneer life in Upper Canada. 971.3

The Earth grid. 526

Easter greetings. 914.7

Easter in Canada. 394.2

The Eastern forest. 599.097

Eating out I. 581.6

Eating out II. 581.6

Echinoderms. 593

Echinoderms. 593

Ecology of the Arctic. 574.509712

Ecology of the Everglades. 574.509759

Economic policy in perspective. 339.5

L'economie forestière. 338.10971

Les ecosystèmes. 574.5

Ecoute bien... 160.76

Edmonton. 917.123

Edmonton, Alberta. 917.123

Education. 379.51

Education and health. 379.51

The Edwardian era. 970.05

Effects of misuse. 613.8

Electrical energy. 621.31

Electrical energy in Canada. 621.310971

Electrical hazards. 644

Electronic fish finding. 639

Electronic politics. 329

L'Electronique en politique. 329

Elementary camping. 796.54

Elementary canoeing. 797.1

Eléments de notre vie quotidienne. 970.3

Elements of brickwork. 693.2

Elements of pottery. 738.1

The Elizabethan era. 820.9

L'Embryon se développe. 612.6

The Emergence (1929-1950). C810.9

Emily Carr. 759.11

The Energy crisis? 333.7

Les enfants de la Grèce. 914.95

Les enfants de la Nigéria du Nord. 916.69

Les enfants de la Thailande. 915.93

Les enfants du Gabon. 916.7

Les enfants du Japon. 915.2

Engines de pêche (câbles et lignes pour la fabrication des fillets de pêch). 639

Environment : biosphere. 333.9

Environment crisis. 333.9

Environment protection. 333.9

L'environnement et la biosphère. 333.9

L'époque de Laurier (1ère partie). 971.05

L'époque de Laurier (2e partie). 971.05

The Era of royal government. 971.01

Eskimo 1 : Arctic village. 917.12

The Eskimo and his work. 970.4

Eskimo carvings. 736

Eskimo heritage. 970.4

Eskimo hunting. 970.4

Eskimo prints. 769

Eskimo sculpture. 736

Eskimos : part 2. 970.4

L'esquimau moderne. 970.4

L'esquimau primitif. 970.4

Et maintenant, tous ensemble. 384.6

Title Index

Etre pubère. 612.6

European Canadians. 325.71

Evergreen trees. 585

Everybody's afraid of something. 152.4

L'Evolution constitutionelle. 342.4

Exercise - a new look. 612

L'expansion du Canada. 971

Les Experts en téléphonie. 384.6

Les exploits de Ti-Jean dans l'Ouest. 440.7

Exploration de l'Arctique canadien. 917.12

Exploration of Arctic Canada. 917.12

Explorations lunaires. 629.45

Explorons la ferme. 630.1

Explorons la forêt. 574.5

Explorons le bord de la mer. 574.92

Explorons le jardin. 635

Explorons l'etang. 574.92

Expo 67 : Montreal, Canada. 607.4

Expo '67 : [Montreal, (Canada)]. 607.4

Fact and fancy. 910

Factors influencing homes. 728

Faire un feu et construire un abri. 613.6

Faire une bannière. 746.3

Faire une cagoule. 746.9

La Famille. 971.3

La famille Huronne-Iroquoise (Indiens des forêts de l'Est). 970.3

Family life. 971.3

The Fantastic world of insects (A). 595.7

The Fantastic world of insects (B). 595.7

Farm chores. 631

Farm life. 971.3

Farming in pioneer Canada. 631.0971

Les faucons. 598.2

Federal government. 328.71

Félins du Canada. 599

Le Festival des phoques. 398.2

The Festival of the seals. 398.2

Film and filters. 771

The Firebird and the magic horse. 398.20947

The Firefighter. 363.3

Fires and cooking. 641.5

First aid in the bush. 614.8

First air aces : first women's liberators (1915). 940.4

The First Chinese communities in British Columbia. 301.450971

The First convoys, and Armistice (1917). 940.4

The First Métis uprising, 1869-70. 971.05

The First salmon. 398.209701

Fish. 338.30971

Fish processing in British Columbia. 639

The Fish processing plant. 639

Fishing gear (ropes and twines for fishing nets). 639

Fishing methods. 639

Fishing town (Port Bickerton, N.S.). 917.16

Five simple wood joints. 694

Flags, coats of arms, and floral emblems of Canada. 929.90971

"Flashy" the fire bug. 614.8

Fleurs sauvages de l'Arctique. 582.09712

Fleurs sauvages diverses : l'est du Canada. 582.0971

Fleurs sauvages diverses : l'ouest du Canada. 582.09712

Title Index

Fleurs sauvages printanières : Colombie-Britannique. 582.09711

Fleurs sauvages printanières : Terre-Neuve. 582.09718

Fleurs sauvages printanières : les Maritimes. 582.09715

Fleurs sauvages printanières : sud de l'Ontario et du Québec. 582.09713

Fleurs sauvages printanières : nord des provinces des Prairies. 582.09712

Fleurs sauvages printanières : nord de l'Ontario et du Québec. 582.09713

Fleurs sauvages printanières : sud des provinces des Prairies. 582.0971

Flin Flon, Manitoba. 917.127

Flossing vs. gum disease. 617.6

Food chains. 574.5

Foods. 971.3

Foolish Bartek : (a Polish tale). 398.209438

Foolish friends : Turkey. 398.209561

The Force keeps the peace. 363.20971

The Force rides west. 363.20971

The Forest economy. 338.10971

Forest industries in B.C. : part 1 : logging. 634.909711

Forest management and lumbering. 634.9

Forestry in the Canadian Shield. 634.9

La forêt des montagnes et la forêt côtière : une comparaison. 581.6

La forêt feuille et la forêt boréale : une comparaison. 581.5

Foreuse sur colonne et tour. 621.9

Forging iron. 671.3

La Forme de la terre. 525

Les formes de relief glaciaire. 551.3

Forming metal by machine. 621.9

Le Fort Langley : carrefour de la côte ouest. 971.1

Fort Langley : gateway to the west. 971.1

Le Fort Walsh dans les collines Cyprès. 971.24

Fort Walsh in the Cypress Hills. 971.24

Fossil fuels : coal. 333.8

Fossil fuels : oil and natural gas. 333.8

The Fourth wave. 325.71

Fowl-like birds. 598.2

France in the New World. 971.01

Fredericton, New Brunswick. 917.15

French Canadians. 301.450971

The Frog. 597

From Europe to Parliament Hill. 301.410971

From fleur-de-lis to Union Jack. 971.01

From franchise to freedom. 301.410971

From mobilization to the battle of the Atlantic. 940.54

From puritan to Augustan. 820.9

From the beginnings to Elizabeth. 820.9

From two to one. 591.1

From war to war. 971.06

Frontenac. 971.01

Frontenac. 971.01

Frontier heritage. 971.2

Frontier mining and grazing (the Outback). 919.4

Fruit Belt preservation and regional planning. 333.7

Fruit farming in British Columbia. 634

Le fumeur est une victime. 613.8

Fundamentals of electricity. 537.2

Fundamentals of make-up. 792

Fur. 338.30971

Title Index

Furniture and household goods. 970

Garden flowers of spring. 582

Garden flowers of summer and autumn. 582

Le gaufre á poches. 599

La Gendarmerie du Nord-Ouest : la rébellion de 1885. 363.20971

La Gendarmerie du Nord-Ouest : la longue marche vers l'Ouest. 363.20971

General electronics. 537.5

Le Général James Wolfe. 971.01

General James Wolfe. 971.01

General shop hazards. 614.8

La générosité. 177

Geography of the Arctic. 917.12

Geomorphologie volcanique. 551.2

Germany : the nutcracker's happy Christmas. 398.20943

Get hooked on fish. 641.3

Get out and vote! election campaigns and issues. 324.71

Getting down to basics about advertising. 659.1

Gifts of the Nile I : farming on the flood plains. 631.0962

Gifts of the Nile II : Cairo, the city. 916.2

Glacial landforms. 551.3

Glacier land deposits. 551.3

Glacier water deposits. 551.3

Les glaciers. 551.3

Glaciers. 551.3

Glaciers. 914.91

Glooscap and the four wishes. 398.209701

Glooscap et les quatre voeux : [légende indienne]. 398.209701

Glooskap brings summer. 398.209701

Go fight City Hall! local decision making. 352.071

Goaltending. 796.9

Goats, goats, goats. 599

The Gobbler. 411

Going to Canada : in the backwoods. 971.3

Going to Canada : Government House. 971.4

Gold refining in Ontario. 622

Gold rush : pioneer mining in British Columbia. 971.1

Good King Arthur. 398.2

Le gouvernement fédéral. 328.71

Le gouvernement local. 352.071

Le gouvernement provincial. 354.71

Gr-r-r-r. 152.4

Grand Manan Island. 917.15

Grand Manan Island : lobster fishing. 639.09715

Grand Manan Island : weir fishing. 639.09715

La grange rouge. 636

The Grasshopper. 595.7

Grassland 1 : animals of the African Grasslands. 591.96

The Grasslands. 599.097

The Great Depression. 971.06

The Great horse contest. 372.6

The Great Lakes - St. Lawrence Seaway. 386.0971

Greece 1 : life in a rural village. 917.95

La grenouille. 597

Grey Owl. 920

Grinders, routers, power saws & jointers. 621.9

The Grocery cart and noise. 177

The Group of Seven. 759.11

Le Groupe des Sept. 759.11

Growing and learning. 612.6

Title Index

Growing up. 176

Growing up. 971.2

Growth and conflict. 973.6

The Growth of Canada. 971

The Growth, the decline. 971.3

La grue blanche d'Amérique. 598.2

La Guerre de 1812. 971.03

La guerre de Sept ans. 971.01

Guilt. 179

Guinea pigs and their care. 636

Gwúshum. 970.3

The Habitant and his home [in the 18th century]. 971.4

The Habitant and his land [in the 18th century]. 971.4

L'habitant et sa maison au XVIIIe siècle. 971.4

L'habitant et sa terre au XVIIIe siècle. 971.4

The Habitants. 333.3

Habitat : key to survival. 639

L'Habitat. 591.5

Habitat : key to survival. 639

Habitat and adaptation. 591.5

Haida argillite carvings. 736

Haida art. 709.01

Halifax - historic seaport. 917.16

Halifax, Nova Scotia. 917.16

Hallowe'en in Canada. 394.2

Hand saws, chisels and files. 621.9

Handmade overhead transparencies and their use. 371.33

Have you a book about? 028.7

Have you a book by? 028.7

Have you a book called? 028.7

Hawks. 598.2

Hearing. 612

Help yourself to good cooking. 641.1

The Heritage puzzle. 917.1

Le hibou et le lemming : une légende eskimo. 398.2

Les hiboux. 598.2

Highland Games. 796.074

Hill and plain communes : North China. 915.1

Histoire de l'aviation au Canada. 387.70971

L'histoire de Manowan : première partie 970.5

L'histoire de Manowan : deuxième partie. 970.5

L'histoire de Pan de Glouton. 398.209701

L'Histoire de Sainte-Marie-des-Hurons : part2 971.3

L'Histoire de Sainte-Marie-des-Hurons : part I. 971.3

L'histoire de Terre-Neuve (1000-1824). 971.8

Historic costumes : part 1. 391.0971

Un historique de la contraception. 613.9

History and geography. 914.91

A history of contraception. 613.9

History of flight in Canada. 387.70971

The History of hockey. 796.9

The History of income tax in Canada. 336.20971

History of Manowan : part 1. 970.5

History of Manowan : part 2. 970.5

The History of Newfoundland (1000-1824). 971.8

History of the Royal Canadian Mounted Police. 363.20971

The History of venereal disease. 616.9

Hitler at bay (1942-43). 940.54

The Hockey coach. 796.9

Title Index

Hockey equipment. 796.9

Hockey I - getting ready. 796.9

Hockey II - the game - offensive play. 796.9

Hockey III - the game - defensive play. 796.9

Home front to victory. 940.54

Home safety. 614.8

Home safety. 614.8

Homer Watson. 759.11

Homer Watson. 759.11

Homes in cold climates. 728

Homes in hot, dry climates. 728

Homes in hot, humid climates. 728

Homes of early day Canada. 728.0971

The Honeybee. 595.7

L'honnêteté. 179

Hoofed mammals of Canada. 599

Un Hôpital pour enfants : examen et urgences. 362.7

Un Hôpital pour enfants : patient hospitalisé. 362.7

L'Hostilité. 179

Hostility. 179

Hot dogs. 664

Hotel : city within a city. 647.

Housing : the Canadian city. 301.5

How a letter travels. 383

How birds adapt to survive. 598.2

How birds find food. 598.2

How birds raise their young. 598.2

How Canada got its flag. 929.90971

How do we make laws? 342

How do you share your library? 024

How does the law work? 340

How homes are adapted to nature : wind and radiation. 728

How it all began. 398.209701

How lobsters grow. 595

How people misuse them. 615

How seeds are spread. 582

How summer came to our land. 398.209701

How the deer got fire. 398.209701

How the leopard got its spots. 398.2096

How to grow crystals. 548

How to make a fire and shelter. 613.6

How will it look? 160.76

How would you use it? 745.5

Human behaviour. 158

The Hunter who went away. 398.2

Hunters of the Arctic. 970.4

Huron Indian Village & Musem. 970.3

Huron Indian Village (reconstructed). 970.3

Hutterite contribution to Canadian society. 301.450971

Hutterite persecution : 1526-1917. 289.9

Hutterite way of life. 301.450971

The Hutterite ways. 301.450971

Hutterites in Canada : 1917 - present. 301.450971

I can see clearly now. 338.988

I come from Jamaica. 301.450971

I was asked to draw this picture : children's views on world development. 330.9

I was born in Portugal. 301.450971

Ice fishing. 799.1

Identifying airplanes. 629.133

Il etait une fois un oeuf. 612.6

L'Ile Grand Manan : la pêche du homard. 639.09715

Title Index

L'île Grand Manan : la pêche à fascines. 639.09715

L'Ile Grand Manan. 917.15

Les Iles de la Madeleine. 917.14

Ilia le Grans : une légende Ukrainienne. 398.20947

Ilia the mighty : a Ukrainian legend. 398.20947

Images d'une ville minière. 917.13

Indian arts and crafts. 709.01

Indian children of the Andes. 918.5

Indian dances and masks. 793.3

Indian snowshoes. 685

Indians : part II. 970.4

Indians : part I. 970.4

Indians I : life on the Plains. 970.4

Indians leaders and centres of renewal. 970.4

Indians of the Great Plains. 970.4

Indians of the Northeastern Woodlands. 970.4

Indians of the Pacific Northwest. 970.4

Indians of the Southwest. 970.4

Indians yesterday and today. 970.4

Les Indiens des Plaines. 970.4

Les Indiens des Régions subarctiques. 970.4

The Industrial city. 917.13

Industrial community 1 : patterns of growth. 301.34

L'industrie du fer et de l'acier au Canada. 338.40971

Influence du soleil sur la terre. 523.7

Initiation à la carte topographique. 912

Initiation á la plongée : tuba et scaphandre autonome. 797.2

Initiation à l'échelle de la carte. 912

Insectivores and bats. 599

Inside outside. 152.4

L'integrité. 179

Integrity. 179

Inter-city train. 385.0971

The Interior Plains. 917.12

International airport. 387.7

The Intrauterine device. 613.9

Introducing map scale. 912

Introducing the Canadian Shield. 917.1

Introducing the postage stamp. 769

Introducing the topographical map. 912

Introduction : the people and the land. 330.971

Introduction : the Western Plains. 917.12

An Introduction to Canada's geography. 917.1

Introduction to energy. 333.7

Introduction to language study. 401

Introduction to maps. 912

An Introduction to snorkel and scuba diving. 797.2

Introduction to the Niagara Fruit Belt. 917.13

The Inuit. 970.4

Inventing a heritage. 394.2

Ireland : O'Reilly's Christmas cap. 398.209415

Irish contributions to Canadian life. 301.450971

Irish cultural heritage. 914.15

Irish feuds and quarrels. 301.4509713

Irish immigration. 325.71

Iron and steel industry in Canada. 338.40971

The Iroquoian people. 913

The Iroquois-Huron Nations (Eastern Woodland Indians). 970.3

Irrigated farming in Alberta. 631.7

It isn't easy. 301.41

L'Italie : la legende de Dame la Befana. 398.20945

Title Index

Jack was every inch a sailor. 784.40971

Jacques Cartier. 971.01

Jacques Cartier. 971.01

J'ai peur. 152.4

James Wilson Morrice. 759.11

Japan I : home life and food. 915.2

Japan II : transportation and communication. 380.5

The Japanese come to Canada. 301.450971

Japanese contribution to Canadian society. 301.450971

Japanese cultural heritage. 915.2

The Japanese during World War II. 301.450971

Je l'envie. 152.4

Je me mets en colère. 152.4

Je me suis trompé de groupe : que suis-je? 160.76

Je ne peux pas. 152.4

Jealousy. 179

Jean-Paul Riopelle. 759.11

Jean-Paul Riopelle. 759.11

Jean Talon. 971.01

Jean Talon. 971.01

Les jeunes Indiens de Andes. 918.5

The Jewish people. 296.4

Jimmie to the rescue. 362.7

June's narrow escape. 362.7

Kandara : life in a Kenyan community. 916.76

A Kibbutz in Israel. 335

Kinds of Canadian communities. 301.340971

Kinds of urban centres. 301.340971

The Kingfisher. 598.2

Knowing your food groups. 641.1

Lacrosse - the Canadian game. 796.34

Land of gold : land of ice : all men explore. 910

Large animals of Africa. 591.96

Latitude. 526

Laurentian winter. 525

The Laurier era : part 1. 971.05

The Laurier era : part 2.

Lawren S. Harris. 759.11

Lawren S. Harris. 759.11

Learning about rocks and minerals. 549

Learning about the fruits we eat. 641.3

Learning about the plants we eat. 641.3

Learning to swim and water safety. 797.2

The Legend of the Christmas tree. F

The Legend of the flying canoe. 398.2

The Legend of the loon. 398.209701

The Legend of the raven who flew backwards. 398.2

La Legende de l'arbre de Noël. F

Lengthy tales. 389

Leroy, Saskatchewan. 917.214

Let's go to the fair. 607.4

Let's serve freshwater fish. 641.6

Let's serve shellfish. 641.6

Let's talk about it. 338.91

Libellules et demoiselles. 595.7

The Library. (Or, how I learned to love Melvil Dewey). 028.7

Life along the waterways. 971

Life in a beehive. 595.7

Life in New France. 971.01

Life in the boreal forest. 599.097

Life in the old Fort. 971.3

Title Index

Life in Upper Canada in the 1860's. 971.3

The Life of Mackenzie King : part II : the final years 1930-1950. 920

The Life of Mackenzie King : part 1 : the formative years 1874-1930. 920

The Life of Sir John A. MacDonald. 920

The Life of Sir Wilfrid Laurier. 920

Life on a Chinese commune : part 2 : building, manufacturing, transport, schools and entertainment. 915.1

Life on a Chinese commune : homes and farming. 915.1

Life on the Barren Lands. 574.509712

Life on the Prairies. 591.5

Light from the sun. 523.7

Une Ligne - une surface. 389

Linear - area. 389

Linear measurement. 389

Linear units. 389

Le lion et le rat. 440.7

Listen for the clues. 160.76

Listen to my world. 152.1

The Little match girl. F

The Living room and clothes. 177

Local government. 352.071

Longitude. 526

Look at my world. 152.1

Looking at the stars. 523.8

Lord Durham's mission. 971.03

Lord Elgin's decision. 971.04

Lord Selkirk : the colonizer. 920

The Lost wisdom (Israel). 398.2095694

Love and marriage. 362.8

Lower Fort Garry : legacy of the fur trade. 971.27

Lowland agriculture in Japan. 631.0952

Loyalty. 179

LSD. 615

LSD. 615

La Lumière du soleil. 523.7

La Lune : ses phases. 523.3

La Lutte pour une terre nouvelle. 971

Macdonald to Borden. 971.05

Magdalen Islands. 917.14

Magnificent Cetewayo. 920

La maison aux fantômes. 372.6

Make something new. 745.5

Making a body mask. 746.9

Making banners. 746.3

The Making of a farm. 970

Making your own microscopic slides. 578

Malacca : gateway to Malaysia. 915.95

Le Mâle - la femelle 591.1

Male and female. 591.1

Les mammifères marins du Canada. 599

The Mandarin and the butterflies. 398.20951

Manitoba. 917.127

Manitoba. 917.127

Manitoba : a broader view. 917.127

Manitoba : the Shield. 917.127

Le Manitoba : vue d'ensemble. 917.127

Le Manitoba : les Plaines. 917.127

Manitoba : the plains. 917.127

Many different me-s. 152.4

Title Index

The Many Faces of Hamilton. 917.13

The Map. 912

Map orientation. 912

Maple syrup. 664

Maple syrup. 664

Marathon, Ontario. 917.13

La marijuana : quelques vérités. 615

Marine mammals of Canada. 599

"Mary Davidson's home". 971.3

Masks. 731

Masks of the North American Indians. 391.09701

Les Masques. 152.4

Masques des Indiens de l'Amérique du Nord. 391.09701

Mass. 389

Mass matters. 389

The Meaning of maturity. 173

The Meaning of puberty. 612.6

Measuring length and area. 389

Measuring mass. 389

Measuring volume. 389

La Mécanisation dans l'expolitation forestière de l'est du Canada. 634.9

Mechanized logging in eastern Canada. 634.9

The Medicine that restores life. 398.209701

Medieval community 1 : the knight. 940.1

Mesure de volumes. 389

Méthodes de pêche. 639

Les Métiers. 971.3

The Metric system : why? 389

The Metric system : a better way .... for all! 389

The Metric system : how?. 389

The Metric system : a better way ... for some. 389

Mets-toi à ma place! 160.76

Meules, toupies, scies éléctriques, et corroyeurs. 621.9

Mexico : the humblest gift. 398.20972

Mexico I : across modern Mexico. 917.2

La Mexique : l'humble présent. 398.20972

The Microscope - a delicate tool. 535

The Microscope - its operation. 535

Milk and ice cream. 637

The Mill. 971.3

Les Millions d'etoiles. 523.8

Minerals. 338.20971

Minerals for Canadians. 338.20971

Mining town (Manitouwadge, Ont.). 917.13

The Miraculous hind : a hungarian legend. 398.209439

La mission de Lord Durham. 971.03

Mixed farming in Manitoba. 631.097127

The Modern Eskimo. 970.4

Moi et mes diverses personalités. 152.4

The Monarch butterfly. 595.7

Le Monde à l'heure du système international. 389

Un monde fermeś. 365

Un Monde nouveau, des méthodes nouvelles. 386.0971

Money : how much do you need? 332.024

Money : planning a budget. 332.024

Money : how to spend it. 332.024

Monuments of the past. 915.1

Moon exploration. 629.45

The Moon's position in space. 523.3

Mosaic Canada. 917.1

Title Index

Mother Earth : an Indian view. 299

La mouette et la baleine. 398.20971

Mount Currie summer camp. 970.3

Mountain environments of Japan. 915.2

The Mountainous West. 330.9711

Moving day mix-up. 372.6

Moving in. 971.2

The Municipal election. 324.71

My birthplace was India. 301.450971

My escape from death. 970.4

My family is Chinese. 301.450971

My father the fireman. 363.3

My Italian heritage. 301.450971

Naba-Cha and the Rocky Mountains. 398.209701

La Naissance. 591.1

La Naissance d'un être humain. 612.6

National Arts Centre. 790.20971

The National Gallery of Canada. 708

National output and its measurement. 339.3

National Research Council. 607

Native and European in North America. 970.1

Native Canadians. 970.1

Native clothing. 391.09701

Native games. 790

Native land claims in B.C. : an introduction (1850-1976). 970.5

The Native peoples of the Great Plains : initial European contact. 970.4

The Native peoples of the Great Plains : European contact to the present day. 970.4

The Native peoples of the Northeastern Woodlands : European contact to the present day. 970.4

The Native peoples of the Northeastern Woodlands : initial European contact. 970.4

The Native peoples of the Pacific Northwest : European contact to the present day. 970.4

The Native peoples of the Pacific Northwest : initial European contact. 970.4

Native picture writing. 411.09701

The Natural ecology of water. 574.5

The Natural environment. 917.13

Natural gas in Alberta. 665

Nature adapts to the city. 574.5

Nature in the neighbourhood. 574.5

The New north. 970.4

New ways in a new land. 386.0971

The Newspaper : part 2. 070

The Newspaper : part 1. 070

The Newspaper business. 971.3

Newsprint in Quebec. 676.09714

Nickel mining in Manitoba. 622

The Night before Christmas. F

Nobel Hercules. 292

Le Noël de la famille Martin. F

Nomadic journey : three nomadic peoples. 910

The North American buffalo. 599

North West Mounted Police : the Klondike Gold Rush. 363.20971

North West Mounted Police : the long march west. 363.20971

The North West Mounted Police - the Rebellion of 1885. 363.20971

Northern development at what cost? 970.5

The Northern territories. 917.12

The Northland. 330.9712

The Northwest Mounted Police. 363.20971

Notre planète : la terre. 525

Title Index

Un nouvel ordre economique international : "parlons-en". 338.91

La Nouvelle-France. 971.01

Nova Scotia. 917.16

Nova Scotia poultry farming. 636.5

Nuclear energy. 621.48

Nurse of Newfoundland. 920

Nursing : the challenge of caring. 610.73

Nutrition - a new look. 641.1

Nutrition and health. 641.1

Nutrition et croissance de l'arbre. 581.3

Objects in our lives. 970.3

Les Objets disparus. 160.76

Observing by hearing, tasting, smelling, touching. 152.1

Observing by seeing : colours purple, orange, green. 152.1

Observing by seeing : colours black, white, brown. 152.1

Observing by seeing : shapes and sizes. 516

Of the farm. 407

Of the horse. 407

Of the land. 407

Ogoki native people visit the city. 370.19

Oil in Alberta. 665

Les oiseaux des villes. 598.2

Old age makeup. 792

The Old map mystery. 372.6

On Canadian roads. 388.30971

On Canadian waters. 386.0971

The One-horned mountain goat. 398.209701

One kitten for Kim. F

Ontario : the north, transportation and recreation. 917.13

Ontario. 917.13

L'Ontario. 917.13

Ontario. 917.13

Ontario's heritage. 971.3

Ontario's heritage. 971.3

Opiates. 615

Orchard City (Kelowna, B.C.). 917.11

Orchids of Eastern North America. 584

Les Organismes et le milieu. 574.5

Orientation & compass. 796.5

L'orientation de la carte. 912

Orienteering. 796.5

Origins and early history of English. 420.9

Oshawa, Ontario. 917.13

Ottawa - the urban community. 917.13

Ottawa - Canada's capital. 917.13

Ottawa and the provinces : issues, choices and values. 342.4

Otter trawling. 639

Our discovery of the universe. 523.1

Our dual heritage. 971.5

Our ever-changing earth. 551

Our five senses of touch. 612

Our journey into space. 523.4

Our place in the universe. 523.1

Our shrinking world. 380

L'ours et les deux compagnons. 440.7

L'ours noir. 599

L'ours polaire. 599

Outdoor cooking. 613.6

Title Index

Outdoor survival kit. 613.6

Outline maps of Canada. 912

Outline maps of the world : part 2 : Europe and Africa. 912

Outline maps of the world : part 3 : Asia and Australia. 912

Outline maps of the world : part 1 : the Americas. 912

An Overview of the Niagara Fruit Belt. 333.7

Ovulation - mammifères. 591.1

The Owl and the lemming : Eskimo legend. 398.2

Painless Parker. 920

Painting a panelled door. 698.3

Le paon de nuit. 595.7

Paper hanging application. 698.6

Le papillon monarque. 595.7

La Parade du Père Noël à Toronto. 394.09713

Parallel line development. 671.2

Paris. 720.944

Parliament : making and changing laws. 328.71

Parliament buildings. 328.71

Parliamentary government. 328.71

Parties and elections. 329.971

Partis et elections. 329.971

Passover. 296.4

Pattern development by triangulation. 671.2

Pattern of embryo development. 612.6

Patterns of life. 574.509712

Paul and Pauline Visit Alberta. 917.123

Paul and Pauline visit British Columbia. 917.11

Paul and Pauline visit Manitoba and Saskatchewan. 917.12

Paul and Pauline visit New Brunswick and Prince Edward Island. 917.15

Paul and Pauline visit Nova Scotia and Newfoundland. 917.16

Paul and Pauline visit Ontario. 917.13

Paul and Pauline visit Quebec. 917.14

Paul-Emile Borduas. 759.11

Paul-Emile Borduas. 759.11

La pêche à la Seine (Ecossaise et Danoise). 639

Pensez "sécurité". 614.8

The People and their work. 914.91

People of the North Pacific Coast. 970.4

People of the Plains. 970.4

People of the sub-Arctic. 970.4

Pepper's Christmas. F

Perching birds. 598.2

Periods, question marks, and exclamation marks. 421

Perseverance. 179

Peru 1 : life in the Andes. 918.5

Peter and the wolf. 398.20947

La Petite marchande aux allumettes. F

Les peuplades de la Côte Nord-Ouest. 970.4

Le Peuple Canadien et son environnement. 769

Phases of the moon. 523.3

Physical setting. 917.12

Pick the picture. 160.76

Pictou, Nova Scotia. 917.16

The Pill. 613.9

Pin point passing. 796.9

Pioneer Christmas. 971.3

The Pioneer community. 971.3

Title Index

The Pioneer community. 971.3

Pioneer entertainment. 971.3

Pioneer family life. 971.3

Pioneer homes and schools in Eastern Canada. 971.3

Pioneer inventions. 971.3

Pioneer life in the Maritimes : part 1. 971.5

Pioneer life in the Maritimes. part 2. 971.5

Pioneer life on the Prairies (1812-1900). 971.2

Pioneer life on the Prairies (1900-1912). 971.2

Pioneers : part 1. 971

Les pioneers des Prairies (1812-1900). 971.2

Les pionniers des Maritimes : 1ère partie. 971.5

Les pionniers des Maritimes : 2e partie. 971.5

Les pionniers des Prairies (1900-1912). 917.2

Les pionniers du Haut-Canada. 971.3

Les piquants du Porc-Epic. 398.209701

Pistons, oil and fuel pumps. 629.22

Pitch, stress and juncture. 421

Places preseving our heritage. 971.0074

The Planet we live on. 525

Planning and preparing meals. 642

Planning for future use. 917.13

Plant communities, wasteland wildflowers. 582

Plant communities, woodlot and wetlands. 581.971

Plants of the Arctic. 581.9712

Plants, sponges, coelenterates. 574.92

Plants, sponges, coelenterates. 574.92

Le plongeon à collier. 598.2

The Pocket gophers. 599

Un Poids - une masse. 389

Point Pelee National Park. 917.13

The Polar bear. 599

The Police force : behind the scenes. 363.2

The Police force : part of the community. 363.2

The Police officer. 363.2

Political life. 320.951

Les poneys : petits et grands. 599

Les populations. 591.5

Populations. 591.5

Port city : Halifax. 387.109716

Port of Halifax. 387.109716

The Port of St. John. 387.109715

Port of Thunder Bay. 386.09713

Port of Toronto. 386.09713

The Port of Toronto. 386.09713

The Port of Vancouver. 387.109711

La position de la lune. 523.3

Pottery : hand building techniques. 738.1

Pourquoi les pieds-noirs ne font jamais de mal aux souris. 398.209701

Pourquoi prend-on de la drogue? 613.8

The Praire provinces. 917.12

Prairie homestead. 301.450971

The Prairie region. 917.12

Pre-natal development. 612.6

The Predators. 598.2

Predators. 598.2

Le premier saumon. 398.209701

Premiers soins en forêt. 614.8

Prince Edward Island National Park. 917.17

Principaux signaux de détresse. 384

Principes de canôtage. 797.1

Title Index

Principles of kitchen management. 640

Principles of magnetism. 538.01

Le Printemps et l'été : ce qu'ils sont. 525

Problems of land use in urban fringe – urban shadow areas. 333.7

Problems of urban environment. 301.34

The Process of reproduction. 591.1

Le Processus de reproduction. 591.1

Producing graphics for slides and filmstrips. 778.2

Producing your own instructional audio-visual programme. 371.33

Producing your own slide program. 371.33

Le projecteur cinématographie de 16 mm : 3e partie. 778.2

Le projecteur cinématographique de 16 mm. : 2e partie. 778.2

Le projecteur cinematographique de 16 mm: 1ère partie. 778.2

Prologue (1759-1867). C810.9

Une promenade en traineau. 372.6

Proper bush clothing. 646

La protection de l'environnement. 333.9

The Province of Quebec : the Appalachian region. 917.14

The Province of Quebec : the Laurentian region. 917.14

The Province of Quebec : the St. Lawrence region. 917.14

Les Provinces des Prairies. 917.12

Les Provinces Maritimes. 917.15

Provincial government 354.71

Puberty : parts 1 & 2. 970.3

Puberty. 612.6

Public transportation in the city. 388.409713

The Puffer. 411

Pulp and paper. 676

Pulp and paper manufacturing in Newfoundland. 676.09718

Puss 'n Boots. 398.20944

Put them in order. 160.76

Pysanky. 914.7

Quand je serai grand. 152.4

Le Québec. 917.14

Quebec. 917.14

Le Quebec : les Applaches. 917.14

Le Quebec : la Plaine du Saint-Laurent. 917.14

Le Quebec : le Plateau laurentien. 917.14

Quebec and Ontario : old colony and new outpost. 971

Quebec City, Quebec. 917.14

Queen Charlotte Islands. 917.11

Queen Charlotte Islands. 917.11

Qu'est-ce que la fumée? 614.7

Qu'est-ce que l'aide au developpement international? 338.91

Qu'est-ce que l'hygiène alimentaire? 641.1

Qu'est-ce qui est blanc ou jaune, et qui fait marcher les doigts? 384.6025

Qu'est-ce qui manque? 160.76

Qu'est-ce qui ne va pas? 160.76

Qu'est-ce qu'on peut faire de ca? 745.5

Qu'est-ce qu'UNICEF? 362.706

Quotation marks and the apostrophe. 421

The Raccoon. 599

Radial line development. 671.2

The Raftsmen. 784.40971

Rail transportation in Canada : the early days. 385.0971

Title Index

Rail transportation in Canada : today. 385

Rails across Canada. 385.0971

Railway city : Winnipeg. 917.127

The Rajah's garden. 398.20954

Raquettes indiennes. 685

Le rat de ville et le rat des champs. 440.7

Rébellion dans le Bas-Canada. 971.03

Rébellion dans le Haut-Canada. 971.03

Rebellion in Lower Canada. 971.03

Rebellion in Upper Canada. 971.03

Recreation : the Canadian city. 301.34

Reform in the Atlantic colonies. 971.5

Les réformistes des colonies de l'Atlantique. 971.5

Regardent les étoiles. 523.8

Le régime parlementaire. 328.71

Regina. 917.124

Regina, Sask. 917.124

Les régions forestières du Canada. 917.1

Le remède de la vie. 398.209701

Remembrance Day. 394.2

Le renard et la cigogne. 440.7

Le renard et le bouc. 440.7

Les Repas et le budget. 641.1

Le repérage électronique du poisson. 639

The Rescue of Julius the donkey. 372.6

The Rhythm and sympto-thermal methods. 613.9

Rice growing in China. 633.0951

Ride safely to school. 614.8

Rideau Canal. 386.09713

Riflery. 799.3

Rio de Janerio. 918.1

The Rise of Socialism in Canada. 320.50971

River city : Montreal. 917.14

Riverina (Murray-Darling Basin). 919.44

Les roches et les minéraux. 549

Rockhounding. 796.5

The Rocky Mountains. 599.097

The Rocky Mountains national parks. 917.11

Rodents, rabbits and hares. 599

The Role of the Public Service. 350.971

Roman provinces and Pompeii. 722

The Romantic era. 820.9

Rongeurs, lapins et lièvres. 599

Royal Canadian Mint. 737.4

Royal Winter Fair. 630.74

Royal Winter Fair. 630.74

Rrrrr. 152.4

The Runaway. 372.6

Rural China. 631.0951

Le sac de M. Danlune. 372.6

Safety on the slopes. 614.8

Safety on the street. 614.8

Saguenay-Lake St. Jean - the river. 971.14

Saguenay-Lake St. John - the Lake Region. 971.14

Saint John - Canada's first city. 917.15

Saint John River Valley - Edmunston to Kings Landing. 971.15

Saint John River Valley - Mactaquac to Saint John. 971.15

Sainte-Marie-among-the-Hurons : part I. 971.3

Title Index

Sainte-Marie-among-the-Hurons. 971.3

Sainte-Marie-aux-Hurons. 971.3

Salmon. 970.3

Salmon fishing in B.C. 639.09711

Sam Slice tells about snack foods. 641.1

Samuel de Champlain. 971.01

Samuel de Champlain. 971.01

Saskatchewan. 917.124

Le saumon atlantique. 597

Le saumon du Pacifique. 597

Scarecrow and pumpkin. F

Scenic wonderland. 917.1

School and recreation. 971.3

School bus safety. 614.8

School safety. 614.8

The Science Centre. 507.4

Scies à main, ciseaux et limes. 621.9

Scraping tools and abrasives. 621.9

Screwdrivers, wrenches, sheet metal, & welding. 621.9

Sculpture esquimau. 736

Les scuptures sur argilite des Haïdas. 736

Seacoast environments of Japan. 915.2

The Seaway. 386.0971

The Seaway and its ships. 386.0971

A Seaway port. 386.09713

The Second Métis uprising, 1885. 971.05

The Secret in the barn. F

Sécurité en hiver. 614.8

Seigneurs and seigneuries. 333.3

Seigneurs et seigneuries. 333.3

Seine netting : Scottish and Danish methods. 639

Selected wildflowers : Western Canada. 582.09712

Selected wildflowers : eastern Canada. 582.0971

Un seul chaton. F

The Seven Years' War. 971.01

Shakespeare : the man, the times and the plays. 822.3

The Shaman goes to the moon. 398.2

Shanghai : city life in China. 915.1

The Shape of the earth. 525

The Shape of things : part 1. 741.2

The Shape of things : part 2. 741.2

Shapes designed by man. 516

Shapes in nature. 516

Shaping the Canadian nation. 769

Sharing heritage. 917.1

Sheep industry. 636.3

Ships and power. 386.0971

Shoot to score. 796.9

The shopping centre. 658.8

A Shopping centre. 658.8

Shorebirds. 598.2

Short cut to trouble. 362.7

The Silliest man in Italy. 398.20945

Sir John A. Macdonald : part 1. 971.04

Sir John A. Macdonald : part 2. 971.04

Sir John A. Macdonald (1ère partie). 971.04

Sir John A. Macdonald (2e partie). 971.04

Skating. 796.9

Sketching the New World : Maritime scenes. 971

Le ski - mise en train pré-saisonnière. 796.9

Le ski - mouvements de base (1ère partie). 796.9

Le ski - mouvements de base (2e partie). 796.9

Title Index

Skiing - pre-season conditioning. 796.9

Skiing : basic skills : part 1. 796.9

Skiing - basic skills : part 2. 796.9

Sleeping Beauty : a French legend. 398.20944

Sleigh ride. 407

Small boat safety. 614.8

Smell, taste and touch. 612

The Smoking epidemic. 613.8

Soldering methods. 671.5

Les solvants. 613.8

Solvents. 613.8

Sources of electricity. 621.3

Sources of power. 333.7

Southern Ontario. 917.13

The Sparkling imagination. 372.6

Spider ecology. 595

Spiders. 595

Spirits and monsters. 299

Sports and recreation. 796

Spring. 525

Spring and summer : what they mean. 525

Spring is coming. 525

Spring journey. 970.4

Spring wildflowers : southern Prairie provinces. 582.09712

Spring wildflowers : southern Ontario and Quebec. 528.09713

Spring wildflowers : northern Prairie provinces. 582.09712

Spring wildflowers : the Maritimes. 582.09715

Spring wildflowers : British Columbia. 582.09711

Spring wildflowers : Newfoundland. 582.09718

Spring wildflowers : Northern Ontario and Quebec. 582.09713

Spring wildflowers of eastern North America. 582.097

Square stories. 389

Squirrels. 599

St. Jean, Port Joli, Quebec. 917.14

St. John's, Newfoundland. 917.18

St. Laurent to the present. 971.06

St. Valentine's Day. 394.2

Stage movement and directing. 792

Staking a claim. 971.2

Standardizing measurement. 389

Stanley Park. 917.11

Starting your own weather station. 551.6

Stone Age man I : an archaeological dig. 913

Stop acting like a baby. 152.4

The Story of Atlantic salmon. 597

The Story of Greedy Pan. 398.209701

The Story of how to eat to grow tall. 641.1

The Story of mammals. 599

The Story of New France. 971.01

The Story of Pacific salmon. 597

The Story of Thanksgiving. 394.2

Strangers to Canada. 301.450971

The Structure of government. 354.712

Struggle for the new land. 971

Les stupéfiants opiacés. 615

Suburban site. 301.34

Les sucres. 664

Sugar and coral coast (Queensland). 919.43

Summary and conclusion. 617.6

Summer. 525

Title Index

Summer - reflections on Lake Blue Water. 525

Summer days. 970.4

Summer survival. 613.6

Summer wildflowers of eastern North America. 582.097

The Sun dance of the Plains Indians. 398.209701

Sunday in the park. 796

Super Jesus. 232.9

The Superlative horse. 398.20951

The Supermarket. 658.8

Surprise adventure. 372.6

Surrender. 940.54

A Survey. 382.0971

Survival in the bush. 613.6

Swimming safety. 614.8

Swimming strokes. 797.2

Sydney. 919.44

The Symbol in Indian art. 709.01

Syria : the little camel. 398.2095691

Un Système de mesure. 389

Team play. 796.9

Techniques antinoyade. 614.8

Teenage father. 301.41

Teenage mother. 301.41

Teeth : a new look. 617.6

The Television receiver. 621.388

Telling stories with puppets and masks. 791.5

Temperature. 389

Temperature and mass. 389

The Terrible mud of Flanders (1916). 940.4

Les Territoires du Nord-Ouest. 917.12

The Test and bottles. 179

Thanksgiving foods. 971.3

Thanksgiving in pioneer Canada. 971.3

Thanksgiving today. 394.2

That's not fair. 152.4

The 16 mm film projector : part 1. 778.2

The Facts about venereal disease. 616.9

Things dangerous to eat. 614.8

Think safety. 614.8

Threatened and endangered wildlife. 639

Threatened and endangered wildlife. 639

Three families of Montreal. 917.14

Three in a haunted house. 372.6

Thunder Bay on tour. 917.13

Thunder Bay's industrial harbour. 386.09713

Ti-Jean and the lumberjacks. 398.2

Ti-Jean et les bûcherons. 440.7

Ti-Jean saves the harvest. 398.2

The Ticker. 411

The Tiger and the rabbit. 398.2097295

Timber. 338.10971

Timber City : Vancouver. 917.11

A Time of migration and troubles. 301.4509711

To be alone. 152.4

To be together. 176

To measure volume. 389

Toads and frogs of Eastern Canada. 597

Tobacco farming in Ontario. 633

Today and tomorrow. 380.5

Too many laws... or too few? 340

Title Index

Toronto - growth, change & progress. 917.13

Totem pole tales. 736

Totem poles. 736

Touch my world. 152.1

Tournevis, clefs, tôle et soudure. 621.9

Tout le monde a peur de quelque chose. 152.4

Toward a new international economic order. 382.1

The Town of Fort Steele. 971.1

Traditional Eskimo life. 970.4

Traffic safety. 614.8

Tragedy and triumph. 910

The Transistor. 621.3815

Transistor application. 621.3815

Transit safety. 614.8

Transportation. 380.5

Transportation. 388.409713

Transportation and communication in Japan. 380

Transportation in the Canadian Shield. 380.5

Transportation in Toronto. 388.409713

Transportation today : by land. 388

Transportation today : by air and water. 380.5

A Trip through early day Canada. 971

Trip to the sugar bush. 664

Trois familles de Montréal. 917.14

Trois repas par jour. 642

The Trouble with alcohol. 613.8

Trousse de survie. 613.6

Trout farming in Manitoba. 639.097127

Trouvons autre chose. 745.5

Trouvons les ressemblance. 160.76

Trucks in Canada. 388.34

Tubal ligation and vasectomy. 613.9

The Twentieth century : 1929 - present. 820.9

The Twentieth century : 1900-1929. 820.9

Two cultures. 325.71

The Two frogs : a Japanese legend. 398.20952

Un de deux. 591.1

Unité de surface. 389

Les Unités de volume. 389

Uranium mining in Ontario. 622

Urashima Taro the fisherlad. 398.20952

Urban culture. 301.34

Urban economy. 330.12

Urban government. 352.071

Urban life in Japan (no. 1). 915.2

Urban life in Japan (no. 2). 915.2

The Urban revolution : the first cities. 301.34

Urbanization : the new accent on cities. 301.34

Using a potter's wheel. 738.1

Using capital letters. 421

Using punctuation marks. 421

Using the drill press. 621.9

Using them safely. 615

Vaginal spermicides and the condom. 613.9

The Value of a boiled egg. 398.2095694

Values : yours and theirs. 174

Vancouver. 917.11

Vancouver Island. 917.11

Vanity. 179

La Veille de Noël. F

La Vérendrye. 971.01

Title Index

La Vérendrye. 971.01

Versailles and Portugal. 728.8
Victoria. 917.11
Victoria, B.C. 917.11
Victoria, B.C. 917.11
Victoria Day. 394.2
The Victorian era. 820.9
La Vie commence - plantes et poissons. 574.1
La Vie commence - grenoiulles. 597
La vie dans la ruche. 595.7
La vie dans le Haut-Canada vers 1860. 971.3
La vie quotidienne d'un petit Indien. 970.3
La vie quotidienne d'une petite Indienne. 970.3
Vient de - devient. 574.3
Le Village. 971.3
The Village broom shop. 971.3
Village de pêche. 917.16
Un village du Haut-Canada. 971.3
Une ville arctique sur un delta. 917.12
La ville de Fort Steele. 971.1
Une ville du bois d'oeuvre. 917.11
Ville ferroviaire (Winnipeg). 917.127
Ville fluviale (Montreal). 917.14
Ville fruitière. 917.11
Ville portuaire (Halifax). 387.109716
Vision. 612
A Visit to a farm. 630.1
A Visit to a garden. 635
A Visit to a pond. 574.92
Visit to a wheat farm. 633.0971

A Visit to the airport. 387.7
A Visit to the seashore. 574.92
A Visit to the woods. 574.5
A Visit with the vet. 636.089
Une visite à l'aéroport. 387.7
Une visite au Palais du Parlement. 328.71
Visiting a pioneer cemetery. 971.3
Visiting an early day Canadian town house. 971.3
Visiting early Canadian churches. 726.0971
Visiting pioneer Canada. 971.3
Vivre ensemble. 176
Vivre seule. 152.4
Volcanic landforms. 551.2
Volcanoes. 914.91
Un Volume - une capacité. 389
Volume - capacity. 389
Volume and capacity. 389
Volume units. 389
Le vote au Canada. 324.71
Voting in Canada. 324.71
Vous et votre personnalité. 155.2

Walls and bonds. 693.2
The War of 1812. 971.03
The War of 1812. 971.03
The War to end war (1914). 940.4
Water rescue. 614.8
Water safety. 614.8
Waterfowl. 598.2
The way things used to be. 970.4
The Way to cook fish. 641.6

Title Index

The Way we live today. 917.12

The Weaver. 971.3

Welding techniques. 671.5

The Welland Canal (historical). 386.09713

The Welland Canal (today). 386.09713

Wet cement and the radio. 179

What are laws? 340

What do they have in common. 160.76

What is a community? 301.34

What is a spider? 595

What is international development assistance? 338.91

What is money? 332.4

What is nutrition? 641.1

What is smoke? 614.7

What is UNICEF? 362.706

What on earth! : a look at plants. 581.97

What pet for me. 636

What the sun means to the earth. 523.7

What they do. 615

What's in a dairy barn. 637

What's missing? 160.76

What's white and yellow and read all over? 025

What's wrong here? 160.76

Wheat. 338.10971

Wheat farming. 633.0971

Wheels and wings. 380.5

When I grow up. 152.4

When the sap runs. 664

Where they come from. 615

Where to find it. 701

Which group will they go to? 160.76

White men in the Arctic. 971.2

The Whooping crane : [a study of a vanishing species]. 598.2

Why a porcupine has quills. 398.209701

Why do people take drugs? 613.8

Why do trees grow? 581.3

Why governments? 342

Why the spider has a narrow waist. 398.2096

Wiggle nose and long ears. 599

Wild flowers of spring. 582

Wild flowers of summer & autumn. 582

Wings over Canada. 387.70971

Winnipeg. 917.127

Winnipeg General Strike, 1919. 331.890971

Winnipeg, Man. 917.127

Winnipeg, Man. 917.127

Winter. 525

Winter - ice fire lights. 525

Winter camp. 970.4

Winter safety. 614.8

Winter survival. 613.6

Wintering in the bush. 796.54

Wire sculpture with a twist. 731

The Wishing bowl (China). 398.20951

Work and trade. 971.3

Working between centers on the lathe. 621.9

Working in a bakery. 664

Working in a meat packing plant. 664

World of Jack Miner : the pioneer naturalist, 1965-1944. 920

The World of microscopy. 578

World War I and disillusionment. 810.9

Title Index

World War II - an increasing conscience.   810.9

Writing systems.   411

A Yangtze rice commune.   915.1

You and your personality.   155.2

Your anger.   152.4

Your envy.   152.4

Your fear.   152.4

Your frustration.   152.4

The Yukon.   917.12

Part Four

Series List

SERIES INDEX

1837 Rebellions : $54.05
    The 1837 Rebellion in Lower Canada.

    The 1837 Rebellion in Upper Canada.

A la découverte de l'écologie : $85.00   M-L.
    Ecology : exploration and discovery
    Les communautés végétales et animales.

    Ecology : exploration and discovery
    Les cycles de nourriture.

    Ecology : exploration and discovery
    Les ecosystèmes.

    Ecology : exploration and discovery
    L'Habitat.

    Ecology : exploration and discovery
    Les Organismes et le milieu.

    Ecology : exploration and discovery
    Les populations.

A Question of values   NFB.
    Points de vue
    To be alone.

Activités de plein air : survie : $85.00   M-L.
    Outdoor survival
    Faire un feu et construire un abri.

    Outdoor survival
    Premiers soins en forêt.

    Principaux signaux de détresse.

    Outdoor survival
    Principes de canôtage.

    Outdoor survival
    Techniques antinoyade.

    Outdoor survival
    Trousse de survie.

Adventures with map and compass : $65.95
                                                UEVA (Can),
    The Compass.

    The Map.

Adventures with map and compass : $65.95   SHN,
                                                UEVA (Can),
    Orienteering.

Africa : $30.00   FMS,
    African meat-eaters.

    Animals together.

    Large animals of Africa.

Agriculture in Canada : $55.65   Sch. Ch.,
    Berry farming in N.B.

    Cattle ranching in Alberta.

    Fruit farming in British Columbia.

    Irrigated farming in Alberta.

    Mixed farming in Manitoba.

    Nova Scotia poultry farming.

    Tobacco farming in Ontario.

Allô! Parlons téléphone : $96.00   Int. Cin.,
    Hello! Getting together with the telephone
    Allô, Monsieur Bell!

    Hello! Getting together with telephone
    Et maintenant, tous ensemble.

    Hello! Getting together with the telephone
    Les Experts en téléphonie.

    Hello! Getting together with the telephone
    Qu'est-ce qui est blanc ou jaune, et qui fait marcher les doigts?

American literature : $158.40   SHN,
    Civil War and second thoughts.

    A Declaration of faith.

    World War I and disillusionment.

    World War II - an increasing conscience.

Series List

Les amérindiens ; $85.00 M-L.
   The Native peoples of North America
     Les amérindiens de la côte du pacifique : jusqu'à
     l'arrivée des europeens.

Les amérindiens : $85.00 M-L.
   The Native peoples of North America
     Les amérindiens de la côte du pacifique : depuis
     l'arrivée des europeens.

   The Native peoples of North America
     Les amérindiens des forêts de l'est : jusqu'á
     l'arrivée des europeens.

   The Native peoples of North America
     Les amérindiens des forêts de l'est : depuis
     l'arrivée des europeens.

   The Native peoples of North America
     Les amérindiens des Grandes Plaines : jusqu'à
     l'arrivée des Europeens.

   The Native peoples of North America
     Les amérindiens des Grandes Plaines : depuis
     l'arrivée des europeens.

Animal adventures with two endings : $49.50 M-L.
   The Adventures of bunny rabbit.

   The Adventures of kitty cat.

   The Adventures of puppy dog.

   Animal pets.

Animal stories from other lands : $85.00 M-L.
   How the deer got fire.

   How the leopard got its spots.

   The Mandarin and the butterflies.

   Peter and the wolf.

   Puss 'n Boots.

   The Tiger and the rabbit.

Animals - a close-up look : $75.00 (S) M-L.
   Les animaux - tableaux réalistes
     Buffalo, buffalo, buffalo.

Animals - a close-up look : $75.00 M-L.
   Les animaux - tableaux réalistes
     Donkeys, donkeys, donkeys.

   Les animaux - tableaux réalistes
     Goats, goats, goats.

Animals of Canada : $72.00 NFB.
   The Beaver.

   The Black bear.

   The Cat family.

   The North American buffalo.

   The Pocket gophers.

   The Polar bear.

   The Raccoon.

   Squirrels.

Les Animaux - tableaux réalistes : $75.00 M-L.
   Animals - a close-up look
     Les Bestiaux de l'ouest.

   Animals - a close-up look
     Les Bisons des plaines.

   Animals - a close-up look
     Les Chèvres en vedette.

   Animals - a close-up loo
     Les poneys : petits et grands.

Les Animaux - tableaux réalists : $75.00 M-L.
   Animals - a close-up look
     Les Anes domestiques.

Applications of electricity : $75.00 (S) M-L.
   Domestic circuits.

Les arbres m'ont raconté : $86.00 Int. Cin.,
   Tales from the treetops
     Le chasseur qui partit.

   Tales from the treetops
     Commencement.

(S) = See also Supplement Series Index.

Series List

Les arbres m'ont raconté : $86.00　　　Int. Cin.,
　Tales from the treetops
　　L'histoire de Pan de Glouton.

　Tales from the treetops
　　Pourquoi les pieds-noirs ne font jamais de mal aux souris.

Archaelogy : $34.50　　　RBM,
　Developing an Iroquoian village site.

　The Iroquoian people.

Arctic portrait : $49.00　　　Int. Cin.,
　Animals of the Arctic.

　Hunters of the Arctic.

　Plants of the Arctic.

The Arctic through Eskimo eyes : $86.00　　Int. Cin.,
　My escape from death.

　Spirits and monsters.

　The way things used to be.

　The Way we live today.

Art : $69.00　　　R.B.M.,
　Elements of pottery.

　Pottery : hand building techniques.

　Using a potter's wheel.

　Wire sculpture with a twist.

L'art indigène　　　NFB,
　Native arts
　　L'art graphique esquimau.

　Native arts
　　L'art sculptural esquimau.

　Native arts
　　Masques des Indiens de l'Amérique du Nord.

　Native arts
　　Les scuptures sur argilite des Haïdas.

Les artistes canadiens [I]　　　NFB. c1961.-
　Artists of Canada : series I
　　Alfred Pellan.

　Artists of Canada : series I
　　Artistes de la côte canadienne du Pacifique.

　Artists of Canada : series I
　　Cornelius Krieghoff.

　Artists of Canada : series I
　　David Milne.

　Artists of Canada : series I
　　Homer Watson.

Les artistes canadiens [II]　　　NFB,
　Artists of Canada : series II
　　Le Groupe des Sept.

　Artists of Canada : series II
　　Jean-Paul Riopelle.

　Artists of Canada : series II
　　Lawren S. Harris.

　Artists of Canada : series II
　　Paul-Emile Borduas.

An Artist's notebook : $27.00　　　B&R,
　The Shape of things : part 1.

　The Shape of things : part 2.

　Where to find it.

Artists of Canada : series I　　　NFB,
Les artistes canadiens [I]
　Alfred Pellan.

　Les artistes canadiens [I]
　　Artists of Pacific Canada.

　Les artistes canadiens [I]
　　Cornelius Krieghoff.

　Les artistes canadiens : [I]
　　David Milne.

　Les artistes canadiens : [series II]
　　Emily Carr.

　Les artistes canadiens [I]
　　Homer Watson.

Series List

Artists of Canada : series II   NFB.
  Les artistes canadiens [II]
    The Group of Seven.

    James Vilson Morrice.

  Les artistes canadiens [II]
    Jean-Paul Riopelle.

  Les artistes canadiens [II]
    Lawren S. Harris.

  Les artistes canadiens [II]
    Paul-Emile Borduas.

Atlantic Canada : $63.00   NFB.
  Le Canada Atlantique
    Atlantic Canada : New Brunswick.

  Le Canada Atlantique
    Atlantic Canada : Nova Scotia.

  Le Canada Atlantique
    Atlantic Canada : Prince Edward Island.

  Le Canada Atlantique
    Atlantic Canada : geography.

  Le Canada Atlantique
    Atlantic Canada : Island of Newfoundland.

  Le Canada Atlantique
    Atlantic Canada : Labrador.

  Le Canada Atlantique
    Atlantic Canada : economy.

Attitudes morales : $75.00   M-L.
  Moral decision-making
    La culpabilité.

  Moral decision-making
    La générosité.

  Moral decision-making
    L'honnêteté.

  Moral decision-making
    L'Hostilité.

  Moral decision-making
    L'intégrité.

Australia : $38.50   VCI.
  An Australian city : Sydney (no. II).

  An Australian city : Canberra.

  An Australian city : Sydney (no. I).

Australia : $79.95   EDU.
  The Aborigine.

  Frontier mining and grazing (the Outback).

  Riverina (Murray-Darling Basin).

  Sheep industry.

  Sugar and coral coast (Queensland).

  Sydney.

Auto mechanics : $75.00 (s)   M-L.
  Care of wheels and tires.

  Driving mechanism.

  Pistons, oil and and fuel pumps.

Basic photography : $69.00 (s)   R.B.M..
  The Camera.

  Film and filters.

Basic punctuation : $85.00   M-L.
  Commas.

  Periods, question marks, and exclamation marks.

  Pitch, stress and juncture.

  Quotation marks and the apostrophe.

  Using capital letters.

  Using punctuation marks.

Bird life of North America : $85.00   M-L.
  Birds and their environment.

  Fowl-like birds.

Series List

Bird life of North America : $85.00   M-L.
  Perching birds.

  Predators.

  Shorebirds.

  Waterfowl.

Birds of Canada : $54.00 (s)   NFB.
  The Canada goose.

  The Common loon.

  Hawks.

  The Kingfisher.

  The Whooping crane : [a study of a vanishing species].

Birds of North America : $56.00 (S)   FMS

Block parent : $20.00   LBE.
  Jimmie to the rescue.

  June's narrow escape.

  Short cut to trouble.

British Columbia : $15.90   VCL.
  Stanley Park.

  Vancouver Island.

British literature : $225.00   SHN.
  The Elizabethan era.

British literature : $255.00   SHN.
  From puritan to Augustan.

  From the beginnings to Elizabeth.

  The Romantic era.

  Shakespeare : the man, the times and the plays.

  The Twentieth century : 1929 - present.

  The Twentieth century : 1900-1929.

British literature : $255.00   SHN.
  The Victorian era.

Canada : a nation built on trade : $60.00   McI.
  Fish.

  Fur.

  Minerals.

  A Survey.

  Timber.

  Wheat.

Canada and its regions : the geography of a changing land :$155.00   Int. Cin.
  Atlantic Canada.

  Central Canada : the people.

  Central Canada : the place.

  Introduction : the people and the land.

  The Mountainous West.

  The Northland.

  The Prairie region.

  Urbanization : the new accent on cities.

Canada and the Second World War : a nation comes of age : $63.25   SHN.
  From mobilization to the battle of the Atlantic.

Canada and the Second World War : a nation comes of age : $82.00   SHN.
  Home front to victory.

Le Canada Atlantique   NFB.
  Atlantic Canada
    Le Canada atlantique : L'Île de Terre-Neuve.

  Atlantic Canada
    Le Canada atlantique : le Nouveau-Brunswick.

Series List

Le Canada Atlantique   NFB.
  Atlantic Canada
    Le Canada atlantique : le Labrador.

  Atlantic Canada
    Le Canada atlantique : économie.

  Atlantic Canada
    Le Canada atlantique : géographie.

  Atlantic Canada
    Le Canada atlantique : l'Ile du Prince-Edouard.

  Atlantic Canada
    Le Canada atlantique : la Nouvelle Ecosse.

Canada : coast to coast with Paul and Pauline $59.50
    Lea.,
  Paul and Pauline Visit Alberta.

  Paul and Pauline visit British Columbia.

  Paul and Pauline visit Manitoba and Saskatchewan.

  Paul and Pauline visit New Brunswick and Prince Edward Island.

  Paul and Pauline visit Nova Scotia and Newfoundland.

  Paul and Pauline visit Ontario.

  Paul and Pauline visit Quebec.

Le Canada en guerre : l'histoire militaire d'un peuple pacifique : $86.00   Int. Cin.,
  Canadians at War : the military story of a peaceful people
  La Canada dans l'Empire Britannique.

  Canadian at war : the military story of a peaceful people
  La Défense du Canada dans un monde en évolution.

  Canadians at war : the military story of a peaceful people
  D'une Guerre à l'autre.

  Canadians at war: the military story of a peaceful people.
  La Lutte pour une terre nouvelle.

Canada : "Il est né d'une race fiée" : $85.00   M-L.
  Canada : "The true north strong and free"
  Les Territoires du Nord-Ouest.

  Canada : "the true north strong and free"
  La Columbie Britannique.

  Canada : "the true north strong and free"
  L'Ontario.

  Canada: "The true north strong and free"
  Les Provinces des Prairies.

  Canada : "the true north strong and free"
  Les Provinces Maritimes.

  Canada : "the true north strong and free"
  Le Québec.

Canada on the move : $76.00   McI.,
  On Canadian roads.

  On Canadian waters.

  Rails across Canada.

  Vings over Canada.

Canada : the true north strong and free : $85.00 (s) M
  Canada : il est né d'une race fière
  The Atlantic provinces.

  Canada : il est né d'une race fière
  The Northern territories.

  Canada : the true north strong and free
  Ontario.

  Canada : il est né d'une race fière
  The Praire provinces.

  Canada : il est né d'une race fière
  Quebec.

Series List

Canada's heritage today : $102.00   McI.,
An Appetite for heritage.

Collecting my own heritage.

The Heritage puzzle.

Inventing a heritage.

Places preseving our heritage.

Sharing heritage.

Canada's living heritage : $86.00   Int. Cin.,
Le patrimoine vivant du Canada
Discovering our heritage.

Le patrimoine vivant du Canada
Frontier heritage.

Le patrimoine vivant du Canada
Ontario's heritage.

Le Patrimoine vivant du Canada
Ontario's heritage.

Le Patrimoine vivant du Canada
Our dual heritage.

Canada's North : $59.40   SHN,
Discovering the land.

Discovering the people.

Canada's Prime Ministers : a matter of style : $75.90   SHN,
Borden to St. Laurent.

Macdonald to Borden.

St. Laurent to the present.

Canadian-American relations : $82.00   SHN,
Canadian-American relations : part 2 : 1914-1963.

Canadian-American relations : part 1 : 1775-1914.

Canadian-American relations : part 3 : 1963 to the present.

The Canadian Arctic : $69.00   R.B.M.,
The Arctic today.

Days of the igloo.

The Eskimo and his work.

Geography of the Arctic.

Canadian cities   NFB,
Port city : Halifax.

Railway city : Winnipeg.

River city : Montreal.

Timber City : Vancouver.

Canadian clothing   VCL,
Clothing design.

Clothing manufacturing.

Canadian communities   NFB,
Arctic Delta town (Inuvik, N.W.T.).

Dairy farming community (Elmira, Ont.).

Fishing town (Port Bickerton, N.S.).

Mining town (Manitouwadge, Ont.).

Orchard City (Kelowna, B.C.).

Three families of Montreal.

Canadian community helpers : $15.90   Sch. Ch.,
A Day in the life of a letter carrier.

How a letter travels.

Canadian community studies ; $55.65   Sch. Ch.,
Flin Flon, Manitoba.

Canadian community studies : $55.65   Sch. Ch.,
Fredericton, New Brunswick.

Leroy, Saskatchewan.

Series List

Canadian community studies : $55.65   Sch. Ch.,
Marathon, Ontario.

Pictou, Nova Scotia.

St. Jean, Port Joli, Quebec.

Canadian community studies : $55.66   Sch. Ch.,
Oshawa, Ontario.

The Canadian flag : $65.00 (s)   Int. Cin.,
How Canada got its flag.
Canadian flags and how they are used.

Canadian folk culture : the Chinese : $79.00   RBM,
Chinese contribution to Canadian life.

Chinese cultural heritage.

Difficulties of Chinese immigrants.

The First Chinese communities in British Columbia.

Canadian folk culture : the Doukhobors : $79.00
    R.B.M.,
Doukhobor contribution to Canadian society.

Doukhobor immigrants in the West.

Doukhobor way of life.

A Time of migration and troubles.

Canadian folk culture : the Hutterites : $79.00 R.B.M.,
Hutterite contribution to Canadian society.

Hutterite persecution : 1526-1917.

Hutterite way of life.

Hutterites in Canada : 1917 - present.

Canadian folk culture : the Irish : $79.00   R.B.M.,
Irish contributions to Canadian life.

Irish cultural heritage.

Irish feuds and quarrels.

Canadian folk culture : the Irish : $79.00   R.B.M.,
Irish immigration.

Canadian folk culture : the Japanese : $79.00 R.B.M.,
The Japanese come to Canada.

Japanese contribution to Canadian society.

Japanese cultural heritage.

The Japanese during World War II.

Canadian history pictures   TBE,
Eskimos : part 2.

Historic costumes : part 1.

Indians : part II.

Pioneers : part 1.

Canadian holidays : $180.00 (s)   B & R,

Canadian Christmas : Christmas decorations.

Canadian christmas : festive foods.

Canadian Christmas : traditions of Christmas.

Christmas today.

Dominion Day.

Easter in Canada.

Hallowe'en in Canada.

Remembrance Day.

St. Valentine's Day.

The Story of Thanksgiving.

Thanksgiving foods.

Thanksgiving today.

Victoria Day.

Canadian Indian people   R.B.M.,
Indian arts and crafts.

Series List

Canadian Indian people   R.B.M.,
     Indians leaders and centres of renewal.

     Indians yesterday and today.

Canadian literature : $140.00   SHN,
     The Beginnings (1867-1929).

     A Coming of age (1950-present).

     The Emergence (1929-1950).

     Prologue (1759-1867).

Canadian mosaic   VCL,
     Calgary stampede.

     Flags, coats of arms, and floral emblems of Canada.

Canadian mosaic : $39.75   Sch. Ch.,
     Totem poles.

The Canadian mosaic : $105.00   M-L,
     Black Canadians.

     British Canadians.

     Chinese and Japanese Canadians.

     Cultures in conflict.

     European Canadians.

     French Canadians.

     Mosaic Canada.

     Native Canadians.

Canadian pioneer days : $128.00   B & R,
     Activities in pioneer days.

     Country life.

     Pioneer Christmas.

     Pioneer entertainment.

     Pioneer family life.

Canadian pioneer days : $128.00   B & R,
     Pioneer inventions.

     Thanksgiving in pioneer Canada.

     Visiting pioneer Canada.

Canadian ports : $31.80   Sch. Ch.,
     Port of Halifax.

     Port of Thunder Bay.

     The Port of Toronto.

     The Port of Vancouver.

Canadian Shield   NFB,
     Forestry in the Canadian Shield.

     Introducing the Canadian Shield.

     Transportation in the Canadian Shield.

Canadian stories and legends series   NFB,
     Légendes indiennes
         Glooscap and the four wishes.

     The Legend of the flying canoe.

     Légendes indiennes
         Naba-Cha and the Rocky Mountains.

     Why a porcupine has quills.

Canadian studies   Sch. Ch.,
     Royal Winter Fair.

Canadians : $27.95   UEVA (Can),
     Changing identity.

     Cities and towns.

     Scenic wonderland.

     Sports and recreation.

Series List

Canadians at war : the military story of a peaceful people : $86.00 Int. Cin.,
  Le Canada en guerre : l'histoire militaire d'un peuple pacifique.
  Canada in the British Empire.

  Le Canada en guerre : l'histoire militaire d'un peuple pacifique
  Defending Canada in a changing world.

  Le Canada en guerre : l'histoire militaire d'un peuple pacifique
  From war to war.

  Le Canada en guerre : l'histoire militaire d'un peuple pacifique
  Struggle for the new land.

Canadians in conflict NCM,
  Bread and roses : the struggle of the Canadian working women.

  Winnipeg General Strike, 1919.

Character awareness : $85.00 M-L.
  Courage.

  Deceit.

  Jealousy.

  Loyalty.

  Perseverance.

  Vanity.

Children of many lands : $54.00 NFB,
  Children of Gabon.

  Children of Greece.

  Children of Japan.

  Children of Northern Nigeria.

Les enfants du monde
  Children of Thailand.

Les enfants du monde
  Indian children of the Andes.

China CFM,
  Contemporary culture.

China : $23.85 Sch. Ch.,
  Life on a Chinese commune : part 2 : building, manufacturing, transport, schools and entertainment.

  Life on a Chinese commune : homes and farming.

  Rice growing in China.

China : $38.50 VCI.
  Hill and plain communes : North China.

  Shanghai : city life in China.

  A Yangtze rice commune.

China : $79.95 EDU.
  City life.

  Commune in the North.

  Commune in the South.

  Craft industries.

  Education.

  Political life.

China : $89.00 CFM,
  Agriculture, industry and transportation.

  Cities of China.

  Education and health.

  Monuments of the past.

  Rural China.

The Christmas classics : $75.00 M-L.
  Les contes de Noël
  The Birds' Christmas carol.

  Les contes de Noël
  Dickens' Christmas carol.

Series List

The Christmas classics : $75.00   M-L.
  Les contes de Noël
    The Legend of the Christmas tree.

  Les contes de Noël
    The Little match girl.

  Les contes de Noël
    The Night before Christmas.

Christmas tales from many lands : $75.00 (s) M-L,

  Les légendes de Noël des pays étrangers
    Germany : the nutcracker's happy Christmas.

  Les légendes de Noël des pays étrangers
    Ireland : O'Reilly's Christmas cap.

  Les légendes de Noël des pays étrangers
    Mexico : the humblest gift.

  Les légendes de Noël des pays étrangers
    Syria : the little camel.

Cities of Canada   R.B.M.,
  Calgary.

  The City of Halifax.

  Edmonton.

  Halifax - historic seaport.

  Ottawa - the urban community.

  Ottawa - Canada's capital.

  The Port of St. John.

  Regina.

  Saint John - Canada's first city.

  Toronto - growth, change & progress.

  Vancouver.

  Victoria.

  Winnipeg.

Cityscapes : $64.00   Int. Cin.,
  City life.

Cityscapes : $64.00   Int. Cin.,
  City moods.

  City patterns.

Common Canadian wildflowers   NFB,
  Les fleurs sauvages communes du Canada
    Arctic wildflowers.

  Les fleurs sauvages communes du Canada
    Selected wildflowers : Western Canada.

  Les fleurs sauvages communes du Canada
    Selected wildflowers : eastern Canada.

  Les fleurs sauvages communes du Canada
    Spring wildflowers : southern Prairie provinces.

  Les fleurs sauvages communes du Canada
    Spring wildflowers : southern Ontario and Quebec.

  Les fleurs sauvages communes du Canada
    Spring wildflowers : northern Prairie provinces.

  Les fleurs sauvages communes du Canada
    Spring wildflowers : the Maritimes.

  Les fleurs sauvages communes du Canada
    Spring wildflowers : British Columbia.

  Les fleurs sauvages communes du Canada
    Spring wildflowers : Newfoundland.

  Les fleurs sauvages communes du Canada
    Spring wildflowers : Northern Ontario and Quebec.

Community close-ups : $192.00   Int. Cin.,
  Children's hospital : in-patient.

  Children's hospital : check-ups and emergencies.

  Hotel : city within a city.

  Inter-city train.

  International airport.

  The Newspaper : part 2.

  The Newspaper : part 1.

  The Police force : behind the scenes.

  The Police force : part of the community.

  The shopping centre.

Series List

The Community helpers : $25.90   FCC.,
  The Firefighter.

  The Police officer.

Community helpers : $36.00   NFB.
  Building a house.

Community studies : $69.00   (s)   R.B.M.
  The Fish processing plant.

  Kinds of Canadian communities.

  What is a community?

Concepts / a series in Canadian studies   G.H.
  Land of gold : land of ice : all men explore.

La conquête du gouvernement responsable : $45.00
                                          NFB.
  Development of self-government
    La décision de Lord Elgin.

  La mission de Lord Durham.

  Development of self-government
    Rébellion dans le Bas-Canada.

  Development of self-government
    Rébellion dans le Haut-Canada.

  Les réformistes des colonies de l'Atlantique.

Les Contes de Noël : $75.00   M-L.
  The Christmas classics
    Le Conte de Noël de Dickens.

  The Christmas classics
    La Legende de l'arbre de Noël.

  The Christmas classics
    Le Noël de la famille Martin.

  The Christmas classics
    La Petite marchande aux allumettes.

  The Christmas classics
    La Veille de Noël.

Contes et légendes d'ailleurs   NFB.
  Stories and legends from other lands series
    La belle au bois dormant.

Contes et légends d'ailleurs   NFB.
  La biche miraculeuse : une légende hongroise.

Contes pour enfants   M-L.
  Reading motivation
    La grange rouge.

  Reading motivation
    Un seul chaton.

Conversational French for beginners : les fables de
la Fontaine : $149.00   CFM.
  La cigale et la fourmi.

  Conseil tenu par les rats.

  Le corbeau et le renard.

  Le cordonnier et le banquier

  Les deux chevres.

  Le lion et le rat.

  L'ours et les deux compagnons.

  Le rat de ville et le rat des champs.

  Le renard et la cigogne.

  Le renard et le bouc.

Cooking and nutrition : $75.00   M-L.
  Cuisine et alimentation
    Help yourself to good cooking.

  Cuisine et alimentation
    Knowing your food groups.

  Cuisine et alimentation
    Nutrition and health.

  Cuisine et alimentation.
    Planning and preparing meals.

  Cuisine et alimentation
    Principles of kitchen management.

Series List

Cuisine et alimentation : $75.00   M-L.
   Cooking and nutrition
      Alimentation et bonne santé.

   Cooking and nutrition
      Connaître les sortes d'aliments.

   Cooking and nutrition
      La Cuisine : un atelier.

   Cooking and nutrition
      Les Repas et le budget.

   Cooking and nutrition.
      Trois repas par jour.

Les débuts de la Confederation : $36.00   NFB.
   Early growth of Confederation
      L'époque de Laurier (1ère partie).

   Early growth of Confederation
      L'époque de Laurier (2e partie).

   Early growth of Confederation
      Sir John A. Macdonald (1ère partie).

   Early growth of Confederation
      Sir John A. Macdonald (2e partie).

Development of self-government : $45.00   NFB.
   La conquête du gouvernement responsable
      Lord Durham's mission.

   La conquête du gouvernement responsable
      Lord Elgin's decision.

   La conquête du gouvernement responsable
      Rebellion in Lower Canada.

   La conquête du gouvernement responsable
      Rebellion in Upper Canada.

   La conquête du gouvernement responsable
      Reform in the Atlantic colonies.

The Diefenbaker-Pearson years : $64.00   SHN.
   The Diefenbaker-Pearson years : part II :
      1963-1968.

The Diefenbaker-Pearson years : $64.35   SHN.
   The Diefenbaker-Pearson years : part 1 :

Discovering life around us : $45.00   NFB.
   A Visit to a farm.

   A Visit to a garden.

   A Visit to a pond.

   A Visit to the seashore.

   A Visit to the woods.

Le Drapeau Canadien : $65.00   Int. Cin.,
   The Canadian flag
      Comment le Canada obtint son drapeau.

   The Canadian flag
      Les Drapeaux Canadiens d'autrefois.

   The Canadian flag
      Les Drapeaux Canadiens et leur usage.

Drugs, medicines, and you : $75.00   M-L.
   Effects of misuse.

   How people misuse them.

   Using them safely.

   What they do.

   Where they come from.

Early Canada : $112.00   SHN.
   The Era of royal government.

   France in the New World.

   From fleur-de-lis to Union Jack.

   Life in New France.

Early day Canada : $96.00 (s)   B&R.
   Homes of early day Canada.

   A Trip through early day Canada.

   Visiting a pioneer cemetery.

   Visiting an early day Canadian town house.

   Visiting early Canadian churches.

Series List

Early growth of Confederation : $36.00   NFB,
Les débuts de la Confederation
  The Laurier era : part 1.

  The Laurier era : part 2.

Les débuts de la Confédération
  Sir John A. Macdonald : part 1.

Les débuts de la Confédération.
  Sir John A. Macdonald : part 2.

Ecology : exploration and discovery : $85.00 (s) M-L,
A la découverte de l'écologie
  Food chains.

A la découverte de l'écologie
  Habitat and adaptation.

A la découverte de l'écologie
  Populations.

Electronics : $85.00   M-L,
  Application of the vacuum tube.

  Basic radio circuitry.

  The Development of the vacuum tube.

  The Television receiver.

  The Transistor.

  Transistor application.

Elementary science   NFB,
  Science à l'éléméntaire
  5 senses + measurement = observation.

Science à l'élémentaire
  How to grow crystals.

Science à l'élémentaire
  To measure volume.

Energy : crisis and resolution : $85.00   M-L,
  Alternatives for the future.

  Electrical energy.

  Fossil fuels : coal.

Energy : crisis and resolution : $85.00   M-L,
  Fossil fuels : oil and natural gas.

  Introduction to energy.

  Nuclear energy.

Energy in Canada : $23.85   VCL,
  Churchill Falls.

  Natural gas in Alberta.

  Oil in Alberta.

Les enfants du monde   NFB,
  Children of many lands
  Les enfants de la Grèce.

  Children of many lands
  Les enfants de la Nigéria du Nord.

  Children of many lands
  Les enfants de la Thaïlande.

  Children of many lands
  Les enfants du Gabon.

  Children of many lands
  Les enfants du Japon.

  Children of many lands
  Les jeunes Indiens de Andes.

Enrichment mathematics : $39.00   R.B.M.,
  Shapes designed by man.

  Shapes in nature.

Eskimo myths and legends : $69.00   R.B.M.,
  The Angekkok of Thule.

  Attituk and the caribou.

  The Legend of the raven who flew backwards.

  The Shaman goes to the moon.

Eskimo stories (s)   RBM,
  Eskimo hunting.

Series List

Eskimo stories   RBM.
    Traditional Eskimo life.

The Everglades : $38.00   FMS.
    Birds of the Everglades.
    Ecology of the Everglades.

An Exchange with people of native ancestry : $18.00   RQM.
    City students visit Ogoki.
    Ogoki native people visit the city.

Exploring our solar system : $86.00   Int. Cin.,
    Our discovery of the universe.
    Our ever-changing earth.
    Our journey into space.
    Our place in the universe.

Facts and feelings   NFB.
Savoir ... sentir
    It isn't easy.

Facts on Canada   R.B.M.
    Antique cars.
    Canadian wildlife - flora.
    Trucks in Canada.

Family living and sex education series A : $75.00   M-L.
    Vie de famille et education sexuelle série A
    The Beginning of life : plants and fish.
    Vie de famille et éducation sexuelle série A
    Birth.
    Vie de famille et éducation sexuelle série A
    From two to one.

Family living and sex education series A : $75.00   M-L.
    Vie de famille et éducation sexuelle série A
    Growing and learning.
    Vie de famille et éducation sexuelle série A
    Male and female.

Family living and sex education series B : $75.00 (s)   M-L.
    Vie de famille et éducation sexuelle : série B
    Pre-natal development.

Family living and sex education series C : $85.00   M-L.
    Vie de famille et education sexuelle serie C
    Human behaviour.
    Vie de famille et education sexuelle serie C
    The Meaning of maturity.
    Vie de famille et education sexuelle serie C
    The Meaning of puberty.
    Vie de famille education sexuelle serie C
    Pattern of embryo development.
    Vie de famille et education sexuelle serie C
    The Process of reproduction.
    Vie de famille et education sexuelle serie C
    You and your personality.

Family planning methods : $85.00   M-L.
    The Diaphragm.
    The Intrauterine device.
    The Pill.
    The Rhythm and sympto-thermal methods.
    Tubal ligation and vasectomy.
    Vaginal spermicides and the condom.

Famous Canadians   R.B.M.,
    Banting and Best : the discovery of insulin.
    Billy Bishop.
    Dr. Norman Bethune.

Series List

Famous Canadians   R.B.M.,
  Dr. Wilder Penfield.

  Grey Owl.

  Nurse of Newfoundland.

  Painless Parker.

Famous stories of great courage : $85.00   M-L.
  Les récits héoïques
    Adventuresome Marco Polo.

  Les récits héroïque
    Commanding Joan of Arc.

  Les récits héroïques
    Good King Arthur.

  Les récits héroïques
    Magnificent Cetewayo.

  Les récits héroïques
    Nobel Hercules.

  Les récits héröiques
    Super Jesus.

Farm life : $35.40   FCC.
  The Chicken or the egg.

  Farm chores.

  What's in a dairy barn.

  Wiggle nose and long ears.

Feelings : $154.00   Int. Cin.,
  Sentiments
    But I don't know how.

  Sentiments
    Everybody's afraid of something.

  Sentiments
    Gr-r-r-r.

  Sentiments.
    Inside outside.

  Sentiments
    Many different me-s.

Feelings : $154.00   Int. Cin.,
  Sentiments
    Stop acting like a baby.

  Sentiments
    That's not fair.

  Sentiments
    When I grow up.

Fieldtrips on filmstrips series   NFB.
  At the zoo.

  Highland Games.

  Sleigh ride.

  Spring is coming.

Finding material in the resource centre : $27.00
                                                                     B & R.
  Have you a book about?

  Have you a book by?

  Have you a book called?

First and Second World Wars : $138.00   R.B.M.,
  Battle of the North Atlantic.

  Classic drama - hero vs. villain.

  First air aces : first women's liberators (1915).

  The First convoys, and Armistice (1917).

  Hitler at bay (1942-43).

  Surrender.

  The Terrible mud of Flanders (1916).

  The War to end war (1914).

Fishing in Canada : $23.85   Sch. Ch.,
  Fish processing in British Columbia.

  Salmon fishing in B.C.

  Trout farming in Manitoba.

Series List

Les fleurs sauvages communes du Canada **NFB,**
  Common Canadian wildflowers
    Fleurs sauvages de l'Arctique.

  Common Canadian wildflowers
    Fleurs sauvages diverses : l'est du Canada.

  Common Canadian wildflowers
    Fleurs sauvages diverses : l'ouest du Canada.

  Common Canadian wildflowers
    Fleurs sauvages printanières : Colombie-Britannique.

  Common Canadian wildflowers
    Fleurs sauvages printanières : Terre-Neuve.

  Common Canadian wildflowers
    Fleurs sauvages printanières : les Maritimes.

  Common Canadian wildflowers
    Fleurs sauvages printanières : sud de l'Ontario et du Québec.

  Common Canadian wildflowers
    Fleurs sauvages printanières : nord des provinces des Prairies.

  Common Canadian wildflowers
    Fleurs sauvages printanières : nord de l'Ontario et du Québec.

  Common Canadian wildflowers
    Fleurs sauvages printanières : sud des provinces des Prairies.

Folk tales around the world : $85.00 **M-L,**
  The Firebird and the magic horse.

  The Silliest man in Italy.

  The Superlative horse.

  Urashima Taro the fisherlad.

  The Value of a boiled egg.

  Why the spider has a narrow waist.

Folktales from the ancient East **Int. Cin.,**
  Foolish friends : Turkey.

  The Lost wisdom (Israel).

  The Rajah's garden.

  The Wishing bowl (China).

Follow your product : $34.50 **R.B.M.,**
  Forest management and lumbering.

  Pulp and paper.

Food processing in Canada : $15.90 **VCL.**
  Working in a bakery.

  Working in a meat packing plant.

Forest industries in Canada : $23.85 **Sch. Ch.,**
  Forest industries in B.C. : part 1 : logging.

  Newsprint in Quebec.

  Pulp and paper manufacturing in Newfoundland.

Fur-trade outposts : $45.00 **Int. Cin.,**
  La traite des pelleteries
  Fort Langley : gateway to the west.

  La traite des pelleteries
  Lower Fort Garry : legacy of the fur trade.

The Game of hockey : $72.00 (s) **R.B.M.,**
  Goaltending.

  The Hockey coach.

  Hockey equipment.

  Pin point passing.

  Shoot to score.

  Skating.

  Team play.

La géographie du Manitoba **NFB,**
  Geography of Manitoba
  Le Manitoba : le bouclier.

  Geography of Manitoba
  Le Manitoba : vue d'ensemble.

  Geography of Manitoba
  Le Manitoba : les Plaines.

Series List

Geography of Manitoba : $27.00
La géographie du Manitoba
  Manitoba : a broader view.

La geographie du Manitoba
  Manitoba : the Shield.

La géographie du Manitoba
  Manitoba : the plains.

Le gouvernement au Canada   NFB.
Government of Canada
  L'Evolution constitutionelle.

Government of Canada
  Le gouvernement fédéral.

Le gouvernement local.

Government in Canada
  Le gouvernement provincial.

Government of Canada
  Partis et elections.

Government in Canada
  Le régime parlementaire.

Government of Canada   NFB.
Le gouvernement au Canada
  Constitutional development.

Le gouvernement au Canada
  Federal government.

Le gouvernement au Canada
  Local government.

Le gouvernement au Canada
  Parliamentary government.

Le gouvernement au Canada
  Parties and elections.

Le gouvernement au Canada
  Provincial government

Voting in Canada.

Hamilton   R.B.M.,
  The Many Faces of Hamilton.

Hamilton : $34.50   R.B.M.,
  The Industrial city.

The Hard times of Louis Riel : $65.00   SHN.
  1870 Rebellion.

  1885 Rebellion.

Health - a new look : $65.00   M-L.
  Cleanliness - anew look.

  Exercise - a new look.

  Nutrition - anew look.

  Teeth : anew look.

Hello! Getting together with the telephone : $96.00 (S)   Int.
Allô! Parlons téléphone
  What's white and yellow and read all over?

High Arctic heritage : $36.00   NFB.
  Autumn hunters.

Spring journey.

Summer days.

Winter camp.

L'Histoire de Sainte-Marie-des-Hurons : $17.50   RQM,
Sainte-Marie among the Hurons
  L'Histoire de Sainte-Marie-des-Hurons : part 2

Sainte-Marie among the Hurons
  L'Histoire de Sainte-Marie-des-Hurons : part 1.

Histoires à dénouements multiples : $75.00   M-L.
Open-ended multiple/endings
  L'aventure de Robert.

Open-ended multiple/endings
  La chasse aux trésors.

Open-ended multiple/endings
  Le déménagement.

Series List

Histoires à dénouements multiples : $75.00   M-L.
   Open-ended multiple/endings
     La maison aux fantôones.

   Open-ended multiple/endings
     Le sac de M. Danlune.

The History of the English language : $65.00
                                          Int. Cin.,
   Introduction to language study.

   Origins and early history of English.

   Writing systems.

Hockey   R.B.M.,
   The History of hockey.

Homes in Canada and around the world : $84.00
                                          B&R.
   Development of Canadian homes.

   Factors influencing homes.

   Homes in cold climates.

   Homes in hot, dry climates.

   Homes in hot, humid climates.

   How homes are adapted to nature : wind and radiation.

Un Hôpital pour enfants : $45.00   Int. Cin.,
   Community close-ups
     Un Hôpital pour enfants : examen et urgences.

   Community close-ups
     Un Hôpital pour enfants : patient hospitalisé.

How Canada is governed : $130.00   Int. Cin.,
   Get out and vote! election campaigns and issues.

   Go fight City Hall! local decision making.

   Ottawa and the provinces : issues, choices and values.

   Parliament : making and changing laws.

How Canada is governed : $130.00   Int. Cin.,
   The Role of the Public Service.

   Why governments?

Huronia : $17.50   Lea.,
   Huron Indian Village & Musem.

   Huron Indian Village (reconstructed).

Iceland : $69.00   R.B.M.,
   Glaciers.

   History and geography.

   The People and their work.

   Volcanoes.

Image Canada : $45.00   NFB.
   Image du Canada
     Fort Walsh in the Cypress Hills.

   Image du Canada
     Grand Manan Island.

   Image du Canada
     Magdalen Islands.

   Image du Canada
     Rideau Canal.

   Image du Canada
     The Town of Fort Steele.

Image du Canada   NFB.
   Image Canada
     Le Canal Rideau.

   Image Canada
     Le Fort Walsh dans les collines Cyprès.

   Image Canada
     L'Ile Grand Manan.

   Image Canada
     Les Iles de la Madeleine.

   Image Canada
     La ville de Fort Steele.

Series List

Impressions : Canada   R.B.M.,
   Alberta.

   British Columbia.

   Manitoba.

   Manitoba.

   Nova Scotia.

   Ontario.

   Saskatchewan.

Indian culture in Canada : $69.00   R.B.M.,
   Indian dances and masks.

   Mother Earth : an Indian view.

   The Symbol in Indian art.

   Totem pole tales.

Indian legends : $85.00   M-L,
   Légendes amérindiennes
     The Festival of the seals.

   Légendes amérindiennes
     Glooskap brings summer.

   Légendes amérindiennes
     How it all began.

   Légendes amérindiennes
     The Medicine that restores life.

   Légendes amérindiennes
     The One-horned mountain goat.

   Légendes amérindiennes
     The Sun dance of the Plains Indians.

Indians and Inuit : the first people of North America
: $105.00   M-L,
   Indians of the Great Plains.

   Indians of the Northeastern Woodlands.

   Indians of the Pacific Northwest.

   Indians of the Southwest.

   The Inuit.

Indians and Inuit : the first people of North America
: $105.00   M-L,
   Native and European in North America.

Inquiry into weather : $85.00 (s)   M-L,
   Starting your own weather station.

Insects and spiders : $54.00   NFB,
   The Cecropia moth.

   Les insectes du Canada
     Dragonflies and damselflies.

   Les insectes du Canada
     The Grasshopper.

   Les insectes du Canada
     The Honeybee.

   Les insectes du Canada
     The Monarch butterfly.

   Les insectes du Canada
     Spiders.

An Introduction to : Ontario Science Centre   RQM,
   The Science Centre.

An Introduction to : sources of power   RQM,
   Sources of power.

It's a metric world : $164.71   ADD,
   Capacity counts.

   Celsius scenes.

   Cubic concepts.

   Lengthy tales.

   Mass matters.

   Square stories.

Japan : $72.00   VCI,
   Lowland agriculture in Japan.

   Mountain environments of Japan.

Series List

Japan : $72.00   VCI.
  Seacoast environments of Japan.

  Transportation and communication in Japan.

  Urban life in Japan (no. 1).

  Urban life in Japan (no. 2).

Journey through early Canada with V.H. Bartlett :
$64.00   Int. Cin.,
  Life along the waterways.

  Quebec and Ontario : old colony and new outpost.

  Sketching the New World : Maritime scenes.

Junior safety   NFB.
  Ride safely to school.

Landforms from the Ice Age. : $32.00   B & R.
  Glacier land deposits.

  Glacier water deposits.

Le drapeau canadien   Int. Cin.,
  Les drapeaux canadiens et leur usage.

Learning about money : $65.00 (s)   M-L.
  Money : how much do you need?

  Money : planning a budget.

  Money : how to spend it.

Learning about our universe : $85.00 (s)   M-L.
  La terre et l'univers
  Light from the sun.

  La terre et l'univers
  The Moon's position in space.

  La terre et l'univers
  Phases of the moon.

  La terre et l'univers
  The Planet we live on.

Learning about our universe : $85.00   M-L.
  La terre de l'univers
  What the sun means to the earth.

Learning about science : $75.00   M-L.
  Les saisons, la terre, l'espace.
  Autumn and winter : what they mean.

  Les saisons, la terre, l'espace
  Looking at the stars.

  Les saisons, la terre, l'espace
  Moon exploration.

  Les saisons, la terre, l'espace
  The Shape of the earth.

  Les saisons, la terre, l'espace
  Spring and summer : what they mean.

Learning about the human body : $85.00 (s)   M-L.
  Hearing.

  Smell, taste and touch.

  Vision.

Légendes amérindiennes : $85.00 (s)   M-L.
  Indian legends
  Au tout début.

  Indian legends
  Le Bouc à une corne.

  Indian legends
  La danse du soleil des Amérindiens de Plaines.

  Indian legends
  Le Festival des phoques.

  Indian legends
  Le remède de la vie.

Les Légendes de Noël des pay étrangers : $75.00 (s)
    M-L.
  Christmas tales from many lands
  L'Italie : la legende de Dame la Befana.

  Christmas tales from many lands
  La Mexique : l'humble présent.

Series List

Légendes indiennes   NFB.
  Canadien stories and legends series
    Glooscap et les quatre voeux : [légende indienne].

  Canadian stories and legends series.
    Les piquants du Porc-Epic.

    Le premier saumon.

Legends of the Micmac : $86.00 (s)   Int. Cin.,
  How summer came to our land.

  The Legend of the loon.

  Telling stories with puppets and masks.

Let's go shopping : $66.00   Fasia.
  The Country store.

  The Department store.

  A Shopping centre.

  The Supermarket.

The Life of Mackenzie King : $65.00   SHN.
  The Life of Mackenzie King : part II : the final years 1930-1950.

  The Life of Mackenzie King : part 1 : the formative years 1874-1930.

The Little people   SHN.
  Maple syrup.

  Scarecrow and pumpkin.

Living and growing   NFB.
  La vie qui pousse
    Backwards is forwards in reverse.

  La vie qui pousse
    Being born.

  Comes from ... grows to.

The Living Arctic :$54.00   Int. Cin.,
  Eskimo heritage.

The Living Arctic :$54.00   Int. Cin.,
  The New north.

  Patterns of life.

  Physical setting.

  White men in the Arctic.

The Living Arctic : $57.00   FMS
  The Arctic animals.

  The Arctic birds.

  Ecology of the Arctic.

Living in the outdoors   MUFL.
  Eating out I.

  Eating out II.

  Elementary camping.

  Wintering in the bush.

Look, listen, discover! : $230.00   Int. Cin.,
  Ouvre l'oeil et le bon...
  Can you find them?

  Ouvre l'oeil et le bon...
  Does it belong?

  Ouvre l'oeil et le bon...
  How will it look?

  Ouvre l'oeil et le bon...
  How would you use it?

  Listen for the clues.

  Ouvre l'oeil et le bon...
  Make something new.

  Pick the picture.

  Ouvre l'oeil et le bon...
  Put them in order.

  What do they have in common.

  Ouvre l'oeil et le bon...
  What's missing?

Series List

Look, listen, discover! : $230.00 — Int. Cin.
  Ouvre l'oeil et le bon...
  What's wrong here?

  Ouvre l'oeil et le bon...
  Which group will they go to?

Looking back — R.B.M.
  The 1920's.

  The Edwardian era.

Make-up for the stage : $66.00 — Fasla.
  Basic makeup.

  Beards.

  Corrective makeup.

  Old age makeup.

Mammals of Canada : $45.00 — NFB.
  Carnivores : the flesh eaters.

  Hoofed mammals of Canada.

  Insectivores and bats.

  Marine mammals of Canada.

  Rodents, rabbits and hares.

Mammals of North America : $40.00 — FMS.
  The Arctic.

  The Eastern forest.

  The Grasslands.

  The Rocky Mountains.

Man in his world — F&V.
  China I : food production.

  China II - transportation.

  Eskimo I : Arctic village.

  Gifts of the Nile I : farming on the flood plains.

Man in his world — F&V.
  Gifts of the Nile II : Cairo, the city.

  Grassland 1 : animals of the African Grasslands.

  Greece 1 : life in a rural village.

  Indians I : life on the Plains.

  Industrial community 1 : patterns of growth.

  Japan I : home life and food.

  Japan II : transportation and communication.

  Medieval community 1 : the knight.

  Mexico I : across modern Mexico.

  Nomadic journey : three nomadic peoples.

  Peru 1 : life in the Andes.

  Stone Age man I : an archaeological dig.

Manowan — NFB.
  Manowan
  L'histoire de Manowan : première partie

  Manowan
  L'histoire de Manowan : deuxième partie.

  Manowan
  History of Manowan : part 1.

  Manowan
  History of Manowan : part 2.

Map skills — NFB.
  Introducing the topographical map.

Map skills : $36.00 — NFB.
  Introducing map scale.

  Introduction to maps.

  Map orientation.

Maturity : options and consequences : $85.00 — M-L.
  Growing up.

  Love and marriage.

Series List

Maturity : options and consequences : $85.00 M-L.
 Teenage father.

 Teenage mother.

 The Trouble with alcohol.

 Values : yours and theirs.

Mes sentiments : $65.00 M-L.
 Your emotions
  C'est frustrant.

 Your emotions
  J'ai peur.

 Your emotions
  Je l'enviè.

 Your emotions
  Je me mets en colère.

Metalwork : hand tools M-L.
 Forging iron.

 Soldering methods.

 Welding techniques.

Metalwork : machine operation : $75.00 M-L.
 Forming metal by machine.

 Using the drill press.

 Working between centers on the lathe.

Metalwork : machine operations : $75.00 (s) M-L.
 Chuckwork on the lathe.

Métis and native uprisings and the land question NC.
 Big Bear, Poundmaker and Crowfoot.

 The First Métis uprising, 1869-70.

Métis and native uprsisings and the land question NC.
 The Second Métis uprising, 1885.

Metric measurement : $65.00 (s) M-L.
 Usage du système international
 Area units.

 Usage du système international
 Linear units.

 Usage du système international
 Volume units.

Metric measurement : $69.00 R.B.M.,
 Linear - area.

 Mass.

 Temperature.

 Volume - capacity.

Metric measurement for primary children : $69.00 R.B.M.,
 Area.

 Linear measurement.

 Temperature and mass.

 Volume and capacity.

Mining and processing in Canada :$39.75 VCL.
 Aluminum processing in Quebec.

 Asbestos mining in Quebec.

 Gold refining in Ontario.

 Nickel mining in Manitoba.

 Uranium mining in Ontario.

Le Monde des oiseaux : $64.00 (s) Int. Cin.,
 The World of birds
 Comment les oiseaux élèvent leur petits.

 The World of birds
 Comment les oiseaux s'adaptent pour survivre.

Moral decision-making : $75.00 (s) M-L.
 Attitudes morales
 Guilt.

Series List

Moral decision-making : $75.00   M-L,
  Attitudes morales
    Hostility.

  Attitudes morales
    Integrity.

National parks of Canada : $30.00   FMS,
  Point Pelee National Park.

  Prince Edward Island National Park.

  The Rocky Mountains national parks.

Native arts   NFB,
  L'art indigène
    Eskimo prints.

  L'art indigène
    Eskimo sculpture.

Native arts : $35.00   NFB,
  L'art indigène
    The Art of the totem pole.

  L'art indigène
    Haida argillite carvings.

  L'art indigène
    Masks of the North American Indians.

Native land claims in B.C. : $40.00   TC,
  Cowichan : a question of survival.

  Native land claims in B.C. : an introduction (1850-1976).

The Native peoples of North America : $85.00   M-L,
  Les Amérindiens
    The Native peoples of the Northeastern Woodlands : initial European contact.

The Native peoples of North America : $85.00   M-L,
  Les Amérindiens
    The Native peoples of the Pacific Northwest : initial European contact.

Nature in the city : $57.00   FMS,
  City habitats.

  Nature adapts to the city.

  Nature in the neighbourhood.

Nature study : $51.00   B & R,
  Deciduous trees.

  Evergreen trees.

  Garden flowers of spring.

  Garden flowers of summer and autumn.

  Wild flowers of spring.

  Wild flowers of summer & autumn.

New children's stories : $65.00   M-L,
  The Great horse contest.

  The Rescue of Julius the donkey.

  The Runaway.

  The Sparkling imagination.

New France : exploration and growth : $54.00   NFB,
  Frontenac.

  Jacques Cartier.

  Jean Talon.

  Sainte-Marie-among-the-Hurons.

  Samuel de Champlain.

  La Vérendrye.

New France : segneurial system : $45.00   NFB,
  The Habitants.

Series List

New France : seigneurial system : $45.00   NFB.
    The Habitant and his home [in the 18th century].

    The Habitant and his land [in the 18th century].

    Seigneurs and seigneuries.

    The Story of New France.

Niagara Fruit Belt : $29.85   FCC.
    Fruit Belt preservation and regional planning.

    Introduction to the Niagara Fruit Belt.

    Problems of land use in urban fringe - urban shadow areas.

Now what : $35.00   PPH.
    The Chocolate bar and the bicycle.

    The Grocery cart and noise.

    The Living room and clothes.

    The Test and bottles.

    Wet cement and the radio.

Ocean bottom dwellers : $60.00   AEU.
    Crustaceans, molluscs.

    Echinoderms.

    Echinoderms.

    Plants, sponges, coelenterates.

    Plants, sponges, coelenterates.

"Of the" : $27.00   NFB.
    Of the farm.

    Of the horse.

    Of the land.

Open-ended multiple/endings : $75.00   M-L.
    The Absent-minded Mr. Willoughby.

Open-ended multiple/endings : $75.00   M-L.
    Histoires à dénouements multiples
    Moving day mix-up.

    Histoires à dénouements multiples
    The Old map mystery.

    Histoires à dénouements multiples
    Surprise adventure.

    Histoires à dénouements multiples
    Three in a haunted house.

The Opening of the Canadian west : $67.00   SHN.
    Growing up.

    Moving in.

    Staking a claim.

Our living pioneer ancestors   B&R.
    "Mary Davidson's home".

Our national capital :$39.75   VCL.
    National Arts Centre.

    The National Gallery of Canada.

    National Research Council.

    Parliament buildings.

    Royal Canadian Mint.

Our native people - customs and legends   ROM.
    Cree syllabary.

    Native clothing.

    Native games.

    Native picture writing.

Outdoor education   R.B.M.
    Canoe Museum.

    Canoeing skills and safety.

    Dressing fish.

Series List

Outdoor education   R.B.M.
  Ice fishing.

  Outdoor cooking.

  Plant communities, wasteland wildflowers.

  Plant communities, woodlot and wetlands.

  Proper bush clothing.

  Summer survival.

  Winter survival.

Outdoor education : no. 910 : $76.00   R.B.M.,
  Learning to swim and water safety.

  Swimming strokes.

Outdoor survival : $85.00 (s)   M-L.
  Activités de plein air : survie
  Elementary canoeing.

  Activités de plein air : survie
  First aid in the bush.

  Activités de plein air - survie
  How to make a fire and shelter.

  Activités de plein air : survie
  Outdoor survival kit.

  Activités de plein air : survie
  Water rescue.

Outline maps   NFB.
  Outline maps of Canada.

  Outline maps of the world : part 2 : Europe and Africa.

  Outline maps of the world : part 3 : Asia and Australia.

  Outline maps of the world : part 1 : the Americas.

Ouvre l'oeil et le bon... : $230.00 (s)   Int. Cin.,
  Look, listen, discover!
  A quoi cela ressemble-t-il?

Ouvre l'oeil et le bon... : $230.00   Int. Cin.,
  Look, listen, discover!
  Classons, classons!

  Look, listen, discover!
  Ecoute bien...

  Look, listen, discover!
  Je me suis trompé de groupe : que suis-je?

  Look, listen, discover!
  Mets-toi à ma place!

  Look, listen, discover!
  Les Objets disparus.

  Look, listen, discover!
  Qu'est-ce qui manque?

  Look, listen, discover!
  Qu'est-ce qui ne va pas?

  Look, listen, discover!
  Qu'est-ce qu'on peut faire de ca?

  Look, listen, discover!
  Trouvons autre chose.

  Look, listen, discover!
  Trouvons les ressemblance.

Le Patrimoine vivant du Canada : $86.00 (s) Int. Cin.,
  Canada's living heritage
  A la découverte de notre patrimoine.

  Canada's living heritage
  La Dualité de notre patrimoine.

The People we are : $95.00   McI.
  I come from Jamaica.

  I was born in Portugal.

  My birthplace was India.

  My family is Chinese.

  My Italian heritage.

The Peoples of Canada - our multicultural heritage :
$82.00 (s)   SHN.
  Changing profile.

  Two cultures.

Series List

Pets and their care : $32.00   B & R.
  Guinea pigs and their care.

  A Visit with the vet.

  A Visit with the vet.

  What pet for me.

Pioneer community : $85.00   M-L.
  La vie quotidienne des pionniers du Haut-Canada
  Crafts.

  La vie quotidienne des pionniers du Haut-Canada
  Family life.

  La vie quotidienne des pionniers du Haut-Canada
  Farm life.

  La vie quotidienne des pionniers du Haut-Canada
  Foods.

  La vie quotidienne des pionniers du Haut-Canada.
  School and recreation.

  La vie quotidienne des pionniers du Haut-Canada
  Work and trade.

The Pioneer community at work : $114.00   McI.
  The Cabinet maker.

  The Mill.

  The Newspaper business.

  The Pioneer community.

  The Village broom shop.

  The Weaver.

Pioneer life   NFB.
  Les pionniers
    The Pioneer community.

Pioneer life : $72.00   NFB.
  Les pionniers
    Early pioneer life in Upper Canada.

  Les pionniers
    Gold rush : pioneer mining in British Columbia.

Pioneer life : $72.00   NFB.
  Les pionniers
    Life in Upper Canada in the 1860's.

  Les pionniers
    Pioneer life in the Maritimes : part 1.

  Les pionniers
    Pioneer life in the Maritimes. part 2.

  Les pionniers
    Pioneer life on the Prairies (1812-1900).

  Les pionniers
    Pioneer life on the Prairies (1900-1912).

Les pionniers : $72.00 (s)   NFB.
  Pioneer life
    Les pioneers des Prairies (1812-1900).

  Pioneer life
    Les pionniers des Maritimes : 1ère partie.

  Pioneer life
    Les pionniers des Maritimes : 2e partie.

  Pioneer life
    Les pionniers des Prairies (1900-1912).

  Les pionniers du Haut-Canada.

  Pioneer life
    La vie dans le Haut-Canada vers 1860.

  Pioneer life
    Un village du Haut-Canada.

Points de vue   NFB.
  A question of values
    Un historique de la contraception.

Points de vue   NFB.
  Vivre ensemble.

  A Question of values
    Vivre seule.

Postage stamps tell Canada's story : $86.00
                                          Int. Cin.,
  Les timbres poste racontent l'histoire du Canada
  Canada : people and environment.

Series List

Postage stamps tell Canada's story : $86.00 — Int. Cin.,
   Les timbres poste racontent l'histoire du Canada
   Canada and its provinces.

   Les timbres poste racontent l'histoire du Canada
   Introducing the postage stamp.

   Les timbres poste racontent l'histoire du Canada
   Shaping the Canadian nation.

Preventive dental health : $72.00 — B&R,
   Awareness of dental problems.

   Dental aids and trends in dentistry.

   Details of brushing, disclosing & flossing.

   Flossing vs. gum disease.

   Summary and conclusion.

Principles of electricity : $75.00 — M-L,
   Current and pressure.

   Fundamentals of electricity.

   General electronics.

   Principles of magnetism.

   Sources of electricity.

Province of Quebec : $27.00 — NFB,
   Le Québec
   The Province of Quebec : the Appalachian region.

   Le Québec
   The Province of Quebec : the Laurentian region.

   Le Québec
   The Province of Quebec : the St. Lawrence region.

Provincial capitals — Sch. Ch.,
   Edmonton, Alberta.

Provincial capitals — Sch. Ch.,
   Charlottetown, P.E.I.

   Halifax, Nova Scotia.

Provincial capitals — Sch. Ch.,
   Quebec City, Quebec.

   Regina, Sask.

   St. John's, Newfoundland.

   Victoria, B.C.

   Victoria, B.C.

   Winnipeg, Man.

   Winnipeg, Man.

Le Quebec — NFB,
   Province of Quebec
   Le Quebec : la Plaine du Saint-Laurent.

   Province of Quebec
   Le Quebec : le Plateau laurentien.

A question of values — NFB,
   Points de vue
   A history of contraception.

   To be together.

Reading motivation — M-L,
   Contes pour enfants
   Big red barn.

   Contes pour enfant
   One kitten for Kim.

Reading readiness : $85.00 — M-L,
   The Bungler.

   The Cowboy.

   The Doodler.

   The Gobbler.

   The Puffer.

   The Ticker.

Series List

Les Récits héroiques : $85.00 (s)   M-L,
    Famous stories of great courage
    Les aventures de Marco Polo.

    Famous stories of great courage
    Cetewayo le magnifique.

Regional studies : $138.00   R.B.M.,
    Cape Breton Island : an overview.

    Cape Breton Island : industrial regions.

    Ontario : the north, transportation and recreation.

    Saguenay-Lake St. Jean - the river.

    Saguenay-Lake St. John - the Lake Region.

    Saint John River Valley - Edmunston to Kings Landing.

    Saint John River Valley - Mactaquac to Saint John.

    Southern Ontario.

Royal Canadian Mounted Police : $69.00 (s)   R.B.M.,
    The Beginning of a new era.

    The Northwest Mounted Police.

Safety : a way of life : $65.00   M-L,
    Home safety.

    School safety.

    Traffic safety.

    Transit safety.

Safety songs and stories : $130.00   Int. Cin.,
    Bicycle safety.

    Home safety.

    Safety on the street.

    School bus safety.

    Small boat safety.

    Swimming safety.

Sainte Marie among the Hurons : $17.50 (s)   ROM.,
    L'histoire de Sainte-Marie-des-Hurons
    Sainte-Marie-among-the-Hurons : part I.

Les Saisons, la terre, l'espace : $75.00   M-L,
    Learning about science
    L'Automne et l'hiver : ce qu'ils sont.

    Learning about science
    Explorations lunaires.

    Learning about science
    La Forme de la terre.

    Learning about science
    Le Printemps et l'été : ce qu'ils sont.

    Learning about science
    Regardent les étoiles.

Sam Slice tells the story of food : $95.00   McI.,
    Learning about the fruits we eat.

    Learning about the plants we eat.

    Sam Slice tells about snack foods.

    The Story of how to eat to grow tall.

    Things dangerous to eat.

Savoir ... sentir   NFB,
    C'est pas facile!

Scarborough Bluffs : $34.50   R.B.M.,
    The Natural environment.

    Planning for future use.

The Scarlet force : the story of the North West Mounted Police : $45.00   Int. Cin.,
    The Force keeps the peace.

    The Force rides west.

Series List

Science   R.B.M.
    The Biology of taste and smell.

    Birds, in wetlands.

    Birds, their upland homes and habits.

    Discovering animals in winter.

    Discovering plants in winter.

    The Fantastic world of insects (A).

    The Fantastic world of insects (B).

    Making your own microscopic slides.

    The Microscope - a delicate tool.

    The Microscope - its operation.

    The Natural ecology of water.

    Our five senses of touch.

    The Predators.

    Spider ecology.

    What is a spider?

    The World of microscopy.

Science á l'élémentaire   NFB.
  Elementary science
    5 sens + mésures = observation.

  Elementary science
    Croissance de cristaux.

  Elementary science
    Mesure de volumes.

Search for the Northwest Passage : $49.00   Int. Cin.
  Discoveries and disappointments.

  Fact and fancy.

  Tragedy and triumph.

Season stories   M-L.
  Summer - reflections on Lake Blue Water.

  Winter - ice fire lights.

The Seasons : a journey through the year : $86.00   Int. Cin.
  Autumn.

  Spring.

  Summer.

  Winter.

Sécurité dans l'atelier : $85.00   M-L.
  Shop safety
    Dangers fréquents en atelier.

  Shop safety
    Foreuse sur colonne et tour.

  Shop safety
    Meules, toupies, scies éléctriques, et corroyeurs.

  Shop safety
    Pensez "sécurité".

  Shop safety
    Scies à main, ciseaux et limes.

  Shop safety
    Tournevis, clefs, tôle et soudure.

Sentiments : $154.00   Int. Cin.
  Feelings
    Ce n'est pas juste.

  Feelings
    Cesse de faire le bébé.

  Feelings
    Je ne peux pas.

  Feelings
    Les Masques.

  Feelings
    Moi et mes diverses personalités.

  Feelings
    Quand je serai grand.

  Feelings
    Rrrrr.

  Felings.
    Tout le monde a peur de quelque chose.

Series List

Settlers of North America : $75.00 M-L.
   Commerce.

   Community life.

   Furniture and household goods.

   The Making of a farm.

   Transportation.

Sex education : $45.00 NFB.
   About V.D. - gonorrhea.

   About V.D. - syphilis.

   Conception and birth.

   Contraception.

Sex education : $45.00 NFB.
   Puberty.

Sheet metal M-L.
   Parallel line development.

   Pattern development by triangulation.

   Radial line development.

Shop safety : $85.00 M-L.
   Sécurité dans l'atelier
     Drill presses and lathes.

   Sécurité dans l'atelier
     General shop hazards.

   Sécurité dans l'atelier
     Grinders, routers, power saws & jointers.

   Sécurité dans l'atelier
     Hand saws, chisels and files.

   Sécurité dans l'atelier
     Screwdrivers, wrenches, sheet metal, & welding.

   Sécurité dans l'atelier
     Think safety.

SI - the metric system : $65.00 M-L.
   Le système international
   Measuring length and area.

   Le système international
   Measuring mass.

   Le système international
   Measuring volume.

   Standardizing measurement.

South America : $69.95 (s) EDU.
   Rio de Janerio.

Special occasions R.B.M.,
   The Day Santa came to town.

   Let's go to the fair.

   Pepper's Christmas.

   The Secret in the barn.

   When the sap runs.

Special occasions and events R.B.M..
   The Canadian and World Plowing Match.

   Royal Winter Fair.

Stories and legends from other lands series NFB.
   Baron Münchhausen in a whale of a tale : a
     German legend.

   Foolish Bartek : (a Polish tale).

   Contes et légendes d'ailleurs
   Ilia the mighty : a Ukrainian legend.

   Contes et légendes d'ailleurs
   The Miraculous hind : a hungarian legend.

   Contes et légendes d'ailleurs
   Sleeping Beauty : a French legend.

   Contes et légendes d'ailleurs
   The Two frogs : a Japanese legend.

Series List

The story of food : $43.00   Int. Cin.,
  Bread and pastry.

  Chocolate.

  Hot dogs.

  Milk and ice cream.

Survival & safety in the outdoors   R.Q.M.,
  Canoeing : the strokes.

  Canoeing : the basic.[Filmstrip]. --

  Riflery.

  Rockhounding.

  Survival in the bush.

Survival & safety in the outdoors : $59.50   RQM,
  Orientation & compass.

Le système International : $65.00   M-L,
  SI - the metric system
  Une Ligne - une surface.

  SI - the metric system
  Un Poids - une masse.

  SI - the metric system
  Un Système de mesure.

  SI - the metric system
  Un Volume - une capacité.

Tales from the treetops : $86.00   Int. Cin.,
  Les arbres m'ont raconté
  Beginnings.

  Les arbres m'ont raconté
  The Hunter who went away.

  Les Arbres m'onte raconté
  The Story of Greedy Pan.

La Terre et l'univers : $85.00   M-L,
  Learning about our universe
  Influence du soleil sur la terre.

La Terre et l'univers : $85.00   M-L,
  Learning about our universe
  La Lumière du soleil.

  Learning about our universe
  La Lune : ses phases.

  Learning about our universe
  Les Millions d'etoiles.

  Learning about our universe
  Notre planète : la terre.

  Learning about our universe
  La position de la lune.

The Native peoples of North America : $85.00   M-L,
  Les Amérindiens
  The Native peoples of the Great Plains : initial European contact.

  Les Amérindiens
  The Native peoples of the Great Plains : European contact to the present day.

  Les Amérindiens
  The Native peoples of the Northeastern Woodlands : European contact to the present day.

  Les Amérindiens
  The Native peoples of the Pacific Northwest : European contact to the present day.

Theatre arts : "bare boards and a passion" : $69.00
                                                 R.B.M.,
  Basic set design and stages.

  Fundamentals of make-up.

  Masks.

Thinking skills : observing (s)   VCI.
  Observing by hearing, tasting, smelling, touching.

  Observing by seeing : colours purple, orange, green.

  Observing by seeing : colours black, white, brown.

491

Series List

Thinking skills : observing   VCI.
    Observing by seeing : colours red, yellow, blue.

    Observing by seeing : shapes and sizes.

This is my world : $27.00   B&R.
    Listen to my world.

    Look at my world.

    Touch my world.

Thunder Bay's historic old Fort William   CP.
    The Growth, the decline.

    Life in the old Fort.

Les Timbres post raconte l'histoire du Canada :
$86.00 (s)   Int. Cin.
    Postage stamps tell Canada's story
    Le Peuple Canadien et son environnement.

Trade unions : the Canadian experience : $65.00
                                            SHN.
    Beginnings.

    Development.

Trades & technology : masonry   M-L.
    Elements of brickwork.

    Walls and bonds.

Trades & technology : painting and decorating   M-L.
    Painting a panelled door.

    Paper hanging application.

La Traite des pelleteries : $45.00   Int. Cin.,
    Fur-trade outposts
    Le Fort Langley : carrefour de la côte ouest.

Transport : l'aventure Canadienne : $86.00   Int. Cin., (s)
    Transportation : the Canadian adventure
    De la terre à l'air.

    Transportation : the Canadian adventure
    De la traction animal à la vapeur.

    Transportation : the Canadian adventure
    Un Monde nouveau, des méthodes nouvelles.

Transportation in Canada   R.B.M.,
    Age of steam and the automobile.

    Airshows in Canada.

    Aviation in Canada.

    Aviation in Canada : the early days.

    Aviation in Canada - today.

    The Great Lakes - St. Lawrence Seaway.

    Identifying airplanes.

    Port of Toronto.

    Rail transportation in Canada : the early days.

    The Seaway and its ships.

    A Seaway port.

    Transportation today : by land.

    Transportation today : by air and water.

Transportation in Canada : $276.00   R.B.M.,
    Rail transportation in Canada : today.

Transportation : the Canadian adventure : $86.00 (s)
                                                         Int. Cin.,
    New ways in a new land.
    Today and Tomorrow.
    Wheels and wings.

Series List

Ukranian Easter : $34.50   R.B.M.
  Easter greetings.

  Pysanky.

The Ukranians-Canadian homesteaders : $34.50   R.B.M.
  Prairie homestead.

  Strangers to Canada.

Understanding the earth grid : $20.00   BH.
  The Earth grid.

  Latitude.

  Longitude.

The United States : "From sea to shining sea" : $65.00 (s)   M-L.
  Growth and conflict.

The Urban community   FCC.
  Public transportation in the city.

Urban studies : $103.50   R.B.M.
  The City : laboratory of history.

  Housing : the Canadian city.

  The Municipal election.

  Problems of urban environment.

  Urban government.

Urbanism in Canada   R.B.M.
  Aging of the urban site.

  Kinds of urban centres.

  Recreation : the Canadian city.

  Suburban site.

  Transportation.

  Urban culture.

Urbanism in Canada   R.B.M.
  Urban economy.

Usage du Système International : $65.00 (s)   M-L.
  Metric measurement
  Le Monde à l'heure du système international.

  Metric measurement.
  Unité de surface.

  Metric measurement
  Les Unités de volume.

Vanishing animals of North America : $38.00   FMS.
  Habitat : key to survival.

  Habitat : key to survival.

  Threatened and endangered wildlife.

  Threatened and endangered wildlife.

Venereal disease : what I need to know : $85.00 (s)   M-L.
  The History of venereal disease.

Victorians : $95.00   NCM.
  Going to Canada : in the backwoods.

  Going to Canada : Government House.

Vie de famille et éducation sexuelle série A : $75.00   M-L.
  Family living and sex education series A
  Le développement et l'apprentissage.

  Family living and sex education series A
  Développement pré-natal.

  Family living and sex education series A
  Le Mâle - la femelle

  Family life and sex education series A
  La Naissance.

  Family living and sex education series A
  Un de deux.

Series List

Vie de famille et éducation sexuelle série A : $75.00
                                                M-L.
   Family living and sex education series A
     La Vie commence - plantes et poissons.

Vie de famille et éducation sexuelle série B : $75.00
                                                M-L.
   Family living and sex education series B
     Les Cellules reproductives.

   Family living and sex education series B
     La Naissance d'un être humain.

   Family living and sex education series B
     Ovulation - mammifères.

   Family living and sex education series B
     La Vie commence - grenouilles.

Vie de famille et éducation sexuelle série C : $85.00
                                                M-L.
   Family living and sex education series C
     Ce qu'est la maturite.

   Family living and sex education series C
     Le Comportement humain.

   Family living and sex education series C
     L'Embryon se développe.

   Family life and sex education series C
     Etre pubère.

   Family living and sex education series C
     Le Processus de reproduction.

   Family living and sex education series C
     Vous et votre personnalité.

La vie qui pousse   NFB.
   Living and growing
     Derriere est evant sens devant derriere.

   Living and growing
     Il etait une fois un oeuf.

     Vient de - devient .

La Vie quotidienne des pioneers du Haut-Canada :
$85.00   (s)   M-L.
  Pioneer community
    La Famille.

La Vie quotidienne des pioneers du Haut-Canada :
$85.00   M-L.
  Pioneer community
    Les Métiers.

  Pioneer community
    Le Village.

The Welland Canal : $19.90   FCC.
   The Welland Canal (historical).

   The Welland Canal (today).

Why do we have laws? : $86.00   Int. Cin.
   How do we make laws?

   How does the law work?

   Too many laws... or too few?

   What are laws?

Why go metric? : man & measurement : $64.00   SHN.
   The Metric system : why?

   The Metric system : a better way .... for all!

   The Metric system : how?.

   The Metric system : a better way ... for some.

Wildflowers of North America : $50.00   FMS.
   Autumn wildflowers of eastern North America.

   Orchids of Eastern North America.

   Spring wildflowers of eastern North America.

   Summer wildflowers of eastern North America.

   What on earth! : a look at plants.

Wildlife of North America : the mammals : $95.00 FMS (s)
   Life in the boreal forest.

Series List

Wildlife of North America : the mammals : $95.00 FMS
   Life on the Barren Lands.

   Life on the Prairies.

   The Story of mammals.

Women in Canada : $63.30 SHN.
   From Europe to Parliament Hill.

   From franchise to freedom.

Woodworking : hand tools (A) : $85.00 (s) M-L.
   Five simple wood joints.

   Scraping tools and abrasives.

The World of birds : $64.00 Int. Cin.,
   Le monde des oiseaux
   How birds adapt to survive.

   Le monde des oiseaux
   How birds find food.

   Le monde des oiseaux
   How birds raise their young.

Your emotions : $65.00 M-L.
   Mes sentiments
   Your anger.

  Mes sentiments
  Your envy.

  Mes sentiments
  Your fear.

  Mes sentiments
  Your frustration.

Your library : how to use it : $75.00 (s) M-L.
   Discovering your library.

   Doing a project.

   How do you share your library?

Part Five

Distributors' Directory

DISTRIBUTORS' DIRECTORY

ADD
    Addison-Wesley (Canada) Ltd.
    36 Prince Andrew Place
    Don Mills, Ontario
    M3C 2T8

B & R
    B & R Products
    380 Esna Park Drive
    Markham, Ontario
    L3R !H5

BAM
    Burbank Audio-Visual Media Ltd
    5707 Burleigh Crescent S.E.
    Calgary, Alberta
    T2H 1Z7

BSC
    The Book Society of Canada Ltd.
    Box 200
    Agincourt, Ontario
    M1S 3B6

CP
    Cornett Productions
    c/o L.D. Hamilton
    R.R. #2
    Lakefield, Ontario
    K0L 2H0

EDU
    Edu-Media
    P.O. Box 1240
    Kitchener, Ontario
    N2G 4H1

ETHOS
    Ethos Ltd.
    2250 Midland Avenue, Unit 9
    Scarborough, Ontario
    M1P 3E6

FASLA
    Filmstrip and Slide Laboratory
    P.O. Box 1022
    Oakville, Ontario
    L6J 1N0

F & W
    Fitzhenry & Whiteside Ltd.
    150 Lesmill Road
    Don Mills, Ontario
    M3B 2T5

FCC
    Filmstik Company of Canada
    89 Greylawn Crescent
    Scarborough, Ontario
    M1R 2V7

G.H.
    Griffin House
    461 King Street West
    Toronto, Ontario
    M5V 1K7

I.T.F.
    International Tele-Film Enterprises Ltd.
    47 Densley Avenue
    Toronto, Ontario
    M6M 5A8

K.M.
    Kevin Moynihan Audio-Visual Services
    144 Front Street West
    Suite 330
    Toronto, Ontario
    M5J 1G2

LBE
    London Board of Education
    Learning Materials Centre
    931 Leathorn Street
    London, Ontario
    N5Z 3M7

LEA
    Leamat
    c/o Mr. R.Q. Millman
    25 Roehampton Avenue
    Toronto, Ontario
    M4P 1P9

MCI
    McIntyre Educational Media Ltd.
    30 Kelfield Street
    Rexdale, Ontario
    M9W 5A2

Distributors' Directory

MHR
McGraw-Hill Ryerson Ltd.
330 Progress Avenue
Scarborough, Ontario
M1P 2Z5

PHM
Prentice Hall Media
1870 Birchmount Road
Scarborough, Ontario
M1P 2J7

PPH
Puckrin's Production House
13025 - 149 Street
Edmonton, Alberta
T5L 2J7

SC
Media Services
Sheridan College
1430 Trafalgar Road
Oakville, Ontario
L6H 2L1

SCH. CH.
Scholar's Choice
50 Ballantyne Avenue
Stratford, Ontario
N5A 6T9

SCH. SER.
School Services of Canada
525 Adelaide Street West
Toronto, Ontario
M5V 1T6

SCO
Scolaire Filmstrips
1411 Willowdown Road
Oakville, Ontario
L6L 1X2

SEC
Sécas Internationale
5275 Rue Berri
Montreal, Quebec
H2J 2S7

SFM
Scarboro Foreign Mission Society
Mission Information Department
2685 Kingston Road
Scarborough, Ontario
M1M 1M4

TBE
Toronto Board of Education
Teaching Aids Department
155 College Street
Toronto, Ontario
M5T 1P6

TC
Target Canada; Research & Production
Group Ltd.
193 East Hastings Street
Mezzanine No. 2
Vancouver, British Columbia
V6A 1N7

VEC
Visual Education Centre
75 Horner Avenue
Toronto, Ontario
M8Z 4X5

WINT.
Wintergreen Communications Ltd.
c/o Hugh Moreland
8481 Keele Street, Unit 8
Concord, Ontario
L4K 1B6

Addendum

The following titles were inexplicably dropped during the automated print-out procedure. They are therefore included as an addendum to the present edition, along with appropriate title and series indexes. These indexes have been manually prepared, but it has proved impossible to generate a relevant PRECIS index for the added titles. The author apologizes for any inconvenience resulting from this 'solution,' and expects to integrate the following titles into subsequent editions of this work.

Classified Catalogue

Addendum

028.7
Using audio-visual resources.
prod. [Toronto] : M-L, 1974. dist.
Sch. Ser. or Wint. 46fr: col:
35mm. & cassette (7 min.): auto.
& aud. adv. sig. & teacher's guide.
$16.50 (Your library : how to use
it : $75.00) j

1. Audio-visual materials.

Photographs are used to describe the
use of A-V material for research, for
pleasure, and by non-readers.
Concentrates on proper use of equipment,
most effective method of viewing
filmstrips for study purposes, using
slides, records, and cassette tapes.

028.7
Where do I go from here?
prod. [Toronto] : M-L, 1974. dist.
Sch. Ser. or Wint. 52fr.: col:
35mm. & cassette (9 min.): auto.
& aud. adv. sig. & teacher's guide.
$16.50 (Your library : how to use
it : $75.00) j

1. Libraries and readers.

Describes uses of card catalogue and
Dewey system to find library materials.
Explains the use of tables of contents,
chapter titles, and indexes of both in
research, emphasizing use of other
materials, vertical file and magazines.
Shows close-ups of real catalogue cards.

152.1
Observing by seeing : colours red, yellow, blue.
prod. [Hamilton, Ont.] : VCI, 1977.
dist. MHR 28fr.: col.: 35mm. & captions
& teacher's guide. $35.00 (Thinking
skills : observing) p

1. Red. 2. Yellow. 3. Blue.

Introduces the basic colours of red,
yellow, and blue, identifies the words
naming these colours, and discusses
the occurrence and meanings of the
colours in everyday life. Produced
in 3 parts.

160.76
Les ensembles.
prod. [Toronto] : Int. Cin., 1976.
dist. VEC 54fr.: col.: 35mm. &
cassette (5 min.): auto. & aud.
adv. sig. & teacher's guide. $24.00
(Ouvre l'oeil et le bon... :
$230.00) pj

1. Reasoning-Study and teaching.

Six cartoon characters group and
re-group themselves according to
different classification principles,
such as colour of clothing and size.
Children are asked to identify type
of classification being used, and
how characters will be split up.
Would be useful for Special
Education students as well.
English title available : WHICH
GROUP WILL THEY GO TO?

177
Generosity.
prod. [Toronto] : M-L, 1973. dist.
Sch. Ser. or Wint. 47fr.: col.:
35mm. & cassette (10 min.): auto.
& aud. adv. sig. & teacher's guide.
$16.50 (Moral decision-making :
$75.00) pj

1. Behaviour.

Dramatic presentation of a situation
involving a young girl who must
decide whether or not to share with
others. Four alternative solutions
to the situation encourage children
to reach their own decision avoiding
simplistic solutions. Of most value
in a classroom situation where
discussion can take place. French
title available : LA GENEROSITE.

179
Honesty.
prod. [Toronto] : M-L, 1973. dist.
Sch. Ser. or Wint. 51fr.: col.:
35mm. & cassette (10 min.): auto.
& aud. adv. sig. & teacher's guide.
$16.50 (Moral decision-making :
$75.00) pj

1. Honesty.

Dramatic presentation of a realistic
situation concerning honesty.
Narrated by a young boy who is over-

Addendum

paid by a paper route customer and must then decide what to do with the extra money. Five different solutions are presented in sequence to allow for class discussion. French title available : L'HONNETETE.

232.9
    Jésus: Homme-Dieu.
      prod. [Toronto] : M-L, 1975. dist. Sch. Ser. or Wint. 72fr.: col.: 35mm. & cassette (12 min. 30 sec.): auto. & aud. adv. sig. & teacher's guide. $16.50 (Les récits héroiques : $85.00) j

      1. Jesus Christ - Biography.

      Outlines the events in Jesus' life from the age of thirty until his death. Includes his entrance into Jerusalem on Palm Sunday, the Last Supper, his arrest, and his death. Stresses Jesus' great courage and kindness. English title available: SUPER JESUS.

292
    Le grand Hercule.
      prod. [Toronto] : M-L, 1974. dist. Sch. Ser. or Wint. 58fr.: col.: 35mm. & cassette (10 min. 30 sec.): auto. & aud. adv. sig. & teacher's guide. $16.50 (Les récits héroiques: $85.00) j

      1. Mythology, classical.

      Uses expressive drawings to tell the story of Hercules, son of Zeus. Describes how Hercules strangles two snakes with his bare hands at the age of one, his victory over King Erginus, and the liberation of Thebes. An interesting introduction to Greek mythology. English title available: NOBLE HERCULES.

299
    Eskimo spirit beliefs.
      prod. [Scarborough, Ont.] : R.B.M., 1974. dist. ETHOS 41fr.: col.: 35mm. & cassette (16 min.): auto. & aud. adv. sig. & teacher's manual. $19.00 (Eskimo stories) ji

      1. Eskimos - Religion.

Uses artwork to present a general introduction to the spirit world of the Eskimo. Discussion covers the roles of the shaman or angekokk and the three most important spirits of the Eskimo: Sedna, spirit of the sea; Pinja, spirit of the sky; and Asiaq, spirit of air and weather.

301.34
    Organizing a community study.
      prod. [Toronto] : B&R, 1976. dist. B&R. 28fr. : col.: 35mm. & cassette (12 min. 55 sec.) : auto. & aud. adv. sig. & teacher's guide. $18.00 (Early day Canada: $96.00) ji

      1. Cities and towns 2. Social surveys.

      Suggest that there are common factors, such as climate and availability of building materials, which influence the construction of buildings in any community throughout the world. Encourages using this method of looking for and identifying common factors to investigate other topics including food, transportation and clothing.

332.4
    Money: what is it?
      prod. [Toronto] : M-L, 1974. dist. Sch. Ser. or Wint. 60fr. : col.: 35mm. & cassette (8 min.) : auto. & aud. adv. sig. & teacher's guide. $16.50 (Learning about money : $65.00) pj

      1. Money.

      Photos depict the historical background and purpose of money, banking, and credit. The basics of barter, currency, cheques, income tax, and inflation are discussed, as well as opening a bank account, writing and cashing cheques.

Addendum

363.20971
Meeting the challenge.
prod. [Scarborough, Ont.] R.B.M., 1976. dist. ETHOS 45fr.: col.: 35mm. & cassette (13 min.) : auto. & aud. adv. sig. & teacher's manual. $19.00 (Royal Canadian Mounted Police : $69.00) ji

1. Canada. Royal Canadian Mounted Police.

Dicusses the modern techniques used by the R.C.M.P. today. Emphasizes its work in the North, and special duties performed in all the provinces except Ontario and Quebec.

363.20971
Modern technology and methods.
prod. [Scarborough, Ont.] R.B.M., 1976. dist. ETHOS 46fr.: col.: 35mm. & cassette (9 min.) : auto. & aud. adv. sig. & manual. $19.00 (Royal Canadian Mounted Police : $69.00) ji

1. Canada. Royal Canadian Mounted Police.

Details modern R.C.M.P. methods involving latest technology in forensic science. Emphasis is placed on diversity of the work and on the training programme.

372.6
Cendrillon.
prod. [Montreal?] NFB,1968. dist. SEC. 38fr.: col.: 35mm. & disc (33 1/3 r.p.m. 9 min. 7sec.) : aud. adv. sig. $18.00 pj

1. French language - Study and teaching.

The well-known fairy tale illustrated by different grade 5 pupils from Montreal includes simple French captions plus an accompanying record. For French language instruction.

380.5
The early days.
prod. [Scarborough, Ont.] R.B.M., 1976. dist. ETHOS 46fr.: b&w : 35mm. & cassette (11 min.) : auto. & aud. adv. sig. $19.00 (Transportation in Canada) ji

1. Canada - Transportation-History.

Examines the various modes of transportation used in Canada from the mid-eighteenth to early nineteenth century. Regional and seasonal variations are included.

380.5
Muscle and steam.
prod. [Toronto] : Int. Cin., 1974. dist. VEC 53fr.: col. & b&w.: 35mm. & cassette (10 min. 30 sec.): auto. & aud. adv. sig. $24.00 (Transportation: the Canadian adventure : $86.00) ji

1. Transportation - History.

Authentic drawings and photographs of early stagecoaches and steam engines illustrate the use of horse and steam power in the development of Canadian overland transportation. French title available : DE LA TRACTION ANIMAL A LA VAPEUR.

380.5
Le présent et le futur.
prod. [Toronto] : Int. Cin., 1975. dist. VEC 59fr.: col.: 35mm. & cassette (14 min. 30 sec.): auto. & aud. adv. sig. $24.00 (Transport: l'aventure canadienne : $86.00) ji

1. Transportation.

Discusses transportation of the future. Describes STOL aircraft, monorails, hovercraft, and SST's. Shows how nature of the environment will be the cause of and remedy for man's transportation problem. English title available : TODAY AND TOMORROW.

382.1
Partners in development?
prod. [Toronto] : K.M., 1976. dist. K.M. 38fr.: col. & b&w.: 35mm & cassette (9 min.): aud. adv. sig. only. $20.00. is

1. International economic relations. 2. Developing areas.

Discusses Canada's role as an exploiter in Guyana's bauxite production. Shows how Guyana, by nationalizing the bauxite industry, hopes to put an end to the process

Addendum

of exploitation. Intended to arouse discussion of the role of exploiting nations in Third World countries.

382.1   Vers un nouvel ordre économique international.
prod. [Montreal?] : NFB, 1977. dist. SEC 57fr.: col. & b&w.: 35mm. & cassette (11 min. 23 sec.): auto. & aud. adv. sig. $18.00. s

1. International economic relations.
2. Developing areas.

An analysis of economic relations existing between wealthy powers and developing nations. Explains how past exploitation of colonies by Europe and North America has led to present trade imbalance. Describes Third World's attempts to control their own resources through nationalization of industry and exportation of manufactured goods. Illustrated with photographs, drawings charts. English title available: TOWARDS A NEW INTERNATIONAL ECONOMIC ORDER.

384   Basic distress signals.
prod. [Toronto]: M-L, 1974. dist. Sch. Ser. or Wint. 47fr.: col.: 35mm. & cassette (10 min.): auto. & aud. adv. sig. & teacher's guide. $16.50 (Outdoor survival: $85.00) i

1. Signals and signaling.
2. Wilderness survival.

Describes basic distress signals to be understood by rescue pilots. Includes using life jackets, reflections of sunlight, fire at night and smoke by day, groupings of three of anything, or shaping peeled logs into symbols to convey needs. Good information for any trek into the bush. French title available: PRINCIPAUX SIGNAUX DE DETRESSE.

384.6   Getting together.
prod. [Toronto]: Int. Cin., 1976. dist. VEC 76fr.: col.: 35mm. & cassette (5 min.): auto. & aud. adv. sig. & teacher's guide. $24.00 (Hello! getting together with the telephone: $96.00) pj

1. Telephone.

A brief look at the communication needs of a community and the role of the telephone in fulfilling these needs. French title available: ET MAINTENANT, TOUS ENSEMBLE.

384.6   Hello, Mr. Bell.
prod. [Toronto]: Int. Cin., 1976. dist. VEC 87fr.: col.: 35mm. & cassette (13 min. 45 sec.): auto. & aud. adv. sig. & teacher's guide. $24.00 (Hello! getting together with the telephone: $96.00) pj

1. Telephone - History.

Alexander Graham Bell, impersonated by an actor, shows us the development of the telephone from his early model to the ones presently used. French title available: ALLO! MONSIEUR BELL.

384.6   Now you're talking.
prod. [Toronto]: Int. Cin., 1976. dist. VEC 80fr.: col.: 35mm. & cassette (10 min. 15 sec.): auto. & aud. adv. sig. & teacher's guide. $24.00 (Hello! getting together with the telephone : $96.00) pj

1. Telephone.

Introduces young children to the proper use of the telephone, teaching them to be both skillful and effective. Includes how to use the telephone in an emergency. French title available: LES EXPERTS EN TELEPHONIE.

Addendum

389
    The metric world.
       prod. [Toronto]: M-L, 1974. dist.
       Sch. Ser. or Wint. 44fr.: col.:
       35mm. & cassette (11 min.): auto.
       & aud. adv. sig. & teacher's guide.
       $16.50 (Metric measurement: $65.00)
       i

    1. Metric system.

    Introduction to International System:
    meters, centimeters, millimeters,
    kilometers, grams, kilograms, hectares,
    etc. Gives examples of everyday
    usefulness for measuring mass, volume,
    area, distance. French title
    available: LE MONDE A L'HEURE DU
    SYSTEME INTERNATIONAL.

389
    Unités de longueur.
       prod. [Toronto]: M-L, 1975. dist.
       Sch. Ser. or Wint. 54fr.: col.:
       35mm. & cassette (16 min.): auto.
       & aud. adv. sig. & teacher's guide.
       $16.50 (Usage du système international:
       $65.00) i

    1. Metric system.

    Introduces the meter, kilometer,
    centimeter and millimeter. Shows
    conversion from one to the other and
    when to use each unit. Defines
    perimeter, circumference, radius,
    diameter, and discusses how to find
    each. Provides classroom activities
    that can be done during the filmstrip.
    English title available: LINEAR UNITS.

398.2
    Le bon Roi Arthur.
       prod. [Toronto]: M-L, 1975. dist.
       Sch. Ser. or Wint. 67fr.: col.:
       35mm. & cassette (11 min. 30 sec.):
       auto. & aud. adv. sig. & teacher's
       guide. $16.50 (Les récits héroiques:
       $85.00) j

    1. Arthur, King.

    The story of King Arthur and his
    courage when facing the Savle Knight
    (King Pellinore). With the sword
    Excalibur, Arthur is able to defeat
    Pellinore and chooses to offer him
    friendship. English title available:
    GOOD KING ARTHUR.

398.209415
    L'Irlande: la casquette de O'Reilly.
       prod. [Toronto]: M-L, 1976. dist.
       Sch. Ser. or Wint. 57fr.: col.:
       35mm. & cassette (9 min.): auto. &
       aud. adv. sig. & teacher's guide.
       $16.50 (Les légendes de Noël des
       pays étrangers: $75.00) pj

    1. Folklore - Ireland.
    2. Christmas stories.

    Colourful hand puppets depict the
    tale of O'Reilly, an Irish Scrooge
    who learns of kindness and
    generosity on Christmas eve. The
    narrator, with his Irish lilt,
    provides a unique voice for each
    character of the story. English
    title available: IRELAND: O'REILLY'S
    CHRISTMAS CAP.

398.20943
    L'Allemagne: le plus beau Noël de
    casse-noix.
       prod. [Toronto]: M-L, 1976. dist.
       Sch. Ser. or Wint. 64fr.: col.:
       35mm. & cassette (14 min.): auto. &
       aud. adv. sig. & teacher's guide.
       $16.50. (Les légendes de Noël des
       pays étrangers: $75.00) pj

    1. Folklore - Germany.
    2. Christmas stories.

    The famous German Nutcracker legend
    is recaptured through colourful
    original drawings. The narrator's
    German accesnt and his ability to
    create a different voice for each
    character capture attention as does
    the familiar background music from
    the Nutcracker Suite Ballet. A
    familiar tale of interest to young
    children. English title available:
    GERMANY: THE NUTCRACKER'S HAPPY
    CHRISTMAS.

398.20943
    Le Baron Münchhausen dans une histoire
    chavirante : un conte Allemand.
       prod. [Montreal?]: NFB, 1975. dist.
       SEC 34fr.: col.: 35mm. & captions.
       $9.00 j

    1. Legends - Germany.

    A humorously exaggerated tale of a
    ship's encounter with a whale, and

Addendum

how the baron saved the day, illustrated with artwork. English title available: BARON MUNCHAUSEN IN A WHALE OF A TALE: A GERMAN LEGEND.

398.20945
Italy - the legend of La Befana.
prod. [Toronto]: M-L, 1976.
dist. Sch. Ser. or Wint. 57fr.: col.: 35mm. & cassette (11 min.): auto. & aud. adv. sig. & teacher's guide. $16.50. (Christmas tales from many lands: $75.00) pj

1. Folklore - Italy.
2. Christman stories.

Portrays the traditional legend of the immortal Christmas wanderer - La Befana. Characters fashioned of wood, cloth, pipe cleaners, spools and other common household materials, are creatively photographed, and the tale is related by a narrator with an Italian accent. French title available: L'ITALIE : LA LEGENDE DE DAME LA BEFANA.

398.20952
Les deux grenouilles: un conte Japonais.
prod. [Montreal?]: NFB, 1974. dist. SEC 41fr.: col.: 35mm. & captions. $9.00 p

1. Folklore - Japan.

Water colour illustrations enhance this tale of two frogs, one from Kyoto and the other from Osaka, who decide to travel and meet each other on a mountain top. English title available: THE TWO FROGS: A JAPANESE LEGEND.

398.2095691
La Syrie: le petit chameau.
prod. [Toronto]: M-L, 1976. dist. Sch. Ser. or Wint. 50fr.: col.: 35mm. & cassette (8 min.): auto. & aud. adv. sig. & teacher's guide. $16.50 (Les légendes de Noel des pays étrangers: $75.00) pj

1. Folklore - Syria.
2. Christmas stories.

A Christmas legend recounting the relationship that developed between the youngest of the three wise men and his tiny camel during their trip to Bethlehem. The tale demonstrates courage and determination. Three-dimensional characters sculpted from clay illustrate the story, and the background music is characteristic of the Syrian setting. English title available: SYRIA: THE LITTLE CAMEL.

398.209701
Glooskap nous a donné l'été.
prod. [Toronto]: M-L, 1975. dist. Sch. Ser. or Wint. 49fr.: col.: 35mm. & cassette (10 min.): auto. & aud. adv. sig. & teacher's guide. $16.50 (Légendes amérindiennes: $85.00) j

1. Indians of North America-Legends.
2. Seasons - Stories.

An allegorical explanation of the seasons. Suitable for classroom discussion of seasons, or discussion of allegory. English title available: GLOOSKAP BRINGS SUMMER,

398.209701
Legend of Mikchik.
prod. [Toronto]: Int. Cin., 1976. dist. VEC 78fr.: col.: 35mm. & cassette (8 min.): auto. & aud. adv. sig. & teacher's guide. $24.00 (Legends of the Micmac: $86.00) pji

1. Micmac Indians - Legends.

Old Mitchik, who was once a famous young warrior, learns that not even magic can restore his youth forever, and he must accept his old age with dignity.

398.209701
Why the Blackfeet never hurt a mouse.
prod. [Toronto]: Int. Cin., 1973. dist. VEC 45fr.: col.: 35mm. & cassette (6 min.): auto. & aud. adv. sig. & teacher's guide. $24.00 (Tales from the treetops: $86.00) pji

Addendum

1. Indians of North America - Legends.

An Indian legend telling why the Blackfeet never hurt a mouse, and why Man is chief of all the animals in the forest. Illustrated with seed collages. Narrated by Chief Dan George. French title available: POURQUOI LES PIEDS-NOIRS NE FONT JAMAIS DE MAL AUX SOURIS.

398.20971
The seagull and the whale.
prod.[Montreal?]: NFB, 1976. dist. McI. 27fr.: col.: 35mm. & captions. $9.00 p

1. Folklore - Canada.

A Maritime legend of the seagull who finds her lost egg in the stomach of a whale. Illustrations add humour. French title available: LA MOUETTE ET LA BALEINE.

407
De la terre.
prod.[Montreal?]: NFB, 1975. dist. SEC 54fr.: col.: 35mm. & printed notes. $9.00 ("De la" : $27.00) pji

1. Language arts - Study and teaching.
2. Canadian Shield - Pictorial works.

Photographs portray the wild landscapes of the Canadian Shield Region of Canada. Emphasizes the order and design found in untouched wilderness. Of most use in a language arts programme to stimulate discussion. No captions. English title available: OF THE LAND.

407
Du cheval.
prod. [Montreal?]: NFB, 1975. dist. SEC 39fr.: col.: 35mm. & printed notes. $9.00 ("De la" : $27.00) pji

1. Language arts - Study and teaching.
2. Horses - Pictorial works.

An experience of form and movement is the photographer's perception of the horse, frozen in moments of changing time. Portrays the beauty of the horse from many unusual angles. Of most use in a language arts programme to stimulate discussion. English title available: OF THE HORSE.

523.8
Millions of stars in the universe.
prod. [Toronto]: M-L, 1973. dist. Sch. Ser. or Wint. 34fr.: col.: 35mm. & cassette (6 min.): auto. & aud. adv. sig. & teacher's guide. $16.50 (Learning about our universe : $85.00) ji

1. Stars. 2. Telescope. 3. Astronomy

Demonstrates the vastness of space and the millions of stars that are present in it. Shows telescope and explains its use for astronomers. The Milky Way Galaxy is featured. French title available: LES MILLIONS D'ETOILES.

551.5
Precipitation and weather.
prod. [Toronto]: M-L, 1974. dist. Sch. Ser. or Wint. 44fr.: col.: 35mm. & cassette (7 min.): auto. & aud. adv. sig. & teacher's guide. $16.50 (Inquiry into weather: $85.00) j

1. Meteorology.

Discusses different forms of precipitation and how precipitation and condensation work in a laboratory, then in the atmosphere. Reviews different types of clouds and their names and function. Defines weather, atmosphere, wind, and the effect of the sun on weather. Good diagrams of air currents.

551.5
Storms, hurricanes and tornadoes.
prod. [Toronto]: M-L, 1974. dist. Sch. Ser. or Wint. 52 fr.: col.: 35mm. & cassette (8 min.): auto. & aud. adv. sig. & teacher's guide. $16.50 (Inquiry into weather : $85.00) j

1. Meteorology.

Addendum

Describes cloud formations and their use in forecasting weather, cold and warm fronts, condensation, positive and negative charges causing lightning; hurricane formations, the eye of the hurricane and its effects over water and land. Also includes tornadoes, where they start, how and when.

551.6
Using your own weather station. prod. [Toronto] : M-L, 1974. dist. Sch. Ser. or Wint. 45fr.: col.: 35mm. & cassette (6 min.): auto. & aud. adv. sig. & teacher's guide. $16.50 (Inquiry into weather : $85.00) j

1. Weather forecasting.

Describes steps necessary to predict weather: kinds of clouds and amount of sky covered; checking humidity (using wet and dry bulb thermometers and special paper) wind direction and speed, and the temperature. Also shows how to interpret weather maps. Good for classroom use after viewing "Starting Your Own Weather Station."

551.6
A visit to the weather station. prod. [Toronto]: M-L, 1974. dist. Sch. Ser. or Wint. 48fr.: col.: 35mm. & cassette (9 min.): auto. & aud. adv. sig. & teacher's guide. $16.50 (Inquiry into weather : $85.00) j

1. Weather forecasting.

A visit to a weather station shows how knowledge of wind direction and speed assists weather prediction. Describes the use of a Stevenson screen, anemometer, barometer, hygrometer, radiosonde, barograph and various other technological aids to weather predicting.

551.6
Weather and what affects it. prod. [Toronto]: M-L, 1974. dist. Sch. Ser. or Wint. 36fr.: col.: 35mm. & cassette (6 min.): auto. & aud. adv. sig. & teacher's guide. $16.50 (Inquiry into weather : $85.00) j

1. Meteorology.

Contrasts a homemade weather station station with a government weather station. Shows how land formations and bodies of water affect weather, explaining the difference between climate and weather. Suggests viewers find answers to why climates vary in different parts of the world.

574.5
Ecosystems. prod. [Toronto]: M-L, 1975. dist. Sch. Ser. & Wint. 51fr.: col.: 35mm. & cassette (6 min. 30 sec.): auto. & aud. adv. sig. & teacher's guide. $16.50 (Ecology: exploration and discovery : $85.00) j

1. Ecology.
2. Man - Influence on nature.

Explores the environmental, physical and organic elements that compose an ecosystem. Encourages viewers to discuss the prevention of the harm done by man to natural habitats and ecosystems. Broad scope allows this to be used as an introduction to man's effect on natural balance of nature. French title available: LES ECOSYSTEMES.

574.5
Organisms and environment. prod. [Toronto]: M-L, 1975. dist. Sch. Ser. or Wint. 57fr.: col.: 35mm. & cassette (8 min.): auto. & aud. adv. sig. & teacher's guide. $16.50 (Ecology: exploration and discovery: $85.00) j

1. Ecology.
2. Adaptation (Biology).

A detailed examination of the ways living organisms interact with and

Addendum

are adapted to their environment. Explains the terms organism, environment, matter, and illustrates conditions for optimum growth of plants and animals. Photos show actual classroom experiments. French title available: LES ORGANISMES ET LE MILIEU.

574.5
Plant and animal communities. prod. [Toronto]: M-L, 1975. dist. Sch. Ser. or Wint. 53fr.: col.: 35mm. & cassette (7 min.): auto. & aud. adv. sig. & teacher's guide. $16.50 (Ecology: exploration and discovery: $85.00) j

1. Ecology.

An exploration of a forest community showing the interdependence of plant and animal populations and the physical elements of their environment. Traces the delicate natural balances which compose an ecosystem. French title available: LES COMMUNANTES VEGETALES ET ANIMALES.

590.74
Helpers at the Metro Toronto zoo. prod. [Scarborough, Ont.]: R.B.M., 1976. dist. ETHOS. 37fr.: col.: 35mm. & cassette (7 min.): auto. & aud. adv. sig. $19.00. pj

1. Metropolitan Toronto Zoo.
2. Zoological gardens.

Introduces the many people employed by the zoo. Photographs feature aspects of zoo maintenance, such as food preparation and distribution, clean-up of grounds, repairs and office work. Discusses veterinary services. Content and photographs add to simple narration.

591
Impreintes d'animaux. prod. [Montreal?]: NFB, 1968. dist. SEC 35fr.: b&w.: 35mm. & captions & teacher's manual. $9.00. pj

1. Tracking and trailing.

Uses black and white drawings to classify common Canadian domestic and wild animals as flat-foots, toe walkers, and toe-nail walkers. Shows detailed illustrations of the tracks they make and how to identify them. English title available: ANIMAL TRACKS.

591.1
Ovulation : mammals. prod. [Toronto]: M-L, 1973. dist. Sch. Ser. or Wint. 30fr.: col.: 35mm. & cassette (6 min.): auto. & aud. adv. sig. & teacher's guide. $16.50 (Family living and sex education series B: $75.00) j

1. Reproduction.
2. Sex education.

Describes the differing female reproductive cycles of several mammalian species. Includes discussion of the fertilization of the egg and growth of an embryo in the uterus of a human mother. Illustrated with photos and graphics French title available: OVULATION: MAMMIFERES.

591.1
The reproductive cells. prod. [Toronto]: M-L, 1973. dist. Sch. Ser. or Wint. 26fr.: col.: 35mm. & cassette (5 min.): auto. & aud. adv. sig. & teacher's guide. $16.50 (Family living and sex education series B: $75.00) j

Addendum

597
　　The beginning of life: frogs.
　　　prod. [Toronto]: M-L, 1973. dist.
　　　Sch. Ser. or Wint. 29fr.:
　　　col.: 35mm. & cassette (5
　　　min.): auto. & aud. adv. sig.
　　　& teacher's guide. $16.50
　　　(Family living and sex
　　　education series B: $75.00) j

　　　1. Frogs. 2. Reproduction.

　　　A detailed discussion of the
　　　reproductive process and the
　　　life cycle of frogs. The stages
　　　of development from embryo to
　　　tadpole to frog are included.
　　　French title available: LA
　　　VIE COMMENCE : GRENOUILLES.

598.2
　　Birds of the eastern forest.
　　　prod. [Georgetown, Ont.]:
　　　FMS, 1973. dist. McI. 48fr.:
　　　col.: 35mm. & captions. $10.00
　　　(Birds of North America : $50.00)
　　　ji

　　　1. Birds - North America.

　　　Presents forty species of
　　　birds photographed in their
　　　Eastern forest habitats. Captions
　　　identify and explain individual
　　　characteristics and how many have
　　　adapted to a changed environment.

598.2
　　Birds of the grasslands.
　　　prod. [Georgetown, Ont.]: FMS,
　　　1973. dist. McI. 48fr.: col.:
　　　35mm. & captions. $10.00 (Birds
　　　of North America: $50.00) ji

　　　1. Birds - North America.

　　　Describes how the grasslands of
　　　central Canada and U.S. provide
　　　various birds with shallow marshes
　　　for nesting sites, water insects for
　　　food, and aspen groves for perching
　　　and cover, while others are
　　　attracted to trees and shrubbery
　　　around farms. Includes photos of
　　　ducks, grebes, hawks, owls,
　　　warblers, and eagles in surrounding
　　　dry hills.

598.2
　　Birds of the northern forest.
　　　prod. [Georgetown, Ont.]: FMS,
　　　1973. dist. McI. 48fr.: col.:
　　　35mm. & captions. $10.00. (Birds
　　　of North America: $50.00) ji

　　　1. Birds - North America.

　　　A close-up look at many varieties
　　　of birds that inhabit the north,
　　　with captions that describe feeding
　　　and nesting habits, and preferred
　　　locations. Points out how fish
　　　from polluted waters are affecting
　　　osprey population.

598.2
　　Birds of the Rocky Mountains.
　　　prod. [Georgetown, Ont.]: FMS, 1973.
　　　dist. McI. 48fr.: col.: 35mm. &
　　　captions. $10.00. (Birds of
　　　North America: $50.00) ji

　　　1. Birds - North America.

　　　Describes the variety of habitats
　　　in the Rockies and how different
　　　kinds of birds are attracted to
　　　the special conditions found in
　　　each area. Photos show jays,
　　　grosbeaks, finches in the forests;
　　　goldfinches, bluebirds, etc. in the
　　　orchard; and grassland birds, such
　　　as ducks, where ponds are located.

598.2
　　Comment les oiseaux se procurent leur
　　nourriture.
　　　prod. [Toronto]: Int. Cin., 1975.
　　　dist. VEC 57fr.: col.: 35mm. &
　　　cassette (7 min. 30 sec.): auto. &
　　　aud. adv. sig. & teacher's manual.
　　　$24.00 (Le Monde des oiseaux:
　　　$64.00) ji

　　　1. Birds - Habits and behaviour.

　　　How and where birds find nourishment
　　　in their natural habitat, and how
　　　each kind of bird is physically
　　　adapted to eat the different types
　　　of food in its environment. English
　　　title available: HOW BIRDS FIND
　　　FOOD.

Addendum

598.2
Les oiseaux communs du Canada.
  prod. [Montreal?]: NFB, 1968.
  dist. SEC 33fr.: col.: 35mm.
  & captions & teacher's manual.
  $9.00 pj

  1. Birds - Canada.

  Detailed drawings portray some of
  the more common birds of Canada,
  presented in the order of the
  evolutionary scale from primitive
  to advanced species. Measurements
  are not metric. Filmstrip only
  provides information on the
  name and size of birds; detailed
  notes are found in the manual.
  Best if used with groups.
  English title available: COMMON
  BIRDS OF CANADA.

598.2
Owls.
  prod. [Montreal?]: NFB, made
  1960:1972. dist. McI. 27fr.:
  col.: 35mm. & printed notes &
  captions. $9.00 (Birds of
  Canada : $54.00) pj

  1. Owls.

  Depicts the environment and
  habits of several species of
  owls including the barn owl,
  snowy owl, screech owl, and
  great horned owl. French
  title available: LES HIBOUX.

598.2
The seabirds of Bonaventure Island.
  prod. [Georgetown, Ont.]: FMS,
  1973. dist. McI. 48fr.: col.:
  35mm. & captions. $10.00
  (Birds of North America:
  $50.00) ji

  1. Gannets.
  2. Birds - Bonaventure Island,
     Que.

  Describes nesting habits of the
  gannet and the raising of their
  young on Bonaventure Island.
  Shows other birds on the island,
  including the herring gull,
  puffin, kittiwake, and common
  murre.

599
Cattle, cattle, cattle.
  prod. [Toronto]: M-L, 1973. dist.
  Sch. Ser. or Wint. 65fr.: col.:
  35mm. & cassette (9 min.): auto.
  & aud. adv. sig. & teacher's guide.
  $16.50 (Animals: a close-up look:
  $75.00) kpji

  1. Cattle.

  Uses close-up photography to
  examine the beef cattle that roam
  the grasslands of the foothills
  of the Rocky Mountains. Describes
  the physical features of beef
  cattle, how they are herded by
  cowboys, and why they are
  branded. Narration on one sound
  track natural sounds and music on
  the other. Would be useful in a
  language arts programme. French
  title available: LES BESTIAUX DE
  L'OUEST.

599
Ponies, ponies, ponies.
  prod. [Toronto]: M-L, 1973. dist.
  Sch. Ser. or Wint. 46fr.: col.:
  35mm. & cassette (7 min.): auto. &
  aud. adv. sig. & teacher's guide.
  $16.50 (Animals: a close-up look:
  $75.00) kpji

  1. Ponies.

  Depicts the physical characteristics
  habits, and environment of Welsh
  ponies. Includes photos of
  competition jumping. Narration on
  one sound track, music and sound
  effects on the other. Would be
  useful in a language arts
  programme. French title available:
  LES PONEYS: PETITS ET GRANDS.

599.097
Life in the western mountains.
  prod. [Georgetown, Ont.]: FMS, 1976.
  dist. McI. 57fr.: col.: 35mm. &
  cassette (13 min.): auto. & aud.
  adv. sig. $19.00 (Wildlife of
  North America: the mammals: $95.00)
  ji

  1. Mammals. 2. Adaptation (Biology)

Addendum

Describes the mountain environment of the Pacific Rim and Rockies as habitats for wildlife, and the factors of altitude, temperature, moisture and sunlight that affect mammals. Focuses on special characteristics of some of the mammals to survive and survival techniques adopted by others. Includes photographs of mountain goats, sheep, caribou, and grizzly bear, and on location sound effects.

599.0971
Les carnivores.
prod. [Montreal?]: NFB, 1976. dist. SEC. 35fr.: col.: 35mm. & captions. $9.00. ji

1. Mammals.

Uses drawings and photographs to describe the habits of the five groups of carnivores - cats, bears, dogs, raccoons, and weasles and their relatives. Examines the various methods of hunting these mammals and their place in the balance of nature. States size and weight of each animal illustrated. Not metric. English title available: CARNIVORES: THE FLESH EATERS.

611
The muscular system.
prod. [Toronto]: M-L, 1976. dist. Sch. Ser. or Wint. 43fr.: col.: 35mm. & cassette (8 min. 30 sec.): auto. & aud. adv. sig. & teacher's guide. $16.50 (Learning about the human body: $85.00) j

1. Muscles.

A comparison of three different muscle groups, examining the way each functions, its importance, its development and care. Cartoons, diagrams and photos.

611
The skeletal system.
prod. [Toronto]: M-L, 1976. dist. Sch. Ser. or Wint. 49fr.: col.: 35mm. & cassette (10 min. 30 sec.): auto. & aud. adv. sig.& teacher's guide. $16.50 (Learning about the human body: $85.00) j

1. Bones.

Description of the three main functions of bones, also their interrelationship with joints, cartilage, ligaments, and muscles. Cartoons, diagrams and photos.

611
The teeth.
prod. [Toronto]: M-L, 1976. dist. Sch. Ser. or Wint. 51fr.: col.: 35mm. & cassette (10 min, 30 sec.): auto. & aud. adv. sig. & teacher's guide. $16.50. (Learning about the human body: $85.00) j

1. Teeth.

A detailed presentation on teeth. Covers the purpose, kinds, functions enemies and care of teeth, as well as outlining the parts of a tooth. Cartoons, diagrams, and photos provide illustration.

612.6
A human being is born.
prod. [Toronto]: M-L, 1973. dist. Sch. Ser. or Wint. 32fr.: col.: 35mm & cassette (5 min.): auto. & aud. áud. adv. sig. & teacher's guide. $16.50 (Family living and sex education series B: $75.00) j

1. Childbirth. 2. Reproduction. 3. Sex education.

Uses diagrams and photos to demonstrate the process of childbirth and to explain the male and female reproductive systems. French title available: LA NAISSANCE D'UN ETRE HUMAN.

Addendum

612.6
    Puberté
       prod. [Montreal?]: NFB, 1975
       dist. SEC   38fr.: col.: 35mm.
       & captions. $9.00 is

       1. Adolescence.
       2. Menstruation.

       Silhouettes of males and females,
       with diagrams of organs, are used
       to illustrate physical external
       and internal changes that occur
       with puberty. The nature of
       menstruation and menstrual
       cycle are shown. English
       title available: PUBERTY.

614.8
    Walk safely on the highway.
       prod. [Montreal?]: NFB, 1974.
       dist. McI. 40fr.: col.:
       35mm. & captions. $9.00.
       pj

       1. Walking - Safety measures.
       2. Accidents - Prevention.

       Drawings portray a boy and a
       scarecrow illustrating safety
       rules for walking on the highway.
       Dialogue for different speakers
       is underlined with different
       colours for use as a play-
       reading activity.

615
    Some known facts about marijuana.
       prod. [Montreal?]: NFB, 1973.
       dist. McI. 58fr,: col. & b&w:
       35mm. & cassette (11 min. 45
       sec.): auto. & aud. adv. sig.
       $18.00. is

       1. Marihuana.

       Photographs show the plant, its
       habitat, history and uses.
       Cartoons provide good coverage of the
       physical, social and emotional
       reasons for the drug's use,
       its known effect on the human body,
       as well as its legal aspects.
       French title available: LA
       MARIJUANA: QUELQUES VERITES.

616.9
    How does V.D. spread?
       prod. [Toronto]: M-L, 1974. dist.
       Sch. Ser. or Wint. 46fr.: col.:
       35mm. & cassette (9 min.): auto. &
       aud. adv. sig. & teacher's guide.
       $16.50 (Venereal disease: what I
       need to know: $85.00) is

       1. Venereal diseases.

       Clearly describes gonorrhea and
       syphilis, symptoms, and how they
       spread. Outlines reasons for
       growing incidence of V.D., stressing
       need for informed and open dis-
       cussion. Illustrated with photos,
       diagrams, sketches.

616.9
    How is V.D. cured?
       prod. [Toronto]: M-L, 1974. dist.
       Sch. Ser. or Wint. 53fr.: col.:
       35mm. & cassette (11 min.): auto. &
       aud. adv. sig. & teacher's guide.
       $16.50 (Venereal disease: what I
       need to know: $85.00) is

       1. Venereal diseases.

       Uses clear, easily understandable
       terms with photos and diagrams
       to describe the symptoms of
       gonorrhea and syphilis, emphasizing
       that, because symptoms may be
       mistaken for something else, treat-
       ment should be sought, even if
       only suspected. Discusses clinical
       detection of V.D. and treatment
       with antibiotics. Effects of
       gonorrhea on a female (sterility,
       infection of fetus) are also
       outlined.

616.9
    Name your V.D. contacts.
       prod. [Toronto]: M-L, 1974. dist.
       Sch. Ser. or Wint. 57fr.: col.:
       35mm. & cassette (8 min.): auto. &
       aud. adv. sig. & teacher's guide.
       $16.50 (Venereal disease: what I
       need to know: $85.00) is

       1. Venereal diseases.
       2. Sexual ethics.

Addendum

Peter faces a dilemma when he learns he is infected with gonorrhea - should he or shouldn't he identify and/or notify his contacts? When he learns of the dangers involved if disease is not treated early, he decides he has a responsibility to name his contacts. Diagrams and photos.

616.9
    What is gonorrhea?
        prod. [Toronto]: M-L, 1974. dist. Sch. Ser. or Wint. 41fr.: col.: 35mm. & cassette (8 min.): auto. & aud. adv. sig. & teacher's guide. $16.50 (Venereal disease: what I need to know: $85.00) is

        1. Gonorrhea.

        Explains how gonococcus germs spread, and the symptoms, characteristics and treatment of the disease. Stresses the need for early diagnosis and treatment, the need to name contacts, and discusses where to obtain help. Diagrams and photos.

616.9
    What is syphilis?
        prod. [Toronto]: M-L, 1974. dist. Sch. Ser. or Wint. 57fr.: col.: 35mm. & cassette (11 min.): auto. & aud. adv. sig. & teacher's guide. $16.50 (Venereal disease: what I need to know: $85.00) is

        1. Syphilis.

        An informative description of the characteristics, symptoms, and treatment of syphilis. Diagrams and photos are used to show the three stages of disease, how it spreads, and the organ and tissue damage caused. Emphasizes need for early diagnosis and treatment, stressing the need for naming contacts.

621.31
    Domestic electricity.
        prod. [Toronto]: M-L, 1974. dist. Sch. Ser. or Wint. 65fr.: col.: 35mm. & cassette (8 min.): auto. & aud. adv. sig. & teacher's guide. $16.50 (Applications of electricity : $75.00) s

        1. Electric power plants.
        2. Electric transformers.
        3. Electric power distribution.

        Presents the role of the electric power plant, transformer, and main electrical panel in distributing power to and in the home. Shows the origin of electrical power, types of power plants, explaining the function of transformers and how they raise and lower voltage power. Describes the main electrical panel in a home, the distribution of power, and the function of circuit breakers and fuses to detect a circuit overload.

621.313
    The generator.
        prod. [Toronto]: M-L, 1974. dist. Sch. Ser. or Wint. 56fr.: col.: 35mm. & cassette (8 min.): auto. & aud. adv. sig. & teacher's guide. $16.50 (Applications of electricity : $75.00) s

        1. Electric generators.

        An explanation of the basic principle of a generator. Shows the relationship between mechanical motion and the electricity that is produced. Photographs and diagrams show parts of the generator, such as coil, sliprings, and rotors. Also identifies and discusses function of different types of generators including AC and DC generators.

621.319
    Switch wiring and low voltage circuits.
        prod.[Toronto]: M-L, 1974. dist. Sch. Ser. or Wint. 60fr.: col.: 35mm. & cassette (9 min.): auto. & aud. adv. sig. & teacher's guide. $16.50 (Applications of electricity: $75.00) s

Addendum

1. Electric switchgear.
2. Electric circuits.

Explains the concept of the electrical switch that controls the power in a home. Discusses different types of switches and their installation for a variety of purposes. Describes low voltage circuits and their application in a house, using a door buzzer as an example.

621.46
The motor.
prod. [Toronto]: M-L, 1974. dist. Sch. Ser. or Wint. 60fr.: col.: 35mm. & cassette (9 min.): auto. & aud. adv. sig. & teacher's guide. $16.50 (Applications of electricity: $75.00)   s

1. Electric motors.

Discusses the production of mechanical motion by an electrically-powered motor. Identifies and explains the parts of a common AC motor, such as field windings, commutator bars, and carbon brushes. Diagrams and photographs illustrate the different types of motors - compound, induction, synchronous - and their functions.

621.9
Planes and planing.
prod. [Toronto]: M-L, 1973. dist. Sch. Ser. or Wint. 57fr.: col.: 35mm. & cassette (11 min.): auto. & aud. adv. sig. & teacher's guide. $16.50 (Woodworking: hand tools (A) : $85.00) is

1. Planes.

Identifies the parts of a common plane. Uses close-ups to introduce and demonstrate jack, smoothing, jointer, block, rabbet and router planes.

621.9
Screwdrivers and screws.
prod. [Toronto]: M-L, 1973. dist. Sch. Ser. or Wint. 37fr.: col.: 35mm. & cassette (6 min.): auto. & aud. adv. sig. & teacher's guide. $16.50 (Woodworking: hand tools (A) : $85.00) is

1. Screwdrivers.

Illustrates a variety of wood screws and screwdrivers and demonstrates how to use them correctly. Includes Phillips and Robertson screws and screwdrivers as well as ratchet, spiral ratchet and offset screwdrivers.

621.9
The sharpening of plane irons, chisels and gouges.
prod. [Toronto]: M-L, 1973. dist. Sch. Ser. or Wint. 39fr.: col.: 35mm. & cassette (9 min.): auto. & aud. adv. sig. & teacher's guide. $16.50 (Woodworking: hand tools (A) : $85.00) is

1. Chisels.   2. Plane irons.
3. Gouges.

Demonstrates techniques for sharpening a chisel and a plane iron, and for grinding gouges with inside or outside bevels. Emphasizes need for care when using equipment.

629.22
Cylinder heads and valves.
prod. [Toronto]: M-L, 1973. dist. Sch. Ser. or Wint. 53fr.: col.: 35mm. & cassette (9 min.): auto. & aud. adv. sig. & teacher's guide. $16.50 (Auto Mechanics: $75.00) is

1. Automobiles - Engines.

Proper removal and replacement of cylinder head, valve and rocker arm assemblies, and manifolds in a one-head engine. Indicates reasons behind each step in procedure, and kinds of tools and equipment needed. Stresses maintenance of parts and tools. Illustrated with close-up photography.

Addendum

629.22
Operation of the running gear.
  prod. [Toronto]: M-L, 1973.
  dist. Sch. Ser. or Wint. 55fr.:
  col.: 35mm. & cassette (12 min.):
  auto. & aud. adv. sig. & teacher's
  guide. $16.50 (Auto mechanics:
  $75.00) is

  1. Automobiles - Transmission devices.
  2. Automobiles - Brakes.

  Shows each part of the running
  gear, its operation and function.
  Parts include springs, shocks,
  and braking system. Includes
  terminology definitions. Clear
  diagrams, photographs illustrate.

641.5
Feux et cuisine.
  prod. [Montreal?]: NFB, 1965.
  dist. SEC. 33fr.: col.: 35mm.
  & captions. $9.00. is

  1. Cookery, Outdoor.

  Photographs show various methods
  of cooking outdoors, as well as
  safety measures, helpful hints
  and ideas. Stoves vary from
  propane and gas to charcoal.
  Fires, such as the altar fire,
  the trench fire, the bean hole
  and teepee fire are shown.
  Directions for making a
  reflector oven are included.
  English title available:
  FIRES AND COOKING.

665
The oil industry in Canada.
  prod. [Montreal?]: NFB, 1974.
  dist. McI. 68fr.: col. &
  b&w.: 35mm. & captions. $9.00.
  ji

  1. Petroleum industry and trade.

  History of petroleum in Canada.
  Compares its use to other sources
  of fuel, the search for oil,
  drilling for oil, and rate of
  production. Location of actual
  and potential oil basins, distillation
  process; oil products and methods
  of coping with oil slicks.

669
Le métal brillant.
  prod. [Toronto]: Int. Cin., 1975.
  dist. VEC 75fr.: col.: 35mm. &
  cassette (10 min. 45 sec.): auto. &
  aud. adv. sig. $24.00 is

  1. Aluminum.

  Explains the various processes
  involved in the manufacturing of
  aluminium. A study in interdependence, from the mining of
  bauxite in tropical countries to
  the processing of the ore in Arvida,
  Quebec, and Kitimat, B.C. Gives
  examples of multi-uses of this
  metal from buses to space blankets.
  English title available: THE SHINY
  METAL.

669
The shiny metal.
  prod. [Toronto]: Int. Cin., 1975.
  dist. VEC. 75fr.: col.: 35mm. &
  cassette (9 min. 45 sec.): auto. &
  aud. adv. sig. $24.00 is

  1. Aluminum industry and trade.
  2. Canada-Industries.

  Explains the various processes
  involved in the manufacturing of
  aluminium. A study in interdependence, from the mining of
  bauxite in tropical countries to
  the processing of the ore in Arvida,
  Quebec, and Kitimat, B.C. Gives
  examples of multi-uses of this
  metal from buses to space blankets.

671.5
Metal fastening methods.
  prod. [Toronto]: M-L, 1973. dist.
  Sch. Ser. or Wint. 48fr.: col.:
  35mm. & cassette (9 min.): auto. &
  aud. adv. sig. & teacher's guide.
  $16.50 (Metalwork - machine
  operations: $75.00) is

  1. Metal work.

  Demonstrates the most common methods
  used to fasten together metal pieces
  Covers a tinner's rivet and blind
  rivetting, bolts, machine screws,
  cap screws used as fasteners, and
  spot welding. Simple step-by-step
  instructions and photographs
  illustrate tools and machinery used,
  as well as how and when to use them.

Addendum

684
Staining and finishing wood.
prod. [Toronto]: M-L, 1973. dist.
Sch. Ser. or Wint. 47fr.: col.:
35mm. & cassette (9 min.): auto.&
aud. adv. sig. & teacher's guide.
$16.50 (Woodworking: hand tools
(A): $85.00) is

1. Wood finishing.

A photographic presentation of the
applications of stains and finishes.
Discusses the use of oil, a wiping
stain, orange and white shellac,
varnish, and wax. The cleaning
of brushes, use of wood filler and
sanding, and cleaning throughout
all stages are included.

759.11
La peinture ancienne au Canada français.
prod. [Montreal?]: NFB, 1967. dist.
SEC 61fr.: col.: 35mm. & captions.
$9.00. s

1. Painting, Canadian (French).

Contains 37 reproductions of paintings
from French Canada, from the 17th -
19th centuries with short introductions
to each section. Identification of the
paintings is also given in the notes.

764
Printing screen prints.
prod. [Oakville, Ont.]: SC, 1971.
dist. SC. 34fr.: col.: 35mm. &
cassette (5 min.): auto. adv. sig.
only. $35.00 is

1. Silk screen printing.

Drawings, diagrams and photographs
examine procedure for screen
printing. Stresses good preparation
procedures and arrangement of utensils.
Describes methods of registration,
and off-contact printing. A detailed,
technical presentation.

764
Setting up your own screen studio.
prod. [Oakville, Ont.]: SC, 1971.
dist. SC. 75fr.: col.: 35mm. &
cassette (7 min 40 sec.): auto.
adv. sig. only. $35.00 is

1. Silk screen printing -
Equipment and supplies.

Close-up photography aids the
concise instruction provided for
screen studio arrangement. Gives
suggestions for ventilation, light,
ink mixing and storage, printing
table and purchasing supplies.
Also useful for art studio layouts
in general.

769
La naissance d'un pays.
prod. [Toronto]: Int. Cin., 1975.
dist. VEC. 60fr.: col.: 35mm. &
cassette (13 min.): auto. & aud.
adv. sig. & teacher's guide.
$24.00 (Les timbres poste racontent
l'histoire du Canada: $86.00) ji

1. Postage stamps.
2. Canada-History-Pictorial works.

Traces Canada's history through
historic and commemorative stamps.
Includes Indians, explorers, famous
battles, Confederation, well-known
politicians, and people in the
field of medicine. English title
available: SHAPING THE CANADIAN
NATION.

769
La présentation du timbre poste.
prod. [Toronto]: Int. Cin., 1975.
dist. VEC. 60fr.: col.: 35mm. &
cassette (12 min.): auto. & aud.
adv. sig. & teacher's guide. $24.00
(Les timbres poste racontent
l'histoire du Canada: $86.00) ji

1. Postage stamps - History.
2. Postal service - Canada - History

Describes history of stamps and the
development of our postal system.
Emphasizes the historical
significance of special issues, the
various types of stamps and their
uses, as well as the value of some
rare examples. English title
available: INTRODUCING THE POSTAGE
STAMP.

Addendum

769
    Les provinces canadiennes.
        prod. [Toronto]: Int. Cin., 1975.
        dist. VEC 65fr.: col.: 35mm. &
        cassette (13 min.): auto. & aud.
        adv. sig. & teacher's guide.
        $24.00 (Les timbres poste
        racontent l'histoire du Canada:
        $86.00) ji

        1. Postage Stamps.
        2. Canada-History-Pictorial works.

        Describes specific aspects of each
        provinces. Includes historic
        events and important landmarks,
        such as Charlottetown Conference,
        the Bluenose, Red River Settlement,
        the development of the West, and
        the Gold Rush. English title
        available: CANADA AND ITS PROVINCES.

770.28
    Picture techniques.
        prod. [Scarborough, Ont.]: R.B.M.,
        1976. dist. ETHOS 68fr.: col.:
        35mm. & cassette (13 min.): auto.
        & aud. adv. sig. & manual. $19.00
        (Basic photography: $69.00) ji

        1. Photography.

        Designed to give the viewer some
        of the basic techniques of taking
        good pictures.

778.2
    The 16mm. film projector: part 2.
        prod. [Montreal?]: NFB, 1961.
        dist. McI. 18fr.: col.: 35mm.
        & captions. $9.00 is

        1. Projectors.

        Illustrates the movement of the
        film and gives threading diagrams.
        35mm, 16mm and 8mm are shown and
        diagrams explain each part of the
        projector involved in movement of
        the film. Includes threading
        diagrams for Ampro, Bell and Howell,
        Eastman Kodak, RCA and Victor
        projectors. Designed for training
        volunteer projectionists. French
        title available: LE PROJECTEUR
        CINEMATOGRAPHIQUE DE 16MM. : 2e
        PARTIE.

778.9
    Photographing people.
        prod. [Scarborough, Ont.]: R.B.M.,
        1976. dist. ETHOS 53fr.: col.:
        35mm. & cassette (8 min.): auto. &
        aud. adv. sig. & teacher's manual.
        $19.00 (Basic photography: $69.00)
        ji

        1. Photography of people.

        Covers some very basic concepts of
        taking pictures of people. Useful
        for the beginning photographer of
        any age.

796.9
    The referee's role.
        prod. [Scarborough, Ont.]: R.B.M.,
        1975. dist. ETHOS 35fr.: col.:
        35mm. & captions & reading script.
        $19.00 (The game of hockey: $72.00)
        ji

        1. Ice hockey.

        Examines the function of the
        referee during a hockey game.

915.95
    Malacca: porte de la Malaysia.
        prod. [Montreal?]: NFB, 1975. dist.
        SEC 101fr.: col.: 35mm. & cassette
        (14 min. 10 sec.): auto. & aud. adv.
        sig. & teacher's manual. $18.00
        ji

        1. Malacca, Malaysia - description.

        A young narrator provides a
        comprehensive description of life
        in Malaysia. Includes colourful
        details about rubber production,
        rice farming, sports, food,
        entertainment, religion, education,
        history, language and the ethnic
        make-up of Malaysia. Part of a kit
        entitled "Spotlight on Development".
        English title available: MALACCA:
        GATEWAY TO MALAYSIA.

916.76
    Kandara: la vie dans une agglomération.
    Kenyane.
        prod. [Montreal?]: NFB, 1975. dist.
        SEC 105fr.: col.: 35mm. & cassette
        (16 min.): auto. & aud. adv. sig. &
        teacher's guide. $18.00 ji

Addendum

1. Kandara, Kenya - Description.

Describes life in Kandara, an isolated village in Kenya. Tribal customs, farming, division of labour, foods, social system, religion, house construction, sports, games, musical instruments, outdoor markets, and the importance of water are all discussed. Narrated by a young Canadian girl whose pen pal in Kandara provides information about the community. English title available: KANDARA: LIFE IN A KENYAN COMMUNITY.

917.11
British Columbia.
prod. [Toronto]: M-L, 1974. dist. Sch. Ser. or Wint. 76fr.: col.: 35mm. & cassette (15 min.): auto. & aud. adv. sig. & teacher's guide. $16.50 (Canada: "The true north strong and free": $85.00) i

1. British Columbia - Economic conditions.

Describes favourable climate of British Columbia and benefits of its natural wealth and geography. Stresses dependence on the Pacific Ocean for fishing industries and trade with the Orient. Shows how British Columbia's economy is diversified with copper, lead and zinc mining, agriculture, and forest industries. Outlines B.C.'s economic and resource development in the past and for the future. French title available: LA COLOMBIE BRITANNIQUE.

917.12
Vue d'ensemble: les plaines de l'Ouest.
prod.[Montreal?]: NFB, made 1961 : 1977. dist. SEC 41fr.: col.: 35mm. & captions. $9.00 ji

1. Prairie provinces - Geography.

A photographic overview of the Western Plains region of Canada. Discusses physical geography, climate, economy, transportation systems, and population. Points out the importance of wheat production, beef cattle, and the petroleum industry. Measurements are not metric. English title available: INTRODUCTION: THE WESTERN PLAINS.

917.12
Le Yukon.
prod. [Montreal?]: NFB, 1963? dist. SEC 41fr.: col. & b&w.: 35mm. & captions. $9.00 ji

1. Yukon Territory - Description and travel.

A general introduction to the terrain, cities and industries of the Yukon. Shows the major cities and industries, stressing the role of transportation in the region's development and expansion. Photographs convey the beauty of the area and the abundance of natural resources.

917.127
Le Manitoba: le bouclier.
prod. [Montreal?]: NFB, 1970. dist. SEC. 37fr.: col.: 35mm. & captions & manual. $9.00 (La géographie du Manitoba) ji

1. Manitoba - Geography.

Photographs and maps illustrate the harsh landscapes of the Canadian Shield, plus development and potential of this area. Specifically studies mining, water power, forestry and economic activities of the people. Includes Thompson and Flin Flon, and describes problems in developing the shield. Measurements are not metric. English title available: MANITOBA: THE SHIELD.

917.16
Lunenburg - a community study.
prod. [Scarborough, Ont.]: R.B.M., 1976. dist. ETHOS 50fr.: col. & b&w.: 35mm. & cassette (11 min.): auto. & aud. adv. sig. & teacher's guide. $19.00 i

1. Lunenberg, N.S. - Description

Addendum

Photographs of today's Lunenburg depict many reminders of its past as a major shipbuilding centre and important fishing community.

918.1
Brasilia.
prod. [Kitchener, Ont.]: EDU, 1974. dist. EDU. 25fr.: col.: 35mm. & cassette (14 min.): auto. & aud. adv. sig. & teacher's manual. $15.95 (South America: $69.95) jis

1. Brasilia, United States of Brazil - Description.

A description of a modern city in a barren setting. Discusses the advantages and disadvantages of building a whole city to a specific plan and includes a tour of the Legislature, the Ministries and the Plaza of the Three Powers. Encourages comparison with other South American cities.

918.2
Buenos Aires.
prod. [Kitchener, Ont.]: EDU, 1974. dist. EDU. 25fr.: col.: 35mm. & cassette (13 min.): auto. & aud. adv. sig. & teacher's manual. $15.95 (South America: $69.95) jis

1. Buenos Aires, Argentine Republic-Description.

Describes Buenos Aires as a very modern and industrial city, discussing its imports, exports, railway and shipping systems, and many businesses related to agriculture. Shows the influence of politics on everyday life, the growth of suburbs, and great prosperity. Tours several communities and describes booming tourist industry.

918.4
La Paz.
prod. [Kitchener, Ont.]: EDU, 1974 dist. EDU. 25fr.: col.: 35mm. & cassette (14 min.): auto. & aud. adv. sig. & teacher's manual. $15.95 (South America: $69.95) jis

1. La Paz, Bolivia-Description.

A view of the little-known mountain capital of Bolivia. Describes colourful dress of the natives, their food, and the very steep and hilly streets. Discusses the political and social problems in this city of both ancient and modern lifestyles.

918.5
Cuzco.
prod. [Kitchener, Ont.]: EDU, 1974 dist. EDU 25fr.: col.: 35mm. & cassette (13 min.): auto. & aud. adv. sig. & teacher's manual. $15.95 (South America: $69.95) jis

1. Cuzco, Peru-Description.

A comprehensive tour of the Inca capital of South America showing the importance of tourism and its influence on the natives. Discusses primitive social habits, poor farming techniques, and meagre education of Indians compared with the white man. Leads to discussion of the problems this city faces and the reasons for them.

920
Jeanne d'Arc: héroine française.
prod. [Toronto]: M-L, 1975. dist. Sch. Ser. or Wint. 59fr.: col.: 35mm. & cassette (11 min. 30 sec.): auto. & aud. adv. sig. & teacher's guide. $16.50 (Les récits héroiques : $85.00) j

1. Jeanne d'Arc, Saint, 1412-1431.

Uses art work to tell the story of a simple peasant girl whose conviction that she is sent by God to drive the British out of France, provides her with the courage to

Addendum

lead her soldiers in the Battle of Orleans. Story does not deal with Joan's ultimate fate, but only with her courage in battle. Has obvious and worthwhile feminist overtones. English title available: COMMANDING JOAN OF ARC.

920
  Stephen Leacock.
    prod. [Scarborough, Ont]: R.B.M., 1975. dist. ETHOS 44fr.: col.: 35mm. & cassette (10 min.): auto. & aud. adv. sig. & teacher's manual. $19.00 ji

    1. Leacock, Stephen Butler, 1869-1944.

    A brief look at the life and career of one of Canada's best known authors and humorists, Stephen Leacock. Illustrated with artwork and photographs.

929.90971
  The flags of Canada's past.
    prod. [Toronto]: Int. Cin. 1973. dist. VEC. 42fr.: col.: 35mm. & cassette (9 min.): auto. & aud. adv. sig. & teacher's guide. $24.00 (The Canadian flag: $65.00) ji

    1. Flags - Canada - History.

    Discusses the origin of flags in general, and shows how the history of Canada affected the development of her national flag. French title available: LES DRAPEAUX CANADIENS D'AUTRE FOIS.

970.1
  The first Canadians.
    prod. [Scarborough, Ont.]: SHN, 1976. dist. PHM. 74fr.: col. & b&w.: 35mm. & cassette (22 min.): auto. & aud. adv. sig. & teacher's guide. $39.60 (The peoples of Canada: our multi-cultural heritage: $82.00) is

    1. Indians of North America - History.
    2. Eskimos - History.
    3. Canada - Immigration and emigration-History.

    Discusses the history and customs of many Indian and Eskimo tribes. Traces pattern of European settlement across Canada and its effect on the native people. Uses historic paintings, etchings, maps, and drawings.

971.1
  La course à l'or.
    prod. [Montreal?]: NFB, 1968. dist. SEC. 41fr.: col. & b&w.: 35mm. & captions. $9.00 (Les pionniers: $72.00) jis

    1. British Columbia - History.
    2. Gold mines and mining - History.

    Describes the struggle of the prospectors on their journey to the British Columbia goldfields in 1858. Depicts the primitive means of transportation and the building of the Caribou Wagon Road from Yale, British Columbia, to Barkerville, British Columbia. Uses photographs of prospectors, local townspeople and the gold mines. English title available: GOLD RUSH: PIONEER MINING IN BRITISH COLUMBIA.

971.2
  Le patrimoine des pionniers.
    prod. [Toronto]: Int. Cin., 1975. dist. VEC. 59fr.: col. & b&w.: 35mm. & cassette (16 min.): auto. & aud. adv. sig. & teacher's guide. $24.00 (Le Patrimoine vivant du Canada: $86.00) ji

    1. The West, Canadian - History.

    A look at the early settlement of the Prairie Provinces and the west coast, including a brief history of the Yukon gold rush and the major early trading companies. Uses paintings, drawings, and photographs English title available: FRONTIER HERITAGE.

Addendum

971.27
Le petit Fort Garry: l'héritage de la traite des pelleteries.
prod. [Toronto]: Int. Cin., 1975. dist. VEC 79fr.: col. & b&w.: 35mm. & cassette (15 min.): auto. & aud. adv. sig. $24.00 (La traite des pelleteries : $45.00) jis

1. Lower Fort Garry, Man. - History.
2. Fur trade - History.
3. Manitoba - History.

Traces Lower Fort Garry from early days of fur trading through the periods of the Riel Rebellion, the Nortwest Mounted Police and the creation of the province of Manitoba. Shows many scenes of the fort today as it is for tourists and students. English title available: LOWER FORT GARRY: LEGACY OF THE FUR TRADE.

971.3
Activities of the season.
prod. [Toronto]: B & R, 1973. dist. B&R 19fr.: col.: 35mm. & cassette (4 min. 45 sec): auto. & aud. adv. sig. $10.00 (Canadian Holidays: $18.00) pj

1. Frontier and pioneer life - Ontario.
2. Thanksgiving Day.

Uses photographs of Black Creek pioneer village to show how the change of season influenced the activities of pioneer families. Thanksgiving activities illustrated include soap and candle-making, the storing of firewood, preserving food, and spinning and weaving.

971.3
L'école et les loisirs.
prod. [Toronto]: M-L, 1972. dist. Sch. Ser. or Wint. 46fr.: col.: 35mm. & cassette (11 min.): auto. & aud. adv. sig. & teacher's guide. $16.50. (La vie quotidienne des pionniers du Haut-Canada: $85.00) ji

1. Frontier and pioneer life - Ontario.

Photos taken at Upper Canada Village depict learning in a one-room pioneer school. A quilting bee and a wedding are shown as forms of entertainment for the pioneers. English title available: SCHOOL AND RECREATION.

971.3
La ferme.
prod. [Toronto]: M-L, 1972. dist. Sch. Ser. or Wint. 48fr.: col.: 35mm. & cassette (12 min.): auto. & aud. adv. sig. & teacher's guide $16.50 (La vie quotidienne des pionniers du Haut-Canada: $85.00) ji

1. Frontier and pioneer life - Ontario.

Emphasizes the importance of farming to the pioneers as each step from preparing the soil for planting to the final harvest is shown. Photos taken at Upper Canada Village include scenes of grinding wheat in into flour and the making of linens from flax. English title available: FARM LIFE.

971.3
Le foyer.
prod. [Toronto]: M-L, 1972. dist. Sch. Ser. or Wint. 46fr.: col.: 35mm. & cassette (11 min.): auto. & aud. adv. sig. & teacher's guide. $16.50 (La vie quotidienne des pionniers du Haut-Canada: $85.00) ji

1. Frontier and pioneer life - Ontario.

Photos taken at Upper Canada Village Ontario, illustrate pioneer cooking methods, the utensils used, the methods of preserving food, and the cutting of meat. Bread making and butter making are discussed in detail. English title available: FOODS.

Addendum

971.3
    Le patrimoine Ontarien.
      prod. [Toronto]: Int. Cin., 1975.
      dist. VEC 55fr.: col.: 35mm. &
      cassette (15 min.): auto. & aud.
      adv. sig. & teacher's guide.
      $24.00 (Le patrimoine vivant
      du Canada: $86.00) ji

      1. Ontario - History.

    Briefly describes the early history of Upper Canada with the use of paintings, drawings and photographs of historic Ontario figures, homes and forts. English title available: ONTARIO'S HERITAGE.

971.3
    Sainte-Marie-among-the-Hurons: part 2.
      prod. [Toronto]: R.Q.M., 1975. dist.
      LEA. 41fr.: col.: 35mm. & captions.
      $9.00 (Sainte Marie among the Hurons: $18.00) ji

      1. Ste. Marie among the Hurons, Ont. - Description.
      2. Jesuits-Missions.

    Provides general coverage of Ste.-Marie-Among-the-Hurons as it is today, including buildings and artisans. For use in conjunction with Part I, or as a prelude to a visit to Ste. Marie. French title available: L'HISTOIRE DE SAINTE-MARIE-DES-HURONS.

973.2
    A new people, a new nation.
      prod. [Toronto]: M-L, 1976. dist.
      Sch. Ser. or Wint. 77fr.: col.:
      35mm. & cassette (15 min.): auto.
      & aud. adv. sig. & teacher's guide.
      $16.50 (The United States: "From sea to shining sea": $65.00) is

      1. United States - History - Colonial period.
      2. United States - History - Revolution - Causes.

    With historical drawings, diagrams, and realistic sound effects in the narration, the development of ideals of American democracy is emphasized in the events that led to the American Revolution.

973.8
    In pursuit of the dream.
      prod. [Toronto]: M-L, 1976. dist.
      Sch. Ser. or Wint. 76fr.: col.:
      35mm. & cassette (15 min.): auto. &
      aud. adv. sig. & teacher's guide.
      $16.50 (The United States: "From sea to shining sea": $65.00) is

      1. United States - History - 1865-1898.

    Uses historical drawings and photographs, to outline the growth of the territories in the United States in the nineteenth century. Explains reasons for westward expansion and the treatment of the native Indians during this settlement. Encourages group discussion and further study of the American Indians today.

973.9
    We, the people.
      prod. [Toronto]: M-L, 1976. dist.
      Sch. Ser. or Wint. 80fr.: col.:
      35mm. & cassette (15 min.): auto. &
      aud. adv. sig. & teacher's guide.
      $16.50 (The United States: "From sea to shining sea": $65.00) is

      1. United States - History - 20th century.

    Presents an overview of American history up to the present time. Examines the age of technology and its effect on growth of the U.S. Traces beginnings of labour unions and big business and involvement in world affairs. Uses many historical photographs.

Title Index

Addendum

Activities of the season.	971.3	Les ensembles.	160.76
L'Allemagne: le plus beau Noël de casse-noix.	398.20943	Eskimo spirit beliefs.	299
		La ferme.	971.3
Le Baron Münchhausen dans une histoire chavirante: un conte Allemand	398.20943	Feux et cuisine.	641.5
Basic distress signals.	384	The first Canadians.	970.1
The beginning of life: frogs	597	The flags of Canada's past.	929.90971
Birds of the eastern forest.	598.2	Le foyer.	971.3
Birds of the grasslands.	598.2	The generator.	621.313
Birds of the northern forest.	598.2	Generosity.	177
Birds of the Rocky Mountains.	598.2	Getting together.	384.6
Le bon Roi Arthur.	398.2	Glooskap nous a donné l'été.	398.209701
Brasilia.	918.1	Le grand Hercule.	292
British Columbia.	917.11	Hello, Mr. Bell.	384.6
Buenos Aires.	918.2	Helpers at the Metro Toronto zoo.	590.74
Les carnivores.	599.0971	Honesty.	179
Cattle, cattle, cattle.	599	How does V.D. spread?	616.9
Cendrillon.	372.6	How is V.D. cured?	616.9
Comment les oiseaux se procurent leur nourriture.	598.2	A human being is born.	612.6
		Impreintes d'animaux.	591
La course à l'or: les premiers mineurs de la Colombie Britannique.	971.1	In pursuit of the dream.	973.8
		L'Irlande: la casquette de O'Reilly.	398.209415
Cuzco.	918.5	Italy: the legend of La Befana.	398.20945
Cylinder heads and valves.	629.22	Jeanne d'Arc: heroine française.	920
De la terre.	407	Jésus: Homme-Dieu.	232.9
Les deux grenouilles: un conte Japonais.	398.20952	Kandara: la vie dans une agglomération Kenyane.	916.76
Domestic electricity.	621.31	Legend of Mikchik.	398.209701
Du cheval.	407		
The early days.	380.5	Life in the western mountains.	599.097
L'école et les loisirs.	971.3	Lunenburg: a community study.	917.16
Ecosystems.	574.5	Malacca: porte de la Malaysia.	915.95

Addendum

Le Manitoba: le bouclier.	917.127	Photographing people.	778.9
Meeting the challenge.	363.20971	Picture techniques.	770.28
Le métal brillant.	669	Planes and planing.	621.9
Metal fastening methods.	671.5	Plant and animal communities.	574.5
The metric world.	389	Ponies, ponies, ponies.	599
Millions of stars in the universe.	523.8	Precipitation and weather.	551.5
Modern technology and methods.	363.20971	Le présent et le futur.	380.5
Money: what is it?	332.4	La présentation du timbre poste.	769
The motor.	621.46	Printing screen prints.	764
Muscle and steam.	380.5	Les provinces Canadiennes.	769
The muscular system.	611	Puberté.	612.6
La naissance d'un pays.	769	The referee's role.	796.9
Name your V.D. contacts.	616.9	The reproductive cells.	591.1
A new people, a new nation.	973.2	Sainte-Marie-among-the-Hurons: part 2.	971.3
Now you're talking.	384.6	Screwdrivers and screws.	621.9
Observing by seeing: colours red, yellow, blue.	152.1	The seabirds of Bonaventure Island.	598.2
The oil industry in Canada.	665	The seagull and the whale.	398.20971
Les oiseaux communs du Canada.	598.2	Setting up your own screen studio.	764
Operation of the running gear.	629.22	The sharpening of plane irons, chisels and gouges.	621.9
Organisms and environment.	574.5	The shiny metal.	669
Organizing a community study.	301.34	The 16mm. film projector: part 2.	778.2
Ovulation: mammals.	591.1	The skeletal system.	611
Owls.	598.2	Some known facts about marijuana.	615
Partners in development?	382.1	Staining and finishing wood.	684
Le patrimoine des pionniers.	971.2	Stephen Leacock.	920
Le patrimoine Ontarien.	971.3	Storms, hurricanes and tornadoes.	551.5
La Paz.	918.4	Switch wiring and low voltage circuits.	621.319
La peinture ancienne au Canada français.	759.11	La Syrie: le petit chameau.	398.2095691
Le petit Fort Garry: l'héritage de la traite des pelleteries.	971.27	The teeth.	611
		Unités de longueur.	389

Addendum

Using audio-visual resources. 028.7

Using your own weather station. 551.6

Vers un nouvel ordre économique international. 382.1

A visit to the weather station. 551.6

Vue d'ensemble: les plaines de l'Ouest. 917.12

Walk safely on the highway. 614.8

We, the people. 973.9

Weather and what affects it. 551.6

What is gonorrhea? 616.9

What is syphilis? 616.9

Where do I go from here? 028.7

Why the Blackfeet never hurt a mouse. 398.209701

Le Yukon. 917.12

Series List

Series List

Animals - a close-up look: $75.00   M-L
    Cattle, cattle, cattle.
    Ponies, ponies, ponies.

Applications of electricity: $75.00   M-L
    Domestic electricity.
    The generator.
    The motor.
    Switch wiring and low voltage circuits.

Auto mechanics: $75.00   M-L
    Cylinder heads and valves.
    Operation of the running gear.

Basic photography: $69.00   R.B.M.
    Photographing people.
    Picture techniques.

Birds of Canada: $54.00   NFB
    Owls.

Birds of North America: $50.00   FMS
    Birds of the eastern forest.
    Birds of the grasslands.
    Birds of the northern forest.
    Birds of the Rocky Mountains.
    The seabirds of Bonaventure Island.

Canada: "the true north strong and free": $85.00   M-L
    British Columbia.

The Canadian flag: $65.00   Int. Cin.
    The flags of Canada's past.

Canadian holidays: $180.00   B&R
    Activities of the season.

Christmas tales from many lands: $75.00   M-L
    Italy: the legend of La Befana.

Early day Canada: $96.00   B&R
    Organizing a community study.

Ecology: exploration and discovery: $85.00   M-L
    Ecosystems.
    Organisms and environment.
    Plant and animal communities.

Family living and sex education series B: $75.00   M-L
    The beginning of life: frogs.
    A human being is born.
    Ovulation: mammals.
    The reproductive cells.

The game of hockey: $72.00   R.B.M.
    The referee's role.

Hello! Getting together with the telephone: $96.00   Int. Cin.
    Getting together.
    Hello, Mr. Bell.
    Now you're talking.

Inquiry into weather: $85.00   M-L
    Precipitation and weather.
    Storms, hurricanes and tornadoes.
    Using your own weather station.
    A visit to the weather station.
    Weather and what affects it.

Learning about money: $65.00   M-L
    Money: what is it?

Series List

Learning about our universe: $85.00   M-L
    Millions of stars in the universe.

Learning about the human body: $85.00   M-L
    The muscular system.
    The skeletal system.
    The teeth.

Légendes amérindiennes: $85.00   M-L
    Glooskap nous a donné l'été.

Les légendes de Noël des pays étrangers: $75.00   M-L
    L'Allemagne: le plus beau Noël de casse-noix.
    L'Irlande: la casquette de O'Reilly.
    La Syrie: le petit chameau.

Legends of the Micmac: $86.00   Int. Cin.
    Legend of Mikchik.

Metal work: machine operations: $75.00   M-L
    Metal fastening methods.

Metric measurement: $65.00   M-L
    The metric world.

Le monde des oiseaux: $64.00   Int. Cin.
    Comment les oiseaux se procurent leur nourriture.

Moral decision-making: $75.00   M-L
    Generosity.
    Honesty.

Outdoor survival: $85.00   M-L
    Basic distress signals.

Ouvre l'oeil et le bon...: $230.00 Int. Cin.
    Les ensembles.

Le patrimoine vivant du Canada : $86.00   Int. Cin.
    Le patrimoine des pionniers.
    Le patrimoine Ontarien.

The peoples of Canada - our multicultural heritage: $82.00   SHN
    The first Canadians.

Les pionniers: $72.00   NFB
    La course à l'or: les premiers mineurs la Colombie Britannique.

Les récits héroïques: $85.00   M-L
    Le bon Roi Arthur.
    Le grand Hercule.
    Jeanne d'Arc: héroïne française.
    Jésus: Homme-Dieu.

Royal Canadian Mounted Police: $69.00   R.B.M.
    Meeting the challenge.
    Modern technology and methods.

South America: $69.95   EDU
    Brasilia.
    Buenos Aires.
    Cuzco.
    La Paz.

Tales from the treetops: $86.00   Int. Cin.
    Why the Blackfeet never hurt a mouse.

Thinking skills: observing.   VCI
    Observing by seeing: colours red, yellow and blue.

	Series List		
Les timbres poste racontent l'histoire du Canada: $86.00	Int. Cin.	Wildlife of North America: the mammals: $95.00	FMS
La naissance d'un pays.		Life in the western mountains.	
La présentation du timbre poste.			
Les provinces canadienne.		Woodworking: hand tools (A): $85.00	M-L
La traite des pelleteries: $45.00	Int. Cin.	Screwdrivers and screws.	
		The sharpening of plane irons, chisels and gouges.	
Le petit Fort Garry: l'héritage de la traite des pelleteries.		Staining and finishing wood.	
		Planes and planing.	
Transport: l'aventure Canadienne: $86.00	Int. Cin.		
		Your library: how to use it: $75.00	M-L
Le présent et le futur.			
		Using audio-visual resources.	
Transportation: the Canadian Adventure: $86.00	Int. Cin.	Where do I go from here?	
Muscle and steam.			
Transportation in Canada	R.B.M.		
The early days.			
The United States: "From sea to shining sea": $65.00	M-L		
In pursuit of the dream.			
A new people, a new nation.			
We. the people.			
Usage du système international: $65.00	M-L		
Unités de longueur.			
Venereal disease: what I need to know: $85.00	M-L		
How does V.D. spread?			
How is V.D. cured?			
Name your V.D. contacts.			
What is gonorrhea?			
What is syphilis?			
La vie quotidienne des pionniers du Haut-Canada: $85.00	M-L		
L'école et les loisirs.			
La ferme.			

Ministry of Education, Ontario
Information Centre, 13th Floor,
Mowat Block, Queen's Park,
Toronto, Ont.   M7A 1L2